NORTH AMERICAN
PINOT NOIR

The publisher gratefully acknowledges the generous contribution to this book provided by the General Endowment Fund of the University of California Press Associates.

NORTH AMERICAN

PINOT NOIR

JOHN WINTHROP HAEGER

University of California Press Berkeley Los Angeles London

University of California Press
Berkeley and Los Angeles, California

University of California Press, Ltd.
London, England

Library of Congress Cataloging-in-Publication Data

Haeger, John Winthrop, 1944–
North American pinot noir / John Winthrop Haeger.
p. cm.
Includes bibliographical references and index.
ISBN 0-520-24114-2 (alk. paper)
1. Pinot noir (Wine)—North America. 2. Wine and wine making—North America. I. Title.
TP557 . H34 2004
641.2'223—dc21 2003013277

Manufactured in the United States of America
13 12 11 10 09 08 07 06 05 04
10 9 8 7 6 5 4 3 2 1
The paper used in this publication meets the minimum requirements of ANSI/NISO Z39.48-1992 (R 1997) *(Permanence of Paper)*.∞

CONTENTS

MAPS

Following page 190

Acknowledgments

Few wine books are possible without the generous cooperation of winegrowers. The men and women who grow and make North America's pinot noirs have offered me time, hospitality, information, expertise, and wines unstintingly and repeatedly, both to educate me and to support this project; I am deeply grateful to them all. My gratitude absolutely extends to dozens of pinot makers whose wines are *not* explicitly profiled in these pages, including many in Burgundy and elsewhere in Europe, as well as to makers of other varieties, whose help and perspective were no less essential to a fair understanding of the whole picture.

In addition to winegrowers, enologists, and viticulturists, and their many assistants and publicists, I have been hugely assisted by several dozen librarians, academic specialists, sommeliers, restaurateurs, and plain lovers of fine wine. Some of these individuals helped me to locate sources, check references, and organize tastings; others provided invaluable introductions and background or facilitated entrée to hugely informative events. A few were kind enough to review drafts of a chapter or two, and to save me from an avalanche of errors both large and small. I owe special thanks to the following individuals, wineries, and organizations.

For assistance with research, sources, and contacts: Bo Simons and the Sonoma County Wine Library; John Skarstad and Alex Borg, in the Shields Library at the University of California, Davis; Elizabeth Diefendorf and the New York Public Library; Jean-Frédéric Jauslin and the Swiss National Library; Carole Moore and Marcel Fortin, in the Robards Library at the University of Toronto; Gail Unzelman at Nomis Press; Deborah Golino and Susan Nelson-Kluk at Foundation Plant Services; Patricia Bowen at the Pacific Agri-Food Research Centre (Summerland, Canada); Eve Mezvinsky; Santa Barbara County Vintners' Association; Nan Campbell and the Carneros Quality Alliance; John Hibble and the Santa Cruz Mountains Winegrowers Association; Monterey County Vintners and Growers Association; Jim Trezise and the New York Wine and Grape Foundation; the Wine Council of Ontario; the Ontario Grapegrowers Marketing Board; Heidi Cusick and the Mendocino County Alliance; Sue Chiverton and the Anderson Valley Winegrowers Association; Sue Horstmann and the Yamhill County Wineries Association; Charles Sullivan; Gerald Asher; Jane Carr and the Institute of Masters of Wine; Jerry DiFalco and DiFalco Vineyard Management; Steve Williams and Anderson Valley Viticultural Services; James Rey Ontiveros and Bien Nacido Vineyards; Nick Peay and Peay Vineyards; and Stephen Cary of Yamhill Valley Vineyards.

For special hospitality: David Graves at Saintsbury; Bob Sessions and Jean Arnold at Hanzell Vineyards; Milla Handley at Handley Cellars; Chalone Vineyard; Greg Brewer at Melville Vineyards and Winery; Ingo Grady at Mission Hill Winery; Dick Reno at Chateau Lafayette-Reneau; Weingut Dr. Bürklin-Wolf; Brian Quinn at the Ivy House Restaurant (Portland); Austrian Wine Marketing; and Kurt Egli at Henri Badoux (Aigle).

For special expertise and answers to queries far beyond the call of duty: Larry Brooks; Brian Talley; Greg La Follette; Mary Hall; Debbie Zachareas; Kermit Lynch; David Adelsheim; Aubert de Villaine; Robert Drouhin and Véronique Drouhin-Boss; Jacques Seysses; Anne Gros; Raymond Bernard; and Patrice Rion.

For hospitality associated with pinotcentric events: Oregon Pinot Camp; World of Pinot Noir; and Pinotfest at Farallon Restaurant (San Francisco).

For assistance in preparing the manuscript for the publisher: Jennifer Porro and Madelyn Homick.

And for patience, support, and encouragement as vacations were turned into wine safaris, and countless dinner menus were redesigned to be pinot-friendly, and as talk of clones and *terroir* invaded the household conversation space: Julianne Frizell.

The usual caveat applies, of course: the responsibility for errors, omissions, and misunderstandings of fact rests with me alone.

Introduction

I wasn't raised around pinot noir or, for that matter, wine of any kind. My parents' libations were Johnnie Walker Red Label before dinner and water or reheated breakfast coffee with meals. On those occasions when guests or other circumstances seemed to require something special with the food itself, my father consulted his whiskey merchant. These interactions generally produced something like Mateus or a shipper's bottling of Médoc. Somehow, in the 1960s, it came to my father's attention that champagne had been served historically in tall flutes rather than shallow saucers. An architect by training, with wonderful taste and a keen interest in industrial design, he then applied himself to collecting antique champagne flutes. This passion occasionally brought sparkling wine to our table, but never an especially good label, since the bubbly's purpose was simply to illustrate the logic of the flute: the long, elegant ascent of bubbles from the top of the stem to the top of the glass.

In 1966, fresh from college, I left the East Coast for graduate school at the University of California, Berkeley. Wine seemed to appear all around me. One fellow student worked weekends as a cellar rat for Napa Valley wineries. Another worked for San Francisco journalist Davis Bynum, himself bitten by the wine bug, who operated a retail wine store not far from the Berkeley campus, selling gallon jugs of Barefoot Bynum brand red and white table wine, and something called Dry Flor sherry. Barefoot Bynum was priced for an academic budget.

There was also Professor Carlo Cipolla. Cipolla taught courses in European economic history during each winter quarter at Berkeley, pursuant to some perpetual time-share arrangement he had negotiated with the University of Padua. He had a well-stocked cellar at home in Padua and was great friends with Louis P. Martini, the Italian vintner whose father had established one of Napa Valley's very best first-generation brands. When the so-called Navy Recruiting Table protest erupted on the Berkeley campus in the winter of 1967—a sequel of sorts to the Free Speech Movement that had shut down the politically sensitive campus in 1964—Cipolla was confronted with a dilemma: honor the strike proclaimed by the antiwar activists or continue teaching economic history? Announcing that as a "guest" in the States, he did not wish to penalize students who felt morally obligated to boycott classes, but that he simultaneously felt obligated to give lectures for students who chose not to strike, Cipolla compromised. For the duration of the strike, he lectured on the history of wine in Europe. So I learned basic politicoeconomic facts about wine—for example, that the northern limits of the cultivation of vines in Western Europe coincide more or less with the northern boundary of the Roman Empire; and that wine being a luxury, vines are planted only where nothing else will grow—while more conscientious students carried protest banners in the gray rain outside.

Then I bought my first book about wine, Frank Schoonmaker's *A Wine Tour of France.* Peers considered Schoonmaker the most influential wine merchant of the post-Prohibition era, but in truth there were not enough wine drinkers in 1960s America to sustain more than a handful of books about wine. I also purchased one each of every wine available in *half*-bottles from Jay Vee Liquors, a supermarket-size emporium exactly one mile from the Berkeley campus—the closest proximity allowed under state law. As systematically as the few books and randomly selected half-bottles allowed, I began to read and taste my way through wine. I spent weekends visiting the dozen or so tasting rooms along Highway 29 in the Napa Valley. When I moved from Berkeley to Southern California in 1968 to take a job teaching Chinese language and history, my frame of reference shifted from California to European wines, thanks primarily to friendly mentoring from the wine manager at Jurgensen's Grocery Company in Pasadena (once a formidable institution but now defunct), who made my vinous education his personal project. Jurgensen's did a large business in Bordeaux, but also imported directly things like minerally white Cassis from Domaine du Paternel and spicy red Bandol from Domaine Tempier, which were then absolutely unknown in the States.

I wish I could say exactly when and where I first tasted pinot noir. It would be even better if I could say that my first pinot experience, whatever it may have been, was ethereal, transporting, and transformational. Notes and memory both fail me, however. Maybe the first pinots failed me too. There may have been a pinot noir or two among my initial purchase of half-bottles, perhaps at least a modest Bourgogne Rouge from Louis Jadot or Louis Latour. According to my oldest notes, I served a Davis Bynum pinot noir with something called *boeuf en mars* at a dinner party in the fall of 1970. The *boeuf en mars* was an obscure, tomato-enriched variation on beef bourguignon, but the Bynum pinot is mysterious. It must have been made from grapes Bynum sourced in Napa, because he had no access to Joe Rochioli's Russian River valley fruit until 1973. My notes say the wine was not vintage-dated.

In truth, I found my way to pinot noir slowly. I drank through a lot of Bordeaux and California cabernet first. I tried relatively obscure wines, like Château La Tour de Mons, Château Guionne, and Château Cantebau-Couhins, that fitted the budget of a young academic; some slightly more exalted properties like Château Gloria and Château d'Angludet; California cabs from Beaulieu, Heitz, and the old Souverain Cellars, before Lee Stewart sold the brand to Pillsbury; a good assortment of Italian varieties made in California by Louis Martini and Samuel Sebastiani; and barbera and grignolino. In the 1970s even zinfandel passed for an Italian variety. I drank Barolos from the 1971 and 1978 vintages for winter dinners at home.

One by one, in the late 1970s and early 1980s, Burgundies show up in my notes. Gevrey-Chambertin Petite Chapelle from Paul Grillot. Nuits-St.-Georges from Jadot and Latour. Clos Vougeot Château de la Tour from Jean Morin. And a case of red Chassagne-Montrachet 1971 from Bachelet-Ramonet that turned more or less to vinegar in a closet while I waited for it to "mature." That red Chassagne was my occasion to discover that pinot noir is unforgiving of poor storage conditions and that spoiled wine is no better for cooking than it is for drinking.

In 1984 I made my wine writing debut, with modest chutzpah and no certifiable qualifications of any kind except that I spoke passable French, with an article for *Connoisseur* magazine about the cabernet-based wine being made 400 miles from cab's ground zero in Bordeaux, at the Mas de Daumas Gassac near Montpellier. "Who could have imagined," Daumas Gassac's eccentric proprietor admitted some years later, "that this unknown writer could get us four pages in America's snobbiest magazine?" But this first story led to a second, and to pinot noir. *Connoisseur*'s editor in chief, the prolific and colorful Thomas Hoving, shared a literary agent with one Kermit Lynch, an ex-hippie and ex-musician who had built a business importing handcrafted wines from France and Italy. To promote Lynch's then forthcoming book, *Adventures on the Wine Route,* the agent persuaded Hoving that an article in *Connoisseur* about wine importers could be useful. I was asked to write the story. I rather quickly discovered that America's then handful of small-scale, hands-on importers—Lynch, Robert Chadderdon, Robert Haas, Neal Rosenthal, and Martine Saunier—all had predilections for Burgundy. Rosenthal was at pains to explain to me, during a late-afternoon tasting in the back of his small retail shop on Lexington Avenue in New York, that pinot noir is "the most intellectual of wines." I imagine this appealed to the academic in me. Shaking off the memory of the spoiled red Chassagne, I bought more Burgundy.

New World pinot, I have to admit, is a far more recent discovery. I reassure myself that there wasn't really much to discover until quite recently—but this perspective, I realize now, maligns a generation of New World pinot pioneers. Awash in red Burgundies, I missed David Lett's early successes with pinot at The Eyrie Vineyards in Oregon. This is puzzling, because I lived for two years in the mid 1970s in McMinnville, just blocks from Eyrie, and even worked occasional weekends at Sokol Blosser Winery's new tasting room, in exchange for an employee discount on its young-vines pinot, sold as Pinot Noir Rosé. I was only dimly aware that Josh Jensen (Calera), David Graves (Saintsbury), Joseph Swan, and Jim Clendenen (Au Bon Climat) had begun to make some very good pinots in California. Or that Davis Bynum, who had crafted my grad school jug wines, was now ensconced near Healdsburg, California, and had made the first pinot noir to carry the words "Russian River Valley" on its label.

It was 20 years later that several revelations struck in rapid succession. A sommelier at the Auberge du Soleil in Napa, young enough to have been barely out of college, sent me in search of El Molino's pinot noir, made by Reg Oliver at a tiny winery just north of St. Helena in the Napa Valley; and Marcassin, the now ultrafamous and unobtainable cult wine made by Helen Turley almost within eyeshot of the Pacific on the Sonoma Coast. In the El Molino I found, more or less to my astonishment, the hints of leather, animal, and forest floor I liked in red Burgundies. I never located the Marcassin, and now I know why. Then there was Iron Horse Vineyards, predominantly a producer of Champagne-method sparkling wines. Iron Horse produced a still, vineyard-designated pinot called Thomas Road in 1996, whose cherry fruit and smoke flavors became a personal favorite. In the course of research for a story on Mendocino's remote and cool Anderson Valley—which I imagined at the outset to be about "endangered" white grape varieties like riesling and gewürztraminer, now mostly driven out of expensive grape-growing areas like Los Carneros by chardonnay—I was amazed by the fine quality of two pinots from Pepperwood Springs, where a former publicist for Southern Pacific railway taught herself, very much on the job, to make wine. And then there was Littorai, the label launched by Ted and Heidi Lemon. A decade earlier, Ted Lemon had been a French major at Brown University studying in Dijon when he became enamored of and inspired by wine. The only American to have become winemaker for a reputed Burgundian producer, Lemon returned to the States in 1990 with a French wine education and matchless Old World experience. He sourced fruit from California's coolest coastal mesoclimates (including Anderson Valley) and began making tiny quantities of awesome pinot noir.

And so, in 1999, the idea for this book was born. There was too much activity, scattered in too many spots from Santa Barbara to Oregon, to be summarized in an article. Too much progress with a grape of almost mythic difficulty to be dismissed as a fluke. Too many new plantings in promising areas to suppose that pinot noir, in North America, was simply a fad. Too many people—not making a lot of money, but nevertheless devoted absolutely to succeeding where others had failed—to be written off as cranks. And too much smart, serious money following in the footsteps of the pioneers, planting large spreads of expensive vineyard in the cool climates where, according to fairly new wisdom, pinot would thrive.

Pinot noir is the latest of the great European grape varieties to achieve distinction in the New World. The two *c* grapes—chardonnay and cabernet sauvignon—came first. Cabs and chards from California's Napa Valley outplaced a list of classified Bordeaux and well-regarded white Burgundies at an infamous blind tasting in Paris in 1976. Syrah, the grape responsible for the great reds of the Rhône Valley, was also successfully transplanted (as shiraz) to Australia. And merlot, the primary grape in Pomerol and St.-Emilion, achieved dubious distinction in the New World for rapid consumer acceptance, a lower price point than cabernet, and a breathtaking growth rate measured in acres planted, tons harvested, and bottles sold.

The evidence that New World pinot noir must now be taken seriously may still be anecdotal, but the anecdotes are ubiquitous. In a 1998 tasting staged by the editors of *Wine Spectator,* the world's largest-circulation wine magazine, three American pinots from the 1994 vintage were bested only by the 1990 and 1993 vintages of Méo-Camuzet's fabulous Richebourg, prompting editor at large Harvey Steiman, a veteran commentator on red Burgundies, to observe that "pinot noirs of the United States are fast closing the gap" with Burgundy. On her first trip to the California vineyards, in 1999, *Irish Times* wine correspondent Mary Dowey, well acquainted with the major wine regions of Europe and plied with every outstanding cab and chard California's wineries could muster, wrote that pinot noir was "the grape that stole my heart." Dowey's "special treat" wine from ten full days of tasting was Saintsbury's 1996 Brown Ranch pinot noir. And in February 2000 Joshua Greene, *Wine & Spirits'* editor in chief, tasted no fewer than 94 newly released American pinots, scored 19 of them 90-plus, talked about the "rush of joy" he got from the best wines he tasted, and observed that while the American equivalents of Burgundy's *grand cru* vineyards are still being discovered, "there is no question that several already exist."

At the beginning of the 1990s, restaurants could barely sell the few pinots they deigned to list, usually in categories headed "Miscellaneous" or "Other Reds." By 2000, pinot had been transformed into every sommelier's dream of the food-friendliest wine on earth. *Wine & Spirits'* 1999 restaurant poll found pinot noir gaining ground against both cabernet and merlot as the wine of choice with red meat, and ranking second to chardonnay as an accompaniment to fish and shellfish. In fact, more pinot noir was ordered to accompany seafood than sauvignon blanc! From Everest in Chicago, chef Jean Joho reported to *Wine & Spirits* that his pinot noir sales doubled in the late 1990s and that it was now ordered by a younger clientele. At Heartbeat in New York City, wine director David Gordon picked Flowers' 1996 Camp Meeting Ridge as his single favorite among the 75 wines of all types and regions on the restaurant's list. Of the pinot noir served in America's restaurants, 81 percent was American made. By 2002 almost 10 percent of the top-selling wines in American restaurants were bottlings of pinot noir.

Just 25 years ago, only a few North American winemakers were nutty enough—or passionate enough—to mess with pinot noir. In the 1970s just a handful of pioneers persevered. Then, in the late 1980s and early 1990s, pinot specialists and "Burgundy" specialists dedicated to the combination of pinot and chardonnay began producing mostly tiny lots of promising wine. For a time, a surplus of fruit from plantings originally intended for sparkling wine encouraged new efforts with still pinot. Almost suddenly, in the 1990s, American pinot noir became not just salable but "hot." Shipments of California pinot noir doubled from 300,000 to 600,000 cases. Supermarket sales of pinot noir from all sources (including Burgundy) surged from $10 million in 1993 to $34 million in 1998. The growth rate (measured in cases of varietal California wine shipped) for pinot rose to nearly 15 percent, second only to the growth rate for the endlessly popular merlot. Harvested acres of pinot noir in Oregon tripled between 1989 and 1998. Some pinots—such as Williams Selyem, Rochioli, and Dehlinger—achieved cult status, selling out to restaurants and to mailing lists so popular that the lists themselves were forced to close.

These successes attracted widespread attention. Dan Duckhorn, who had built his reputation on merlot and sauvignon blanc in Napa, bought the old Obester property in Mendocino's Anderson Valley. Chuck Wagner of Caymus Vineyards, another terrifically successful cabernet specialist who had renounced pinot noir two decades earlier, planted a nine-acre pinot vineyard in western Sonoma and contracted to manage one of the oldest pinot vineyards in Santa Barbara County. Beringer, Cakebread, Patz & Hall, and Simi all released pinots for the first time (or for the first time in a long time) in 1997. Sparkling wine houses like J Wine Company, Domaine Carneros, Gloria Ferrer, and Codorníu Napa embarked on programs to make still pinot noir. Napa's Steve Girard, who was known for fine cabernet and chardonnay, sold out, moved to Oregon, and launched himself into pinot. Gary Andrus, the former Olympic skier who had founded Napa's Pine Ridge Winery in the 1970s, bought land in Oregon for a new venture focused on pinot noir. Even small-scale specialists in other varieties, like Dry Creek Valley's Doug Nalle, could not resist the temptation to make a barrel or two of pinot. Wine giants like Kendall-Jackson, Gallo, and Mondavi made huge acquisitions of cool-climate land and planted pinot aggressively, though admittedly a bit less aggressively than they did chardonnay. The land rush drove prices for unplanted potential vineyard land to unprecedented heights.

Bottle prices for New World pinots edged up too. At the end of the 1990s, prices in the $30 to $50 range were common, especially for limited bottlings; a few wines, like single-vineyard releases from Williams Selyem and Saintsbury's Brown Ranch wine, were priced between $75 and $100. While such prices were modest by comparison with those asked and paid for California's cult cabernets and for the very finest examples of *premier cru* and *grand cru* Burgundy, it remains true that pinot noir is, in general, an expensive variety. *Wine Spectator*'s calculations showed that the average bottle price of pinots scored 90-plus was about $32 in 1998, versus an average $24 for similarly scored cabernets or chardonnays. The average production for pinots scored 90-plus was also fewer than 600 cases; for cabernets in the same range, the average production was almost 4,000 cases; and for chardonnay, nearly 8,000. So-called supermarket pinot noir barely exists. Good cabernets and chardonnays priced from $6 to $8 exist; good pinots in the same price range do not. The absence of "entry-level" wines among New World pinots—or among red Burgundies, for that matter—means that pinot lovers are almost always converted from another passion, not made from scratch.

This book is not intended as a hymn to the wondrousness of pinot noir, nor as a recitation of its vagaries. All the prose we need about the fragrance, finesse, delicacy, sensuality, and magic of pinot noir has been written already. A lot of it is true; some of it is silly; but there is enough already. Nor is this book a claim of victory for North American pinot—a sort of flag raising by victorious winegrowers in a newly conquered land. Only publicists for large wineries and their trade associations make such claims with apparently straight faces. California, Oregon, New York, Ontario, and British Columbia have not overtaken Burgundy in their few years of effort, however concerted; but neither is it the case that pinot in North America is so fundamentally a different beast that comparisons to Europe are irrelevant. Nor will this book argue that North American pinots are always better value than red Burgundies. A decade of relative price stability in Burgundy and huge progress to reverse a generation of ruinous farming practices have revived Burgundy since 1988 and substantially re-equilibrated price and value. Finally, this book is not primarily a buying guide. There are no scores, stars, or puffs. Tasting notes on individual wines are intended mainly to illustrate the properties of *terroirs* and the stylistic choices of winemakers, and to provide a prose description for consumers.

This book is intended as a survey of the landscape. I describe those areas where, as of the date of writing, the best pinot fruit is grown. As far as possible, I try to say why particular sites have distinguished themselves. A great deal of fascinating evidence exists because, at least in California and Oregon, many of the very best pinot makers own little land. For many reasons, they buy in most or all of their fruit and make small lots of vineyard-designated wine. Conversely, many growers sell fruit from a single parcel to several winemakers. Even when pinot makers own a vineyard, they often choose to sell part of their harvest to other makers of high repute, or to trade fruit, simply to gain experience with *terroir* (which can be defined as all of the physical properties of a site). This non-estate approach is, for the moment at least, much more widespread with pinot than with other varieties and contrasts rather markedly with the largely estate-based practices that prevail with high-end cabernet sauvignon. Whenever possible, I cross-reference sites and makers so that stylistic proclivities, winegrowing choices, and the mark of *terroir* can be recognized and compared.

The book does not shrink from comparing North American pinots with red Burgundies, and sometimes also with pinots grown in Alsace, Switzerland, the Loire valley, Italy, Germany, or Austria. With most of a millennium's experience in making pinot in Europe and barely a generation of serious effort thus far in the New World, with winemakers now traveling more like jet-setters than peasant farmers to exchange their experience, and with identical plant materials being introduced in both theaters, it is scarcely credible to pretend that the quest to produce great wine from the pinot noir grape is just a disconnected array of purely local efforts, subject to evaluation by local standards only. At the same time, I do not assume that "Burgundian" character (whatever the term may actually mean) defines great pinot or that a New World pinot is unsuccessful simply because it does not taste like a Burgundy.

This book seeks to identify trends, both promising and worrisome. Pinot noir in North America is nothing if not a work in progress, but pinot noir in Burgundy is also, to some small but important extent, reinventing itself. Some of the change has a "back to the future" character, in which it is difficult to tell progress from degeneration. Critics will argue that it's much too early for a book about North American pinot. The fundamentals aren't sorted out yet in North America, they will say; the ostensible best sites have been planted for only a decade or two; the cast of winemaking characters changes constantly; everything will be different in five years. They are right, of course. But change is not peculiar to pinot noir. Of the 3,000 entries in the first edition of Jancis Robinson's landmark *Oxford Companion to Wine,* half were updated for the second edition five years later and 500 brand-new entries were added. From the historian's perspective, the value of a snapshot is enhanced, not eroded, by change.

This book is for red Burgundy drinkers who have wondered what sort of wine pinot noir might give if its makers were liberated from a few regulations and relieved of annual autumn anxiety over rain and ripening fruit. It is for cabernet drinkers who have allowed themselves to lust for a kinder, gentler mouthfeel and for wines better adapted to savory pork, woodsy mushrooms, and grilled salmon. It is for merlot drinkers, seduced by the promise of "soft" wines, who got mostly insipid wines instead. It is for pinotphiles curious to know more about wines they like and about other wines related by style or provenance; for connoisseurs frustrated by the short supply of a few cult wines and seeking terrific alternatives; and for consumers wondering if those easy generalizations about the "cherry" in Russian River valley pinot, the "strawberry" in Los Carneros pinot, and the "tomato" in southern Central Coast pinot really stand up. It is for any wine drinker who has had a first bottle of pinot from someplace in North America and has been tempted to try another. And it is for everyone interested in the epic evolution of wine culture in the New World.

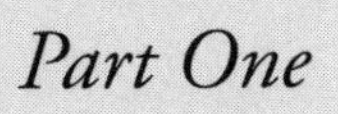

Part One

THE GRAPE, THE WINE, AND THE HISTORY

Chapter 1

THE BASICS

The names of wine grape varieties, from albariño to zinfandel, have become the bedrock vocabulary of wine talk worldwide. Nearly everyone who buys or drinks wine in the New World knows the names of ubiquitous varieties like cabernet, chardonnay, and merlot. The Alcohol and Tobacco Tax and Trade Bureau (TTB; formerly the Bureau of Alcohol, Tobacco and Firearms), which regulates the labels of wine sold in the United States, recognizes about 260 varietal names, but its rather odd list includes quite a number of names that are not true varieties, as well as many hybrids. Spain, a country of surprising varietal idiosyncrasy and diversity, claims more than *600* varieties under cultivation. Botanists and viticulturists estimate up to several thousand varieties worldwide, grown in some 25 million acres of vineyard. Many more varieties have come and gone over the centuries, leaving just documentary traces. Even in those Western European wine lands where wine nomenclature is still rooted firmly in geography, nearly all producers and many consumers can recite, more or less without hesitation, the varietal identities behind the wines of Sancerre and Hermitage, the Rheingau, and the Rioja.

The plethora of wine grape varieties is believed to be descended from a single plant species, identified botanically as *Vitis vinifera*—though some knowledgeable viticulturists have been known to wonder if certain additional species, now extinct, might not lurk in the pedigree of some modern varieties. *Vitis* covers a group of thornless, dark-stemmed, shreddy-barked plants, most of them grapes of some sort, sporting stem tendrils opposite the set of their leaves. They grow as climbers on other plants and manmade structures, not unlike Virginia creeper and Boston ivy, to which the genus is related. Vinifera, the wine-worthy species, is a deciduous plant, tending toward thicker shoots and more deeply indented leaves than other grapes, and is generally more vulnerable to fungi and parasites. It is distinguished primarily for its fruit, which is thinner-skinned than other species of *Vitis.* Its fruit is also more tender, sweeter, and more delicately flavored than other grapes, but needs more heat and sunshine to ripen.

The varieties of vinifera are largely—perhaps entirely—the product of cultivation. Varieties are thus often described as cultivars, which is simply a contraction of the English words *cultivated varieties.* Before humankind intervened, sometime between 10,000 and 7000 B.C., all vinifera grew wild, and identifiable varieties, for all practical purposes, did not persist longer than the lifetime of a single vine plant. In fact, stable varieties *could not* exist in the universe of wild vinifera, because the wild species is dioecious—meaning that unisexual flowers grow on separate male and female plants. Since fruit is thus produced only by the female plants, and then only when a female flower is cross-pollinated by some helpful insect, every instance of cross-pollination between wild grapevines is a matter of what geneticists call obligate outcrossing. This process inevitably reshuffles the genes in each resulting seedling, guaranteeing that every new vine is genetically different from its parents—perpetuating heterogeneity in the population of wild vines, and effectively precluding persistent varietal differentiation.

The domesticated version of vinifera, by contrast, is a reliable hermaphrodite. Its bisexual flowers are capable of self-pollination, and every flower can produce fruit. For at least 7,000 years and perhaps longer, domesticated vinifera has been propagated vegetatively. People, interfering with nature, have taken buds or cuttings from individual vines, and grown new vines from the cuttings. In this process, no genes are reshuffled. Instead, each new plant is a genetically identical copy of its individual parent. Genetic consistency and varietal identity have thus been maintained, with help from human beings, across multiple plant generations, as long as the relevant vine population was derived from a relatively small number of parent plants, which were chosen with an eye to similarity of leaves, clusters, and berries.

PINOT'S EARLIEST TRACES

No one knows how early vinifera vine populations displayed recognizable varietal character. Although archaeologists have been able to assemble a good many facts about the early history of wine production and consumption, early viticulture is stubbornly obscure. The paraphernalia of prehistoric wine production have been unearthed, primarily in the form of pottery wine jars and drinking vessels. Grape remains have been found at various Neolithic sites around the eastern end of the Mediterranean and along several tributaries of the Tigris River in modern Iran and Iraq. Chemical residues in wine jars, dating to the fourth millennium B.C., have been positively identified as fermented grape juice. But the growing of grapes has left fewer traces than the making and consumption of wine. In Egypt, hieroglyphic writing from the third millennium gives us an isolated glimpse into contemporaneous vineyards. The glyph for grapevines is the recognizable image of a vinelike plant trained along something resembling a trellis or arbor. Otherwise our first insights into early viticulture come from Greek and Roman documents of the first millennium B.C. It is certainly fair to presume that the first evidence of substantial, regular wine production cannot antedate the first cultivated vineyards. It is, however, an open question whether vinifera was domesticated once, and cuttings of domestic vines then carried, carpetbag style, around the ancient world; or whether a ubiquitous wild vinifera species, widely distributed throughout Europe and western Asia 10,000 years or more B.C., was the object of multiple domestications.

For most of the twentieth century, the accepted opinion of most wine historians and paleobotanists was that *all* vinifera had a common geographic origin—in Transcaucasia, between the Black and Caspian Seas, where modern Turkey, Iraq, and Iran share borders. This view, which originated with the work of Russian botanists at the end of the nineteenth century, was embraced by French viticulturist Pierre Viala, whose *Traité général d'ampelographie* was published in 1909 (ampelography is the science of vine description and identification). It is repeated in Jancis Robinson's classic *Vines, Grapes, and Wines,* which recasts Viala's work for an anglophone readership. Viala believed that vinifera had been transported, presumably along the same vectors traversed by other cultural indicators, across the ancient Near East to both Egypt and Greece, and thence to Rome and Western Europe. The picture of Greek and Roman settlements along the western Mediterranean littoral, with its well-known legacy of ceramic wine jars, is consistent with this scenario, and with much of what is known about the spread of both wine and culture into Western Europe.

This view of events is not, however, without problems. There is some evidence to indicate that grapes were cultivated and wine made in some parts of France *before* the first Greek settlements could have had any impact. Several varieties of vinifera grown during the Middle Ages in northern Europe, including pinot noir, seem not to have resembled the grapes grown in the southern parts of Europe. In addition, there is the inconvenient fact that *Vitis vinifera* grew wild throughout the Mediterranean basin, as far north as Belgium and Luxembourg and east into Austria, Hungary, Bulgaria, and Romania as recently as the end of the nineteenth century—before it succumbed to phylloxera—and that small populations of wild vinifera persist today in the Pyrenees, as well as in parts of Italy, Greece, Turkey, and Iran. Since it is not likely that migrants from the eastern Mediterranean would have transported *wild* vine cuttings in their saddlebags, the extensive and persistent populations of wild vines throughout large parts of Western Europe may be one more indication that some wine grape varieties were not imports at all, at least in the sense that we usually think about imports executed by the known couriers of classical civilization. "It is not unthinkable," writes Raymond Bernard, longtime chief of the Office Interprofessionnel des Vins in Dijon, "that wild vines could have existed in the vast forest of Gaul" long before the Greeks or Romans arrived, and that "local *Vitis vinifera silvestris*" could have become "*Vitis vinifera sativa*" in situ, with a bit of human intervention. If this is true, pinot noir is a likely candidate for indigenous European origin, and perhaps even Burgundian origin, for reasons we will see momentarily.

Searching across the centuries for the first traces of modern grape varieties is treacherous business, given the imprecision of textual descriptions and the lack of detail in early drawings—when drawings of any kind have survived at all. There are indications that vineyards may have flourished in what is now the Côte d'Or at least as early as the second century B.C. The earliest surviving description of these plantings—and this may be a secondhand report—is found in *De re rustica* by one Lucilus Junius Moderatus Columella, a farmer's son from the area around modern Cadiz, in Spain, and dates from the first half of the first century of the common era. Columella, who was knowledgeable about viticulture, insightful about matters of quality, and an early student (it appears) of Italian grape varieties, describes "the smallest and best" of three grapes types found in Burgundy in terms that are not inconsistent with the properties of pinot noir. This type, according to Columella, had "the roundest leaf of all," was "tolerant of drought and cold," and produced an age-worthy wine. For no less an authority than Jacques Lavalle, whose classic *Histoire et statistique de la vigne et des grands vins de la Côte d'Or* was published in 1855, Columella's description was sufficient evidence that something akin to pinot existed in the northern half of France at the beginning of the common era. In fairness, however, vastly more detail would be required to clinch the case objectively. Additional documentation does accumulate during the medieval period, as the monks of Cluny gained control of most of the vineyards in modern Gevrey-Chambertin and the monks of St.-Vivant acquired and cultivated vineyards in modern Vosne-Romanée. *Noirien* and *morillon* seem to emerge at this time as the monikers of choice for the local pinotlike red wine grape.

The first mentions of pinot by name—sometimes spelled *pynos* or *pineau*—show up during the last quarter of the fourteenth century in *actes* and other civil documents associated with the dukes of Burgundy. The first, widely cited by wine historians, was an *acte* of Philip the Bold ordering the shipment to Flanders—which Philip had acquired by marriage—of "six queues and one poinçon" (about 11 modern barrels) of "vermilion pinot wine" in 1375. Even better known is a second *acte,* dated 1395, in which the same Philip orders gamay vines, which he describes as "vile and noxious," uprooted from the Côte d'Or in favor of "pinot."

The great French wine historian Roger Dion believes that "pinot" was used to designate wine—in fact, Burgundy's best wine—*before* it was accepted as the name of a grape variety. Dion found its first application to grapes in 1394, two decades after Philip's "vermilion pinot" was sent off to Flanders, in the pardon of a *maître de la vigne* who beat to death a child who had failed to keep "pinots" separate from other grapes at harvest. Dion then found numerous references to "morillon dit pinot" and "morillon appelé pinot" in documents from the first quarter of the fifteenth century, as if pinot were being used to denote a subset of some larger type or class of red grapes. Some of these references imply that the pinot vines were newly planted. Dion permits himself to hypothesize that pinot was used to denote a grape variety or subvariety somehow superior to other related cultivars, that Philip the Bold may have coined the new name personally, and that Philip may also have been the patron of this instance of subvarietal selection. However that may be, the name *pinot* coexists persistently, following its first appearance in 1375, with a host of apparent paranyms (variant names, including nicknames, for what appears to be the same grape variety): *noirien, franc noirien, plant à bon vin, plant fin, plant noble, franc bourgignon, franc pinot, petit pinot,* and always *morillon.* Many of these names remained in common use within the memory of living Burgundians. To this day, there is special fondness for the *morillon* moniker in the commune of Morey-St.-Denis. Locals, who call themselves Morillions, like to assert that the name is evidence that pinot itself originated in Morey. They do not say why pinot is also called *morillon* in the department of Loir-et-Cher, 200 miles to the west.

WHAT DNA REVEALS

It is not likely that a complete genetic tree for *Vitis vinifera*—beginning with one or many instances of domestication and then traversing vine generations to the varietal population with which we work today—can ever be reconstructed. Written descriptions and surviving images, as we have seen, are insufficient for conclusive varietal identification, and many varieties crucial to the species tree have disappeared entirely in the course of time, leaving what amount to blank spaces in the pedigree of modern varieties. Carole Meredith, a viticulturist and plant geneticist recently retired from the University of California, Davis, has nonetheless pioneered techniques that have revolutionized our understanding of wine grape varieties. Since 1996, Meredith has used DNA fingerprinting—the same technology that is used to connect criminals to crime scenes and to establish paternity among humans—to determine the correct identities of modern grape varieties that have come to be known under multiple names, and to identify the parents and even grandparents of some varieties—at least where the parent varieties have themselves survived in cultivation or in collections. Meredith's extraordinary work has established, inter alia, that petite sirah is not syrah but durif; that zinfandel is identical to Croatian crljenak kastelanski, and that cabernet sauvignon, the most respected grape in Bordeaux, is the offspring of sauvignon blanc and cabernet franc.

Meredith's DNA-based work on northern French varieties has recently established that pinot noir is one of the genetic parents of chardonnay, gamay, aligoté, and at least 13 other varieties, including melon, the grape of Muscadet, and auxerrois, sometimes described as the "true" pinot blanc of Alsace. The other parent of all these progeny is gouais, a white variety once widely grown in northern France but now almost extinct except for a few specimens that survive in plant collections. This finding is hugely significant on several counts. First, and tantalizingly, the finding suggests that, for some unknown reason, pinot and gouais were an uncommonly "good parental combination," perhaps because they were relatively genetically dissimilar. Conversely, none of the progeny of pinot and gouais seem to have spawned successful progeny of their own, perhaps because they lacked the genetic distance necessary to birth stable offspring. Could this be evidence that vinifera was in fact domesticated several times over, in quite different locations, birthing "families" both closely and distantly related? Second, given that textual mentions of chardonnay and gamay occur as early as the thirteenth century, it is possible to conclude with certainty that both pinot noir and gouais are older, at least, than that, and conceivably as old as the dawn of French viticulture. Finally, that no cultivar has yet been identified as a parent of either pinot or gouais at least leaves open the possibility that the parents of one or both may have been wild vines—perhaps the *Vitis vinifera sativa* about which Bernard has speculated. Beyond any doubt, Meredith's DNA work leaves intact the conventional wisdom that pinot noir, whatever its origins, is very old indeed.

Conventional field observation and DNA fingerprinting both indicate that pinot noir has a strong proclivity toward spontaneous mutation in the vineyard. Pinot gris and pinot blanc, the red-grayish and green-yellowish versions of pinot, are generally grown as distinct varieties, but their DNA profiles are genetically indistinguishable from pinot noir, and they almost certainly originated as spontaneous field mutations from red-berried vines. In 1936, according to Clive Coates, Nuits-St.-Georges grower Henri Gouges noticed that some of the old pinot noir vines in his Clos des Porrets vineyard had begun to produce white grapes. Having propagated cuttings from these mutated vines and planted them in the nearby Les Perrières vineyard, Gouges began making (and still makes today) several barrels of white pinot noir. Now Gouges has propagated this white pinot, which Coates calls "pinot Gouges," back into the Clos des Porrets vineyard where he first found it, so there is now also a dribble of Clos des Porrets blanc, and he has shared cuttings of pinot Gouges with other vintners in the Côte de Nuits.

Pinot meunier, the staple grape of Champagne, which is occasionally made into a still wine, is taken to be a "chimera." "A mutation exists in the outer layer of cells," according to Meredith—causing the distinctive "floured" leaf that gave the variety its name—"but if you isolate an inner layer of cells and regenerate a plant from those cells, the new plant resembles a typical pinot noir." One Austrian scientist advances a different view, however. Ferdinand Regner, of the Federal College of Viticulture in Klosterneuburg, published research in 1999 claiming that pinot meunier (known in German-speaking countries as schwarzriesling) is actually a parent rather than a mutation of pinot noir, and that pinot noir represents the crossing of schwarzriesling with traminer. This research is not accepted outside Austria, and Regner's results have not been replicated in other studies. The mutability of pinot noir is generally thought responsible for the profusion of its clones, sometimes called stable mutations (of which more in chapter 5).

PINOT'S HABITAT EXPANDS

Whether pinot noir arrived in France with the Romans or the Greeks, or was domesticated in situ from indigenous *Vitis vinifera,* and whether its first appearance is put as early as five or six centuries B.C. or as late as the European Middle Ages, there can be no doubt that pinot made Burgundy famous, and vice versa. Many wine historians believe that the alliance of pinot and Burgundy was an explicit policy of Burgundy's Valois dukes, whose duchy extended from the Alps to Flanders, and whose power and influence rivaled those of the kings of France until the seventeenth century. Roger Dion in particular, extending his hypothesis about Philip the Bold's seminal role in the propagation and promotion of pinot noir, argues that the reputation of Beaune wines as "the finest in the world" was a "propaganda triumph of the Valois dukes of Burgundy." In any case, as the variety was transported northward to Champagne, west to the Loire, eastward to Alsace and Germany, and southward across what is now Switzerland to Italy, its Burgundian pedigree was respected. The name *pinot* took firm hold in France, and the grape emerged in Italian as pinot nero. In German-speaking areas, it became known as Burgunder, Blauburgunder, and Spätburgunder. When pinot gris and pinot blanc emigrated to Germanic lands, they were dubbed Grauburgunder and Weissburgunder, respectively, testifying to the presumed Burgundian origins of these color mutations as well. In parts of France, *pinot* was sometimes mistakenly applied to unrelated varieties, as in pineau de la Loire, a paranym for chenin blanc; we are told that the *pinot* spelling was not made official until the end of the nineteenth century, and then only to protect the word from mispronunciation by Burgundian peasants, who had a tendency to render *pineau* as something like "peen-yew."

Today there are about 11,000 acres of pinot noir in the Côte d'Or, the celebrated strip of east-facing slope between Dijon and Chalon-sur-Saône that is home to Burgundy's finest wines. There are another 10,000 acres in southern Burgundy, in the districts called the Côte Chalonnaise and the Mâconnais, where no small quantity of pinot is blended with gamay to make Bourgogne Passetoutgrains. But Champagne is home to more pinot noir than the Côte d'Or, and more pinot is crushed for champagne than is made into still red Burgundies. Pinot noir is also grown and made as a varietal wine in Alsace and Sancerre, and grown primarily for blending in Lorraine, the Jura, Savoie, Menetou-Salon, and St.-Pourçain. Pinot noir is the fourth most planted variety in Germany (after riesling, Müller-Thurgau, and sylvaner), mostly in Baden, but also in the Pfalz and the Rheingau, and in pockets like Assmannshausen and the Ahr, near Bonn, where it has been a specialty for a century. It is Germany's only significant red variety. In Switzerland, 1,500 acres of pinot are grown in the Valais, where it used to be blended with gamay to make Dôle but now stands increasingly on its own; near Neuchâtel, where it accounts for half of total vineyard surface and makes mostly a pale red wine known as Oeil de Perdrix; around the lakes southeast of Zurich; and in small appellations (like Bündner Herrschaft) near the border with Liechtenstein. In 2000, Austria accounted for just over 1,000 acres of pinot noir, about evenly divided between Niederösterreich and Burgenland. In Italy, there is pinot in Breganze, the Alto Adige, and Friuli, as well as in isolated vineyards throughout the country's northern half—notably in Oltrepò Pavese and the Arno valley, downstream from Florence. Macedonia, Serbia, Bulgaria, Slovakia, the Czech Republic, and Hungary all grow pinot noir. In at least one case, a Burgundy *négociant,* Charles Thomas of Nuits-St.-Georges, has become involved with a Franco-Romanian venture to produce pinot noir in the appellation called Dealu Mare.

In the nineteenth century and with some gusto in the twentieth, thanks to immigrants, plant collectors, and a growing number of serious vintners, pinot was also transplanted to various parts of the world outside Europe, including South Africa, North America, Chile, Australia, and New Zealand. North America is now home to more pinot noir than Burgundy. Somewhat confoundingly, especially for those who believe that grape varieties have well-established *terroir* preferences, pinot is successfully grown alongside chardonnay in Burgundy, alongside sauvignon blanc in Sancerre, alongside chasselas in Switzerland, cheek-by-jowl with riesling in Alsace and Germany, and not far from syrah in some parts of California and Australia.

THE GOOD, BAD, ETHEREAL, AND PERVERSE

As a vining plant, pinot noir is not especially vigorous and has a tendency to throw relatively slender trunks and willowy branches. Its leaves generally measure about five inches in each dimension—slightly larger than syrah but smaller than cabernet sauvignon. Leaves are usually three-lobed but only slightly indented, and thicker than in some varieties, with a surface that is sometimes described as bubbly. Viticulturists observe, however, that pinot noir actually exhibits a wide variety of leaf shapes. Sometimes the leaf is lobed on one side only; sometimes it is grossly asymmetrical; sometimes the lobes are so understated that the leaf seems almost round, or even square. The ripe fruit cluster is typically small, compact, and almost cylindrical—like the pinecone for which it is presumably named. Individual berries also tend to be small, almost perfectly round, and the color of midnight blue. Cluster morphology and berry size vary by clone, however, with some highly regarded clones distinguished for their comparatively smaller berries and tighter structure. And despite the recurrent description of cylindrical clusters, pruning in the vineyard to remove "wings" and "shoulders" from clusters is a common practice, so not all untrimmed clusters look very cylindrical to the untrained eye.

Pinot noir has the reputation of being fiercely difficult to grow, and many growers who have experimented with pinot in the New World have abandoned it. Robinson calls pinot "a minx of a vine" that "leads [growers] on a terrible dance." Burgundians admit that it is delicate, needing in Henri Jayer's words "sunshine but not too much and water but not too much," but spend relatively little time cataloging its liabilities. Among the common varieties of vinifera, pinot does seem especially susceptible to mildew and botrytis, as well as to several viral diseases, including leaf roll and fanleaf. Because it buds early, it is often at risk in cooler climates from spring frosts, though some sources indicate that it resists cold temperatures tolerably well. Like wild vinifera, and possibly testifying to a close relationship with wild vines, pinot appears sensitive to hard rain and abrupt temperature changes after budbreak, birthing clusters with a large percentage of stunted grapes or clusters that fall from the vine unfertilized. Pinot is a relatively shy-bearing variety under most circumstances, so fecundation failures can cause catastrophically small harvests. In addition, pinot noir's small berries have relatively thin skins that are easily broken by rough handling at harvest. The thin skin's tannins comprise only about 1.7 percent of the grape's weight—as compared to 3 percent to 6 percent in most red varieties—and pinot's anthocyanins, the soluble pigments that give most red wines their color, are present in less than half the quantity as in, for example, syrah. Serious winegrowers in all areas are now meticulous about their pinot noir, lavishing it with intensive, vine-by-vine attention throughout the growing season, and (when their experience permits) contrasting it with syrah, which some say more or less grows itself. "God made cabernet sauvignon," André Tchelistcheff, the father of modern California winegrowing, is supposed to have said, "whereas the devil made pinot noir."

No variety of vinifera has a more exalted reputation for making fine wine, however—when all has gone well in both vineyard and cellar. "Good pinot noir," say *Wall Street Journal* wine columnists Dorothy Gaiter and John Brecher, with a fair degree of objective sobriety, "has an elegant, velvety taste that tends to be less intense, less tannic and more berry-like than cabernet sauvignon." An "official" description by the Austrian Wine Marketing Board involves "elegant, soft tannins [and] a very fine bouquet which is difficult to describe [but is] reminiscent of raspberries and almonds." Attempting in 1981 to capture pinot's "personality," veteran California wine critic Robert Finigan allowed that pinot is "at once elegant and earthy, musty and fresh, pungent and expansively fragrant." Visually, it is neither thick nor dense, and black is not its color. "You must be able to see through a glass of it," explains Henri Jayer, who has made some of Burgundy's most respected exemplars. "The Pinot has a pretty robe," he continues, "glistening and shimmering like a cat's eyes, [and] sparkling like a diamond."

Many Burgundians insist that pinot's greatest appeal is aromatic. The smell of a fading rose is one classic description, but the spectrum of floral properties associated with pinot noir is actually quite broad, ranging from rose across lavender and lilac to violets, in combinations that sometimes remind people of potpourri. Fruit-driven examples of pinot noir can display everything from raspberry and strawberry to cherry, cassis, plum, and various black fruits. In North America, a variety of intense local berries joins the list, including lingonberry, whortleberry, and gooseberry. A host of tarlike, resiny, woody, and woodsy smells and flavors (including mushrooms and truffles) are common and wholly acceptable, as are overtones of meat and animal, ranging from charcuterie to wet fur and leather, and sometimes extending into the realm of organic wastes. Minerality is common, and usually appreciated. Still, Jayer insists, "the wine must be clean and pure." In fact, it must be "full and fleshy, fat and concentrated, but discreet, supple and soft at the same time, and it must have definition." For Anne Gros, a generation younger than Jayer, the model is not hugely different. "Harmonious, balanced, ample and concentrated," she says, "but also elegant." Ken Burnap—a onetime restaurateur who has made some excellent pinots at Santa Cruz Mountain Vineyard—said to *Connoisseurs' Guide* in 1977, "Pinot noir is the only red grape variety that is totally honest, totally clean, no gimcracks; no little fancy hints and fringes that never come through. Pinot noir is a strong, hard-hitting, clean red wine. In my experience of drinking wine, it is the one wine that keeps your taste buds alive and perking through dinner. It cuts through all the cream sauces and thick tastes."

Pinot's fans are so enthusiastic about "their" variety that efforts to create straightforward description often turn poetic, and are sometimes transformed into panegyrics. Contrasting pinot with "blockbuster versions" of syrah, cabernet, and merlot, Sarah Kemp, publisher of Britain's *Decanter* magazine, likens pinot noir to a Merchant-Ivory movie—"refined, beautiful, ethereal and intellectually appealing." Its flavors, according to wine writer Oz Clarke, "are sensuous, often erotic, above rational discourse, and beyond the powers of measured criticism." Joel Fleischman wrote ten years ago in *Vanity Fair,* "At their best, pinot noirs are the most romantic of wines, with so voluptuous a perfume, so sweet an edge, and so powerful a punch that, like falling in love, they make the blood run hot and the soul wax embarrassingly poetic." California wine writer Richard Paul Hinkle talks about pinot's "raw, succulent and fleshy textural sensuality" balanced with "inherent elegance and grandeur." Pinot is "a righteous grape," according to Master Sommelier Madeline Triffon, director of wine and beverages for Unique Restaurant Corporation, "chock full of incredible texture and hedonistic pleasures"; it is "sex in a glass," so seductive that "it's very, very hard to say 'no' to." "The king of natural wines," concluded George Saintsbury, 80 years ago, in *Notes on a Cellar-Book,* reflecting on the red Burgundies it had been his privilege to enjoy.

The enthusiasm for pinot noir qua wine is far from universal and unqualified, however. Makers and commentators articulate their models and pen their descriptions, but pinot's broad range of acceptable hues and color density, and its wide organoleptic bandwidth (the range of sensory impressions it conveys to the nose and the palate), still generates confusion even among experienced tasters, whether the wine was grown in Burgundy, North America, or somewhere else. For Jayer, thinking only about Burgundy, "the diversity of styles from one cellar to another" is an essential part of the genius both of grape and of place, and he has professed concern lest the diversity be lost to "vins standards" that are "perfect and perfectly neutral," which he sees looming on Burgundy's horizon. Some winemakers on this side of the Atlantic seem to agree with Jayer, arguing that pinot is the only variety—thus far—to have escaped being "defined" by wine critics, and therefore to remain a safe haven for a relatively broad range of interpretations and styles. But others find that mischief lurks in diversity. John Baxevanis, in *Wine Regions of America,* blames the "passionate opinions" and "lack of consensus" about pinot noir's ideal expression on pinot's intrinsic "lack of varietal identity." This diversity has the baleful effect, he argues, of making pinot "the subject of considerable manipulation either through winemaking processes, or by the addition of other wine to add color, flavor, alcohol, longevity, etc." For wine writer Norm Roby, charged to create tasting panels on a variety-by-variety basis for *Vintage* magazine in the early 1980s, the lack of consensus emerged as a practical problem. He cited major intrapanel rifts over acceptable levels of body, tannins, and volatility, with some tasters preferring a light, delicate style while others privileged intensity of flavor. "For many pinot noirs," Roby reported, "two tasters loved it, two hated it and two felt it was just average in quality." Similar results are reflected in the published notes of San Francisco's Vintners Club, covering tastings held over a 14-year period between 1973 and 1987. Repeatedly, only two or three tasters out of a dozen could agree which wine in each flight was the "best" pinot, and some wines emerged from the tastings ranked simultaneously at the top and the bottom of the heap. Although genuinely pathological disparities of opinion about pinot are less common today than they were 20 years ago, wine juries are rarely unanimous in their assessments of pinot noir, winemakers themselves often disagree on qualitative issues, and individual wines are still rewarded, in the same tasting, with both rave reviews and punishing scores.

Critics and consumers, and sometimes even pinot noir's most avowed fans, complain that pinots can be stubbornly inconsistent, unpredictable, and often downright disappointing. They contrast this misbehavior with the better "manners" shown by fine Bordeaux, syrah-based wines, and reds grown in Northern Italy. These brickbats are cast equally against red Burgundies, North American pinots, and pinots made elsewhere. Several hobgoblins are at work. First, pinot noir makes an unstable wine. There is no nice way to say this, though adjectives like *moody* and *capricious* take off some of the edge. Pinot can show beautifully from barrel and then suffer an acute case of bottle shock. It can taste ethereal one day, but then close down to a shadow of its former self. California wine writer Dan Berger calls pinot "enigmatic," complaining that the same wine is "flamboyant and engaging" at one moment and "acerbic and angular" at another. Pinot is certainly more susceptible than gutsier varieties to damage from excessive heat, and it can be traumatized by rough transport.

Kermit Lynch, the California-based importer of fine Burgundy, remembers his experience with the 1972 vintage of Hubert de Montille's Volnay Champans, which arrived dumb in California, having suffered from its oceanic traverse. "Put it in a cool cellar for six months," de Montille counseled the worried importer. Lynch did, and the wine recovered, but Lynch wisely used refrigerated containers for future shipments, in an effort to mitigate pinot's mood swings.

Conversely, pinots can improve spontaneously and unpredictably when they are three, five, or eight years old. Five years after the vintage, Iron Horse Vineyards' first edition of vineyard-designated pinot noir, from the Thomas Road Vineyard—a slightly lightweight but very charming wine in its youth—inexplicably put on weight in the bottle and gained layers of complexity not at all associated with age.

Second, there is substantial discontinuity between really good pinot noir, wherever it is grown, and lesser wines made from the same grape. Everything short of really good seems irretrievably mediocre. This curse, which may be rooted in pinot's legendary transparency and fragility, along with its extreme sensitivity to being overcropped, explains why so much Bourgogne Rouge offers only the palest hint of a fine Gevrey, Echézeaux, or Volnay, and why large lots of industrial North American pinot noir echo fine vineyard-designates and microblends only faintly. It also explains why so-called entry-level pinot, priced inexpensively, is so hard to find. It is also the best available answer to Jim Clendenen's otherwise reasonable plaint, in a 1998 address to the Napa Valley Wine Library, that consumers and critics reserve a special onus for pinot noir, demanding that *all* pinot noir be conceived as "the ultimate in greatness." Consumers permit a majority of cabernet sauvignon, zinfandel, syrah, and nebbiolo to exist respectably as "delicious, serviceable, and tremendously versatile wines," Clendenen observed accurately, while they obstinately hold pinot to a higher standard. The inconvenient fact is that when pinot noir is *not* held to a higher standard, it is usually much less than delicious. *Serviceable pinot noir* is not quite an oxymoron, but it comes close.

Finally, pinot noir, in all its manifestations, suffers from the scarcity of *individual* wines. The total acreage planted to pinot noir in the Côte d'Or is not much less than the total vineyard acreage in the Haut-Médoc and St.-Emilion combined, and there is only a little less *grand cru* Burgundy made in an average year than there is first-growth Bordeaux. But of *each* first-growth Bordeaux (except Château Ausone) 12,000 to 33,000 cases are made, against a paltry couple hundred (and sometimes less) by most producers lucky enough to own a slice of Le Chambertin, Bonnes-Mares, or Clos du Tart. Burgundian patterns of landholding do not constrain the North American scene, but individual benchmark pinots on this side of the Atlantic are very often produced, with uncanny similarity to *grand cru* Burgundy, on an almost Lilliputian scale, usually because the output of a small vineyard is deliberately divided by its owner among several client wineries. In Burgundy, the multiplicity of small producers leads to huge differences between the best wine made from Bonnes-Mares (for example) and the worst, and to disappointed consumers who forswear Burgundies entirely after mistakenly spending a lot of good money on the worst. North America largely escapes the good-and-bad Bonnes-Mares problem, but increasingly shares with Burgundy the downside of very many wines produced in very small quantities of each. The basic law of very small supply and modestly large demand sends prices soaring and creates offensive discontinuities between price and value.

Under the circumstances, it is perhaps not surprising that wine literature is awash in bittersweet love-hate vocabulary about pinot noir. For every superlative, there is a countervailing reservation; for every rapturous evaluation, there is somewhere an angry critic or disappointed consumer. Burgundians have lived long enough with pinot noir to have become accustomed to its ways and to accept its foibles as the price of sometimes stunning wine. But on this continent, aspiring winemakers and unhappy critics have embraced an odd vocabulary redolent of epic strife and operatic drama without which, it seems, no story about pinot noir is ever complete. The variety is said to be capricious, petulant, tantalizing, and even quixotic. Dan Berger says it is "cursed with a personality so sour it would make the grinch look like Santa Claus." Its makers are said to be "lunatic-fringe" questers after "the Holy Grail." Marc de Villiers's book about one of North America's pinot pioneers is titled *The Heartbreak Grape.* This is all good fun, but in the following pages, I will attempt a slightly more sober approach.

Chapter 2

THE BURGUNDIAN CONNECTION

Burgundy lies about 170 miles southeast of Paris, astride the main medieval trade routes linking the Mediterranean with the "new" cities of northern Europe, and bisected now by the high-speed rail line from Paris to Lyon. Defined as the Région Bourgogne, it covers just over 12,000 square miles, or about three times the area of Los Angeles County. Burgundy is mostly green fields and woodland, sustaining dairy farming and an assortment of field crops—including seeds for Dijon's famous mustards. France's Charolais beef takes its name from the town of Charolles, near Mâcon in the southern part of the region; and the cheeses made at St.-Florentin in the Yonne, and at Cîteaux, where the Cistercian monks set up shop at the end of the eleventh century, are known throughout France. The region's name is perpetually linked to *boeuf à la bourgignonne,* beef cooked with vegetables in red wine; *muerettes,* a generic form of food preparation with a thickened red wine sauce; and escargots, which are a local specialty. Burgundy's towns are mostly tiny; scattered hamlets are common; and even the administrative capital at Dijon boasts a smaller population than Eugene in Oregon.

Apart from Chablis in the north, vineyards are important mostly along the region's eastern edge, where the Saône River flows south from its origins in Champagne to its confluence with the Rhône at Lyon. Pinot noir is grown almost the full length of the Saône valley, but for pinotphiles worldwide, the focus of attention is a 30-mile strip of mostly east- and southeast-facing slopes on the Saône's west bank, beginning (at the north end) where Marsannay gets disentangled from the suburban fringes of Dijon and ending in the picturesque hills around Santenay. Santenay is a minor hot-spring-fed spa west of Chagny. Throughout this area, since the middle of the nineteenth century, village names have been hyphenated with the names of the greatest local vineyards, and nearly everyone earns a living, directly or indirectly, from wine. The typical vintner lives powerfully close to his product, occupying the upper floors of a house whose street and basement levels are dedicated to crushers, fermentors, tanks, and barrels.

The French name for this area, and for the administrative jurisdiction that encloses it, is the Côte d'Or or, more commonly, just La Côte. The section from Beaune north is also called the Côte de Nuits, for the town of Nuits-St.-Georges; the southern section is also called the Côte de Beaune. Unfortunately, French commentators and French-English translators have taken the *or* in Côte d'Or a bit too literally, birthing renditions such as Golden Slope and Gold Coast in English. But as Richard Olney has demonstrated in his impeccably researched book on Romanée-Conti, Côte d'Or is actually a contraction of Côte d'Orient, meaning simply the east-facing side of the hills. The only gold in these hills lines the pockets of its wealthiest winemakers.

TERROIR, VITICULTURE, AND NOMENCLATURE IN THE CÔTE D'OR

The Côte d'Or straddles the 47th north parallel, putting it on the same latitude as Olympia, Washington, and (astonishingly) St. Johns, Newfoundland—and giving Beaune 15.5 hours of daylight on the longest day of each year, a full hour more than pinot regions on California's Central Coast. Its climate, often described as continental, is actually transitional. Summers are warm but rarely hot, with summer daytime high temperatures in the low 80s; and winters, though dusted with snow, are neither long nor bitter. Alfresco lunches are often possible in February and March. Hills protect the vineyards from westerly winds and inclement weather, creating a climate that is slightly warmer and drier than that of the surrounding countryside. Rainfall is spread throughout the year. May and June both have a tendency to be wet, confounding many tourists. Budbreak for pinot noir normally occurs in early April, flowering in early June, veraison (the point in the growing season when grapes develop color) in mid August, and harvest in late September, though year-to-year variations can move the typical dates by 20 days in either direction.

The bedrock of the Côte d'Or consists of various types and ages of limestone, some of which, around Comblanchien north of Beaune, is quarried for marble. But the surface soil is only unevenly laced with limestone debris, the balance being flint, nonlimestone gravels, and clay. Generally and unsurprisingly, the upper slopes exhibit thinner surface soils and more omnipresent limestone than lower elevations, making them more suitable, it is usually thought, for chardonnay than for pinot noir.

The main challenge in Burgundy, in most vintages, is coaxing the grapes to ripen fully. This challenge is endemic to so-called marginal climates, where heat accumulation is barely sufficient to ripen the fruit, and the final stage of ripening falls at the very end of the growing season. Sometimes Mother Nature gets the job done alone, combining a warm summer with a long, dry autumn. Sometimes rigorous yield management in the vineyard is sufficient to turn the trick: grapes ripen faster when fewer bunches are left on each vine. But six years out of ten, Burgundian vignerons harvest grapes containing less sugar than they need to make the kind of wine they want, compelling them to add sugar during fermentation. Whether a thus chaptalized pinot is any better or worse than a pinot whose sugar was produced wholly in the vineyard is not entirely clear. Most Burgundians argue simply that chaptalization does no harm. Others explain that, if performed incrementally throughout the fermentation, it can be beneficial, extending the fermentation's overall length. But no less an authority than Lalou Bize-Leroy, producer of some of Burgundy's most respected wines, waxed enthusiastic about her 1999 Corton-Renardes precisely because it reached an astonishing (for Burgundy) 14.9 percent alcohol *without chaptalization,* saying she was impressed by "how the alcohol seemed balanced" because "it did *not* come from added sugar." Whatever the truth, chaptalization is a fact of life in Burgundy more than half the time. Winemakers and viticulturists on both sides of the Atlantic also comment on an inexplicable curiosity of Burgundy: that Burgundian pinot may taste riper at lower levels of sugar than pinot grown in North America. The green flavors of underripeness are said to be less pronounced, and the best flavors are produced against a backdrop of less sugar. This phenomenon is no better understood than the qualitative impact, if any, of chaptalization.

The complexity of the Côte d'Or's viticultural map is legendary. More than 1,000 site names are recognized, almost half of which are *lieux-dits* (rural sites with recognized names) within the territories that produce the Côte's two dozen so-called village wines. The list also includes 476 vineyard sites officially classified as *premier crus,* and 32 *grand cru* vineyards, which, in theory, produce Burgundy's greatest wines. Almost all these sites are very small. Of the *grand cru* vineyards owned by Domaine de la Romanée-Conti, for example, only Romanée-St.-Vivant is larger than 20 acres; La Romanée-Conti itself is just 4.5 acres. In the commune of Vosne-Romanée, six of the ten *premier cru* vineyards are smaller than ten acres, and only one is larger than 20. Of the 19 *premier cru* sites in nearby Chambolle-Musigny, 13 are smaller than ten acres, and none is larger than 15. Two flyspeck vineyards in Chambolle, Derrière-la-Grange and Les Combottes (not to be confused with the larger Aux Combottes vineyard), have a surface of less than two acres each.

This mosaic of tiny pieces contrasts so dramatically with wine appellations in North America that comparisons on this score are almost meaningless. In the United States, all names of states and counties may be used as appellations of origin for wine, as may the names of American viticultural areas approved by the TTB. The smallest of the last is Cole Ranch in California's Mendocino County (which does not produce pinot noir); but at 150 acres, it is still twice the size of Echézeaux. American viticultural areas most associated with pinot noir, like Russian River, Los Carneros, and Oregon's Willamette Valley, each cover many tens of thousands of acres, of which multiple thousands are planted to wine grapes. The Burgundian arrangement, whose decoupage is finer than in any other part of France, is generally taken as evidence of pinot noir's legendary transparency—that it is hugely sensitive to site and produces quite different results in soils or exposures that, despite proximity, are subtly different. But vineyards now planted exclusively to chardonnay are no less finely delineated than those dedicated to pinot, and chardonnay is generally believed to show less the influence of specific sites.

Of all of France's wine regions, according to Alexis Lichine, "Burgundy was the first to have close attention paid to its subtle differences from vineyard to vineyard." Close attention to effects of site on the organoleptic properties of wine is said to have begun with the Cistercians, whose involvement with Burgundian viticulture was intimate. It is said, though not very reliably documented, that the Cistercian monks "tasted the soil" in an effort to understand how site became imprinted on wine. Whatever the Cistercian role, the tradition of tiny *lieux-dits* associated with wine production was well established by the eighteenth century. Many *lieux-dits* are part of the controlled appellation laws drafted in 1936.

To compound matters further, more than 3,000 growers till the Côte d'Or's 14,000 acres of vineyard. Of these, 2,700 own less than 12 acres each; fewer than 200 own more than 25 acres. Since almost no vineyard, no matter how tiny, is owned in its entirety by a single proprietor—the handful of exceptions are called *monopoles* and are clearly and proudly announced as such on wine labels—the mosaic of site names is overlaid and subdivided once again by the fact of multiple ownership. Clos de Vougeot is famous for its division among, at last count, 73 owners. At Chambertin Clos de Bèze, 37 acres are divided among 25 owners. This circumstance—which results from land division at the time of the French Revolution, Napoleonic prohibitions against primogeniture, and the economic burdens imposed, even today, by the French system of inheritance taxation—leaves most Burgundian vignerons with an interesting combination of assets and liabilities. Even those owning fairly substantial acreage overall hold a patchwork quilt of lands: a few rows of vines here and there, scattered across several communes and many *lieux-dits.* This situation means trips in many directions to tend one's vines year-round, and much hauling of grapes at harvesttime. It also means plenty of opportunity for errors if an improperly supervised picker misidentifies rows. It could generate a rich palette of components if the vigneron were inclined to blend wines, but the typical Burgundian will not, having too much respect for small distinctions among sites. On the other hand, scattered holdings are excellent insurance against accidents of nature, especially summer hailstorms. The typical vigneron may not cultivate enough Vosne Aux Brûlées, for example, to make than one or two barrels of wine.

To appreciate how stunningly fine-grained Burgundy's vineyard and ownership divisions really are, consider the following: if every grape in Burgundy were harvested by the vine's owner; if every owner bottled his own wine; and if every wine were labeled for the most specific geographic designation to which it is entitled (none of which is the case), there would be less than one case of finished wine made per proprietor per vineyard. The countervailing truth, however, is this: no less than 53 percent of Burgundy's wine production is "generic" wine—Bourgogne Blanc, Bourgogne Rouge, or Bourgogne Grand Ordinaire—which the Burgundy wine establishment must work hard to sell for a respectable price.

CENTURIES OF TRADITION, CENTURIES OF EVOLUTION

The oft-repeated generalization about winemaking in Burgundy is the fact of its antiquity. North American vintners often cite Burgundy's "centuries" of winemaking experience as a sort of apologia for their own shortcomings. The Burgundians, they observe, have been making pinot much longer than anyone in North America, so it follows logically that they should be the variety's acknowledged masters. (Curiously, the same argument is rarely made about chardonnay, though the circumstances are nearly identical.) For Burgundian vignerons, the region's long history is often brandished as a competitive advantage. In this view, Burgundies should have nothing to fear from New World upstarts. Whether one believes that pinot noir is native to Burgundy or that it was imported sometime during the Middle Ages, it obviously has been tended in Burgundy for many centuries.

It is also inarguable that most of Burgundy's currently practicing winemakers are the sons or daughters, grandchildren, or great-grandchildren of winemakers, whereas there is barely even a second-generation winemaker to be found anyplace in the New World. It is, however, easy to overestimate the weight and significance of history in Burgundy. The French Revolution changed everything, of course, as vineyards were confiscated from the church and the aristocracy, ownership was redistributed to bourgeois families, and wine expertise was transferred to a new social class. Before the Revolution, entire vineyards were the property of single families—Burgundy was, in other words, composed mostly of *monopoles*—and it was the Revolution's aftermath that created the modern patchwork quilt of fragmented ownership and cultivation. The fragmentation of ownership, in turn, enabled Burgundy's great merchant houses, founded in the eighteenth and nineteenth centuries, to dominate its wine business for a century and a half, and to monopolize the expertise associated with winemaking (or at least blending and *élevage*) until the middle of the twentieth century. Most of the grandfathers and great-grandfathers of today's winemakers did not make any finished wine; instead they sold grapes or partially finished wine to *négociants.*

Meanwhile, in the vineyard, even varieties ebbed and flowed. Philip the Bold's fourteenth-century *acte* reserving the best vineyard sites for pinot was by no means universally observed, and several varieties other than pinot and chardonnay thrived, even in the Côte d'Or, until quite recently. Aligoté was important within the memory of many living winemakers, and there is still a bit of aligoté in production around Meursault. Entire appellations changed color, in some cases more than once.

Beaune's vineyards were primarily planted to white grapes in the nineteenth century; and Chassagne, in the eighteenth century, was famous for its red wines. Alexis Lichine tells us that one bottle of red wine from Chassagne Morgeot was then worth two bottles of white Montrachet. In Puligny, the vineyards of Les Pucelles, Clavaillon, and Les Caillerets were also red-wine producers. Lavalle wrote in 1855 that Puligny's reds were as good as the best anywhere in the Côte de Beaune. Beaune's vineyards were not shifted from a majority presence of chardonnay to a 95 percent dominance of pinot noir until the beginning of the past century. And in Chassagne, as recently as 1979, the ratio of pinot noir to chardonnay was 55 to 45; now the only pinot in Chassagne is a few plots of old vines.

Phylloxera, which all but completely destroyed European vineyards at the end of the nineteenth century, did not spare Burgundy, and it changed local viticulture fundamentally. If the modern Burgundian vineyard is planted two to five times more densely than its modern New World counterpart, Burgundy's vineyards were denser still before phylloxera, approximating 5,000 vines per acre. Nor were the vines arranged in today's modern rows, each plant a grafting of budwood to rootstock. Instead, vines were propagated by bending and burying the cane of an adjacent vine until the buried segment self-rooted, guaranteeing the genetic identity of new plants with old, but creating a wild jumble of vegetation in the field, scarcely recognizable as a vineyard by today's standards.

Vinifications and wines, too, changed completely over the centuries. In the eighteenth century, Savigny was described as a "delicate pink wine"; Nuits-St.-Georges made wines "to keep for the following year"; and Volnay's reds were prized *en primeur,* much like modern Beaujolais. A century later, rosés were out of fashion and the marketplace had begun to demand darker and longer-fermented reds. Even a wine like Romanée-Conti was not exempt from changing tastes. In the eighteenth century, it was made with 20 percent white grapes (pinot blanc and pinot gris), fermented just 12 to 36 hours, and kept three years in (old) barrels before it was bottled. By 1850, the percentage of white grapes blended with pinot noir at Romanée-Conti was down to 6 percent, the fermentation had been drawn out to four days, and the wine was barreled for four to five years.

At the beginning of the twentieth century—before the controlled appellation laws were drafted, much less enforced—red Burgundies were routinely adulterated with fat, coarse, warm-climate wines from the Languedoc, Algeria, and Spain. Lichine tells us that Pommard in particular was a "label umbrella" for these blended reds, generating the "thick, typical Burgundies for which the Belgians, Dutch and English were clamoring." Thus began, he explains, "the misleading cliché that Burgundies are thick, mouthfilling wines"—an association that probably explains why post-Prohibition "Burgundy" made in California was a big red blend based on zinfandel, and typically heavier than what was sold as "claret." Even after controlled appellation enforcement ended the worst abuses of adulteration, Burgundies remained, in the 1940s and 1950s, "sturdier" than they are today, a fact that Clive Coates attributes to low yields and the old age of the first generation of postphylloxera vines. Yields then marched upward, increasing from a typical one ton per acre to two tons in the 1960s, and to 2.5 tons in the 1970s.

The point is clear enough. No one should imagine that Burgundy is a story of patient, incremental improvements in viticulture and winemaking, with each new generation learning from the last. On the contrary, Burgundy's historical landscape is littered with U-turns, the pursuit of fleeting changes in consumer preferences, and wholesale alterations to the structure of its wine business. On the other hand, the sites themselves do have remarkable continuity, and the advantage of having grown grapes in persistent sites for centuries is incontrovertible. North American vintners, hard pressed to find more than a handful of sites where pinot has been planted for even half a century, ought to envy the Burgundian vigneron's ability to discover, for example, just when grapes were harvested from a given site in a warm year at the end of the previous century, or to consult a surviving father who can remember how long his Pommard Les Epénots was vatted in, say, 1938.

No change in Burgundy is more important to the story of pinot noir in North America than the renaissance that swept Burgundy in the 1980s. In one sense this renaissance was the culmination of a revolt with origins in the 1930s, when a handful of gutsy, farsighted growers turned against the Beaune and Nuits-based *négociants.* Growers like Armand Rousseau, the marquis d'Angerville, and Henri Gouges began to finish, bottle, and sell their own wines, offering them primarily to importers like Gerald Asher in England and Frank Schoonmaker in the United States. The *négociants* attempted unsuccessfully to isolate the mavericks by refusing to purchase any grapes, must, or wine from any of them. Still, as late as the end of the 1940s, according to Lichine, only "a few hundred cases from the whole Côte d'Or" were sold by producers *directly to consumers.*

Gradually, this picture changed. Estate bottling and estate merchandising became the Burgundian rule. Growers sold not only to foreign importers but also to French restaurants and retailers, as well as to a growing stable of individual consumers. Lichine paints a colorful picture of this revolution: "Our erstwhile artisans have become little retailers, transforming Burgundy into an enormous wine bazaar. Beginning at Easter and continuing in an ever-increasing stream through the summer, the small courtyards of the growers in Chassagne, Meursault, Pommard, Vosne, and Gevrey are filled with wine-thirsty customers, eager to meet the proprietor directly." Lichine dubbed the new grower-producer "Monsieur Vente-Directe." Only a handful of the old *négociant* firms survived this epochal redistribution of talent and resources, primarily because they had the genius to purchase substantial vineyard land of their own—a trend that continues.

But there was much more to the Burgundian renaissance than estate bottling and estate-based sales. There were also hugely important advances in enology, better equipment, and (for the first time in Burgundy) handsome profits from wine. These profits bought university educations for the baby-boom generation of winemakers and their children; airplane tickets to viticultural conferences and wine fairs; and internships around the world. Growers' children, armed with degrees in enology from the universities at Dijon and Montpellier and certificates from the Lycée agricole in Beaune, returned to their home villages eager to assume responsibility for vineyards and vinifications, and to bask in the prosperity that had come to simple agriculture. They abandoned the postwar reliance on chemical fertilizers and herbicides, which had nearly wrecked Burgundy's fine vineyards, and turned with enthusiasm to sustainable, organic, and even biodynamic agricultural practices. In the cellars, they embraced (perhaps a trifle too enthusiastically) a preponderance of new oak barrels, state-of-the-art crusher-destemmers, gentle membrane presses, and better hygiene. Insatiably curious in ways their fathers never were, they tasted in one another's cellars, comparing notes on methods and sites, and were not above tasting a few wines from overseas as well, the better to understand the global marketplace for fine wine.

At least two outsiders played a huge role in the renaissance. Jacques Seysses, a Parisian with experience as a banker in New York and wealth inherited from his family's Belin biscuit business, purchased a little-known *domaine* at Morey-St.-Denis in 1966. Armed with experience working at Volnay's esteemed Domaine de la Pousse d'Or, Seysses created the Burgundian rarity: a new *domaine.* Not only did Domaine Dujac soar rapidly into the ranks of Burgundy's most respected producers, but Seysses also mentored an entire generation of young winemakers and catalyzed dialogue among pinot makers around the world.

The other outsider of note is Jean-Pierre de Smet, a Niçois by birth, who worked the 1977 vintage at Dujac and subsequently studied enology at Dijon. In 1987, de Smet helped the French insurance giant AXA purchase the Vienot family's estate in Nuits-St.-Georges, which he and AXA have run since under the name Domaine de l'Arlot, sharing a talented vineyardist with Dujac until the latter's untimely death in 2001.

Many of Seysses's other protégés have taken family *domaines* throughout the Côte d'Or to international levels of quality prominence. Christophe Roumier in Chambolle, Denis Mortet in Gevrey, Anne Gros and Etienne Grivot in Vosne, and Patrick Bize in Savigny all come to mind. Some of the old *négociants* have passed from the scene, of course, having been deprived of grapes and wine by the triumph of estate bottling. But others—such as Joseph Faiveley and Joseph Drouhin, led by sons François and Robert, respectively—have reinvented themselves, purchasing distinguished vineyard sites in appellations throughout the Côte and dedicating themselves to the pursuit of the highest quality.

The renaissance has also affected, in its turn, the stylistic parameters of red Burgundy. At Romanée-Conti, vatting times were extended from the short nineteenth-century norm to as much as three weeks. Seeking more forward fruit, several good producers adopted cold macerations. But there is no consensus on these matters. Louis Latour, for one, is skeptical. On the eve of his retirement in 2001 from the venerable (and successful) *négociant* house that bears his and his grandfather's name, Latour inveighed against Burgundy's contemporary "infatuation" with long vattings and "gadget-vinifications." The "norm," he insisted, should be the six- to seven-day vatting "introduced" in the nineteenth century.

Postrenaissance Burgundy is so dramatically different from the Burgundy of half a century earlier that a prewar Burgundian, reborn and dropped today into a village of the Côte de Nuits, might recognize nothing more than the steeple of his village church. And no evolution has had a more profound impact on pinot in the rest of the world than this rebirth of pride, dedication, and the pursuit of excellence in the variety's historic heartland. We shall see, in the next chapter, how it is fundamental to the rise to prominence of pinot noir in North America.

Chapter 3

THE RISE OF PINOT NOIR IN NORTH AMERICA

Pinot noir, we are told by Jancis Robinson, "travels sullenly." In a memorable and oft-repeated phrase, Robinson contrasts pinot's alleged aptitudes with those of cabernet sauvignon, which "happily packs its bags and travels about the world." One could be excused for assuming that pinot noir was an especially rare or tardy import to North America, or that it failed here more persistently than did other varieties of vinifera. Unsurprisingly, the real story, inevitably woven in and around the whole history of wine in North America, is rather more complex. Pinot noir was present almost from the beginning of North America's adventures with vinifera, and it received attention almost second to none.

There is no evidence that pinot figured among the persistent efforts of the eastern colonists and early republicans to propagate vinifera, which began as early as 1619 in Virginia and continued, in various locations east of the Mississippi River and in Missouri, until the early part of the nineteenth century. There were hundreds of documented trials during this period, and doubtless many more for which documentation has disappeared—some involving named varieties, others dealing more or less anonymously with "European" or just "foreign" grapes. The bottom line is that all those trials succumbed, often before the vines had fruited for the first time, to various combinations of climate and disease, of which endemic phylloxera was the most relentless, having no known remedy until the end of the nineteenth century. It is therefore of only academic interest whether pinot noir was among the varieties imported by would-be viticulturists in the eastern states. If it was, it perished quite democratically alongside all other vinifera, leaving no progeny. The early wine industry of the eastern states was built instead on native American grape varieties until, in the second half of the nineteenth century, it shifted toward newly developed hybrids.

CALIFORNIA'S FIRST PINOT NOIR

On the West Coast of North America, the environment was entirely different. There the climate was hospitable to vinifera, disease pressure was low, and phylloxera (until the 1860s) was nonexistent. The first vinifera in what is now California was the so-called mission grape, imported from Mexico by the Franciscan padres who, beginning in 1715, established the chain of missions that stretches from San Diego to Sonoma. Mission is genetically identical to Chilean pais and to at least one subvariety of what the Argentines call criolla, the Old World parents of which have not yet been identified.

Following the start of the California Gold Rush in 1848, California viticulture entered a new phase, driven by an unprecedented wave of immigration from Europe and the first serious development of agribusinesses. French and German orchardists and vineyardists seem to have imported many of the major European varieties during the 1850s. The first importer of pinot noir may have been Pierre Pellier, a native son of La Rochelle, who is said to have landed in California for the first time about 1852, and then again in 1856, bearing vines on both occasions. Secondary sources say that pinot noir was "perhaps" among Pellier's imports, which, along with some fruit trees, were apparently the foundation for a successful family farm and nursery business in California's Santa Clara Valley. Or the first importer may have been the infamous Colonel Agoston Haraszthy de Mokcsa, the founder of Sonoma's Buena Vista Winery. Haraszthy, who seems to have been a shameless self-promoter, claimed to have no less than 158 grape varieties under cultivation at Buena Vista in 1858. Four years later, he was also the kingpin in a subscription scheme to import an even wider array of grape varieties, offering subscribers 25 varieties for $25, 50 varieties for $50, or "two cuttings of every grape variety now in cultivation in the civilized world" for a mere $500. Armed with a commission from the governor of California and its legislature, Haraszthy toured Europe's wine regions, including "Dijon, Gevrey, Chambertin, and Clos Vougeot," returning in 1862 with cuttings from some unknown number of "varieties." In *A History of Wine in America,* Thomas Pinney observes that Haraszthy first claimed to have imported 1,400 varieties, then reduced his claim to 300, and finally published a catalog offering 492 varieties for sale—including pinot noir. But Haraszthy's venture was surrounded by a jumble of confusion. Many of his vine cuttings were collected not directly from European vineyards but rather from intermediaries. Their identities were garbled in transshipment, or they were simply mislabeled, and the preponderance seem not to have been successfully propagated.

A third candidate for first importer of pinot noir is Charles Lefranc (1824–1887), whose name still figured, albeit in small type, on bottles of wine produced under the Almaden label in the 1960s. Lefranc, who emigrated from France in 1850 and founded New Almaden Vineyards later in the decade, is said to have imported "from the Champagne country of France" the pinot vines that were the foundation for the early successes of the Paul Masson Champagne Company in the 1890s. But Lefranc and New Almaden were famous primarily for their Bordeaux-type wines, and the story about pinot from Champagne cannot be confirmed in contemporaneous sources.

In any case, whether the first importer was Pellier, Haraszthy, Lefranc, or some less documented vineyardist may be of only academic interest. Pinot noir attracted little attention in the 1850s. Neither, for that matter, did cabernet sauvignon. Among red vinifera varieties, only zinfandel—for reasons completely unrelated to its obscure European pedigree—seems to have gained a significant toehold in California at the time.

In the 1880s, when Americans began to realize how gravely European vineyards had been devastated by phylloxera, it occurred to entrepreneurs bloated with pioneer hubris that California might have an opportunity to *replace* Europe as the world's main source for good wine. Assessing the baseline from which this enterprise would need to be launched, Charles A. Wetmore, chief executive officer of the Board of State Viticultural Commissioners, which he had helped to found, did not exude optimism in 1884. "Not a single bearing vineyard [is] planted systematically with the varieties necessary to reproduce the types of Bordeaux clarets, Burgundies, Sauternes, Hermitage, Portuguese port, Spanish sherry, Madeira or Cognac," he wrote to the legislature. Of pinot noir, he observed that it "is not yet cultivated in any quantity sufficient to give token of its merits in this state." But a series of articles about wine and brandy production in France that Wetmore had written in the 1870s fanned his contemporaries' interest in vinifera, and a small varietal fever gripped California regardless.

Hiram Crabb, an Ohioan who had begun growing grapes near Oakville in the Napa Valley in 1865, developed one of the largest vine collections in the world during the 1880s, primarily by grafting "foreign varieties" onto rootstocks of mission and zinfandel. His catalog of cuttings for sale, published in 1882, includes pinot noir. Crabb subsequently became famous for a variety called Black Burgundy, sometimes dubbed eponymously Crabb's Black Burgundy, which some of Crabb's contemporaries appear to have mistaken for pinot noir, probably on the basis of its name. (In fact, Black Burgundy was mondeuse—known in Italy as refosco—the variety responsible for the light red wines of the Savoie.)

The *Merchant,* a San Francisco newspaper that covered agricultural matters regularly during this period, reported in April 1883 that John H. Drummond, an "enthusiastic vigneron" whose Dunfillan Vineyard (near Glen Ellen in Sonoma) "will be known by its products to every connoisseur of wine in the United States," had obtained some vines within California from both Wetmore and Crabb, but had also imported "truly named cuttings of every variety of vine that promises to be adaptable to the soil and climate of Glen Ellen." Among Drummond's imports, according to the *Merchant,* were "Franc Pinot," "Norien," and "Pinot de Pernand"—all legitimate paranyms for pinot noir—brought from "the Bourgogne" in 1881; and "Pinot Noir d'Epernay," brought from Champagne in 1883. Apparently European plant collectors also figured among the sources for American importers, because Drummond is also said to have imported "Pinot de Coulanges" from "the collection of Mr. Henry Vilmorin in Paris" in 1883. Coulanges is a village about four kilometers northeast of Beaune, so Pinot de Coulanges was almost certainly another paranym for pinot noir. Drummond made a still, blush-colored wine from one or more of his pinot selections, called Oeil de Perdrix, which seems to have enjoyed a good reputation.

Drummond and Wetmore also appear to have exchanged cuttings. On October 10, 1884, the *Merchant* reported that Drummond had sent Wetmore "a splendid collection of grapes grown at his Dunfillan Vineyard. . . . It is the largest collection that has ever been received and displayed at the offices of the State Viticultural Commission" and "has been seen and admired by hundreds of visitors." Pinot noir, in the form of the aforementioned Pinot de Pernand and Pinot Noir d'Epernay, figured explicitly on the list of 93 varieties that Drummond supplied to Wetmore. On October 23, 1885, Drummond advertised "Important Vine Stocks for Sale" in the *Merchant,* including Franc Pinot "from Vougeot and Beaune in the Bourgogne," which was described as "a fair bearer" that "yields the most famous wines of Burgundy"; and Pinot de Pernand, here described as "a good bearer, giving a wine of high-class Burgundy character."

Wetmore, Crabb, and Drummond were by no means the only actors in the varietal drama of the 1880s, nor the only pioneers with pinot noir. A "special correspondent" to the *Merchant* reported in 1885 that "Messrs Guthrie and McCartney," the owners of the Los Guilicos Ranch eight miles south of Santa Rosa in the Sonoma Valley, "have imported 3000 vines from France," among which "Pinot Noir Fin," "Pino Noir Gross," Pinot Blanc, Mondeuse, and Caesar were said to have come "from Burgundy." Just north of Santa Rosa, at the end of the 1870s, an unlikely cast of characters—including a viticulturist from Missouri, a mystical prophet from New York, and a "prince" from Japan—planted 400 acres of vineyard to some combination of cabernet sauvignon, zinfandel, and pinot noir, but the source (or sources) of the plant materials for this so-called Fountaingrove Vineyard does not seem to have been recorded. In 1886, the *Merchant* reported on a "very valuable collection" of grapes placed on exhibition by a "Mrs. Warfield of Glen Ellen," the proprietor of Ten Oaks Vineyard, which included Pinot de Pernand ("a great bearer of fine Burgundy type and high keeping quality"), Franc Pinot ("the celebrated wine of Clos Vougeot"), something called Black Pinot "from the Champagne," and Gamay Teinturier "from Beaune in Burgundy." Whether Mrs. Warfield obtained these varieties from her neighbor Drummond or imported them separately is not known.

In Napa, the legendary Captain Gustav Niebaum, founder of Inglenook, is reported to have visited European vineyards extensively and repeatedly, to have collected a huge library on wines and vines, and to have imported no small number of grapevines. There is no incontrovertible evidence that he imported pinot noir, but Robert Lawrence Balzer, the dean of California wine writers immediately after World War II, reports in his 1948 book *California's Best Wines* that John Daniel, the post-war owner of Inglenook, served him a bottle of estate-bottled Inglenook Pinot Noir from the 1892 vintage, described as "one of Niebaum's first fine vintages." Balzer found the wine "delicate, fruity and undeniably pinot." Not far away, on Spring Mountain, one Tiburcio Parrot, the son of a San Francisco businessman and millionaire, was apparently growing pinot at the end of the 1880s; his Miravelle estate (now Spring Mountain Vineyard) produced a "pinot noir labeled Chambertin." In Los Carneros, it is possible (but not certain) that Judge John Stanly, whose La Loma ranch was planted in the 1880s, included pinot noir.

Nor was the action confined to Napa and Sonoma. At Chateau Bellevue in the Livermore valley, Alexander Duval, a Bordelais by birth who is said "to have passed his early years in the Burgundy district," "personally superintended the planting of 160 acres and has only the choicest French varieties, including the Sauterne as well as the Côte d'Or grapes." Nearby, a Mr. A. B. Henderson, managing editor of the *San Francisco Examiner,* "followed the bent of his neighbors" by planting "high-grade grapes" including "Petite Pinot." In her 1889 book, *Wines and Vines of California,* Frona Wait observes that "superior wines are being and will continue to be made [in Livermore] from the well-known stocks . . . including the Burgundy family." Wait goes on to accept Crabb's Black Burgundy into this family, observing (perhaps accurately) that it was "more prolific than the Noirien or Pinot Moir [*sic*] of the Côte d'Or and better suited for wines destined for transportation," but suggesting inaccurately that it was a type of pinot noir.

Jean-Baptiste Jules Portal was almost certainly another early importer of pinot noir. Portal established the Burgundy Vineyard near Cupertino in 1872, propagating vine-stocks he imported from France. Portal seems to have used his pinot noir in various red blends. Farther south, on Santa Cruz Island off the coast of Santa Barbara, San Francisco merchant Justinian Caire planted pinot noir alongside cabernet sauvignon, petite sirah, and zinfandel in the 1880s, and his wines are said to have enjoyed a good reputation.

Clearly, pinot noir was part of the minitempest of enthusiasm for European varieties that washed over California in the 1880s. It was never excluded from lists of varieties offered for sale, or from hymns to California's potential to grow fine wines. But just as clearly, almost from the outset, pinot noir had the character of an also-ran variety: impossible to ignore because of the great wines made from it in Burgundy, but never attracting the same attention that was lavished on varieties from Bordeaux. For all his work with pinot noir, Drummond remained primarily interested in cabernet and merlot, and these varieties were the basis for Dunfillan Vineyard's most successful wines. The same can be said, apparently, for most of the growers in Napa.

It has been widely assumed, in the light of subsequent history, that California's lesser interest in pinot stemmed from difficulties growing it, but this is true only in part. In the second half of the nineteenth century, Bordeaux was infinitely more visible than Burgundy. Then, as now, there was a lot more of it available. Owing to centuries of English and Irish involvement in Bordeaux, its wines were well established in London, which was already the most important wine marketplace in the world. In 1853, the Paris-Bordeaux railway was opened for business, bringing Parisians to Bordeaux and clarets to Paris in unprecedented numbers. The growing popularity of Médoc wines was enshrined in the famous classification undertaken for the Paris Exhibition in 1855. Paris bankers, most visibly the Rothschilds, purchased Bordelais châteaux, enhancing their prestige with their own well-known names. Burgundy, by contrast, languished in relative obscurity. Even the best of Burgundy's growers were poor, and the *négociants* of Beaune and Nuits were no match for the international firms that grew up along the Quai des Chartrons in Bordeaux. It is scarcely surprising that California's wine pioneers, who were four parts entrepreneur to every one part connoisseur, and very anxious to establish themselves as the prime beneficiaries of the decimation of Europe's diseased vineyards, focused their attentions first and foremost on the varieties behind clarets and Sauternes, treating pinot noir more or less as an afterthought.

It was no help to pinot's reputation that California's early efforts to coax fine wine from its fruit were fraught with difficulty. In an effort to assist the state's nascent wine industry, the University of California's College of Agriculture had established trial plots of many varieties in various locations around the state, notably at Cupertino, Mission San Jose, and Fresno. Wine was made from trial-plot grapes in the university's "experimental cellars," and the results were published in reports to the Regents of the University. These reports, published in the late 1880s and 1890s, were generally discouraging about pinot noir. There are repeated references to "unevenly ripened" fruit, "overripe bunches with dried berries," musts with "suspicious" smells, and samples that "deteriorated in bottle" because of secondary fermentations. The secondary fermentations were attributed primarily to "the poor condition in which the grapes have been received, it being almost impossible to ship such delicate grapes without crushing them and allowing them to be attacked by injurious organisms, before they can be put into the fermenting vat." Some of the references to dried and overripe berries described grapes received from the university's trial plot in Fresno. The university recognized this problem, saying that "for the hot interior localities, the Pinots must be unhesitatingly rejected." Less helpfully, the university recommended "blending in the fermenting vat [with pinot] some more acid and more robust variety," but admitted this would entail some "sacrifice of [pinot noir's] smooth Burgundy character." The bottom line, the university argued, was that "Bordeaux and Italian varieties" have given "universally . . . much better results than those of Burgundy." In 1889, it concluded about pinot as follows: "Under the conditions of wine-making in California, it is next to impossible to make and keep a perfectly sound wine of Pinots alone. In some locations it is doubtless possible to make a Pinot wine of high quality and to age it, but only with a minute attention to detail and an elaborate care, which no price that is likely to be obtained at present would justify. The grapes would have to be picked at exactly the right degree of ripeness, handled with the greatest care to avoid breaking the berries, and then fermented and kept in a perfect cellar, where the conditions of temperature, ventilation and cleanliness were under perfect control."

Evidence suggests, however, that the university's experimental work on varieties, Drummond's dialogue with Wetmore, and the fulsome catalogs of numerous plant collections and nurseries were a relatively thin veneer atop an industry with quite different preoccupations. Most of California's winegrowers were more concerned with prosaic matters like unspoiled wine, profitable crop yield per acre, and penetration of the lucrative markets in the eastern United States, from which New York and Ohio-based producers, still working with native varieties, sought to exclude them. It is true that by 1893, California wines displayed at the Columbian Exposition in Chicago bore varietal names or appropriated European geographic names hiding varietal identities, but the overwhelming preponderance of the state's production carried proprietary names, such as Garnier Lancel & Company's Nectarubi red. Or it was labeled as "claret" or "Burgundy," both of which rubrics applied, often interchangeably, to zinfandel-dominated red blends. At the end of the 1880s pinot noir was still barely a footnote in the California wine business, represented by a few bottles sold as Chambertin, and even these were probably not pure pinot noir. The Bordeaux varieties, buoyed a bit by the attentions of Crabb, Wetmore, and others, good press from the university, and the huge prestige of their homeland, did better than pinot noir, especially in the form of blends sold as Medoc. The overwhelming beneficiary of a decade's fascination with vinifera, however, remained zinfandel—the same variety that had unseated mission a generation earlier.

In the end one is left to conclude that despite the infatuation of some pioneers with Europe's great varieties of vinifera, including pinot noir, virtually all of Europe's classic varieties were doomed to marginalization in North America until varietal wine could enter the marketplace at a premium price. A census of Napa County in 1887 counted 16,661 acres under vine, up from just 3,500 seven years earlier, of which fully one-third was zinfandel, while red Bordeaux varieties accounted for barely 800 acres, and pinot noir was not mentioned. In 1891, a directory of growers and wine grape acreage in the Sonoma viticultural district showed nearly everyone growing zinfandel, but contained just scattered references to "French varieties," "mixed varieties," and "Burgundy." Only two growers in the entire district listed pinot among their crops; only one mentioned cabernet by name.

Some vines of pinot noir, progeny of 1880s imports, seem to have survived phylloxera, presumably because they were grafted onto resistant roots. (The replacement of self-rooted vines with "compound" vine plants consisting of vinifera budwood grafted to resistant American rootstocks was the accepted remedy for phylloxera worldwide by 1890.) At Inglenook, Captain Niebaum seems to have been especially sensitive to the importance of grafting vinifera onto resistant American rootstocks, so it is quite possible that the pinot he is said to have imported in the 1880s, and which produced the 1892 vintage that Balzer was served in 1948, were the same vines that survived in front of the old winery building on Highway 29 until the 1940s. (Eventually, these vines became the basis for the so-called Martini clones of pinot, discussed in chapter 5.) It is also likely that the pinot planted at Fountaingrove in the 1880s survived. The planting was directed by a viticulturist-winemaker with experience in New York, so it is not unlikely that the vinifera cuttings were established, from the outset, on resistant rootstocks. Certainly Fountaingrove was producing varietal pinot noir in the 1930s. Although some new planting and replanting was done at Fountaingrove after Repeal, it seems likely that the anchor, at least, for the property's 1930s pinots was pre-Prohibition vines. In 1941 Fountaingrove's hillside vineyards were said to "include plantings of pinot noir which are among the largest of the state." Some of Lefranc's plantings at New Almaden may also have escaped phylloxera; "pinot" from Champagne is said to have been the secret behind the much-ballyhooed success of the 1892 "champagne" made by Lefranc & Masson.

Other pinot noir survived phylloxera, and subsequently also Prohibition, via an interesting detour. Among the experimental vineyards established in the 1880s by the University of California under the indefatigable leadership of its chief professor, Eugene Hilgard, was a site in the foothills of the Sierra Nevada near the town of Jackson, first planted in 1889. The choice of this site seems to have involved the closing of the silver mines at nearby Placer and a desire to find agricultural employment for ex-miners, but agriculture at this elevation was not an easy proposition, and the experimental station was closed in 1903. The vineyard survived, however, preserving no less than 132 cultivars of vinifera, most of them transferred to Jackson from test plots elsewhere in the state, until they were rediscovered by a plant pathologist working for the United States Department of Agriculture in the 1960s. Jackson's isolation had kept both phylloxera and viral infections at bay, and the vines were found to be remarkably disease-free. They are the source of the so-called Jackson clones of pinot noir (see chapter 5).

FROM PHYLLOXERA TO PROHIBITION

After phylloxera and before Prohibition, more pinot noir vines seem to have been imported into California. Paul Masson, the Burgundian who married Charles Lefranc's daughter and subsequently entered into a sparkling wine–based partnership with Lefranc's son Henry, is said to have sent off to France for cuttings of good Burgundian varieties in 1896. In other tellings, Masson brought cuttings personally from Burgundy, where he seems to have returned several times during the 1890s and the early years of the twentieth century. In some versions of the story, Masson obtained his cuttings from Louis Latour, in others from Domaine de la Romanée-Conti; but Latour's archives contain no correspondence with Masson, and there is no record that Latour sold him plant material. Masson and Latour were friends, however, so a gift of vine cuttings is not implausible. Whatever the real source of Masson's pinot, the cuttings were propagated at La Cresta, a mountaintop ranch near Saratoga that Masson acquired during the 1890s. This vineyard became the foundation for subsequent plantings by Martin Ray, from which the so-called Mount Eden selection of pinot noir is derived (see chapter 5).

Meanwhile, in Napa, Beaulieu founder Georges de Latour, who had come to California from the Périgord in 1883, imported large quantities of bench-grafted vines from France in 1906, 1907, and 1908. These imports are well documented in the *St. Helena Star.* The *Star* also tells us that de Latour planted pinot noir to support the production of sparkling wine in 1909. Historians have generally assumed that the pinot de Latour planted in Rutherford consisted of the bench grafts he had personally imported, but there is some conflicting testimony and no unambiguous record, even in the *Star,* that pinot figured on the list of varieties de Latour imported. In a 1976 interview with Richard Paul Hinkle published in *Redwood Rancher,* André Tchelistcheff, Beaulieu's chief winemaker from 1938 to 1973, is quoted as saying that de Latour obtained his cuttings "during the first decade of this century" from the "reputable old firm of Salomon Nursery in central France." But Philip Woodward, one of the cofounders of Chalone Vineyard, remembers Tchelistcheff telling him that de Latour's pinot came from Paul Masson. Yet another version of the story has de Latour's pinot sourced virtually next door, from his neighbor and friend Gustav Niebaum. Without specific archival records at Beaulieu, it is impossible to be sure.

Several wineries throughout California are said to have made pinot-based Burgundy (as opposed to the more commonplace zinfandel-based Burgundies) before Prohibition. Writing in *Wines and Vines* in 1942, Leon Munier reported that "thirty and forty years ago, a number of California wineries produced Burgundy from the pinot noir," including Moulton Hill in Cloverdale, Inglenook and Stanly in Napa, Linda Vista in Mission San Jose, and Palmtag in Hollister. If Munier's ex post facto judgment is to be believed, these were "true to type and desirable" pinot-based Burgundies. There are also at least two documented instances of "Chambertin" produced by California vintners before the turn of the century, one by Jacob Gundlach at the Rheinfarm estate east of the village of Sonoma, the other by Tiburcio Parrot at Miravalle, already mentioned.

THE POST-PROHIBITION DECADES

Prohibition, which outlawed the commercial production of alcoholic beverages in the United States from 1920 to 1933, is regarded by most historians as a graver blow to its fledgling fine-wine business than epidemic phylloxera had been 40 years earlier. Some vineyards were grubbed up by discouraged vintners. Others survived, but "noble" varieties disappeared from them, replaced by gutsy, sturdy, well-colored grapes that shipped well. Home winemaking was legal during Prohibition, and home winemakers across the country became the main market for California's wine grapes. Many vineyards were converted to interplanted field blends. With few exceptions, grape growing was divorced from winemaking. Repeal, when it finally came in 1933, occurred in an environment of global economic depression, and California was flooded with small entrepreneurs seeking to get rich quick on the presumed pent-up demand of thirsty American consumers. "The cold reality," summarizes James T. Lapsley, a historian and vintner, "is that winemaking in California [in 1933] was a poorly organized, highly competitive, undercapitalized industry attempting to meet the unknown demand of a fragmented national market from an oversupply of low quality grapes, all in the depths of the Depression."

Considering the circumstances, the fine-wine segment of the American wine business, small but important before Prohibition, recovered with remarkable speed. Within a few years of Repeal, quality-oriented producers who had survived Prohibition—such as Inglenook, Beaulieu, and Beringer—doggedly dedicated small fractions of their resources to the production of dry varietal table wines. Determined to raise the technical quality of Beaulieu's wines, in 1938 Georges de Latour recruited André Tchelistcheff, a Russian émigré with formal training in both chemistry and agriculture, to take charge of production at Beaulieu. A year before Repeal, the prescient Louis M. Martini made 40,000 gallons of dry red table wine in a rented Napa Valley facility, and then began construction of his own state-of-the-art winery—the first to have the equipment necessary to manage temperature-controlled fermentations. In just two years, between 1934 and 1936, Napa acreage devoted to petite sirah and alicante, darling varieties of the shipping business during Prohibition, was cut by two-thirds. Inglenook grafted dozens of acres to cabernet and pinot noir; Beaulieu grafted palomino and petite sirah to pinot noir and chardonnay; and Beringer replaced a mixed red vineyard with cabernet and pinot noir. A 1936 survey showed almost 800 nonbearing vineyard acres—presumably new plantings.

The University of California, whose College of Agriculture had played a key role in the state's first fine-wine boom during the 1880s, joined the fine-wine campaign from its new campus at Davis, near Sacramento. Albert Winkler and Maynard Amerine, young professors in the new Department of Viticulture, worked tirelessly with the infant industry, "giving lectures, short courses and training programs designed to disseminate viticultural know-how to the state's grape growers, and to encourage the upgrading of grape varieties." Winkler focused his attention on what he called the North Coast—by which he meant nearly all regions west of the Central Valley—arguing for a focus on dry wines and on the selection of varieties well adapted to "cool climates." (In this context, anything cooler than the Central Valley passed for cool.) He recommended cabernet sauvignon and pinot noir for midvalley Napa, along with charbono, mondeuse, and zinfandel. Cabernet sauvignon, he said, "is given first place among red wine grapes by common consent," and pinot "warrants its place in this list of varieties" by virtue of its "smoothness and character." Not content simply to recommend grape varieties, the university also undertook, though a bit later, to assist in identifying healthy vine specimens, and eventually became a distributor of disease-free, true-to-variety cuttings. This story, as far as it affects pinot noir, is told in chapter 5.

Dry varietal wines, often vintage-dated, began to appear within a few years after Repeal. Wente Brothers in Livermore produced vintage-dated sauvignon blanc as early as 1935. Beaulieu made a "Madame de Latour Private Reserve" cabernet sauvignon in 1936. Fountaingrove bottled pinot noir, said to have been 100 percent varietal, beginning no later than 1936. Although Leon Adams, in *The Wines of America,* says the first post-Repeal Fountaingrove wines were "moldy and sour," most of these early varietal wines were, apparently, quite good. The Wente sauvignon blanc went on to win a gold medal and grand prize at the San Francisco World's Fair in 1939, and to feature in a tasting of "appropriate white wines" with Long Island oysters, organized by the Wine and Food Society in February 1940 in New York. Beaulieu's 1936 Madame de Latour cabernet apparently lasted well enough to be served at a banquet of the Lucullus Society in New York's Waldorf-Astoria Hotel 17 years after the vintage, in 1953. And if the first post-Repeal vintages of Fountaingrove were unsatisfactory, the problem was apparently short-lived. No less an expert than Joseph Swan is said to have found this property's 1937 zinfandel to be "one of the best wines ever produced in Sonoma County," and Fountaingrove's 1939 pinot noir was served at a Wine and Food Society tasting at New York's Pierre Hotel in 1945. Virtually all of the varietal pioneers grew and made pinot noir—Beaulieu, Inglenook, Martini, Wente, Martin Ray, Fountaingrove, and even, in several vintages, Italian Swiss Colony. The first boutique wineries to appear in the 1940s—Chafee Hall's Hallcrest Vineyards in the Santa Cruz Mountains, Lee Stewart's Souverain Cellars in Napa, and Freemark Abbey, also in Napa—beginning a trend that was to transform the state's fine-wine business within a generation, all joined the pinot parade.

Pinot noir had an excellent reputation at this point. Tom Marvel and Frank Schoonmaker, writing the first post-Prohibition assessment of American wines in 1941, called pinot the one serious rival to cabernet sauvignon "in Napa, Sonoma and the Santa Cruz Mountains. . . . True pinot noir," they wrote, "is beginning to yield, under favorable conditions, as good wines as it yields in general in France. . . . It is possible to make out of the great traditional European grapes—the Cabernet, the

Pinot Noir and the Pinot Chardonnay—grown on foothill vineyards, cultivated, picked, sorted, crushed and fermented in the slow, meticulous European way—wines which will, in a few short years, be able to hold their own against the better Classed Growths of the Medoc, and against all but the very best red Cortons, for example, and white Meursaults." In 1945, the *Wine Review* listed pinot, along with sémillon and cabernet, as a beneficiary of "the definite move to improved varieties," and Napa County's agricultural commissioner remarked a "definite trend to the high class wine grapes such as cabernet and pinot." Several accounts suggest that Tchelistcheff was especially proud of the 1946 edition of his Beaulieu pinot noir, though winemakers who worked with him later in his career, and discussed pinot with him extensively, do not recall that he was hugely fonder of the 1946 than of other vintages in the same decade.

Books about premium American wine and growing connoisseurship reinforced each other during the 1940s and 1950s. Schoonmaker not only wrote about wine; he also imported it and played a key role, as merchant, in the promotion of American varietal wines. San Francisco and New York chapters of the London-based International Wine and Food Society had been established soon after the end of Prohibition, and they now staged regular wine tastings and food-and-wine dinners. A San Francisco–based Medical Friends of Wine group was also founded in 1941. A 1942 Italian Swiss Colony pinot noir, glossed as "not clarified or filtered," figured in a 1947 Wine and Food Society tasting in New York, along with a "fruity, rich, velvety and matured" nonvintage Paul Masson pinot and Fountaingrove's 1942 pinot noir, which was described as "a very fine and velvety, full-bodied vintage red wine made from the Pinot grape of Burgundy fame"—"one of the finest red wines produced in America."

POWER WINEMAKING AND PINOT NOIR

Wine judgings were a regular feature of the California State Fair when this event was revived after the end of the Second World War. Pinot noir was a category of its own in these competitions right from the outset in 1947. Guidelines for judges about permissible styles and varietal character were furnished by the Technical Advisory Committee of the Wine Institute, a trade organization created by leaders of the California wine industry after Repeal. In the pinot noir category, the judges were told, "heavier-bodied and darker-colored wines should be on an equal basis with the lighter-bodied and lighter-colored wines," and "the varietal flavor and aroma of the Pinot Noir grape must be pronounced." In 1947, Italian Swiss Colony won the fair's gold medal for pinot noir, Lee Stewart's tiny Souverain Cellars took the silver, and Beaulieu was awarded the bronze. In 1948, no gold was awarded, but Beaulieu and Inglenook shared the silver, while Louis Martini took the bronze. Despite the prominence of the category, quantities produced were small. Beaulieu and Inglenook accounted for only 450 cases of wine between them; Martini managed to produce 1,000 cases. Slowly, the varietal wines found their way onto the wine lists of restaurants and private clubs in major metropolitan areas across the country. In 1949, San Francisco's Bohemian Club had four pinot noirs on offer with meals: 1943 Beaulieu, 1943 Fountaingrove, 1945 Souverain Cellars, and 1942 Inglenook. The prices for these ranged, incidentally, from a low of $1.50 for the Fountaingrove to a princely $2.60 for the Inglenook.

Growing interest in varietal wines was bedeviled throughout the 1940s and 1950s, however, by what one wine buyer, for Macy's in New York, called an "abracadabra" of "confusing," "misleading," and "semi-varietal" names. Pinot noir seems to have suffered disproportionately in this regard, having been obliged to fight identity wars on three fronts. In the first theater, pinot needed to be distinguished from Burgundy, which (as we have seen) was sometimes a blend of pinot noir with one or more other red varieties, and sometimes a red blend containing no pinot noir whatsoever. Second, pinot noir was confused, both in the vineyard and in the bottle, with unrelated varieties, notably Red Pinot and Pinot St. George, both of which are paranyms for negrette, and with Black Pinot, which was actually mondeuse. But the third and most pervasive confusion, which is still not completely unraveled, involves pinot noir and soi-disant gamay, sometimes also called Gamay Beaujolais. The gamay of Beaujolais, properly designated gamay noir à jus blanc, barely existed in California, then or now. Instead, what has been called gamay, Gamay Beaujolais, or Napa Gamay has been either valdiguié, a minor variety grown mainly in southwestern France, or (more commonly) a clone of pinot noir, which most viticulturists and winemakers still call the "Gamay Beaujolais clone" of pinot (see chapter 5). It is often alleged that Paul Masson is responsible for the original confusion of gamay and pinot, having erroneously imported and redistributed some cuttings of "pinot" that were actually gamay, but the facts do not seem to fit the accusation.

Although the true identity of so-called Gamay Beaujolais as a clone of pinot noir was clear to ampelographers as early as the 1950s, wineries showed a perverse determination to use both names inaccurately. Throughout the 1960s and into the 1970s, Beaulieu and Mirassou made Gamay Beaujolais from pinot noir grapes; at the same time, Beaulieu was producing trade-named Beaumont from 100 percent pinot noir. Until 1973 Inglenook made Gamay Beaujolais from a near equal blend of pinot and Napa Gamay (i.e., valdiguié); thereafter its Gamay Beaujolais was made "primarily" from pinot noir. Almost unbelievably, the TTB, which regulates American wine nomenclature, *still* permits the use of the Gamay Beaujolais name on bottles of pinot noir and on bottles of valdiguié, as well as on blends of the two, though this permission is finally scheduled to expire in 2009. Through the midcentury period, Gamay Beaujolais was mysteriously more marketable than pinot noir, perhaps because it sounded French—perhaps because it was relatively euphonious, and easier for the American voice box to say.

By 1960, pinot noir was firmly if still marginally established in the production portfolios of California's premium wineries. Most of the planted acreage was in mid-valley Napa, cheek by jowl with the best vineyards of cabernet sauvignon—in the backyards, more or less, of the premium producers. About half as much acreage was planted to pinot noir as to cabernet—and both were still dwarfed by zinfandel, which remained the anchor for most of the state's red wine blends. Louis Martini pioneered pinot noir plantings in Los Carneros in the 1940s, when he acquired part of Judge Stanly's Riverdale ranch. The first trial blocks of pinot noir there date to 1946. Martini's plantings grew to about 70 acres in the 1950s, and probably constituted the state's largest single investment in pinot noir before 1960. Fountaingrove, which Marvel and Schoonmaker had taken to be California's largest pinot vineyard in 1941, ceased operations in 1953, and its 400 acres of vines (not all of them pinot) were uprooted to make room for postwar suburban housing on the northern edge of Santa Rosa. Outside of Napa and Sonoma, pinot was confined until the 1960s to a few acres of heavily virus-infected vines at Wente Brothers in Livermore, some surviving acreage at Paul Masson, and Martin Ray's hilltop vineyard overlooking Cupertino.

In 1963, Albert Winkler surveyed varietal acreage in the so-called coastal counties. "It is heartening to note," he wrote in the preface, "how the plantings of cabernet sauvignon, chardonnay, pinot noir and white riesling are being extended in this area." He counted 438 new and as yet nonbearing acres of pinot noir, in third place behind colombard and cabernet sauvignon. At about the same time, the Mondavis began to acquire vineyard property in Napa, beginning with Hiram Crabb's venerable To-Kalon vineyard, which had been substantially redeveloped during World War II by Martin Stelling. This ranch was said to include "significant acreage" in cabernet sauvignon and pinot noir, as well as a handful of white varieties. New, relatively well capitalized wineries sprang up in Napa like weeds after spring rain, joining the post-Prohibition "old" guard. The new entrants included Chappellet, Diamond Creek, Spring Mountain, Cuvaison, and Sterling. Joe Heitz, who had made wine for Beaulieu, set up shop on his own. Robert Mondavi, separated from the balance of his family by a famous quarrel, constructed the first entirely new, purpose-built winery in Napa since Louis Martini's in 1933. Ridge Vineyards was created on Montebello Ridge, overlooking Cupertino. Disease-free plant material for new vineyards was made available by the University of California's Foundation Plant Materials Service (FPMS), first to nurseries and then to growers, beginning in 1959. Most important, perhaps, the very best bottles produced in the 1960s, which seem to have been cabernet sauvignon almost without exception, were suddenly able to command prices from $5 to $8, about double the $3 to $4 range that had prevailed in the previous decade. But only Martin Ray, isolated on a mountaintop near Cupertino within eyeshot of Paul Masson's La Cresta ranch, and Hanzell, Ambassador James Zellerbach's bid to excel with Burgundian varieties, located just outside Sonoma, were bold enough to ask premium prices for pinot noir.

American per-capita wine consumption doubled from less than one gallon in 1966 to two gallons in 1979. (Eventually it peaked at 2.43 gallons in 1986.) California's production of table wine soared. Money flowed into the wine business, packing cellars with spiffy stainless steel tanks; state-of-the-art French, German, and Italian destemmers, crushers, and wine presses; and thousands upon thousands of French oak barrels. Winemaking came to be associated with an elegant and genteel style of life, attracting investments and refugees from other businesses and professions, as well as from Europe. For the first time since the 1880s, wine grapes became a major crop in Sonoma. For the first time ever, Mendocino and Monterey counties were planted extensively to grapes. Farmers in Santa Barbara County saw wine grapes emerge as an attractive alternative to strawberries and set out the first important vineyards there since the middle of the nineteenth century.

Across the state, even in sites that were less than ideal, cabernet sauvignon emerged as the king of California red wines. Beaulieu's and Inglenook's flagship wines had been cabernets from the first days after Repeal. Now Heitz, Mondavi, Caymus, Stags' Leap Winery, Stag's Leap Wine Cellars, Sterling, Clos du Val, and others staked their reputations on cabernet as well. Even at Ridge, where the preponderance of energy in the 1970s was invested in single-vineyard zinfandels made from purchased fruit, the premium-priced estate wine was a Bordeaux blend dominated by cabernet sauvignon.

The concentration on cabernet owed a great deal to the international prominence of Bordeaux, which gained star billing among wine regions for the first time since World War II. A string of fine vintages—in 1959, 1961, 1962, 1966, and 1970—generated excitement throughout the world's wine trade. Investment poured into Bordeaux's vineyards and cellars. Not just *grands crus* but wines from several score of less grandly classified châteaux were imported into North American markets, absorbing the attention of connoisseurs and attracting new customers from the ranks of war and postwar veterans, who had discovered wine during their time in Europe. California's new premium vintners recognized the magnetism of Bordeaux. They coveted the American customers who were flocking to buy Margaux, Mouton, and their modestly priced siblings, seeking to tempt those customers with California wines made from the classic grape varieties of Bordeaux.

California's focus on cabernet sauvignon, especially for an industry overwhelmingly based in the Napa Valley, made eminent economic sense. And the wisdom of the choice seemed confirmed by the results of the famous tasting organized by Steven Spurrier in Paris in 1976, in which Stag's Leap Wine Cellars' 1973 cabernet sauvignon, only the second vintage the winery had produced, placed first in a blind tasting judged by French winemakers and journalists—ahead of Château Mouton-Rothschild, Château Haut Brion, and Château Montrose from the well-reviewed vintage of 1970.

Initially, premium wine's rising tide was sufficient to raise all varietal boats. Alongside cabernet, virtually every aspirant to the production of premium wine throughout the 1960s tried his or her hand at pinot too, almost as if it were an obligatory exercise. All of the champions of varietal wine from the 1930s, 1940s, and 1950s persevered with pinot. Pedroncelli, Inglenook, Buena Vista, Beaulieu, Martini, Beringer, Simi, Charles Krug, Almaden, and Wente all made pinot noir. But so did the newcomers—Freemark Abbey, Robert Mondavi, Veedercrest, Sutter Home, Sterling, Souverain Cellars, and Ridge. On the strength of this interest, acreage planted to pinot noir increased more than tenfold from 1961 to 1971.

Pinot noir seems not to have lagged cabernet qualitatively in this period, though a reliable picture is difficult to reconstruct from the meager documentary record. Writing in *Notes on a California Cellarbook* in 1988, veteran journalist and wine judge Bob Thompson recalled his pleasure with four pinot noirs from the 1968 vintage, which recalled for him Louis Martini's successful 1957. "The Heitz and Robert Mondavi bottlings," he wrote, "had most of the same fruit flavors as their Martini predecessor, but amplified." Thompson also liked the 1968s from Beaulieu and Martini. "Each of the four," he continued, "had substance enough to hold a peak for a good ten years and plenty of subtleties to admire in between the bouts of euphoria brought on by their essential flavors." Robert Gorman *(Gorman on Premium California Wine)* liked Sebastiani Bin #121 pinot noir, a special bottling for Esquin Imports said to have been made primarily from the 1964 vintage; Hanzell's 1966; and Beaulieu's 1968. The Sebastiani, he wrote, "looks very much like a Côte de Nuits Burgundy," has "a peacock's tail of bouquet," "lots of fruit," and a "rich and appetizing" mouthfeel. The Hanzell manifested an "intense silky red," "classic Pinot Noir fragrance," and "dark and exotic aroma" and was "soft, well-bred and civilized." He characterized the Beaulieu as a "masterpiece," citing "huge bouquet" and "very ripe pinot character."

Systematic tastings conducted by San Francisco's Vintners Club, organized in 1973 for the specific purpose of evaluating wines in comparative blind tastings, paint a much less consistent picture of pinot noir in the 1960s, however. In five tastings (of 12 wines each) held in the first half of 1974, covering pinots made from 1963 through 1972, the "best" wines scored about 14 points on the Davis 20-point scale (dramatically below the standard of 17 points set for outstanding quality). They attracted consensus descriptors consistent with Thompson's and Gorman's unscientific notes—"good varietal character," "long, rich finish," "deep ruby red," and "rich, spicy nose." But many other notes were numerically low and terminologically pejorative: many wines were criticized, variously, for "thin edges," "bitterness," "oxidized" appearance, "weediness," "vegetable aromas," "harsh and biting" flavors, and even in one case a "bluish-green color"! The average score for pinots in these five tastings was just 13.02 points out of 20, barely above the threshold for "good commercial wines." Worse, perhaps, nearly half the tasted wines, 29 out of 60, scored less than 13 points, meaning that they showed "a noticeable defect." These results were vastly worse than the Vintners Club's evaluation of cabernets from the same period. In a cabernet tasting held in July 1974, for example, cabernet sauvignons from the 1964 through 1971 vintages managed an average score of 15 out of 20—two full points higher than the running average for pinot noir.

Outside the Vintners Club circle, as the 1960s gave way to the 1970s, comments about California pinot noir turned decisively negative across the board. For Thompson, who had enjoyed the 1968s, "one Pinot Noir of the 1970s after another was alcoholic, raisiny, tannic and flavored mostly by wood." *Connoisseurs' Guide,* a new consumer-oriented publication, reviewed 1970s pinots in 1977 with frequent resort to descriptors like "dull" and "short." Beaulieu's Beaumont bottling in 1973, the year of Tchelistcheff's retirement, was said to have a "briary, burnt quality" and a "cloying woody nose." Three years later, the *Guide's* assessment had not improved, with numerous references to "volatile off-odors," "pungent" aromas, and "slightly varnishy" and "dirty" notes.

While there are too many wines at issue and too few surviving, reliable tasting notes to reconstruct what happened to pinot in the 1960s and '70s, it seems clear that it did not enjoy the same "onward and upward" trajectory traced by cabernet and chardonnay. The language of the tasting notes that have survived, especially from the Vintners Club, strongly suggests that many of the pinots made in this period were not just disappointing or mediocre; on the contrary, they were plainly flawed and actively unpleasant. This evolution cannot reasonably be explained, as some have suggested, by claims that grapes were grown in areas that were a bit too warm or from "inferior clones." The same clones had been grown in many of the same sites for some time, and were used in earlier years to make, apparently, quite good wine—if evaluations by observers like Thompson, Schoonmaker, and Balzer are to be believed. Much more likely, bad pinots were the consequence of winemaking techniques ill adapted to pinot's special needs.

The villain, almost certainly, was a winemaking recipe, applied indiscriminately to all red varieties, that was rooted in new technology, heavy-handed intervention, and risk minimization. Josh Jensen, who later founded Calera Wine Company, recalls that when he returned from Europe in 1972 and began learning about California wine, "most wineries had a standard red wine method," which they applied equally to all red varieties. Thompson remembers an era of "more-is-better winemaking," buttressed with fancy crushers, destemmers, and presses, the first widespread use of temperature-controlled fermentors, and the beginning of a vogue for new, unseasoned French oak barrels of Burgundian and Bordelais dimensions. California red wines of the period were being pumped, processed, and seasoned, as booming business enabled wineries to stuff their cellars with new equipment and to purchase almost limitless quantities of new French oak *barriques.* Cabernet and zinfandel tolerated this treatment reasonably well. But pinot noir, underendowed with tannins and anthocyanins, suffered. In the cellar, it tended to lose color, display off flavors, and maderize (oxidize and turn brownish). Compounding one error with another, vintners tried to rescue their hollow shells of would-be pinot from complete ignominy by blending in small percentages of darkly colored and deeply flavored varieties like carignane, zinfandel, and petite sirah.

The Wine Institute, testifying to the depths of confusion, even issued a press release in 1976 explaining that "virus-free stock," "low fermentation temperatures," "frequent racking" (to make the wine "progressively clearer"), and additions of "small amounts" of "other varieties" were responsible for recent *improvements* in California pinot noir. "Many California winemakers," according to the Institute, "feel they have turned the corner [on pinot noir]," based on California's position as the "world leader in the technology of winemaking," many of whose "innovations" have been "especially applicable to the production of Pinot Noirs." On the contrary, bad wines, negative reviews, and consumer disaffection drove winery after winery to drop pinot from their offerings during the late 1970s and early '80s—Sterling, Caymus, Freemark Abbey, Heitz Cellars, and even Louis Martini left the field—and tarnished pinot's reputation for another decade. Pinot noir could not be made well in the New World, it was said—and repeated, over and over.

THE RENAISSANCE BEGINS

While these disappointments bred mostly more of the same, all dark clouds, almost by definition, have a bit of silver lining. For a tiny band of contrarians, the dismal condition of 1960s and 1970s pinots was a call to arms. One after another, small wineries dedicated specifically (if not always exclusively) to succeeding with Burgundian varieties were established across California and in Oregon. The first of the Burgundian specialist operations, Hanzell Vineyards near Sonoma, had been created a decade earlier by San Francisco forest-products magnate James Zellerbach, who planted pinot noir and chardonnay in 1952. But Hanzell's first pinots, though they eschewed the standard red wine recipe, were distinctive and controversial, and Hanzell was better known in the early years for its chardonnay.

Other pioneers emerged beginning at the end of the 1960s. There was Chalone, the reincarnation of Francis William Silvear's vineyard, off the power grid on the edge of the Pinnacles National Monument near Soledad, where Bordeaux- and Montepellier-trained Philip Togni made a remarkable string of old-vine pinots beginning in 1965. Chalone's owner, Harvard-educated Dick Graff, also became involved in the early 1970s with Mount Eden Vineyards in Saratoga, in its turn the reincarnation of Martin Ray's hilltop vineyard from the 1940s. Beginning in 1973, first Graff and then Merry Edwards, an incredibly talented young winemaker fresh from Davis, turned out exceptional pinots from Ray's old plantings.

Another early Burgundian specialist was Carneros Creek, the first winery to be established in the Carneros district of Napa since Repeal. There Francis Mahoney, a veteran of the retail wine trade, made a variety of wines beginning in 1972, but focused his energies on pinot. Mahoney was fascinated by pinot noir's many mutations, and he invested considerable energy in a ten-year test, then unprecedented, of 26 clones and selections of pinot, taken from the University of California's vineyards at Davis and from plantings around the state. The university was his active partner in the effort to identify those "subvarieties" of pinot, commonly known as clones or selections, which had the best chance to produce fine still wines.

Yet another pioneer was Joe Swan, a commercial airline pilot fascinated with wine, who bought a dying zinfandel vineyard near Forestville, in Sonoma, in 1968. Encouraged by André Tchelistcheff, whom he had befriended some years earlier, Swan planted pinot noir in 1969. Swan's first two vintages of pinot, 1972 and 1973, were well received, in part because Tchelistcheff, who liked them a lot, acted as their informal and unpaid champion. Finally, there was Josh Jensen, who had discovered the charms of fine Burgundy when he read anthropology at Oxford. Jensen searched California for veins of limestone soil, believing that limestone might be the key to growing fine pinot noir. He found his grail on a remote hilltop in San Benito County, near the farm town of Hollister, where he planted 12 acres of pinot in 1975 and produced his first vintage, to considerable acclaim, in 1978.

While these lights were keeping the quest for really good pinot alive through the dark ages of California's wine boom, something hugely significant happened 800 miles to the north. David Lett, a Utah native who had arrived in California some years earlier to study dentistry but discovered wine instead, reinvented himself as a winemaker. Enthralled with French Burgundies and convinced that a climate genuinely cooler than anything in California was the indispensable key to success with pinot noir, he moved to Oregon in 1965 and planted cuttings of pinot he had brought up from California. Others followed Lett's lead, attracted by affordable land and an attractive, honest, low-glitz lifestyle, but mostly by a passionate conviction that Oregon's climate, with its cooler springs and falls and greater rainfall, was friendly to their chosen variety. By the end of the 1970s, Oregon's Willamette Valley, southwest of Portland, supported a modest wine industry focused overwhelmingly on pinot noir, with just marginal attention to chardonnay, riesling, and pinot gris, and no attention at all given to Bordeaux varieties.

The smallish scale of Oregon's wine enterprise appealed to Burgundians, a few of whom allowed themselves to take Oregon seriously. In 1979, Lett's 1975 Eyrie Vineyards Pinot Noir placed third in an international wine Olympiades orchestrated by the French gastronomic magazine *GaultMillau* in Paris, outperforming quite a number of fine French Burgundies. In 1980, in a rematch of Olympiade winners organized by Beaune-based *négociant* Robert Drouhin, the same wine finished second only to Drouhin's own Chambolle-Musigny from the legendary 1959 vintage. Roy Andries de Groot, who published *The Wines of California, the Pacific Northwest and New York* in 1982, wrote that "the news of the Oregon success flashed around California as if it were the discovery of a new gold strike at Sutter's Mill." De Groot appears to argue that Jensen, Edwards, and several early pinot makers in Santa Barbara were inspired by Oregon's competitive triumph, but this claim puts the cart before the horse. Nonetheless, Oregon's enterprise did attract critical attention and established incontrovertibly that the history of pinot noir in North America, from this point forward, was a tale of two states, at least.

Fortunately for California winemakers interested in rescuing pinot from the dismal failures of the 1970s, the supply of grapes did not decline as dramatically as the reputation of the wines they made. The grapes remained available almost entirely thanks to the emergence during the 1970s wine boom of a healthy business in sparkling wines made from pinot noir and chardonnay. The success of Jack and Jaime Davies's reconstruction of the old Jacob Schram winery in Calistoga, rechristened Schramsberg, dedicated to world-class sparkling wine made from the classic varieties used in Champagne (and poured in the national spotlight when President Nixon traveled to mainland China in 1973), attracted huge attention. Within a few years, many major French Champagne producers, led by the venerable Moët & Chandon, had developed a business interest in California wine, and a handful of domestic aspirants had emerged as well, generating a large and stable demand for pinot noir and chardonnay grapes. New pinot vineyards were planted specifically to satisfy that demand, especially in Los Carneros and along the lower course of the Russian River, but also in Monterey and in the Anderson Valley of Mendocino County. Combined with the new estate plantings undertaken by the small tribe of quality-oriented pinot pioneers and their neighbors, these vineyards were sufficient to keep the total of California acreage dedicated to pinot growing at least through 1978, when it peaked at just over 10,000 acres.

The interest of the sparkling-wine producers also helped reduce the risk of transferring pinot from the relatively warmer sites in midvalley Napa, inland Sonoma, and Mendocino, where a few pre-Prohibition plantings had survived and where new plantings were concentrated before World War II, to sites newly classified by Davis viticulturists as Region I—which refers to areas in which the heat accumulation is sufficient to ripen only the most precocious of varieties. Although it is de rigueur to argue, with 30 years' hindsight, that the transition of pinot into cooler climates was a necessary condition for real success with still wine, planting grapes of any kind in places like Los Carneros and Anderson Valley was still regarded as akin to folly in the early 1970s. Some of the university's farm advisers stubbornly advised growers like Donald Edmeades in Anderson Valley and Francis Mahoney in Carneros against grapes. But pinot (and chardonnay) destined for sparkling wine did not need to ripen completely, so the cooler climates could be exploited without increased risk as long as sparklers were the end product.

THE RENAISSANCE TAKES HOLD

By the tail end of the 1970s and the early 1980s, the stage was set for pinot's renaissance. In Los Carneros, Acacia and then Saintsbury emerged, focused on pinot noir. In the Russian River valley, Tom Dehlinger, Davis-trained and briefly experienced at Hanzell, began to make well-regarded pinots from his family's farm south of Forestville. The wines Davis Bynum made from Joseph Rochioli's grapes got better and better. Gary Farrell, who had become Bynum's winemaker is 1978, made two vintages of pinot noir for Rochioli's own label and launched Gary Farrell Wines in 1982. In Santa Barbara County, a coterie of talented winemakers, fanatically devoted to pinot noir and chardonnay, worked briefly at Zaca Mesa, which became virtually a finishing school for local winemakers, and then set up shop on their own, as Au Bon Climat, Byron, and (a bit later) Daniel Gehrs. In the Anderson Valley, Navarro Vineyards founder Ted Bennett began making estate-bottled pinot noir in 1978. In the Santa Cruz Mountains, the first vintages of pinot noir from Ken Burnap's Santa Cruz Mountain Vineyard were well reviewed, as were the 1978, 1979, and 1980 wines made by David Bruce. And in Oregon, David Lett, who had been joined in the quest for great pinot by Dick Erath and Dick Ponzi almost from the outset, now had additional company. Myron Redford founded pinotcentric Amity Vineyards in 1976, Bill and Susan Blosser created Sokol Blosser in 1977, and Adelsheim Vineyard made its first pinot noir in 1978.

At the beginning of 1982, two landmark articles about California pinot noir appeared in *Vintage* magazine. The first—by Joel Butler, who later became one of America's first Masters of Wine—featured detailed tasting notes on then recent vintages of pinot—mostly 1978, 1979, and 1980—from Acacia, David Bruce, Calera, Carneros Creek, Chalone, Firestone, Mount Eden, Martin Ray, Joseph Swan, Santa Cruz Mountain Vineyard, and St. Francis. The 1980 Estate Reserve Chalone, tasted from barrel, got Butler's highest score—18 out of 20—recognized for an "intense" aroma of "spice, chocolate and berry overtones," "rich yet elegant" flavor, "lush fruit," and a "velvety mid-palate. Reminiscent," wrote Butler, of "a young Jayer Burgundy." More than two dozen other pinots received scores above 14, with approving and sometimes enthusiastic comments about their "deep" and "brilliant" colors; "lovely" aromas redolent of cherries, black pepper, herbs, raspberries, anise, spice, and even coffee; "rich mid-palate"; "good acidity"; "complexity"; "balance"; and "elegance." Comparisons with fine Burgundy were common. Just two months later, Norman Roby, who later became London-based *Decanter* magazine's California correspondent, declared categorically that "Pinot Noir has experienced a rebirth." He recalled that "elder statesmen" of the California wine business had told him as recently as five years earlier that pinot was "a real problem child." Now, he assured readers, thanks to a "turnabout" that has "proceeded at a dizzying pace," "Pinot Noir is the hottest wine type around, and is the most exciting and controversial wine topic since the Haraszthy legend was put to rest." Because Roby and his fellow panelists attempted to taste "every bottle of pinot noir known to exist at the end of 1981," the collected notes were less uniformly enthusiastic than Butler's, who had concentrated on the best bottlings he could find. But the contrast with tasting notes from just eight years earlier, when the Vintners Club had staged its comparative tastings, was still dramatic.

Dorothy Gaiter and John Brecher, the husband and wife who were later to become the *Wall Street Journal*'s wine columnists, say they "discovered" good California pinot noir in 1981. The object of their revelation was the 1978 Raymond Winery pinot noir, which sported a "fantastic, chocolate-liqueur nose," and was "big, luscious, rich [and] very much American, [but] definitely a Pinot." *Gourmet* magazine wine editor and veteran wine merchant Gerald Asher told me that he became aware of California's potential to make fine pinot when he tasted Saintsbury's first releases in 1983 and 1984. "Saintsbury was not trying to make a wine that would age," he recalled, "but their wine was *gouleyant*"—a French term, used almost exclusively to describe wine, connoting "tasty" and "agreeable."

A key feature of the pinot renaissance was a preoccupation, on the part of winemakers and critics alike, with site. For the most part, the mantra was simple: cooler is better, because cooler is more like Burgundy. Pinot noir vineyards gradually disappeared from their erstwhile home in midvalley Napa, migrating to foggy, windswept Carneros. When cabernet sauvignon systematically refused to ripen in the Santa Maria and Anderson valleys—at least to the very ripe standard that had come to be accepted for this variety in America—cabernet was largely abandoned, first for chardonnay, but then also for pinot noir. Oregonians brandished weather data illustrating how closely, they said, their climate resembled the Côte d'Or's, and California-trained winemakers smitten with pinot moved north in noticeable numbers. Except in Oregon, however, the march toward cool sites was slow and incremental. Pinot around Russian River was planted mostly in the region's warmer section, along the river's western bank between Healdsburg and Wohler Bridge. Until the 1990s, the Sanford & Benedict vineyard was virtually the only pinot planted in the cool, western end of the Santa Ynez Valley. And only one unbonded winemaker, Marin refugee Daniel Schoenfeld, planted pinot noir in the "true" Sonoma Coast, on ridges above the fog, almost within smelling distance of the ocean.

The lure of cooler sites, and the enthusiasm for them expressed by much-respected veterans like Tchelistcheff, was not the only force moving pinot away from the warmer valleys. Economics was also at work. The winemakers who drove the pinot renaissance knew absolutely that high-yielding vines produced diluted, bland pinot noir. As yields were forced down by rigorous pruning and crop thinning, and sometimes also by virus-infected vines, pinot could not compete with cabernet sauvignon in midvalley Napa, where cabernet made an excellent wine at between two and three times the yield.

Considering that the practitioners of renaissance pinot were generally well schooled in Burgundian perspectives, however, it is interesting that aspects of site other than climate were conspicuously neglected. Pinot noir was planted on both flat land and hills, and even in the floodplains of rivers. Soil properties were neglected almost entirely. The exceptions were Calera, where the site was chosen explicitly for its limestone subsoil, and Oregon, where the red volcanic soils near Dundee and in the Eola Hills were favored for their ability to hold enough water that vines could be grown without irrigation. The Oregonians also confined their vineyards to hillsides, in part because the flatlands were in use for other lucrative forms of agriculture and in part because, in a marginal climate for viticulture, they needed sloping land, facing south, to gather in early- and late-season heat.

Although it is widely argued that pinot's renaissance was the child of better sites and decreased yields, better winemaking was unquestionably the true key factor. Almost without exception, the second-generation pioneers of the 1970s turned their backs on the red wine recipe that wine technology and prosperity had birthed at the end of the 1960s. They removed stems from their fruit, as far as possible, without crushing the berries, or dumped whole clusters straight from the vineyard into their fermentors. They made their wines in open-top tanks, often repurposed from some nearby dairy, or in plastic-lined picking boxes, so they had constant access to their fermenting musts, day and night. They home-manufactured ersatz plungers to punch down the cap of skins and stems that fermentation pushed to the surface of the tanks, or they just hopped into the tanks and punched the cap down with their feet. They allowed the must temperature to rise naturally, rather than attempting to manipulate it. They found ways, using buckets, or forklifts, or gravity if they were lucky, to get the fermented must pressed and barreled without using pumps, which eviscerated the wine. Then they learned to leave the wine alone, except for topping each barrel religiously, to be sure it had only the tiniest interaction with the surrounding air.

This approach had the advantage that it could be executed on a shoestring, which was all most of them had, and even without electricity, which was sometimes not available. But it also made better wine. The washed-out colors, limp flavors, smells of acetone, and oxidized behaviors that afflicted pinot in the late 1960s and early 1970s were eliminated by *removing technology* from the cellar, and by following a recipe conceived specifically for pinot noir. When the new recipe was combined with better fruit, farmed to lower yields and picked before it could raisin, pinot not only emerged unflawed and varietally correct; it also began (once again) to make nuanced, complex, and interesting wines.

At the end of the 1970s and in the early 1980s in California, the ranks of pinot makers had a bit the character of a revolving door. A number of wineries, especially those that had not made it any kind of specialty, gave up on pinot noir entirely. Surprisingly, many of these apostates appear to have quit not in frustration but after producing one or more quite successful vintages. Sterling Vineyards' well-reviewed 1971 pinot noir was its last effort. Caymus Vineyards made a string of well-reviewed pinots in the early 1980s, notably a 1981 Special Selection praised for its balance, length, and intensity; then it severed pinot from its portfolio. Smith-Madrone, which had planted pinot in 1970, left the game late in the 1980s, saying that pinot noir had made "their best and worst wines." The largest number of defectors were Napa-based wineries, but even Randall Graham, who had founded Bonny Doon Vineyard near Santa Cruz in 1979 for the avowed purpose of making the Great American Pinot Noir, turned his efforts to Rhône varieties after a string of, in his own opinion, less-than-successful wines. The defections in Napa had a great deal to do, of course, with Napa's increasingly stellar success with cabernet sauvignon and cabernet-based Bordeaux blends, as well as the lofty price that cabernet grapes grown in the Napa Valley were then able to command. When the difference between cabernet sauvignon and pinot noir in price per ton was compounded with the requirement that, to produce quality wine, pinot's yields had to be managed to half or less the yield for good cabernet, the economic contrast between the varieties became too stark to ignore.

For every maker that abandoned pinot, however, there was at least one newcomer to the ranks, and in Oregon there were only newcomers. Pinot noir was the keystone of nearly every new producer's portfolio in the Willamette Valley. By the early 1980s, serious pinot makers in the two-state area reached critical mass. There were enough pinot-oriented practitioners in each of the main regions—Santa Barbara, the Russian River valley, Los Carneros, and Oregon—to talk with one another meaningfully and regularly. In the summer of 1980, a group of Oregon vintners gathered, in true Oregon style, at a hostelry dedicated to fly-fishing called the Steamboat Inn, on the Umpqua River in the southern part of the state. They did fish, but they also brought wines, which they tasted, compared, and critiqued. "Steamboat" became an annual event, and it continues to this day, dedicated entirely to conversations among winemakers about pinot noir, with no public and no press allowed. The Oregonians began to invite California winemakers too, promoting interregional dialogue. Winemakers brought experimental lots and problem wines. They returned a second year to show off progress and new problems. Eventually Burgundian winemakers, Australians, New Zealanders, Canadians, and aspirants to pinot from other states were included at Steamboat. Many winemakers believe that the communications fostered at Steamboat played a key role in the pinot renaissance.

Still, really good pinot noir remained scarce. The bad and mediocre wines produced in the 1970s, many of which persisted into the new decade, took an inevitable toll on consumer attitudes. Diana Lett, David Lett's wife and partner on the Oregon "frontier," remembers that "the wine market had little to no interest in pinot noir" in the late 1970s and early 1980s. She recalls that on early nationwide marketing trips by Oregon producers, "There was hardly any interest even in great vintages from famous Burgundian *domaines,* scarcely any interest in California pinot noirs, and certainly none for those from . . . Oregon."

The impact of the bad wines was probably magnified by very modest pronouncements made by some of the best new-generation pinot makers, who seemed happy to give the impression that they were still groping their way forward, battling a difficult, capricious, and temperamental variety, defeated more often than they were successful. When Joe Swan reflected on his first 14 vintages of pinot noir for the

Vintners Club in 1987, he allowed that he did not have "all that many wines which I think are outstanding." He permitted himself to say that he did think his 1973 was "very good" and that he had "always liked" his 1977 as well, but qualified this faint praise with the observation that the 1977 had "its lovers and haters."

Happily for pinot, however, the first phase of its renaissance coincided more or less with what Michael Bonadies, founding partner in one of the country's most successful restaurant groups, calls "the birth of the new American restaurant." Bonadies observes that "for the first time, a large number of Americans were focused on what they ate and where they ate it. The country was talking food and restaurants. There were new food and wine magazines, newspaper sections and columns and TV shows." Not only did chefs become celebrities, but restaurants hired wine directors and sommeliers. Sommeliers loved Burgundy, and they were early adopters of American pinot noir when the first good exemplars appeared in the marketplace. "By the late 1980s," Bonadies recalls, "sommeliers were bumping cabernets to make room for the hot new pinots, [and] began to preach the gospel to their customers, praising pinot and winning some converts."

The 1988 vintage seems to have been the turning point. Larry Brooks, who made pinot noir at Acacia beginning in 1979, remembers 1988 as the "first vintage of low supply and great demand." Brooks cites the existence, by 1988, of a sufficient number of makers, a succession of vintages uncompromised by weather either in California or in Oregon, and the especially successful pinot vintages in 1984 and 1985. These factors led, he recalls, to "a feeding frenzy when the 1988s hit the market in the early 1990s." Bottle prices increased. Because the best wines tended to be made in lots of only a few hundred cases, pinot noir—a sluggish seller just a few years earlier—joined cult cabernets, Meritage blends, and a few vineyard-designated zinfandels in the hallowed ranks of "allocated" wines.

Winegrowers rushed to plant additional pinot, using newly available plant material from France, along with newly discovered verities about planting density and trellis configuration, and to replant older vineyards imperiled by phylloxera. Pinot acreage in Oregon exploded from less than 1,000 acres in 1990 to more than 5,000 acres a decade later. In California, acreage more than doubled in the same time, from approximately 9,500 acres in 1990 to more than 19,000 acres in 2000, and the percentage of this acreage harvested for sparkling wine plummeted. In British Columbia's Okanagan valley, 500 acres of pinot were planted, about 100 in the Finger Lakes district of New York, and lesser amounts in Maryland, Virginia, Ontario, Ohio, Michigan, Colorado, Texas, and the Four Corners region of the Southwest.

The average price paid for California pinot noir grapes, having trailed "king" cabernet sauvignon in most years before 1986, soared from $804 a ton in 1991 (when cabernet clocked in at $918) to $1,849 a ton in 2001, against only $1,062 for cabernet sauvignon. These numbers are misleading, however, because cabernet sauvignon's average price is depressed by the existence of substantial plantings in the Central

Valley, where nonpremium fruit brings perennially lower prices, while pinot noir is grown almost entirely in premium-priced North Coast counties. Still, comparing North Coast cabernet to North Coast pinot, cabernet sauvignon's historic premium disappeared after 1990. By 2002, pinot noir from the state's most reputed vineyards, such as Pisoni in the Santa Lucia Highlands and Hirsch in Sonoma Coast, figured among the most expensive wine grapes anywhere, topping $6,000 a ton. A shift from per-ton to per-acre pricing, originally embraced by small-volume producers to garner control over yields and to protect their qualitative aspirations, can push the effective per-ton price even higher in low-yield years.

Producers who forsook pinot in the 1980s—Caymus and Louis Martini, for example—sought reentry paths, leasing existing vineyards or planting new ones in prime areas. Cabernet-based producers like W. H. Smith, Joseph Phelps, and Duckhorn invested in pinot noir. Dozens of new pinot-only labels were created, producing just a few hundred cases each, often by winemakers whose day job was assisting in a larger establishment or consulting. A few picture-perfect vintages, both in California and in Oregon—notably 1994 and 2000—added fuel to the fire.

Inevitably, this activity and excitement attracted the attention of the wine press, which began comparing North American pinots with red Burgundies for the first time since Eyrie's 1975s had precociously bested *grand cru* and *premier cru* Burgundies in 1979. After casting a quick retrospective glance over the preceding two decades of pinot noir in California and Oregon, *New York Times* columnist Frank Prial reported in 1998 on a tasting of four 1995 pinots: Corton Pougets and Beaune Clos des Ursules made by Louis Jadot, and Allen Ranch and Olivet Lane bottlings by Williams Selyem. "Great pinots," he concluded, "every one." And *Wine Spectator,* which emerged during the 1990s as the world's largest-circulation wine magazine, could not resist organizing a Pinot Noir Challenge that year, arguing quixotically that although "few wine aficionados seriously question the age-old premise that Burgundy is home turf to world's best pinot noirs," they wanted to "test this assumption anyway." Quite a lot of the 20 North American pinots tasted against top Burgundies from the 1990 and 1993 vintages showed well enough that the magazine could conclude that "the pinots of the United States are fast closing the gap" with Burgundy's.

In fact, the resurgence of North American interest in pinot noir during the last quarter of the twentieth century owes a great deal to the nearly simultaneous renaissance in Burgundy, just as California's earlier infatuations with cabernet, first in the 1880s and again in the 1960s and '70s, turned on contemporaneous stirrings in Bordeaux. When Robert Finigan, who launched one of America's first wine newsletters in 1975, began covering American pinot noir in 1978 and 1981, he was scarcely less critical of Burgundies than of "most" California pinots. "A pretty sad lot overall," he summarized, "but then so are their contemporary opposite numbers from Burgundy." Finigan slammed the Burgundians, with a few notable and expensive exceptions, for making wines "not vinified for extended cellaring," for "barnyardy and undrinkable" products, and for "dirty and impossible flavors." Many observers say that robust demand in the 1960s was the culprit, leading Burgundy's growers to embrace chemical fertilizers and defoliants in order to boost output. Clive Coates, in *Côte d'Or,* confirms that Burgundy at the time was "on its knees," ruined by overfertilization and the introduction of inferior, high-yield clones that led to "thin, pallid, fruitless and short-lived wines." Additionally, many of the producers responsible for Burgundy as we know it today were not bottling their own wines. Some, who were early adopters of estate bottling, were far from quality-oriented at the outset. In Morey-St.-Denis, Denis Mortet did not begin bottling his wines until 1982. All the production of Méo-Camuzet was sold in bulk until 1983, as was most of Jean-Jacques Confuron's as late as 1988. In some cases small-scale, hands-on British and American importers, seriously active in Burgundy for the first time in the late 1970s, were the instruments of revolution, giving producers like Jean-François Coche-Dury and Jean Pichenot (in Savigny) an outlet for wine finished and bottled in their own cellars. Finally, the 1970s were also a miserable decade meteorologically, leading to difficult and often unsuccessful vintages in 1972, 1973, 1974, 1975, and 1977.

In light of pinot's poor performance on its home turf during the 1970s, it is scarcely surprising that North American efforts lagged. The North Americans lacked good and credible models of current excellence, and were forced to rely for inspiration on a small stock of old bottles, like the 1950s Burgundies Josh Jensen had tasted at Oxford in the 1960s. When good young Burgundies began to arrive in the 1980s, selected by a new generation of brokers and importers who insisted on unfiltered products transported in refrigerated containers; and when a new generation of Burgundian vignerons—college- and *lycée*-trained, tempered with New World internships, and often anglophone—began interacting with their American counterparts at home, at Steamboat, and elsewhere, the cause of pinot noir in North America was substantially advanced. Nor did it hurt that Robert Drouhin, leader of the house of Joseph Drouhin, one of Beaune's most respected *négociants,* set up shop in Oregon in 1986, creating Domaine Drouhin Oregon a stone's throw from the Letts' pioneer pinot vineyard at Eyrie.

In fact, the renaissance in Burgundy was felt not only in North America; it reverberated around the world. Close to home, the first really good red wines were made in Sancerre in the 1985 vintage by winegrowers who had studied in Dijon or Beaune, and who used oak cooperage to finish their previously tank-raised wines. Alsatian pinot noir took a quantum leap forward at about the same time, shedding the limitations of a hitherto rosé-driven style, increasing fermentation temperatures, and adopting small cooperage. Across the Rhine, in Baden and the Palatinate, young winemakers like Karl-Friedrich and Steffen Christmann in Gimmeldingen were impressed with the "new" Burgundies they tasted when they made visits to the Côte d'Or. They came home, expanded their plantings of pinot noir, adopted "traditional" Burgundian cellar practices, and began to produce pinots of exceptional depth and character. At Fläsch, in the Swiss canton of Graubunden, Daniel Gantenbein acquired new clonal material from Burgundy and set a new standard for pinot in northeastern Switzerland. In fact, Switzerland's pinot renaissance was widespread, touching the area around Lake Neuchâtel previously known almost exclusively for pale, *oeil de perdrix*–style pinots, as well as the Chablais Vaudois, where serious varietal pinots began to displace traditional blends of pinot and gamay. Around the Neusiedler See in Austria, there were numerous pinot-related stirrings. Josef Umathum took the reins of his family wine estate in 1985, concentrating a substantial fraction of his attentions on pinot noir, which he believes has been cultivated in Pannonia since the thirteenth century. Several mostly young producers near the town of Gols organized themselves into an association called Pannobile in 1995. A good many Pannobile producers now make serious pinots with intensely fruity aromas, good structure, and the marks of *élevage* in barrel.

The pace of this change only increased through the balance of the 1990s, as Burgundy was finally able to combine some fine vintage years with a mastery of yields and enological science. Eyes around the world turned to Burgundy. North America's contemporary infatuation with pinot noir was far from an isolated or peculiarly American phenomenon. On the contrary, it was part of a global evolution with roots in pinot's heartland—in Burgundy itself.

Chapter 4

WHERE IT HAPPENS

Across North America, there are about 30,000 acres of pinot noir. This translates to about 6 percent of the acreage devoted to all red wine grapes. By a different yardstick, it is a surface slightly larger than the borough of Manhattan, but smaller than the District of Columbia. If it were all bearing and made entirely into varietal table wine, 30,000 acres would be enough to produce about 7.6 million cases in an average year. With allowances for nonbearing acreage, sparkling wine, and the pinot noir that disappears into red blends, North America's pinot vineyards now turn out closer to 2.8 million cases of varietal pinot—which is less than 2 percent of total American wine sales.

Of those 30,000 acres, 90 percent are concentrated on the continent's western coast, between the mouth of the Columbia River and the Santa Barbara Channel, in a narrow swath of territory no more than 25 miles from the Pacific Ocean. This area, which I call the Pacific Pinot Zone for convenience, enjoys a marine climate largely without extremes of winter cold or summer heat, and with precipitation confined almost exclusively to the winter months. At the zone's southern end, pinot noir flourishes primarily within sniffing distance of salt water, where the primary determinant of climate is the onshore spread of marine weather during the growing season, sucked east from the ocean by convection in California's hot inland valleys and landlocked deserts. At the northern end, in Oregon, where latitude truncates the growing season, viticulture requires some protection from unmitigated marine influence, and is therefore concentrated on the inland side of the Coast Ranges. Night and morning overcast, low clouds, and fog are the almost constant companions of pinot noir in most of California, except in a few genuine coastal sites in the Santa Cruz Mountains and north of San Francisco. In these places, coastal fog is so persistent at sea level that vineyards must be planted *above* the fog line, on ridge tops, where the fog burns off by midday. In Oregon, to compensate for its latitude, midslope and south-facing hillsides are preferred to minimize the risks associated with frosts on the valley floor and inadequate heat on the hilltops, and to strike a balance between overly vigorous bottomland soils and hopelessly thin soils at the highest elevations.

The balance of the North American pinot vineyard is widely scattered. There are now about 500 acres of pinot noir in the Okanagan River valley of British Columbia, straddling the 50th parallel. The Okanagan is the unexpected extreme northern end of the American southwestern steppe and desert that begins on the eastern shore of the Gulf of California and continues north through Nevada, eastern Oregon, and Washington. It is sealed off from marine influence in British Columbia by the Cariboo Mountains, yet saved from extreme winter cold by the deep waters of Okanagan Lake. Another 500 acres of pinot noir are found on the greater south shore of Lake Ontario, which includes Canada's Niagara Peninsula and the Finger Lakes region of upstate New York, where the lakes' influence is an indispensable buffer against vine-killing winters and a moderator for continental summer heat. There are also isolated plantings of pinot on the southern shore of Lake Erie in Ohio and on the eastern shore of Lake Michigan, where circumstances are similar to the greater south shore of Lake Ontario. The rest of the continent's pinot noir is in high-altitude vineyards in Colorado, New Mexico, Arizona, and Texas, where winegrowers rely on the chill of altitude to protect the vines from growing-season temperatures that would otherwise be prohibitively hot, and in a few pockets elsewhere in New York, Pennsylvania, Idaho, Washington, Maryland, Virginia, and North Carolina.

The Pacific Pinot Zone includes the regions that have become synonymous with fine pinot noir in North America—especially Los Carneros, the Russian River valley, Santa Barbara, and the Willamette Valley—which account for the overwhelming majority of plantings. It also includes a number of areas in which attention to pinot noir has a shorter history, or plantings have occurred thus far on a smaller scale, or plantings have actually been reduced by disease. Additionally, there are subdivisions of the major areas that are in the process of developing distinct identities. In some cases regions coincide quite precisely with the boundaries of American Viticultural Areas, or AVAs, proposed by vintners and approved by the TTB. In other cases, the AVAs, at least for now, have less currency with consumers than do preexisting political designations.

As a matter of purely arbitrary convenience, this book will approach the Pacific Pinot Zone from south to north, one AVA at a time, except that some neighboring AVAs are grouped together for convenience of discussion. The southern Central Coast is defined to include the Santa Rita Hills, Santa Maria Valley, Arroyo Grande, and Edna Valley AVAs. The Salinas Valley is defined to include the Santa Lucia Highlands, Chalone, and Mount Harlan AVAs, and parts of the Monterey AVA. The Santa Cruz Mountains, Los Carneros, Russian River valley, and Anderson Valley are each treated independently. The "true" Sonoma Coast is defined without reference to the much larger AVA of the same name; and Oregon's Willamette Valley is handled for the moment as a single AVA, though applications are pending to superimpose smaller AVAs on the larger canvas, creating distinct identities for the Eola Hills, the Dundee Hills, Ribbon Ridge, the Chehalem Mountains, the Yamhill-Carlton District, and the McMinnville foothills. British Columbia's Okanagan River valley is treated independently. The Finger Lakes region of New York and Ontario's Niagara Peninsula are treated together as the greater south shore of Lake Ontario.

THE SOUTHERN CENTRAL COAST

Geographically, California's Central Coast is a long stretch of discontinuous coastal hills running primarily northwest to southeast from Morro Bay to Point Conception, and marine-ventilated valleys oriented mostly east-west. These valleys are a bit like Napa and Sonoma rotated clockwise 90 degrees; the landlocked ends are warm during most of the long growing season, while marine air keeps the valley mouths cool. Because the Pacific coastline turns from north-south to east-west at Point Conception, the southern end of the Central Coast region is surrounded by ocean on two sides, making it cooler still. Away from the coast, the countryside is mostly grass- and chaparral-covered ranch land; closer to the ocean the chaparral gives way to strawberry, broccoli, lima bean, cilantro, and tomatillo fields. In the south, close to the tile-roofed beachfront city of Santa Barbara, the land has attracted a noticeable population of movie stars and their horses, plus the occasional llama and ostrich ranch. The main population centers are the cities of Santa Maria, whose economy depends on agriculture, ranching, oil, and service to nearby Vandenberg Air Force Base; and San Luis Obispo, founded as one of the California missions. The epicenters for wine tourism are the quaint Victorian village of Los Olivos in the south, which offers a number of tasting rooms, plus inns, restaurants, art galleries, and antique shops; and the mission city of San Luis Obispo in the north.

History There was some viticulture associated with the Spanish missions at Santa Barbara, La Purísima, near Lompoc, Santa Ynez, and San Luis Obispo; some commercial viticulture around San Luis Obispo in the second half of the nineteenth century; and a few noncommercial vineyards established by ranchers and homesteaders in the Santa Ynez and Arroyo Grande valleys, where a bit of centenary zinfandel survives to this day. But the serious viticultural history of the southern Central Coast did not begin until the 1960s.

In 1964, Uriel Nielson and Bill DeMattei planted 30 acres of wine grapes on the Tepusquet Bench overlooking the Santa Maria River. Nielson, the son of table-grape growers in the San Joaquin Valley and a graduate of the University of California, Davis's new viticulture program, had become convinced that the Santa Maria Valley was a hugely promising environment for wine grapes, and that Northern California wineries would purchase whatever he could grow. When Nielson and DeMattei's first harvest was sold in 1968 to the Christian Brothers for a price equal to the highest being paid for fruit in Napa Valley, their success immediately generated an avalanche of interest and promotion. The county's main newspaper, the *Santa Barbara News-Press,* ran an article trumpeting the county's "newest and perhaps most glamorous crop," and the Pacific Gas and Electric Company then circulated the article to its agricultural customers in pamphlet form. Bank of America forecast annual growth rates of more than 10 percent for the wine industry and offered loans for vineyard development. In an evolution unique to the southern Central Coast, the entire region's viticulture was then built by farmers intent on growing fruit for large winemaking operations located 300 miles north, and by commercial investors prepared to bankroll the farmers. Virtually all of the names then big in California wine—the Christian Brothers, Paul Masson, Almaden, Geyser Peak, Beringer, Gallo, and Mondavi—were early and enthusiastic buyers of Santa Barbara grapes.

However, when the rapid increase in national per-capita wine consumption that fueled the wineries' appetites flagged in the mid 1970s and the prices paid for wine grapes fell, the Santa Barbara County vineyards were affected. Without an indigenous winemaking industry, grape growing in the area was vulnerable. As late as 1975, according to Otis L. Graham Jr. et al.'s *Aged in Oak: The Story of the Santa Barbara County Wine Industry,* there were only four producing wineries in the county, of which one had yet to release its first vintage. Vineyard acreage grew from just over 2,000 acres in 1972 to nearly 7,500 acres in 1979. At the end of the 1970s and in the 1980s, the county's winery and winemaker population finally began to grow, but now the large, exogenous wine corporations, which had bought Santa Barbara grapes during the earlier boom, became major purchasers of land and developers of the county's vineyards. In 1987, Kendall-Jackson bought Cambria, including 1,000 acres of vineyard, and Robert Mondavi acquired Byron, including 400 acres of vines. Wine World Estates, then the parent of Beringer and Chateau Souverain, bought the Estrella River Winery in 1988, including 515 acres of vineyard, and followed this purchase with 2,500 acres on White Hills Road and 375 acres in Cat Canyon. Within a few years, a huge percentage of the county's vineyards changed ownership, throwing the area's small coterie of landless boutique winemakers into a crisis from which they did not recover until the 1990s.

As in other regions, little attention was paid to the appropriate marriages of mesoclimates and grape varieties at the outset. Nielson and DeMattei planted a shotgun assortment of cabernet sauvignon, sylvaner, riesling, sauvignon blanc, and chardonnay. A similar menu was chosen when the Miller brothers put grapes on a parcel around the Tepusquet adobe in 1968. In both locations, the cabernet refused to ripen reliably, or produced wine with a decidedly green edge. Because of changing consumer tastes, the market for both sylvaner and riesling shriveled. In general, cool-climate varieties like pinot noir were neglected at the outset. Bob Woods, who managed a ranch adjacent to the Nielson-DeMattei parcel, is credited with planting the county's first few acres of pinot in 1969, though it is not clear in retrospect whether he was prescient or lucky. Richard Sanford and Michael Benedict, respectively a geographer and a botanist at the University of California, Santa Barbara, were apparently the second planters of pinot, in 1970, in the vineyard that still carries their names, on Santa Rosa Road between Buellton and Lompoc. But even these Burgundy-oriented pioneers hedged their bets: in addition to pinot and chardonnay, they set in cabernet and riesling vines, and several years passed before they were satisfied to graft these to the successful Burgundian varieties.

Chardonnay was Santa Barbara's first success story, emerging as the area's best-selling variety. Very gradually, however, a fragile association of the Central Coast valleys with good pinot noir was also established. In 1976, Hugh Johnson and Bob Thompson's *California Wine Book,* quoting "some skilled observers," identified Santa Maria Valley as, perhaps, "*the* place in all California for pinot noir." Two years later, when the first vintage of Sanford & Benedict's pinot was released, Dan Berger, writing in the *Los Angeles Times,* called it "a wine of cult proportions." Slowly, pinot noir emerged as the privileged red grape variety in the Santa Maria and western Santa Ynez valleys, and plantings of it spread into neighboring San Luis Obispo County.

In San Luis Obispo County, the first vineyards went into the ground in the 1970s, in the Edna Valley. The first grape farmer here was the county's farm adviser, who planted vines as a proof of concept. Then, within the space of a single year and less than one mile apart, commercial plantings were undertaken at Chamisal Vineyard and Paragon Vineyards, southeast of San Luis Obispo on Orcutt Road. The spotlight fell on chardonnay, but both enterprises put in pinot noir as well. Some of Paragon's pinot, purchased and vinified by Chalone, was private-labeled in 1977 and 1978. In 1979 it was released as Edna Valley Vineyard pinot noir, the child of a joint venture between Paragon and Chalone.

In 1981, Don Talley, a second-generation vegetable farmer in the Arroyo Grande Valley, set out that valley's first wine grapes since the 1880s, on an experimental basis. Both his experimental planting and subsequent commercial plantings included pinot noir. Maison Deutz, the California offshoot of Champagne Deutz, followed with 60 acres of pinot noir, and more of chardonnay—destined for sparkling wine—in 1984. In the 1990s, plantings of pinot noir finally exploded throughout the southern Central Coast, surpassing even chardonnay in rate of increase.

There were only five wineries in Santa Barbara County in 1973. By 1992 the number had grown to 34, and by 1998 to 56. Although the ten largest now produce four-fifths of total volume, 60 percent are boutique producers bottling fewer than 5,000 cases a year. Gradually Santa Barbara is also using more of its own fruit. In 1998 46 percent of harvested grapes were crushed by local wineries, up from barely a third in 1992. In 2000, the most recent year for which data are available, no less than 3,000 acres were planted to pinot noir, up from 1,200 acres in 1997 and barely 900 in 1992. In 2000, San Luis Obispo County had an additional 1,100 acres. In the Santa Rita Hills and Arroyo Grande Valley AVAs, pinot is the most widely planted variety.

Terrain, Terroir, and Vineyards The largest concentration of vineyard in the southern Central Coast, and also the largest of pinot noir, is found in the Santa Maria Valley AVA, a lopsided hexagon extending east from the urban boundaries of Santa Maria and Orcutt, where the land is low and relatively flat, to the first peaks of the San Rafael Mountains. Pinot noir is planted primarily along a 12-mile south- and southwest-facing crescent of the San Rafael foothills and Santa Maria River benchland, about 15 miles from the ocean, called the Tepusquet Bench; and on flattish, sandy mesas between Foxen Canyon Road, Telephone Road, and Clark Avenue, almost touching the eastern city limits of Santa Maria and Orcutt.

For all practical purposes, the true benchland portion of the Tepusquet Bench is now planted corner to corner, and pinot noir accounts for about one-fifth of its total planted acreage. Northwest to southeast, this surface is exploited by Bien Nacido, developed and still owned by the Miller family, farmers for three generations in Santa Barbara and Ventura counties; Cambria, now owned by Jackson Family Farms; and Byron, which now belongs to Robert Mondavi. Byron's land includes the 120-acre parcel originally planted by Nielsen and DeMattei in 1964. Cambria's property—1,400 planted acres, of which 235 are devoted to pinot noir—includes a parcel planted in 1971 by Louis Lucas and Dale Hampton, some of which was dedicated to pinot noir from the beginning.

At Bien Nacido, pinot noir now represents 250 acres in a total vineyard surface of just over 800 acres. The oldest pinot at Bien Nacido was set out in 1973; the youngest was planted in 1997. The letter-designated blocks, of which F, G, H, N, Q, R, S, and T are pinot noir, were planted in 1973, except that F was replanted in 1997; the number-designated blocks 1 through 3 and 7 through 10 are also pinot noir but represent younger plantings. The original plantings are true benchland sites below the toe of the foothills, all roughly rectangular and southwest-facing; the numbered vineyards are smaller, irregular hillside parcels with various southern and western exposures. The foothill sites, where the soils are a bit rockier and thinner, are increasingly favored for pinot noir, not only at Bien Nacido, but also at Cambria and Byron, but many winemakers who work with Bien Nacido fruit, and several who purchase small quantities of pinot noir from Cambria, still have well-developed preferences for some of the older, mature blocks on flatter benchland. In all, about two dozen producers, including boutique producers with astral reputations for fine pinot noir, source pinot from Bien Nacido, and at least one—Chris Whitcraft, who obtains fruit from more than one block—keeps even the blocks separate from each other, sometimes producing more than one block-designated Bien Nacido pinot in a single vintage. (See the profiles on Lane Tanner, Gary Farrell, Foxen, Testarossa Vineyards, The

Ojai Vineyard, Sanford, and Au Bon Climat in part II for additional information about pinots made from Bien Nacido fruit.)

A small coterie of Santa Barbara County winemakers (Foxen and Lane Tanner inter alia) also source pinot from Cambria's so-called Julia's Vineyard, a name applied to six blocks of low-lying benchland on the south side of Santa Maria Mesa Road, where a mix of sandy loam and fractured quartz-rich shale overlays cobbly subsoil. Otherwise, neither Cambria nor Byron sells fruit, though some Cambria pinot is used in other Kendall-Jackson pinot programs, and some deselected Byron fruit goes to other Mondavi programs.

The mesas on the southwestern side of the river are the AVA's other main concentration of vineyard. Because this area is a few miles closer to the ocean, it is slightly cooler than the Tepusquet Bench, and its soils are sandier. This combination makes, in general, for more elegant and less tannic wines. The total planted surface on the mesas is about 1,000 acres, of which a substantial percentage, but less than half, is pinot. The historic vineyards are Santa Maria Hills, a thin east-west strip of land between Dominion and Telephone Roads where ten acres of cabernet sauvignon and white riesling were planted in 1970, followed by 135 acres of pinot noir in 1973 and 1974; and Sierra Madre, on Dominion Road, originally planted by the same vineyardists who undertook what is now Cambria's section of Tepusquet, in 1974. The western section of the vineyard was planted with scion material from Wente's increase block (an area of vineyard grown primarily to produce budwood for new plantings) in Arroyo Seco, making it some combination of UCD 1A, 2A, and 4. (For more information on the University of California, Davis, pinot selections, see chapter 5.) The eastern section used a "heat-treated clone from Cal-Vine Nurseries," which was probably UCD 5. From the 1970s into the 1990s, fruit from both vineyards was sold to many makers, and a good many well-respected Santa Maria Valley pinots were made wholly or partially from Sierra Madre or Santa Maria Hills fruit.

In the 1990s, however, pieces of both vineyards changed hands. An 80-acre area of Sierra Madre was sold to Fess Parker in 1995, who renamed it for his wife, Marcella. The rest of the ranch was sold to Robert Mondavi in 1996, at which point fruit sales to independent winemakers ceased. At Santa Maria Hills, 78 acres were carved out for Cottonwood Canyon Winery in 1988, which converted 18 acres of erstwhile chardonnay to pinot noir. The rest of Santa Maria Hills was then divided between Caymus Vineyards, which leases and manages the vineyard's western side, and Lucas & Lewellyn Vineyards, the 1990s reincarnation of Louis Lucas's pioneering vineyard ventures.

Elsewhere on the mesas, additional acreage was planted to grapes in the 1990s, including the Dierberg Vineyard, which came on-line in 1999. Foxen, Tantara, and Fess Parker all made vineyard-designated pinots from Dierberg in 1999 or 2000, or both. At this writing, vineyards on the mesas still coexist with a majority population of flower farms and berry fields, so there is more land to plant there in due season.

Second to the Santa Maria Valley AVA in acreage devoted to pinot noir is the new Santa Rita Hills AVA, approved in 2001. This AVA overlays the western end of the Santa Ynez Valley AVA, which appellation vineyards in this area may also use; it encompasses about 30,000 acres north and south of the Santa Rita Hills, extending from a few miles east of Lompoc to a few miles west of the Buellton flats. It is a roughly bell-shaped appellation, with the bell's crown located where Highway 246 crosses the 200-foot elevation contour, and the bell's lip approximately in Drum Canyon, five miles west of Highway 101. The eponymous Santa Rita Hills are, effectively, the bell's clapper. Vineyards in this east-west maritime throat are concentrated along Highway 246 on the north side of the hills, where the topography is fairly gentle, with a dominance of eroded, grassy, rolling hills; and on the steeply contoured hillsides of the Santa Ynez River valley proper, between the Santa Rita Hills and the Santa Ynez Mountains. Vineyards are sited on both sides of the river, offering all possible aspects and exposures and a preponderance of fairly steep hillside locations.

Vineyard development in the Santa Rita Hills area lagged development in the eastern Santa Ynez Valley and the Santa Maria Valley by two-plus decades, however, despite the pioneering planting at Sanford & Benedict in 1970. The consensus in the 1970s and 1980s was that Sanford & Benedict was misguided. When Bryan Babcock's family purchased what is now their vineyard on Highway 246 in 1978, they were attracted by the cheaper price of land, not by its potential for vines.

Visually, this region is quite different from the Santa Maria Valley and more attractive, mixing picturesque horse ranches and bean fields with neat rows of vines. Arresting panoramas emerge one after another along Santa Rosa Road, especially overlooking vineyards like Sea Smoke that have claimed buttes on the northern side of the Santa Ynez River. Vineyard holdings are small, rarely exceeding 100 contiguous acres, and numerous small four- and five-acre parcels, meticulously farmed by pinot noir fanatics, were planted at the end of the 1990s. The Santa Rita Valley has been home to Babcock Winery since the early 1980s; now Babcock has been joined by Clos Pepe and Melville, and by large plantings undertaken by Fess Parker and Foley. On the southern side of the appellation, new vineyards (primarily pinot noir) have been planted by Lafond, Gainey, Sea Smoke Cellars, and a partnership of Fiddlehead Cellars and Beringer. Sea Smoke is the creation of Bob David, a developer of computer games who divides his life among Reno, the Caribbean, and the Santa Ynez Valley; his winemaker is Kris Curran, a native daughter trained at both Davis and Fresno, who previously worked at Cambria. Sanford, which had made its wines in a Buellton warehouse since the original Sanford-Benedict partnership was dissolved in the early 1980s, completed construction of a new winery adjacent to the old Sanford & Benedict vineyard in 2002. This spectacular complex, fashioned from copious quantities of field rock and repurposed old timber, is the most ambitious winemaking facility in the new AVA.

When the petition to establish the Santa Rita Hills AVA was submitted in 1998, there were about 500 planted acres in the appellation-to-be, mostly pinot noir. This surface at least doubled between 1999 and 2001, guaranteeing that most of this appellation will be young-vines territory for the foreseeable future. Making allowances for topography and for ridge-top locations that are too windy for vines, sources estimate that as much as half of the appellation's total surface could eventually be planted to grapes but expect most new vineyard development to be concentrated on the AVA's south side, given the recent designation of the Highway 246 corridor as critical habitat for the endangered California tiger salamander.

Pinot noir's other homes in the southern Central Coast are in San Luis Obispo County. They are the western end of the Arroyo Grande Valley AVA, between the Lopez Lake Recreational Area and Highway 101, and the Edna Valley AVA. The western end of the Arroyo Grande Valley is a relatively narrow east-west throat whose fertile bottomland is intensively farmed for vegetables. There are only two growers of pinot noir there. The larger by far is Laetitia, the mostly still-wine successor to Maison Deutz, which owns almost 2,000 hillside acres within sight of the Pacific Ocean, just east of Highway 101, of which about 450 acres are planted to pinot. Farther inland, Talley Farms tends another 56 acres of pinot noir on the hills above its vegetable fields.

The Edna Valley—larger, broader, and windier during the growing season and colder in the winter than the western end of the Arroyo Grande Valley—almost touches the midpoint of the Arroyo Grande Valley at its own southeastern end. Oriented northwest to southeast, sandwiched between the Santa Lucia Mountains on its northeastern side and the San Luis Hills on the southwestern side, it is cooled by marine air from Morro Bay, which sweeps first across Los Osos Valley west of San Luis Obispo. Vineyards are planted on the valley floor and in the foothills on both sides of the valley, up to the 600-foot contour on the Santa Lucia side and the 400-foot contour on the San Luis side. Various sandy clay loams, clay loams, and clay-based soils prevail here, many of which are calcareous at some level of the topsoil or subsoil. Since 1995, vineyard plantings have exploded in both valleys, more than tripling the planted surface in the Arroyo Grande Valley to 918 acres and nearly doubling the surface in the Edna Valley to 2,288 acres. In the Arroyo Grande Valley, pinot noir is the majority tenant, as it is in the Santa Rita Hills farther south, covering about 55 percent of total vineyard acres; but chardonnay is still king in the Edna Valley. There, pinot noir represents only one-quarter of the total vineyard area, but this fraction is up dramatically from 1995, when pinot accounted for only about 6.5 percent of the planted surface. There is still plenty of room for more vineyard in both AVAs, though the valley's bottomlands are too fertile for good wine grapes, and the steeper hillside sites may be too expensive to farm. For the moment, Arroyo Grande's pinot vineyards are almost entirely devoted to estate production, though both Talley and Laetitia sell small quantities of fruit to Au Bon Climat. Independent growers have dominated historically in the Edna Valley, but Chamisal Vineyard was reborn in 1998 as an estate winery called Domaine Alfred, and several boutique-size producers (Stephen Ross, Windemere, and Kynsi inter alia) now devote part of their energies to pinot noir made from estate-grown fruit.

THE GREATER SALINAS VALLEY

The Salinas Valley is by far the largest of California's coastal valleys, extending from the southern shore of Monterey Bay almost to the city of Paso Robles, by which point the Salinas River itself flows underground. At the northwestern end, during the growing season, the valley is a giant wind tunnel about ten miles wide, bounded on its northeastern side by the grassy Gavilan Range and on the southwestern side by the rugged Sierra de Salinas. Noticeable wind is clocked during most of each summer day after midmorning, and midday wind speeds can easily exceed 25 miles per hour. The valley's temperature gradient is steep, with peak growing-season temperatures in the low 60s at the bay shore but closer to 100 degrees at Paso Robles. Agriculture is the valley's main business, with head and leaf lettuces dominating the northwestern end of the valley floor, giving way to broccoli, onions, and field crops farther south and inland. The main population centers—Salinas, Greenfield, and King City—are heavily involved with agricultural processing. The Salinas Valley accounts for most of Monterey County's extensive vineyards, which topped 41,000 acres in 1999. The vineyards are concentrated in midvalley, on both sides of the valley, between Soledad and Greenfield. The Scheid Vineyard may be the single largest spread, farming about 5,000 acres of grapes in Monterey and San Benito counties and supplying customers ranging from Canandaigua and Heublein to Joseph Phelps and the Hess Collection.

History As elsewhere along the California mission trail, the valley's first vines were planted at the end of the eighteenth century by the Franciscan friars, around the mission at Soledad. The first commercial viticulture was apparently high on the eastern side of the valley, at what is now Chalone Vineyard, where an Oregonian by the name of Francis William Silvear planted several varieties, including pinot noir, in about 1919. As late as 1955, however, there were barely 100 acres of wine grapes in the entire valley.

The modern history of Salinas Valley viticulture began in the 1960s in response to the same growth in wine consumption that fueled the planting boom on the southern Central Coast. In Salinas, however, the prime movers were the four largest wine producers in neighboring Santa Clara and Contra Costa counties—Paul Masson, Almaden, Mirassou, and Wente Brothers—whose historic vineyards were under pressure from massive urban and suburban growth at the southern end of San Francisco Bay. These giants did not buy Monterey grapes from local growers, as the Christian Brothers did from Nielson and DeMattei; they bought land and planted their own vineyards. Aware that they were planting grapes in virgin territory and working closely with the University of California, the big four agreed that they would plant only clean, disease-free vines in Monterey, using budwood sourced from the FPMS at Davis. By the middle of the 1960s, Wente Brothers' certified increase block at Arroyo Seco had become a principal supplier of cuttings to growers in other parts of the state. Several early growers of pinot noir in the Russian River valley obtained their budwood from Wente's Arroyo Seco parcel. On the heels of the Santa Clara County producers, some large-scale investors and several medium-size wineries (notably the Monterey Vineyard and Monterey Peninsula Winery) pumped capital into new vineyards in Monterey, creating many vast spreads. More than 25,000 acres were planted in just two years between 1972 and 1974.

Unsurprisingly, this feverish expansion saturated the market, creating huge losses and investor bankruptcies, so planted acreage shrank dramatically after 1976. Pinot noir suffered disproportionately, its planted surface falling from a peak of 2,370 acres in 1976 to just 1,365 nine years later. This situation did not substantially improve until the 1990s, when Kendall-Jackson and Robert Mondavi became substantial purchasers, planters, and replanters of Salinas Valley vineyard, motivated in part by losses to phylloxera in the North Coast counties. About the same time, growers finally matched varieties to the valley's hugely different microclimates, a few longtime lettuce farmers got interested in grapes, and boutique producers demanded better fruit from established growers. Paraiso Springs, which had planted and grown grapes, including pinot noir, for Mirassou and Wente in the 1970s and 1980s, found itself selling instead to Morgan Winery, a local high-end producer, to Los Carneros–based Saintsbury, and most recently to Larry Brooks's new label, Campion.

Terrain, Terroir, and Vineyards For good pinot noir, the main area of interest is the Santa Lucia Highlands AVA, though some pinot noir is also grown in the neighboring Arroyo Seco AVA, as well as in the Monterey AVA, which covers considerable surface on the eastern side of the Salinas River. The Santa Lucia Highlands AVA is an 18-mile-long crooked finger of land on the valley's western side, hugging River Road, Foothill Road, and Paraiso Springs Road and separated from the valley floor by a quite visible fault. Its southeast-facing terraces are actually a series of alluvial fans composed primarily of very well drained loam, sandy loam, and gravelly loam. It is somewhat ironic that the prime movers behind the creation of the Santa Lucia Highlands AVA were not pinotphiles but advocates for cabernet sauvignon. Smith & Hook winemaker Art Nathan, who was one of them, argues that the Highlands "may be the coldest area in California where we can still ripen cabernet." Nowadays, the largest stand of pinot noir in the appellation (about 80 acres) belongs to Paraiso Springs. Most of it is mature vineyard, but significant quantities of newer plantings are farmed by Robert Mondavi, Smith & Lindley, Sleepy Hollow, Estancia, Cloninger, and Morgan.

That this AVA has begun to emerge as an area of great promise for pinot noir can be credited mostly to Gary Pisoni, the colorful and voluble son of a local farming family. In 1982 Pisoni, who had become passionate about wine in college, planted six acres of wine grapes, including pinot noir, on land his father had purchased for cattle ranching. Fortuitously, the ranch was a wind-protected site tucked behind folds in the mostly southeast-facing hills; it enjoyed temperatures a few degrees warmer than most of the AVA and consisted primarily of decomposed granite soils, with varying admixtures of sandy loam and rock. This Old Block is still in production, and Pisoni has since planted six additional blocks, all of which are 100 percent pinot noir. Tessa Block, the largest at 17 acres, was planted in 1991, just a bit more tightly spaced than Old Block; Hermanos Block, Camper Block, and Tina Block—five, 2.5, and 1.2 acres, respectively—followed in 1994; Elias Block, 4.5 acres of steep slope and especially poor soil, was set out in 1995; and Mommies Block, 2.5 acres of fairly rich loam where topsoil washes down from higher elevations, was planted in 1999. Tina Block was an experiment to see if quality pinot could be grown on a lyre-shaped trellis and at consequently higher yield. Elias Block has the distinction of having been planted on its own roots (as was Mommies later), and is reserved for the production of Pisoni's estate wine, made by Gary's son Jeff. Vine spacings, rootstocks, and row orientations vary. The scion material is a matter of some controversy; see chapter 5 for details. Pisoni sells his fruit, except for Elias Block, to a small stable of highly reputed, boutique-size pinot makers around the state, including Patz & Hall, Longoria, Arcadian, and Tandem, all of whom vineyard-designate most of it, making Pisoni easily the best-known vineyard in the AVA. In 1997, Pisoni teamed up with his longtime friend and neighbor Gary Franscioni to plant Garys' Vineyard about six miles north of Pisoni, in a less wind-protected and more typical Santa Lucia Highlands location. Garys' began producing in 1999 and has joined Pisoni on the short list of much-coveted Santa Lucia fruit. In 2001, the AVA was estimated to contain about 8,000 total planted acres, of which about 1,100 are pinot noir.

The other AVAs of consequence for pinot noir in this area are Chalone and Mount Harlan. Both are mountain appellations in the Gavilan Range, on the valley's eastern side. Chalone is at about 1,800 feet above sea level, in wild, chaparral-covered land near Pinnacles National Monument, overlooking (albeit distantly) the town of Soledad. Mount Harlan is higher still, averaging 2,200 feet, and clings to the mountains' northeastern face, overlooking La Cienega Valley rather than Salinas Valley. Geologically, climatically, and historically, these AVAs have little in common with the Salinas Valley, and are treated here based solely on their proximity. Both AVAs were created around preexisting wineries, Chalone and Calera. Chalone encompasses a total surface of about 8,600 acres, of which only a few hundred are planted. A few of these do not belong to the Chalone Vineyard, notably vines owned by the Brosseau family, but the Brosseaus' holdings depend on Chalone Vineyard for their access to water. There are 108 acres of pinot noir owned by Chalone Vineyard in the Chalone AVA, plus ten acres owned by the Brosseaus and a few more owned and farmed by Michael and Carol Hastings Michaud. Michaud was the winemaker at Chalone Vineyard in the early 1990s. Historically, Chalone made one of the first North American pinot noirs to be widely acclaimed and compared favorably with fine red Burgundy, in 1969. Much the same can be said for Calera, beginning with the 1982 vintage.

At Mount Harlan, Calera expected to have company in the AVA, but the remote site has thus far attracted no other vineyardists or vintners. The Mount Harlan AVA covers a surface of about 7,400 acres, but only about 55 are planted, of which 45 are pinot noir.

A key feature of both appellations, distinguishing them not only from the Salinas Valley proper but also from most of California, is a calcareous subsoil reminiscent of European wine lands. Although altitude tempers growing-season high temperatures slightly, both sites rely for their suitability for pinot noir on huge diurnal temperature variation, peaking midafternoons in the 90s but falling into the 50s overnight.

THE SANTA CRUZ MOUNTAINS

Geographically, the Santa Cruz Mountains are the piece of California's coastal range that extends between San Francisco and Monterey Bay. By convention, the designation is applied to the southern end of these hills, where the peaks are relatively impressive and the terrain fairly rugged, from approximately Crystal Springs in the north to Mt. Madonna, about six miles northwest of Watsonville. The Santa Cruz Mountains are a significant weather break, draining precipitation from maritime weather systems as they cross the coastline, and are therefore largely responsible for the mild climate of the Santa Clara Valley. This means that the western side of the mountains, facing the Pacific, receives 60 to 80 inches of winter rain, but the ocean also moderates air temperatures, generating mild winters and coolish summers. Dense fog and wind are common. The lee side of the mountains is much drier, with cooler winters and warmer summer days. The area is sparsely populated, except for the littoral along the north shore of Monterey Bay. The mountains' redwood forests were the object of a considerable logging industry in the nineteenth century and cattle were run where the terrain was not too rough, but agriculture is now confined primarily to the low land on the coastal side, where a great concentration of flower bulbs, strawberries, and brussels sprouts are grown. Redwood forest still dominates the higher terrain, which remains sparsely settled. The expansion of Silicon Valley has birthed minor concentrations of high-technology industry in Scotts Valley and Santa Cruz. The main artery across the mountains is Highway 17, but wine tourism requires forays onto narrow secondary roads, where hairpin turns offer often spectacular vistas but require speeds not much greater than that of molasses in winter.

History The first serious vineyards were planted on the eastern side of the Santa Cruz Mountains in the 1850s, when grape growing in the Santa Clara Valley spread uphill, seeking poorer soils and cooler temperatures. A decade later, after loggers had cleared land on the western side, vineyards were planted in what came to be called the Vine Hill district, above the town of Scotts Valley, near Ben Lomond, and in the hills above Soquel. More than 2,000 acres were then dedicated to wine grapes in the 1870s and 1880s, and Santa Cruz wines frequently won prizes in national and international competitions. An important development was the establishment of the Sacred Heart Novitiate in the hills above Los Gatos in 1886, incorporating a few acres of producing vineyard that had previously belonged to the Wilcox Ranch. The novitiate planted additional vines in the 1890s.

Pinot noir does not seem to have figured in any of Santa Cruz's earliest plantings, but the variety cut a southward path across the mountains beginning in 1896, after Paul Masson imported budwood from France to plant the hilltop site he called La Cresta, in the hills overlooking Saratoga. Martin Ray—a onetime stockbroker and real estate agent legendary for his eccentric personality and irascible behavior who had befriended Masson as a child—purchased La Cresta from Masson in 1936. About the same time, the novitiate expanded its vineyards once again, this time planting some pinot noir, but the source of its plant material is not known. In 1944, Ray sold La Cresta to the Seagram's Company but took cuttings from Masson's vineyard to start a vineyard of his own on a neighboring hilltop. Ray made pinot noir from his second-generation cuttings of Masson's budwood throughout the 1950s and 1960s, but lost control of all but a few acres of his property in the early 1970s following an acrimonious battle with dissident investors. Mount Eden Vineyards succeeded Ray and made some of California's most acclaimed pinots in the 1970s.

Meanwhile, David Bruce, a Stanford-trained dermatologist who had become enamored of Ray's wines, much as Ray had been smitten with Masson's a generation earlier, took cuttings to plant his own vineyard, this time on the western side of the mountains, just beyond the summit, on Bear Creek Road. Eventually Bruce became involved with other vineyard projects on the western side of the summit, including a 17-acre parcel of pinot noir he sold to ex-restaurateur Ken Burnap in 1976, which Burnap rebirthed as Santa Cruz Mountain Vineyard. Mount Eden Vineyards also became an important source of budwood for new pinot noir vineyards in other parts of California.

Unfortunately, one of the assets of the Santa Cruz Mountains—the range's rugged, timbered hillsides laced with streams—was transformed into a serious liability for its wine industry, and perhaps especially for pinot noir, in the 1990s. The region's ecology is hospitable to a bacterium that causes Pierce's disease, which is fatal to grapevines, and to an insect called the blue-green sharpshooter, which transmits the bacterium. Many dozens of acres of vineyard succumbed to Pierce's disease at the end of the decade.

Terrain, Terroir, and Vineyards The Santa Cruz Mountains AVA, created in 1981, encompasses about 350,000 acres in three counties. A genuine mountain appellation, it excludes land below the 400-foot contour on the Pacific side and below the 800-foot contour on the lee side. Its soils are generally thin and stony, and underlain with shale and sandstone. This is a natural damper on yields and has a tendency to increase the wines' concentration, but it can also make for tannic wines and for angular structure. At lower altitudes on the Pacific side, ocean fog is a persistent morning influence, but in higher-altitude vineyards the fog tends to burn off by midmorning, and sites near the summits escape the fog entirely. In general, the eastern side of the appellation is warmer, being protected from marine influence by the mountain spine itself.

In the entire AVA there are now just over 700 acres of vines, divided among more than 80 vest-pocket-size vineyards. This total is up very slightly from the numbers reported in the Santa Cruz Mountains Winegrowers Association's 1995 vineyard directory, which lists 61 vineyards covering 680 acres, but this AVA is barely growing, owing to a combination of rampant Pierce's disease and the expense of farming aggressively steep terrain. Because of the terrain and the "loner" ethos of the area, the typical vineyard size is tiny—less than five acres—though a few larger holdings drive the average size to 11 acres. Vineyards are typically owned by growers, but a few of the larger spreads belong to wineries, and many growers sell fruit to wineries located within the AVA. Demand for Santa Cruz Mountains fruit is intense thanks to the very short supply, and at least one local winery (Clos La Chance) has created a vineyard-management subsidiary specifically to plant and farm tiny backyard-size plots for individuals owning suitable land, in return for purchase rights to the grapes produced.

Pinot noir was believed to account for 151 of the AVA's 700-plus planted acres in 2001, up from 115 in 1995. The most noteworthy of the pinot vineyards are the estate vineyards at Mount Eden, David Bruce, Santa Cruz Mountain Vineyard, and Thomas Fogarty, but a few grower-owned sites have developed sufficient identity to emerge as non-estate vineyard-designated wines. Peter Martin Ray's five acres of pinot, just below the older Martin Ray vineyards now exploited by Mount Eden, are an example; Cronin Vineyards bottles a vineyard-designated pinot from Peter Martin Ray's fruit. On the Pacific side, Santa Cruz Mountain Vineyard and Salamandre Wine Cellars have made numerous vineyard-designated pinots from the Ciardella Vineyard, which was called Matteson Vineyard until the ownership changed in 1997. Ciardella's 3.5 acres of pinot noir were planted in increments during the 1980s at an altitude of 1,600 feet, above Watsonville. The surrounding eucalyptus appears to imbue these wines with resinous aromas.

A new, high-profile all-pinot project began to wend its way through Santa Clara County's permits and approvals process in 2000, attracting considerable attention from the local press. T. J. Rodgers, the chairman of Cypress Semiconductors, has proposed to plant 70 acres off Skyline Drive not far from the Thomas Fogarty Winery, spending "whatever it takes" to exploit the site. The plans include a custom-built funicular tractor to gain access to the steep slopes, excavation of three caves to house a gravity-flow winery, and full solar power. If and when Rodgers's plans are fully approved and realized, his venture would constitute the largest (and most expensive) pinot project in the entire AVA.

LOS CARNEROS

The main route from San Francisco to the Napa Valley wine country runs across the Golden Gate Bridge, north through the posh suburbs of Marin County, then east along the sparsely settled shoreline of San Pablo Bay. At Sears Point, where the Sonoma Mountains, reduced to grassy knolls, meet the bay, a dogleg of road now called the Carneros Highway takes off north into the Sonoma Valley but then turns east itself, winding through the rolling hills at the southern end of the Mayacamas Range into Napa County. This is Los Carneros, the mouth ends of two northwest-southeast-oriented valleys, where the climate is determined not by the valleys' mountain rims but by the proximity of San Pablo and San Francisco bays, the huge Sacramento River delta, and the open ocean beyond the Golden Gate. There is persistent morning fog and afternoon wind. Vineyards share Los Carneros's higher elevations with dairy farming, a bit of declining orchard, and some minor commerce, but there are no commercial centers here, and no centers of population. Much of the bay front is marshland laced with sloughs, now set aside as refuge for various shoreline birds, fish, and invertebrates. There is now a generous handful of tasting rooms in Los Carneros, and visitor services are in ample supply nearby, in Napa and Sonoma.

History The nineteenth-century history of Los Carneros revolves mostly around the northernmost of the California missions, established at Sonoma in 1823, and Los Carneros's easy maritime access to San Francisco from wharves built along Sonoma Creek and the Napa River. The land was used primarily for sheep and cattle ranching, and for pear, plum, apple, and apricot orchards. Los Carneros's wharves were the main point of embarkation for fruit, hay, and grain destined for San Francisco and points beyond.

Some wine grapes were planted here as early as the 1840s, however. The first documented planting seems to have been done by Jacob Leese along Huichica Creek, just west of what is now the Napa-Sonoma county line, on land now owned (and once again planted to grapes) by Robert Mondavi. Leese, who was a son-in-law of General Mariano Vallejo, the area's military commander under Mexican rule, may also have been the first person to make wine in Carneros, reportedly using "a soft cow hide and strong-legged Indians" (according to Ernest Peninou's *History of the Sonoma Viticultural District*) to press his grapes. In the mid 1850s, Leese sold a huge chunk of his land grant to William Winter, a native of Indiana, who built Carneros's first winery. Later in the century, additional vineyard was planted, especially on the eastern edge of the modern appellation, along what are now Cuttings' Wharf Road and Buchli Station Road. Wineries were built on Judge John Stanly's ranch on Stanly Lane, and north of the Carneros Highway in what is now the Winery Lake vineyard. In the 1880s, this was the James Simonton estate, called Talcoa, managed by George Husmann, the viticulturist who devised and championed vine grafting as a remedy for phylloxera. Another winery, Garetto, established in 1899 on Buchli Station Road, remained in use throughout Prohibition—according to some accounts, the winery even possessed a truck-mounted still that was driven safely underwater whenever federal agents staged a raid—and is now home to Bouchaine Vineyards.

There is considerable confusion about the varietal identity of the pre-Prohibition grape plantings in Los Carneros. No less than André Tchelistcheff is apparently (and perhaps unintentionally) responsible for much of it. In his oral history he testifies that Carneros "was known in the old days before Prohibition as a fine quality region of Pinot Noir and the Chardonnays" and cites both the Stanly ranch and "the southernmost portion" of Haraszthy's property—presumably Buena Vista—as spots where these varieties were supposed to have been grown. In another part of the same interview, Tchelistcheff remembers tasting "a Cabernet and a Burgundy of 1918 with Georges de Latour," both apparently from the Stanly ranch. The Burgundy, he says, was "a combination of Cabernet and Pinot Noir" that he "considered . . . as even much greater wine than the Cabernet straight." Separately, he told wine historian Charles Sullivan that he had tasted "a 1918 Pinot noir from the Stanly Ranch." This testimony is, at best, problematical. Did Tchelistcheff actually taste both a Burgundy and a pinot noir from the 1918 vintage—both necessarily sometime after his arrival in California 19 years later in 1937? Or were these the same wine, differently identified in two tellings of the story? How did Tchelistcheff know the source or the varietal identity of the grapes vinified two decades earlier? Stanly's La Loma name had been sold—perhaps as early as the 1890s but certainly by 1910—to the California Wine Association, which owned no fewer than 50 wineries and was the state's main producer and distributor of blended wine. If the wine Tchelistcheff says he tasted was in fact the CWA ("CALWA") brand of La Loma "Burgundy," there can be no assurance that it contained pinot noir at all or that any of the fruit, whatever its variety, had been grown on Stanly's ranch.

A separate and slightly more persuasive bit of evidence that pinot noir may have been grown in or near Carneros before Prohibition is J. Gundlach and Company's 1901 Chambertin, presumably made from grapes grown on Jacob Gundlach's Rhinefarm Estate, east of Vineburg and just north of the current boundary of Los Carneros. Wine historians, as we have seen, believe that the wines labeled "Chambertin" at the end of the nineteenth century were pinot-based, just as those called "Médoc" were mostly varietal cabernet sauvignon, so the Chambertin could have been made from estate-grown pinot noir. At best, however, Tchelistcheff's ex post facto testimony and Gundlach's Chambertin establish only the *possibility* that some pinot noir was grown someplace in or near Carneros before Prohibition, and this is not a certainty by any means. More likely, the few vineyards that existed in this area in the late nineteenth and early twentieth centuries were dedicated primarily to mondeuse and to three varieties native to the French southwest—tannat, negrette, and abourieu—plus the riesling and chasselas planted by the German farmers who clustered south and east of Sonoma. There are numerous references to all of these red varieties in the contemporary record. The monikers by which they were commonly known in California may explain why various commentators (and perhaps even Tchelistcheff) were led to believe that Carneros was awash in pinot noir before Prohibition, since negrette was called Pinot St. George and abourieu was dubbed Early Burgundy.

The well-documented history of pinot noir in Los Carneros begins after World War II. In 1948 Louis M. Martini planted it on the former Stanly ranch, part of which he had purchased in 1942. Martini's first plantings at Stanly—which he renamed for Stanly's winery, La Loma—were cabernet sauvignon, however, demonstrating that even in this period, Carneros was not regarded as a natural home for pinot noir. Martini's plant material was taken from an old block of pinot at Inglenook (see chapter 5 for details), and his initial plantings, carried out in collaboration with Davis viticulturist Harold Olmo, were explicitly experimental. It is not known how much acreage Martini eventually dedicated to pinot noir at La Loma, but it was apparently substantial, and the firm made varietal pinot from these plantings during the 1950s. Sometime later—probably about 1962—Louis M.'s son Louis P. Martini purchased additional land in Carneros, about four miles from La Loma, on Las Amigas Road. Approximately 110 acres were dedicated to pinot noir at this site, a small piece of which is still in production—see the Acacia Winery profile for details.

While the Martinis were making the first sustained commitment to pinot noir in Carneros, Tchelistcheff emerged as the region's most visible cheerleader and as an enthusiastic proponent of its suitability for chardonnay and pinot noir. The handful of vintners who began, in the 1960s, to take Carneros seriously report that Tchelistcheff encouraged them. He seems also to have made repeated efforts to persuade Hélène de Pins, who controlled Beaulieu Vineyards after de Latour's death in 1940, to invest in Carneros; but these were not successful until 1965, when the firm finally purchased the land now known as BV 5. In fact, it appears that it was Beaulieu's acute need for grapes following the sale of Martin Stelling's To-Kalon vineyard to Charles Krug in 1962, and not the cool charms of Carneros, that clinched the acquisition of BV 5. Meanwhile, the Beautour pinots Tchelistcheff produced at Beaulieu during the 1940s and 1950s were made not from Carneros fruit (as some writers have alleged) but from the firm's home vineyards in Rutherford. Tchelistcheff explains in his oral history that it was only after BV 5 was planted (to chardonnay and pinot noir) in 1965 that he "moved all the Burgundy varieties out" of the Rutherford vineyards.

The coincidence of the premium wine boom and the introduction of modern drip irrigation technology led to more plantings of wine grapes in Los Carneros during the 1960s and 1970s. The triumph of cool-climate varieties was no more instantaneous there than it was in the southern Central Coast or the Russian River valley, however. Growers and wineries alike persisted in planting pinot noir cheek by jowl with varieties requiring warmer sites, especially cabernet sauvignon. Buena Vista planted 84 acres of cabernet between 1969 and 1971 and 48 more acres in 1978, both before and after the brand invested in more than 400 acres of Carneros pinot noir, chardonnay, gamay, riesling, getwürztraminer, and merlot. In the 1960s, when Rene di Rosa planted his Winery Lake Vineyard on land he had originally intended to use for hay or sheep ranching, pinot noir was only one among many varieties he chose to grow.

Very gradually, however, several factors combined to ensure that Los Carneros focused increasingly (and finally overwhelmingly) on pinot and chardonnay. As the value of midvalley land in Napa increased, its use for low-yield and lower-value varieties like pinot noir became economically disadvantageous. Pinot came to make better sense where the land was cheaper, as it was in Carneros. Simultaneously, wine drinkers learned to prefer Bordeaux-type wines with very ripe flavors, so the cool Carneros-style cabernets fell from favor. And the sparkling-wine business boomed, creating a brisk demand for pinot noir and chardonnay grapes. Finally, a handful of visionaries stubbornly dedicated to making pinot noir that could rival Burgundy focused their attentions on Carneros.

Francis Mahoney, who figures among the visionaries, founded the Carneros Creek Winery in 1972, beginning clonal trials of pinot noir and building the first wine production facility to be sited in the Carneros area since the turn of the century. Two years later, Domaine Chandon, the California venture of Champagne giant Moët & Chandon, purchased and planted its first parcels in Carneros, dedicated to pinot noir and chardonnay destined for sparkling cuvées. Acacia Winery, another enterprise oriented to Burgundian varieties, broke ground in 1979. Acacia owned no vines, but purchased the best grapes it could find from local growers, and pioneered vineyard designation. Acacia was followed in 1980 by Bouchaine, which reclaimed the old Garetto Winery from Beringer (which had used it only as a barrel and storage facility), and in 1981 by Saintsbury. Three more European sparkling houses followed Moët into Carneros during the 1980s—Freixenet and Codorníu from Catalonia and Taittinger from Reims. Between 1983 and 1986, more than 500 acres of pinot noir and chardonnay were planted in Carneros by Buena Vista, Carneros Creek, Cuvaison, Domaine Chandon, Gloria Ferrer, Louis Martini, and independent growers Lee Hudson and Tony Truchard. Robert Mondavi, formerly content to source most of the fruit required for its pinot noir program in midvalley Napa, purchased a large ranch on Duhig Road in 1988 and planted that firm's first 15 acres of Carneros pinot noir in 1989.

In all, about 1,800 acres of Carneros land changed hands between 1985 and 1989, of which 70 percent were acquired by so-called up-valley wineries, including Grgich Hills, Mondavi, St. Clement, Shafer, and Silverado Cellars. Martini sold the former Stanly ranch to an investment group called CVI (Carneros Valley Investors), which expanded the Martini plantings and sold fruit to numerous wineries. From the eastern slope of the Sonoma Mountains to Highway 29 in Napa, hundreds of acres were converted from orchard and pasture to pinot and chardonnay vineyard, and the last graveyards of rusting automobiles and junk were removed from the landscape. Of the new vine plantings in Carneros, 85 percent were either chardonnay or pinot noir; other varieties virtually disappeared from local radar. By the beginning of the 1990s, Los Carneros, now very serious wine country, was the largest producer of pinot noir in North America—a position it maintained until it was overtaken by the Willamette Valley and the southern Central Coast at decade's end.

Terrain, Terroir, and Vineyards The Los Carneros AVA, established in 1983, is shaped a bit like a lumpy, horizontal hourglass. The narrow neck of the appellation is squeezed between the southern end of the Mayacamas mountains and the bay and coincides with the Napa-Sonoma county line. The western lobe, in Sonoma County, extends across the flat southern end of the Sonoma Valley into the foothills on the valley's western side. The eastern lobe, mostly in Napa County, is bounded on the north by the 400-foot contour of the Mayacamas Range and on the east by the Napa River; it consists mostly of gently rolling terrain with few flats. The southern boundary of both lobes and the neck follow railroad tracks laid in the 1880s as close to the marshland as the land was firm, which also defines the outer limit of land suitable for grapevines. All of the high ridges in Carneros have views of San Pablo Bay, and the Richmond–San Rafael Bridge is visible on a clear day from the highest spots, like the terraced gardens of the ultramodern Artesa Winery on Dealy Lane.

The AVA covers about 36,000 acres of land surface, of which a bit less than half are deemed plantable. Of this, just over 8,000 acres of vineyard are under cultivation. In 1998, 36 percent was pinot noir, up from 32 percent in 1988. Cabernet acreage, 6 percent of total vineyard surface in 1988, has shrunk to 3 percent, but plantings of merlot have increased, and syrah has made a measurable appearance.

Vineyards are concentrated on the relatively flat land on the western side of Sonoma Creek close to the western edge of the appellation, and on the rolling hills bisected by the Carneros Highway that extend from approximately one mile east of Schellville to the intersection with Highway 29 south of Napa. Vineyards also extend northward on the Napa side of the AVA into the canyon along Dealy Lane and Henry Road, and along Old Sonoma Road; but these areas, known locally as Carneros's banana belt, are a bit warmer than sites closer to water, so a significant percentage of the AVA's merlot and syrah has been planted there. There is also a sparse scattering of vineyards on flat land between the two lobes of the appellation, southeast of the town of Sonoma, around the crossroads called Vineburg. These flatland vineyards belong almost exclusively to independent growers. Vineyards are now also beginning to creep up the eastern slopes of the Sonoma Mountains.

On the western side of Sonoma Creek, the Sangiacomo family is the main owner of vineyard. Their customers are a virtual who's who of the most important makers of cool-climate varieties in California, many of whom produce vineyard-designated pinots from Sangiacomo fruit. Gloria Ferrer and Sebastiani also have substantial vineyard holdings on this side of the AVA, and MacRostie has pioneered new plantings on Wildcat Ridge, behind Gloria Ferrer. Buena Vista Winery has major holdings just west of the Napa-Sonoma line, south of the Carneros Highway.

In Napa County, the largest single owner of Carneros vineyard is Domaine Chandon, but many up-valley Napa houses own significant parcels, including Robert Mondavi, Beaulieu Vineyards, Clos du Val, Seagram's (which owns both Sterling and Mumm), Robert Sinskey, and Cuvaison. Carneros-based wineries also own considerable acreage, especially Domaine Carneros, which owns two parcels in addition to its home vineyard behind the château at the corner of Duhig Road and Carneros Highway. Other locally based wineries are Saintsbury, which purchased the Brown Ranch on Old Sonoma Road in 1995, and Mont St. John, which owns more than 160 acres at the corner of Carneros Highway and Old Sonoma Road. On the Napa side of the appellation, independent growers like Lee Hudson, Larry Hyde, Ira and Shirley Lee, Andy Beckstoffer, and Jim St. Clair sell fruit to up-valley wineries, to land-poor or landless Carneros wineries, and to winemakers domiciled in other parts of California, spawning a large number of vineyard-designated bottlings. The St. Clair Vineyard is Acacia's flagship bottling and is the only vineyard-designated pinot the brand has produced continuously in every vintage since its founding. Hyde Vineyard pinot has been made by Steele Wines, Etude, Whitethorn, Paul Hobbs, Patz & Hall, and at least a dozen others.

No one knows the head count for sure, but well-informed sources estimate that when wineries and independents are tallied, there are fewer than 60 growers of pinot noir in the entire appellation. This concentration of relatively large holdings in relatively few hands makes Los Carneros demographically quite different from other major pinot regions except the Santa Maria Valley. Partially the concentration is the consequence of gentle topography, which favors large-scale exploitation, but Carneros is also the backyard of some of the richest and best capitalized wine interests in North America, who have had the resources to buy and develop its land in relatively large pieces.

Los Carneros's soils divide between two main types, both formed in the past two million years of geological time, when the waters of San Pablo Bay retreated to more or less the present shoreline. Soils that are predominantly yellow-brown, and frequently laced with bits of seashell, belong to the so-called Haire series. Owing to the remnants of marine organisms and salt marsh vegetation, these soils tend to be relatively high in calcium. Diablo soils, which are predominantly black, are mostly fossil-free and more acidic. Both series have high clay content and form only a shallow layer on top of a hard clay pan. The high clay makes for very muddy vineyards after winter rains, and for relatively high water retention during the growing season. Because Carneros gets less than 20 inches of rainfall annually, many viticulturists believe the clay topsoil is at least a mixed blessing. The hard clay pan is more controversial. Its upside is that it makes the topsoil shallow, which discourages vine vigor and naturally limits yields, but some observers think the pan under Carneros's shallow soils prevents deep rooting of vines, which interferes with their access to subsoil components thought to be associated with complexity in wine. Some local winegrowers advocate using drain tile in the vineyard to increase soil permeability. Some viticulturists describe a trend to privilege the Haire soils for pinot, leaving Diablo soils for chardonnay; others favor planting pinot in the thinnest, best-drained soils available, regardless of geological series, to get the best control over vigor. A few winemakers with long Carneros experience argue that it's essential to be very choosy about site. They are partial to sites where an old streambed has left some sedimentary loam or surface rock, like parts of Saintsbury's Brown Ranch.

There are a few blocks of very old pinot noir still producing in Carneros. Some of Louis P. Martini's Las Amigas plantings, now owned by Andy Beckstoffer's Napa Valley Vineyard Company, have already been discussed. Some 1960s plantings have also persisted at Winery Lake, in the Hyde Vineyard and at Beaulieu's BV 5 vineyard. But most Carneros pinot noir is now made from new plantings or from replanted vineyards. Some of the replanting has been driven by losses to phylloxera and eutypa, but vineyard consultant Mary Hall says that a lot of vines have been pulled out in Carneros just because "they don't make good wine," and because the economy has been healthy enough to sustain the ensuing cost. In part this trend reflects the declining utilization of Carneros's pinot for sparkling wines, more tolerant of higher yields and less-fastidious quality. The sparkling houses buy less fruit now from independent growers and have repurposed substantial parts of their estate vineyards for still-wine programs. Gloria Ferrer, Domaine Carneros, and Domaine Chandon all produce significant quantities of high-end still pinot noir, and Codorníu Napa quit the sparkling business entirely, spawning a new winery called Artesa dedicated entirely to still-wine production. The new and replanted vineyards have taken advantage of "modern" tight spacing, new plant material from France, and very finely tuned irrigation systems, as well as resistant, devigorating rootstocks, which are all the signature of the new Carneros, as they are of new pinot vineyards elsewhere in North America.

THE RUSSIAN RIVER VALLEY

The upper course of the Russian River drains a succession of inland valleys in Mendocino and Sonoma counties before reaching Healdsburg, a pretty centenary town that claims to be Sonoma's wine country capital. It is the river's middle and lower course, south and west of Healdsburg, that is famous for pinot noir. There the river first traverses a relatively broad valley, then cuts a narrow gorge through the coastal mountains, and empties into the Pacific between Goat Rock Beach and the town of Jenner. Throughout the growing season, ocean fog swirls around the mouth of the river, chilling ill-prepared tourists who think the summer in California is always and universally warm. Marine air snakes up the valley, affecting the weather as far upstream as Windsor, just west of Highway 101 and about four miles south of Healdsburg. In fact, the penetration of coastal fog owes as much to the Petaluma Gap, a significant break in the coastal hills between Bodega Bay and the Point Reyes Peninsula, about 20 miles farther south, as it does to the river valley proper. Combined, these gaps create more than 100 square miles of mesoclimates (the climatic conditions of a vineyard or small appellation) that work well for cool-climate grapes: cool nights, persistent morning fog, and daytime high temperatures six to 15 degrees lower than the neighboring and more protected Dry Creek and Alexander valleys.

The lower Russian River is also something of a geological oddity. California's rivers generally follow the natural contours of its hills, emptying into the Pacific in genuinely coastal valleys or at natural inlets like San Francisco Bay. Geologists now think the Russian River once behaved like those other rivers, following a southward course from the southeastern end of the Alexander Valley across Knights Valley into the Napa Valley, and thence to San Pablo Bay. In other words, what is now the Napa River may once have been the lower course of what we now call the Russian River. Roughly a million years ago, give or take a half-million years, some massive upheaval, probably volcanic, forced the river to change course. This explains its contemporary meanderings around Black's Peak, Fitch Mountain, and Healdsburg; then its southward flow toward Wohler Bridge; and finally the sinuous gorge that transports it through the coastal mountains to the sea.

Although wine grapes are now the area's largest crop, prunes, hops, and an early-ripening apple called the Gravenstein dominated the landscape for the first two-thirds of the twentieth century, and grapes still share the land with sheep and cattle ranches, apple orchards, berry farms, and market gardens. Wine tourism is decentralized throughout the area. There are inns, restaurants, galleries, wineries, and tasting rooms in Healdsburg, Guerneville, Sebastopol, a handful of smaller towns, and in between them.

History The Russian River valley was the scene of a booming wine business in the second half of the nineteenth century. Until quite recently, students of viticultural history believed that the first wine grapes in this area were planted in the 1850s, northwest of Santa Rosa. Now documents uncovered by wine historians suggest that settlers from the Russian coastal colony at Fort Ross, driven to agriculture after they had substantially exhausted the local seal and sea otter populations, planted ranches near the western edge of the Russian River Valley AVA, near the villages of Graton and Freestone, in the 1830s. The Yegor Tschernick ranch near Freestone seems to have specialized in vegetables and fruits, including wine grapes. (See the section on the true Sonoma Coast, below in this chapter, for a further discussion of Russian viticulture in Sonoma County.)

Widespread grape farming along the Russian River did not begin until English, German, Swiss, French, and Italian entrepreneurs, drawn to California by business opportunities that proliferated in the wake of the Gold Rush, settled there in the 1870s and 1880s. These were ex-miners and stockbreeders, carpenters and contractors, grocers and feed merchants. One or two doubled as physicians and lawyers. Only a few had any prior experience with wine. In the early 1870s hundreds of vineyard acres were planted on flat to rolling land in the southeastern quadrant of the appellation near Santa Rosa, and around the towns of Windsor and West Windsor, as well as in the much hillier southwestern quadrant near Occidental, close to the sites of the early Russian vineyards. The initial concentration in these areas probably owes a good deal to the new railroad lines. The tracks of the Northwestern Pacific Railroad, completed in 1871, are still in evidence at Healdsburg, Windsor, and Santa Rosa. About the same time, the North Pacific Coast Railroad provided links to Bay Area markets from the western end of the county. In the 1880s vineyard sites multiplied in both areas and between them, along Laguna Road near the now extinct village of Trenton (currently the site of the Joseph Swan Vineyards), in Green Valley around Forestville and Graton, and along the Russian River near Guerneville. Wineries, many of quite significant size, were erected at Fulton, Windsor, Trenton, and Forestville. An 1891 directory of grape growers, winemakers, and distillers published by the Board of State Viticultural Commissioners lists well over 300 grape growers in townships that fall within the boundaries of the modern Russian River appellation, accounting for about 7,000 acres and half a million gallons of wine production. This high tide of viticulture succumbed to phylloxera and Prohibition, of course, and was not regained, much less surpassed, until a century later.

The red variety of choice during the nineteenth century in the Russian River townships was zinfandel, though the mission grape persisted there too, as it did elsewhere. To produce white wine, the farmers planted riesling, chasselas, and so-called Burger, which was a California name for French montbadon. There are, however, a few references to "Burgundy," collectively to "French varieties," and one reference, in Sebastopol, to pinot. California wine historian Ernest Peninou also cites the case of Jean Garnier, whose family is said to have been "vineyardists" for several generations "near Beaune," who brought vines for 75 acres of "fine French varietals" to the Beausejour Winery at Occidental about 1880. Given the proximity of known plantings of pinot noir in the Sonoma Valley and at Fountaingrove, on the outskirts of Santa Rosa, it would be surprising if some pinot had not gotten established here and there in the Russian River townships. But the record does not suggest that any grower made a specialty of it, or that any Russian River winery produced varietal wine from pinot noir.

The first well-documented planting of pinot around the Russian River occurred in the 1960s, as it did in the southern Central Coast area. Early in the decade Bob Sisson, the University of California farm adviser for Sonoma—mindful of the heat summation studies done by Albert Winkler and Maynard Amerine in the 1940s—began advising Russian River growers to try chardonnay and pinot noir in place of zinfandel. Several growers heeded Sisson's advice, including Charles Bacigalupi, who owned vineyard on Westside Road. Bacigalupi had never heard of chardonnay or pinot noir before Sisson brought them to his attention, and claims he had to write down the names to keep from forgetting them. Eventually, he obtained pinot noir budwood from Karl Wente, probably from Wente's new increase block in Arroyo Seco, but Bacigalupi remembers Wente telling him that the stock had come from France via the family's old vineyard in Livermore. Three years later, in 1968, Bacigalupi's neighbor Joseph Rochioli Jr., who had hitherto farmed hops, hay, and Blue Lake beans for cash, and then colombard and cabernet sauvignon, also planted pinot noir. His budwood came partially from Wente too, and from "a vineyard in mid-valley Napa." And in 1969, acting on the advice of André Tchelistcheff, Joe Swan planted pinot noir at his small farm on Laguna Road.

As elsewhere, success with pinot was far from immediate. Rochioli reports selling his first crops of pinot to Martini & Prati, who passed them on to Gallo, where they ended up ignominiously in Hearty Burgundy. Many of the early plantings were used to make sparkling wines—at Korbel, Iron Horse, and Piper-Sonoma. But in 1973 Davis Bynum, a onetime San Francisco newspaperman who had built the first winery on Westside Road in 1965, made a varietal pinot from Rochioli's fruit, and Swan's inaugural vintage of pinot noir attracted considerable attention from connoisseurs. The 1970s market, however thin, was sufficient to sustain the pioneers, and much of the acreage they planted remains in production today.

More pinot was planted in the 1980s, as Russian River winemakers acquired a reputation for success with pinot. By the end of the 1980s, Rochioli's own label, Gary Farrell, Williams Selyem, and Dehlinger had joined Joe Swan and Davis Bynum in the firmament of Russian River pinot noir. Steve Kistler had relocated to Russian River from the Sonoma Valley, and La Crema had been created to specialize in pinot noir. Jeff Cox, writing in *Global Vintage Quarterly,* asserted that "by the mid to late '80s" you could "draw a line between Sebastopol and Healdsburg and be pretty sure the consistently best pinot noir in North America came from vineyards within a few miles on either side of the line."

In the 1990s, the growing popularity of pinot, the prestige of some Russian River labels, and the relative accessibility of roads, power, and other infrastructure compared to the true Sonoma Coast and Anderson Valley, combined to unleash an unprecedented land rush in the Russian River area. Local winemakers including Williams Selyem and Gary Farrell, previously content simply to purchase grapes, decided that prudence required them to acquire vineyards of their own. Large wine firms with significant Russian River holdings like Gallo and Kendall-Jackson expanded. A who's who of Napa wineries—Joseph Phelps, Beringer, Caymus—signed contracts with Sonoma real estate firms to locate potential vineyard property around Russian River. Along the Gravenstein Highway north of Sebastopol, apple orchard gave way to acre upon acre of grapevines. In 1997, E. and J. Gallo's purchase of the MacMurray Ranch on Westside Road, one of the last remaining large blocks of plantable ranch land in the plain south of Healdsburg, was the catalyst for events sometimes characterized as "the Gallo Affair." In order to exploit the MacMurray Ranch efficiently, Gallo obtained a grading permit to relocate more than 2 million cubic yards of dirt, using equipment said to have been repurposed from construction of the Alaska pipeline. West of Sebastopol, near Freestone, Joseph Phelps obtained permission to clear-cut 100 acres of hillside forest so their recently purchased parcel could be planted more or less corner to corner. These and other similar events incited conservationists, who were then successful in imposing a variety of new regulations and strict enforcement on new vineyard projects, and in forging alliances with some smaller-scale winegrowers.

Terrain, Terroir, and Vineyards The Russian River Valley AVA encompasses 96,000 acres, of which just over one-tenth, or about 10,000 acres, is now planted to grapes. The appellation is shaped rather like a squashed diamond, wider than it is high, its apex located just south of Healdsburg, its bottom angle anchored in the foothills of the Coast Ranges west of Sebastopol. The western angle of the diamond is near Guerneville, where Korbel has made sparkling wines since the early years of this century; the eastern angle touches the northwestern outskirts of Santa Rosa's banal urban sprawl. A bulging protrusion on the northeastern side of the diamond incorporates two areas of overlap with the neighboring (and generally warmer) appellations of Chalk Hill and Alexander Valley. Overall the area is often described as "bucolic," characterized by alternations of rolling hills, redwood forest, and apple orchards. Vineyards vary considerably in size, from several hundred acres to small parcels, but since the estimated 10,000 planted acres are divided among about 200 growers and many growers own multiple, noncontiguous parcels, the average Russian River vineyard size is small. The best-informed estimates suggest that about one-third of the AVA's grapes are pinot noir, and that acreage devoted to pinot noir is increasing faster than acreage devoted to any other variety.

The greatest concentration of vineyard is in the wide plain south of Healdsburg, for which the name "Middle Reach" is gaining currency. This is splendidly beautiful country, apart from a few disfiguring gravel quarries that operate on the river's edge. Most of the "easy" bottomland and benchland has long since been planted, leaving only the hills on the western side of the valley, rimmed with redwoods, for new vineyards. Many of the most respected names in Russian River pinot (Bynum, Rochioli, and Williams Selyem) are found in the Middle Reach, primarily along a five-mile stretch of Westside Road just north of Wohler Bridge. A good deal of pinot noir is also grown on the eastern side of the river, though it is concentrated a bit farther upstream than the best west-side ranches. Apart from J Wine Company's Nicole's Vineyard, which occupies an unusual hilltop site, most of the east-side vineyards are sited on alluvial lowland where pinot tends to ripen early, and most fruit from this area is used to make sparkling wine.

Due south of the Middle Reach, straddling the north-south axis of the AVA, lies an area of rolling hills called Vine Hill in the nineteenth century, for which the designation "Laguna Ridge" has now been proposed. This area is sometimes described as the banana belt of the appellation, with warmer temperatures and earlier harvest dates. The largest vineyards in Laguna Ridge belong to Sonoma-Cutrer and Gallo, but it is also home to important small houses like Joseph Swan, Kistler, Dehlinger, and Lynmar, which have made pinot a specialty, and to the Pellegrini family's Olivet Lane vineyard, which has provided fruit to Williams Selyem, Gary Farrell, and Merry Edwards, among others.

East of Laguna Ridge, a flattish plain extends to the northwestern outskirts of Santa Rosa. This area used to be known as the Laguna de Santa Rosa, for the lakes—now drained and farmed—that once laced the countryside. Guerneville Road, which bisects this area east to west, sits on a levee six to ten feet above the adjacent fields. The Martinelli, DeLoach, and La Crema wineries are in this area, and vineyard is extensively planted on the north and south sides of River Road, and between River Road and Guerneville Road. Although a number of good pinots are made from fruit grown in this area, the water table is naturally high, and expensive farming is required to maintain a good environment for fine wine grapes. The heroic water channels and drain works constructed at the Kunde family's Saralee's Vineyard are a good illustration of what is needed to get superior fruit in this terrain. The appellationists have proposed calling this part of the AVA "Los Molinos," to commemorate the windmills that were once used to drain the former swampland, but "Santa Rosa Plain" is also used.

Green Valley—home to Iron Horse Vineyards, Marimar Torres Estate, and Hartford Court, along with a number of blocks of vineyard owned by the Dutton family—occupies hillier land west of Laguna Ridge, where Green Valley Creek drains northward into the Russian River. Green Valley is actually a separate AVA, all but a few acres of which are contained within Russian River or Sonoma; Green Valley wines are entitled to both appellations. Green Valley's vineyards consist almost entirely of redeveloped orchard and berry farms just ten miles from the coast as the crow flies. This coastal proximity makes Green Valley substantially cooler than either Middle Reach or Laguna Ridge, leading to a predominant concentration on pinot noir and chardonnay. (A few stands of old zinfandel survive, mostly on steep hillsides and thin soils, where naturally low yields help to hasten its ripening.) Several makers, including Tandem, Flowers, DuNah, Failla Wines, and Patz & Hall, are using fruit from Green Valley's Keefer Ranch, a 1996–1998 planting of the UCD 2A, 4, 5, and 23 selections of pinot noir, about one mile northwest of Graton on the northern bank of Green Valley Creek. The 14 acres of pinot at Keefer are on a gentle, south-facing slope. Row orientations vary as a function of prevailing steepness.

Apart from the Middle Reach and the Santa Rosa Plain, the topography of the appellation is aggressive, and vineyard parcels tend to be scattered: a few acres of vine here and there, surrounded by unplantable forest or scrub. The topography and new environmental regulations designed to prevent erosion have combined to reinforce the locals' aversion to large-scale exploitation of the land. But the hilly and cool western part of the appellation, along Salmon Creek near Freestone and just east of Occidental, is so desirable for pinot noir that it has become a magnet for pinotphile growers despite its inconveniences. "Even if," says one winemaker, "you can plant only 30 or 40 acres in 1,000, there are plenty of attractive sites left. But you have to plant them three to five acres at a time."

Soil types vary widely in the Russian River valley, owing to its fairly large size and active geological history. Soils close to the river can be very porous and well drained, but sometimes also quite vigorous combinations of riverborne alluvium, sand, and gravel. Beyond the river's floodplain, the benchland soils contain more clay. Weathered sandstone- and granite-based soils dominate in the Laguna Ridge and Green Valley areas. The depth of these soils varies, but most are relatively low in clay. The best known of these—so-called Goldridge sandy loam, which extends from Forestville to Sebastopol—can be so finely pulverized at the surface that the ground looks like talcum powder. Josephine soils, found on the northwestern side of Green Valley Creek, are redder, rockier, and a bit more plastic, containing both iron and clay. In the Santa Rosa Plain, decomposed volcanic material has given most soils a high percentage of clay. W. H. Wright, who teaches geology at Sonoma State University, argues that the best pinot seems to come from soils laced with at least a modicum of clay, but many winegrowers disagree, maintaining that nothing is better than the best possible drainage.

In 1997, a committee organized and sponsored by the new Russian River Valley Winegrowers Association began work on a petition to adjust the boundaries of the AVA. The petition, submitted to the TTB at the end of 1999, argued that the basis for the appellation remained as it was in 1983—the area in which the penetration of coastal fog has a dominant influence on climate—but that "errors" had been made in 1983, from ignorance, "inclusionary bias," and "local political gerrymandering."

They might have added that measuring fog is not easy, even though the first maps of the so-called fog intrusion zone were drawn as early as the 1970s by farm adviser Robert Sisson. In 1999, the association proposed to eliminate the AVA's overlap, east of Healdsburg, with the neighboring Alexander Valley AVA; to eliminate half of the overlap, east of Windsor, with the Chalk Hill AVA; to delete areas in the AVA's northwestern quadrant that escape maritime influence because of altitude; and to annex a considerable area south of Sebastopol and west of Santa Rosa that falls within "the historic coastal cool fog line." The net effect of the changes, if approved, would be to shrink the AVA by 15 percent to 20 percent. The last of the changes is probably the most significant, since a good many new vineyards dedicated to pinot noir and chardonnay were established south of the current boundary, in an area being called "Sebastopol Hills" (located, as things stand today, in the Sonoma Coast AVA), during the 1990s. The other changes are more a matter of ecological consistency but would not substantially affect the way producers in the area label their wines, since not much pinot noir is produced in the overlap areas with Alexander Valley and Chalk Hill. But Russian River's petition represents the first time that any party has ever requested the government to *change the boundaries of an existing AVA.* Elsewhere and previously, modifications have taken the form of overlays, creating a new AVA, with a new name, entirely within or partially overlapping an existing AVA, with the earlier one remaining untouched. This feature of the Russian River application has apparently delayed regulatory action, and the petition was still pending in mid 2003.

In addition to the boundary adjustment, the petition asked to "submit into record" certain *subappellational* designations—Laguna Ridge, Los Molinos, Sebastopol Hills, and Middle Reach—which gained currency during the committee's work. If the petition is eventually approved, it is possible that these designations could begin to appear on bottles of Russian River valley wine in conjunction with the Russian River Valley AVA designation, giving consumers a much better idea where their wine was grown and a potentially useful tool to help interpret vineyard-specific nomenclature.

THE TRUE SONOMA COAST

North and south of Jenner, where the Russian River meets the ocean, the Coastal Ranges assume the form of low mountainous terrain with relatively narrow valleys, deep canyons, and mildly sloping summits. Several mountain ridges with summits above 1,200 feet roughly parallel the coast, which places them approximately perpendicular to prevailing airflows. In this configuration the ridge closest to the ocean is generally too cold for grapes, but it blocks the inland spread of the omnipresent coastal fog bank, which in its turn is perpetually re-created by the passage of moist marine air over an area of especially cold surface water. Thus the second and third ridges from the coast are an ideal environment for cool-climate grapes. The proximity of a very large body of quite cold water moderates temperatures throughout the growing season, while altitude (and the first coastal ridge) hold the fog at bay even in the morning hours, maximizing solar radiation. A summer's morning drive from fog-engulfed Jenner up Meyers Grade Road into brilliant sunshine amply illustrates the situation. Unlike summers, winters on the true Sonoma Coast can be very wet, averaging 80 inches of rain.

The southern edge of the true coast is less than two hours from San Francisco's Golden Gate Bridge, but the area is very sparsely settled and is accessible only via narrow, twisting, and often unpaved roads that turn relatively short distances into hours-long trips. Many farms and vineyards remain off the power grid and beyond the reach of postal and courier services. The predominant vegetation consists of coastal redwoods and Douglas fir trees that have been intermittently logged, and the tiny economy, such as it is, depends mostly on ranching sheep. The only population center of consequence is the town of Bodega Bay, at the area's southern end, which supports day-boat fishing and coastal tourism, though Fort Ross—the California settlement established to feed the Russians' Aleutian whaling aspirations in the eighteenth century—is also a tourist attraction.

History The first wine grapes were planted in the true Sonoma Coast, as they were in the western part of the neighboring Russian River valley, by the Russians who settled Fort Ross. Wine historian Charles Sullivan has documented vine plantings just inland from the fort as early as 1817, and a first small harvest in 1823. The plant material seems to have included at least two varieties of vinifera, one red and one white, both imported from Peru. The record does not say if the Russians made wine from their grapes, nor is it clear whether their enterprise had any impact on the subsequent history of winegrowing in western Sonoma County. A master's thesis written by Ynez Haase in 1949 at the University of California, Berkeley, asserts that General Mariano Vallejo, who is usually credited with having established California's first commercial winery, visited at least one of the Russians' vineyards and "counted" its vine plants, but we do not know whether Vallejo took cuttings or, if he did, whether the cuttings were propagated elsewhere. According to Sullivan, no less than Charles Krug sourced cuttings from a vineyard "within the enclave" at Fort Ross—supposedly palomino, the main grape of Jerez, often incorrectly identified in California as Golden Chasselas. These seem, at least for the moment, to be the only traces of intersection between the Russians' grape-growing ventures and the rest of the California wine industry. Russian viticulture, such as it was, apparently disappeared when the Russian settlers left California in the middle of the nineteenth century.

Following their departure, about 1880, English settlers seem to have planted a bit of zinfandel—perhaps as much as several hundred acres—in the Bodega, Salt Point, and Ocean townships, in modern coastal Sonoma between the mouth of the Russian River and the Mendocino County line, and to have made wine for local consumption. Sullivan interviewed several current residents of the Sonoma Coast with personal memories stretching backward into the early years of the twentieth century. These interviews suggest that several small wineries may have operated in the greater Fort Ross area before Prohibition. Whatever vineyard remained by the 1920s, however, seems to have been converted to orchard.

Modern winegrowing started again, more or less from scratch, in the 1970s. Michael Bohan, whose family had been running sheep on their ranch east of Fort Ross since the middle of the nineteenth century, was apparently the area's first winegrower. Bohan planted a few acres of zinfandel on a 1,400-foot ridge in 1971. In 1973, Donnie and Linden Schatzberg, fresh from overseas Peace Corps experience in sustainable agriculture, planted six acres of dry-farmed vineyard just east of Fort Ross, on Creighton Ridge. The Schatzbergs set out pinot noir, gewürztraminer, white riesling, and two hybrids, but eventually grafted the hybrids and most of the riesling to pinot noir, which has been sold to Williams Selyem since 1996. Right from the beginning, Bohan's fruit attracted some attention from established winemakers inland, who purchased most of what he grew; and wine made from his grapes by a tiny local winery called Sea Ridge, on Bohan-Dillon Road, won a gold medal at the Sonoma County Fair in 1981. Daniel Schoenfeld, a self-avowed ex-hippie who had been involved with the 464 Magnolia restaurant in Larkspur, was the third viticultural pioneer in the area. His first vines (zinfandel and pinot noir) went into the ground in 1980, on land he had purchased seven years earlier as an "escape from San Francisco."

David Hirsch, a clothing-business veteran from Santa Cruz who had "never grown a tomato," bought a thousand-acre sheep ranch not far from Sea Ridge in 1978 "because it was remote and cheap." Hirsch commissioned a resource survey to ascertain what uses might be promising. The area, he remembers, "was like Appalachia—there was no visible economy. Coyotes had finished the sheep. The land had been stripped by foresting." The survey examined the possibility of farming shiitake mushrooms. Then Hirsch brought his friend Jim Beauregard, a winegrower from Santa Cruz, up to have a look. "Plant pinot noir," Beauregard is supposed to have told Hirsch.

By this time, Bohan had supplemented his zinfandel with a bit of pinot noir, and Schoenfeld planted several acres of pinot in 1981. Lee Martinelli began purchasing grapes from the Charles family, who were neighbors of the Bohans, and Martinelli was interested in pinot noir. He hooked up with Helen Turley, not yet famous, who became involved with the declining Sea Ridge winery, and purchased land near Hirsch in 1985 that became the basis for Turley's Marcassin brand. In 1989 Hirsch began planting his eponymous vineyard to riesling and pinot noir, and sold his fruit to Kendall-Jackson. Suddenly, within the space of a single month in 1993, Hirsch says, he had calls from Williams Selyem, Whitcraft, Littorai, and Kistler, and the Hirsch Vineyard was unexpectedly launched as the flagship of pinot noir in the true Sonoma Coast.

Joan and Walt Flowers followed, on Camp Meeting Ridge a bit closer to the coast, building the area's first modern winery. Then came a parade of wine world luminaries, including Bill Smith of La Jota, Jason Pahlmeyer, and Peter Michael, planting vineyards and "considering" wineries. Anne-Marie Failla and Ehren Jordan purchased land near the Schatzbergs' Precious Mountain vineyard in 1995, but they elected to plant syrah and chardonnay, so Failla Wines pinot noir is sourced elsewhere.

There was also activity south of the Russian River mouth, on the westernmost ridge overlooking Bodega Bay. Taylor Lan planted a vineyard there in 1980, called Summa. In 1989, Kendall-Jackson planted the first six acres of its Seascape Vineyard on Fredricks Lane. Coastlands and Theriot went into the ground early in the 1990s, eventually selling their grapes to Williams Selyem, Littorai, and Siduri, among others.

Terrain, Terroir, and Vineyards The true coast is part of the Sonoma Coast AVA, approved in 1987. The AVA boasts a gargantuan 750 square miles, more than all of Burgundy including Chablis, the Côte d'Or, the Côte Chalonnaise, and the Mâconnais. The true coast coincides with the northwestern corner of the AVA, but the AVA bulges eastward to encompass a huge territory that extends from north of Russian River to the Marin County line, and from the coast itself to east of Healdsburg, the town of Sonoma, and a corner of Carneros. The true coast accounts for something less than 10 percent of this surface. The inland portions of the AVA are, generally, "coastal cool" areas not dissimilar to the Russian River valley, but they are quite different from the true coast, where cool is the product of altitude in close proximity to the coast. Within the true coast region, vineyards have now come to be concentrated in three small areas. The first is the area southeast of Fort Ross where the first coastal vineyards were set out in the 1970s. This includes Camp Meeting Ridge, Bohan-Dillon Ridge, Smith Ridge, King's Ridge, and Skyline Ridge, each of which is separated from the next by the south fork of the Gualala River and its tributary creeks. The second, aforementioned, is the area south of the Russian River and north of Bodega, between Occidental and Bodega Bay. This area consists of the ridges that are separated by the various tributaries of Salmon Creek. And since 1997, a new coastal area has emerged north of the first two, within a few miles of the hamlet called Annapolis. This area, which is north of King Ridge Road and west of Skyline Ridge, includes the ridges surrounding the Wheatfield fork of the Gualala River, and the Buckeye and Grasshopper Creek drainages. The largest holdings in this area belong to Hartford Court and Artesa. Smaller vineyards have been set out by Peay Vineyards and Ridgetop Partners. Peay consists of 48 acres, of which 30 are pinot noir, farmed by Nick Peay and Vanessa Wong, the winemaker at Peter Michael from 1996 to 2001.

Soils in all three areas are typically well drained and moderately deep, ranging from as little as 14 inches of topsoil to about five feet. Gravelly loam soils weathered from sandstone and shale, tinted reddish-brown with decomposed organic material, predominate in the corridor between Fort Ross and Cazadero, but the second and third of the three aforementioned areas display mostly sandy clay-loam soils quite similar to the well-known Goldridge series found in the western part of the Russian River Valley AVA. In general, the Annapolis area is the warmest and driest of the three, while the Bodega area is most dominated by marine influence, owing primarily to lower elevations.

The main challenges to viticulture in the true coast are rain and fog during the flowering season in the spring and early summer, which can shatter incipient clusters and drive down yield. As late as the middle of the growing season, however, gale-force winds and hailstorms can develop unexpectedly, so viticulturists often plan for the worst and farm conservatively. Birds are also voracious, so most vineyards must be netted after the fruit begins to color. Because of the rugged topography and the need to privilege south-facing slopes to compensate for the cool mesoclimate, vineyards are generally small and sometimes isolated. Coastlands amounts to a total of only 15 planted acres on a 40-acre site; Hirsch has planted 47 acres on his spread of 1,100. Even those 47 acres are divided into several noncontiguous blocks, which many winemakers find so different that they amount to separate vineyards. A few slightly warmer sites have been planted to Rhône varieties or to zinfandel, but the true coast is overwhelmingly and increasingly devoted to pinot noir, with chardonnay cast in a supporting role. Sources estimate that there are currently about 600 planted acres in the true coast, most of which are pinot noir. In the area around Annapolis, where all but a handful of vineyard is new since 1998, pinot accounts for more than 230 of about 260 vineyard acres. Pinot is a bit less dominant in the Fort Ross area and south of the Russian River, but still overwhelmingly the main object of interest.

Environmental concerns, and especially local opposition to the further conversion of land use from forestry to agriculture, is a serious impediment to viticultural expansion. Permits to build new winery facilities are hard to obtain, and only a few sites have access to paved roadways. Nor is it easy to persuade winemakers that they should want to take up residence as far from civilization as Fort Ross or Annapolis. Still, Hirsch (who was able to obtain a winery permit in 2002) estimates that the Fort Ross area could expand eventually to between 700 and 900 planted acres, and the Annapolis area seems poised to double in size, from the present circa 260 acres to at least 480 by 2005. Meanwhile, new vineyards have been planted at Marcassin, on Bohan-Dillon Road; along Tin Barn Road between the south fork of the Gualala River and Haupt Creek; at Flowers' "new" ranch on Fort Ross Road; along Seaview Road adjacent to Camp Meeting Ridge; and just north of Bodega, where Lewis Platt, the former CEO of both Hewlett-Packard and Kendall-Jackson, has set out chardonnay destined for Steve Kistler and pinot noir already contracted to Littorai and Scherrer. New vineyard plantings seem destined to continue for the foreseeable future, despite obstacles, and are likely to derive encouragement if and when the petition for a new AVA, submitted by growers in the Fort Ross area, is approved by the TTB.

THE ANDERSON VALLEY

The Anderson Valley, about three hours north of San Francisco, is the northernmost of the Pacific coastal valleys that is warm enough to ripen wine grapes. Farther north, where California's Mad and Klamath rivers meet the ocean, and in Oregon, heat accumulation in genuine coastal valleys is insufficient for grapes, and viticulture is forced to the lee side of the coastal hills. Anderson Valley, the drainage of the Navarro River, is a long throat oriented northwest to southeast, open to the Pacific through a narrow canyon at its northwestern end. Hills hug the valley tightly, leaving little floodplain or bottomland except immediately around the valley's main population center at Boonville. The hills rise steeply to the ridgelines on both sides, peaking almost 2,000 feet above the valley floor.

Although Highway 128, which bisects the valley, is the favored route from San Francisco to the inns, restaurants, antique shops, and galleries on the northern Mendocino coast, the valley revels in its relative isolation and maintains a staunchly antidevelopment bias. Sheep ranching, apple farming, and logging are still the area's main businesses, though viticulture is gaining ground, and Boonville offers only limited visitor services. There are fewer than three dozen guest rooms in the valley, no hospital, no dry cleaner, no supermarket, no Burger King, and nothing at all open 24 hours. The Schmitt family, which moved there 20 years ago from Napa, manages most of the valley's hospitality. John Schmitt operates the ten-room Boonville Hotel; his parents run the Apple Farm, which offers four rooms—when they are not occupied with enrollees in Sally Schmitt's cooking classes.

History Anderson Valley's earliest European settlers arrived in the 1850s, mostly from northern Europe. The surnames etched into the valley's geography—Gowan, Johnson, McGimpsey, Hiatt, and Anderson itself—are decidedly British. Before the beginning of the twentieth century, a few Swiss and Italian homesteaders planted small vineyards, mostly on Greenwood Ridge, that may have amounted to as much as 200 acres in toto. On the lower slopes just above the valley floor, the Pinoli family is said to have begun planting zinfandel and alicante about 1911. There is some suggestion that the Pinolis may have been granted a winery bond, but it is not clear that the bond was exercised, and whatever dribble of commercial winemaking may have existed was snuffed out with the beginning of Prohibition. In 1946 Italian Swiss Colony, then a small winery located across the hills in Asti but looking to expand, made an effort to grow colombard and ugni blanc near Boonville, and contracted with landowners who would plant grapes. Italian Swiss Colony's Anderson Valley ventures were defeated, however, when these and other low-demand, warm-climate varieties refused to ripen reliably. The valley then got a reputation for being too cold for grapes of any kind, and nothing much happened for another 20 years.

The modern history of winegrowing in Anderson Valley began with a handful of well-educated refugees from city life who arrived there in the 1960s, attracted by the area's ranches, unspoiled scenery, inexpensive real estate, and relative remoteness from "civilization." Donald Edmeades, a Pasadena, California, cardiologist who vacationed regularly at the valley's dude ranches, is credited with the first wine grape planting since the Italian Swiss Colony fiasco. He ignored the neighbors and farm advisers who counseled against grapes, stubbornly erected a sign on his barn celebrating "Edmeades's Folly," and planted 11 acres just west of Philo to cabernet, gewürztraminer, and colombard. Five years later, Tony Husch, a Harvard-educated urban planner, planted the valley's first pinot noir (and the first riesling) less than a mile from Edmeades and established the valley's first bonded winery in a disused sheep shed. Along with Hans and Theresia Kobler's Lazy Creek Vineyard and Navarro, founded by Ted Bennett and Deborah Cahn in 1973, this fledgling group was the alpha and omega of the Anderson Valley wine establishment until the 1980s. Some professional winemaking talent was attracted to Anderson Valley early on, primarily Jed Steele and Milla Handley, both then fresh from Davis, but the first pioneers survived more by trial and error than by expertise. They did not make distinguished wines.

In 1982, the French Champagne house of Roederer changed Anderson Valley both quietly and fundamentally. Jean-Claude Rouzaud's family-held firm had scoured California and Oregon for *terroirs* enough like Champagne to grow pinot and chardonnay for sparkling wine. It probably helped the case for Anderson Valley, which might otherwise have seemed impossibly remote, that Rouzaud was a licensed pilot who could land the company's small plane on Boonville's bare-bones airstrip. It also helped that in 1982, Anderson Valley land was dramatically cheaper than similar land in Los Carneros and the Russian River valley. Carefully and very politely, Roederer acquired land, imported clonal material from France (see chapter 5), built housing for prospective employees, and almost literally folded a 200,000-case winery into the side of a hill, so unobtrusively that only its gabled roofline is visible from Highway 128. Roederer and John Scharffenberger, whose eponymous sparkling-wine brand was subsequently sold to luxury conglomerate LVMH and eventually renamed Pacific Echo, then put Anderson Valley on the map as a premium source of Champagne-method sparkling wine, which reputation it still enjoys.

But Roederer's impact did not stop with name recognition. Roederer's winemaker, genial Michel Salgues, former professor at Montpellier's wine and viticulture school, became the valley's informal viticultural and enological consultant, indefatigable cheerleader, and magnet for attracting new winemaking talent. Roederer's plantings more than doubled the acreage devoted to grapes between 1983 and 1990, and the winery supplied both fruit and budwood to other vintners and growers in the valley. Roederer's and Scharffenberger's commercial success with sparkling wine in the 1980s laid the foundation for a tremendous concentration of effort on still pinot in the 1990s.

Although Edmeades, Husch, Navarro, and Lazy Creek all made pinot noir from estate-grown fruit in the 1980s, local wineries did not put much energy into this variety until the 1990s, and much of the demand for high-quality pinot fruit came, even then, from wineries based outside the valley. Williams Selyem and Littorai were early champions of Anderson Valley pinot, joined more recently by a host of boutique makers, including Siduri, Peterson, Skewis, Copain, and Adrian Fog. Kendall-Jackson also purchases significant quantities of excellent pinot from valley growers for its La Crema brand.

Terrain, Terroir, and Vineyards The Anderson Valley AVA, approved in 1983, is a slightly irregular rectangle bounded mostly by arbitrary straight lines drawn between hilltops and reference points, except at the appellation's northwestern corner, where the boundary follows Greenwood Creek. It extends from just southwest of Boonville to about one mile downstream from Navarro and includes hillsides on both banks of the river. The ridge tops on the southern side of the valley are now also included in another and newer AVA, called Mendocino Ridge. Anderson Valley encompasses about 20,000 acres, of which approximately 2,000 are now planted. A survey undertaken in 2000 by the Anderson Valley Winegrowers Association put actual vineyard acreage at 1,793, but insiders believe this figure was understated by at least 10 percent, so the higher figure reflects a compensatory adjustment. There are about 50 growers, of which Roederer and Pacific Echo are the largest, but most holdings are much smaller, with 20 to 30 acres being typical, and vest-pocket vineyards not uncommon. Of the 1,793 acres enumerated in the survey, almost 1,000 were pinot noir, so 1,100 acres of pinot noir is probably close to the true mark. Although reliable historical data are not available, informed sources estimate that the acreage figures have approximately tripled since 1985. About one-third of the valley's pinot is picked for sparkling wine; the balance is used for still wine.

Most of the vineyard is concentrated in the valley's so-called Deep End, northwest of Philo. This is also the coolest part of the AVA and the most favored for pinot noir. Navarro's estate vineyards, most of Roederer's land, Handley, Lazy Creek, Claudia Springs, and Christine Woods, as well as the Wiley vineyard (used by Edmeades) and Floodgate (owned by Bill Hambrecht until it was sold to Dan Duckhorn in 2003), are in the Deep End. There are, however, important pinot vineyards on the valley floor between Boonville and Philo, notably additional vineyards planted by Roederer, and some distinguished vineyards can be found as high as 1,400 feet above the valley floor in the Boonville area, including Rich Savoy's Deer Meadow Ranch, whose fruit goes to Littorai and La Crema; Cerise, which includes an unusual modern planting of Martini selection; and Demuth, which has eight acres of pinot and sells fruit to Skewis and Adrian Fog, among others. Afternoon wind can make hillside sites cooler than valley floor sites during much of the growing season, but if the site is protected by a ridgeline or transverse fold, or if it faces southwest, phenological development may not be very different than for sites on the floor. At this writing, the only pinot noir vineyards on the south-side ridge tops, where the Mendocino Ridge AVA has been overlaid on the Anderson Valley AVA, are DuPratt, where one acre was planted in the 1980s, and Greenwood Ridge Vineyards, which planted four acres of pinot in 1996.

How much room exists for further expansion of the valley's vineyards is a matter of some disagreement among insiders. Some, like Lazy Creek founder Hans Kobler, think there is plenty more space, as long as it's exploited in small chunks, in what he calls "the European style." Others point to the myriad regulations surrounding use of water and the valley's strong bias against development. Most agree, however, that whatever expansion does occur will be driven primarily by pinot noir, and will probably be concentrated on the still-underexploited hillsides. Land values in Anderson Valley, once understated in comparison to Russian River and Carneros, have now almost reached parity with areas much closer to San Francisco. This increase favors varieties, like pinot, that command high prices per ton of fruit. In-valley producers depend heavily on their tasting rooms, which flank Highway 128, to sell their wines. Some of these are grand, as at Roederer and Handley, and some rustic, like Husch's tiny cabin, but they are an important outlet for the valley's smaller wineries, which sell very little wine through conventional distribution channels.

Anderson Valley soils display more heterogeneity than Los Carneros or the Santa Maria Valley, but less than the Russian River valley. On the rolling hills near Philo, which are in fact river terraces and onetime floodplain, relatively deep clay loams with varying admixtures of gravel predominate. The so-called Pinole series is the best drained of these, and generally regarded as the best adapted to viticulture. Other soil series contain more clay and may demand that French drains be installed in the process of vineyard development. On the hills and mountains that rim the valley, thinner soils are the rule, generally ranging in depth from 20 to 40 inches; these are generally well-drained loams weathered in place from the underlying sandstone. It is harder to establish vineyards in these soils, which helps explain why the bottomland was planted first; but once established, the hillside and higher-elevation vineyards produce excellent wines.

THE WILLAMETTE VALLEY

The Willamette Valley is one of America's richest agricultural areas and home to 85 percent of Oregon's population. Geologically, it is the southern end of an intermountain trough that extends from Puget Sound through the western part of Washington State, and then follows an elbow of the Columbia River before spreading over a wide plain nearly 60 miles broad and more than 150 miles long. This plain covers the entire distance between Portland and Eugene, plus a few miles farther south. It is bounded on the west by the Coast Ranges and on the east by the Cascade Range. The Coast Ranges block the inward spread of most oceanic moisture, leaving the valley with an annual average of about 50 inches of rainfall. The Cascades cut off the valley from the continental cold-winter, hot-summer climate that prevails in the eastern half of the state, as the Sierra Nevada does for the landlocked central valleys of California.

Vineyards now share the landscape with a wide array of agriculture, ranging from succulent berries, market crops, and dairies to grass seed, nursery stock, and Christmas trees. Vineyards have been confined almost entirely to hillsides, however, where they have expanded primarily at the expense of pecan, hazelnut, peach, and apple orchards, some of which have been forced out of business by California-based competition. The densest concentration of vineyard is at the valley's northern end, and especially along Highway 99W between the outskirts of suburban Portland and the town of Amity. Highway 99W has become Oregon's main wine route, studded with tasting rooms, restaurants, and wine-related amusements. The heart of wine country is less than an hour's drive from Portland, but visitor services are plentiful in Newberg, Dundee, and McMinnville, and in Salem and Eugene farther south.

History While some grapes were planted in Oregon by the pioneers who settled the Willamette and Umpqua River valleys in the nineteenth century, and there is some evidence that Oregon wines were appreciated in the 1890s, the fledgling industry was not large enough to compete effectively with California. It died at the beginning of Prohibition and was not revived until the 1960s.

In 1965, Charles Coury and David Lett separately planted wine grapes in the Willamette Valley for the first time since Prohibition. Coury was a native of Los Angeles trained in climatology at UCLA, who learned winemaking at the University of California, Davis, and in France. He chose a site west of Forest Grove for his Oregon venture, which was bonded as Charles Coury Vineyards. Lett is a Utah-born winemaker also trained at Davis. He discovered pinot noir there, listened carefully when the faculty said there were few if any sites in California where pinot could be grown successfully, scoured the globe for sites that *would* be suitable for it, and finally put down roots near Dundee, in the heart of the Willamette Valley. Lett and Coury were soon joined by Dick Ponzi and Dick Erath, both Californians, and by Myron Redford, all of them specifically seeking the perfect place for pinot noir. Lett insists that this "purpose orientation" makes Oregon unique among the North American regions where pinot now thrives. "We came specifically here," he says, "to find the place we could grow pinot best." No accident, Lett asserts, that the Willamette Valley was already known for succulent berries, citing the commonplace horticultural theory that slow ripening preserves the flavors of all fruit, which can be "boiled out" by too much heat.

The pinot pioneers of the 1960s, and a second wave who began planting in the 1970s, were people of limited financial resources who could barely afford $200 for an acre of bare land, or orchard land that had first to be cleared of trees. They bought used equipment or cobbled together their own, sometimes built their own houses by hand, and worked other jobs to make ends meet. In 1970, even the state's Department of Agriculture thought Oregon was a crazy place to grow grapes, and banks refused to lend money for vineyard development or wineries. The early winegrowers were forced to rely on one another for encouragement, and to share both information and equipment.

Despite the bootstrapping, they seem to have been very conscious that their work was establishing the foundation for a new industry. In 1972, they took an active role in the creation of county-by-county land use plans, persuading planners to redesignate for vineyard hillside land that had previously been zoned for "view property" development. They pressed the legislature for state-specific wine labeling rules that were more stringent than federal standards, and they succeeded both in prohibiting the use of meaningless wine names like Rhine and Burgundy and in setting a 90 percent minimum content standard for varietally designated wines. Oregon growers and vintners elected to tax themselves at the highest rate in the world—per ton of wine grapes grown—to support a viticultural research program at Oregon State University and to promote Oregon wines in the national and international marketplaces.

While the time lines and pedigrees of various vineyard and cellar practices are hard to reconstruct reliably, it appears that Oregon pinot makers were early adopters in the New World of vertical trellising, relatively tight spacing, low yields, Dijon clones of pinot noir, and rigorous fruit sorting at harvest.

In 1979, The Eyrie Vineyards' 1975 South Block Reserve pinot noir finished second in two blind tastings in France. The first of these competitions was sponsored by the country's first mass-market magazine about wine and food, *GaultMillau;* the second was held under the auspices of Burgundy *négociant* Maison Joseph Drouhin. Although Eyrie's triumph was not loudly echoed in the mainstream press, it was certainly noticed in the wine world, and had a surreptitiously galvanizing effect on Oregon's other pinot producers. A bit of attention from Hugh Johnson, who came over from London to visit, and subsequently also from Robert M. Parker Jr., who went on to establish an Oregon vineyard in partnership with his brother-in-law (see the Beaux Frères profile in part II), also reassured the emerging industry. In 1987 Robert Drouhin, who had orchestrated the 1979 tasting, became the first Burgundy *négociant* to invest in the New World, purchasing 100 acres adjacent to Eyrie and Sokol Blosser in the Dundee hills. Gradually Oregon pinot noir, which had been virtually unsellable at the outset, gained acceptance in the marketplace.

Harry Peterson-Nedry, who co-owns Chehalem Wines in Newberg, identifies three waves of succession to the pioneers: "romantics" like the Adelsheims and Blossers, inspired in part by the pioneers' passion for pinot noir but questing also after a congenial lifestyle away from urban centers; successful professionals transplanted from other fields, able to invest exogenous resources in the wine business; and "apprentices" who worked for first-generation wineries and then set out to create their own, new labels. In addition, there was a slow but continuous northward trickle of California-trained winemakers who found Oregon, in the end, a better place to work with pinot noir. From seven wineries in 1973 (of which six produced pinot noir), the Oregon industry grew to 32 wineries, 115 vineyards, and 1,200 total planted acres in 1980, of which 33 percent were pinot noir. Then, from 1980 to 2001, the scene genuinely exploded, growing to 156 wineries, 520 vineyards, and 11,000 planted acres. Over the same two-decade period, universally dry-farmed vineyards gave way to an increasing proportion of vines on drip irrigation, a huge increase in the average planting density from about 700 vines per acre to more than 2,000, and widespread interest in organic and biodynamic viticulture. And unlike California, which is perpetually unable to resist the lure of "new" grape varieties, Oregon has intensified its historic focus on pinot gris among whites and pinot noir among reds.

Terrain, Terroir, and Vineyards The Willamette Valley AVA, created in 1983, covers virtually the entire valley, including downtown Portland; it extends as far south as the Calapooya Mountains, which divide the Willamette Valley from the neighboring Umpqua River valley. The northern boundary is the Columbia River, into which the Willamette empties at Portland; most of the eastern, western, and southern boundaries are indented and irregular, following elevation contours in the surrounding mountain ranges. Planted vineyard is located overwhelmingly on the western side of the Willamette River, between the river and the lee slopes of the Coast Ranges, and mostly north of Salem. But there are a few vineyards in the south Salem hills, in the hills northwest of Eugene, and in the foothills of the Coast Ranges the full length of the valley.

Almost without exception, vineyards have been planted on hillsides, at altitudes that range from 200 to 700 feet above the valley floor, partially because the true valley soils are too vigorous to produce good grapes, but primarily to keep clear of valley frosts while simultaneously avoiding the cooler average temperatures prevailing at the highest elevations. The aspect of south-, southeast-, and southwest-oriented hillsides also acts as a powerful receptor of solar energy, husbanding heat to ripen the fruit.

Three geological events determined the area's prevailing soil types and carved it into subregions relevant for winegrowing. Sedimentary soils left from the retreat of seawater when the southern end of the Puget Sound trough was uplifted are the main surface layer in the foothills of the Yamhill and Chehalem valleys. This is primarily shallow, sandy, well-drained gray-white dirt. Volcanoes that erupted through the sedimentary floor then created the Red Hills of Dundee and the Eola Hills, where the base rock is basalt while the topsoil is moderately deep, clay-laden loam tinted red with iron. The red color evokes frequent though not especially apt comparisons with soils in the Côte de Beaune, but the dirt's greater capacity to retain moisture can be an advantage where grapes are dry-farmed, as they were in most of the Willamette Valley until quite recently. The northwestern valley's somewhat crenellated topography and complex surface soils were also influenced by the great Missoula floods, which carved gorges and valleys and scattered Canadian debris across thousands of square miles in the Pacific Northwest.

Until the late 1990s, local vintners discussed the subregions of the Willamette Valley as matters of local interest, but universally supported the Willamette Valley AVA as their sole appellation. Now, however, petitions are pending at the TTB to superimpose no fewer than *six* new AVAs on the northwestern quadrant of the Willamette Valley AVA. These form, very roughly, a crescent of partially contiguous hillsides anchored by the towns of Newberg in the northeast, Yamhill in the northwest, and McMinnville in the southwest, plus the Eola Hills between McMinnville and Salem.

To begin in the northeast, Chehalem Mountains is the largest of the proposed areas, encompassing almost 70,000 acres of watershed between the Tualatin and Chehalem valleys. Sedimentary soil series predominate on the southwestern side of the mountains; wind-borne loess is more common on the northeastern side. There are about 80 vineyards totaling approximately 1,100 acres in this area, including Ponzi's historic estate vineyard, planted in 1969. These figures include Ribbon Ridge, a distinct geological formation in its own right, nestled against the southwestern edge of the main spine of the Chehalem range. This islandlike ridge, approximately three and a half miles long and one and three-quarters miles wide, accounts for 14 of Chehalem Mountains' 80 vineyards and just short of 300 acres of its planted surface. Bounded by Chehalem Creek and Dopp Creek and transected by Ribbon Ridge Road, the area displays uncommonly consistent, fine-textured marine sedimentary soils at all plantable elevations. In addition, the air and water drainage on all four sides of the ridge top appear to have created a mesoclimate that is slightly warmer and drier than the immediately surrounding areas. Chehalem's Ridgecrest Vineyard, planted in 1980, is the oldest vineyard on Ribbon Ridge, but other well-known properties include Brick House and Beaux Frères.

Due west of Ribbon Ridge is a 30,000-acre region, shaped roughly like the state of Rhode Island, for which the name "Yamhill-Carlton District" has been coined. This area, basically, is made up of the hillsides associated with the north fork of the Yamhill River and its associated drainages. There are now 26 vineyards totaling 650 acres in the region, which is defined by its sandy, sedimentary soils entirely devoid of volcanic experience and its relative warmth, owing to wind protection on three sides. The area has huge potential for additional vineyard development but is already home to Willakenzie Estate and a number of independent vineyards, planted mostly in the late 1980s and early 1990s. One of the largest and best known of the independent vineyards is Shea, 200 acres of former hazelnut orchard and pastureland ranging in elevation from 350 to 620 feet, where 140 acres were planted beginning in 1989. Pinot noir accounts for 29 of Shea's 33 blocks and is sold to a who's who of fine local vintners plus California's Sine Qua Non, which carts grapes south each

October in a refrigerated truck. Most wineries make vineyard-designated wines from the Shea fruit. Ken Wright, whose brand has lived entirely from purchased fruit since it was established in 1994, has made vineyard-designated wines from several independent vineyards in the Yamhill foothills, including Guadalupe, McCrone, and Wahle. Recently he has planted two estate vineyards on the eastern side of the proposed AVA.

Adjoining the Yamhill-Carlton District on its southeast edge is the birthplace of the modern Oregon wine industry, the Red Hills of Dundee, where David Lett planted the first of the Eyrie vineyards in 1965. The Red Hills are a series of north-south ridges in a five-mile parallelogram bounded by Highway 99W, Highway 240, and Abbey Road north of Lafayette, ranging from about the 200-foot elevation contour to below 1,100 feet. This area is the most intensively planted of the currently proposed AVAs, with 80 vineyards in a 6,500-acre area, almost one-fifth of the included surface currently in vine, and more than half of the plantable acreage already planted. The soils, eponymously red with iron-rich clay, are uncommonly deep for hilly sites, sometimes measuring six feet or more from surface to bedrock. Relatively abundant clay helps retain moisture until late in the growing season, contributing to later harvest dates in the Red Hills than in surrounding sedimentary areas. Home to Lett's original planting and subsequently to Erath Vineyards and Sokol Blosser, these hills are the site of Domaine Drouhin Oregon, Archery Summit, Domaine Serene, and Stoller Ranch, plus numerous smaller wineries and distinguished independent vineyards. The oldest of the independents is Abbey Ridge, first planted in 1977, the majority of whose fruit now goes to Cameron Winery; but Nysa Vineyard and DePonte Vineyard supply various small vintners, including Panther Creek and Ken Wright Cellars.

About ten miles due west of the Red Hills, touching the Yamhill-Carlton District at its southwestern corner, are the McMinnville Foothills, a 40,000-acre area of which just over 500 acres are currently planted. This area is a series of north-south ridges at the gateway to the so-called Van Duzer Corridor, the main throat linking the northern Willamette Valley with the Pacific Coast. Here substantial marine influence drops the average daytime high temperature, extending hang time. Sedimentary topsoil overlays marine basalt and sandstone but contains less sand than the related sedimentary soils in the Yamhill-Carlton District. Although the area's first vineyard, Hyland, was planted in the mid 1970s, it is a mostly new area viticulturally, whose potential has not been fully explored. Besides Hyland Vineyard, the largest holdings are Yamhill Valley Vineyards and Momtazi Vineyards. Youngberg Hill Vineyards, a 12-acre parcel planted on a steep, south-facing slope in 1989, produces an estate-bottled pinot and sells fruit to Panther Creek Cellars. In 2001, Ken Wright Cellars began sourcing fruit from the 16-acre Meredith Mitchell Vineyard, planted in 1988.

South of McMinnville—which is the county seat and the immediate area's main commercial center—lies the southernmost of the newly proposed AVAs, the Eola Hills. The hills rise up like volcanic islands from the valley floor on the western side of the Willamette River. The hills run north-south from about five miles northeast of Amity to State Highway 22, north of the Willamette River at West Salem, with highest peaks at about 1,100 feet. Numerous lateral ridges run east to west on both sides of the main north-south ridge. The main period for vineyard development here began in the mid 1970s, and continues. The largest concentration of vineyard now is around the hills' midpoint, where Bethel Road connects Highway 99W with Spring Valley Road. The estate vineyards of Bethel Heights, Cristom, and Witness Tree are here, along with the large and well-known Temperance Hill Vineyard. There are, however, important estate and independent vineyards throughout the Eola Hills, on both the east and west sides, from Canary Hill and Carter in the southwest to Seven Springs and Elton in the northeast; and new vineyards continue to be planted, mostly at the expense of onetime apple orchard. The western sides of the hills are substantially influenced by marine air flows through the Van Duzer Corridor, so vineyards on that side are typically cooler and later-ripening sites. East-side vineyards are buffered from the marine influence. The main soil series is so-called Nekia, which is basically a thinner version of the iron-rich, red-toned Jory soils that typify the Red Hills; but there are also sedimentary soils on the western side of the main ridge and some alluvial silt-loam at lower elevations. Although the epicenter of the Willamette wine country is in the polygon anchored by the towns of Yamhill, Carlton, Lafayette, Dundee, and Newberg, the Eola Hills enjoy an enviable reputation among vintners for well-structured and deeply flavored pinot, and many blended Willamette Valley pinots use substantial quantities of Eola Hills fruit. The area now encompasses about 1,250 planted acres.

Pinot noir is Oregon's most extensively planted variety, accounting in 2001 for 49 percent of the state's total vineyard surface. If the counties outside the Willamette Valley are disregarded, pinot's share rises to more than 55 percent, and it is the only red variety of statistical significance. Acreage devoted to pinot was up 14 percent in 2001 over 2000, and harvested acres lag total planted acres by more than a quarter, so the variety's momentum is tremendous. Acreage continues to expand rapidly, with only about 75 percent of planted acreage currently bearing. The state faces considerable replanting in the years ahead, however, since almost two-thirds of its vineyards are own-rooted, and phylloxera has begun to appear. A high percentage of the plant material for pinot noir in Oregon is so-called Pommard clone (UCD 4 and/or 5) and Wädenswil (UCD 2A). Willamette Valley pinot has therefore been more homogeneous, at least in terms of plant material, than California's, at least until the Dijon clones became popular in both states in the 1990s. Oregon has made a virtue of climatic necessity, rigorously limiting yields to ensure ripe fruit. This practice has kept the statewide average yield for pinot noir to less than two tons per acre, which is dramatically lower than the California average, though individual California vineyards, especially those tending older vines, are in the same range or lower. Oregon sites with substantial marine influence often limit yields even further to ensure full ripening.

The low yields and the marginal climate probably have something to do with the paucity of investment in Oregon wine from outside sources. Apart from Domaine Drouhin Oregon, Argyle Wine Company, and Archery Summit (since 2001), the area's wineries are overwhelmingly locally, individually, or family owned and relatively small. King Estate, the state's largest winery at 820 acres and 90,000 cases, is domiciled just beyond the perimeter of the Willamette Valley but uses a good deal of Willamette Valley fruit. With that exception, a production level of 30,000 cases constitutes a very large winery by local standards, and many producers make only a few thousand cases.

THE OKANAGAN

Just north of the U.S.-Canadian border, about halfway between Vancouver and the Continental Divide, lies what Canadians call the Okanagan. This long, north-south-oriented, steep-walled, and poetically beautiful valley extends about 120 miles from around Vernon, at the north end of Okanagan Lake, to Osoyoos on the Washington State line. It is simultaneously the course of the Okanagan River, home to three deepwater lakes of glacial origin, and the extreme northern end of the Sonoran Desert. Straddling the 49th and 50th parallels and well buffered from marine influence by the extreme northern end of the Cascade Range, the valley manages a growing season of about 185 days, ideal for the apples that made the area famous in the first half of the twentieth century. It also has an extremely dry climate, which has appealed to Canadian retirees. In fact, the valley's midsection—home to Kelowna, the area's only real "city"—is a good deal colder than the valley's extreme southern end, on the U.S. border. The topography around the main lake is aggressive, with much of its eastern shore inaccessible by paved road. Vineyards, many of them clinging to steep slopes, are now scattered the entire length of the valley, creating stunning vistas reminiscent of Switzerland that combine vines with shimmering lakes, sheer cliffs, and forested hilltops. There is a predictable concentration on early-ripening grape varieties in the north, but significant investment in merlot and the cabernets near the towns of Osoyoos and Oliver.

History Apart from a few vines planted by Oblate missionaries in the 1860s, there was no viticulture in the Okanagan until the 1920s, when a visiting winemaker from Hungary encouraged a local farmer to plant wine grapes. Some local wine was made from apples during the 1930s, and a few small-scale entrepreneurs tried making "real" wine from grapes they trucked north from California. In 1952, William Bennett, a onetime participant in these wine-from-imported-grapes schemes, was elected premier of British Columbia. No longer invested in grape imports, Bennett ordered the province's liquor control board to establish rules that would require the use of local grapes for local wine, which set off a frenzy of planting.

By the end of the 1960s, the Okanagan was home to about 3,000 acres of grapes, but virtually all of them were native labrusca varieties or hybrids. Although vinifera varieties were introduced tentatively in the 1960s and 1970s, and the province's first estate wineries were established at the end of the 1970s and the beginning of the 1980s, the landscape did not change fundamentally until Canada signed the North American Free Trade Agreement in 1988. Suddenly, vintners who had enjoyed guaranteed access to the local marketplace and preferential treatment if they bought local grapes faced the prospect of having to compete against a flood of cheap jug wine that could be imported from the States, more or less without restriction. To level the playing field, the Canadian government agreed to finance a one-time program to pull out labrusca and hybrid vines and replace them with vinifera varieties. British Columbia's vintners rushed to replant, to establish new wineries dedicated to low yields of carefully farmed fruit, to hire experienced winemakers from around the world, and to pass some of the most exigent wine legislation anywhere on earth. The Vintners Quality Alliance was established in 1989 to provide standards for wine, certification criteria including taste panels, and market development support. The British Columbia Wine Institute, created by an act of the provincial legislature, followed in 1990. Laws were passed to require that any Canadian wine sporting an appellation name must be made *entirely* from grapes grown within that appellation; that a vintage-dated wine must contain no less than 95 percent of wine from that year; and that varietal wine must be made from at least 85 percent of the named variety. A new wave of superpremium producers like Burrowing Owl near Oliver and Cedar Creek just south of Kelowna joined the vinifera-oriented pioneers of the 1970s and 1980s, while wineries like Mission Hill, founded in the early 1970s to produce an appalling but commercially successful product called Fuddle Duck, were reborn as ultrapremium vinifera operations.

No one knows for sure when the first pinot noir was planted in the Okanagan. The oldest planting I have discovered is a tiny block measuring only one-fifth of an acre set out in 1975 in the Quails' Gate Vineyard, just south of Westbank. The next may have been Ian Mavety's planting ten years later at Blue Mountain, overlooking Skaha Lake south of Penticton. Both of these plantings are still in production.

Terrain, Terroir, and Vineyards A horticultural surface of approximately 100,000 acres is included within the Okanagan and neighboring Similkameen delimited viticultural areas (DVAs), of which about 10,000 acres are deemed plantable to wine grapes. Thanks to a state-of-the-art project funded in 1999 by Agriculture Canada and the British Columbia Wine Institute and based at Agriculture Canada's Pacific Agri-Food Research Centre in Summerland, fabulously detailed information on viticulture in the Okanagan is currently in the process of being compiled. Using geographic information systems technology, a map-based data model has been created, incorporating block-by-block data on terrain, slope, aspect, soil, microclimate, planting density, variety, clone, rootstock, and yield. Every vineyard block in the Okanagan and Similkameen valleys is included in the project, except for about ten acres belonging to growers who could not be contacted, two wineries and two independent growers who asked not to be included, and a few holdings of less than two acres each. All blocks have been mapped using global positioning technology, and soils information has been imported from a survey conducted by the British Columbia Ministry of Environment in 1986. Weather sensors have been installed in selected vineyards, and growers have been surveyed to obtain information on cultivation practices and yield. Efforts to correlate site-specific information with qualitative data about the resulting wines are still in the future, but an enviably specific picture of the Okanagan vineyard is already emerging.

Half of the plantable acreage had been planted by 2001, up from slightly more than 25 percent in 1997. Pinot noir accounts for about 11 percent of the 5,000 planted acres. Most of it lies north of Penticton, but Burrowing Owl, Blue Mountain, Tinhorn Creek, and Inniskillin are all farther south, and Mission Hill has planted some pinot on a north-facing slope overlooking Osoyoos. About 420 acres of pinot are farmed by wineries, while the balance belongs to independent growers. Independent growers tend to operate on a very small scale, with an average vineyard size of less than ten acres; winery-owned vineyards are larger, averaging just over 40 acres. The total picture features small fragments, however. Of the 220 so-called vineyard operations in the Okanagan, 72 grow at least small amounts of pinot noir, making the average pinot holding of any single operation less than eight acres.

With the overwhelming majority of vineyard very young, it is not surprising that the most common vineyard spacing is relatively tight at four feet by eight, and that 95 percent of vineyards grow pinot on a vertical-shoot-positioned trellis system, which is increasingly standard everywhere. Dijon clones account for nearly three-quarters of total plantings, and Dijon 115 by itself accounts for one-third. A third of the pinot vineyard consists of own-rooted vines; this constitutes a substantial liability, though many of the own-rooted plantings are in sandy soils where phylloxera does not seem to spread.

The largest players in Okanagan pinot noir are Vincor International, which owns the Hawthorne Mountain, Sumac Ridge, and Inniskillin brands, and Mission Hill Family Estate in Westbank, owned by Vancouver native Anthony van Mandl since 1981; but neither of these, nor any other producer in the Okanagan, qualifies as a real pinot specialist. A few wineries like Cedar Creek and Quail's Gate, which have produced a few exceptional bottlings, say they have made a "commitment" to pinot noir and expect it to represent a growing percentage of their total production. Most, however, are in the position of Mission Hill, where management is at the point of trying to decide "whether to get really serious" about pinot. So far, the valley's most serious track record has been assembled by Blue Mountain (see its profile in part II). Pinot noir has been made there since 1991 from estate-grown fruit and currently represents a third of the winery's total production, with additional vines planted in 2001.

THE GREATER SOUTH SHORE OF LAKE ONTARIO

Two related viticultural areas—one in upstate New York, the other in Canada's Ontario province—are the most important venues for pinot noir in the eastern half of the North American continent. These are, respectively, the Finger Lakes region and the Niagara Peninsula. In macrogeographic terms, both are part of the Allegheny Plateau, sometimes called the Niagara Escarpment, about 40,000 square miles of New York, Pennsylvania, Ohio, and Ontario. The plateau consists primarily of rounded hills, ridges, broad valleys, and deepwater lakes in areas where glacial action was important, and of rougher, more mountainous, and more heavily forested topography in areas that were spared from glacial passages. While the areas are quite different in significant ways, the proximity of Lake Ontario shapes both, mostly by mitigating the continental winter cold that would otherwise doom vinifera vines. The triangle formed by the cities of Rochester, Syracuse, and Corning frames New York's Finger Lakes, a quintet-plus of long, narrow, and picturesque north-south-oriented lakes. The glacial action that carved the lakes deposited a layer of moderately fertile, well-drained till around the lakes' northern ends and middle, creating land well suited to various forms of agriculture. Corn, beans, and soybeans, plus Amish settlement and a modest peppering of dairy farms, share the landscape with vineyards and small, historic towns. Although the main population centers are at the northern end of each lake, visitor services are widely distributed, and wine tourism is now a substantial business. A generous hour westward, the Niagara Peninsula is bounded on its northern side by the Ontario lakeshore, on the east by the Niagara River, and on the south by the Welland River. The Niagara Peninsula's wine tourism is concentrated around the town of Niagara-on-the-Lake, at the peninsula's northeastern end, but extends westward to St. Catherines, Vineland, Beamsville, and Grimsby.

History The first vineyard in the Finger Lakes area is said to have been planted by the Reverend William Bostwick in the rectory garden of the newly founded Episcopal church at Hammondsport in 1829, but the gesture may have been primarily symbolic, because there is no record that Bostwick actually made wine. His viticultural example was apparently followed by a few neighbors, however. Other small vineyards were planted near the southern end of Keuka Lake in the 1830s, 1840s, and 1850s, driven in part by the arrival of German immigrants with viticultural experience. The area's first commercial winery, the Hammondsport and Pleasant Valley Wine Company—eventually distinguished for its Great Western brand of sparkling wine—was founded in 1860; the second pioneer firm, the Urbana Wine Company (later known as Gold Seal Vineyards), followed in 1865. The exclusive object of winegrowing in the Finger Lakes region, however, was native labrusca varieties until, nearly 70 years later, Gold Seal hired Charles Fournier, then the chief winemaker at Veuve Clicquot Ponsardin in Champagne, to restore the company's pre-Prohibition reputation. Fournier introduced French-American hybrids, which underpinned the first revolution in New York's wine industry.

Another 20 years after that, in 1953, Fournier began New York's second evolution. At a conference that year at the New York State Agricultural Experiment Station in the nearby town of Geneva, Fournier met Konstantin Frank. Frank was a Ukrainian immigrant with a doctorate in viticulture and special expertise in very cold climates. Possessed of a messianic determination to promote European varieties in his adopted country, he convinced Fournier that vinifera could be grown successfully in upstate New York. Fournier then hired Frank, who was immediately made Gold Seal's chief viticulturist. Working together and with the government's plant quarantine facility at Beltsville, Maryland, Fournier and Frank imported several European varieties, including pinot noir. Gold Seal, whose main product was sparkling wine, made a still pinot noir at least as early as 1960, and Dr. Frank's Vinifera Wine Cellars—founded while Frank was still employed at Gold Seal—began production, including pinot noir, in 1962.

For almost another two decades, however, vinifera varieties remained the stuff of a lunatic fringe in the Finger Lakes region. Agricultural experts at Geneva advised everyone against planting them, and only a few farmers were brave enough to disregard their "professional" advice. Very gradually, a few acres at a time, vinifera spread northward and eastward from the southern end of Keuka Lake, first to the western shore of Seneca Lake, and then around both Seneca and Cayuga lakes. Thanks to the Farm Winery Act, passed by the New York Legislature in 1976, the number of wineries then exploded statewide. Almost all of them are very small garage-scale enterprises and depend overwhelmingly on direct sales to the public from on-site tasting rooms. Quite a number of the Finger Lakes region's 61 wineries make at least some wine from vinifera varieties, but all vinifera taken together account for less than 10 percent of the region's vineyard surface.

Viticulture in the Niagara Peninsula, based on labrusca varieties, began in the third quarter of the nineteenth century. The first winery in the area is said to have been Barnes, founded in 1873 just outside the town of St. Catherines. The second, T. G. Bright and Company, set up shop the following year, and about two dozen wineries were in operation by the century's end. After World War II, Bright's became the first winery to work seriously with both hybrids and vinifera. The pioneer in this work was a French chemist by the name of Adhémar de Chaunac, who had made the company's first dry table wine at the end of the 1930s, against the backdrop of a portfolio otherwise based entirely on ports and sherries. In 1946, de Chaunac imported vines from France—a decade before the better-known imports orchestrated by Fournier and Frank in New York. Most of de Chaunac's imports were French hybrid varieties, but 100 vines were said to have been some mix of chardonnay and pinot noir. There is no evidence that the pinot was used to make still wines, but Bright's did produce award-winning sparkling wines from various combinations of pinot and chardonnay during the 1950s.

Not much more was done with vinifera in the Niagara Peninsula until the 1970s, however, when a nurseryman with a degree in horticulture from the University of Guelph teamed up with an economist and home winemaker from Austria to plant 25 acres of vinifera on a farm just north of Queenston called Inniskillin. In 1974, using a repurposed fruit-packing shed as a winery, Inniskillin produced the Niagara's first estate-bottled, vintage-dated wine from hybrid and vinifera varieties, though pinot noir was not in the lineup. In a replay of the circumstances in British Columbia, Ontario turned vigorously to vinifera after Canada joined the North American Free Trade Agreement in 1988, and by the mid 1990s, two-thirds of the province's vineyards had been replanted to vinifera and French hybrids.

Terrain, Terroir, and Vineyards The Finger Lakes AVA, established in 1982, covers about 4,000 square miles, arbitrarily bounded on its northern side by the Erie Canal and the New York State Thruway, and on the east, south, and west by a succession of state and interstate highways and county lines. Less than half of 1 percent of the included surface is actually planted to vineyard, and nearly all of that hugs the lakes' shores fairly tightly.

The lakes themselves are crucial to successful viticulture. Very cold winters, with average low temperatures 20 degrees below freezing in January and February, are dangerous for grapevines, as are spring frosts, which are commonplace in April and can easily occur into late May. The lakes' deep water, which ranges from about 200 to more than 600 feet at Seneca Lake's deepest point, holds summer heat through the autumn and into the winter, sucking cold air off the surrounding slopes and eliminating "pools" of killer cold air. It also retains winter cold in the spring, delaying budbreak and reducing the risk of destruction from spring frosts. Most vineyards have therefore been planted within eyeshot of the lakes, at altitudes between 200 and 500 feet above lake level. In general the "lake effect" is strongest where the lake water is deepest, so the most favored sites are on the shores of the Seneca and Cayuga lakes and tend to be concentrated near each lake's north-south midpoint. The more generalized moderating effect of Lake Ontario, whose southern shore is about 25 miles from the Finger Lakes' northern ends, also diminishes as one travels southward along each lakeshore. As well, soils suitable for viticulture seem to favor the slopes overlooking each lake's midpoint. At the lakes' northern ends, the soils are sometimes too deep and vigorous for wine grapes, while the southern ends often display exposed bedrock with insufficient topsoil for any form of agriculture.

For the purposes of wine tourism, producers have organized themselves into lake-specific groups, so that it is customary to speak about Keuka Lake wineries, Seneca Lake wineries, and the like. Some of the producers around Cayuga Lake, claiming that the lesser altitudes of Cayuga's surrounding hillsides and Cayuga's larger water surface have combined to create an especially moderate microclimate and longer growing season, carved out a separate Cayuga Lake AVA in 1988, but this designation is rarely seen on labels. A 1997 survey found 86 acres of pinot noir in the Finger Lakes; reliable sources believe this figure had grown to just over 100 acres by 2001. The parcels are universally small, and scattered among the three main lakes. Owing to the pioneering work at Gold Seal by Dr. Frank, the oldest plantings are on the western shore of Keuka Lake. Dr. Frank's original estate planting of pinot here dates to 1959, making it probably the third-oldest pinot noir vineyard in North America still producing, after Chalone's 1946 block and the 1953 block at Hanzell. The oldest planting on Seneca Lake is apparently in Hermann J. Wiemer's vineyard near Dundee, set out in 1979. On the eastern side of Seneca Lake, the first pinot may have been planted by the Wagner family early in the 1980s; a 20-year-old block is now farmed by Mark Wagner at Lamoreaux Landing Wine Cellars near the village of Lodi. Serious producers of pinot noir now include—in addition to Frank, Wiemer, and Lamoreaux Landing—Lakewood Vineyards just north of Watkins Glen, Chateau Lafayette Reneau and Red Newt Cellars in Hector, Fox Run near Penn Yan, and Sheldrake Point, a new venture right on the Cayuga lakeshore near Ovid.

Unsurprisingly, many vineyards have been planted with budwood taken from Dr. Frank, most of which is known locally as Clone 7. What is called Geneva clone may also have come from Dr. Frank's vineyard, but the budwood has been distributed from the experimental vineyard at the New York State Agricultural Experiment Station in Geneva. Small amounts of UCD 13, 29, and 23 have also been used, and the Dijon clones have recently become popular in the Finger Lakes, as they have elsewhere. Thomas Henick-Kling, who directs the enology program at Geneva, thinks that pinot noir is still too sparsely distributed in the Finger Lakes region to allow for any conclusions about sites to which it is especially well suited. Because riesling has emerged as the area's flagship variety of vinifera, it seems likely that the work to align varieties with various site specificities may begin with riesling, and move rather later to pinot noir. That said, pinot noir is now attracting considerable attention from local vintners, culminating in the organization of a Finger Lakes Pinot Noir Alliance in 1999, which has sponsored winemaker visits to Burgundy, and a so-called Eastern Pinot Noir Conference, loosely modeled on the Steamboat seminars held in Oregon.

The Niagara Peninsula, about an hour's drive west of the Finger Lakes, is often described as Canada's banana belt. Geologically, it is the extreme western end of the continuous benchland on the southern shore of Lake Ontario, whose eastern end runs parallel to the northern boundary of the Finger Lakes AVA. The Niagara region is warmer than the Finger Lakes area owing to the greater size and closer proximity of Lake Ontario's deepwater mass, which virtually eliminates the danger of cold-weather damage to grapevines and ensures that even Bordeaux varieties can usually be ripened successfully. Ripening pinot noir is as straightforward on the Niagara Peninsula as it is chancy around the Finger Lakes. In both regions, however, the main threat to pinot noir is disease pressure associated with all-season rain and relatively high humidity.

In general, the Niagara Peninsula is farther along than the Finger Lakes in the transition from juice and hybrid wine grapes to vinifera, thanks largely to the vineyard conversion subsidies offered when Canada joined the North American Free Trade Agreement. Of the area's 20,000 acres of grapes, about three-quarters are now used to make wine, and between 65 percent and 70 percent of the annual grape crush is vinifera varieties. Fifteen percent of the vinifera—or about 450 acres—is pinot noir. Vineyards are concentrated hard by the lakeshore, on the plain between the shore and the lake escarpments, and on slightly higher benchlands. Most of the area's vinifera vineyard is less than ten years old.

The main producers of serious pinot noir are Inniskillin, which makes several vineyard-designated wines as well as a blended bottling, Thirteenth Street, and Vineland Estates, but 42 pinots were submitted to Vintners Quality Alliance Ontario for permission to use the VQA designation in 2001, and 31 of them were approved. Viticulturists attribute the growing interest in pinot—acreage dedicated to pinot doubled from 1997 to 2000—to better clones (and Dijon 115 is the single most widely planted selection), to later cluster thinning, and to better fungicides; but pinot noir is by no means a dominant variety here. Among reds, cabernet franc and merlot are much more widely planted, and the self-proclaimed flagship of Ontario wine is icewine made from white varieties and hybrids.

OTHER REGIONS

Although the regions described above account for more than 96 percent of North America's pinot noir and for virtually all of the enthusiasm that now radiates around this variety, pinot is grown and made elsewhere, and some of it is of more than routine interest. Indeed, given how short and recent most American experience with pinot really is, it makes sense to assume that at least some of the plantings outside what are now regarded as mainstream pinot regions have great potential, and may turn out to make wine as good as or better than many sites in high-profile regions.

The Pacific Pinot Zone Within the Pacific Pinot Zone but outside the aforementioned regions, there is pinot noir north of San Luis Obispo, around the towns of

Paso Robles and Templeton. Sixty acres of vineyard, including some pinot noir, were planted at Hoffman Mountain Ranch (now Hidden Mountain Ranch) northwest of Paso Robles as early as 1964, and some well-regarded pinots were made there under the guidance of André Tchelistcheff during the 1970s and 1980s. A few miles to the southeast, where the Templeton Gap in the Coast Ranges moderates temperatures, Wild Horse Winery, created by Ken Volk in 1983, has made pinot a persistent specialty. The Wild Horse pinot program relies heavily on fruit purchased from other vineyards, however, with which the estate fruit is blended. More recently, pinot has been planted in southern Santa Clara County.

North of San Francisco, there are a few vest-pocket pinot vineyards in western Marin County (see the Dutton-Goldfield and Hartford Court profiles in part II), as well as substantial plantings in parts of the Sonoma Coast AVA that cannot be classified as "true" coast. Gallo of Sonoma's Stony Point Vineyard, which includes pinot noir, is clearly visible from Highway 101 south of Santa Rosa. Although most of the neighboring Sonoma Mountain AVA is regarded as cabernet country, the north-facing slopes, which overlook Bennett Valley, are home to about 60 acres of fine pinot noir that has attracted the attention of pinot-oriented producers in Los Carneros, Sonoma Valley, and the Russian River valley. There, the combination of northern exposure, marine influence via the Petaluma Gap, and elevations generally above 1,000 feet create a hospitable environment for pinot noir. Martin Van der Kamp, who once specialized in sparkling wine, presides over the single largest pinot vineyard in the AVA and sells his grapes to a passel of luminaries including Landmark Vineyards, Tandem, Talacoat, Byington, and Flowers. This vineyard, originally planted in the late 1950s or early '60s, was expanded in 1986 using budwood from the first planting. Dave Steiner's nearby vineyard supplies pinot to Ancien and (until recently) Joseph Swan. Pinot is also grown in the Wolfspierre and Jewell vineyards. Although the Sonoma Valley (on the lee side of Sonoma Mountain) is usually considered too warm for good pinot, Chateau St. Jean grows it successfully near Kenwood. Hanzell (see the profile in part II), nestled in the Mayacamas Range overlooking Boyes Hot Springs, is one of North America's oldest specialty producers. Just north of the Carneros boundary, Gundlach-Bundschu tends the historic Rheinfarm Vineyard, which is the Sonoma Valley's southernmost stand of pinot noir. In Napa—defying the prevailing view that the valley north of Carneros is too hot for good pinot noir—pinot has been grown for many years at Newlan and Trefethen, just north of Napa's city limits, and Reg Oliver (see the profile of El Molino Winery in part II) has planted a few acres at Rutherford, not far from the pinot vineyards farmed at Beaulieu in the 1940s and 1950s. There are also several small pinot vineyards in the Mount Veeder AVA, southwest of Oakville. Mayacamas Vineyards farms a tiny stand of vines in its estate vineyards, and an early 1990s planting near Oakville Grade Road is now made into varietal pinot noir by Lewis Cellars.

Farther north, in Mendocino County, there were 60 reported acres of pinot noir in the Yorkville Highlands AVA in 2002, up from 27 when that appellation was created in 1996. Yorkville Highlands sits astride Highway 128 between the Anderson and Alexander valleys, along the headwaters of Dry Creek and Rancheria Creek. Although more cabernet sauvignon than pinot is grown in Yorkville Highlands, pinot still accounts for almost one-fifth of total planted acreage, and at least four vineyards are dedicated exclusively to pinot noir. Williams Selyem makes a vineyard-designated pinot from the Weir Vineyard, seven bearing acres on a south-facing slope overlooking Highway 128. Outside the Yorkville Highlands and Anderson Valley AVAs, the county accounts for another plus-or-minus 700 acres of pinot. Although much of this is grown in areas imperfectly suited to the variety and the fruit is used primarily in lower-priced bottlings, several well-respected producers have identified very promising new plantings. Patz & Hall, for example, makes an extremely interesting and exotically aromatic pinot from the Alder Springs Vineyard, a 1994 planting of Dijon clones in decomposed sandstone at an altitude of more than 2,000 feet near Laytonville, at the county's northern end.

Although the Willamette Valley accounts for most of Oregon's pinot noir and nearly all of its producers, pinot was actually being grown in the Umpqua River valley, south of the Willamette and about one-quarter its size, before the Willamette pioneers set out their first vines in the mid 1960s. In 2001, fewer than 200 acres were growing in the Umpqua area, which is generally drier and warmer than its northern neighbor, but this was still more vineyard acreage than is dedicated to any other variety. Some Umpqua fruit is vinified by Willamette-based producers in the form of Oregon blends; the balance is made locally by Hillcrest Vineyard, Henry Estate, and Girardet Wine Cellars, among others. Farther south, another 200 acres of pinot are found in the western part of the Rogue River valley, primarily at Bridgeview Vineyards and Foris Vineyards Winery. Another dribble of pinot is grown in the Columbia River valley, on both the Oregon and the Washington sides of the river. Because this is warm country, pinot is generally confined to higher altitudes, where cool nights refresh the fruit and maintain decent levels of acid. Elsewhere in Washington there are another plus-or-minus 150 acres of pinot noir, used mostly for sparkling wine; but on Bainbridge Island, a 30-minute ferry ride from Seattle in Puget Sound, Gerard Bentryn, a trained climatologist, grows a single acre of pinot noir that is regularly vinified into still wine.

Outside the Pacific Pinot Zone, the Okanagan, and the greater south shore of Lake Ontario, very small plantings of pinot noir are concentrated in three main areas. These are, first, high-altitude sites in New Mexico, Arizona, Texas, and Colorado; second, lake-effect sites in the Great Lakes region; and third, well-ventilated sites in several Mid-Atlantic states. The logic of these areas is fairly plain. In the desert and semidesert Southwest, altitude is the only refuge from temperatures that would otherwise be prohibitively hot. Near the Great Lakes, proximity to large bodies of water moderates potentially lethal winter cold, as it does in upstate New York and the Niagara Peninsula. Finally, in the Mid-Atlantic region, good air circulation is the indispensable antidote to excessive rain and high humidity, which are hostile to vinifera in general and often fatal to pinot noir.

The Southwest Although they were eclipsed in the nineteenth and twentieth centuries by California, the southwestern states are home to the oldest continuous winemaking tradition in North America, dating from as early as 1626. Wine grapes were widely grown in colonial New Mexico (which included all of Arizona and part of what is now Texas) in the seventeenth, eighteenth, and nineteenth centuries. Nowadays Gruet, a Champagne house, is the main wine producer (and the main grower of pinot noir) in the state of New Mexico. Gruet farms about 50 acres of pinot noir (alongside 70 acres of chardonnay) on the eastern shore of Elephant Butte Lake, about 150 miles south of Albuquerque. This vineyard, planted beginning in 1983, is at about 4,200 feet above sea level. Gruet's pinot supports primarily a large sparkling-wine program, but the firm has also produced small quantities of medium-hued, cherry-scented, spicy still pinot noir since 1998. A few additional acres of pinot are farmed northwest of Albuquerque, in the Ponderosa Valley on the southern slopes of the Jemez Mountains, at an elevation of about 5,800 feet.

In Colorado, on the western side of the Rocky Mountains, Steven Rhodes planted another tiny vineyard of pinot in 1996 near the town of Hotchkiss, in a new AVA called West Elks. West Elks is a surprisingly temperate area, historically devoted to apple and peach trees, and displays a phenology not dissimilar to that of pinot-friendly regions in Northern California. In extreme southern Arizona, within 20 miles of the Mexican border, Sonoita Vineyards farms another tiny enclave of pinot near the town of Elgin. Sonoita is at about 5,000 feet above sea level, in red, high-clay soils that support high-plains grasslands and a sprinkling of white oak trees. The principal is Gordon Dutt, a soil scientist who coauthored *Grape and Wine Production in the Four Corners Region* in 1980—an exploration of the Southwest's suitability for viticulture.

In the so-called high plains of west Texas, about 45 miles northwest of Lubbock and not far from the New Mexico border, there is another 100 acres of pinot noir, most of it farmed by Messina Hof Winery. Messina Hof's pinot vineyards, planted beginning in 1985, are on a flat plateau at 3,400 feet.

The Great Lakes Area The Grand River Valley AVA, on the southeastern shore of Lake Erie about 20 miles from Cleveland, is home to St. Joseph Vineyards, a boutique winery bonded in 1997 that specializes in pinot noir. Rocky loam soils, deposited in the wake of glaciers, are exceptionally well drained and well adapted to storing and radiating heat. St. Joseph's dry-farmed pinot noir vineyard was planted in 1986 to a combination of Dijon clones and UCD 2A, 4, 13, and 23. My experience with St. Joseph wines from the 1999 vintage was tantalizing, suggesting that this vineyard, and perhaps the AVA, enjoys special potential.

In Michigan, about 30 acres of pinot noir are cultivated by at least three wineries in the Upper Peninsula, in an AVA northwest of Traverse City called the Leelanau Peninsula. The producers are Ciccone Vineyards, Good Harbor Winery, and Bel Lago Vineyards and Winery.

The Mid-Atlantic States In the Mid-Atlantic states, there is pinot in Maryland, Virginia, and North Carolina. Elk Run Winery, northwest of Baltimore in Mount Airy, Maryland, appears to be that state's only producer of pinot noir, working with about 2,000 vines that have been planted in phases since 1995.

In Virginia, the state viticulturist estimates that there are "less than 12" producers, located mostly in the scenic central part of the state. State statistics recorded 29 acres of pinot noir in 1999, which represented about 1.5 percent of the state's total vineyard surface. The earliest planting was probably at Barboursville Vineyards, in about 1982; the largest single stake is now farmed by Rockbridge Vineyards, north of Lexington, at an altitude of about 2,000 feet.

North Carolina's only pinot noir, as far as I know, grows in 1.5 acres of red clay, at about 1,200 feet above sea level, near Dobson in the Yadkin valley. The fruit has been vinified by Chatham Hill Winery since 1999.

THE REGIONS COMPARED

It is surprisingly difficult to collect genuinely comparable data about the main regions in which North America's pinot noir is grown. Even the acreage under vine in the areas with a substantial investment in pinot is not known for sure. The best data are collected by state or provincial agricultural departments, but such data are typically organized by county, and county boundaries do not correspond to the viticultural areas around which, in general, this book has been organized. In some viticultural areas, trade associations of winegrowers have surveyed their members to generate acreage and production statistics, but the associations' confidence in their numbers varies, sometimes because growers respond imperfectly to questionnaires, and sometimes because a significant number of growers or makers remain outside the association's membership. There is also the problem that in the past five years, planting and replanting have increased at such breakneck speed that numbers can be superseded even before they are reported. Climatic data are even more troublesome. Temperatures and rainfall are not consistent across large AVAs. Government-operated weather stations are not always near vineyards, and in-vineyard sensors are too recent to have generated reliable time-series data. And when it comes to the all-important matter of the wines themselves, region-based generalizations are easily frustrated by a host of site-to-site variations, as well as by the subjectivity that tasters and taste descriptions inevitably bring to wine. Data on pinot vineyards outside the main regions present other difficulties. Typically, only small and isolated plantings exist in these areas, and the experience of a single grower can be idiosyncratic.

With these caveats, here are some broad-brush comparisons.

Size Oregon's Willamette Valley now contains the largest planted surface of pinot noir in North America. In 2001, this was approximately 4,800 acres. California's southern Central Coast, if it is aggregated to form a single region, can claim second place in overall size, with approximately 4,300 acres of pinot noir in the ground. The best estimates for the Russian River valley and Los Carneros hover around 3,000 acres each, with Russian River probably the larger by a few hundred acres. The greater Salinas Valley includes virtually all of the pinot noir in Monterey County, which was reported at 2,600 acres in 1999. If the sums are done by county, however, California's Sonoma County wins, claiming acreage in Russian River, Los Carneros, Sonoma Coast, Sonoma Mountain, and Sonoma Valley.

The remaining areas with a substantial and successful investment in pinot noir are all much smaller. Anderson Valley is the largest of the remainder, with about 1,100 acres believed currently planted to pinot noir. California's true Sonoma Coast, following a frenzy of new planting since 1998, now accounts for about 600 acres, though the total rises to more than 1,200 acres if the entire AVA is counted. There are 550 acres in British Columbia's Okanagan valley; Ontario's Niagara Peninsula checks in just slightly smaller. Local sources estimate that there are now about 150 acres planted in the Santa Cruz Mountains and 100 in New York's Finger Lakes region. The Texas Hill Country may have as much as another 100 acres of pinot. Everything else is really dribs and drabs.

These acreage tallies should be roughly consistent with a scan of retail shelves, where Oregon, Santa Barbara, Los Carneros, and Russian River pinots are almost always easier to find than bottlings from Anderson Valley, Santa Lucia Highlands, or the Santa Cruz Mountains; but allowances must also be made for Oregon's lower yields per acre, and for the substantial percentage of Carneros, Russian River, and Anderson Valley pinot noir that is made into sparkling rather than still wine.

Climate Since the early 1970s, nearly all pinotcentric grape growers in North America have fixed their sights on so-called cool-climate areas. In California, this has generally meant the cooler sites in what is, on balance, a relatively warm climate; in Oregon, British Columbia, and New York, it has meant privileging slightly warmer, better-exposed sites in what are generally cool climates. When the subject is pinot noir, the cool-climate mantra is so often repeated that winegrowers seem determined to out-cool each other. Much of the public relations released by regional trade associations emphasizes just how very cool each region is, how much it is like Burgundy, and how closely "cool," "cooler," and "coolest" correlate with wine quality.

In Los Carneros, some winegrowers will intimate, off the record, that the region's main downside is that it may not be cool enough. In the Russian River valley, the winegrowers' ongoing effort to redraw the appellation's boundaries is focused on obtaining a better match of boundaries with cool-weather influence.

There is, however, huge disagreement over how to measure "cool," and what kind of cool really makes a difference. Is the best cool a low total accumulation of heat during the growing season, as defined by Davis professors Winkler and Amerine back in 1944? Is it relatively low daytime high temperatures during the growing season? Alternatively, are high daytime maximums fine as long as overnight temperatures remain cool? Is the cool produced as wind chill just as good as ambient cool? Is a cool climate necessarily associated with late springs and early autumns? And is a climate still cool if its winters are temperate, so that grapevines (and other plants) never experience a true dormant season?

Even if there were agreement on what to measure, it is hard to obtain reliable and comparable data. Vineyards are intensely mesoclimatic and microclimatic, meaning that even in a single vineyard temperature can vary substantially within a few tens of feet, so that official weather stations, sometimes miles away at an airport or post office, may not reflect vineyard-specific realities. On the other hand, in-vineyard sensors have been deployed for only a few years and are therefore unable to provide useful time-series data.

There *are* major climatic differences among the main pinot regions within the Pacific Pinot Zone, and huge differences between regions within this zone and pinot-friendly regions elsewhere in North America. These differences are not especially evident in heat summation figures, which are measured in degree-days. Most heat summation numbers calculated for North America's main pinot regions fall between 2,400 and 2,600 degree-days when averaged over a multiyear period. Typical numbers cited for the southern Central Coast are about 2,450; for Los Carneros, about 2,640; for the cooler parts of the Russian River valley, about 2,500; for the Willamette Valley, about 2,475; for the Finger Lakes region, about 2,350; and for the warmer end of the Okanagan valley, about 2,560. These figures compare to about 2,400 for Beaune, in Burgundy.

A good deal of ink has been spilled to make a case that the "best" climate for pinot noir is the climate most closely approximating Burgundy's. At least in terms of average heat accumulation, this argument appears to make the southern Central Coast and the Willamette Valley the best-chance regions for good pinot in North America, much to the satisfaction of vintners invested in these areas. However, year-to-year variations within any single region dwarf the plus-or-minus 200 degree-days of average difference that separate the warmest and coolest of the major American regions from one another. Consider, for example, that in 1997 (a warmish year), the southern Central Coast clocked about 2,750 degree days, while in 1999 (a cool year) it managed barely 1,850—a staggering 900 degree-days of difference. Or that the

Russian River valley was 500 degree-days warmer in 1997 than it was in 1998. Or that year-to-year variations at Camp Meeting Ridge on the Sonoma Coast have ranged over just a few years between a low of 2,200 and a high of 3,000. Or, for that matter, that Savigny-les-Beaune, in 1999, was warmer than any major pinot-producing region in North America, and 1999 is considered an excellent vintage! Given that the averages are much closer than the year-to-year variations, a good argument could be made that the differences among regions, measured in heat summation terms, are insignificant. Weather, not climate, may be determinative for pinot noir.

Alternatively, if one compares average high temperatures, average mean temperatures, and average diurnal variation for July and August—generally the two warmest months of the growing season everywhere—the main regions look very different. The Salinas Valley (measured at Gonzales) shows the lowest average daytime high temperatures (71 and 72 degrees for July and August, respectively), the lowest mean temperatures (62 and 64, respectively), and the smallest diurnal variation (18 degrees). Numbers from Santa Maria (for the southern Central Coast region) are almost identical, with daytime high temperatures just a tad higher and an average diurnal variation of 21 degrees. The true Sonoma Coast (measured at Camp Meeting Ridge) clocks in slightly warmer, but still comparatively cool, with an average July high temperature of 75, an average August high of 79, July and August means of 65 and 68, respectively, and diurnal variations of 20 and 24 degrees. The Sonoma Coast's July and August mean temperatures turn out to be in the same range (66 to 68) as the mean temperatures in the Okanagan (measured at the cool end in Kelowna), the Finger Lakes region (measured at Hammondsport), the Russian River valley (measured at Graton), and the Willamette Valley (measured at Dundee)—but these areas all show higher average daily high temperatures and greater diurnal variation. Of this group, the highest highs and greatest diurnal variation are experienced at Graton, in the cool Green Valley corner of the Russian River valley, where average daytime highs in July and August are 84 and 83, respectively, and the diurnal variation runs a hefty 36 degrees. Interestingly and somewhat surprisingly, the Vine Hill district near Graton is said to be cooler in midsummer than Hirsch or Camp Meeting Ridge on the Sonoma Coast, because Vine Hill, being lower, is more influenced by fog. All of these regions rely on slightly warmer days and cooler nights to achieve the same average heat. Los Carneros (measured at Vineburg), Santa Cruz Mountains (measured at Scotts Valley), and Anderson Valley (measured at Philo) are warmer still, both in terms of summer average daily high temperatures and daily mean temperatures, but Los Carneros and Anderson Valley also show very high diurnal variation, meaning that overnight lows are perceptibly chilly. Average daytime high temperatures at Vineburg in July and August are 90 and 89 degrees, respectively, but average lows are 49 and 50; at Philo, average highs are 92 and 91, with average overnight lows of 55 and 54. Rather surprisingly, these numbers for Philo are quite similar to numbers for the West Elks AVA in Colorado, where summer daytime highs typically break 90, and lows hover in the mid 50s.

If one thinks carefully about when and how grapes ripen, a reasonable case could be made that temperatures during the last month—or arguably even the last two weeks—before harvest are the *most* important, at least to style, and perhaps to wine quality. In fact, Andrew Reynolds, who teaches cold-climate viticulture at Brock University in Ontario, argues that even heat accumulation should more properly be measured for the last month before harvest than for the whole of the growing season. Clearly, grapes tasted a month before harvest are seriously sour and have almost no flavors desirable in finished wine, and this situation does not change dramatically until the very last weeks before crews are sent into the vineyards to pick. Since it is well understood that low temperatures are crucial to the maintenance of acidity and structure in finished wine, average overnight lows at the tail end of the season could be an important determinant of wine style, especially in a "transparent" variety like pinot noir. Within the Pacific Pinot Zone, the southern Central Coast, the true Sonoma Coast, the Santa Cruz Mountains, and Anderson Valley all show average low temperatures in the last three weeks before harvest of 51 to 52 degrees. Los Carneros, even adjusted for the earliest average harvest date of any major region, displays slightly cooler low preharvest temperatures of 49 to 50 degrees. The cool parts of the Russian River valley are slightly cooler still, with average overnight lows around 48 degrees. The Finger Lakes region and the Willamette Valley, which harvest respectively the first week in October and the fourth week in September, experience average low temperatures of 46 degrees in the last weeks before harvest. The northern Okanagan, which has the latest average harvest date of all, sees average overnight lows below 40 degrees at the end of September and beginning of October.

In general, these preharvest low minimums correlate better with certain stylistic parameters of pinot noir than do most other elements of climate. Low minimums equate to a bright-fruit, high-acid style of pinot, as long as allowances are made for sugar accumulation, which varies a good deal from region to region. Of course, where chaptalization is permitted and practiced, the effects of late-season temperatures can be obscured. In addition, site-to-site variations within regions interfere with generalizations—on this matter as on most others.

In terms of rainfall, the wettest regions are the Russian River valley, Anderson Valley, Willamette Valley, and true Sonoma Coast, with annual precipitation totals ranging between 37 and 40 inches. The Finger Lakes region, Santa Cruz Mountains, and Los Carneros get between 23 and 30 inches total. The driest regions are the southern Central Coast, the Salinas Valley, and the Okanagan, which get barely 15 inches in a year. The wet and dry seasons vary considerably, however. In the Okanagan and the Finger Lakes region, rainfall is spread rather evenly throughout the year, as it is in Burgundy. In the Okanagan there can be occasional hard showers at any time of year, but never very much; in the Finger Lakes region, rain is a constant hazard that can interfere with ripening and harvests, produce rot and mold, give the winemaker endless headaches, and sometimes ruin a vintage. In fact, moisture overall—defined as the combination of rain and relative humidity—is the greatest enemy of viticulture in the eastern third of the continent, and it is especially troublesome for pinot noir, whose thin skin is particularly vulnerable to mildew-related diseases. The Willamette Valley can count on only two genuinely dry months each year, July and August, but June and September average barely more than one inch of rain each, so harvests have a fair chance of escaping precipitation unless they are delayed into October. Some Oregon winemakers say they simply "won't deal with harvest rain" and pick early to avoid it, even if it means chaptalizing the must. Much the same can be said of Anderson Valley and the true Sonoma Coast, where the optimal harvest date can stray into the beginning of the fall rainy season; but Indian summers are also more typical at lower latitudes and chaptalization is not permitted in California in any case. Elsewhere rainfall poses few problems for grape growers.

Wind is also a variable among regions. Typically, California's coastal valleys are all wind tunnels, especially during summer afternoons. Since the direction of the wind flow is usually onshore, the winds have a cooling effect, but rapidly moving air by itself, irrespective of temperature, has a tendency to slow the rate at which grapes ripen. Because the inland areas these tunnels connect with the ocean are large, the Salinas Valley and Los Carneros are the pinot regions most affected by wind, but exposed sites can be problematically windy even in the Santa Rita Hills.

Growing Season Winegrowers care about weather because it affects *how* grapes ripen, which in turn affects both the flavors and the chemistry of the resulting wine. Growers and viticulturists call this process *phenology,* and distinguish four main markers to measure it: the vine's awakening, called budbreak; bloom, which also sets the first tiny berries; color change or veraison, when hard green berries soften and turn red; and harvest, when the grapes are picked for wine. Phenological development varies significantly across the main pinot-producing regions. The earliest budbreak occurs in the southern Central Coast, typically in the last week of February or the first week of March, as a reflection of the southern Central Coast's exceedingly mild winters. Most of California's North Coast wakes up next, during the second, third, and fourth weeks of March, though Calera's Mills Vineyard, on Mount Harlan, can be delayed until mid to late April. The second or third week of April typically sees budbreak in the northern Willamette Valley; and the Finger Lakes area sees the last North American pinot vines to bud out, typically in the first week of May. The main determinant of budbreak is, of course, how long winter temperatures have lasted into spring.

While budbreak varies enormously among the regions, bloom occurs within a much smaller window. In the southern Central Coast, bloom typically reaches midpoint during the second week in May; Russian River and Carneros vineyards pass the same point during the third or fourth week of the same month; the true Sonoma Coast gets there in the first week of June. The second or third week of June is typical for the Anderson Valley, the Willamette Valley, and the Finger Lakes region.

Los Carneros and the warmer parts of the Russian River valley are the first regions to harvest, typically during the first or second week of September. Then very quickly, pickers fan out in the cooler parts of the Russian River valley, the true Sonoma Coast, Anderson Valley, the Willamette Valley, and even the Finger Lakes—in the third or fourth week of September, or early October—but the sugar levels the grapes have achieved by harvest can be very different from region to region. In most of California's pinot regions, 24, 25, or even higher on the Brix scale (a percentage measurement of solutes—mostly sugar—in grapes) is not unusual. Oregon growers are usually very happy with 23 but get much less in cooler years; in the Finger Lakes region, 23 represents a very warm year indeed.

Sugar aside, the grapes have spent more time on the vine (known as hang time) in some regions than they have in others. The longest average hang time is about 18 weeks in the southern Central Coast, followed by 16 or 17 weeks in the cooler parts of the Russian River valley and the true Sonoma Coast; 14 to 16 weeks on Mount Harlan; and 13 to 14 weeks elsewhere. Two correlations are potentially significant. First, long hang times occur where summer daytime maximums remain absolutely cool. These regions are the southern Central Coast, the Salinas Valley, the true Sonoma Coast, and the cool end of the Russian River valley. In other words, high maximums during the growing season shorten hang time, no matter how much cool nights jigger the averages. Second, those regions with the coolest overall climates, measured as mean temperature throughout the *full calendar year*—the Finger Lakes region, the Okanagan, and the Willamette Valley—also experience the shortest hang times for pinot noir. In these high-latitude regions, the growing season cannot start early or last late. At the other end of the spectrum, the southern Central Coast, which displays the mildest winter, the mildest summer, overall the least seasonality, and the lowest latitude, sustains the longest hang time for pinot noir. In between, the regions in California's North Coast, with annual mean temperatures barely different from those of the southern Central Coast but much higher than those of the high-latitude regions (57 to 59 degrees versus 45 to 51 degrees), experience hang times covering the entire intermediate range, from 14 to 17 weeks. These are also the regions in which hang time displays the greatest year-to-year variation. At higher latitudes, vintage variation depends largely on the grapes' sugar content when the harvest must occur because the growing season has definitively ended. In Oregon, the curtain often comes down abruptly with the arrival of the autumn's first significant rain. At lower latitudes, vintage variation is more likely to be a function of heat accumulation after bloom, which can compress the growing season or stretch it out. In these regions, pinot noir, because it is an early ripener, is often picked before the growing season has definitively ended—several varieties are picked after pinot noir, virtually side by side—simply because the grapes have become, by one measure or another, fully ripe. Winegrowers typically argue that longer hang time produces grapes with deeper and more intense flavors—at lower levels of sugar accumulation. Plenty of evidence supports this view, but there is also a basis for some skepticism—at least within the range of 14 to 18 weeks. Inside this range, aspects of *terroir* and viticulture other than temperature and hang time may be dramatically more significant than an extra week or two for grapes on the vine.

Soils Many people believe that the French word *terroir,* which has entered the vocabulary of nearly all discussions about pinot noir, actually connotes dirt or soil, given the obvious linguistic link among *terrain, terroir, terre,* and *territory.* Actually, *terroir* is better understood to encompass *all of the physical properties of a site,* including its mesoclimate, orientation, and aspect; but it is nonetheless fair to assert that the European view of site is substantially soil-centric. This fact helps to explain the nearly microscopic subdivision of Burgundy into small appellations and *lieux-dits,* even though there is relatively little objective evidence linking the chemical composition of particular soils to the organoleptic properties of the wines they produce.

North America, for many reasons, is less concerned with soils in vineyards. Some people say the reason is that Americans are more quantitatively oriented, and climate is easier to measure and compare than soils. Others argue, with perhaps more justice, that the relation between soils and wine quality is subtler than the influence of climate and requires the experience of centuries to understand—experience that is obviously missing from North American viticulture. In any case, the larger of the North American pinot regions are far too large and are superimposed on terrain that is far too geologically active to display any semblance of geological uniformity. Intraregional soil differences are therefore as important in the larger regions as year-to-year weather differences. Smaller appellations like Mount Harlan and Chalone are a bit easier to characterize: both of these are distinguished for their limestone subsoil, which differentiates them from all other American pinot regions, save for Edna Valley and Arroyo Grande, whose soils contain substantial, though not dominant, limestone. Sonoma Mountain is also relatively uniform, being a single volcanic formation. In Oregon, the Willamette Valley is a classic example of the heterogeneity that also typifies the Russian River valley, Anderson Valley, Los Carneros, and the southern Central Coast, but Oregon's vintners—perhaps because they have maintained a more active dialogue with the Burgundians than their Californian colleagues—have been substantially more dirt oriented from the outset. David Lett recalls that, as an aid to his initial search for vineyard sites in the 1960s, he "drove around with an augur in the back of [my] car" for spur-of-the-moment investigations into subsoil composition. With the exception of Chehalem Mountains, where political considerations seem to have intervened, all of the six new AVAs that have been proposed within the Willamette Valley are strongly soil-based, and the Oregonians firmly believe that soil-based differences show up in their pinot noirs.

Across North America, there is agreement on only one soil-based point: that the main influence of soils on wine quality is the porosity of the ground. Good wine, and especially good pinot, comes from soils that are well drained. Heavy soils that hold a lot of water are considered hard to manage, even in arid climates with sophisticated drip irrigation systems, though some Carneros-based producers have made great strides in recent years refining exactly when and when not to irrigate vines. Heavy soils risk making the vines grow too much and too fast, producing an excess of leaves to fruit, boosting yield, bloating berries, and diluting flavors. In North America, there are two main alternatives to heavy soils: the sandy-loam soils that predominate in the valleys of the southern Central Coast, the Russian River valley, and parts of the northwestern Willamette Valley; and the thin, rocky, montane soils found in the Gavilan Range, the Santa Cruz Mountains, the hillsides of the Anderson Valley, Sonoma Mountain, and Oregon's Eola Hills. Volcanic soils appear to work well for pinot. The Eola Hills and Sonoma Mountain, along with the Mayacamas Range on the east side of the Sonoma Valley, are all thin volcanic soils; the Red Hills of Dundee are also volcanic, but deeper.

Perhaps the most controversial soils in the pinot-friendly regions occur in Los Carneros. Both of the two main soil types there contain substantial clay and a fair amount of organic material. The clay is sufficient to turn vineyards seriously and persistently muddy during the rainy season. Proponents of Los Carneros argue that the water-holding capacity of these soils is an asset in a low-rainfall region, and that the hard clay pan that underlies the topsoil is naturally devigorating to grapevines; critics respond that these soils remain problematically heavy. Some winegrowers suggest that the best soils in Los Carneros are coarser sedimentary soils washed through the region in old creekbeds, but these are scarce, accounting for less than 10 percent of the region's planted surface.

Altitude In *Viticulture and Environment,* John Gladstones explains that altitude appears to affect viticulture primarily through its impact on air temperature, though there are theoretical reasons to believe that the lower atmospheric pressure at higher altitudes may adversely affect the chemical composition of grapes. Nearly all of North America's pinot noir is grown below 1,800 feet, apart from a few higher-elevation vineyards in the Santa Cruz Mountains and inland Mendocino County, and genuinely high altitude sites in the Four Corners states. In the California portion of the Pacific Pinot Zone, a counterintuitive but useful correlation generally exists between higher elevations and temperature—higher sites are warmer, not cooler, owing to the impact of the infamous Pacific marine layer. In Oregon, the more normal relationship typically prevails, with higher-elevation vineyards being cooler and ripening later. In the Four Corners states of the American Southwest, relatively high altitude is a major boundary condition for pinot noir. At the 1,000-foot elevation in Arizona, the growing season tops 250 days. At 7,000 feet, it is barely 100 days, which is insufficient, even for an early-ripening variety. Between 4,000 and 7,000 feet, mean July temperatures drop from 80 degrees, which is on the warm side, to 65, which is low. Vintners have found arguably propitious sites within this range, mostly between 4,000 and 5,800 feet.

The Wines Nearly everyone who has attempted to step back from the details has been tempted to generalize about the flavors, weight, and mouthfeel of pinot noirs grown in each of North America's main regions, and to contrast the regions with one another. Pinots grown in the southern Central Coast are said to have a tendency to spicy sappiness with strong highlights of flowers and herbs, and sometimes hard-edged acidity. Within this area, Santa Maria Valley pinots are usually lighter-weight than their Santa Rita Hills cousins and emphasize floral and tea-leaf characteristics, leaving the Santa Rita Hills wines to vaunt brilliant fruit and dark juiciness. Critics of these wines, and of some Salinas Valley pinots, sometimes identify flavor properties redolent of stewed tomatoes and silage, however. A bit farther north, Santa Lucia Highlands wines, of which there are a growing number, are often distinguished for their strong perfume and "racy" character.

Los Carneros wines are said to emphasize strawberry, raspberry, and bright cherry flavors, while the nearby Russian River valley gets the nod for ripe Bing cherries, deep, spicy fruit, and midpalate richness. Mary Hall, a viticulturist who works primarily in Carneros, finds that Carneros pinots are "more reliable year on year," with "more elegance and a sweeter mid-palate," while Russian River wines seem darker, riper, fatter, and more layered. Larry Brooks, who has made pinots in Los Carneros for a quarter-century, finds them "subtle, serious, and well-mannered."

Rather parenthetically, in a tasting designed to determine how American pinots from the 1994 vintage stacked up against red Burgundies from 1983, the *Wine Spectator's* Harvey Steiman wrote that the Russian River valley entrants were impressive for their "rich, full mouthfeel, lush fruit [and] smooth tannins." Rod Smith, writing in *Wine & Spirits* in 2000, said the Russian River valley wines have a "simultaneous concentration and clarity, with hidden power that works something like the bass booster on a top-end stereo." A bit less poetically, Frank Prial finds that Russian River valley pinots share "compactness and a core of strength" with the best red Burgundies. Steve Kistler, who works with fruit from the Russian River valley and the true Sonoma Coast, has been quoted as saying that color and tannins are both so "much, much more pronounced" in Sonoma Coast grapes that shorter vatting times are necessary to avoid making excessively tannic wines. He also finds that the aromas and flavors of Sonoma Coast fruit are "wilder," while Russian River pinot displays mainstream black cherry and cola. Rod Smith, in *Wine & Spirits,* finds that the true coastal pinots display "juicy minerality that is something like sucking on fruit-flavored gravel" plus "briskness and high-toned intensity." My tasting notes confirm a high incidence of "wild" and gariguelike flavors in many Sonoma Coast wines.

Quite different from all the foregoing, Anderson Valley pinots often seem distinguished for their purity of fruit, akin to the expression of fruit in fruit-based eaux-de-vie. Van Williamson, who has made pinot both at Greenwood Ridge and at Edmeades, also argues that Anderson Valley wines tend to be "tighter and lean when they are young," and to both "soften" and "broaden" with age. This generalization is consistent with my experience tasting verticals of pinots from Husch and Edmeades. Many vintners argue that wide diurnal variation, as in Anderson Valley and the western Russian River valley, tends to produce spicier-tasting grapes, but if this is true, diurnal variation is clearly not the only genesis of spicy flavors.

Nearly all writers and some winemakers leap to differentiate California's pinot noir from Oregon's, some claiming that Oregon's wines often lack the sap, richness, velvety texture, and suppleness that characterizes the best Californian exemplars. Others *like* Oregon for its typically lower alcohol, higher acidity, greater elegance, and Burgundian complexity. Ponzi Vineyards' winemaker, Luisa Ponzi, describes the difference between California and Oregon pinots as "the difference between ripe fruit and fresh fruit." The fresh fruit flavors, she argues, come from cooler harvest weather in most years. When Oregon's winemakers convoked several hundred members of the trade for a seminar on Oregon pinot noir in 2000 and polled them for buzzwords describing California and Oregon pinots, respectively, *fruity, full,* and *lush* topped the California list, while *elegant, complex,* and *bright* were the descriptors of choice for the Oregon wines.

Regions even cooler than Oregon, notably the Finger Lakes and the Niagara Peninsula, have historically exhibited light to medium mouthweight, low alcohol even with chaptalization, high acid, and at worst greenness. But these problems are changing as more is learned about grape growing in cool climates, and as earlier-ripening clones are introduced into vineyards. In a tasting early in 2002, several Finger Lakes pinots from the 2000 vintage displayed mocha, black fruit, butter, and jam flavors, along with a pepper-dominated spiciness conventionally associated more with California, plus sweet chewiness in the mouth. Sean Wood, wine columnist for the Halifax (Nova Scotia) *Chronicle-Herald,* who tastes Canadian pinots annually for the Canadian Wine Awards program, argues that both Niagara and Okanagan editions of pinot fall into two groups: impressively structured wines with simultaneously high acid and strong tannin profiles, and "straightforward" wines with "pleasant varietal character." Many Okanagan wines from normal to warm years seem to fall into the first category, leading some tasters to mistake them in blind tastings for true Sonoma Coast or Santa Rita Hills wines.

In the mid 1980s, Los Carneros's trade group, the Carneros Quality Alliance, made a serious effort to determine if Carneros pinot noir could be said to have a distinctive taste. Using a panel of 12 judges and 28 pinots spanning two vintages, of which ten were made from Carneros fruit, the CQA study, which was directed by a Davis specialist in sensory perception, found that four flavor descriptors—*fresh berry, berry jam, spice,* and *cherry*—correlated strongly with the ten Carneros wines. Five other descriptors—*mint, prune, vegetal, smoke/tar,* and *leather*—were found to have no correlation with the ten Carneros wines, and the non-Carneros wines did not correlate at all with one another. This study was the origin of considerable publicity about a so-called Carneros Style of pinot noir, which was widely repeated in wine publications throughout the 1990s. Recently, despite the regions' power in marketing wine, the tide has turned against regionwide generalizations—especially in the larger ones. In Carneros, many makers now distance themselves from the 1986 study, arguing that the Carneros Style, also known as appellation flavors, is now dead. It existed in the 1980s, they say, because Carneros's vineyard was then planted almost entirely to the Martini (UCD 13 and 15) clones, and various viticultural practices were uniform. Now, with a greater diversity of vineyard practices and a richer mix of plant material, they say Carneros's pinots resemble one another less and less.

In 2001, a committee of the Russian River Valley Winegrowers Association began a project designed to show how wines from different parts of their appellation are *dissimilar.* In the first iteration, a Middle Reach wine displayed high intensity of black cherry, cola, coffee, tar, and spice aromas; a Laguna Ridge wine, similarly high in black cherry, showed much less tar and spice, but much more blackberry and raspberry; and a Green Valley wine was characterized by intense cranberry, blueberry, and red cherry. In a coordinated mouthfeel evaluation, the same Middle Reach wine showed intense concentration, smoothness, and long aftertaste; the Green Valley wine showed a less intense aftertaste but more tannin and a tad less smoothness. Two Laguna Ridge wines were enormously different from each other, however, one showing high tannins and intense earthiness, while the other displayed little earth, subtler tannins, but even greater smoothness than the Middle Reach wine.

Many Oregon pinot makers say that marked flavor and mouthfeel *differences* were the impetus for their petitions, in 2001, to superimpose new AVAs on the humongous Willamette Valley. The volcanic soil districts, they say—notably the Red Hills and the Eola Hills—have a tendency to ripen late and to produce fruit-driven wines, while the areas dominated by sedimentary soils produce consistently earthier wines with the aromatic properties of cedar, tobacco, and anise. The petitioners for a Ribbon Ridge AVA find that their wines are characteristically briary, with full, round black fruit flavors conjoined with earthiness. Generally, high tannins are associated with Oregon's sedimentary soils, as they are also with California's montane soils—on Sonoma's coastal ridges, on Sonoma Mountain, and in the Santa Cruz Mountains especially.

Much of the shift in perspective, even among winemakers themselves, from regional generalizations to subregional or even vineyard-by-vineyard specificity is the consequence of a sea change in the presentation of pinot noir in the marketplace. In the 1980s, blends of purchased fruit were the norm, estate wines were unusual, and vineyard-designated non-estate wines were a rare exception. More often than not, blending was executed along the lines of AVAs newly established in the early 1980s. This practice virtually *created* regional typicalities and simultaneously obscured intraregional and vineyard-specific particularities. Better wines may have resulted, or not; but the eccentricities of individual parcels and *terroirs* were known only to winemakers, who tasted the components, and not to consumers, whose experience was confined to the finished blends. Many winemakers, who staked their early reputations on judicious blending, are suspicious of the "new" trend to vineyard-designated pinots, which, they say, flood the marketplace with tiny lots of wine sold for high prices per bottle. The converse proposition, however, is that vineyard designation is the handmaiden of *terroir* properly understood and the main reason some of the large pinot-friendly appellations are beginning to fracture into more homogeneous units.

Consumers of pinot noir, who have somehow learned to cope with the merciless complexity of Burgundy, can surely learn to understand and appreciate a slightly more complex landscape in North America. As this happens, larger appellations, perhaps akin to contemporary AVAs, may evolve into useful designations for blended wines, while vineyard names, or perhaps even block names, become the pinot consumer's best tool for locating wines of indelible personality and year-to-year consistency.

Chapter 5

CLONES AND SELECTIONS OF PINOT NOIR

Clone, the *c* word, ranks second only to *terroir,* the *t* word, in the conversations that winegrowers, retailers, and even consumers have almost constantly about pinot noir. Cloning plants has nothing in common with the cutting-edge technology and ethical dilemmas associated, even in lay discourse, with cloning animals like Dolly the sheep. For once etymology is a friend: English *clone* is based on the Greek word for a twig and refers to nothing more complicated than the age-old practice of generating a new plant, genetically identical to its parent, by taking and propagating a cutting. Anyone who has rooted a plant cutting in a glass jar on the kitchen counter has cloned a plant. In viticulture, a clone is any population of vines propagated asexually from a single mother vine. On the one hand, this definition means that virtually all cultivated grapevines are clones, since all were propagated asexually from some parent vine. On the other, clone chat is not very useful unless the progeny are linked unambiguously with a *single* mother vine and have demonstrated consistent properties and behaviors across several viticultural generations.

In some ways, clonal selection as a process is easier to grasp than clones as things. As a matter of routine, growers, viticulturists, and scientists choose the parents for new grapevines. How they choose is consequential. If a grower elects to privilege consistency of properties and performance, he or she will select budwood (for a row or block or vineyard) from a single parent vine, or from children of the same parent, or purchase it from a nursery that has played by the same rules. This choice is then said to be a matter of *clonal selection,* and the grower is said, albeit imprecisely, to have planted a *clone* or *clones.* Conversely, if a grower elects to privilege diversity, he or she will select budwood from an assortment of parent vines that did not themselves have a common parent. Such a choice is said to be an instance of *mass selection,* and the grower is said to have planted *selections* or *field selections.*

Nowadays, nearly all wine grapes are recognized as displaying some variation within the bandwidth of a single variety. These differences are genetic, although, inconveniently, they are not reflected in the fingerprinting techniques currently used to study grape varieties. Clones are thus a matter of interest to most viticulturists, and there is now a considerable literature on the clones of chardonnay, sauvignon blanc, and cabernet sauvignon, among others. The clones of pinot noir, however, inspire special passions. Pinot, by virtue of its genetic instability and its predisposition to spontaneous mutation, and perhaps also because it seems to be more susceptible to certain viral diseases, which *may* trigger intravarietal mutation—this is a controversial point—displays a very broad range of phenotypes. Several hundred clones of pinot noir are thought to exist. Adjacent vines of pinot noir in the same vineyard, to say nothing of vines in different vineyards, if they were not propagated from the same mother vine, can be very different. They can bud earlier or later; ripen earlier or later; flower more or less reliably; produce grape clusters that are smaller or larger, tighter or looser; produce berries with thicker or thinner skins; and (perhaps most important) make wines that *taste* quite different. Acutely conscious of this variation, the contemporary pinot grower pays enormous attention to choosing, planting, and propagating the "right" clones for each site.

CLONAL SELECTION IN BURGUNDY

The preoccupation with grapevine clones is, in fact, a very recent phenomenon. On both sides of the Atlantic, it developed as one by-product of a more fundamental interest in growing healthy vine plants capable of producing commercially viable quantities of good fruit, in the face of growing threats from viral and other diseases. Most viticulturists and plant scientists believe that the spread of these diseases in the first half of the twentieth century is attributable primarily to the nearly universal practice, following the ravages of phylloxera, of grafting vinifera-based scion material to nonvinifera rootstocks, and to consequent contamination of plant material. In Europe it seems likely that various forms of viticultural neglect during the war years also played a role. In any case, by the 1950s, Burgundy was on the brink of crisis. Mass selection had deteriorated into a downward spiral of rampant viral disease, derisory yields, and vines requiring replacement when they were barely ten years old. The white wine communes of the Côte de Beaune, especially Puligny and Meursault, were facing ruin, barely able to eke a quarter-ton of fruit from an acre of chardonnay.

In 1955, Raymond Bernard—a scientist who had studied ampelography with the illustrious Pierre Galet at Montpellier and had worked a bit on grapevine virus—was put in charge of a regional team to address the viticultural crisis in Burgundy, Alsace, and Lorraine. Bernard, who became the father of clonal selection for chardonnay and pinot noir in France, devoted his first attentions to the embattled chardonnay. He searched throughout Burgundy for visibly healthy vines, which he found particularly in the walled vineyards the Burgundians call *clos;* tagged hundreds individually; and followed each tagged vine in situ for three years, to be sure it did not develop any telltale signs of disease. When he turned his attention to pinot noir, whose viral problems were mercifully less acute, he was fascinated by the enormous variety of phenotypes the trained eye could distinguish in a single vineyard, even when the vines were not visibly diseased. Bernard tagged healthy vines of pinot noir at Domaine Ponsot in Morey-St.-Denis and in the communes of Flagey-Echézeaux and Pommard, taking care that vines expressing different growth patterns, cluster morphologies, and berry sizes were included. If the tagged vines still looked healthy after several years' observation, he grafted cuttings from individual mother vines to new rootstock and followed the sibling vines for several more years in controlled environments. He made sure that each population of siblings was descended from a single mother vine and was never mixed or confused with siblings of another parent. When the sibling vines came into bearing, wine was made separately from each sibling population by the enological station in Beaune and tasted by panels three-quarters of whose members were hands-on winemakers by trade. In parallel, cuttings were transferred to ENTAV (Etablissement nationale technique pour l'amélioration de la viticulture), the French government agency in Montpellier charged with viticultural welfare, where they were planted in sand on their own roots, tested for virus, and assessed for both performance and health. Overlaid, the two parallel processes produced Burgundy's first "clonal" selections, chosen when absence of disease, productivity, and organoleptic quality coincided. These selections rescued chardonnay from the brink of disaster and became a hot topic of conversation among growers of pinot noir, some of whom became early believers in and adopters of clones.

CLONES AND SELECTIONS IN NORTH AMERICA

California's vineyards also displayed a high incidence of viral infection in the 1940s and 1950s. As in Europe, the base cause was almost certainly contamination in the course of widespread vine grafting, but there were also two special circumstances in North America. The first was the end of Prohibition, which had created a sudden large demand for vine cuttings, both to regraft Prohibition-era vineyards to fine varieties and to plant new vineyards capable of satisfying the emerging market for dessert and table wines. Vine cuttings that were imported from Europe without restriction during the late 1930s were found to have carried virus. Alongside the imported cuttings, the Californians had also attempted to cull "heritage" selections from the considerable population of surviving pre-Prohibition vines. Virus was spread in the course of this work as well. Worse, however, it was hard to be sure that the heritage selections were what they were supposed to be. Many heritage vineyards had been planted with misidentified cuttings, or with phantom varieties invented by freewheeling importers or unscrupulous nurserymen. Similar things were growing in these vineyards under different names.

To address these problems, and to ensure that a financially viable wine industry, based on healthy vineyards and high yields, could flourish in the decades after Repeal, the University of California resumed the work it had begun in the nineteenth century. The university operated experimental vineyards, conducted research on various viticultural issues, and disseminated information and advice to the industry. Harold Olmo, a plant geneticist with a doctorate from the university's Berkeley campus, was hired to work on post-Prohibition viticulture at the university's experiment station in Davis. In his oral history, Olmo describes the process of sourcing budwood from pre-Prohibition vineyards, the first of which was Charles Kunde's vineyard north of Glen Ellen. In the 1880s this had been J. H. Drummond's Dunfillan Vineyard, discussed in chapter 3. Olmo mapped individual vines and rows and then transferred budwood to the Larkmead Vineyard north of St. Helena in Napa, which served as a kind of open-air laboratory for Olmo's further work.

In the 1940s Olmo also worked with Louis M. Martini specifically on pinot noir, apparently selecting budwood from a plot of heritage vines at Inglenook, which may itself have represented survivals from Gustav Niebaum's nineteenth-century imports and from other sources. The budwood Olmo and Martini selected was propagated in a trial block at Martini's new Carneros property, which was part of Judge John Stanly's historic ranch. Even as he carried on this work, the coincidence of viral infections and misidentifications seems to have convinced Olmo that a full palette of healthy, true-to-variety plants could not be reconstructed entirely from California's heritage vineyards. He became an early proponent of aggressive reimportation from Europe, and toward the middle of the 1940s he personally made several trips there to prospect for vines. His oral history records that his first trip was to Montpellier, where he was impressed with the "variety collection" at what is now ENTAV. He is supposed to have made several subsequent trips, acquiring vine cuttings, including pinot noir, "from vineyard sites in France, Germany, and Switzerland."

By the end of the 1940s, scientists' concern with the sanitary status of imported plant material became so acute that the entire process of importing vines and cuttings was formalized. The United States Department of Agriculture banned "uncontrolled" plant imports in 1948 and required a government permit, a postentry quarantine period, and supervision by a professional plant pathologist as conditions for further work with imports. University-based scientists, regulators, growers, and winemakers agreed that the University of California should be the conduit for a program conforming to the government's new rules, the main venue for research on grape viral disease, and the vehicle for distributing certified grape selections to nurseries and growers. It was also agreed that the university would resume Olmo's earlier work to verify the varietal identity of vines culled from heritage vineyards. Known informally as the clean stock program, this cluster of activities emerged at the end of the 1950s as the Foundation Plant Materials Service (FPMS), which was renamed Foundation Plant Services (FPS) in 2003. Its various mandates made FPMS the main vector for introducing European vine material to American vineyards for the rest of the twentieth century, save for a few years at the end of the 1980s and early in the 1990s. (Some vine material also seems to have been imported through the Department of Agriculture's facility in Beltsville, Maryland, and at Geneva, New York, under a permit held by the New York State Agricultural Experiment Station; for the last, see the profile of Dr. Konstantin Frank's Vinifera Wine Cellars in part II.) The main actors at FPMS were Olmo, sometimes dubbed the Plant Explorer, who continued to gather budwood from likely and unlikely locations around the world; Austin Goheen, a plant pathologist employed by the Department of Agriculture who devoted much of his professional time to FPMS, whose job was to test vines for disease; and William Hewitt, who handled basic research on grapevine viruses. Some of this research led to the development of techniques for eliminating virus from infected plants. The first of these methods, employed at the end of the 1950s and early in the 1960s, involved the use of a superheated environment to grow vine plants faster than the virus could replicate, creating so-called heat-treated selections.

When FPMS began to make certified, healthy grapevine cuttings available to growers and nurseries in 1958, several selections of pinot noir imported from France and Switzerland were among the first offerings. Additional selections of pinot culled from California heritage vineyards, including Olmo's vine collection at Larkmead, the Martini trials in Carneros, and the university's old experimental vineyard near Jackson in the foothills of the Sierra Nevada, were quickly added to the FPMS list, as were heat-treated selections released in the second half of the 1960s. Each of these selections was a clone, or instance of a clone, having been carefully propagated from a single piece of budwood taken from a single mother vine. Each was also assigned a number, by which it was identified in FPMS lists.

But in these years FPMS scientists and their teaching counterparts on the Davis faculty were not especially interested in clonal selection for, in a phrase Goheen used later, "optimal plant performance." On the contrary, they were primarily concerned with what Goheen called "sanitary selection for disease freedom." This preoccupation led, at least for a period of time, to an American view of wine grape clones that was quite different from the sensitivity evolving in Europe. In this view, clonal variation was not fundamentally genetic. Instead, it was a function of the degree to which the selection had been infected by virus. In other words, a clone was a disease status, not a subvariety. Many viticulturists trained at Davis in the late 1960s and early 1970s remember being raised with this view.

In light of this orientation, it is perhaps unsurprising that California's growers and nurseries were not encouraged to be sensitive to the merits and shortcomings of individual selections. With few exceptions, they asked simply for "pinot noir" when they placed orders for budwood, making no mention of the clone-specific selection numbers in FPMS's lists. Even FPMS kept no record of which selections it supplied until 1962. Thereafter, although FPMS kept selection-specific records, its customers continued to ignore the distinctions among selections. Many selections, or combinations of selections, consequently came to be known by the names of intermediaries, creating confusion that persists to this day. Growers and vintners who obtained cuttings of pinot noir from, for example, Wente Brothers' so-called increase block in Arroyo Seco referred loosely to a supposed "Wente clone" or "Wente selection" of pinot noir. In fact, Wente's increase block, by specific agreement with FPMS, was planted exclusively to certified clones, initially those known as UCD 1A, 2A, and 4, but later also UCD 5 and 13. The same thing happened with pinot noir acquired from Smith Madrone Winery in Napa. Smith Madrone, like Wente, was a certified increase block. Its records were destroyed in a fire, but Stewart Smith remembers that his choice from FPMS was "something heat-treated from Beaune," so the Smith Madrone selection of pinot, to which growers in Los Carneros still refer today, is almost certainly nothing more or less than UCD 5 or 6.

Similar mysteries were perpetuated in distributions outside California. Virtually all of the pinot noir planted in Oregon during the 1960s and early 1970s was derived from California nurseries and vineyards for which the upstream source was FPMS. Confusion persists about whether the so-called Pommard clone of pinot sold into Oregon was UCD 4 or its heat-treated cousin, UCD 5. Oregon's Wädenswil could be UCD's 1A or 2A, or both. In some cases the Wädenswil may be UCD 30, a supposedly heat-treated version of 2A that has subsequently disappeared from the FPMS register. Compounding confusion, the numbering schemes used in FPMS's early years were inconsistent: UCD 1 was originally a Jackson clone, but this number subsequently disappeared from use, while UCD 1A, unrelated to 1, was one of the Wädenswil clones. Additionally, for a period in the 1970s, the staff in Davis's Department of Viticulture and Enology used an idiosyncratic three-digit system to identify selections, meaning that the same selection, even at Davis, sported two numerical designations. Clone 103 seems to have been the department's alternative designation for what FPMS called UCD 4, but extramural publications (see *Connoisseurs' Guide*'s March–April issue in 1977) also equated it, imprecisely, with the Wente rubric. Clone 104 is supposed to have been identical to UCD 13. According to *Connoisseurs' Guide,* Clone 105 was a "productive" clone "brought over from the Beaujolais District by Dr. Olmo." Some of these three-digit numbers found their way onto wine labels in the 1970s before being retired in favor of the FMPS scheme.

Very slowly, small segments of the North American wine industry became clone-savvy in the 1970s, and the focus of attention gradually shifted from clones as clean stock to clones as qualitatively different instances of a variety, as the Europeans had believed from the outset. When Francis Mahoney founded the Carneros Creek Winery in 1971, with the specific goal of making pinot noir as good as Burgundy, he organized the first serious effort to evaluate the performance of the clones and selections of pinot noir that were then available to the industry. Arguing that the various clones of pinot noir available from FPMS had not been tested "either viticulturally or enologically" since the beginning of the clean-stock program, and that "some California growers believe their own vines [not from the clean stock program] make a superior Pinot noir wine," Mahoney undertook to collaborate with Davis-based specialists to compare the performance of 20 selections of both types, both in the vineyard and in the cellar, across a ten-year period. One and a half acres were planted to tiny replications of each selection, 11 of which were taken from the foundation vineyard at Davis. The balance came from other producing vineyards: Joseph Swan's planting near Forestville, the nearby Carneros vineyards of Louis Martini and Beaulieu, and Hanzell and Chalone. Comparative phenological data were collected for each selection through each growing season. Cluster weights and berry sizes were measured. Tiny lots of wine were made, simultaneously at Davis and at Carneros Creek, from each selection, beginning in 1983. The wines were then evaluated by "university and industry experts." In the end, seven of the 20 selections "proved consistently better." Five of these were clean-stock selections from the university's foundation vineyard—UCD 5, 12, 13, 18, and 23. Two were heritage selections—Swan and Chalone. (See below in this chapter for details on all of these.)

Although the Carneros Creek trial was closely watched by other pinot makers when it began, events in Europe overtook it rather quickly. According to David Adelsheim, Oregon pioneer Charles Coury was among the first to recognize the significance of the French work with clones, in 1973. Coury sent his son to work at the French government research center in Colmar (the Centre de recherche de Colmar of the Institut national de la recherche agronomique, in Alsace) in 1974. Adelsheim himself spent part of the same year at the Lycée agricole in Beaune, where he met Raymond Bernard. Several Californians followed the Oregonians, walked vineyards with European researchers, and returned mesmerized by the amplitude of clonal variation. Philip Freese, then a viticulturist for Robert Mondavi, described his 1977 visit to Bernard's experimental vineyard, said to have contained 125 clones of pinot noir, as a "great 'aha.'" A wave of interest in clonal selection swept through the pinot-oriented winemaking communities in both states. Wineries submitted clone-specific orders to FPMS. Conscious, however, that FPMS did not have the newly available French clones on offer, they also pressured FPMS to take a more active role in the importation of new material. In spite of his personal conviction that clonal variation was the result of viral infection, Goheen agreed to import many of the new European clones, but he did not move rapidly enough or aggressively enough to satisfy many vintners, especially Oregonians. Goheen encouraged the Oregonians to obtain their own import permit, which they did in 1975. Their first import was CTPS 162, also known as Colmar 538.

Deborah Golino, FPS's current director, remembers the California and Oregon import programs of the late 1970s and early 1980s as "pretty cooperative" efforts despite Goheen's skepticism about clones, and reports that "Oregon made sure California got all the Dijon clones as soon as possible after they received them." The Oregonians appear to remember more tensions and disagreements, especially when "benign" viruses were found in some of the newly imported clones. When Goheen retired in 1986, the issue became moot. At this point FPMS's import permit lapsed, leaving Oregon as the only active importer. Less than a decade later, the tables were turned when Oregon's permit holder (Oregon State University plant pathologist Ronald Cameron) retired, ending the Oregon program. In 1993, imports were resumed at FPMS, and plant material (including many clones of pinot noir) quarantined in Oregon was transferred to Davis.

In the background, illicit imports of grapevine budwood seem to have thrived, primarily in California, but also in Oregon. As far as pinot noir was concerned, these were the work of individual vintners convinced that the best way to make a wine tasting like a real red Burgundy was to grow fruit from cuttings taken from real Burgundy vineyards with acceptable pedigrees. These imports were usually not clones, but field selections; they involved multiple pieces of budwood taken from multiple vines. The stories of their collection are borderline cloak-and-dagger, sometimes including theft under cover of darkness from one or another of Burgundy's famous vineyards, and sometimes canes snatched from piles left on roadsides after farmhands had pruned the vineyards. A suspiciously high number claim that budwood was obtained or taken from Romanée-Conti, conjuring up images of American vintners in trench coats hovering on the periphery of Burgundy's most illustrious vineyard, waiting for an opportunity to snatch a cutting unobserved. Many of these stories are, at best, only marginally credible.

Other "suitcase" selection stories are more plausible, however. This category involves well-documented and long-standing friendships between individual Burgundian vignerons and individual American counterparts, and selections made in broad daylight from vines that at least *looked* healthy to a more or less educated eye. For some time the Burgundians did not object publicly to these transfers of plant material to aspiring Americans, and the Americans were content to fly under the radar. Some Burgundians were even complicit in the covert operations. For the Americans, the only risks were the small chance of a fine if they were caught violating federal plant quarantine law, and virus in their vineyards if they mistakenly imported diseased wood. Since many of them were beginning to think, heretically, that a little virus in the vineyard was not necessarily a bad thing, the latter disincentive was not powerful, and the former was never especially expensive.

In the mid 1990s, however, the rules of the game changed. Some American growers trumpeted the origins of their "clones" rather loudly, causing French vintners and government authorities to worry that their own reputations could be besmirched by American claims. French producers and the Institut national des appellations d'origine, whose responsibility is the protection of French appellation nomenclature, engaged American law firms to warn American growers and producers that claims to be using plant material from Romanée-Conti and La Tâche, among others, might be a violation of French intellectual property law, even if the source information were correct. This warning had its intended effect. There are still numerous references to "suitcase" and "Samsonite" clones in winery literature and the wine press, but growers or wineries are now circumspect about their claims. Many will admit to having suitcase clones in their vineyards, but very few will say exactly where the budwood was obtained.

In 1996, the plot thickened again. ENTAV, the French government agency responsible for the propagation and distribution of clones identified in the course of programs like Bernard's in Burgundy, decided to trademark "authentic" clones emanating from their collections and to rely on licenses to ensure that those clones were distributed outside France via handpicked commercial nurseries. In this scenario, nurseries choosing to work with ENTAV or INRA were required to pay license fees for each authenticated vine sold and to require nonpropagation agreements from their own customers. Because commercial nurseries in the United States are not permit holders, however, the trademarked clones, like their generic predecessors, were imported, tested, and registered at FPMS. Once again at center stage, FPMS found itself in the interesting position of simultaneously distributing trademarked and "generic" versions of what were presumably the same clones—the former only to a few licensed nurseries, but the latter to all comers. ENTAV, which contends that the generic clones may not be the genuine article, asked FPMS to desist from distributing generic material. At this writing, FPS continues to demur, so generic and trademarked versions of the same French clones persist. In a laudable stab at simplification, however, FPMS decided in 2002 that the trademarked versions of French clones will be assigned *matching* FPMS numbers. This means, for example, that trademarked Pinot Noir 115 (a.k.a. Dijon 115) will henceforth be carried in FPMS lists as FPMS/UCD 115.

All the chat about "French" clones is a bit of a misnomer, of course, since it implies that non-French clones of pinot noir also exist. More likely, once upon a time, *all* pinot noir came from France. Certainly every vine of pinot noir planted in North America is descended, one way or another, from European stock, for the obvious reason that neither pinot noir nor any other variety of *Vitis vinifera* is indigenous to this side of the Atlantic. Every vine, its parent, or some earlier ancestor was imported at some point from Europe—perhaps as early as the 1830s, perhaps as recently as the current year, legally or illegally, its origin known, obscure, or deliberately falsified.

In the vineyard, ampelographers and viticulturists can often make good guesses about the a vine's clonal identity based on the physical appearance of the vine, but some clones and selections show differently in different sites, so this science is imperfect at best. In the laboratory, clones cannot be distinguished from one another by the DNA fingerprinting techniques currently employed to differentiate varieties, though Davis scientists are working on ways to examine "actual DNA sequences," which might be more revealing.

SPECIFIC CLONES AND SELECTIONS

The following is a snapshot of information about most of the clones and selections of pinot noir currently planted in North America—where they came from and when, how they are different, and why winegrowers express preferences both pro and con.

Dijon Clones Dijon clones are the most recent and best documented imports from France. As explained above, they are the products of Raymond Bernard's 30 years of work on clonal selection in Burgundy. The Dijon rubric, no longer used by the French themselves, arose in an early phase of the clonal selection work in Burgundy to distinguish selections made by the Délégation régionale de l'ONIVINS de Dijon from other selections—a criterion that roughly differentiates Bernard's work from other French projects. In fact there are hundreds of so-called Dijon selections with provisional numbers, and French growers who know the numbers can order many of these selections from ENTAV. The most widely propagated in Burgundy, however, and the only Dijon clones to be imported into North America, are those designated by numbers assigned by the Comité technique permanent de la sélection (CTPS)—the French group charged by the Ministry of Agriculture with managing the official catalog of species and varieties of cultivated plants—CTPS 113, 114, 115, 667, 777, and 828. Each one exists as a generic selection, received via various paths at FPMS and identified variously as UCD 44, 45, 46, 47, 71, 72, 89, and 93, and as a trademarked selection (received directly from ENTAV) for which FPMS has reserved the UCD numbers 113, 114, 115, 667, 777, and 828. Because the two-digit UCD numbers for these selections are virtually unknown outside FPMS and the practice of assigning three-digit UCD numbers identical to the CTPS numbers is new, this book follows conventional common practice: *Dijon* plus the CTPS number.

According to Bernard, the original budwood for most of the Dijon clones was taken from Domaine Ponsot in Morey-St.-Denis. None was treated in any way before being distributed although, as we have seen, they were *very* carefully selected. Without any doubt, the Dijon clones have been the hottest budwood in North American pinot culture since they were introduced here in 1987 and 1988. Almost all newly planted vineyards in California, Oregon, British Columbia, New York, and elsewhere include some blocks of Dijon clones, and many vineyards have been planted exclusively to these selections. Dijon 115 is said to have been selected in Burgundy primarily for its consistency of production. In North America, it is the most widely planted of the Dijon family, and is found desirable for its brilliance and perfume. Many winemakers argue that, of any single clone currently available, Dijon 115 has the best chance of making a complete wine, and clonal tastings in which I have participated seem to confirm this claim.

At present, however, greater enthusiasm attaches to the more recently available Dijon clones with higher numbers—667, 777, and 828—which winemakers prize for their impressive concentration, great intensity, and depth of black fruit flavors. In the very limited time North American vintners have worked with them, they have also shown a tendency to taste more like themselves, and less like their site, than some earlier selections; but this property may recede as average vine age increases. Dijon 667, 777, and 828 are also, in principle, the earliest to ripen; but at several California sites they have sometimes been "out-earlied" by non-Dijon selections. Navarro Vineyards in Anderson Valley reports that the Dijon clones do better in cooler seasons, while the field selections (from other California vineyards) do better in warm years. Some California growers express quiet concern that precisely because the Dijon clones were selected to privilege early ripening, they may not be the ideal choice for all California mesoclimates, but the rush to plant them seems unaffected by this reservation. In Burgundy, about 75 percent of vineyards have been replanted, in whole or in part, to one or more of the Dijon clones, and Dijon clones have also been propagated in Switzerland, Germany, Austria, Italy, South Africa, Chile, Australia, and New Zealand, making them the most ubiquitous exemplars of pinot noir in the world.

Roederer Clones When Champagne Louis Roederer set up its American operation, Roederer Estate, in the Anderson Valley in 1982, the firm invested considerable time and money importing plant material from Champagne, especially for pinot noir. These imports followed all applicable quarantine requirements and passed through FPMS, so CTPS 386, 388, and 389 became, respectively, UCD 32, 33, and 41, and were introduced in 1984. (If trademarked versions are eventually introduced, however, these will be known as UCD 386, 388, and 389, in accordance with FPMS's newly adopted numbering policy.) Of these, UCD 32 was sourced originally from a vineyard in Ay, across the Marne River from Epernay; UCD 33 from Verzenay, on the northern side of the Montagne de Reims; and UCD 41 from Ambonnay not far from Bouzy, east of Epernay. It is sometimes said that the original vineyard sources of these clones were Roederer's own Champagne vineyards, but viticulturists at Champagne Louis Roederer cannot confirm this claim. In any case, these selections anchored Roederer's new Anderson Valley vineyards and were widely purchased for other vineyards dedicated, at least in the beginning, to sparkling wine. In general, the Roederer clones have not been much appreciated for still pinot noir, but UCD 32 may be an exception. At both Gloria Ferrer and Greenwood Ridge, UCD 32 has been planted for still-wine programs. There, allowed to ripen fully, it gives complex wine, saturated with dark fruit nuanced with jam, tar, and leather.

Pommard Clones In the 1940s, Harold Olmo is said to have imported cuttings from the Château de Pommard, the largest single property in the commune of Pommard, on the northern edge of the commune. One of these cuttings apparently became the basis for UCD 4 and its heat-treated cousins, UCD 5 and 6 (which are technically *one* clone, since they are all descended from the same mother vine). If the story is true, Pommard is the *only* selection in the Davis repertoire whose origin is cuttings taken directly from a producing European vineyard. All other selections imported from Europe seem to have been taken from plant collections maintained by government-operated experimental stations, or they stem from suitcase imports subsequently culled from California vineyards.

Pommard was among the first selections distributed by FPMS in the 1950s and was widely planted in the 1960s and 1970s. It was the basis for most of the pinot planted in Monterey County during this period, and for part of many vineyards set out in Santa Barbara County. From the certified increase blocks in these areas and elsewhere, it migrated into the Russian River and Anderson valleys. Its most visible success, however, was in Oregon, where it accounted for almost two-thirds of all pinot noir until the introduction of Dijon clones in the 1980s and remains the workhorse of the Oregon pinot industry. It is respected for good color, intense fruit, and considerable spice, and has made stunning wines both on its own and as a component in blends. It also appears to produce wines with good midpalate complexity and luxurious mouthfeel, contributing some of the velvety character that many producers prize in pinot noir. Gerald Asher describes the flavor of Pommard-based pinots as "somber." The original clone, UCD 4, probably accounts for all or most of Rochioli's West Block as well as for the Allen Ranch, which has produced flagship wines for Rochioli, Williams Selyem, and Gary Farrell, among others. Even today, with dozens of selections available and huge enthusiasm for the Dijon clones in nearly all quarters, many growers continue to plant at least some Pommard when setting out new vineyards.

Other Clones from French Selection Programs After Bernard's pioneering work got under way in the 1950s, other clonal selection programs followed suit in other parts of France. At least 27 clones of pinot are now recognized by CTPS and distributed by ENTAV. In addition to the so-called Dijon and Roederer clones listed above, CTPS 111, 236, 375, and 583 were sourced from various vineyards in Burgundy, and CTPS 521, 665, 666, 668, 743, 780, 792, 870, 871, and 872 from vineyards in Champagne. In addition, CTPS 779 and 792 were sourced from a vineyard in Bué, a commune of Sancerre in the upper Loire valley; CTPS 292 and 459 from the Jura; and CTPS 162 (usually known on these shores as Colmar 538) from Alsace. Many of these have been imported, either through the Oregon State University program or by the Canadian plant import and quarantine facility at Saanichton, on the southeast tip of Vancouver Island in British Columbia. Some have ended up at FPMS and been assigned FPMS selection numbers, with cross-references to the CTPS designations—on the supposition that the identities reported in Oregon and Saanichton records are accurate. Thus UCD 31 and UCD 40 are both reported to be CTPS 236; UCD 38 to be CTPS 459; UCD 39 to be CTPS 386; UCD 48 to be CTPS 162; UCD 51 to be CTPS 665; UCD 54 to be CTPS 871; and UCD 64 to be CTPS 780. The various Champagne-sourced clones have gotten some attention from the sparkling houses, but otherwise American vintners have shown only spotty interest in them: CTPS 162 has been planted at Gloria Ferrer, where it gives an attractive and distinctively gingerbread-scented pinot noir. Babcock Vineyards has planted a bit of CTPS 459, but the vines are not yet bearing.

Wädenswil Clones Wädenswil is a town on the southern shore of the Zürichsee about half an hour by suburban railway from the center of Switzerland's largest city. Since 1890 it has been home to the Eidengenössische Forschungsanstalt für Obst-, Wein- und Gartenbau, a government-operated research station with responsibility for viticulture in German-speaking Switzerland, whose first director was Hermann Müller-Thurgau. (Müller-Thurgau gave his name, among other things, to the Müller-Thurgau wine grape variety.) Cuttings from Wädenswil's extensive species gardens, imported in the 1950s, were the source of UCD selections 1A, 2A, 3A, and 30. Of these, 1A and 2A were different clones, having been propagated from different vines in the Wädenswil collection; 3A seems to have come from the same mother vine as 2A; and 30 was a heat-treated version of 2A. Neither 3A nor 30 is any longer listed in the FPMS catalog, and neither developed much of a following among winegrowers, though a few Oregon growers claim to have a bit of UCD 30 in their vineyards.

In Switzerland, the Wädenswil facility is best known for a clone locally called 2/45, which is very widely planted throughout the country and dominant in German-speaking Switzerland. Clone 2/45 generally displays moderate vigor and moderate to high yields, compact cylindrical clusters, good color, a fair tolerance for a variety of mesoclimates, and good resistance to humidity-induced bunch rot. It is probably a fair guess that the Wädenswil clones are somehow related to 2/45, though specialists at Wädenswil say the American numbers are unfamiliar to them, so there is no way to be completely sure.

In North America, 1A showed itself, like 2/45, to be a fairly heavy bearer. As such it seems to have attracted limited interest, but 2A became, and remains, an important selection. In Oregon it accounts for almost one-third all pinot plantings. In California that figure is much lower, but still substantial. In Oregon and most of Northern California, 2A is prized mostly for brilliant, high-toned berry fruit and impressive perfume, and is therefore used primarily as a blending component, adding finesse to wines that would otherwise be darker, heavier, and more monochromatic. The Eyrie Vineyards in Oregon uses a high proportion of Wädenswil in its wines, however, and J Wine Company's flagship Nicole's Vineyard wine is made entirely from 2A. In the southern Central Coast, where 2A accounts for *all* of the pinot noir in Talley's Rincon Vineyard, the selection shows quite differently, producing a much darker and more black-fruited wine that stands impressively on its own.

Mariafeld Clones Wädenswil was also the source, in 1966, for two selections of pinot noir that have come to be identified not with the Wädenswil name but variously as Mariafeld, Klevner Mariafeld, and Clevener Mariafeld. *Klevner* is a German paranym for *pinot*. The mother vines for the various Mariafeld clones are said to have come, about 60 years ago, from the Mariafeld estate of General Ulrich Wille, commander in chief of the Swiss armed forces in World War I, which was on the north shore of the Zürichsee, near Feldmeilen. In Switzerland, the Mariafeld clones are known for a blueberrylike color in the vineyard, an open cluster architecture, and (perhaps because of the open clusters) considerable resistance to bunch rot.

In North America, the Mariafeld cuttings became the basis for UCD 17 and 23. Their Swiss properties have persisted in American vineyards. They remain relatively high-yielding, large-berried selections that generally show higher acid and a combination of strawberry and farmyard aromas. Logically, they are much favored in the Finger Lakes region of New York, where bunch rot is a considerable problem. The Mariafeld selections are not without their partisans even in California, however. Morgan has planted some UCD 23 in its new Double L vineyard in the Santa Lucia Highlands, as have Greenwood Ridge in Anderson Valley and several growers in Edna Valley.

Jackson Clones In 1889, the University of California established an experimental five-acre grape vineyard near the town of Jackson, in the foothills of the Sierra Nevada, apparently to test the feasibility of grape production as a substitute for the area's declining fortunes with gold mining. Professor Eugene Hilgard appears to have been the inspiration behind this facility, as he was behind earlier experimental vineyards at Berkeley and Cupertino. Between 1889 and 1899, cuttings for more than 150 varieties of wine, table, and raisin grapes were apparently transferred to Jackson from the other two vineyards, which in their turn had been planted with cuttings gathered from various privately held vineyards, including H. C. Crabb's To-Kalon Vineyard near Oakville and vineyards belonging to the Natoma Vineyard Company near Folsom. The Natoma cuttings were then-recent French imports, according to Hilgard's unpublished autobiography. Most of the plantings at Jackson occurred in 1889 and 1890 and were documented in a handwritten notebook that has survived in the university library at Berkeley. According to these records, the pinot noir at Jackson, called Pinot Noirien, was set out in row 5 of block L in 1889, using cuttings from Berkeley, and in row 7 of block B, using cuttings from Cupertino. The Jackson station was closed in 1903, having apparently proved that the foothills were less suitable for agriculture than bottomland closer to Sacramento and San Francisco, and the experimental vineyard was abandoned.

When it was rediscovered in 1963 in the course of some remarkable detective work by Austin Goheen, the surviving vines were found to be relatively disease-free, presumably owing to their isolation, and cuttings were gathered for transfer to the university's foundation vineyard at Davis. Contemporaneous handwritten records indicate that two selections of pinot noir were thus derived, called simply selections 1 and 2, both (supposedly) from the Cupertino plantings in row 7 of block B. The FPMS records show that selection 2 was ultimately released as UCD 9 and selection 1 as UCD 16, but two other Jackson clones were also distributed as UCD 1 and UCD 29, both of which have subsequently been withdrawn from the FPMS Grape Register. In clonal trials in Oregon in 1979 and 1980, UCD 1 and UCD 29 were found to be "very similar," with large clusters and berries but good color, dark, wild flavors, and considerable intensity. New York State trials found that UCD 29 had the advantage of cold-hardiness, perhaps because it had earlier adapted to winters in the Sierra Nevada. A trial was also conducted with UCD 29 at Carneros Creek in the 1970s, but it did not emerge as a favorite.

Despite this interest, the Jackson clones have not been widely planted in North America. There is some in Martin Van Der Kamp's Sonoma Mountain vineyard, and Lane Tanner has planted both UCD 9 and 16, along with 2A, in her custom-farmed block at Melville in the Santa Rita Hills. Michel-Schlumberger has also planted some UCD 9 and 16 in Dry Creek Valley, believing that these selections show full flavor development at relatively low levels of sugar. Whatever their virtues, the Jackson clones have the distinction of being the earliest documented imports of pinot noir still under cultivation in North America, having unarguably been imported before 1890—and perhaps considerably earlier, if Crabb's To-Kalon vineyard was in fact their original American source. Neither UCD 9 nor UCD 16 was heat-treated at FPMS.

Martini Clones The Martini clones are descended from the experimental plantings on which Louis M. Martini and Harold Olmo collaborated, on the former Stanly ranch in Carneros. The budwood for most of these plantings is supposed to have come from a small block in front of the old Inglenook Winery on Highway 29 in Rutherford, where Niebaum-Coppola's barrel building now sits, though some budwood may also have been sourced from the University of California's old experimental vineyard in Berkeley. According to Michael Martini, the Inglenook block was laid out in separate rows of visibly different selections, from each (or most) of which his grandfather and Olmo took cuttings for use in Carneros. Niebaum-Coppola's longtime vineyard manager Rafael Rodriguez does not recall that the block was laid out in separate rows of visibly different selections, but he thinks it may well have been a field blend of different selections. Either way, the block is said to have been planted in the 1930s and to have been pulled out in the 1970s. Whether the wood for the 1930s planting was taken from yet older plantings on the Inglenook estate, perhaps dating as far back as Gustav Niebaum's alleged imports in the nineteenth century, or whether those earlier plantings were lost to phylloxera, is now impossible to say for sure.

In any case, Martini and Olmo created a genuine clonal test block on Stanly's ranch, apparently numbering the selections taken from Inglenook sequentially, starting at or about number 40. Two of these selections, transferred to Davis, became UCD 13 and 15 following testing and heat treatment (UCD 13 is said to be Martini's selection no. 58). But a large amount of pinot noir was also propagated directly from Martini's Carneros vineyards by field selection in the late 1960s and early 1970s—Jim St. Clair's vineyard is a case in point—and this process can be presumed to have involved selections in addition to those that became UCD 13 and 15. For the clonal trials at Carneros Creek in the 1970s, Francis Mahoney took three additional selections from Martini's test block: numbers 44, 54, and 56. In the 1990s, before the clonal trial block at Carneros Creek was pulled, FPMS director Deborah Golino transferred selected cuttings from that trial to Davis. One of those, Martini selection no. 56, tested negative for virus and was released in 1999 as UCD 66.

Throughout the 1970s and 1980s, and into the 1990s, UCD 13 and 15 were among the most widely planted of UCD pinot selections. They accounted for an enormous percentage of the planted surface in Carneros and spread into the Russian River valley, Anderson Valley, Monterey, and the southern Central Coast. They are now held responsible (though perhaps undeservedly) for the consistent, slightly monochromatic flavors Carneros pinot noir was said to show in the 1980s. Farmed to relatively high yields and picked early, the Martini clones were used extensively for sparkling wine, especially in Los Carneros and the Russian River valley. Gradually and unfairly, they gained the reputation of making undistinguished still wine, largely because they were farmed undemandingly. Jim St. Clair's vineyard of dry-farmed Martini clone, yielding parsimoniously, made two decades of superb pinot noirs under the Acacia label, and Martini clone, now vertically trellised and narrowly spaced, is giving excellent results in many vineyards, including Lingenfelder in the Russian River valley and Cerise in Anderson Valley. Gerald Asher has written that wine made from the Martini clones has "a sinewy elegance" derived from the overlay of "muscle" and "grace."

Mount Eden Selection and Mount Eden Clone In 1895 or 1896, Paul Masson is supposed to have brought cuttings of pinot noir from Burgundy to California and to have planted them at La Cresta, the mountain vineyard he was then developing in the hills above Cupertino. In one version of the story, he obtained these cuttings from grower-*négociant* Louis Latour. In another, they came from one of the Domaine de la Romanée-Conti vineyards. In a third version, the cuttings came from Romanée-Conti via Latour, but this makes little sense because Latour never owned any piece of Romanée-Conti. It is at least plausible that Masson may have sourced cuttings from Latour, taken from one or another of the firm's many vineyard holdings in the Côte d'Or. The present Louis Latour, grandson of the Louis whom Masson knew, confirms that his grandfather was one of Masson's Burgundian "friends and colleagues" and that Masson returned to Beaune "many times" after he had emigrated to California. But Maison Louis Latour's archives, according to Latour *grand-fils,* contain no correspondence between Masson and Latour *grand-père* and no record that the firm sold any plant material to Masson. In fact, Latour *grand-fils* says he does not believe that Masson demonstrated much interest in moving budwood from Burgundy to California, being more focused on the "creation of an indigenous viticulture based on locally grown varieties." However, he does not exclude the possibility that Masson might have received vine cuttings as a gift.

Whatever the source of Masson's budwood, La Cresta provided cuttings, more than four decades later, for Martin Ray's new vineyard on a neighboring hilltop. Ray's hilltop eventually became Mount Eden Vineyards after being wrested from the Ray family in a legal battle with disaffected investors in 1971. In the most likely scenario, what is called Masson selection is the same thing, more or less, as Martin Ray selection, and therefore also the same as Mount Eden selection. Since the Mount Eden rubric is the most widely used of the three, and since Mount Eden was the source of numerous other plantings in California, it makes sense to adopt Mount Eden as the selection's preferred name. David Bruce took budwood from Martin Ray's vineyard before the transition to Mount Eden occurred, but there is no reason to assume that his selection was substantially different from what remained at Mount Eden after 1971.

In the 1980s, Merry Edwards transferred cuttings from a single vine at Mount Eden to FPMS, where it was heat-treated and released as UCD 37, misleadingly glossed as the Rae [*sic*] clone. This is the only instance of Mount Eden that can properly be called a clone. Mount Eden selection has a fine reputation for small berries and clusters, and for deep, intense flavors. It has been widely propagated in California, and a few vines, transported illicitly, have been introduced from time to time in Oregon. There is not yet much experience with UCD 37, but Merry Edwards, who selected it, has also planted it in her new vineyards near Sebastopol.

Swan Selections and Swan Clone Almost from the time Joseph Swan planted pinot noir in his small estate vineyard near Forestville in 1969, it has been a favored source of cuttings for other plantings, presumably because Swan's pinots showed extremely well right from the outset. Neighbors in the Russian River valley planted "Swan."

So did King Estate in Oregon, Franscioni in the Santa Lucia Highlands, Bruce Newlan in Napa, and countless others in several states. Mahoney took cuttings from Swan's vineyard for the Carneros Creek clonal trials, where they made very tasty wines and became a preferred selection. Swan selection cuttings from Carneros Creek were propagated at Casa Carneros, which became a source of choice for other vintners, especially in and around Carneros.

In spite of Joe Swan's general meticulousness, however, it has been hard to establish the source—or sources—of his original budwood. It has been alleged, variously, that Swan is a suitcase clone, flown in from Burgundy, that it is another instance of Mount Eden, and that it came from the University of California's experimental vineyard in Oakville. Because Swan appears to have kept no written records of his own, the best evidence of his sources comes from Mahoney's handwritten notes when he and Curtis Alley collected the budwood used for the trials at Carneros Creek in 1974. These contain the following, which Mahoney interprets now as a budwood "chronology": "a. R. Conti, b. Paul Mason [*sic*], c. Martin Ray, d. Oakville—1959." And sure enough, in remarks about pinot noir made to the Vintners Club in 1987, Swan testified that he "got some pinot noir cuttings from the University of California Experimental Station at Oakville in 1959," which he then planted on property he owned in the Sierra Nevada. One Keith Bowers, he continued, who was then in charge of the vineyards at Oakville, "had gotten the original budwood from Martin Ray, who had brought it up to Mount Eden from the old Paul Masson vineyards." The story, Swan concluded, "is that the original cuttings came from Romanée-Conti, which is enthralling whether it is true or not." Swan did not say explicitly that he took cuttings from his own Sierra property to plant the Forestville vineyard, but he implied as much. Mahoney's notes and Swan's remarks, overlaid, strongly suggest that Swan's own Sierra vineyard, and then the Oakville experimental vineyard, were the proximate sources of budwood for the Forestville vineyard, but that the "true" upstream source was Mount Eden.

There is, however, good evidence that some additional plant material was introduced at Forestville after the initial planting, including vines quietly given to Swan by a Burgundian vintner. Cuttings from some of these later introductions may have been included in distributions made at later dates from Swan's estate. In the main, it is fair to assume that *some* of what is called Swan is the same as *some* of what is called Mount Eden, but both are field selections, not clones, so the overlap is less than perfect. At the end of the 1990s, cuttings were taken from the Swan-sourced vines in the Carneros Creek trial plot and transferred to FPMS, where one has now been designated UCD 97.

Gamay Beaujolais Clones It is perhaps not surprising, in the confusion of the late nineteenth and early twentieth centuries, that at least one, and perhaps several, of the pinot selections imported into California turned out to have the appearance Burgundians call *pinot droit,* often translated as "upright pinot." This means that the vine's shoots grow straight upward from its trunk rather than at an angle, into the alleys between the vine rows, like most of Burgundy's better selections. (The latter are known informally as bent pinot or *pinot tordu.*) Unfortunately, although the upright growth habit is a viticultural convenience, requiring less aggressive trellising, most *pinot droit* vines are generous bearers of fairly mediocre wine grapes.

In California, the peculiar growth habit and different performance of *pinot droit* were apparently sufficient to convince growers that the selection was not pinot noir at all, so these pinots came to be called gamay, and eventually (to distinguish them from another alleged gamay, which was actually valdiguié) Gamay Beaujolais. In fact, California's Gamay Beaujolais was and is completely unrelated to gamay, except that once upon a time—as genetic studies have demonstrated since—pinot noir was one of gamay's two parent varieties. Leon Adams blames Paul Masson for the Gamay Beaujolais clones, but this accusation is inconsistent with other stories about Masson's imports. Perversely, the TTB still permits pinot noir (made from *any* clone of the variety) to be sold as Gamay Beaujolais, and many nurserymen and winemakers are still confused about the facts.

Cuttings from so-called Gamay Beaujolais in California vineyards, propagated at Davis, are the source for five selections of pinot noir, UCD 18, 19, 20, 21, and 22, which—to honor history but confuse normal mortals—are still called the GB or Gamay Beaujolais clones. At least three of the five (18, 19, and 22) descend from the same mother vine; UCD 22 was heat-treated; 20 and 21 have now been withdrawn. Interestingly, despite the generally bad reputation *pinot droit* has in France, these clones have performed fairly well in North America, and a number of growers raise at least a bit of them. In the Carneros Creek trials, UCD 18 was among the seven clones preferred; UCD 22 also underwent trial in Oregon. In Australian tests, UCD 20 is said to have performed well. In general, however, these clones throw large clusters with above-average yield and are used exclusively for blending in still-wine production, or for sparkling wine.

Suitcase Clones and Their Progeny Because unsupervised grapevine importation has been illegal in the United States since 1948, and because French authorities have become sensitive to trademark infringement when the names of French properties or appellations are used in connection with American wines, it is nearly impossible to untangle the web of stories that circulate about illicitly imported cuttings of pinot noir. Charles Coury, the Oregon pioneer, is said to have imported pinot cuttings from Burgundy in the 1960s. Gary Pisoni, whose eponymous vineyard in the Santa Lucia Highlands is a much-prized source of fruit for many boutique makers of pinot noir, is reported to have planted most or all of his vineyard to cuttings from La Tâche, some of which have since been made available to other growers. But Pisoni is now circumspect on the issue, and some well-informed sources say that Pisoni's budwood came not directly from France, but via a vineyard in the nearby Carmel Valley. There are persistent allegations that some of the vines at Calera came directly or indirectly from one of the Domaine de la Romanée-Conti vineyards. This is a credible proposition, given Calera owner Josh Jensen's long and friendly relations with the owners of Romanée-Conti, but Jensen says that his plant material came from nearby Chalone. Gary Andrus, the former owner of Archery Summit in Oregon, claims to have brought in vines from an impressive handful of well-respected Burgundy properties, including Le Musigny and Les Amoureuses, but these stories are impossible to substantiate, and the new owners of Archery Summit say they cannot confirm them. A few well-respected vintners admit off the record to having imported cuttings from France, including some of the Dijon clones, when they had reason to believe that the supposedly certified material available from North American nurseries was not as advertised.

In a few cases, cuttings from plant material that can be presumed to have entered the country without a permit have *reentered* the mainstream of certified clones. One example is the recently released UCD 90, which is derived from the so-called P selection in the Carneros Creek trials, the budwood for which came from five vines in Chalone's so-called New Block. This block was presumably the MacWood block, planted in 1972 and 1973, just before the Carneros Creek trial began. The FPS calls UCD 90 the Carneros Creek/Chambertin clone, which is highly suggestive of a specific European origin for scion material in Chalone's MacWood block, though officially the source of the latter is not known. Also, in 1996 Byron Vineyard and Winery took cuttings from a vine in the "high-density experimental block" of its Nielsen vineyard, whose origin was said to be "the Chambolle Musigny area of Burgundy, France." These cuttings were transferred to FPMS for testing and custom treatment, in the anticipation—according to a press release—that "a certified Byron clone" would become available "in 2003."

Generally, viticulturists who specialize in pinot noir find that clones are usually true to type wherever they are planted, making it possible to select clones that correspond to a winemaker's organoleptic preferences. Certainly this was the general conclusion of posttrial plantings at Carneros Creek and Casa Carneros. There are exceptions, however. Clones planted on very shallow or very deep soil can perform quite differently. Aside from soil depth, there also seem to be regional eccentricities. The performance of UCD 2A on the southern Central Coast is a good example, and Australian researchers are reported to disagree in principle, finding that pinot noir clones behave quite differently in different *climates.* In addition, some growers think they can detect pinot's famous predilection for spontaneous mutation within a single vine generation, making clones true to type for only short periods in the vineyard; but this is a minority opinion. Given the host of opportunities that exist, at every stage of selection and distribution, to mistake one vine for another, one cannot exclude the possibility that many instances of idiosyncratic performance rest on errors rather than oddities.

In the end, most pinot makers temper their enthusiasm for clonal selection with three caveats. First, as Melissa Moravec argues, "the impact of clones may be somewhat minimized by changes in rootstock, spacing, and trellis." Second, it is widely, though not universally, felt that a *combination* of clones makes better wine than any single clone vinified by itself. For this reason, almost all new vineyards are being planted to some mix of clones and selections. To the extent that this view is correct—and exceptions do exist—it is confirmation of the traditional Burgundian practice of mass selection, as far as this practice can be reconciled with concerns about healthy and diseased vines. The third caveat is that clones never overtake site in overall qualitative importance. The "best" clones can never compensate for a poor site, nor will the "wrong" clones, whatever that may mean, completely obscure the potential of a great site. Moravec, who oversaw the clonal trials at Carneros Creek, testifies that "if required to choose, [Mahoney and I] would rather have a great site with a less suitable clone than a poor site with a great clone." Barney Watson and Steven Price, who supervised the Oregon trials in the 1980s, concluded similarly that "clones won't make a bad site better." So for pinot noir, despite all the passion for clones and clonal selection, the mantra remains the old adage about real estate: location, location, and location.

Chapter 6

WINEGROWING AND WINEMAKING

The basics of growing red-wine grapes and turning them into wine are relatively straightforward. Tens of thousands of growers, professional winemakers, and amateur practitioners do the trick every year around the world. Healthy fruit is harvested properly ripe. Yeasts transform sugar into alcohol. Before, during, and after fermentation, the stuff of red wine is extracted from the grapes' skins. The wine is then "raised," finished, and bottled. And many millions of bottles of more or less sound red wine, crafted from many varieties of vinifera, are then sent to market.

When the object of attention is *fine* wine, however, the basics rapidly decompose into hundreds of individual processes, discrete choices, and complex decisions involving a bewildering array of variables. There are literally thousands of variations on the basic theme, and virtually every choice is consequential. Fine winemaking, unlike basic winemaking, is about specifics—not formulas, recipes, or generalizations.

The number of variables and the complexity of choices are not greater for pinot noir than for other varieties, but the impact of winegrowing and winemaking choices can be greater, largely because pinot—owing to the transparency discussed in previous chapters—shows the fingerprint of every process, intervention, and manipulation, as well as of every neglect, both in the vineyard and in the cellar, more noticeably than do other grapes. Nor are these links between choice and effect always straightforward. Most pinot makers say they cannot reconstruct the choices made during winemaking simply by tasting the finished wine. The impact of individual choices is complicated by their multiplicity and by what computer programmers like to call elbow effects—indirect and often unforeseeable consequences of any modification to a line of code.

Nor do winemakers agree with one another. Most will say that they can and do agree on whether a wine is sound or flawed or good or bad, and that their disagreements are confined to matters of style; but in practice the boundary between quality and style is fuzzy. Winemakers do not agree on how much volatile acidity in a wine is good or on how much more is a flaw, or on other questions. How much funkiness makes a pinot taste desirably complex, and how much more really is *too* much? Is a pinot good if it does not taste more like fruit than stones? Is a pinot great if it tastes ravishing in its youth but does not age attractively? Each of these parameters has a stylistic dimension, to be sure, but each impinges on quality as well, and consensus is elusive. The producer profiles in the second part of this book record the choices, sensitivities, and stylistic objectives of individual producers; this chapter summarizes, as best I can, those points on which they agree or diverge.

WINEGROWING

Sites It is hard nowadays to find a winemaker who quarrels with the proposition that good wine, and especially good pinot noir, is made in the vineyard. Larry Brooks, Acacia's founding winemaker, says 90 percent of a red wine is made in the vineyard; Merry Edwards claims 75 percent of her job is done before the grapes are picked. Many makers assert that if the grapes are good, their job is "to let the wine make itself," to "stay out of the way," and to avoid "subtracting" from the grapes' potential. A few, including Iron Horse's David Munksgard, find such claims a bit hyperbolic, arguing that plenty of hands-on attention in the cellar is the essential partner to careful farming. Vineyards, for their part, are the sum of site, age, and farming; and site in its turn is the combination of weather, soil, and aspect.

A vineyard's location, most winegrowers agree, is the key to its quality and personality. Nine times out of ten, however, when a North American winegrower talks about location, location turns out to mean *climate.* Axiomatically, good sites for pinot noir are said to be cool sites. This wisdom seems to have been received at the end of the 1970s, though really warm sites, like California's hot central valley, were counterindicated as early as the 1880s. But as chapter 4 shows, sites can be cool in very different ways, and the impact of those differences is poorly understood, and in some circles much debated. Many Californians, especially those with large stakes in Los Carneros and the Russian River valley, argue that a large differential between daytime high and overnight low temperatures is just what pinot needs to thrive: daytime highs drive maturation, while overnight lows preserve acidity. John Gladstones, an Australian agronomist who has reviewed the relatively limited scientific literature on this matter and whose book *Viticulture and Environment* is revered by some winemakers, argues to the contrary that high maximums and low minimums both produce undesirable results.

According to Gladstones, the high highs can "inhibit enzymatic activity" and "accelerate the evaporative loss of volatile aroma compounds," while cold nights can retard "physiological ripening and quality development" and actually *increase* the accumulation of sugar since they inhibit all metabolism during the overnight period. If true, this is the exact opposite of cool climates' presumed advantage, which is to decelerate sugar accumulation until other physiological processes in the grape can catch up. Gladstones argues that "relatively constant intermediate temperatures" are what the doctor ordered for wine grapes, because they "specifically favour the biochemical processes of colour/flavour/aroma development in the berries." Gladstones's main object of attention is Australia; one presumes that if he looked particularly at pinot noir in North America, he would expect better pinots from the southern Central Coast, the Santa Lucia Highlands, and the Sonoma Coast than from Los Carneros, the Russian River valley, or even Oregon, since relatively high diurnal variation characterizes all of the latter. Proponents of diurnal variation (a category that includes quite a number of Burgundians promoting what they call *amplitudes*) argue the opposite, however.

Apart from temperature, there is the matter of daylight hours, which vary hugely among the North American regions, from a low of 14 hours and 34 minutes on June 21 in the southern Central Coast to a high of 16 hours and 26 minutes on June 21 in the Okanagan. In a 1988 paper, Oregon winemaker David Adelsheim called sunlight "the saving grace for western Oregon," helping to "compensate for lower temperatures." On this point, Gladstones thinks sunshine hours have little independent effect, contributing to physiological ripeness "largely through their effect on temperature."

It is worth noting that, for all the testimony that cool, somehow defined, is paramount, even André Tchelistcheff—who was a huge champion of "cool" Carneros—reminded an interviewer in 1990 that his best Beaulieu pinot noir had been made from grapes grown in Rutherford, where the summer weather is almost always warmer. He also suggested that pinot noir might "do excellently" in high-altitude sections of Dry Creek Valley and above Schramsberg, between St. Helena and Calistoga. Indeed, some very superior pinots were made in relatively warmer locations in the late 1970s and early 1980s, including Caymus's Napa Valley bottling, Kenwood's Jack London vineyard-designate, a Mill Creek bottling from the southern end of Dry Creek Valley, and Hacienda's Sonoma Valley wine. El Molino gets good results from a new (1990s) planting of pinot noir near Rutherford, and the first vintages of Dry Creek Valley pinot noir made by Michel-Schlumberger are promising. Few would argue that a site's microproperties—whether it faces south or southeast, whether it is flat or steeply sloped, whether it is shielded from prevailing winds by a rise or hillside, and its altitude—can have a profound effect on temperature in the vineyard and on the way its grapes behave. These are crucial matters in Oregon, where a suboptimal choice in aspect, altitude, or orientation can compromise a vineyard in all but the warmest years, making it impossible to ripen even an early-to-ripen variety like pinot noir.

Soils are the other main measure of a site, and a matter of even lesser consensus than climate, probably because they are harder to measure and describe. Because Americans have always looked to Burgundy for the "right" answers on pinot, some winegrowers have searched the American landscape for soils resembling the Côte d'Or's limestone. Calera's Josh Jensen is the archetypical example, expounding a theory that "limestone engenders complexity in the grapes" and telling an interviewer in 1997 that "the only magic bullet [for good pinot] is the soil." Chalone founder Dick Graff was another partisan of limestone, asserting in 1993 that "to date, no great pinot noir has come from non-limestone soil." For a time limestone was so widely accepted as a key factor in making good pinot noir that Randall Graham, who was smitten with pinot before he shifted his focus to Rhône varieties, amended the soil of his Santa Cruz Mountains vineyard with 300 tons of dolomitic limestone and sugar beet lime, to give himself a better shot at success. In the end he concluded that the lime had made no difference, and he gave up on pinot for unrelated reasons. Others believe that limestone soil's main virtue is being a bit more alkaline than grapevines really like, and hence limiting their vigor. In some parts of France, grapevines actually die of chlorosis, an iron deficiency induced by excessively alkaline soil. A few vintners say limestone soils in Burgundy are important not for their chemistry but for their physical properties. Burgundy's limestone soils seem to hold water in a sort of "perfect hydrostatic balance" similar to conditions in a drip-irrigated vineyard. Ancien Wines' Ken Bernards thinks California's volcanic ash can have the same effect: it "wicks" subsoil moisture to the vines. Most North American viticulturists see no reason to be fixated on limestone soils. Pinot noir does well, they say, in any well-drained loamy mix of sand, clay, and organic matter, as long as it is not too rich or deep.

Limestone aside, vines feed on their soil in complex, mysterious, and poorly understood ways, drinking mineral cocktails created when water dissolves various chemical compounds from the soils and adjacent parent rocks, and eventually passing some of these elements into their fruit. It is not just the palpably flinty flavor of some white wines that is soil-derived; it is the weight, coherence, and nonfruit concentration of red wines, including pinot noir. There is no other explanation for the personality and expression of certain wines and appellations, especially when these features persist across vintages that display radically different weather patterns. When, eventually, the really great sites for pinot noir have been as well cataloged in North America as they are now in Burgundy, it seems likely that a long list of physical and chemical soil properties will be recognized as key determinants of styles and quality in winegrowing.

Farming the Vineyard Just a generation ago, farming a vineyard meant little more than planting vines and picking grapes. So much more attention is now paid to cultivation that North American vineyards have changed fundamentally in appearance, and viticulturists commonly contrast "old-style" or "traditional" vineyards, dating mostly from the 1970s, with "modern" vineyards, which have been more or less standard practice since the 1990s.

The traditional vineyard was planted in widely spaced rows with plenty of distance between adjacent vines. Vines were tied to a single wire, or two wires, and thereafter allowed to flop at will. If this meant that a vine's foliage shielded the grape clusters from most sunlight, no one cared. The modern vineyard is denser, with three, four, or even seven times as many vines in every acre. For pinot noir, a three-wire trellis is now standard, eliminating most of the erstwhile "flop." Vines are carefully pruned and shoots hand-positioned on the wires, and leaves are removed to ensure that some moving air and some sunshine can touch every cluster of grapes.

Along with these changes, many growers have been attracted to organic or quasiorganic farming, or even to so-called biodynamics, minimizing or eliminating the use of chemical fertilizers, herbicides, and pesticides. French agronomist Claude Bourguignon, who advises many top French producers, including many Burgundians, argues that the key consideration is that the soil stay alive, meaning that it remain rich in healthy microorganisms. These organisms seem to be an essential agent in the interaction between the chemical components of soil and subsoil on the one hand, and the vine plant on the other. They may be vitally important in the process that makes wine "taste" like a particular piece of soil. Bob Cantisano, a California viticulturist and tireless promoter of organic grape farming, says winemakers tell him that they can make "fuller-bodied, more flavorful, and more intense wines from organic grapes."

Modern grape farming, especially for pinot noir, is dramatically more labor-intensive and expensive than the old plant-and-pick formula; only a huge increase in the market price of grapes has made it affordable. While no grower, anyplace in North America, would plant a new vineyard to look like an old one, there are still raging debates about many parameters of new vineyards. There is also the matter of the "right" clones, discussed in chapter 5.

In most vineyards, scion material is grafted to unrelated rootstock, since all varieties of vinifera are vulnerable to phylloxera. The rootstocks—all derived from resistant American species of *Vitis* and identified with alphanumeric-soup names only growers have any reason to memorize—differ in their rooting habits, their resistance to viral disease and nematodes, their tolerance for specific soil chemistries, and (most important) the degree of vigor they transmit to the vine. Proving that nothing in viticulture is beyond debate, however, many Oregonians and a few Californians have planted vines on their own roots, staring phylloxera in the face, on the theory that own-rooted vines make better wine. In a few cases, mostly by happenstance rather than design, pinot noir has even been planted on the roots of some *other* vinifera variety; see Sanford Winery for an instance of pinot noir on cabernet and merlot roots, and Talley Vineyards for an instance of pinot on what was once own-rooted sauvignon blanc.

Irrigation is another matter for debate. In California nearly all vineyards are irrigated, and the practice is gradually spreading to Oregon, where dry-farmed vineyards were the norm until the 1990s. (In Burgundy, irrigation is not permitted by law, but Burgundy gets more summer rain than any North American region except the Finger Lakes.) As more is learned about how grapes ripen, most growers like having the flexibility to manipulate the vines' behavior by adding or subtracting water; they also like insurance against drought. But some of North America's greatest pinots have come from dry-farmed vineyards. The St. Clair Vineyard in Carneros and Abbey Ridge in the Red Hills are just two of many examples. Partisans of dry-farming argue that irrigated vines develop shallower roots, adversely affecting soil-derived flavors and (in Oregon) leaving the vines vulnerable to quicker water uptake in case of a preharvest rainstorm, while dry-farmed vines are self-regulating, yielding a similar crop year in and year out, regardless of rainfall. The dry-farmed vineyard is not much more likely than the own-rooted vineyard to proliferate, however, because the economic risks, in most of North America outside the Finger Lakes region, are prohibitive.

Growers and vintners also debate whether old vines, dry-farmed or not, make better wine, and especially better pinot noir, than younger vines. By tradition and regulation, Burgundians exclude young vines' fruit from the best bottlings—fruit from vines less than three years old is not permitted in controlled appellation wines—and generally hold that a vine is not "qualitatively adult" until it is past age 25. Now a few Burgundians say that new clones produce top-notch fruit at an earlier age than conventional mass selections, making this segregation unnecessary; but this is a minority position. In North America the average age of pinot vines is much lower, owing both to the explosive rate of new planting in recent years and to forced replanting of phylloxera-infected vines in the early 1990s. Some new vineyards have produced delicious grapes in the very first harvest, though it is an open question whether these vines will subsequently descend into a middle-age trough. Still, many old-vines pinots display aromatic and flavor complexities that are rarely found in wines from younger vines. Hanzell pinots are a good example, as are the reserve wines made from 1992 to 1997 at Husch from that property's oldest vines, and the extraordinary final vintage from Martin Ray's 1940s planting on Table Mountain, released by Mount Eden Vineyards as a special *vieilles vignes* bottling in 1997. There is considerable evidence that old vines minimize the problem of sugar-based ripening outrunning full flavor development (see below).

Tight vine spacing, one hallmark of the so-called modern vineyard style, has been the subject of especially heated debate. Tightly spaced vineyards are expensive. They cost more on a one-time basis to plant, trellis, and irrigate, and a dense planting is more expensive to maintain, year in and year out, than a vineyard planted to fewer vines. On the other hand, tightly spaced vineyards produce more crop per acre, which makes them more profitable. Historically, most European vineyards have been quite densely planted, though exceptions exist, especially in parts of Italy, Spain, and Portugal; while the New World, at least until recently, has sported very loose spacings. There is abundant evidence that European vineyards used to be planted even more densely than they are today, partially because many vineyards were propagated by layering, which dictated close proximity among vines.

As North Americans interested in pinot noir contemplated their circumstances in the 1980s and 1990s, looking for the keys to good pinot, no contrast was more obvious than the tight vine spacing in Burgundy, against the wide alleys and intervals that had come to prevail in America. Many North American viticulturists convinced themselves that tight vine spacing was a qualitative parameter. Archery Summit's founder, Gary Andrus—and many others—came to argue that fewer pounds of fruit per vine translated to better and more intense flavors. Viticulturists buttressed this argument with another: higher-vigor soils demanded tighter spacing to create competition among vines and to decrease fruit production per vine. The more vigorous the soil, it was said, the more important it might be to plant vineyards densely.

Experiments with tightly spaced vineyards were undertaken across California and Oregon, but the results (at least with pinot noir) were mixed. At Domaine Drouhin Oregon, 86 of 90 planted acres were set out in 4.3-foot rows with one meter between vines; the remaining four acres were planted in seven-foot rows with the same intervine spacing. The winery reported that year after year, the seven-foot rows produced their least favorite wines. At Flowers Vineyard on the Sonoma Coast, a 1997–1998 trial of wine from vines planted meter-by-meter against wine from those planted in eight-foot rows with five feet between vines produced the opposite result. The meter-by-meter blocks produced more tannic wines with discernibly herbal and vegetal flavors, while the medium-dense plantings yielded better color, fruitier flavors, and higher levels of large-molecule tannins, which are generally associated with weightier, softer, and more viscous wines. Steve Kistler, who ran another planting-density experiment at about the same time, found that it was "hard to see any [qualitative] difference" between the wines from meter-by-meter plantings and wine from eight-by-five-foot blocks.

At best these results—combined with the vine spacing data reported in this book's producer profiles—suggest no consistent correlation between vine density and wine quality. In fact, there is no correlation in Burgundy, either. Meter-by-meter spacing is universal in the Côte d'Or: in the *grand cru* and *premier cru* vineyards that produce Burgundy's gems and in the much larger surface that is exploited for Bourgogne Rouge and Bourgogne Grand Ordinaire. It is permissible to believe that planting density may be more an economic than a qualitative issue, rooted in efficiency and then codified by region. Given that the cost of inputs in North America differs substantially from the cost in Europe and that North American *terroirs* are rather unlike *terroirs* in Burgundy, there is little reason to suppose that the efficient planting density in one place bears any relation to the efficient density in the other.

Yield With pinot noir, the vineyard's yield is overwhelmingly important. In North America, yield is usually expressed as tons of fruit per acre of vines, though some viticulturists—especially those who advocate very tight spacing—think it makes more sense to talk about pounds of fruit per vine, or even pounds of fruit per running foot of wire trellis. Generally, lower yields (by whatever measure) are associated with better wines; but Richard Smart, a prominent viticulturist, cautions that it is "the factors which created the low yields, and not the low yield itself" that are important. In this context Smart points especially to low vine vigor and its consequence, less opulent foliage.

In addition, lower yields are usually associated with more (and looser) clusters of smaller berries, which have a higher ratio of skin to juice. Smaller berries, often the consequence of spring drought and low soil moisture, normally translate into wines with deeper flavors and more concentration. In this respect, pinot noir appears to be much less forgiving of greed than most varieties, probably because it is ungenerously endowed, relative to other varieties, with anthocyanins, tannins, and other components that are flavor's sources in the grape. "At six tons per acre," explains Zach Berkowitz, one of Carneros's most experienced growers, "pinot noir makes an ordinary red wine. At three to four tons per acre, it makes a good wine. There is just no great pinot noir at six tons per acre." Many vintners would put the threshold number for good pinot much lower than four tons per acre. Yields at Hanzell, in Joseph Swan's estate vineyard, in Porter Creek's Hillside Vineyard, and in the older blocks at Chalone, to name just a few examples, can be as low as a single ton per acre. In Oregon, the statewide average for pinot noir is only two tons per acre. In truth, a low yield is not absolutely better than a somewhat higher yield, and the optimal yield for pinot depends on its site. Climate is a key determinant of what's possible. Vines can ripen more fruit successfully in warmer sites; in cooler sites, the growing season may end before a large crop can ripen fully. Conversely, a warmer site may ripen fruit too fast if the crop load is too light, risking high accumulations of sugar before the grapes have developed full flavor. And climate is not the only issue. Older vines produce less fruit than younger vines; thin, rocky soils are a parsimonious production medium; and some clones consistently underproduce others.

In some sites, especially when the vines are old, yield is naturally limited to just the right level. More often, especially in North America, where many vineyards have been planted in excessively fertile soils, yield is a matter of farming. Springtime pruning is the main tool, after budbreak and before bloom, to ensure that a finite number of buds is left on each vine shoot. But growers have a second chance later in the season. After the crop has set, they can cut some clusters off the vines, leaving them to rot on the ground. Most careful growers will remove imperfect clusters in this fashion, even if they are not making an effort to reduce yield, or remove clusters that seem to be lagging the ripening process, in an effort to achieve more uniform levels of ripeness when the time comes for harvest. These operations are scarcely scientific, however. Growers must guess, as winter ends and the vines wake up, whether spring wind, rain, hail, or late frost will interfere with bloom; and in summer they must guess again whether the growing season will end warm and dry, or cool and wet. They end up where they want to be only when they predict Mother Nature correctly.

Timing the Harvest Deciding when to wait, and when to pick the grapes, is either the last element of grape farming or the first element of winemaking, depending on one's point of view. If consumers were better educated by wine writers, they would understand that this choice is, after site itself, the single most important determinant of a wine's quality *and its style,* and that no variety is more marked by this choice than pinot noir. A generation ago, we are told, winemakers picked "by the numbers." More accurately, a generation ago, winemakers waited by the cellar door and left growers to pick by the numbers. The relevant numbers measure sugar (expressed in degrees on the Brix scale) and acid (expressed both as grams per liter and as a logarithmic value called pH). While there is no evidence that the contemporary winegrower has discarded any of the tools available to measure these numbers, there is now a tendency to wax poetic about the "art" of picking wine grapes, especially about picking pinot noir.

The most common formulation is to say that one is picking by taste, meaning that the berries ought to taste good—to be sweet rather than sour, and not too astringent. But at least a dozen other indicators are also said to be in play: whether the stems taste green or ripe, whether the seeds taste nutty, whether the grapes' skin is just beginning to pucker, whether berries can be pulled away from their stems easily, and more. Some winemakers say they have learned to "read flavors" from visual cues; see the profile of Flowers Vineyard and Winery in part II for an example. Others pay careful attention to the vine plant, looking for signs that it has finished its work for the year and has "nothing more to give." Cessation of shoot-tip growth and leaves with autumnal colors are typical end-of-season indicators.

In many situations, of course, winemakers cannot have their druthers, however such druthers are determined. Most Oregon winemakers will pick early to avoid imminent rain, even if the flavors or the numbers are not ideal. In high-latitude areas where long Indian summers are rare, grapes sometimes get picked less than optimally ripe, just because temperatures are falling fast and the growing season is over—the alternative could be to produce icewine. Conversely, in some parts of California, a brewing September or early October heat wave can launch the picking crews early—in this case the alternative could be wines with overripe, pruny flavors. And there are logistical complexities. Picking crews are not always available on the precise day they are desired, and vineyards do not always ripen evenly, necessitating multiple passes through the vines, days or even weeks apart. Typically, in most of California save for the Salinas Valley, the southern Central Coast, and the true

Sonoma Coast in cool years, and in Oregon in warm, dry years, most pinot is picked as and when the vintner chooses—unconstrained by Mother Nature.

Back now to the numbers. Grapes picked at less than 23 degrees Brix will produce a finished wine containing less than 12.5 percent alcohol, unless sugar is added to the must. Grapes picked much above 26 degrees Brix will yield a wine containing more than 14.4 percent alcohol, unless something is done to remove or dilute the alcohol. These numbers pretty much bracket the acceptable range for North American pinot noir. Pinots in the lower half of the range are usually perceived as lighter and sometimes as more elegant wines; those with more alcohol are usually perceived as bigger and richer. In Oregon it is perfectly permissible to add sugar, which reinforces the winemaker's inclination to pick early. In 1981, picks at 21 Brix were normal, to beat the rain; in 1984 "decent" wine was made from grapes "salvaged" at just 18.5 Brix. In 1986 and 1987, Oregon vintners picked pinot again at 21 Brix, but this time (unusually) to avoid overripeness owing to a California-style heat wave. In all cases, even with chaptalization, the resulting wines were near the lighter end of the pinot spectrum. André Tchelistcheff used to argue, in the 1970s, that Californians should pick pinot "at 22.5–23 Brix," to be sure of avoiding pinot's "tendency to raisin up." But in California today, and in other North American regions when the weather permits, the picking norm is 24 to 26 Brix, which is why many California pinots clock in above 14 percent alcohol. The Ojai Vineyard's Adam Tolmach argues that 24 is always "plenty" sugarwise, and that having to wait until the sugars reach 25.5 "is a clear sign that you are dealing with grapes planted in the wrong spot. . . . The coolest sites," he explains, "can be picked at lower sugars because they have had longer to mature on the vine, but conversely you can also wait longer, because you are not as concerned about escalating pH. But basically you have to pick the warmer climate pinots with too much sugar to achieve properly ripe flavors."

In fact, winegrowers rarely say how ripe the fruit is when they actually pick it. Some makers pick above 26 Brix, making the argument that "full flavor development" demands the late pick and the high sugars. To fix the resulting wine, however, requires voodoo. Water additions to dilute the must are common, though rarely admitted. In extreme cases, the wine may even be chemically or physically dealcoholized. This practice is so controversial that it is generally debated only off the record. Dealcoholization technologies usually involve resort to third parties, who will process a batch of wine, or of grape must, to remove part of the alcohol. Only a few firms do this, and they are *very* tight-lipped about their clients. On the one hand, it is clear that "bigger" wines—whether pinot noir or some other variety—show better in comparative tastings and are rewarded with higher scores, and this is often *simply* because of their size, and not because they are more flavorful. This tendency has driven many Oregon makers, who displayed a stylistic preference for elegant, medium-weight wines in the 1980s, to press the picking envelope when they can and employ their own forms of voodoo to obtain more concentration. On the other hand, some winemakers have begun to worry that fruit really is getting picked too ripe. Part of the problem, according to some viticulturists, is that younger, healthier vineyards, impeccably farmed and planted to virus-free vines, actually ripen sugarwise faster than older, virused selections, throwing the high sugar versus full flavor dichotomy into bold relief. The alleged ability of Dijon clones to produce fuller flavors at lower sugars does not seem to compensate. No less than Tim Mondavi is concerned. "We don't sell leaves, vines, or grapes," he says, "we sell wine. I worry that we are harvesting wine that would be better characterized as port."

Full Flavor Development "Full flavor development" has become such a mantra among pinot growers during the past decade that it makes sense to pause briefly to be sure we understand what is meant. The phrase *full flavor development* is often used interchangeably with the terms *physiological ripeness* and *physiological maturity,* though Stag's Leap's Warren Winiarski—not a pinot grower by any means, but incontestably successful as a vintner—prefers to define full physiological ripeness as "equal outcomes in all clusters," overcoming what he calls "the vine's natural tendency to create a hierarchy for clusters and ripeness." The full flavor idea is that ripeness as measured by classical metrics associated with sugar and pH can sometimes precede ripeness as measured by the berry's color, texture, and flavor. And flavor, which ought to be the key, is actually tricky, because there is no clear and simple connection between berry flavors and the flavors that emerge in the finished wine.

It is important to realize that "full flavors"—whatever this really means—are very much on the palate of the taster. In the first place, when several producers share fruit from a single, more or less homogeneous block of a single vineyard—as, for example, at Bien Nacido and Pisoni—these producers typically pick on quite different dates, because their definitions of full flavor are not the same. At Bien Nacido, Lane Tanner is famous for being an early picker; other vintners say they *begin* to watch the fruit after Tanner has *finished* picking. By contrast, Siduri is a notoriously late picker, especially at Pisoni. In the second place, some flavors give way to others as the ripening process proceeds. Black fruit flavors typically emerge after red fruit flavors, for example, though *terroir* can make grapes taste redder or blacker independently of their degree of ripeness. Also, some flavors are more intense than others, and more intense flavors and aromas can easily overpower those of lesser "size" or intensity. Very deep fruit and strong spice can cover up, sometimes permanently, more delicate floral properties. Compost can cover up mushrooms and underbrush. James Hall (see the Patz & Hall profile in part II) argues persuasively that pure and simple flavor development is overrated as a picking criterion. Since most late-season flavor development is simply a perception of declining acids, "allowing more flavors to be noticed," it follows that "most vineyards that are picked only on flavors are almost always picked overripe." The bottom line: full flavor development is not objective or absolute; it reflects a vintner's stylistic preferences. In the worst case, it can even reflect a vintner's appetite for critical acclaim, or his view of consumers' tastes.

THE VATTING

Vatting, or *cuvaison,* is not familiar terminology for most consumers. Derived from vat or *cuve*—the vessel in which wine is born—these terms denote the entire process of red-wine making, from the time the picked berries are dumped into the box or bin or tank in which they will ferment until the moment the new wine is pressed off the residual skins, stems, and seeds. The length of the vatting stage is the sum of the time allowed for prefermentation maceration; the duration of the active, alcoholic fermentation; and any time dedicated to extended (i.e., postfermentation) maceration. The key business of the vatting is, of course, the transformation of sugar into alcohol. But vatting choices and vat management are also crucial determinants of a wine's size, style, and structure. Vatting choices, acting on the fruit, determine what gets extracted from the grapes in the background while sugar is being converted into alcohol. Color, density, and texture all flow from these choices, which predominantly involve time, temperature, and manipulation.

Whole-Cluster Fermentation Before the vatting can begin, winemakers must decide what goes into the vat. Specifically, they must decide if any portion of the fruit enters the vat as whole grape clusters or if the whole lot is run through a machine that separates berries from stems. The arguments in favor of whole clusters are that when stems are retained during fermentation, they add important spicy aromatics and complexity to the wine; and that the presence of stems during fermentation slows the process down, which has other advantages. Patz & Hall's James Hall goes further, arguing that in some vineyards, such as Pisoni, some whole clusters can "bring out" bright fruit flavors. The arguments against whole clusters are that stems, in most of North America, are rarely "ripe," do not taste good, and impart either green flavors or harsh tannins, or both, to the wine. It is widely alleged, largely without evidence, that stems are routinely riper in Burgundy; in fact, Burgundians argue just as passionately as North Americans about the advantages and disadvantages of stem use. North Americans have also argued the matter for decades, sometimes even to the point of destemming the fruit and then adding back some fraction of the removed stems into the fermentor. In the dark days of bad pinot, when winemakers were actually *pumping* a fruit and juice mix between the destemmer-crusher and the fermentor, the only way to include stems in fermentations was to chop them up and add them back; whole stems and clusters would have clogged the pumps. André Tchelistcheff is said to have advocated stem utilization in the 1970s, but in a 1977 interview he was guarded, arguing that "stems alone are not the answer," though "all Burgundy winemakers use [some] stems."

For the moment, the pendulum has swung against whole clusters in North America. Most makers destem completely or use only a small fraction of whole clusters, and many say they have cut back over time. Some very fine pinots are made with 100 percent whole clusters, however, and the best of these (Broadley and Brewer-Clifton, for example) do not, in my experience, exhibit especially aggressive tannins or allegedly telltale greenness.

Prefermentation Maceration However the stem issue is settled, the winemaker's next consequential choice is how long the fruit should macerate, in increasing amounts of its own juice, before the alcoholic fermentation begins. This is sometimes called prefermentation maceration; more commonly, it is just known as cold soaking. During a cold soak, water is the only functioning solvent, leaching what it can of color and flavors from the grapes. Because water is a less aggressive solvent than alcohol, it is argued that conducting part of the extractive process with water only maximizes the extraction of "good stuff" while minimizing the extraction of harsh or undesirable elements. Short cold soaks occur naturally and almost inevitably, as long as the grapes are cold when they arrive on the crushpad or the cellar is kept chilled, and they have always been part of the process of making pinot noir worldwide. In the 1980s, however, a Lebanon-born enologist named Guy Accad gained some notoriety in Burgundy for advocating longer maceration times, not primarily by keeping the must cold, but by adding strong doses of sulfur dioxide to forestall fermentation. His objective, in large measure, was to deepen the color of the wines. By the time Accad's advice rubbed off in North America, the sulfur dioxide had largely been replaced by enforced cold, using either the chilling jackets on the fermentation tanks or, in lower-tech scenarios, by layering dry ice among the grapes. At present, nearly all American pinot makers take some steps to ensure that fermentation does not start until there have been at least two or three days of prefermentation maceration, and some take steps to extend the process for longer periods. Every possible variation on the theme is someone's favorite, and the impact is primarily stylistic, not qualitative. In my experience, longer cold soaks and shorter active fermentations are usually associated with gentler extractions and more modestly framed wines, but very long cold soaks can lead to very fruit-forward wines; in extreme cases the wines can even take on a tutti-frutti character.

Other front-end choices involve changing, or not, the natural ratio of solids to juice, either by removing juice (called bleeding, or *saignée*) or by adding water; and changing the ratio of acid to sugar. *Saignée* operations are rare, and generally counterproductive, in California, and they increasingly have a bad reputation in Burgundy. In Oregon they occur a bit more frequently, especially if the end of the growing season is wet. Adding water is a more common practice in California, though rarely admitted; see the discussion above about timing the harvest. Adding acid is fairly common in slightly warmer regions, and in vineyards in which the grapes have naturally high levels of potassium, but it is controversial. Makers like Merry Edwards insist that acid additions are the necessary handmaiden of very ripe fruit. Others, like Adam Tolmach of The Ojai Vineyard, do not like the flavors imparted by added acid and avoid whole clusters (which increase the pH of grape must) specifically to avoid having to acidify.

Fermentation and Extraction The first question about fermenting pinot noir is how to get the process started. Basically, there are two choices: rely on the native vineyard and cellar yeasts, or inoculate the must with cultivated yeast. Strong believers in the minimalist, "do no harm" school of pinot making cleave to reliance on resident yeasts. They argue that resident yeasts work more slowly, and that slower fermentations produce more complex wines. Tandem founder Greg La Follette goes much further. He maintains that a good fermentation is a "multiorganism event" in which several "generations" of different yeasts each do their bit, die off, and are succeeded by another generation. Not only does this process produce complexity and personality in the wine; it also improves the wine's ratio of fructose to glucose. "Struggling" yeast cells, straining to do their piece of the fermentation before they die off and hand the torch, will eat glucose first; flourishing yeast consumes fructose more easily. A high-fructose wine "feels more generous in the mouth," according to La Follette; glycoproteins manufactured by the aforementioned "struggling yeasts" also make the wine feel more viscous in the mouth. The case for laboratory yeast is usually built on risk reduction. Laboratory yeasts have predictable behaviors. And because they act faster, fewer "bad" things can happen while the little organisms are waking up.

In the end, the winemakers must be guided by what Joseph Swan's Rod Berglund calls an "invisible hand." They weigh risk and benefit and decide how much of each is comfortable. Many makers, in fact, do a few lots each way, use half the recommended concentration of laboratory yeast, or let resident yeast get the action started before adding "help" and "insurance" from a can.

How fast grapes ferment and what gets extracted from the skins simultaneously are largely functions of temperature and manipulation. Generally, the higher the temperature and the greater the manipulation, the greater the extraction—of color, tannin, and flavor—and the "bigger" the resulting wine. Traditionally, in Burgundy, fermentation temperature has tended to set itself, based on the cellar's ambient temperature, the percentage of whole clusters, the size of the vat, and the type of yeast used. The impact of ambient temperature is obvious. All other things being equal, larger vats, having greater mass, build higher temperatures; and high percentages of whole clusters tend to slow both temperature and fermentation speed.

In recent years, as jacketed vats and other thermal devices have appeared on both sides of the Atlantic, giving makers control over temperature, debate has erupted over optimal temperature. In the 1970s, very cool fermentations were briefly in vogue. It was thought that lower temperatures favored freshness and fruit flavors, while higher temperatures yielded a fatter wine at the expense of aromas. André Tchelistcheff suggested a maximum temperature of 70 to 75 degrees Fahrenheit, arguing that "excess heat burns [pinot], combusts [it], and gives [it] complete neutrality." But experiments conducted at the University of California, Davis, at the end of the 1970s showed that tasting panels preferred wines that had been fermented at 85 to 92 degrees, and Ken Burnap, at Santa Cruz Mountain Vineyard, championed hot fermentations, arguing that pinot noir "is not meant to be fruity; it is meant to be a big, heavy, gutsy, slightly volatile wine." Don Blackburn, a Dijon-trained winemaker who recently launched the Talacoat label, developed the view that heat gives "more color and more stable color, and flavors so focused that you can see them in 3-D." He says, "It is a myth that you blow off flavor with heat." Nowadays most makers try to maintain relatively high fermentation temperatures, though a few say they have recently "backed off" a few degrees to lessen extraction.

Fermentation generates carbon dioxide, of course, which pushes grape skins, seeds, and stems (if any) to the top of the vat, where they form what is called a cap. A dry cap is both dangerous (it can harbor vinegar-producing bacteria) and useless, because color and flavor cannot be extracted from a perpetually floating cap. Winemakers generally use one of two methods to keep the cap in contact with the juice: they pump juice over the cap, or they plunge the cap with their hands, feet, a tamping device called a *pige,* or a mechanically assisted plunger. So-called rotary fermentation—in which the entire vat is moved mechanically—is another approach, but it is rarely used in making pinot noir. Some makers are now working with mesh devices that are inserted at the top of a vat and left in place throughout the fermentation, effectively holding the cap permanently under the surface level of the juice, a method called submerged-cap fermentation. Plunging, usually called punching down in North America, is the traditional Burgundian approach to making pinot noir, but it requires an open-top tank that is not too deep.

Whether it is better to punch down than to pump over is still a matter for some debate, however. Some makers do a bit of both. Larger-volume producers like Gallo of Sonoma, Rodney Strong, and Kent Rasmussen (for his Ramsay label) feel they have no choice but to pump over, or to use rotaries. A few makers argue that punchdowns are needlessly labor-intensive and that pumpovers work just fine. Overwhelmingly, however, North American makers have elected to respect the traditional Burgundian method—one way or another, they punch the cap down. Most believe punchdowns are gentler, achieve better extraction of better flavors, minimize oxidation, and have the least chance of crushing pits, which contain the berries' bitterest tannins. Label references to *méthode à l'ancienne* or "traditional method" usually refer to manual punching.

After Fermentation The end of the vatting stage is the pressing. The most common choice is to press when the must is, more or less, dry—that is to say, when all the grapes' sugar has been converted into alcohol. A few makers like to press a bit earlier, so that the tail end of the alcoholic fermentation is postponed until after pressing and can take place in a barrel. If a large percentage of whole clusters was retained, the fermentation usually cannot finish until after pressing. More commonly, makers leave the juice and skins together for a few days after the fermentation is complete. This option, called long vatting, extended maceration, or postfermentation maceration, used to be avoided like the plague. Tchelistcheff, in 1977, called it "too dangerous." The Burgundians generally eschew more than two or three days of extended maceration, arguing that the wine can lose color and, as Christophe Tupinier describes it, "veer toward more evolved aromas like *eaux-de-vie* fruit and chocolate." Proponents believe, on the contrary, that long vatting helps to polymerize tannins, which makes them seem softer in the finished wine. Within the past decade, some Burgundians have begun to experiment with *hot* postfermentation maceration, raising the must temperature to about 100 degrees for 24 hours after the end of alcoholic fermentation. French reports suggest that this process can increase tannins and deepen color, and that these properties will persist as the finished wine ages. As far as I know, this technique has yet to be adopted in North America.

ELEVAGE

Getting newly made wine into barrels and tending it for a year or two until it is ready for bottling make up the process the French call *élevage,* or "raising" the wine, much as one raises a child or a dog. To start *élevage,* a few staunch traditionalists move their wine directly from the press into barrels, retaining a large percentage of the fermentation's leftovers. This stuff, called gross lees, is mostly spent yeast. Makers who keep it say their wines go to barrel "dirty." More often, makers allow the pressed wine to settle in a tank for one or several days so that the gross lees can fall to the bottom and be substantially eliminated. The case for retaining gross lees is usually made in terms of greater complexity in the finished wine. The spent yeast cells are said to interact with the wine and the barrels' wood surfaces to create complex flavors and aromas.

The second step in *élevage* is the wine's secondary, or malolactic, "fermentation." Since malolactic fermentation (ML) produces carbon dioxide but no alcohol, it is really better understood as natural deacidification, whose main function is to transform malic acid into lactic acid, which is less tart. Some makers like to make ML happen early and quickly, adding cultured malolactic bacteria to the must as soon as the wine is in barrel, or even before. Others rely on resident malolactic bacteria to get the job done and are content to wait patiently until it happens of its own accord. Left to its own devices, ML may not occur until the cellar warms up in the spring after the vintage.

The gentle-handling mantra is also important in *élevage.* Most red varieties are manipulated aggressively in the cellar, moved often from one barrel to another or from barrel to tank and back to barrel, in the interest of keeping the wine clean, eliminating "off" odors, and softening it. This practice is called racking. But pinot noir tolerates such handling poorly, rapidly losing character, color, and flavor. At worst, it can oxidize visibly, turning from red to terra-cotta or brown. This was certainly the greatest problem with pinots made in the late 1960s and early 1970s: they were pumped, splashed, and manipulated into hapless mediocrity, mostly during *élevage.* Nowadays there is almost universal agreement that pinot, once in barrel, is best left alone. Unless they have an especially troublesome lot, most makers rack pinot once at most, usually after ML has finished, and they move the wine from barrel to tank only when necessary to make a final blend or as a preface to bottling. When they do move pinot, most makers avoid conventional pumps. An ingenious wandlike device called the Bulldog Pup (Pup, not pump)—invented about 1980 by Don Othman, who now runs Kynsi Winery in Edna Valley—is used instead, effectively "pushing" the wine out of the barrel with the aid of compressed nitrogen, argon, or air. This method, explains Oregon's David Adelsheim, "helps to preserve the long-string phenolic structure of the wine and reduces the chance of oxidation." Cristom's Steve Doerner explains the underlying logic of the minimal-movement approach: "Since pinot noir starts out as a delicate wine without a strong backbone, every time you do something to it, you strip more of the body out of it. So if you are striving for a rich, complex wine, the less you handle it, the closer you will come."

The centerpiece of modern *élevage,* of course, is the oak barrel. Hugely convenient containers, barrels have been used for more than two millennia to store and transport various liquids, including wine. Their shape makes them relatively easy to move, even when they are full, and a barrel's bilge collects fermentation detritus naturally. Burgundy's version of the wine barrel, called a *pièce,* is a wee bit squatter and trivially larger than the Bordelais *barrique* and is coopered from staves that are substantially thicker. One *pièce* has a capacity of 228 liters, which translates almost exactly to 25 cases containing a dozen 750-milliliter bottles apiece. Until the mid twentieth century, *pièces* were coopered primarily from the wood of Burgundian forests and were kept in service for decades—or as long as a village cooper could maintain each barrel's physical integrity. The great Burgundies from the 1929, 1937, 1945, 1949, and 1959 vintages were made and sold in more or less well-aged barrels, even at top estates like Domaine de la Romanée-Conti. Beginning in the 1960s, however, Burgundy's *négociants* and vignerons noticed that *new* barrels seemed to have positive effects on pinot noir. They helped to clarify the wines, stabilized their color, and softened the tannins. Winemakers who could afford it stuffed their cellars with new and nearly new barrels, creating a windfall business for coopers and a huge supply of old, disused *pièces,* many of which finished their lives, sawn in half, as patio planters.

The demand for new oak then drove coopers to seek wood much farther afield than local forests. Burgundian coopers ventured west to the forests of central France and east to the Vosges Mountains, between Lorraine and Alsace. In the space of two decades, wine barrels, which had hitherto been nothing more than containers and units of sale, were transformed into *environments* in which newly fermented wines were finished and *flavored.* The source of the wood and the cooperage techniques became elements of a new connoisseurship among winemakers, and the stamp of new oak became an inseparable part of the profile associated with fine red wine in Burgundy and elsewhere.

In North America before the 1960s, small oak cooperage was virtually unknown. Red wine was made not in small barrels, but in large and more or less inert tanks—usually of redwood. The exceptions to this rule were Martin Ray, who is said to have bought Burgundy barrels from Louis Latour as early as the 1940s, and Hanzell, which purchased barrels from Tonnellerie Sirugue, in Nuits-St.-Georges, beginning in 1956. In the 1960s, Robert Mondavi, Louis Martini, and Chalone all began to import French barrels and to mimic the new French barrel protocol. Like the contemporaneous French, these vintners used barrels for just three or four vintages before discarding them, marking their wines very perceptibly with flavors derived from oak and char.

In the years since, winemakers on both sides of the Atlantic have developed considerable expertise with barrels and strong preferences about wood sources, coopers, precooperage stave-drying times, and just how much "toast" is applied to the barrel's inner surface during its manufacture. Today, barrel selection is a matter of seasoning wine, in much the same way that cooking on a cedar plank flavors a side of salmon or grilling over mesquite charcoal imparts distinctive tastes to meats. Most North American pinot makers say they prefer French to American or Hungarian oak, citing subtler flavors, less "balsamic" character, and "prettier" matches between barrels and wine. Among French oaks, however, preferences vary. Barrels coopered from the forest of Tronçais, in the Allier, are said to have the tightest grain and therefore to mark the wine with the subtlest stamp of wood. Many winemakers say that the tight grain typical of the Allier means that oak flavors are leached into the wine more gradually, lessening the impact of new oak in the first vintage but increasing it in the second, third, and fourth. Other forests in central France are said to impart floral aromatics to the wine. Some winemakers like Vosges wood, taken from the mountains between Alsace and Lorraine, for flavors said to be sweet or "meaty." From all regions, barrels coopered from staves that have first been air-dried over three winters, rather than two, are more subtly influential and less likely to make the wine taste as if it had been kissed with walnut shells. Heavily toasted barrels impart more flavors of smoke and charred wood than do lightly or moderately toasted versions. Merry Edwards, in an opinion piece written for the Vintners Club in 1988, said the "small Burgundian cooper" she first patronized shaped his barrels by soaking the staves in a giant cauldron, "so that there was zero charring." The cooper, who was not named, later converted to a brazier but still generated "a very low amount of char." Edwards added, "I always say I like my toast in the morning with jam, not in my chardonnay."

Two cooperages—Burgundy-based François Frères and Bordeaux-based Séguin Moreau—now divide the lion's share of the North American barrel market. A third, Tonnellerie Remond, has focused on high-end pinot noir as its special niche, but at least a dozen others are used in substantial quantities by pinot makers. Although a few producers (see the profiles of Williams Selyem and Hanzell, for example) buy all their barrels from a single cooper, creating an association between cooperage and house style, most prefer to spread the qualitative and supply-related risks associated with natural products across multiple coopers. Many argue that a mix of barrels from several makers (or several forests) helps to add complexity to their wines and that an assortment of barrels should be regarded as a blending tool.

Winemakers honestly disagree about the most flattering combinations of wines and barrels, and many experiment ceaselessly. Some "power winemakers" display addictions to heavily toasted new barrels, using 100 percent new wood each year if they can afford it. In extreme cases, they even use "200 percent new wood," racking wine from one set of new barrels to a second, as yet unused, set after malolactic fermentation is over. These gyrations are rarely appropriate for pinot noir. At the other extreme, imitating Burgundy's prewar practices, The Eyrie Vineyards is still using some barrels dating from its first vintages in the early 1970s.

Now that the use of young, small oak cooperage has become virtually universal both in Burgundy and in North America, one is forced to taste red Sancerre, or pinots made in Switzerland's Chablais Vaudois, to rediscover the taste of traditional Burgundy and of most North American pinots made before the late 1960s. This can be a very instructive exercise, especially when the same wine is made in both barrel-raised and tank-raised styles. In my experience, barrel-raised wine often displays more charm when it is young, while tank-raised wine sometimes evolves more elegantly.

FINISHING THE WINE

Thanks to several American wine writers and well-respected importers of European wines, the *last* steps taken by winemakers before the finished wine is bottled have been more closely scrutinized than any of the winemaking choices discussed in the preceding pages. These last steps are fining and filtration.

Fining involves the introduction of a substance, such as egg white, that attaches to particulate matter in the wine and drags it out. The main reasons to fine are to clarify a wine that is stubbornly hazy at the end of *élevage* and to take the edge off harsh tannins, though many winemakers think the latter use is actually futile.

Filtration is what it sounds like: passing wine through some kind of screen, membrane, sheet, pad, or cartridge to strain out undesirable stuff, including bits of detritus from fermentation, yeast, or bacteria. It is another way to achieve visual clarity, but it can also serve to eliminate organic material that poses a risk of spoilage in the bottle. This can be a significant issue if the wine contains any residual sugar (which could referment), brettanomyces yeast (which could bloom in the bottle and manifest itself as strong farmyard aromas), or lactic acid bacteria (which could induce out-and-out spoilage). The downside of filtration is that some good stuff inevitably disappears with the bad. Critics assert that any filtration can rob the wine of aroma, flavor, texture, or color and impair its ability to age. Fred Scherrer (see the "Producers to Watch" section at the end of part II) argues in favor of retaining the "colloidal material built during vinification" for its importance as the finished wine ages. No less a critic than Robert M. Parker Jr. has emerged as an implacable enemy of filtration, claiming "credit" if there are now several hundred producers in Burgundy who *do not* filter their wines, versus a "handful" when he began writing at the end of the 1970s. The pinots made at Beaux Frères in Oregon, which Parker co-owns, are said to be unfiltered. Berkeley-based importer Kermit Lynch has championed unfiltered wines relentlessly and has more than once refused to consummate purchases of lots that were filtered by the vigneron against his contrary instructions and prior agreement.

Wine writers take sides, too. Andrew Jefford, writing in *Decanter* in 2002, characterized filtration as analogous to "insisting your child only ever leaves the house in handcuffs, just in case he or she does anything naughty while they're [*sic*] out." From this quarter, hair-raising tales of wines "ruined" by filtration—"black" wines turned to rosé, for example—are legion. This testimony has led many consumers to assume that unfiltered wines are invariably better than their filtered cousins and that the difference can be profound when the object of filtration is a "sensitive" variety like pinot noir. In their turn, producers (especially producers of pinot noir) have responded to consumer perception by trumpeting "unfiltered" (or sometimes "unfined and unfiltered") on their labels, and a number of pinot makers have become skittish about discussing filtration with consumers and wine writers.

In the course of the research for this book, I asked every producer if she or he practiced filtration. A substantial minority claimed never to filter. A larger number hedged, saying that they filter "rarely," "occasionally," or "as necessary." Some opened Socratic discussions, asking in their turn what *kind* of filtration should be considered *real* filtration, intimating that "coarse" or "gentle" filtrations should not be considered filtrations in the narrow (and presumably pejorative) sense of the term. More than a few makers argued that filtration is just one of a winemaker's tools, the use of which it makes no sense to deny. Only a handful admitted to filtering routinely and enthusiastically. Kent Rasmussen maintained that filtration "always" improves pinot in the long run; Domaine Carneros's Eileen Crane asserted boldly that "filtration is a very good thing." Larry Brooks, who made many unfiltered pinots in his years at Acacia, said filtration is now his "default decision" because so many unfiltered pinots (in his experience) developed problems in bottle. Brooks admitted that "you always lose a little something with filtration," usually "aromatics and flavor" rather than "structure," but said that these losses are relatively minor if the filtration is "well done." In Brooks's definition, "well done" could mean cross-flow filtration if the producer can afford the technology; otherwise it means that the wine makes only a single pass through a cellulose pad filter that has been neutralized first. (As far as I know, among North American pinot makers, only Saintsbury and Robert Sinskey have so far invested in cross-flow filtration equipment.) As an alternative, Brooks conceded that it is possible to devise a low-risk nonfiltration regimen for pinot, including a high-tannin, high-alcohol recipe, yeast that would take the wine bone dry, long barrel time with little new oak, and a generous application of sulfur dioxide before bottling. "But why," he queried rhetorically, "would you want to bend your entire winemaking style simply to avoid filtration?"

If one had to discern a consensus on the basis of what pinot makers *say* about filtration, one would probably conclude that most practitioners believe that, in the absence of a good reason to filter, there is a powerful reason *not* to. But there is ample anecdotal evidence that many makers, bowing to their perception of consumers' opinions, do not behave as they say.

ISSUES WITH PINOT NOIR

The Hierarchy of Importance Asked to rank all the choices they make, from the time grapes arrive at the winery's crushpad to the time finished wine is put into bottles, in terms of impact on the wine's quality and its style, most winemakers argue that the front-end choices are vastly more significant than the choices made later on in the process. Thus matters like sorting and destemming, along with various parameters of fermentation, are ahead of barrels and filtration in the hierarchy of importance. Front-end choices often constrain the winemaker's options downstream. For example, a fermentation that is highly extractive of tannins drives some winemakers to fine the wine before bottling it.

Gentle Handling All successful makers argue forcefully that whenever there is a choice between a rough or aggressive procedure and a gentle one, or between doing something and doing nothing, the better choice for pinot noir is the less-intrusive course. This perspective is peculiar to pinot noir among red varieties. Cabernet, zinfandel, and syrah all tolerate more intervention and processing than pinot, presumably because as grapes they all contain vastly more "stuffing." Some makers of these other varieties argue that they actually *benefit* from being "beaten up"; others maintain that even cabernet would prefer to be treated like pinot noir, but does not suffer miserably if and when it is abused. A few, like Fred Scherrer, say that their winemaking is now "gradual" and "gentle" for all the red varieties they make. Scherrer asserts that he is "nonplussed how a gentle hand with zinfandel is ignored, and how cabernet sauvignon ignores it, yet with pinot it is applauded."

Gentle handling has many manifestations. Whole grapes reflect a gentler approach than crushed grapes. A gravity-flow winery, or a winery in which forklifts are used to mimic gravity, enables gentler handling than do pumps. The gentlest press is the best press. Leaving wine in the same barrel for its entire *élevage,* or pushing it gently between barrels using inert gas or compressed air, is better than frequent racking. Ideally, no fining or filtration is preferable to any form of physical clarification. And so on. What wine writer Bob Thompson calls "more-is-better winemaking," much in vogue during the 1970s, is the opposite of gentle handling and probably responsible for most of the bad pinot noir made at that time. "There is a reason," explains Acacia's founding winemaker, Larry Brooks, "why winemakers should go on vacation in the winter. If they are not around, they are not tempted to intervene."

Small versus Large Producers Pinot noir appears to be the great democratizer among wine grape varieties. It is made equally well by very small *garagiste* producers, using nothing fancier than plastic-lined fruit bins as fermentors, and by very large firms, working with high technology and cellars full of stainless steel. This truism seems to have been with us for at least two decades. In 1980, *Connoisseurs' Guide* observed that while "widely distributed producers such as Beaulieu, Robert Mondavi, Fetzer, Kenwood, Phelps, Burgess and Firestone are in the quality pinot class . . . still the excitement in pinot noir has been substantially the province of the small scale producer." The *Guide* argued that the small producer's "patience, interest and marketing" were assets in offering "small lots of wine that capture distinctive varietal nuances"—whether from a small vineyard "or even a section of a vineyard." The natural affinity for pinot noir of small producers with small lots of wine is an inescapable piece of the variety's story in North America—from Martin Ray, Hanzell, and Joseph Swan to Williams Selyem, Littorai, and Siduri. It is also in stark contrast to the trend for other varieties, with which the stellar successes have usually been painted on a larger canvas—at least until the advent of cult cabernets.

Boutique producers are largely responsible for the emergence of vineyard-designated pinots, made in small lots, though a few tiny landless operations (Hamacher and McKinlay in Oregon, for example) have staked their reputations on well-constructed blends instead. Larger-scale producers have tended to dominate in the blended wine arena for the obvious reason that they can assemble large palettes of blending components with relative ease. Even so, the market success of prominent small producers has driven larger houses, one after another, to launch one or more special bottlings of vineyard- or block-designated wine. In fact, pinot noir more often raises the obverse question: whether it can be made really well on a really large scale. Tim Mondavi makes a good case that large wineries ought to work hard on the best possible pinot for the simple reason that large wineries have the resources to experiment; La Crema has tried to mimic small-scale winemaking on a larger scale. Doing so means maintaining large farms of small-size fermentors, along with armies of cellar rats to tend them and the huge barrel rooms that follow; but there are practical limits on the number of vessels any one winemaker can follow effectively.

Blending Pinot with Other Varieties While the reputation of red Bordeaux was built unabashedly on blending three or four or five varieties, Burgundy aspired, at least from the fourteenth century, to make its red wine from pinot noir and nothing else. *Aspired* is the right word here, because the record is actually imperfect. In the first place, Burgundy's vineyards before the middle of the nineteenth century were usually field blends of pinot noir with its pink and yellow mutations, namely pinot gris and pinot blanc, and cofermentations of all three were standard winemaking practice. Blends of pinot noir and gamay also have a long history in Burgundy, and Bourgogne Passetoutgrains is still made today, even by good producers. In addition, for most of the past two hundred years, some mourvèdre from Bandol, grenache from the Languedoc, or syrah from the Rhône (or some combination of these) has now and then been added to red Burgundies by numerous makers to give the wines more color and deeper flavors than one could squeeze from pinot by itself. Such practices were not specifically illegal until the *appellation d'origine contrôlée* laws were promulgated in the 1930s.

In California, even though allegedly varietal wine has been the object of considerable interest from connoisseurs since the end of Prohibition and most premium wine is sold today under varietal names, a great deal of this so-called varietal wine actually contains a hefty percentage of something else. In America this practice is quite legal. Most pinot noirs made in California during the 1960s and 1970s seem to have been blends of some sort. According to Robert Gorman *(Gorman on Premium California Wines),* Charles Krug, Wente Brothers, and Sonoma Vineyards "traditionally made their pinot noirs with some Petite Sirah blended in," giving the Napa-based wines a "very nice Rhône-type character" but producing "surprisingly stylish" pinots at Sonoma Vineyards, owing (in Gorman's opinion) to the cooler, Russian River valley origins of the petite sirah. Bob Thompson claims to prefer early Martini pinots made with an addition of Pinot St. George to Martini's later vintages, which were made from 100 percent pinot noir. Pedroncelli pinots from the 1960s have a good reputation; however, John Pedroncelli reports that they were invariably made with a substantial addition of zinfandel. The early Beaulieu "Beaumont" pinot noirs are said to have been "produced exclusively from pinot noir grapes," though Beaulieu blended pinot, gamay, petite sirah, and mondeuse to produce the wine sold as Burgundy.

Nowadays, only a few serious producers will admit to playing with less than pure pinot, though some inexpensive pinot noirs contain as much as 25 percent something else. Au Bon Climat's Santa Barbara County bottling is a blend of up to 25 percent mondeuse with pinot noir; Lane Tanner's short-lived Santa Maria Valley cuvée contained 5 percent syrah "to make it different"; Rodney Strong pinots range between 2 percent and 5 percent syrah; Nalle Vineyards blends less than 5 percent zinfandel into its tiny production of Russian River valley pinot noir; a few bottlings here and there contain tiny percentages of pinot meunier. More interesting, perhaps, than these instances of introducing other red varieties into final blends of pinot noir is the process of cofermenting pinot noir with white varieties. Several makers add the lees of a white-wine fermentation (most often chardonnay) to vattings of pinot, sometimes for flavor enhancement and sometimes to tame aggressive tannins. Larry Brooks has gone further. He has revived the old Burgundian practice of cofermenting whole white grapes with pinot, using between 5 percent and 8 percent pinot gris in several cuvées of Campion Wines' Edna Valley, Santa Lucia Highlands, and Carneros pinot noir in 2000, 2001, and 2002, arguing that the technique heightens the wines' aromas without compromising color in any way.

Outside of California, the exceptions are even fewer. Allegations that many American pinots are adulterated with other grapes persist but are impossible to confirm, and they seem increasingly unlikely. Much of the historical impetus for blending, both in Burgundy and in California, was to compensate for pinot's natural shortcomings—low concentrations of tannins and anthocyanins especially—and its tendency to oxidize prematurely, even before bottling. With better viticulture generating better fruit with deeper colors and plenty of tannin, along with simple adjustments to winemaking that overcome the pressure toward oxidization, there really is no longer much reason to blend other varieties into pinot noir. Nearly all contemporary producers, in fact, argue the contrary: they hold that blending pinot noir is anathema, since pinot's delicacy is easily overpowered, or denatured, by even small additions of other varieties.

Is Pinot Noir Hard to Make? Pinot noir's reputation as a hard grape to grow has been addressed in chapter 1. Its equally stubborn and pervasive reputation for being hard to make has more obscure roots, but seems largely tied to efforts outside Burgundy to make wines that resemble, match, or even outshine the best that Burgundy can do. Within Burgundy, most makers have little or no experience with any other red grape, so the problem set associated with pinot noir is accepted with reasonable equanimity. In North America, however, during the last quarter of the twentieth century, pinot developed a reputation as the bad boy of red grapes, challenging winemakers like no other variety, and regularly visiting worry, insomnia, dyspepsia, and even heartbreak on hapless pioneers. André Tchelistcheff told *Connoisseurs' Guide* as early as 1977 that "Pinot Noir is a big problem." The *Guide* then contrasted "recent successes" with cabernet, chardonnay, and even white riesling with pinot, which was characterized as "one of the last frontiers in California winemaking."

For two decades, winemakers have been happy to confirm and embellish this characterization, cataloging lists of bad pinots, reciting the names of producers who have given up and moved on, and assuring everyone that, at best, pinot was and is capricious, irregular, and unpredictable. Colorful contrasts between pinot making and cabernet making have become ubiquitous in American winemaking lore. Talacoat's Don Blackburn likens cabernet to a "tapestry quilt." Pinot noir, he says, "is more like jumping off a high board." Wine writers, naturally attracted to a good American story of intrinsic difficulty, pain, persistence, and hard-won success, have forged a mythic, operatic score around pinot. "Not easy to grow or make into good wine anywhere," intoned Charles Olken in the *Los Angeles Times* as recently as 2002, citing its "caprice" as an explanation for its relatively high cost. A "difficult grape to grow and ferment," said Frank Prial in the *New York Times* in the same year. This reputation is a bit hard to square with the guidelines for making good pinot, embraced by nearly all of the best producers, which (as outlined above) are founded largely on minimalist handling and on doing nothing whenever possible. It is also hard to square with the inescapable fact that very good pinots are now made by vintners who have had little prior experience with the allegedly tricky grape.

In fact, pinot has at least one fundamental chemical peculiarity: its anthocyanins are not linked to glucose units as they are in most other red varieties. This peculiarity is responsible for pinot's strong propensity to oxidize, and therefore to lose color, as well as for its low tolerance for sulfur dioxide, which is very commonly used in winemaking as a preservative and disinfectant. Because the different chemical structures of grape varieties were not well understood until fairly recently, the pioneering North Americans who worked with pinot noir in the period between the introduction of modern winemaking technology in the 1960s and the reintroduction of low-tech approaches to winemaking in the 1980s did in fact suffer case after case of frustration, exasperation, and spoiled or mediocre results. But in the past 15 years, the previously elusive truth has been widely recognized. Gentle handling, minimal manipulation, and a generally noninterventionist mind-set really are the pinot maker's staunchest allies, and they do minimize the liabilities that are caused by its chemical structure. Followed and respected, these principles do compensate, very largely, for pinot's special chemistry. "People tell you pinot noir is the most difficult wine to make," Argyle Winery's winemaker, Rollin Soles, told the *San Francisco Chronicle* in 2003, "but that's a sound bite. Once you find the perfect spot [to grow it], it's just like making any other wine."

It is still true, however, that pinot is inexplicably moody in the cellar. It passes in and out of phases that are borderline unpleasant. This property of the variety vexes winemakers, tempts them to intervene against their better judgment, and keeps the reputation of winemaking difficulty alive despite a quarter-century of progress. Pinot's transparency is also a perennial issue. Pinot does showcase flaws that tougher varieties hide. It's like "a wrong note in a flute concerto," according to Manfred Krankl, a veteran restaurateur whose Sine Qua Non brand now includes both pinot noir and syrah: "In the context of the concerto the error reverberates, where the same mistake is barely perceptible in a steel-band rock-n-roll concert." When winemakers repeat now the old truth that pinot is hard to make, it's fair enough to challenge them. But it is important to remember that a lot of sweat and tears were shed to get pinot making to where it is today, and that even today, there are many easier ways to earn a living.

Chapter 7

BURGUNDIES AND NORTH AMERICAN PINOTS COMPARED

Everyone asks: How is North American pinot noir different from red Burgundy? Is it a fundamentally different beast? Is it fair to compare them? Which is better? Which is better value? Which lives longer? Which ages more gracefully? Should a consumer expect the same flavors, textures, satisfactions, and pleasures from both families of wine, or should these wines satisfy in quite different ways? Alternatively, beginning with the presumption that Burgundy has the advantage of history and accumulated experience, are the best pinots grown in North America as good as the greatest red Burgundies? Are American pinots comparable to Burgundy's lesser wines, but not to its *grands crus?* Are Oregon pinots, or even New York State pinots, more like red Burgundy than wines grown in the Russian River valley, Los Carneros, or Santa Barbara? Is there a track race, and is North America "catching up"? Are North American pinots more like Burgundies now than they were at the end of the 1970s? Conversely, are Burgundies beginning to act and taste more like North American pinots, for whatever reasons? There are endless forms of these basic questions, and the questions have been around for a quarter-century at least.

It is easy enough to catalog the differences between Burgundy and North America's main pinot-producing regions. The Côte d'Or is farther north than any region except the Okanagan. Burgundy's average summer high temperatures are higher than those of the southern Central Coast and the Salinas Valley, but cooler than everywhere else. Average winter low temperatures are warmer than those of the Finger Lakes and Okanagan regions, but colder than everywhere else. Rain falls throughout the year in Burgundy; in North America it is almost entirely confined to the winter months, except around the Finger Lakes, where the precipitation pattern is much like Burgundy's. In the Okanagan valley, there is scarcely any rain at all. The soils of the Côte d'Or are rich in limestone, mostly formed in situ from ancient marine deposits; North American pinot is grown in almost every soil type *except* sedimentary limestone. Even in the Gavilan Range on the east side of the Salinas Valley, the indigenous limestone is quite different from its Burgundian namesake, being harder, higher in silica, and less organic. Burgundian vineyards are never irrigated; North American pinot vineyards are usually irrigated, except in Oregon and New York, where the utility of irrigation is just beginning to be recognized.

In Burgundy, appellation laws govern which varieties a grower is permitted to plant, how the vines are pruned, how old the vines must be before grapes are harvested for controlled appellation wines, the maximum yield per hectare, the minimum level of sugar at harvest, and the earliest date a grower is permitted to pick. In North America, all of these matters are a matter of winegrower discretion. Côte d'Or vineyards are typically planted to a density of 4,050 plants per acre; a medium-density vineyard in North America is typically about one vine every five feet by eight, or 1,100 plants per acre, and many older vineyards are less than half as dense. Côte d'Or vines are trained low to the ground, with the first trellis wire only about 15 inches from the earth's surface, in order to derive maximum benefit from soil-stored heat; the North American norm is closer to 25 inches.

Burgundian vintners chaptalize their wines three years out of four, either because they must add sugar to obtain sufficient alcohol, or because they prefer a longer fermentation, which chaptalization facilitates. Among major North American regions, chaptalization is permitted only in Canada, New York, and Oregon, but is far from normal even in those locations and is forbidden entirely in California, where it is generally the last thing a vintner would want to do in any case. On the contrary, California pinot makers are more inclined to add acid than sugar, which is not permitted in Burgundy, and would be counterproductive even if it were legal. Burgundian cellars are naturally cold, but not as cold as Americans imagine, and harvest often (but not always) occurs when there is a distinct chill in the autumn air. In some North American regions in some years, it can still be pretty toasty when pinot noir is picked from the vine. A good, finished red Burgundy containing 14 percent alcohol by volume is very rare; well over 14 percent is common in California, and frequent even in Oregon and the Okanagan, especially in warm years.

Faced with differences of these sorts, many observers, including American winemakers, have concluded that the best defense is to avoid comparisons entirely. "We are not trying to make Burgundy," says Saintsbury's David Graves. "We don't smoke Gauloises, and the French make the best French wine in the world." And Joe Heitz, who dabbled a bit in pinot noir before getting focused on cabernet sauvignon, told an interviewer in the late 1970s that America, even then, made good pinots. "Just because it doesn't taste like Burgundy," he said, "doesn't mean there is anything wrong with it!"

The oranges-and-apples defense is not entirely satisfying, however, nor is it completely honest. As Frank Prial observed in the *New York Times* in 1996, Oregon and

California winemakers "insist with straight faces that the Burgundy style is not their ideal. Like true denizens of the West Coast, they will lapse readily into New Age blather about the need to protect their own inner selves. But comments like 'this has Chambertin written all over it' are not exactly unacceptable." The adjective *Burgundian* is a commonly used descriptor for North American pinots, though there is no consensus on its meaning, and quite a number of winemakers on this side of the Atlantic reach even deeper into the pot of Burgundian appellations to describe their wine. Oregonians often characterize the Red Hills of Dundee as their "Pommard," and one maker in Ohio distinguishes his regular and reserve bottlings by asserting that one is more like Pommard, while the other more closely resembles Volnay. Josh Jensen, queried by an interviewer about his frequent references to Burgundy in 1997, admitted that he "keep[s] mentioning the place" but didn't think he had "compared one of [his] wines to a Burgundy for at least a year." Jensen then argued that Burgundy–North American comparisons were on the wane, which a scan of the wine press and winery publicity would be hard pressed to confirm.

For their part, the Burgundians often shy from comparisons by alleging that they "do not make pinot noir." When Andrew Barr told Aubert de Villaine, co-owner of Domaine de la Romanée-Conti, that he was writing a book about pinot noir, de Villaine replied that pinot was "the opposite of what Burgundy is about." The virtue of pinot, de Villaine pointedly explained to Barr, "is that it has no taste of its own" and therefore "shows the *terroir* more than any other variety." "It is," he summarized, "a sort of ghost." Although most Burgundians have now learned to *talk* about pinot, at least to the outside world, it is true that their preoccupations revolve around their individual villages and vineyards. They are not being entirely disingenuous when they say that they make Morey-St.-Denis or Musigny or Beaune Clos-des-Mouches, not pinot noir. Declassifying a barrel of vineyard-designated wine into a village appellation, or a village wine into Bourgogne Rouge, is not just a matter of economic loss; it is an admission that *terroir* has failed, at least in one vintage, to leave its distinguishing mark. Indeed, it is one of the genuine black-and-white contrasts between Burgundy and North America that in Burgundy the very best wines are invariably small lots of a vineyard-designated product, and almost always from sites classified as *grands crus,* while in North America the best wines can be blends and often are. Véronique Drouhin-Boss, who has responsibility for Domaine Drouhin Oregon, calls this the big difference in winemaking between Burgundy and North America. Serious Burgundies are always *terroir*-focused. In Oregon, Drouhin is "trying to make the very best pinot noir that we can."

After having hundreds of conversations on both sides of the Atlantic and tasting thousands of bottles, not only in Burgundy and the States but also in Canada, Sancerre, Alsace, the Rheinpfalz, Switzerland, Austria, and the Alto Adige, I am convinced that careful comparisons of pinot in the New World and the Old are fair and illuminating—for consumers and winegrowers alike. Pinot noir spread from Burgundy into its newer homes for one of only two reasons: either its ability to ripen early made it a grape of choice in other cool climates, or the quality of the wine it made in Burgundy inspired emulation. Suitability was the dominant issue in the variety's early distribution to other regions in northern France, Switzerland, and Germany. But overwhelmingly and unarguably, it is the reputation of Burgundy's wines—and the pleasure they have given to connoisseurs around the world—that explains why (and when) cuttings of pinot have been hauled farther afield. It also explains the renaissance of interest in pinot in various regions, as well as the increased plantings, since the mid 1980s. All of North America's pinot pioneers and most of its current practitioners discovered pinot noir through Burgundy or Burgundies, and almost without exception their models for the greatest possible success are Burgundy-based. Absent some epiphany with a bottle, nearly every one of these vintners would be working instead with some other variety, or would simply have chosen another career. Burgundy remains, according to Chehalem's Harry Peterson-Nedry, the "gold standard" for pinot noir. "In terms of finesse, structure, and expression of *terroir,*" he says, "it is the standard against which all other regions measure themselves."

Furthermore, the apples-to-oranges contrasts between Burgundy and North America can easily be overdone. On a ten-year average basis, heat accumulation during the growing season in Burgundy is only trivially lower than on the southern Central Coast, in the Willamette Valley, and in the western Russian River valley. In 1997, Savigny-les-Beaune was actually much warmer than the Eola Hills; in 1998 it was warmer than Los Carneros; and in 1999 it was warmer than *any* major pinot region in North America. The very different patterns of rainfall can be substantially manipulated with irrigation, so one contrast *may* alter the significance of another. There is no arguing that Burgundy's soils are radically different from those of any major North American region, but the significance of these differences and their impact on wines in the bottle are far from clear. As Mary Hall, a Carneros-based viticulturist, has observed, "if pinot noir had been planted first in the New World rather than the Old, we might be wondering if the variety could really flourish in an alkaline environment like Burgundy." On both sides of the Atlantic, winegrowers are working with quite similar plant material—as far as anyone knows, all pinot noir came from Burgundy at some point, whatever the route and the date of traverse—especially as the Dijon clones occupy an increasing share of pinot's acreage everywhere. Fermenting wine in those cool Burgundian cellars may not be all that different from a few days of cold soak in a slightly warmer cellar in California. Aside from vine density, which remains controversial, and trellis height, viticultural practices are now quite similar. Nearly everyone uses some form of vertical shoot positioning, prunes short in the spring, and adjusts the crop load downward, at least a bit, after veraison. Everyone pulls leaves to ensure that the fruit gets some exposure to direct sun. Astonishingly, given the very different densities of planting, yields aren't really very different. Mature vineyards, farmed to make the best possible wine, hover at or below two tons per acre in both Burgundy and North America, with the exception that some quite warm sites in California may hang up to three or even four tons—simply to slow the ripening process and extend the growing season.

In the cellar, there is no significant methodological difference between Burgundy and North America, though individual variations on the main theme exist in all camps. There are so-called traditionalists and so-called new wave winemakers in both theaters. The traditionalists, in both places, cleave to heavier use of whole clusters, longer fermentations, and generally longer barrel times; new wave winemakers, more oriented to preserving the primary flavors of fruit, favor shorter barrel times and more intensive use of new wood. If it were possible to ignore cultural paraphernalia, a bit higher humidity, and mold, it would be impossible to distinguish many Burgundian cellars from North American wineries—even to equipment purchased from the same manufacturers.

A generation ago, the typical Burgundian vigneron and the typical American winemaker were entirely different cultural types. The vigneron learned most of what he knew from his father, made wine by a combination of habit and instinct, appealed to enologists only to fix problems, and almost never tasted any wine other than his own. The American winemaker was university trained, risk averse, fanatical about cleanliness, and interventionist by instinct. When the first pinot-oriented Americans trekked to Burgundy at the end of the 1960s, they were content to work a harvest, picking and crushing grapes. Later on some went to school in Burgundy and earned winemaking credentials from the Lycée agricole in Beaune. Talacoat's Don Blackburn even became a prefect at the famous wine school, rousing younger students from their dormitory beds each morning; he now counts many of the younger generation of French winemakers among his close friends. Littorai's Ted Lemon, who won a postgraduate fellowship to study winemaking in Dijon, at what is now the Université de Bourgogne, became the first and only American actually to make wine in Burgundy, for the house of Guy Roulot in Meursault. Now most of Burgundy's younger generation is also university trained, well-traveled, and often anglophone. These winemakers are veterans of internships in California, Oregon, Australia, or New Zealand. They have been mentored by the same handful of internationalist pioneers (notably Jacques Seysses at Domaine Dujac) who have guided the young Americans. They have tasted widely in their own villages and up and down the Côte d'Or, and they have been active participants in international conferences, cool-climate viticultural symposia, and the so-called Steamboat Conference, held annually in Oregon.

North America intrigues many young Burgundians. While organic farming has roots on both continents, a good many Burgundians saw organic and quasiorganic vineyards first in Oregon and have learned the art of comparative tasting in America. "In American vineyards," says Véronique Drouhin-Boss, "you are free to do essentially anything you want; in France you have the pressure of history, *mentalité,* and regulations." This difference has made North America, in some sense, a "laboratory" for Burgundy. In New York, Canada, Oregon, and California, Burgundians can see what happens when the lowest trellis wire is fixed higher above the ground, and when vines are planted less densely.

Burgundian and American makers share a remarkably similar image of good pinot noir. A good vintage is preceded by a rainy winter, and warm and sunny weather is the best environment for bloom. Burgundians need a hot, dry summer with just a few rains in late August or early September. Californians could do with a slightly cooler summer to slow down the vines, but they are learning to interrupt irrigation during the main part of the growing season and then restore it at the very end, just as the Burgundian looks for a bit of rain in late August, to relieve what could otherwise turn into drought-induced stress. On both sides, the ideal pinot is nuanced and balanced, with complexities extending beyond pure and primary fruit. The California maker would prefer not to acidify if given the choice; the Burgundian would like to chaptalize only a little, believing that, as Lalou Bize-Leroy told the International Pinot Noir Celebration in 2000, "natural sugar" is better than added sugar.

Jacques Seysses, asked about differences between Burgundian and American approaches to winemaking, said he thought the Americans he knew best, Ted Lemon and Josh Jensen, if they were given Domaine Dujac's fruit with which to work, would make wines quite similar to his own. In 1999, Ancien Wines' Ken Bernards conducted the experiment for real. He arranged to purchase 1,500 pounds of grapes from a parcel of Les Cognées vineyard in Morey-St.-Denis owned by the firm of Arlaud Père et Fils. Picked in the early morning on September 22, the grapes were chilled with frozen carbon dioxide and trucked to Satolas Airport in Lyon, whence they were airfreighted to Los Angeles, trucked to San Francisco's produce market, and finally, 66 hours after picking, destemmed and fermented in the Napa Valley. Bernards found that his Les Cognées fruit behaved a lot like the pinot he buys from Sonoma Mountain. It displayed something he calls "reverberating flavors" and considerable minerality, and retained a lot of color at the end of fermentation. Bernards made the wine conventionally, with no chaptalization and no cold soak, a warm fermentation, and seven days of postfermentation maceration; and he raised it for 15 months in one new Remond barrel and one three-year-old François Frères barrel. The result was a medium-colored wine with an explosive nose of rich earth, wet slate, truffle, violets, and a hint of licorice; bright huckleberry and *griotte* (a type of cherry) in the mouth; a very long mineral-edged finish; and medium weight. It could have been a Morey-St.-Denis, which of course it was; but it was not radically un-Californian either, except for lower alcohol and fruit that was less overt and opulent than California sometimes gives.

In fact, it is often hard to distinguish red Burgundies from North American pinots when the wines are tasted blind. Seysses, who has pinots from around the world in his cellar and often tastes them blind, readily admits that he is frequently deceived, even failing to recognize his own wine in a flight of others. To have the best crack at identifying a North American pinot, he tries to guess "how much sunshine the wine has seen." At the International Pinot Noir Celebration (IPNC) in 1999, a panel composed of two Portland-based sommeliers, two Oregon winemakers, and one importer of Burgundies was asked to identify the provenance of five pinots: two from Oregon, one from Los Carneros, one from Martinborough in New Zealand, and one from the firm of Fougeray de Beauclair in Marsannay. Although every panelist had definite opinions based on classic descriptors, no panelist correctly identified more than two of the five wines; and two wines (the Martinborough wine and one of the Oregon wines) were misidentified by *all* the panelists. The results were not much better when *Wine Spectator* set its senior European editor and New York–based editor at large, both well versed in Burgundies and North American pinot noirs, to work on 20 red Burgundies and 20 American pinots, from known and semimature vintages, in 1998. Even these experts could correctly distinguish the Burgundies from the American wines only three times out of four.

The confusion is often blamed on an increasingly "international" style of winemaking, which some Burgundians, in particular, decry. "We have changed in Burgundy since the 1980s," says Patrice Rion, of Domaine Daniel Rion in Prémeaux-Prissy. "In part through the influence of the journalists, our wines of lace and polish have given way to more structured wines marked with tannin and fruit. We used to say in France that the customer should adapt himself to the wine. Now we see French wines being influenced by the market—just as they are in the New World." But Etienne de Montille, tasting older vintages of red Burgundies and Oregon pinots at the 2000 edition of IPNC, thought even these were hard to tell apart. "It's time to end this fight between the New and Old Worlds," he proclaimed diplomatically. "The real fight is between good and mediocre wines."

More nonsense is written about the comparative age-worthiness of Burgundies and American pinots than about any other single subject. The received wisdom is that, however charming or delicious an American pinot may be in its youth, it will not age like a Burgundy. This fallacious generalization is sometimes hurled against the ensemble of North American pinots, or reserved, depending on the speaker, either for Oregon or for California exemplars. Burgundians are fond of repeating the allegation, especially in the wake of some tasting in which one or more young American pinots have bested one or more young red Burgundies. American winemakers are frequently all too willing to go along, responding that they are not trying to make wines that will age, but wines that give immediate pleasure instead. How quintessentially American! Writers complicate the issue by presuming that any good red Burgundy will age flatteringly—they write *approvingly* that a hard, young Burgundy "needs time." And they make the converse presumption about a North American pinot: if it is not good young, it will never be good, so they are critical and mark the wine down comparatively.

Average American consumers (unlike their English counterparts) drink so little mature wine that they do not know what such wine is supposed to taste like. Misled by writers and sometimes also by winemakers, consumers then define *age-worthy* as "does not change with age." When they encounter an older bottle that displays changed color and secondary aromas that are gradually replacing the primary fruit flavors of the wine's youth, they conclude that it has not aged well, which is the exact opposite of the truth. These attitudes have led some observers, like Véronique Drouhin-Boss, to assert that ageability is fundamentally subjective. Regarding a Domaine Drouhin Oregon wine from the late 1980s, tasted in 2000, she said simply, "If you are French, you drink the wine today. If you are British, in ten years time. But if you are American, you really should have drunk it ten years ago."

Age-worthiness, especially where pinot noir is concerned, has recently become a favored topic for winemaker panels. It was the main theme for the IPNC in Oregon in 2000 and a subject for debate at the World of Pinot Noir in 2001. Many winemakers with some sympathy for age, on both sides of the Atlantic, argue that acidity is the key to age-worthiness, especially for pinot noir; and they contrast pinot with cabernet, which (they say) must have good tannin to age well. Others argue for "balance" among acid, tannin, and alcohol. An incomplete consensus emerged at the World of Pinot Noir around the proposition that high-alcohol wines are naturally age-challenged. Drouhin-Boss asserts that *yield* is the key to age, and that the winemaker must "understand the vintage." Too much extraction in a lighter vintage will always, she believes, come at the expense of finesse and ageability.

The cold, hard facts are simply these: a pinot that ages gracefully is better than one that disintegrates only because it gives different pleasures at different times in its life, and is thus more complete. No one knows exactly how wine ages, and no one can predict the evolution of any wine precisely. Pinot noir, because of its moodiness, is more difficult to predict than most. It may seem to decline for a time, and then unexpectedly improve. Its color can even *darken* with age, and it can put on weight. Pinot's evolution is a bit like the stock market, however: long-term trends are easier to foresee than short-term movements. There is plenty of red Burgundy that has commenced an irreversible decline ten years after the vintage, and plenty of American pinot that does the same. But the vertical tastings reported in this book (see the profiles of Husch Vineyards and Hanzell Vineyards especially, but also notes on older vintages of Ponzi, Eyrie, Chalone, Joseph Swan, McKinlay, and Calera) make clear that good North American pinot ages just as rewardingly as Clive Coates's benchmarks for fine red Burgundies do—namely, six to 15 years after the vintage for most village and *premier cru* wines, and ten to 25 years for *grand cru* wines. *Connoisseurs' Guide* appears to have reached a similar conclusion, especially as California pinot noirs have gotten better. In a 1977 tasting of wines from the period 1957 through 1970, the *Guide* found "a large number of tired wines, a small group of interesting wines, and a handful of extremely lively, well-made wines," including 20-

year-old pinots that "displayed good form . . . retained aroma, balance and varietal distinction." Writing in the *Los Angeles Times,* the *Guide*'s Charles Olken found it "striking" how many "supposedly short-lived" pinots from the 1980 to 1991 vintages, tasted in 2002, had held up "amazingly well."

North American pinots are not so different from red Burgundies that comparisons are ill-conceived or meaningless. Neither are they so similar that consumers should have identical expectations of both. Each category is a spectrum of wines crafted by hundreds of makers in at least the same number of distinctly different sites. But the spectra do overlap, and the area of overlap is significant. They overlap because pinot noir is, in the end, still pinot noir. Because Burgundy's very best wines are, once again in the 1990s as they were in the 1950s, worthy of worldwide emulation. Because makers on both sides of the Atlantic have forged an ongoing dialogue about models and methods. Because there is more agreement about models and methods between Burgundian and American practitioners of pinot noir than there is between Burgundy and Bordeaux. Because weather is actually more important than climate—year-to-year variations within each region mark wines much more dramatically than relatively small differences between statistical averages. And because the nonweather attributes of *terroir* are so finely granular, and so complex, that they distinguish Pommard Les Boucherottes from adjacent Beaune Clos des Mouches, and Santa Rita Hills Rozak Ranch from nearby Santa Rita Hills Melville Vineyard, more dramatically than they differentiate between the Côte d'Or as a whole and North America as a whole.

There are, however, a few very general differences. Most North American pinots have a tendency to display more—and more intense—primary fruit flavors than most red Burgundies. Said another way, fruit takes up more of the wine's aromatic and flavor bandwidth in North America. In Burgundy, other aromas and flavors, especially floral, woodsy, and animal-related elements, share more of the wine's space. Some observers think the "gamy" flavors of Burgundy have more to do with winemaking than with *terroir,* deriving from extended lees contact. Others think barrels tend to explain development of gamy flavors; but barrels from the same cooper and forest, used to raise wines in Burgundy and wines in North America, produce different results. Red Burgundies often display a dominance of minerality, ranging from dusty and chalky properties to slate, graphite, Carborundum, and plain wet stone. In North America, these same mineral components of flavor usually play the role of supporting actors.

An entire cosmetics case of aromas is characteristic of Burgundy. Burgundians often say Burgundy is *about* perfume; Americans are more likely to say that pinot is about mouthfeel. A supposedly typical Burgundy tends toward slightly higher acidity and lower pH than what is considered a typical North American wine, which can create the impression of greater angularity and structure. The same properties occur in North America, but less frequently, and are most often associated on these shores with wines grown in very thin soils, or in years and regions in which the temperature has fallen rapidly during the last month before harvest.

Higher alcohol is a hallmark of North American pinot noir, except for those grown in New York State; it contributes to an impression of comparative warmth, generosity, and fullness of body. Many observers find that North American pinots, especially those grown in California, have a thicker texture than Burgundy. Burgundy made from fine sites in warm years has the ability to display concentration and exuberance within a wiry, sinewy frame; North American wines are more likely to express the same concentration as "fat" and "chewiness." The vocabulary North American makers use to describe their target pinot includes descriptors like *opulent* and *hedonistic;* Burgundians are more likely to talk about elegance and finesse. Some of those who have made pinot noir in both places, like Drouhin-Boss, argue that "elegance comes naturally in Burgundy," while in North America, "you have to struggle for elegance." My own tasting notes for Burgundies contain many more references to nuance and layers than my notes on North American wines. It is not entirely clear why so-called elegance should be easier to achieve, or more often achieved, in Burgundy, but it is permissible to suspect that it has something to do with the oft-repeated allegation that full flavor development—whatever that really means—seems to occur in Burgundy at lower levels of sugar accumulation than most of North America is able to manage. It would be more accurate to say, perhaps, lower levels than most North American pinot makers are prepared to tolerate.

A further wrinkle in the comparison of Burgundies and North American pinots is this: a majority of North American wines, even those from Oregon and New York in warm and dry years, are in terms of chemistry more like *grand cru* Burgundy than like the majority of Burgundy's village and *premier cru* wines. The reason is that in Burgundy, *grand cru* sites have the greatest potential for ripeness if Mother Nature cooperates at all. But in Burgundy, *grand cru* sites also show legendary *terroir*-driven complexity. In these comparisons, similar weights and concentrations can be put side by side with perfect fairness, but the Burgundies usually have an edge when it comes to nuance, layers, and complexity. On the other hand, if nuance, layers, complexity, and flavor are optimized and set at par, North American wines can seem to have an edge because their weight and concentration are comparatively impressive.

And which, for now, is "better"? It is difficult to imagine parsing this question so that the answer could be accurate, definitive, meaningful, or helpful. Better how? Better grown? Better made? Better to drink now, or made to age better? Better in front of a roaring fire on a rainy winter afternoon, or better company for seared lamb medallions or braised quail at the table? And which wines should be chosen to compare with which others? Wines selling for about the same price? The most expensive wines on each side regardless of absolute price? Wines only from "well-regarded producers"—if there were any consensus on who is and who is not well regarded? Only bottles taken directly from the producers' own cellars and more or less undisturbed since bottling? Wines from the same vintage, or from comparable vintages—however *comparable* is defined? How many wines have to be tasted to yield a fair picture of Burgundy, or of American regions scattered from Southern California to upstate New York? Who is to taste these wines on our behalf, that we should regard their judgments as definitive? Makers, writers, merchants, sommeliers? All of the above? And how many palates must be enlisted on our behalf, in order to compensate for inevitable differences of experience, perspective, and just plain taste, even among seasoned professionals? And at the end of the day, even if there were generally acceptable answers to all of these question pieces, what end would be served if everyone involved could agree that the "best" red Burgundies are "better" than the "best" North American pinots, or vice versa? That a free market should recalibrate prices? That even more consumers should chase after tiny quantities of essentially unobtainable wine? That wine magazines and newsletters should sell more copies when they report the results? That producers have new copy for press releases, trade briefings, and sales calls to wine shops and restaurants? That consumers have new bragging rights for the contents of their personal cellars?

Wine competitions are now a way of life and commerce, however, so the underlying question persists in spite of its problems and its intrinsic wrongheadedness. It is in the American character to perfect, outdo, overtake, and keep score—and winemakers are not exempt. The same is not in the French character, but defense of honor is. And Americans and Burgundians alike have no small amount of wine to sell into international markets, where the reputation of the "best" wines can easily help to sell less extravagant offerings. As far as I know, the first shot involving pinot noir was *GaultMillau*'s Olympiades du Vin in 1979, in which The Eyrie Vineyards 1975 Oregon Pinot Noir finished second to Joseph Drouhin's 1959 Chambolle-Musigny, creating a minor stir on both sides. Its main effect, perhaps, was to legitimate the comparative question. If an unknown Oregon pinot could show competitively against fine Burgundies from respected producers in stellar vintages, pitting other Burgundies against other American pinots was suddenly fair game.

Other taste-offs followed. I have already alluded to *Wine Spectator*'s version of the Olympiades, the so-called Pinot Noir Challenge, organized in 1998. Twenty red Burgundies, 17 of them *grands crus,* were tasted blind against 20 North American pinots, all of which had been well reviewed by *Spectator*'s editors when they were newly released. Half of the 40 wines were selected from the 1990 vintage, and were thus approaching middle age; the others were 1993s (in the case of Burgundy) and 1994s (in the case of North America). There were two tasters only, both *Wine Spectator* editors. The magazine's bottom line: slightly higher scores for the red Burgundies in both flights, but many accolades for Gary Farrell's Allen Ranch bottlings, Kistler's Cuvée Catherine, and Broadley's Claudia's Choice. Various editorial comments were made about Burgundy's "solid franchise" and North America's "huge progress" since the dark days of the 1970s and 1980s, as well as its "watershed" performance in 1994.

Two years later, to prove a point about price, Calera Wine Company's Josh Jensen began pitting his own wines against expensive Burgundies from well-regarded producers in a roadshow of blind tastings, organized for wine writers and sommeliers. Only wines from the same vintage were tasted together, and Burgundy's weaker vintages were avoided. Happily for Jensen, since the point of his exercise was to justify an across-the-board price increase for his wines, most tasters in most tastings preferred the Calera wines to the selected Burgundies, though contrary opinions surfaced with sufficient regularity to keep things interesting. For the record, the Burgundies included such luminary wines as a 1996 Richebourg from Domaine de la Romanée-Conti, and a 1988 Mazis-Chambertin from Domaine Maume.

Comparative studies are a legitimate form of inquiry. All the social sciences are implicitly comparative, and both comparative literature and comparative linguistics are widely taught. Art history is never taught with only a single work in view. If all great literature were confined to a single tradition, comparative literature would be a fairly dismal and pointless field. Conversely, if all the world's literatures were more or less the same, comparing them would be a matter of little interest. If, whenever red Burgundies and American pinots were tasted side by side, experienced tasters ranked all of the one or the other somehow better, the case for interesting comparability would not be strong.

The compelling fact that emerges from tasting Burgundies alongside American pinots in the 1990s and at the beginning of the new millennium is that they are (finally?) *genuinely comparable.* Side by side, the best of each illuminates the best of the other. My cellar is full of red Burgundy and a fair selection of American pinots. When a red Burgundy and a North American pinot are removed from the cellar together, the nod can go in either direction, or I may detect no significant qualitative difference between the wines. A 1995 Pommard Les Rugiens from Hubert de Montille was infinitely blander and less interesting recently than a 1997 Arcadian Sleepy Hollow Vineyard, which was nuanced, layered, and spicy. But a 1993 Estate from Joseph Swan and a 1989 Nuits-St.-Georges Les Boudots from Jean Tardy were more or less a qualitative draw. I liked them both, and I was surprised by how similar they seemed. Tasting them side by side raised questions about how they were similar and how different, how *terroir* and winemaking overlapped and intersected. If the wines had been qualitatively very different, if one had been much better than the other, comparing them would have been boring, irrelevant, or both. This should be the *real* bottom line: we all win when wine from both camps can be open on the same table, enjoyed by the same palates, judged by the same standards *without handicap*—but appreciated for their respective and individual virtues, hallmarks, and personalities.

Chapter 8

REFLECTIONS

When we take stock and look forward, the proverbial glass (of North American pinot noir in 2003) is certainly more than half full. The gravely flawed wines of the 1970s are gone. The basic truth that pinot *cannot* be made successfully if it is treated like any other red grape is well understood. Several hundred producers are at work on the variety in at least 13 states and two Canadian provinces. Many dozens of them are turning out very good wines, and newly minted labels of exceptional quality enter the market with each successive vintage. The best North American pinots can be compared with the top tier of red Burgundies, without handicap or apology. Restaurateurs and connoisseurs have supported pinot's renaissance with almost boundless enthusiasm, making pinot the only red variety to have increased its share among top-selling restaurant wines almost every year since 1992.

There is still some distance to go, however, and a few clouds on the horizon. In the short term, 2003 marked the third year in a row that American vineyards produced more grapes than its wine business could use or sell. Predictable consequences ensued. Some of the crop went unpicked, some was sold for derisory prices, some vineyard land was converted to other uses, and some wineries were sold or bankrupted. Through 2002, this gloom barely touched pinot noir, which for the most part cheerfully inhabits uncontested space between commodity fruit at the base of the wine market and vanity vineyards at the top. In 2003, however, even pinot was affected by oversupply. Vintners who once queued at growers' doors, eager for an opportunity to buy prime fruit, found the tables turned, with growers more than willing to sell, often at much-reduced prices, and to give vintners their choice among blocks. Vineyard managers in Anderson Valley reported that substantial quantities of top-quality pinot noir went unpicked for the first time in recent memory. Several well-respected vineyards—Floodgate in Anderson Valley and the historic Sierra

Madre Vineyard in Santa Maria, for example—were offered for sale or actually changed hands. The prices asked for pinot grapes from the best-known vineyards in California, like Hirsch and Pisoni, did not soften, but several vintners wondered aloud if even these Grail-like names would not be affected if the fruit glut persisted into 2004 or 2005—especially as more and more fastidiously farmed vineyards planted at the turn of the millennium began to bear. If consumers are lucky, prices for the least available and most stringently allocated North American pinots will remain flat for a few years, while prices for larger-production wines may soften slightly. A few good midpriced pinots may also come to market, made from premium-quality fruit momentarily cheapened by oversupply. Opportunities of this sort are likely to be short-lived, however. Because it is a shy bearer, pinot cannot survive if prices stay depressed for very long.

In the longer term, I believe that two stylistic and qualitative issues need attention in order for North American pinot noir to fulfill the balance of its promise. Entirely too many pinots currently are being made as if the only model for really fine pinot noir were offered by Romanée-Conti in the most perfect of all possible years. Put another way, the model for too many American pinots is too large a wine, made from grapes that are picked too ripe, sporting too much alcohol, struggling for balance in a space in which balance is, in fact, hard to achieve. How much of this phenomenon is attributable to the "Romanée-Conti effect" is not entirely clear. Certainly other factors are at work, including the tendency of critical scores to reward size and intensity at the expense of elegance and finesse, and the legitimate taste preferences of some winemakers, whose palates are simply not satisfied unless the wine has been somehow stuffed with early-gratification hedonism. All these factors have been wrapped into a catechism about the need to delay harvest until the grapes are physiologically mature, and then to accept as a feature (or as a necessary evil) that the accumulated sugar will yield a finished wine approaching or exceeding 15 percent alcohol, plus lush black fruit flavors that obscure other and subtler aromatics. I look forward to a day when only a few North American pinots are made this way, and only those few that are genuinely better this way than any other—which is far fewer than are made this way now. Alongside those wines, the continent needs a spectrum of acceptable styles with this most expressive of grape varieties to justify the effort and relatively high cost that are associated with meticulous farming and low yields.

Mother Nature may provide some relief in time. Most of the North American pinot vineyard is still painfully young, and young vines seem to throw fruit in which sugar accumulation races. As today's three- and five-year-old vines approach a Burgundian standard of maturity after 2020, they may develop entirely satisfying flavors with a bit less sugar. It might not be an entirely bad thing, in addition, if today's antiseptically healthy vines were touched with just a bit of virus, as they may well be in time. Virus, like age, seems to slow down sugar accumulation. There may be other solutions as well. Greg Bjornstad of Tandem Winery has written a tantalizing paper suggesting that, at least in some vintages, viticultural practices can be adapted to "control alcohol in the vineyard."

A separate (though sometimes overlapping) problem is that too many of North America's pinot vineyards are, even today, mislocated. The problem is not, as many winegrowers and viticulturists intimate in muffled tones, that pinot is still grown in areas too warm for it. On the contrary, the drive to relocate pinot from allegedly warm sites like midvalley Napa to cooler mesoclimates like the true Sonoma Coast and Oregon has been so successful that some perfectly satisfactory pinot-friendly sites have been abandoned to other varieties, largely for economic reasons. The problem of location, in my opinion, has two aspects. First, too much pinot noir (and other varieties, for that matter) is being grown where the soil is too deep and rich. Most of Europe avoided this circumstance because good agricultural land was so needed for food crops that it was rarely consecrated to vineyard. (Could this be the true significance of tight spacing in European vineyards? Would fewer vines per unit of surface area in very low-vigor soil produce economically unsustainable yields?) But the North American breadbasket is vast by comparison, and the commercial value of wine grapes is now so high that land plainly too good for wine grapes is used for vineyard regardless. In these sites vine plants produce too much crop and too much foliage—too much, that is, if the object is really fine wine. Too many North American vineyards try to compensate for excessively rich sites by aggressive crop thinning and canopy management. The best canopy, as one grower put it insightfully, is "one that does not need to be managed." And the best fruit, by the same token, comes from more or less self-regulating, low-yield vines in sites too poor to sustain anything grander than wine grapes.

Second, when all is said and done, not all low-vigor sites in acceptable mesoclimates are capable of producing great wine. No matter how the winegrower intervenes, some will never produce wine of more than routine interest. This happens for a whole host of reasons, all imperfectly understood. Geology is at work, no doubt: various types of rock are layered, eroded, and decomposed in different ways, are more or less permeable to vine roots, handle moisture differently, leach different mineral cocktails into the vine's root environment, and establish a different symbiosis between the life of the earth and the life of the vine. North American pinot growers may wish their circumstances were as predictable as in the Côte d'Or, where the best vineyards line up almost end to end or side by side, and the next best nearby, until one is either too high on the hill or too low, and the vineyards have become relatively mediocre. But there is no Côte d'Or in North America; the geology here has been jumbled by more complex and recent activity in the earth's crust. The significance of different exposures and altitudes is also less obvious and consistent. Many of our best sites for pinot are certainly located in the areas now deemed pinot-friendly, but a lot of ordinary sites are cheek-by-jowl with the best, and some of the very best may still be unplanted, or even undiscovered. All will be sorted out in due season, but it is not likely to take less time in the New World than it did in the Old, and it may well take longer.

Meanwhile, if we can manage to embrace good pinots when we taste them, to abandon mediocre efforts when they cannot be improved, and to marvel at the truly great when they emerge, we can have a lot of fun with a wonderful variety.

MAPS

A NOTE ON THE MAPS

One schematic map of North America and ten regional maps have been developed for *North American Pinot Noir.* The regional maps portray the most pinot-intensive areas on the continent, while the locations of other pinot-oriented activity can be found on the general schematic map. The regional maps are intended to give readers a visual sense of each area—especially topography, intensity of vineyard development, geographic distribution of vineyards within the region, and approximate locations for each winery and vineyard mentioned in the text.

Wineries co-located with their vineyards are represented as wineries; vineyards where there is no winemaking facility are represented as vineyards. As far as possible, every known vineyard in each region is represented with a light green or dark green square dot, regardless of whether pinot noir is planted in that vineyard, but the pace of new planting and inaccuracies in source data mean that this aspiration is imperfectly realized. The color values associated with elevation are accurate within each map but are not consistent from map to map. With the exception of the Okanagan River valley map, all the regional maps are based on United States Geological Survey 1:100,000 digital line graphs and 7.5-minute series digital elevation models; the Okanagan River valley map relies on 1:50,000 digital elevation data supplied by DMTI Spatial, Inc.

Vineyard location data were derived from many sources. For the Santa Rita Hills and Santa Maria Valley, most were taken from sheet maps previously commissioned by the Santa Barbara County Vintners' Association, supplemented by interviews with growers and vintners. For the Santa Lucia Highlands, the main source was a sheet map previously commissioned by Caymus Vineyards. For Los Carneros, a sheet map commissioned by the Sonoma County Grapegrowers Association, GPS-based data from Vestra Resources, Inc., and information provided by individual wineries were all used. For the Russian River valley, the main source was a sheet map commissioned by the Sonoma County Grapegrowers; individual growers provided supplementary information. For the Sonoma Coast and Anderson Valley, most data were obtained through interviews with local experts. For the Willamette Valley, Alan Campbell of NW Vineyards provided vineyard location data as points on USGS digital orthoquadrangles, which were in turn based on vineyard boundaries drawn, revised, and confirmed by local experts. For the Okanagan, the vineyard data were entirely GPS-derived and come from a project funded by Agriculture Canada and the British Columbia Wine Institute at the Pacific Agri-Food Research Centre in Summerland, British Columbia.

The cartographers for all the maps were Mark Chambers of Petaluma, California, and Bill Nelson of Accomac, Virginia.

Map 1. Pinot noir in North America.

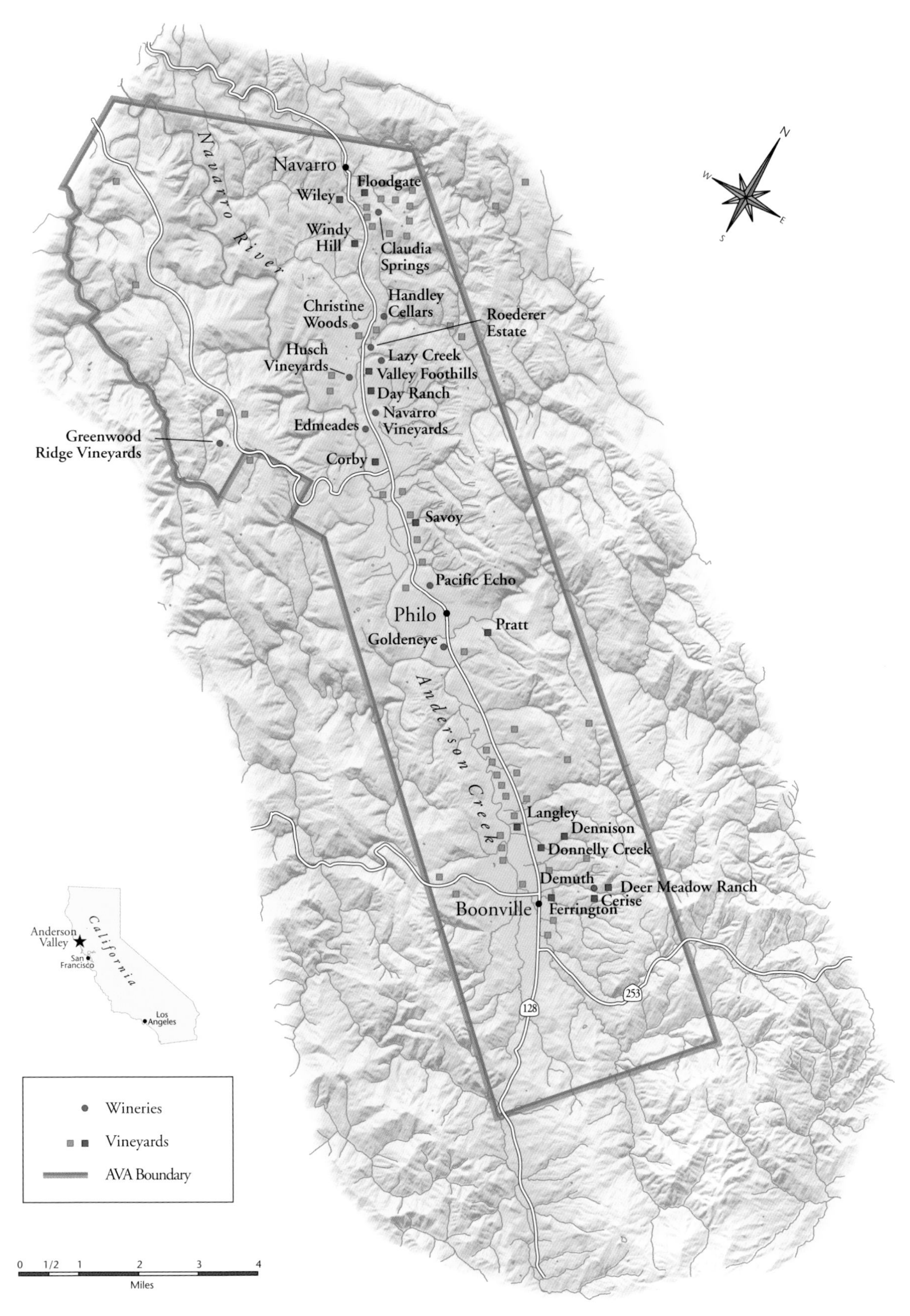

Map 2. Anderson Valley.

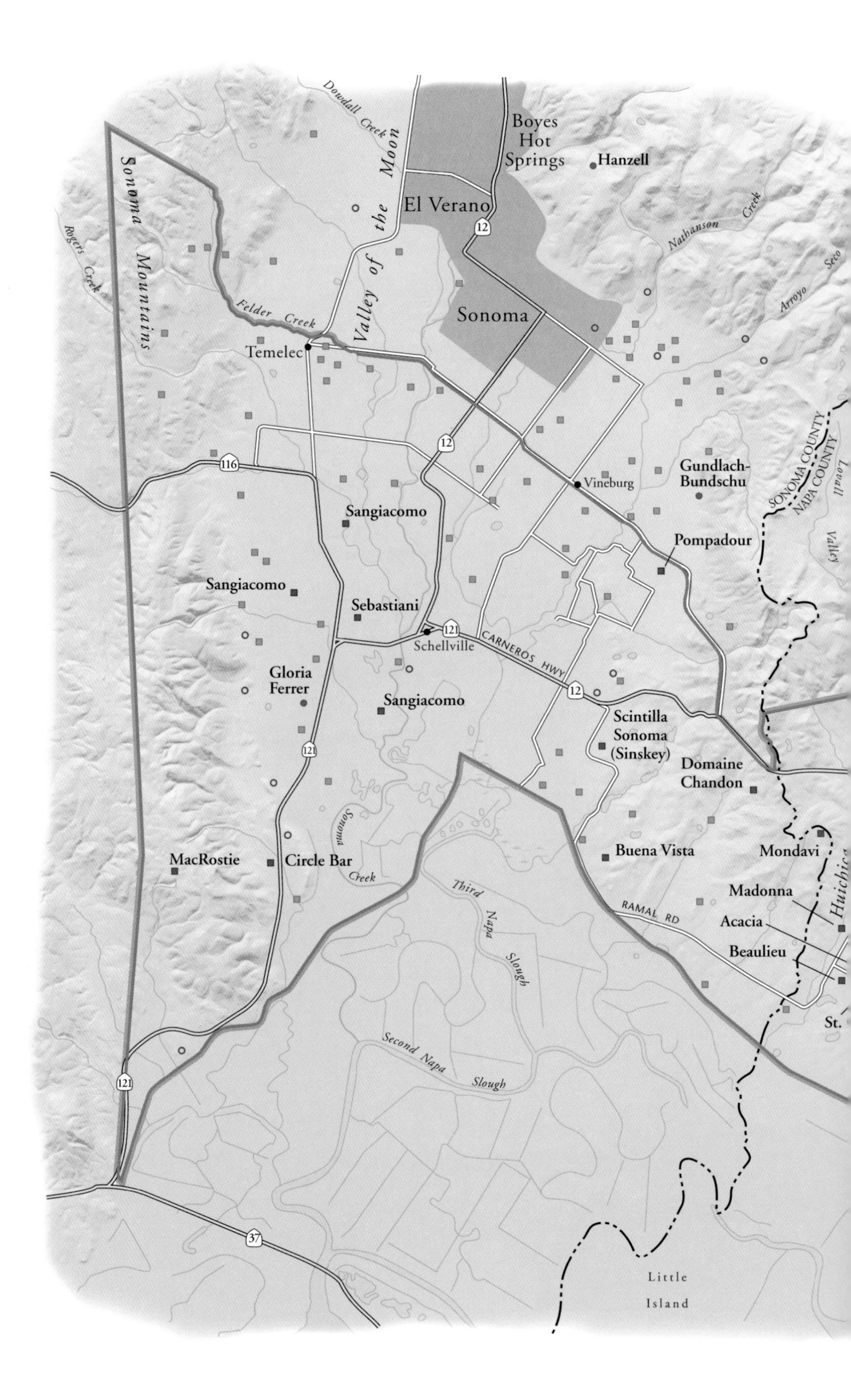

Dowdall Creek
Valley of the Moon
Boyes Hot Springs
Hanzell
El Verano
Sonoma Mountains
Rogers Creek
Nathanson Creek
Arroyo Seco
Felder Creek
Sonoma
Temelec
116
12
Vineburg
Gundlach-Bundschu
SONOMA COUNTY
NAPA COUNTY
Lovall Valley
Sangiacomo
Pompadour
Sangiacomo
Sebastiani
121
Schellville
CARNEROS HWY
Gloria Ferrer
Sangiacomo
Scintilla Sonoma (Sinskey)
Domaine Chandon
Sonoma Creek
MacRostie
Circle Bar
Buena Vista
Mondavi
Third Napa Slough
RAMAL RD
Madonna
Acacia
Beaulieu
St.
Second Napa Slough
37
Little Island

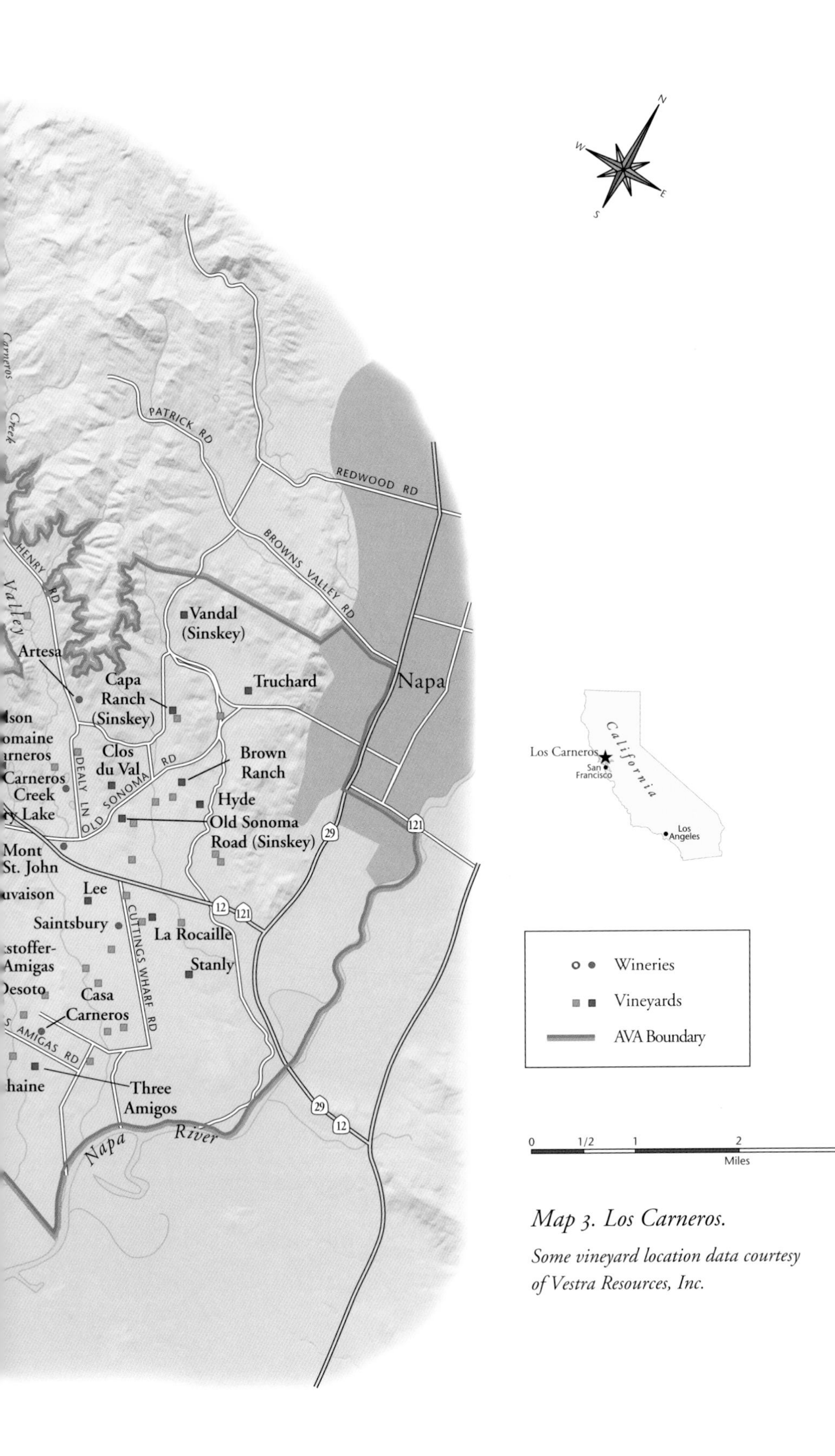

Map 3. Los Carneros.

Some vineyard location data courtesy of Vestra Resources, Inc.

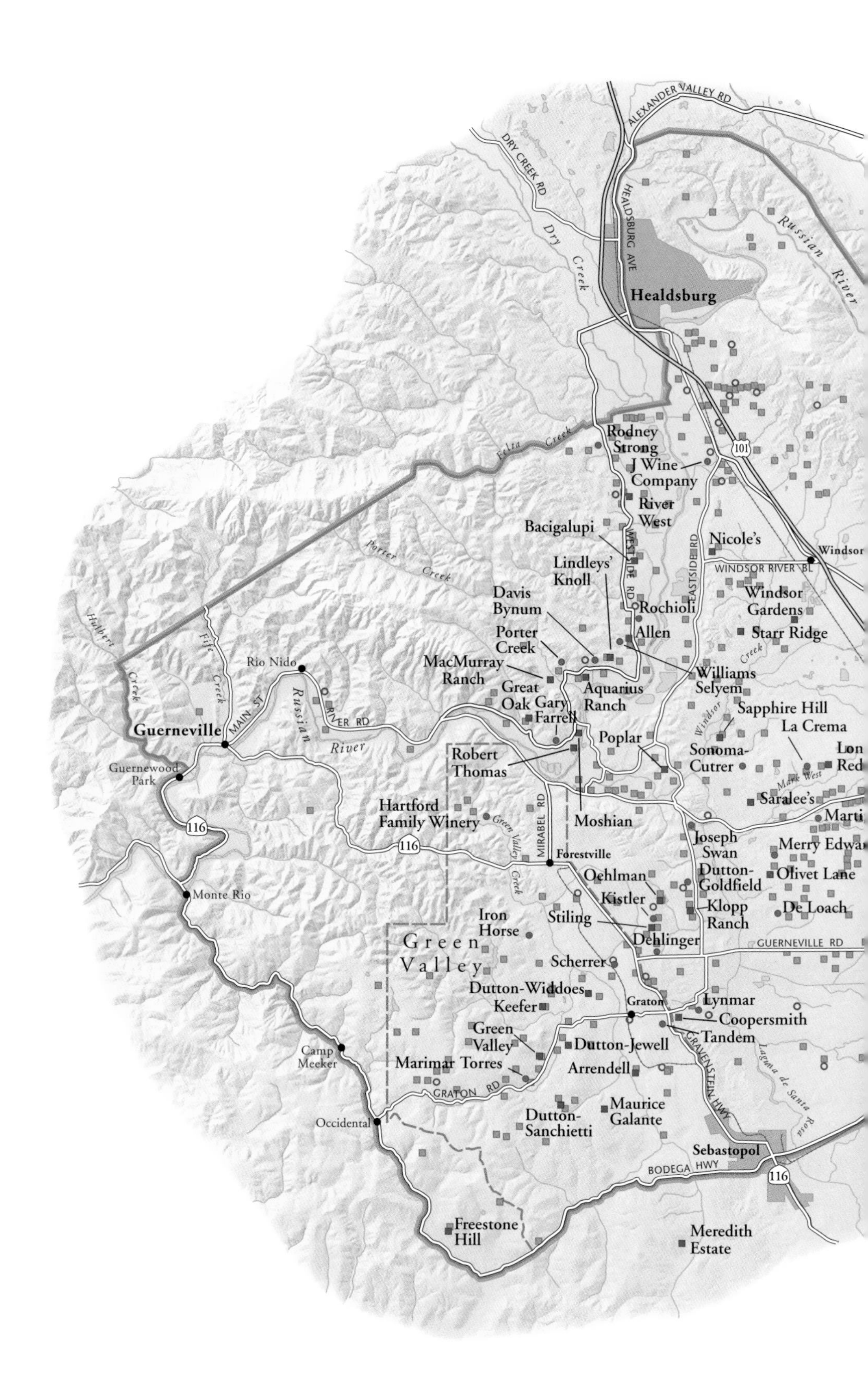

Healdsburg
ALEXANDER VALLEY RD
DRY CREEK RD
Dry Creek
HEALDSBURG AVE
Russian River
Felta Creek
Porter Creek
Hulbert Creek
Fife Creek
Rio Nido
MAIN ST
RIVER RD
Russian River
Guerneville
Guernewood Park
116
Monte Rio
Camp Meeker
Occidental
Rodney Strong
J Wine Company
River West
Bacigalupi
Nicole's
Windsor
WINDSOR RIVER BL
WESTSIDE RD
EASTSIDE RD
101
Lindleys' Knoll
Davis Bynum
Rochioli
Allen
Windsor Gardens
Starr Ridge
Porter Creek
MacMurray Ranch
Williams Selyem
Great Oak
Gary Farrell
Aquarius Ranch
Sapphire Hill
La Crema
Windsor Creek
Poplar
Sonoma-Cutrer
Mark West
Saralee's
Robert Thomas
Hartford Family Winery
Green Valley Creek
MIRABEL RD
Moshian
Joseph Swan
Merry Edwa
Forestville
Oehlman
Dutton-Goldfield
Olivet Lane
Kistler
Klopp Ranch
De Loach
Iron Horse
Stiling
Dehlinger
GUERNEVILLE RD
Green Valley
Scherrer
Dutton-Widdoes
Keefer
Graton
Lynmar
Coopersmith
Tandem
Green Valley
Dutton-Jewell
GRAVENSTEIN HWY
Laguna de Santa Rosa
Marimar Torres
Arrendell
GRATON RD
Maurice Galante
Dutton-Sanchietti
Sebastopol
BODEGA HWY
Freestone Hill
Meredith Estate

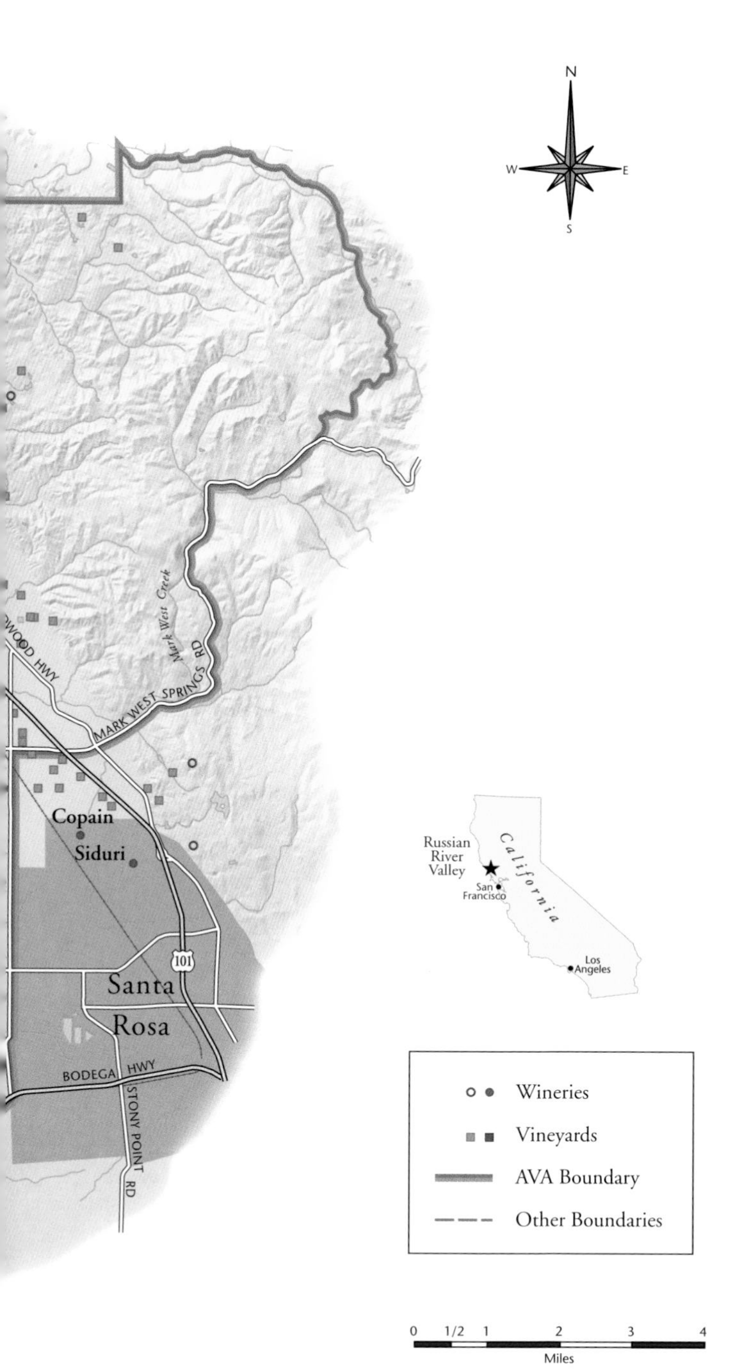

Map 4. Russian River valley.

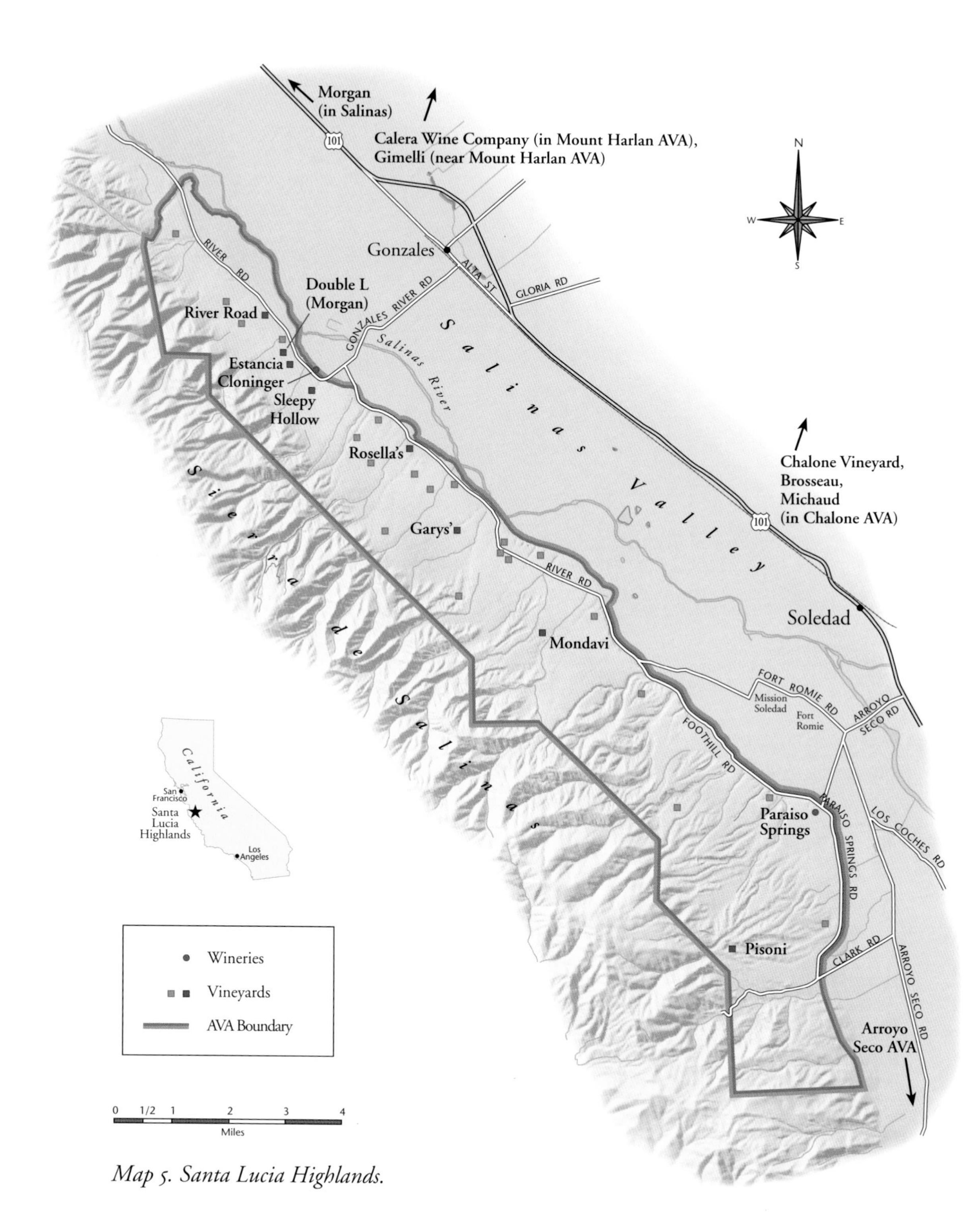

Map 5. Santa Lucia Highlands.

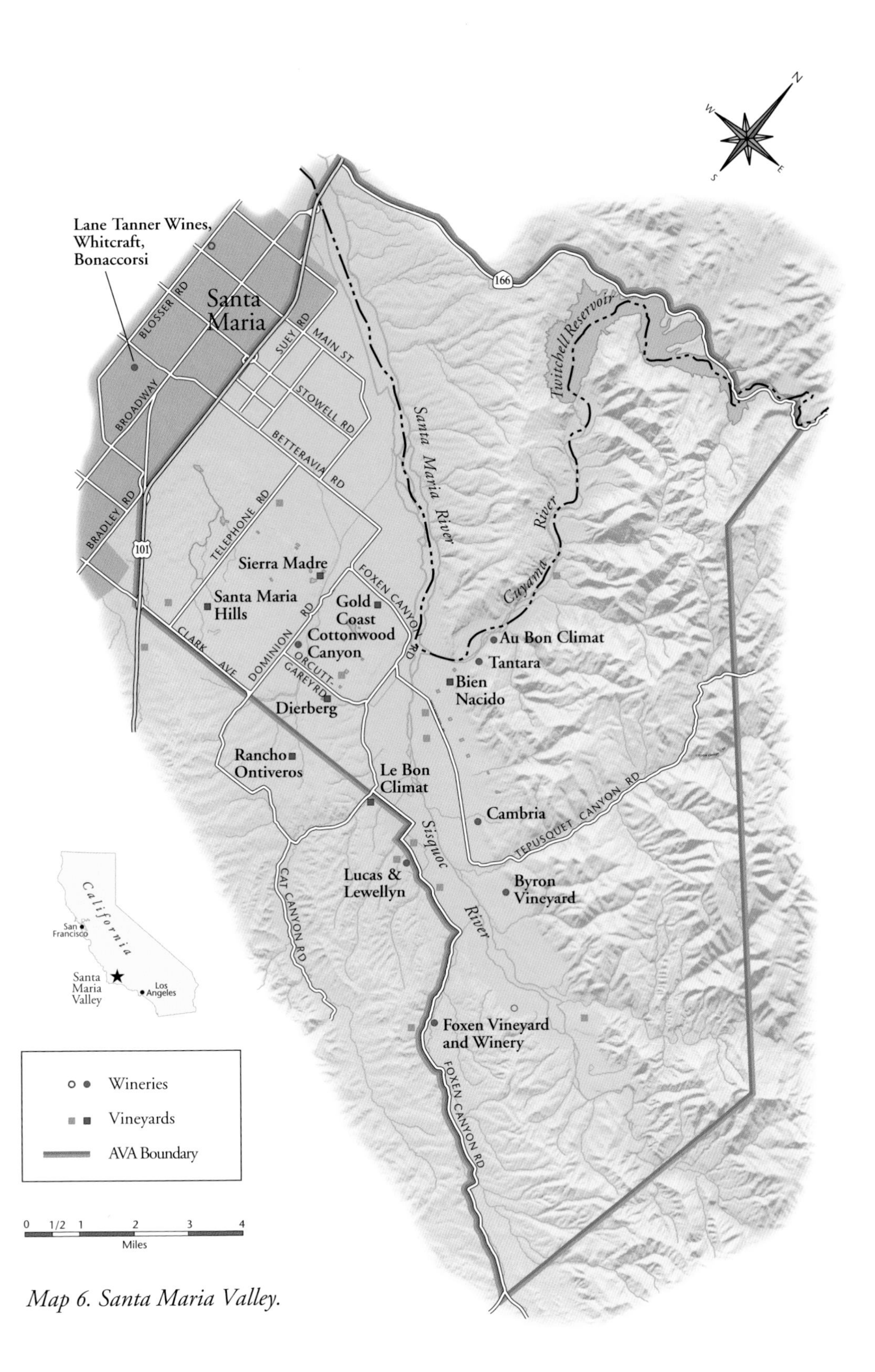

Map 6. Santa Maria Valley.

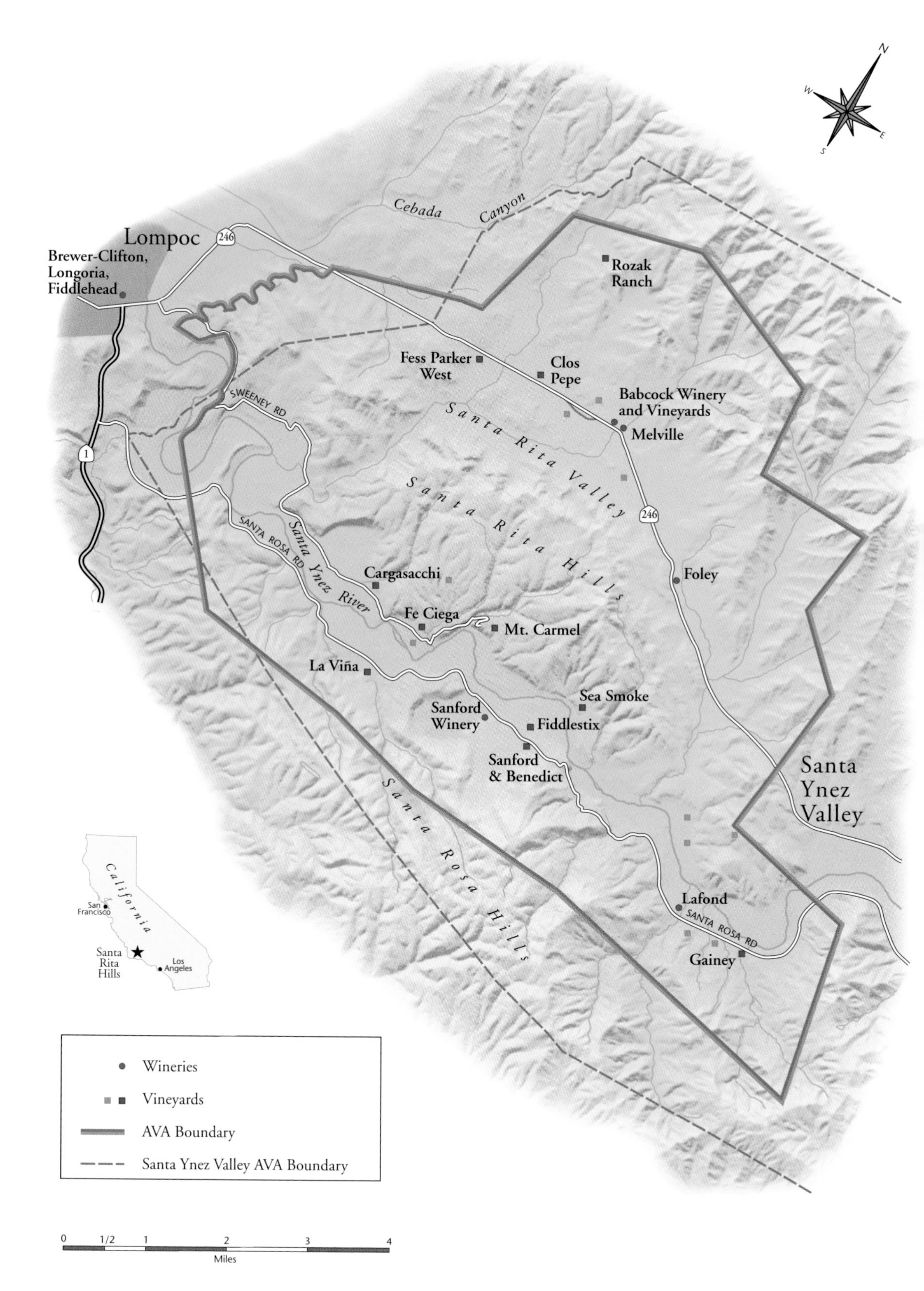

Map 7. Santa Rita Hills.

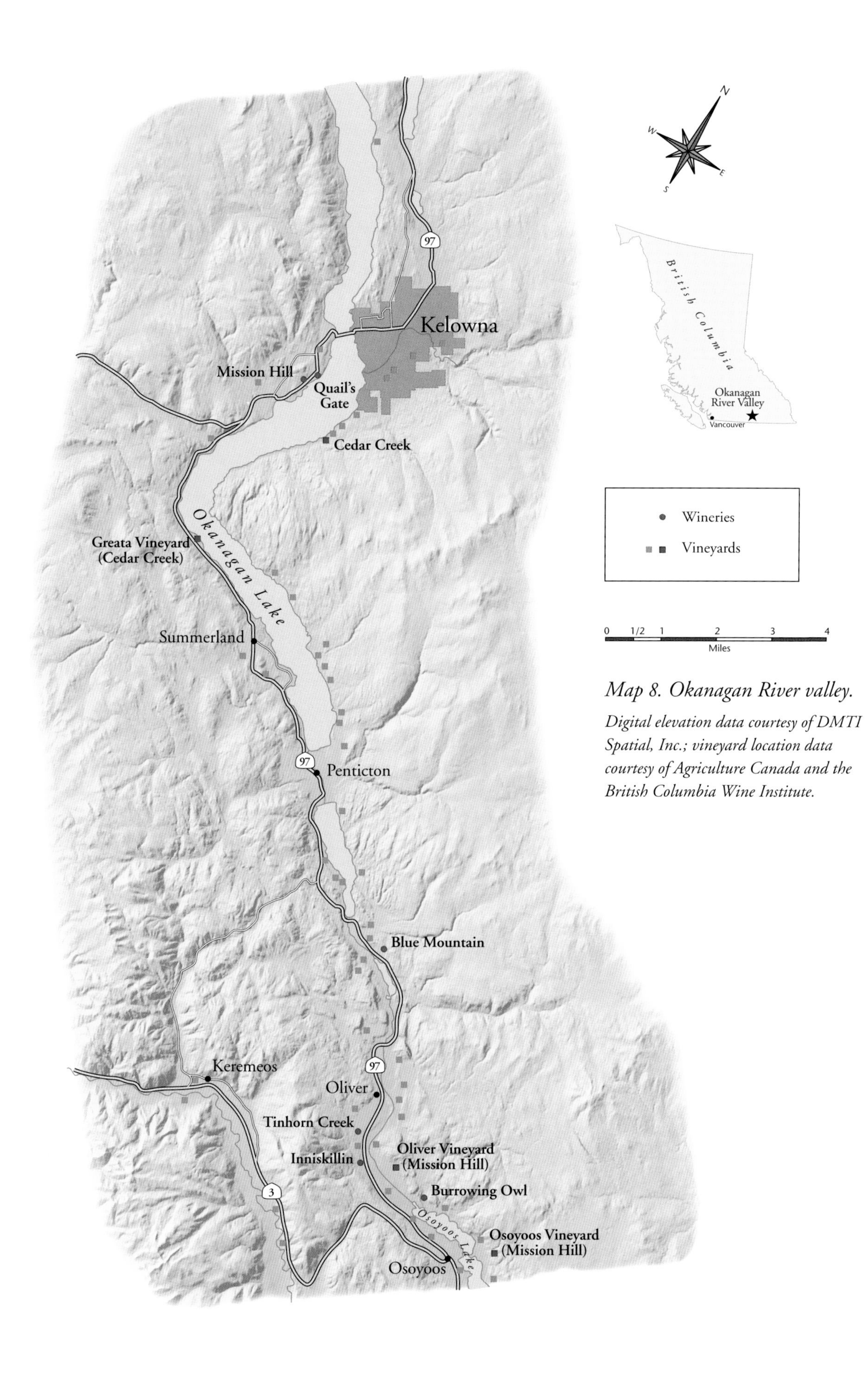

Map 8. Okanagan River valley.

Digital elevation data courtesy of DMTI Spatial, Inc.; vineyard location data courtesy of Agriculture Canada and the British Columbia Wine Institute.

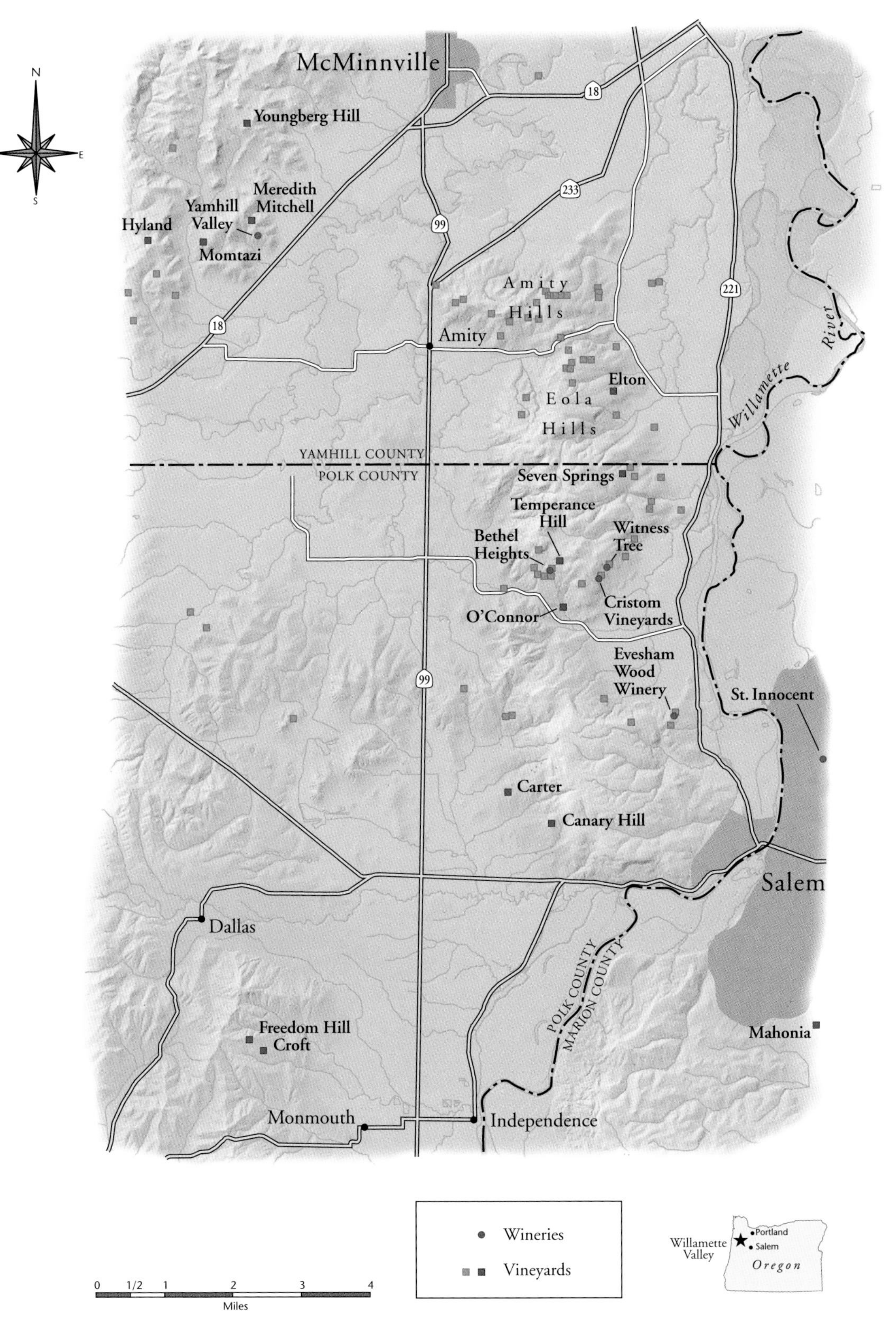

Map 9. Willamette Valley (central).

Vineyard and winery location data courtesy of NW Vineyards.

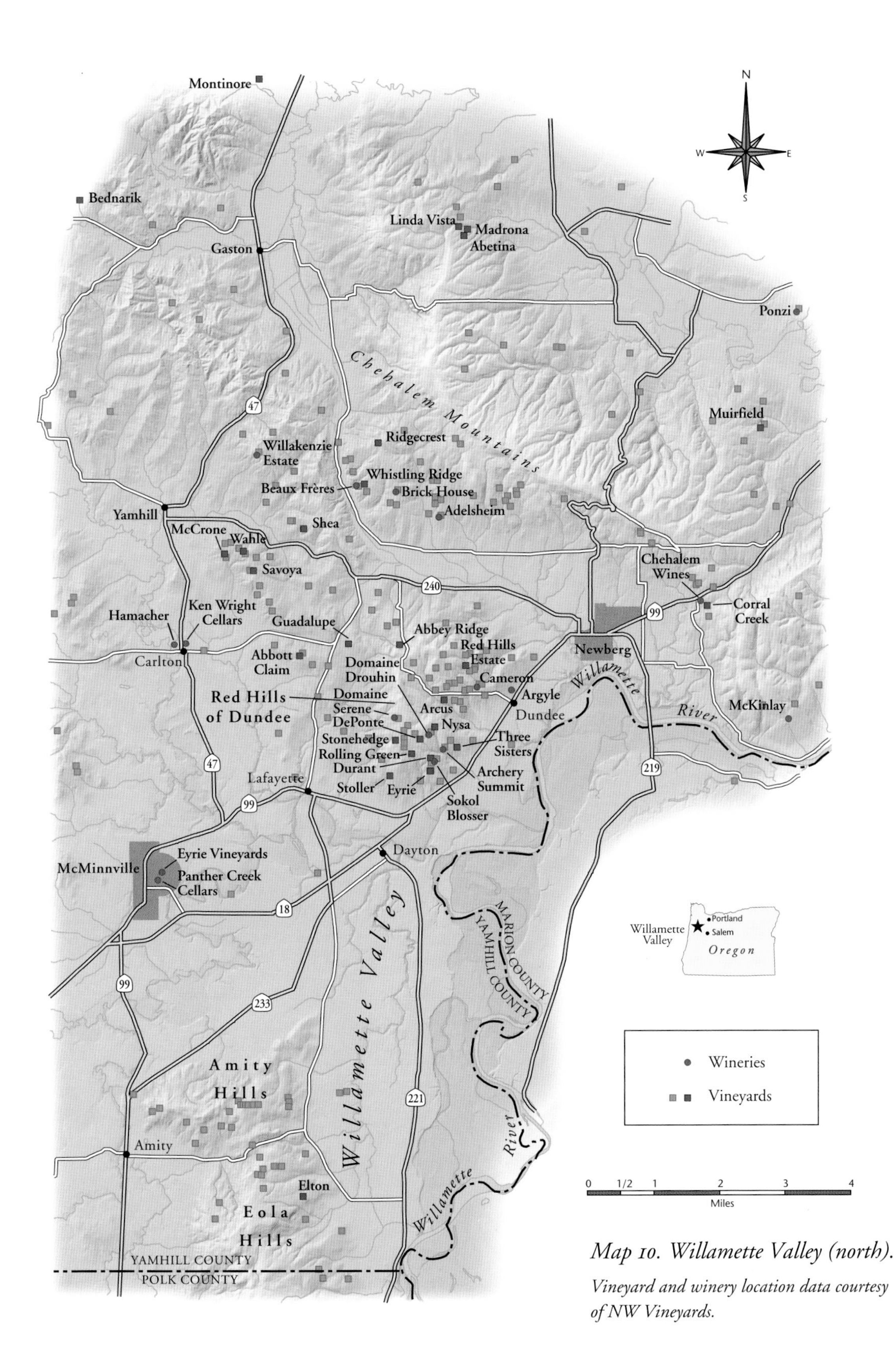

Map 10. Willamette Valley (north).

Vineyard and winery location data courtesy of NW Vineyards.

Map 11. Sonoma Coast.

Part Two

PROFILES OF KEY PRODUCERS

Introduction

The six dozen producers profiled in the following pages vary enormously in size, style, program, and personality. Some are bona fide boutique producers; others make up to 40,000 cases of pinot annually. Pinot noir is the raison d'être for some; for others it qualifies, *almost,* as a sideline. Some producers make only a single pinot noir in each vintage; others have complex portfolios extending to a dozen or more wines, made from grapes sourced from widely scattered regions. Taken together, they represent a fair picture of pinot production in the United States and Canada at the beginning of the new millennium.

No one can say for sure exactly how many wineries across North America make pinot noir. For that matter, given that several producers can share a single winery bond, and that a single business entity can spawn multiple wine brands, it is not easy even to define *winery* for counting purposes. New wineries are born every year; existing ones add pinot noir to their offerings; others are consolidated, sold, or disappear into bankruptcy. A fair estimate is that somewhere between 400 and 450 wineries make pinot noir. Several huge wine corporations, not profiled in these pages, account for the overwhelming majority of total pinot production, including Sebastiani, Constellation Brands, Bronco Wine Company, and Beringer-Blass.

Are the six dozen producers profiled in these pages "the best" of the rest? This is a fair question and deserves a serious answer. On the one hand, I think that most observers familiar with American pinots, if asked to list the best producers, would generate lists overlapping substantially with mine. On the other hand, "best" lists of almost any stripe are methodologically suspect. What was the universe from which the "best" were selected, and by what criteria?

In my case, the universe was all producers I could identify who have a *substantial stake* in pinot noir and *track records* covering at least four vintages made and released by press time. Additionally, since a picture of North American pinot noir was my objective, I was as interested in significance as in raw quality. But biases lurk even in simplicity. Producers domiciled in major pinotcentric regions were more visible than outliers, and producers who could afford to invest in publicists sometimes found *me,* while others were undeservedly missed. Oregon presented a special challenge: approximately 140 of the state's plus-or-minus 180 wineries make pinot noir. To adjust for these phenomena, I asked trusted producers to name other, less-visible producers worthy of attention; and I compared my evolving list of producers with producers who received *consistently* high marks across several vintages in more than one of the following: *Wine Spectator, Wine & Spirits, The Wine Advocate,* and *The Vine.* This was a useful approach but obviously imperfect. Within the universe, I selected for a preponderance of well-made wines showing complexity and personality; for influence on other winemakers; and for contribution to the successful evolution of American pinots, regionally or nationally.

As far as possible, I did not consider, in making my selections, whether a producer was large or small, was widely or narrowly distributed, or offered good value for money. In fact, I ignored prices entirely. I also tried to maintain neutrality with respect to style, avoiding bias toward or against fruit-forward wines, highly extracted wines, lightly colored wines, high-acid wines, and so forth, as long as the wines were excellent exemplars of their style and type.

No one should imagine, however, that this book was built on large, systematic blind tastings, with benchmark wines carried forward from one flight to the next. It was not. In that sense, my list of producers, in the pages that follow, is based on impression rather than science. In addition, several producers whom one would expect to find in any list of "best" achievers were reluctantly omitted because they declined to provide the access needed for inclusion, provided seriously incomplete information, were unable or unwilling to arrange appointments, or specifically opted out.

A word about the winemaking notes in the profiles that follow. They are based entirely on conversations with principals and winemakers. While I have made every reasonable effort to get the story right, the details of winegrowing are not always easily summarized, and mistakes occur. Wineries also make changes, so what was true at the time of writing may no longer be accurate at the time of reading. It is also impossible to verify that things are as described. Many winemakers are skittish about certain protocols—notably the addition of water to reduce the percentage of alcohol, high-tech dealcoholization, fining, and filtration. I have reported neither more nor less than what I was told by the principals, even when additional third-party information came to my attention and was credible. *Caveat lector.*

Also, a few words are necessary about the tasting notes. All wine tasting is, I believe, essentially existential. Sensations and perceptions are personal. Furthermore, they exist only at one time and one place, and for one bottle of a particular wine.

Different bottles of the same wine are not identical. The same wine tastes different at different times, even to the same taster. Mouth chemistry and disposition change with time and place; temperature and handling play a role; and adjunct food has a profound effect. Most of the tasting notes in these pages describe wines tasted only once. If the wine was tasted more than once, that fact is noted, along with observations on any significant differences in perception.

Almost without exception, the wines were *not* tasted blind. Some wines were tasted in the company of their makers in winery or professional settings; others were tasted in a variety of comparative environments. Many were tasted in my home, in what might be described as a quasiprofessional setting. Some were tasted with meals; most were tasted alone, or in a small series, in "clean palate" circumstances. Whenever the wines were first tasted with food, they were retasted a few hours later by themselves. As far as possible, I tasted them from Riedel Vinum Burgundy glasses; unhappily, it was not always possible to do so. Notes describing clearly flawed wines have been omitted. The calendar year (or years) of tasting is always given in the notes. When a wine was tasted before its release, this fact is indicated. And although I have tasted thousands of barrel samples as well as finished wines, the barrel sample notes are not reported—too much can change twixt barrel and bottle.

Some producers with substantial libraries of older wines generously provided the basis for extensive vertical tastings. Even though these wines have disappeared from the marketplace and show up only rarely at auction, I believe the notes are a useful window on the evolution of older vintages of North American pinot noir, and they are therefore reported. Overall, the tasting notes will be most useful to consumers as a reference, and *in the aggregate* as a picture of pinots made by each producer; they are not intended as a buying guide to individual wines or vintages.

As far as possible, I have tried to write descriptive rather than judgmental tasting notes. The idea is to paint a picture of the wine as and when I tasted it. Most tasters use terminology that has been personalized to some extent, and I am no exception. Nevertheless, most of the descriptors used in the notes are described, at least comparatively, in the Wine Aroma Wheel developed at the University of California, Davis (see http://wineserver.ucdavis.edu/anoble/waw.html and other sites), and in the Mouthfeel Wheel devised at the University of Adelaide in Australia, several versions of which are also Web-accessible. Note that descriptors like *medium-weight* and *medium-length* do not connote deficiencies as compared to wines that feel heavier in the mouth or last longer—many critics might reasonably argue that medium is just the right weight and length for a perfect pinot noir. Similarly, a saturated color is not better than a transparent tone, and "brilliant" can be very rewarding visually. Fruit flavors are not the only virtue in a wine, and earthiness, cooked vegetables, resin, mint, and sarsaparilla can all add interest, complexity, and depth. The whole point of fine wine is personality, and pinot noir without personality is usually quite dull.

ACACIA WINERY

Napa, California

The creation of Acacia was the second seminal event of the 1970s in Los Carneros, after the debut of Carneros Creek Winery. A large group of investors underwrote the early years of the project, which was dedicated exclusively to pinot noir and chardonnay. Michael Richmond was Acacia's evangelist, and Larry Brooks was the founding winemaker. The 1979 and 1980 vintages were made at Kenwood in Sonoma, but a large, barnlike winery was built on Las Amigas Road in time for the 1981 harvest.

Within a few years, however, amid rumors of mismanagement and misappropriation of funds, and with some cabernet sauvignon and merlot bottled under the Acacia name without the knowledge or consent of key partners, the winery was put up for sale. In July 1986 it was acquired by Chalone, Inc., California's first publicly held wine producer. Although their titles and responsibilities changed several times, Richmond and Brooks remained close to Acacia for most of the next decade. After tours elsewhere on Chalone's behalf, Richmond returned to Acacia as general manager from 1998 to 2002. Brooks's fingerprints are on every Acacia pinot noir made between 1979 and 1996, when he left to work as a consultant and to launch his own label. In 1996, Michael Terrien, an enologist trained at the University of California, Davis, joined Acacia as a harvest worker. Named enologist in 1997 and winemaker in 1999, Terrien became Acacia's general manager and director of winegrowing in 2002.

Acacia was the first California winery to establish a reputation for vineyard-designated pinot noir based on purchased fruit. Three of these wines were made in Acacia's inaugural vintage, from the Iund Vineyard, east of the winery; the St. Clair Vineyard, across Las Amigas Road to the south; and Ira Lee's vineyard, less than a mile away, near Saintsbury. Vineyard-designated wines from the Madonna and Winery Lake vineyards debuted in 1980. Of these five, only St. Clair has remained an uninterrupted source of vineyard-designated wine to the present day. Winery Lake and Lee were made until 1983, Madonna until 1987, and Iund until 1992.

Worries about phylloxera-induced interruptions of supply then drove Acacia to curtail its vineyard-designate program in favor of a reserve wine, which was made from 1993 to 1996. (Even the St. Clair vineyard-designate carried the word *reserve* on its label—in addition to the vineyard-designation—for several years in the early 1990s.) But later in the decade, after Lee's vineyard and parts of the Iund Vineyard were replanted on resistant rootstock, vineyard-designation was revived. An SVS (for Single Vineyard Selection) wine was made from Beckstoffer–Las Amigas vineyard in 1995. Lee's vineyard was replanted in 1992, in east-west-oriented 11-foot rows with five feet between vines. The scion material is primarily Swan selection and Dijon 115. An SVS edition of Lee was resumed in 1997; DeSoto yielded its first SVS wine in 1998. Vineyard-designated pinot was once again made from the Iund Vineyard in 1999 and 2000. St. Clair, Acacia's heirloom non-estate vineyard, was planted in 1973 to a field selection from Las Amigas Vineyard. Now substantially virused but lovingly dry-farmed by Jim St. Clair, the vineyard's wide, 12-foot rows with six-foot intervine spacing now yield barely one ton to the acre but generate the most elegant and least flamboyant of Acacia's SVS bottlings, generally picked at a lower Brix than the others. Beckstoffer–Las Amigas was originally planted by Louis P. Martini in 1963 and is the only part of Martini's pioneer Carneros plantings still in production. Beckstoffer is dry-farmed like St. Clair and yields parsimoniously at about 1.3 tons per acre.

In addition to the vineyard-designated wines and the short-lived reserve program, Acacia made and released a Carneros blend every year except from 1980 to 1983. The Carneros wine, like the vineyard-designates, relied almost entirely on purchased fruit until very recently. The sources—in addition to parcels that are also used, or have been used, in the single-vineyard program—are CVI (Carneros Valley Investors purchased the Stanly ranch about 1980), Truchard, Hudson, and Ahollinger.

During the second half of the 1990s, Acacia took several steps to anchor its pinot program with estate vineyards and to reduce its dependence on purchased fruit. In addition to 15 acres of mature pinot just east of the winery that were acquired from Andy Beckstoffer's Napa Vineyard Company in 1994, new vines were set out to replace older, failing vines on the remainder of the former Beckstoffer land in 1997 and on a contiguous 20-acre parcel acquired in 1993. In 2000 and 2001, more pinot noir was planted on a 50-acre parcel at the corner of Las Amigas and Duhig roads that was purchased in 1999. More or less simultaneously, the chardonnay vineyard planted around the winery building in 1979 was ripped out, and it is now in various states of replanting to pinot noir.

The above-mentioned parcels, all contiguous and now collectively called Acacia Estate, cover the eroded foothills at the extreme southern end of the Mayacamas Range, near the east-west midpoint of the Carneros appellation. Terrien has chosen to farm this land organically and at the time of writing was in the process of identifying "extraordinary" sites from which a new generation of estate-grown and block-designated wines could be made beginning in 2003. Meanwhile, an estate pinot was made in 2001 and 2002, and the 2002 edition of Acacia's Carneros wine was so dependent on estate fruit that its label carried an Estate Bottled designation for the first time in the history of the brand.

WINEMAKING

Terrien believes that pinot noir should be picked "when the fruit isn't improving any longer." The visual clues are skins that begin to slacken, seeds that are "nutty" rather than "seedy," and color that "bleeds freely from a torn skin." Grapes are completely destemmed, but the ratio of crushed fruit to whole berries is varied from year to year as a function of the perceived strength of tannins. (Crushed fruit, because it releases sugar quickly into the must, ferments at a higher temperature than whole berries, extracting more tannin.) Fermentors are jacketed stainless steel cylinders seven feet in diameter with three-foot top openings. There is no cold soak. Instead, a "fast and furious" fermentation is started with "a hefty punch" of cultured yeast, and peak fermentation temperatures reach about 90 degrees Fahrenheit. Nontraditionally, Terrien prefers pumpovers to punchdowns during fermentation, but he uses a high-volume, low-velocity displacement pump that still assures, he says, relatively gentle handling of the must. Pressing is done before the must is dry. (Acacia avoids postfermentation maceration in the belief that such treatment attenuates the fruit and risks compromising lush texture.) The press fraction is kept separate, but is typically reintroduced into the blend after evaluation.

For the Carneros blend, 40 percent new barrels are used; the ratio for the SVS wines ranges from 40 percent to 60 percent. François Frères is the predominant cooper; others are also used. Barrel lots destined for the SVS program are selected in March following each vintage, at which time the first blend for the Carneros wine is also done. The wines stay in barrel eight to nine months, are racked once, and are cartridge filtered (but not fined) before bottling. In some respects, Terrien's protocols are new. Vintages before 1996 typically relied on some proportion of whole grape clusters—Larry Brooks believed that stems were contributors to complexity—and longer vattings, including at least a week of postfermentation maceration.

THE WINES

Acacia pinots are generally ripe-picked, rich, high-tannin wines with considerable aging potential. Terrien thinks recent vintages are "darker, richer, and spicier" than earlier editions and refers to them as products of "the new Carneros." Hallmarks of the new Carneros are increased clonal diversity, better-oriented plantings, trellising designed to increase the berries' exposure to sunlight, and early-season soil moisture deficit followed by late-season irrigation. Terrien believes that delaying irrigation until late in the growing season tends to produce smaller berries with a higher skin-to-juice ratio; Richmond felt the protocol was useful in avoiding "high-acid and high-pH wines" that had a tendency to taste "tomato-ey." Terrien, like Richmond before him, is fanatical about wine texture. The ideal pinot noir, he explains, has "plush mouthfeel" and substantial, "caressing" palate weight. Terrien thinks of pinot's flavors as the reflection of a life cycle, beginning with the "fresh and delicate flavors of new life" manifest in fruit and flowers, but continuing through "the flavors of decay, roasting meat, forest, and truffle."

Tannin management is a persistent issue at Acacia—hence the practice of complete destemming and the fairly heavy use of new wood. Some tasters found early vintages of Acacia pinot excessively oaky, and some of the earlier vintages now display toasty and soylike properties that *may* be left over from heavy use of wood at the outset; but recent vintages seem well-enough balanced.

TASTING NOTES

2001 Beckstoffer Vineyard (tasted in 2003): Transparent, deep black-red; aromas of root beer and flowers; more mint, pepper, and minerality than fruit in the mouth; very structured, full-bodied, and long.

2001 Carneros (tasted in 2003): Transparent, dark black-red; cedar, balsam, and black fruit aromas; sweet, dark black fruit, barrel char, and fine-grained tannin in the mouth; large-framed, grippy, mouthcoating, and medium-long.

2001 DeSoto Vineyard (tasted in 2003): Ripest of the 2003 SVS wines; transparent, dark blackish-red color; root beer, blackberry jam, and baked-rhubarb aromas; cedar, slate, graphite, and clove in the mouth; medium-weight but very concentrated and grippy, with a texture midway between fine emery and suede.

2001 Lee Vineyard (tasted in 2003): Brilliant, medium-dark black-red; black fruits, evergreen, and forest-floor aromas; pepper and clove in the mouth; sweet and full-bodied, heavyish, long, and emery-textured.

2001 St. Clair Vineyard (tasted in 2003): Transparent, medium garnet; distinctive nose of geranium, peppermint, and bay laurel; complex palate of red berries, mint, resin, tobacco, licorice, and white pepper; medium-weight, concentrated, and grippy.

2000 St. Clair Vineyard (tasted in 2002): Transparent, medium-dark black-red; aromas of shoe polish and dark fruit; infused violets, cassis, blackberry, and black fruit on the palate, with overtones of tobacco and merbromin; viscous, unctuous wine with a sweet core, medium-length, and a suedelike finish.

1999 Carneros (tasted in 2003): Deep brick-red; aromas of very ripe fruit and beetroot with a hint of prune; rich, resinated ultraripe plum flavors in the mouth; sweet, concentrated, slightly heavy; slightly grippy, with fine-grained tannins, medium-length.

1999 St. Clair Vineyard (tasted in 2002): Medium-dark black-red; aromas of earth and black tea with a hint of nuts; infused violets, black fruits, mocha, tree bark, and cola, plus black pepper, in the mouth; slightly sweet, full, and chewy, concentrated and long, with a texture between velvet and suede.

1997 Beckstoffer–Las Amigas Vineyard (tasted in 2000): Transparent, black-red; aromatically complex wine marked by cherry, dried fruit, earth tones, and tree bark with touches of gamy meat and cocoa; brooding, tannic, and rich; needs time.

1997 Lee Vineyard (tasted in 2000): Transparent, black-red, with some tiling at the edge; aromas of menthol, eucalyptus, and resin; some meat, licorice, cedar, and smoke on the palate; grippy, rich, and long.

1997 St. Clair Vineyard (tasted twice, in 2000 and 2002): Transparent, medium-dark black-red; nose of blackberry pie and root beer with a whiff of rose petal; jam, mint, resin, evergreen, tobacco, and black pepper on the palate; very sweet, concentrated and grippy; long and emery-textured.

1996 St. Clair Vineyard (tasted in 2002): Nearly saturated, medium-dark black-red; unassertive nose reminiscent of tea and prunes; resin, tar, eucalyptus, and tobacco in the mouth; chewy, tannic, concentrated wine with a sweet core, long finish, and emery texture.

1995 St. Clair Vineyard (tasted in 2002): Saturated, black-red with just a hint of tile; black fruits, smoke, fig, and citrus on the nose; briar, bark, black pepper, and cola in the mouth; stuffed, sweet, grippy wine with considerable concentration, medium-length, and velvety texture.

1994 St. Clair Vineyard (tasted in 2002): Medium-dark black-red color, slightly tiling and slightly hazy; aromas of mushroom and tobacco; black fruits, blackberry jam, leather, black pepper, cedar, and briar in the mouth; sweet, concentrated, and grippy, with a long finish and emery texture.

1993 St. Clair Vineyard (tasted in 2002): Transparent, medium black-red with terracotta highlights; aromas of resin, tar, and mint; vibrant flavors of cassis and blackberry, with highlights of mocha, tobacco, pepper, cinnamon, smoke, and cedar; full-bodied and medium-weight, slightly sweet, long, suede finish. A personal favorite.

1992 St. Clair Vineyard (tasted in 2002): Again, transparent, medium black-red with terra-cotta tones; tea and dried flower petals on the nose; cherry, cassis, resin, mocha, black pepper, and clove and cinnamon on the palate; concentrated, chewy, sweet wine, suede-textured, medium-long finish.

1991 St. Clair Vineyard (tasted in 2002): Transparent, medium black-red with terracotta; aromas of tea and faded raspberry fruit; candy, resin, earth, licorice, clove, cinnamon, and mocha in the mouth; full, chewy, medium-weight wine, medium-length with a silky-suede finish.

1990 St. Clair Vineyard (tasted in 2002): The lightest-colored of the middle-aged vintages, and tiling; huge, seductive nose of dried flowers, wild strawberry, raspberry, and cherry, plus hints of cashew and hazelnut; cherry, cassis, and chocolate on the palate; sweet, full-bodied, slightly chewy but silken, long and charming. Drinking beautifully.

1989 St. Clair Vineyard (tasted in 2002): Transparent, medium terra-cotta; dried rose petals and faded strawberry on the nose; earth, tobacco, black pepper, and merbromin in the mouth; sweet, viscous, medium-weight, long suede finish.

1988 St. Clair Vineyard (tasted in 2002): Transparent, medium terra-cotta with an orange rim; slightly funky nose of dried leaves and plankton; flavors of raspberry, cherry, mint, and tobacco with an overtone of smoke; medium-weight, slightly grippy, long, emery finish.

1987 St. Clair Vineyard (tasted in 2002): Transparent, medium-hued, red-cored, and orange-rimmed; aromas of violets and raspberry; red fruits, black pepper, cedar, and smoke on the palate; concentrated and slightly sweet, with some chewiness and a slightly chalky finish.

1986 St. Clair Vineyard (tasted in 2002): Transparent, medium-dark, red-cored, and orange-rimmed; earth, mushrooms, resin, cedar, and tobacco on the nose; well-defined and brilliant flavors of cherry, cassis, and licorice, plus game, meat, and cinnamon; slightly chewy, sweet, and concentrated, with a silken finish.

1985 St. Clair Vineyard (tasted in 2002): Transparent, medium terra-cotta, slightly hazy; nose of potpourri; earth, resin, tobacco, raspberry, evergreen, and faded cinnamon in the mouth; stuffed and grippy; medium-long and velvety.

1984 St. Clair Vineyard (tasted in 2002): Brilliant, medium terra-cotta; nose of potpourri and dried leaves, with a touch of resin; tobacco, leather, truffle, white pepper, chocolate, briar, and soft Indonesian spice on the palate; slightly sweet and concentrated, full, and chewy, long and velvety.

1983 St. Clair Vineyard (tasted in 2002): Brilliant, medium, orange-rimmed terra-cotta; preserves of old raspberry, strawberry, and cherry on the nose; chocolate, evergreen, and briar in the mouth; medium-weight, full-bodied wine with a slightly sweet core, a medium to long finish, and a suedelike texture.

1982 St. Clair Vineyard (tasted in 2002 from magnum): Dark, saturated black-red with some terra-cotta and a slightly orange rim; aromas of rose petal and dried leaves; earthy, mineral flavors in the mouth, with white pepper, cinnamon, merbromin, and soy; slightly sweet and grippy, texture of rough velvet.

1981 St. Clair Vineyard (tasted in 2002): Dark, saturated, orange-rimmed terra-cotta; slightly vegetal nose that mixes compost and dried flowers, plus a hint of wild raspberry; mint, earth, leather, licorice, white pepper, evergreen, and merbromin in the mouth, with an aftertaste of clove; medium-weight and full-bodied, stuffed, long, and suedelike.

1980 St. Clair Vineyard (tasted in 2002): Saturated, medium-dark tile red with an orange rim; nose similar to the 1981 but with a complement of resin and sarsaparilla; earth, leather, forest floor, with hints of clove and chocolate in the mouth; medium-weight, moderately long, suede-textured.

1979 St. Clair Vineyard (tasted in 2002): Dark, saturated, black-red core with terra-cotta highlights and an orange rim; aromas and flavors of tar, earth, tobacco, leather, soy, and merbromin; medium-weight, stuffed, sweet, and concentrated, long velvety finish.

PRACTICAL INFORMATION

Acacia's total production of pinot noir is between 20,000 and 30,000 cases annually. The Carneros blend and three of the SVS wines are nationally distributed. For others, consult the tasting room. The latter is open seven days, but visits are by appointment only; 707-226-9991.

ANCIEN WINES

Napa, California

Ken Bernards grew up in what is now the heart of the Oregon wine country, surrounded by cellar rats and pinotphiles. Armed with a degree in flavor chemistry from Oregon State University, he began his winemaking career at Domaine Chandon in 1987, working first as a research enologist and later as associate winemaker. In 1989 a trip to Burgundy solidified his enthusiasm for pinot noir, and a road sign near Dijon, pointing the way to an archaeological site, provided the name he was to use a few years later for wines of his own. Ancien Wines was created in 1992 as a personal side project. It followed Bernards when he left Domaine Chandon to become winemaker at Truchard Vineyard in 1994. Then, in 1997, Ancien moved to a tiny shared-space winery on the eastern edge of Napa, where it blossomed into a nearly full-time passion, subsidized by Bernards's consulting work as close as Carneros and as far away as the coastal valleys of Chile.

In 1992, Ancien's Carneros pinot noir was produced entirely from a single knoll in the first of Domaine Chandon's Los Carneros vineyards: an especially well drained, low-vigor site planted in 1973 to UCD 13 on St. George rootstock. The fruit from this site was deemed too intense for Chandon's sparkling program and was therefore made available for Bernards's personal project. The Ancien Carneros pinot became a blend in 1998, when Bernards added fruit from Ferguson Ranch—also a well-drained knoll, virtually identical in vine age and planting density, and also planted to UCD 13. In 2000, Bernards began sourcing fruit from a third Carneros site: a small parcel of Buena Vista's Donum Estate, not far from the Ferguson Ranch parcel. The surface soil in this block is black clay—not usually promising for pinot noir, but on this site the subsoil is well-drained gravel, which seems to compensate for the liabilities of the topsoil. Although Bernards originally intended to blend the Donum fruit into his Carneros bottling, he subsequently decided to release it separately. In 2001, it was the source for a small release of so-called Diablo Cuvée.

In 2001, Bernards harvested the first crop from the Toyon Farm Vineyard, which overlooks the Hyde vineyard on the north side of the Carneros Highway. Bernards was involved in the layout of Toyon Farm and in the choice of plant material, which is a combination of Swan selection (from Carneros Creek via Casa Carneros) and Dijon 115, planted quite densely in seven-foot rows with five-foot inter-vine spacing. As of this writing, Bernards had not yet decided whether the Toyon Farm fruit would be used in Ancien's Carneros blend or be separately vineyard-designated.

Meanwhile, in 1996, the Ancien pinot program was expanded to include a non-Carneros wine "as different as you can get" from the Carneros bottling. This wine, labeled Sonoma Mountain, comes from Swan selection vines in Dave Steiner's vineyard on the northwestern side of Sonoma Mountain overlooking Bennett Valley. The cool site is cursed with late budbreak and poor set, but these factors also help limit yield and reinforce intensity. Late budbreak notwithstanding, the site ripens slowly and harvest rarely occurs before October 10. Until 2000, the balance of Steiner's pinot went to Joseph Swan (see the profile later in this section).

With the 1999 vintage, Bernards added two more non-Carneros pinots to his portfolio. The first takes advantage of fruit from a newly planted vineyard adjacent to the production facility he now shares with Whitford Cellars off the Coombesville Road in East Napa. Called Mink Vineyard, this is 2.5 acres of Dijon 115 and Swan selection from Casa Carneros planted to Bernards's specifications in a surface soil of cobbly alluvium underlaid with white volcanic ash. (Bernards argues that the layer of volcanic ash operates like the limestone in Burgundy: it is a wick for deep moisture.) The second is a Russian River Valley pinot from Kent Ritchie's Poplar Vineyard at the intersection of Eastside Road and the Trenton-Healdsburg Road. Poplar is a 1973 planting of UCD 13 on a well-drained hillside where the surface soil is powdery loam and the subsoil consists mostly of volcanic ash.

Total Ancien production in 1999 was about 950 cases of pinot noir, plus a dribble of Carneros chardonnay.

WINEMAKING

Although Bernards varies his winemaking practices to suit each vineyard and vintage, he does not diverge far from what he describes as his "default mode." Very small lots are fermented in one-ton fruit bins. He likes the surface-to-volume ratio of these bins and their cap depth, which enable good extraction. The clusters are destemmed directly into the bins and the stems entirely discarded "nine vintages out of ten." A four-day cold soak at 55 to 58 degrees Fahrenheit is followed by seven to nine days of hot (94 to 95 degrees) fermentation, which is jump-started with RC 212 and Assmannshausen yeasts. (The Sonoma Mountain wine takes longer to ferment and is generally allowed a postfermentation maceration of approximately six days.) Punchdowns are performed throughout the cold soak and fermentation processes. The must is lightly pressed with a bladder press; press fraction and free-run juice are combined, and the wine goes into barrel dirty. Bernards inoculates about half of his barrels to induce malolactic fermentation but is happy to wait until May or June of the year following the vintage for this process to spread to the balance of lots and to complete.

Barrel regimes are tailored to each wine. One hundred percent Remond barrels, of which about 55 percent are new, are used for the Sonoma Mountain wine. (Bernards likes the marriage of the Remond wood with the Sonoma Mountain fruit for its "seamless" support of the wine's palate from attack through finish, and for its "respect" for the floral and sage perfumes that characterize this fruit.) The Russian River wine takes all François Frères. Mink Vineyard seems to work well with Cadus barrels; the Carneros blend gets a combination of François Frères and Billon, of which about 25 percent is new. Bernards is reluctant to stir the lees in barrel, citing research that plenty of autolysis occurs without manipulation and arguing that stirring "can strip a wine of lively fruit and 'muddy' it." The Mink Vineyard wine spends the least time in barrel (about ten months), followed by the Carneros (11 months), the Russian River (11 to 12 months), and the Sonoma Mountain (16 months). All the wines are normally racked once in the spring and are generally not fined. Pinots may be pad filtered before bottling if Bernards has any reason to be concerned about stability in bottle.

THE WINES

Ancien pinots are medium-weight, distinctive wines from sites chosen because they are somehow special, sometimes even atypical of their region, and they are explicitly crafted to be quite different from one another. Bernards says he "enjoys blending" but prefers "interesting, eccentric wines" to "necessarily complete" wines. The Carneros wines, fairly true to type, have a tendency to display primarily red-toned fruit and to be fruit-forward, while wines from the Poplar Vineyard are usually more complex and layered. Ancien's Sonoma Mountain wine is the most exotically aromatic of the three and the slowest to evolve. In the ultimate quest for eccentricity and comparative wisdom, Bernards had three tons of freshly picked grapes from Morey-St.-Denis in Burgundy airfreighted to Napa in 2000 so that he could have the chance to make a New World pinot from Old World fruit! (See chapter 7 for additional information on this project, called Par Avion.)

TASTING NOTES

1999 Carneros (tasted prerelease in 2000): Transparent, medium garnet color; strong (and atypical) dominance of earth and forest floor on the nose; cherry, blackberry, cola, and vanilla in the mouth; good balance and linenlike mouthfeel, substantial grip and chewiness at the end.

1999 Napa Valley Mink Vineyard (tasted

prerelease in 2000): Dark black-red; aromas of earth, gingerbread, blackberry, and boysenberry; very spicy palate; rich body and quite tannic.

1999 Par Avion (tasted in 2001): Transparent, medium reddish-black; explosive nose of rich earth, wet slate, truffles, and violets; *griotte* and huckleberry in the mouth, focused in a narrow bandwidth of fruit flavors, surrounded with considerable minerality; bright, elegant, medium-weight, and long.

1999 Russian River Valley Poplar Vineyard (tasted prerelease in 2000): Transparent, black-red color; black fruit and leather; notes of licorice, black pepper, clove, vanilla, and chocolate; moderately tannic mouthfeel with flavors of slate and tree bark; substantial length.

1999 Sonoma Mountain Steiner Vineyard (tasted in 2001): Transparent, medium ruby; nose of very ripe fruit with a hint of raisin, plus plums and wet earth; sage, herb, bay laurel, and bramble overlay dark fruit in the mouth; mocha on the finish; moderately tannic, slightly chewy, long, and mineral.

PRACTICAL INFORMATION

Ancien wines have limited distribution in 12 states, primarily to restaurants. The winery's mailing list is the individual consumer's best source. Visits by advance appointment only; 707-255-3908.

ARCHERY SUMMIT ESTATE

Dundee, Oregon

Archery Summit is the Oregon venture initiated by Nancy and Gary Andrus, who had founded Napa's Pine Ridge Winery in 1978. Gary Andrus discovered wine during travels related to his first career, as an Olympian and professional skier. He worked harvests in Bordeaux in the off-season for skiing, studied enology at Montpellier in France, and used the proceeds from his share in the Copper Mountain, Colorado, ski resort to finance the purchase of Pine Ridge. Drawn eventually by the challenge of pinot noir, finding that he liked Oregon pinots best in comparative tastings, and emboldened by Robert Drouhin's investment in Oregon, Andrus bought property immediately adjacent to Domaine Drouhin in 1992, as well as the Fuqua vineyard on Red Hills Road.

In 1993 and 1994, the first Archery Summit pinots were "prototyped" at Pine Ridge, and this experience informed the design of the onsite winery: a no-expense-spared, state-of-the-art, gravity-fed facility designed to handle 14,000 cases annually. Construction of the winery, including an extensive network of barrel cellars dug into the hillside, was begun in 1994, and it was ready for the 1995 harvest. In 1991 Andrus and his wife sold a 90 percent share in Pine Ridge LLC, which included both the California and the Oregon properties, to Leucadia, a New York–based investment house; in 2002 Leucadia acquired the Andruses' remaining share. Andrus then purchased property in New Zealand's Central Otago region for a new pinot project, and in 2003 acquired Lion Valley Vineyards near Hillsboro, Oregon, just southwest of Portland.

Archery Summit owns four pinot vineyards currently in production, all in the Red Hills of Dundee, and in 2000 began development of a fifth, on Ribbon Ridge. The easternmost of the Red Hills sites—the former Fuqua vineyard, now renamed Red Hills Estate—anchored Archery Summit's pinot program during the 1990s. There are 17 acres of pinot noir on this site, of which two were planted in 1977 and three in 1988. These old vines are own-rooted UCD 4, now affected by phylloxera, but they have the advantage of maturity, and the old-vines fruit is divided between the Red Hills and Premier cuvées.

Andrus added UCD 2A and Dijon 113, 114, 115, and 777 on this site. He also says he imported budwood from La Tâche, Romanée-Conti, and the comte de Vogüé's holdings in Le Musigny, but the winery's current staff cannot confirm this claim from either documentary evidence or field inspection. Andrus was fanatical about planting with very tight spacing, arguing that "the more vines per acre, the less fruit per vine, and the less fruit per vine, the better the wine." He was also a proponent of low-to-the-ground pruning and trellising, as is the norm in Burgundy, so that the vines could take advantage of ground warmth.

Just west of Red Hills Estate is Archery Summit's Arcus Vineyard, a steep, bow-shaped (hence the name) parcel formed by fusing two adjacent vineyards, previously known as Archibald and Marsh, that were purchased simultaneously in 1993. Andrus cannily redeveloped Arcus. Only the east-, south-, and southeast-facing blocks were retained for pinot. An old six-foot by nine-foot block of UCD 4 was interplanted and intraplanted so that the vines are now spaced three feet by four and a half, close to the meter-by-meter density favored in Burgundy. The whole array of Dijon clones was then added, along with (again according to Andrus) field selections from Le Musigny and Roumier's holdings in Les Amoureuses.

The third estate vineyard, on the winery site at Archery Summit Road, is a steep, south-facing slope spanning elevation contours from about 260 to 770 feet. There Andrus planted, entirely from scratch, 27 acres of pinot noir—UCD 2A and 4, along with Dijon 113, 114, 115, and 667—on a variety of rootstocks. Touching this so-called Archery Summit Estate vineyard at the high, northeastern corner is a separate, ridge-top vineyard called Renegade Ridge. Once again, Andrus claims to have planted a six-acre block of this vineyard to the field selections from La Tâche, Romanée-Conti, and Le Musigny; once again this claim cannot be corroborated. The Ribbon Ridge site, between Brick House and Beaux Frères, began bearing in 2002.

Andrus functioned as executive winemaker for both Archery Summit and Pine Ridge until his departure in 2001, but most day-to-day winemaking at Archery Summit was done by Sam Tannahill from 1995 until 2002, when Anna Matzinger, who came to Archery Summit in 1999, was named winemaker. Tannahill was a onetime student of Japanese history who first learned wine by working the floor at Wally's Wines and Spirits in Los Angeles. He spent two years working at Domaine de l'Arlot in Nuits-St.-Georges while simultaneously studying enology in Dijon. Matzinger is a graduate of Washington State's Evergreen State College with a background in environmental studies and Soviet studies whose wine training was, more or less, on the job. She worked at Beringer and Preston (of Dry Creek) in California, as well as in New Zealand and Australia, before her appointment at Archery Summit.

WINEMAKING

Andrus was a curious combination of old-world training, prodigious curiosity, endless experimentation, and strong, sometimes simple-sounding opinions, and his mark on Archery Summit is—so far at least—indelible. The vineyards are carefully tended, leaves are pulled routinely to ensure that the clusters color well from some exposure to direct sun, and decisions regarding whole-cluster usage are made in the vineyard before harvest. The winery picks in small, 40-pound bins that are not consolidated in the vineyard. Each one goes directly to the destemmer as picked. Rigorous sorting is done with custom-built equipment to eliminate mold in wet years, and to privilege grapes with dark skins. Pectolytic enzymes are added to increase extraction, and oenotannins are "in the toolkit" if they are needed. In recent vintages, whole-cluster utilization has increased and now averages between 30 percent and 40 percent. High tech is used to control what Andrus liked to call "the thermodynamics of fermentation." He argued that "you have to manage fermentation so the fermentation does not manage you." First there is a four- to eight-day cold soak, enforced by the tanks' chilling jackets, with manual punchdowns once a day. Then the jackets are used to warm the must to between 70 and 80 degrees Fahrenheit, at which point fermentation begins with resident yeasts and punchdowns accelerate to three times a day. In the first part of the primary fermentation, from around 24 to 20 Brix, Archery Summit sets the upper chilling jacket on the dual-jacketed tanks to maintain a temperature between 85 and 90 degrees. For the last one to two days of the primary fermentation, the must temperature is raised to about 85 degrees by reversing the chilling jackets, if necessary, until the must goes dry. The final burst of heat is intended to increase polymerization of the tannins, and the must is usually pressed at dryness, but some tanks are left for four or five days after they go dry, with daily tasting, until the tannins "feel right." Free-run juice may go directly to barrel, or may be settled for a very few hours in tank; either way it goes to barrel dirty. The press fraction is evaluated. If it is to be used, it is settled; if not, it is eliminated.

New oak only is used for the estate wines; Premier Cuvée (see below) sees a somewhat lower percentage of new wood. Barrels are mostly heavy-toast François Frères with toasted heads, from the Tronçais and Châtillon forests, or Rousseau heavy-toast. Malolactic fermentations typically finish the May after the vintage, and the blends are done in July; but the wines are returned to barrel until bottling, which occurs, roughly, as follows: Arcus and Renegade Ridge are bottled in September, Premier Cuvée in November, Red Hills in December, and Archery Summit Estate early in the new year. The wines are not filtered and generally not fined either, but a bit of the lees is sometimes added back, and light fining with skim milk or egg whites happens occasionally.

THE WINES

Archery Summit's portfolio consists of an eponymous cuvée from each of the three main estate sites—Red Hills, Arcus, and Archery Summit—plus a Red Hills appellation wine called Premier [*sic*] Cuvée, and a block-designated bottling based on the Renegade Ridge vines. Until 2000, Archery Summit bought fruit from the Shea vineyard and bartered fruit from Arcus vineyard for fruit from Cristom's Marjorie and Louise vineyards, which were then made as vineyard-designates. But fruit purchases ended after the 2000 harvest, and the brand became 100 percent estate. Premier Cuvée is the main nationwide release, at 3,000 to 4,000 cases annually. The other estate wines are made in lots of 1,200 cases or fewer. The old 1977 vines at Red Hills Estate are divided between the Red Hills Estate bottling and Premier Cuvée, both of which debuted in 1993. The division is made in the vineyard, with the "best" section of the block going to the Premier Cuvée. The first vintage for Arcus Estate was 1994; Archery Summit Estate followed in 1996. Jeunesse was made only in 1996 and 1997, using first- and second-crop fruit from Red Hills, Arcus, and Archery Summit. Jeunesse and Archer's Edge were made simultaneously, but Archer's Edge used primarily third-, fourth-, and fifth-crop fruit; now Archer's Edge is the only young-vines wine. Because Archery Summit has a dynamic planting program, the fruit sources for Archer's Edge are in constant flux. This situation did not concern Andrus during his tenure. He believed (with some justice) that *terroir* is pretty elusive when the vines are very young.

Archery Summit wines are usually dark and saturated, and often more purple than red. Typically, they are complex, concentrated, and very tannic in their youth. At tastings, the winery often decants the young wines to moderate the sensory impact of their tannins.

TASTING NOTES

1999 Archer's Edge (tasted in 2001): Transparent, medium black-red; notes of violets; very bright strawberry and red cherry fruit in the mouth; strong accent of cinnamon and allspice; medium-long, linen-textured wine.

1999 Arcus Estate (tasted twice in 2001): Transparent, medium-dark black-red; cherry, violets (on one occasion), and rose petal (both times); complex array of berry fruit on the palate; flavors of mint, cinnamon, and anise, with slate and mineral highlights; tannic and grippy, very structured, medium-long finish.

1999 Premier Cuvée (tasted early 2001): Transparent, medium-dark black-red; strong nose of violets and roses; cherry, resin, tar, and tobacco on the palate; a slightly sweet core, balanced and long.

1999 Red Hills Estate (tasted early 2001): Transparent, dark black-red; rose petal on the nose, but also smoke, black pepper, licorice, and black fruit; dark cherry and black fruits dominate on the palate; earth, cinnamon, and vanilla; high concentration, very firm tannins, long and velvety, almost voluptuous.

1998 Archery Summit Estate (tasted twice in 2001): Transparent, very dark black-red wine; dark, slightly sweet, brooding black fruit core with smoke; hints of violet petal; tobacco, orange peel, clove, cinnamon, and allspice joined with coffee and chocolate flavors; very concentrated, grippy, highly structured wine, long.

1997 Red Hills Estate (tasted in 2001): Transparent, medium black-red; dense nose of animal, tree bark, cinnamon, and leather; rich, red-black fruit in the mouth; earthy and quite fleshy, especially considering the vintage; medium-long velvety finish.

PRACTICAL INFORMATION

The Premier Cuvée, Red Hills Estate, and Arcus Estate wines are nationally distributed, though Red Hills and Arcus are released at different times of the year, so that they do not compete directly with each other. The other wines are more easily available directly from the winery, which operates a direct-mail wine club for customers in reciprocal states. Tours of the winery can be arranged by advance reservation; 800-732-8822.

AU BON CLIMAT

Los Olivos, California

Jim Clendenen is one of the authentic pioneers of fine pinot noir in North America. Famous for his substantial physical stature, wild coiffure, occasionally outlandish dress, and outspoken opinions about wine, he could more justifiably be appreciated for his fundamental enological and viticultural curiosity, his encyclopedic familiarity with the best makers in Burgundy (built on a gregarious personality and fluent French), and his honest, no-nonsense wine craftsmanship. Born in Ohio to (by his own description) "gastronomically impoverished parents during the culinary Dark Ages of the American 1950s," Clendenen studied prelaw at the University of California, Santa Barbara, played third-division basketball in Bordeaux, more or less memorized Edmund Penning-Rowsell's *Wines of Bordeaux* before graduating from college, and visited Burgundy and Champagne during the 1977 vintage. Having thereafter abandoned his remaining enthusiasm for legal studies, he made his first pinot noir as assistant winemaker for Zaca Mesa Winery in 1979, returned to Burgundy to work for

Domaine Duc de Magenta in 1981, and founded Au Bon Climat (with fellow Zaca Mesa alumnus Adam Tolmach and a paltry $50,000 in capital) in 1982. The project was named for a hill just in front of the dairy barn at Los Alamos Vineyards, where Clendenen and Tolmach made their first vintages of pinot noir and chardonnay. The hill looked to Clendenen like a good Burgundian *mi-côte climat.*

The 1982 through 1986 vintages of Au Bon Climat pinot were made exclusively from Los Alamos Vineyards fruit, which was entirely UCD 5 clone, except for one lot of fruit trucked down from Oregon in 1985 and crafted as a separate bottling. But pinot noir was a hard sell in the early 1980s, and by 1986 Au Bon Climat had reduced its production to a mere 300 cases—against 3,000 cases of chardonnay. In 1987, however, Clendenen was able to purchase pinot noir grapes from the Sanford & Benedict vineyard, which then became a staple in his portfolio and initially the high-end anchor of Au Bon Climat's revived and expanded pinot program. In 1988, with the "home" Los Alamos vineyard up for sale, Clendenen made a deal with the Millers of Bien Nacido. The Millers built Clendenen a no-nonsense metal warehouse of a winery on the northwestern corner of the Bien Nacido ranch, and Au Bon Climat began to purchase Bien Nacido grapes. Fruit from Brian Talley's Rincon and Rosemary's vineyards debuted in Clendenen's pinot program in 1991.

In 1992, Clendenen and the François Frères cooperage established a new company and pinot label called Ici/Là Bas. Ici/Là Bas pinots were initially made entirely from Oregon's Montinore vineyard, raised in 100 percent new heavy-toast François Frères barrels, explicitly designed to demonstrate that such cooperage was not—as many Oregon winemakers alleged at the time—"too strong" for Oregon fruit. Subsequently the Ici/Là Bas label has also been used for blends of California and Oregon wine, and for California North Coast bottlings. Meanwhile, under the Au Bon Climat label, Clendenen created three prestige cuvées of pinot (see below) and a Cold Heaven bottling. The Cold Heaven label belongs to Clendenen's wife, Morgan, and is otherwise devoted to viognier.

In 1998, Clendenen was finally able to purchase and plant vineyard of his own: 44 acres due south of Bien Nacido and due west of Byron on Palmer Road, called (as if to evoke the Holy Grail found at last) *Le* Bon Climat. Here he has planted Dijon 113, 115, and 667, UCD 5, Swan selection, Mount Eden selection from Sanford & Benedict, and UCD 2A from Talley. Le Bon Climat fruit from the third leaf vintage in 2000 went to Cold Heaven—its "soft" properties match Morgan Clendenen's style—replacing Bien Nacido G Block, and debuted in Au Bon Climat wines in 2001.

WINEMAKING

Clendenen is first and foremost a champion of natural winemaking—no concentrators, no mega-red, no spinning cones. He also insists that pinot should be picked "early" and "not too ripe." For him, La Tâche 1962 is an example of great wine from ripe fruit, whereas La Tâche 1971 is a great wine from less-ripe fruit. "Early" means 23 to 24.5 Brix. "Fruit at 25 Brix is nothing but a problem for us," he asserts. "The fermentation tends to get too warm and to stick, and the wine then ends up sweet and unstable." Au Bon Climat picks early in the morning so the fruit is guaranteed cold, and a "natural" cold soak follows. Primary fermentation is allowed to begin spontaneously with resident yeast, but the must is then inoculated "as a security blanket." Clendenen likes to build slowly to "a lot of heat"—peak temperatures reach 95 to 99 degrees Fahrenheit—and advocates pump-overs rather than punchdowns on the front end "to keep seeds inside the grapes," hold the pH down, and preserve balance. By day six, he moves to a combination of punch-downs and pumpovers, or entirely to punch-downs. Although he began making pinot using 100 percent whole clusters, he has now backed off to zero on stem retention, but about one-quarter of the fruit is retained as whole berries. Fermentors are five-ton, six-foot by six-foot open-top stainless steel cylinders, not temperature controlled.

The must is generally pressed when dry, consolidated in tank, then barreled in 35 percent to 100 percent new François Frères cooperage, but with an interesting wrinkle. From each fermentor, on day four of the vatting, Clendenen "bleeds" a small fraction of highly pigmented juice, which is then fermented in barrel and reassembled, either at first racking or (more recently) in the consolidation tank after pressing. The press fraction is also consolidated. Clendenen finds that these barrels are quite prone to develop special aromatic properties, notably chocolate, coffee, and mocha. Au Bon Climat pinots then spend 12 to 20 months in barrel, and are racked once malolactic fermentation has finished in the spring. Fining is routine, but only about one pinot in 20 is filtered.

THE WINES

Clendenen now makes a dizzying array of pinots under three labels, from fruit sourced as far north as Forest Grove in Oregon and as far south as the western Santa Ynez Valley. If there are any common characteristics to the whole family of Clendenen pinots, they would be varietal character (which Clendenen calls "pinocity") and a high tolerance for the foresty flavors that are sometimes described as "Burgundian funk." In Au Bon Climat's lineup, the main volume until 2001 was associated with two blended wines: a Santa Barbara County bottling and a Santa Maria Valley cuvée. Because of the rising price of fruit, the Santa Maria Valley wine was not made in 2002 or 2003, but production of the Santa Barbara County wine increased. (The Santa Barbara County wine is a blend of pinot noir and mondeuse—the former widely sourced, the latter from Bien Nacido.) A vineyard-designated wine from Le Bon Climat effectively replaced the Santa Maria Valley cuvée in 2002, at a higher price point.

Among the high-end Au Bon Climat pinots, the Sanford & Benedict is a genuine vineyard-designate, made in every vintage since 1987 except 1990. The 1987, 1988, and 1989 vintages were made from dry-farmed vines. Since 1991, Sanford & Benedict has been farmed as an irrigated vineyard, with (in Clendenen's view) a negative impact on quality between 1991 and 1996.

The fruit Clendenen purchases from Brian Talley's Arroyo Grande vineyards travels various paths. Sometimes lots of Talley pinot are made as *single*-vineyard designates, labeled either Rincon or Rosemary's. In 1996 and 1998, Rincon fruit was blended with fruit from Laetitia, also in the Arroyo Grande valley, to create a Laetitia and Rincon bottling. In 1994, 1997, 1999, and 2000, lots of Rincon and Rosemary's were blended with each other, appearing as Rincon and Rosemary's. In most years Talley fruit also goes into the Isabelle bottling; see below. The Talley vineyards are planted entirely to UCD 2A, but in this site UCD 2A gives a deeply colored, lush wine, quite different from its performance in Los Carneros, the Russian River valley, and Oregon.

Clendenen's vineyard-designated pinot from Bien Nacido is called La Bauge au Dessus. The name is vintage Clendenen. *Bauge* is French for a pigsty. By extension it denotes filthy accommodations, sordid spots, and brothels. When Clendenen determined, in 1990, that the upper portion of Bien Nacido's Block Q (23 acres of UCD 4 planted in 1973) produced a wine with strong barnyard aromas and intense flavors, he appealed to French slang for its moniker. La Bauge au Dessus has been made every year since 1990, but fruit from Block 2 (a 1994 planting just above Q on Bien Nacido's main south-facing bench) and Block 11C (a small hillside parcel custom-planted in 1997) has now entered the Bauge blend.

As if this array of wines were not enough, Clendenen decided to celebrate the conception of his daughter in 1994 and his son in 1998 by creating two additional Au Bon Climat pinots, eponymously designated Isabelle and Knox Alexander, respectively. Both are barrel-select cuvées. Isabelle consists of "the best barrels from the best sites" available to Clendenen, generally including some Rosemary's and some Sanford & Benedict, but often extending to barrels from as many as eight or nine sites. The first vintage of Isabelle, in 1994, was anchored with grapes from John Dyson's Vista Verde vineyard in Monterey County. Knox Alexander, which debuted in 1998, is an even blend of the best lots of wine from Dijon clone plantings at Bien Nacido with the best non-Dijon lots. The 1999 was made from young vines of Dijon 115 and UCD 2A; the 2000 is a combo of Dijon 777 with Swan selection and UCD 16.

Recent editions of Ici/Là Bas, which are made in lots of roughly 500 cases, include 1999 wines from the Montinore Vineyard in Oregon and the Elke Vineyard in Anderson Valley, and a 2001 wine dubbed White Rose, made from a vineyard high in the Dundee Hills above Archery Summit Estate. The early vintages of Ici/Là Bas pinots were subtitled La Cagoule ("the mask") to honor the otherwise unheralded partnership with François Frères; a 1997 blend of Elke (California) and Montinore (Oregon) fruit was dubbed La Détente; currently the submoniker of choice is Les Révélés. For Clendenen, these wines are still made to prove a point, and he likes to see them as "revelations" of what's possible with pinot.

Morgan Clendenen would like her Cold Heaven label to be known for viognier, but her 300 cases of pinot noir persistently command attention. The 1996 through 1999 releases were made from Bien Nacido's Block G (planted in 1973); in 2000 she began using young-vines fruit from Block G at Le Bon Climat, which is planted to Dijon 113. The stylistic objective with Cold Heaven pinot is medium-weight, "feminine" wines.

TASTING NOTES

2000 Santa Maria Valley (tasted in 2002): Transparent, medium garnet; ripe berry fruit, soft spice, cooked vegetables, and a hint of barnyard on the nose; raspberry and cherry on the palate with black pepper, graphite, red licorice, and a hint of allspice; very slightly spritzy and edgy in the mouth with a canvas-like texture, medium-weight and medium-length.

1999 Cold Heaven (tasted in 2000): Transparent, medium black-red; strong aromas and flavors of meat and fennel, like spicy Italian sausage; tree bark and hard spice; considerable length.

1999 Ici/Là Bas Elke Vineyard–Anderson Valley (tasted in 2001): Transparent, medium black-red; dominant flavors and aromas of raisined currants, toast, and vanilla; medium-weight.

1999 Ici/Là Bas Oregon (tasted in 2001): Transparent, light to medium ruby with terra-cotta highlights; berry fruit plus black pepper, slate, and mint; some unresolved tannin; full-bodied wine with the texture of rough linen.

1999 Isabelle (tasted in 2001): Saturated, black-red color; violets on the nose; sweet, chewy core with notes of tree bark and iodine; medium-weight and very long finish. Made from predominantly Talley fruit.

1999 Knox Alexander (tasted in 2001): Saturated, black-red; sweet berry-fruit core with flavors and aromas of licorice, slate, cinnamon, and star anise; highlights of herbs and brambles; powerful wine with substantial weight and length.

1999 Rincon and Rosemary's (tasted in 2001): Saturated, dark black-red with mahogany tints; core of sweet cherry on the nose and palate; considerable spice, especially clove; rich and long.

1999 Sanford & Benedict (tasted in 2001): Dark black-red wine with saturated pigmentation; predominance of nonfruit aromatics, including merbromin, tree bark, leather, tar, and earth; some hard spice; large-framed, chewy wine made from a yield of just 0.8 ton per acre; atypically concentrated, very long, fine.

1998 Laetitia and Rincon (tasted in 2002): Transparent, light to medium garnet; pungent nose of very ripe fruit, smoke, compost, and meat; dark cherry, infused flowers, and white pepper in the mouth; light- to medium-weight, medium-length, texture of rough silk.

1995 Isabelle (tasted in 2001): Medium-dark brick-red; nose of animal and leather; sweet fruit with licorice on the palate; inky, structured wine with fine-grained tannins, medium-weight and persistent.

1993 La Bauge au Dessus (tasted in 2002): Transparent, medium mahogany; nose of well-tanned leather and mushrooms with undertones of resin; more leather in the mouth with very ripe black fruit and white pepper; elegant, evolved silken wine with a long finish.

PRACTICAL INFORMATION

All Au Bon Climat, Cold Heaven, and Ici/Là Bas wines are nationally distributed to a combination of restaurant and retail accounts. There is no Web site, mailing list, or direct sales from the winery. The winery is closed to the public except for open houses on the third Sundays of April and October; 805-937-9801.

BABCOCK WINERY AND VINEYARDS

Lompoc, California

The same year that Bryan Babcock entered Occidental College in the Los Angeles area, his parents purchased 110 acres of ranchland on Highway 246 between Buellton and Lompoc, as a retreat from careers in dentistry and restaurants. Two years later, in 1980, having observed the preoccupations of their new neighbors, the Babcocks converted 25 acres of their ranch to vineyard. When Bryan graduated from college in 1982, the lure of the vineyard was strong enough to overcome his fascination with "ideas, goods, services, and the marketplace." Instead of pursuing an M.B.A., he enrolled at the University of California, Davis, in food science and enology. In 1984, he stayed home for the first crush at the family's new, small winery, and "forgot about school altogether." The once-small winery now turns out 25,000 cases annually, and the vineyard surface on the ranch has grown to 75 acres.

Although the ranch was originally planted entirely to white varieties and the brand is best known for fine sauvignon blanc, Babcock has been involved with pinot noir from the outset. Early vintages of pinot noir were made from grapes purchased from the Sierra Madre Vineyard; later on, and until 1997, fruit was also purchased from Bien Nacido's Block G. In 1987, the first vines of pinot noir were set out in the estate vineyard, and the first commercial release of estate pinot was made in 1989. Over the years, as phylloxera forced Babcock to replant blocks of own-rooted vines, the commitment to pinot noir increased. In

2002 there were 32 acres of pinot, of which 28 were bearing. Vine spacing is an unusual pattern of 11-foot rows with three feet between vines. Babcock likes the wide rows for ease of farming and because, oriented north to south, they allow more sunlight on the exposed fruit at the beginning and end of the day. "Planting density," he argues, "is not fundamental." His 1980s experience with phylloxera led to experiments with a number of rootstocks. Scion material includes all of the Dijon clones, a "Calera selection" obtained from a vineyard in Carmel Valley, as well as UCD 2A, 4, and 38. (The last, an unusual choice, is CTPS 459, originally imported by Oregon State University.) Yield in Babcock's sandy-loam soils averages about two tons per acre, but is increasing as the vines mature, except that the hilltop parcel gives only about 1.5 tons per acre. Following the 1997 vintage, Babcock stopped purchasing pinot fruit from the Santa Maria Valley, arguing that he "likes to be closer to pinot noir, because it is a trickier deal."

WINEMAKING

Babcock's winemaking, at least as far as pinot is concerned, is straightforward and low-risk. He says that his wines are "not forced," but the natural product of their fruit. "You can predict the wine from the fruit," he asserts. "Pinot noir that starts off nice and rich and dark in cluster samples will make a great wine." He finds that he is usually able to pick Santa Rita Hills pinot between 24 and 25 Brix, which corresponds to pH levels around 3.25 in the berries, or 3.6 to 3.7 in the finished wine. Lower pH levels, he believes, make the wine "too sharp." (Eventually, as the vines get older, however, Babcock thinks the uptick in pH may come at lower Brix, dropping slightly the percentage of alcohol in the finished wine.) Grapes are picked cool, completely destemmed, and inoculated within 24 hours. Fermentors are 1,500-gallon jacketed stainless steel open-tops. Fermentations move quickly and usually finish in eight or nine days, with once-daily punchdowns. Temperature, according to Babcock, is not a big concern, as long as it does not get above 100 degrees Fahrenheit. In his view, the 85- to 95-degree range produces "silky" wines, while temperatures above 100 can yield excessively tannic results. Whenever fermentation temperatures rise into the high 90s, he turns on the chilling jackets. He prefers to press the must when there is just a bit of sugar left and to inoculate for the malolactic fermentation immediately after pressing, in tank. Gentle press fractions usually taste good and are reunified with the free-run juice. Harder press fractions are evaluated. If they pass a taste test, they go into Babcock's Santa Barbara County bottling (see below); otherwise they are bulked out.

Remond and Marsannay are the favored coopers, and Babcock has a preference (in pinot noir) for tighter wood grains (e.g., wood from the Tronçais and other Allier forests) and lighter toasts. Anywhere between 30 percent and 60 percent new barrels are used; 40 percent to 50 percent is "good." All Babcock pinots spend nine to 11 months in barrel. Babcock thinks the pinots can "lose their edge" if they are kept much longer in wood. "If you stay longer in barrel," he argues, "growing brettanomyces can force you to filter, or to add more sulfur dioxide." There is no use of enzymes and no fining, but filtration is another matter. Babcock thinks filtration is "not such a bad thing": he says that "a great wine on the near side of the filter is still a great wine on the far side." He will filter for clarity, stability, or to remove excessive concentrations of brettanomyces. After bottling, Babcock pinots are generally held for only two or three months before release.

THE WINES

From 1984 through 1988, Babcock's only pinot noir was a Santa Barbara County bottling, made initially from Sierra Madre fruit and then from Bien Nacido. Beginning in 1989, when the first estate fruit came onstream, the best lots of estate grapes were used to make a pinot labeled Estate Grown, while the balance was blended into the Santa Barbara County wine. Occasionally, when the Bien Nacido fruit was "extraordinary," it was made as a vineyard-designate. After the 1997 harvest, Babcock decided to concentrate on the estate vineyard and on his immediate neighbors in the Santa Rita Hills, so he discontinued the purchase of Santa Maria Valley grapes and changed the composition of the Santa Barbara County wine. A vineyard-designate from the Mount Carmel vineyard, a close neighbor to Babcock's estate, debuted in 1997 and has been made since, except in 1999, when an excruciatingly small harvest interrupted the program. In 1998, the Estate Grown wine was renamed Grand [*sic*] Cuvee. In 1999, to compensate for the aforementioned tiny harvest, only one wine was made, on a one-time-only basis, called Tri-Counties Cuvee. This wine was a blend of estate and other Santa Rita Hills wine made at Babcock, with near-finished wines made elsewhere from Los Carneros, Sonoma, and Mendocino fruit. The 2000 releases were a one-time-only Central Coast wine made in part from Paso Robles fruit, a Santa Barbara County wine, the Grand Cuvee, and the Mount Carmel bottling; in 2001 another Santa Rita Hills vineyard-designate was added to the lineup, from the Cargasacchi Vineyard. Cargasacchi is a 14-acre parcel of pinot noir overlooking the Santa Ynez River that was planted in 1999. It is mostly Dijon 115 on 3309 rootstock, in very rocky clay-loam soil. Also in 2001, Babcock repurposed the Grand Cuvee designation as his best blend from the Santa Rita Hills. Although estate fruit is still its core, the 2001 edition also includes fruit from Mount Carmel and Cargasacchi.

In general, Babcock pinots are fruit-driven wines with plush textures, though some older vintages also show strong minerality.

TASTING NOTES

2001 Cargasacchi Vineyard (tasted prerelease in 2002): Saturated, deep black-red with violet hues; black fruit, tar, and violets on the nose; huge, sweet mouth of dark cherries, blackberry, rich hard spice, some barrel char, and black pepper; full-bodied and concentrated, medium- to heavyweight, very slightly grippy, long.

2001 Grand Cuvee (tasted prerelease in 2002): Transparent, dark black-red; aromas of black fruits; very peppery in the mouth, with copious sweet cassis and cherry, black licorice, and clove; concentrated, stuffed, slightly grippy, and long.

2001 Mount Carmel Vineyard (tasted prerelease in 2002): Barely transparent, nearly saturated, medium-dark black-red with purple highlights; explosive nose of very ripe dark Italian plum with bramble; very sweet, coffee-laden blackberry and loganberry that is almost jammy; notes of white pepper and infused violets; full, rich, and concentrated, with a suedelike texture, very slightly mineral, and long.

2000 Grand Cuvee (tasted twice, in 2001 and 2002): Transparent, ruby-red; cherries, expansive nose of smoky cherry, with leather and animal notes and a hint of camphor; more ripe cherry in the mouth, with clove, allspice, chocolate, and vanilla; medium-weight, soft, silken, and long.

2000 Mount Carmel (tasted twice, in 2001 and 2002): Barely transparent, medium to dark oxblood-red; earth, black fruits, pine-tar, and India ink aromas with mocha and hints of game and sausage; spicy blackberry and black cherry with dark chocolate and evergreen in the mouth; rich, concentrated, mouthcoating, and long, with a suedelike finish and a hint of spearmint at the end.

2000 Santa Barbara County (tasted in 2001): Transparent, medium black-red; aromas of cherries, plums, leather, and nuts; creamy fruit in the mouth, with hints of licorice and cinnamon; medium body, medium-length, silken.

1994 Estate Grown (tasted in 2001): Transparent, dark reddish terra-cotta; leather and animal aromas; sweet core of chewy plum fruit with accents of milk chocolate and sweet spice; long and velvety.

1993 Estate Grown (tasted in 2001): Medium-deep reddish terra-cotta; nose of old cherry furniture and furniture wax; dark plum fruit on the palate, with toasty cinnamon and slatelike minerality; still some grip, medium-weight and medium-length.

PRACTICAL INFORMATION

Pinot noir currently accounts for about one-quarter of Babcock's total production, which covers a wide range of varieties, including several Italian and Spanish grapes that are relatively scarce on the American landscape. The wines are nationally distributed in most markets, but the vineyard-designated wines are best obtained directly from the winery. An onsite tasting room is open Fridays through Sundays; 805-736-1455.

BEAUX FRÈRES

Newberg, Oregon

Beaux Frères is a well-known, all-pinot-noir project owned by Michael Etzel; his world-famous (in wine circles) brother-in-law, Robert M. Parker Jr.; and a Canadian wine lover and investor, Robert Roy. It is in the Ribbon Ridge area of Oregon's Willamette Valley. Etzel and his wife found the property, which was then an 88-acre pig and dairy farm, in 1986. The first five acres of vines were planted in 1988, and the first fruit, harvested two years later, was sold to Ken Wright (see the Ken Wright Cellars profile) and Dick Ponzi (see Ponzi Vineyards). Etzel, who was then working for Ponzi as a cellar rat, was impressed with the Ponzi wine made from Beaux Frères' fruit. At the same time Parker, according to Etzel, grew "tired of dumping money" into the unprofitable grape-growing venture. The brothers-in-law sold a one-third share in the property to Roy, whose investment was sufficient to transform the farm's pig barn into a winery and to launch the Beaux Frères brand. Three barrels of Beaux Frères pinot noir were made in 1991; 1992 was the first serious commercial release. As a matter of policy, Parker does not review Beaux Frères wines.

The Beaux Frères estate vineyard is laid out on south- and southeast-facing hillsides above the pig barn turned winery, between the 400- and 500-foot contours. The rows—which are oriented 19 degrees east of north-south to accommodate the prevailing slope—are six feet apart with one meter between vines, which yields a very dense 2,200 vines per acre. The scion material for the 1988 planting was own-rooted UCD 2A and 4 sourced from a nursery. and for the 1989 and 1990 plantings was budwood from nearby vineyards, for a total of 16 acres. Beginning in 1992, eight more acres were planted to nursery-sourced Dijon clones on a combination of 3309 and 101–14 rootstocks. Some of the early own-rooted plantings have since been replaced, owing to phylloxera infection. The first Dijon-clone fruit appeared in Beaux Frères wines in the 1997 vintage. In addition, an 11-acre southeast-facing hilltop parcel called the Upper Terrace was planted at the end of the 1990s, entirely to Dijon 113, 114, 115, 667, and 777; it produced its first crop in 2002.

Viticultural practices are fastidious, with spring pruning to a single cluster per shoot, vertical shoot positioning, leaf-pulling on the east side of each row, and green harvesting before veraison to achieve a target yield of approximately two tons per acre. No synthetic treatments except for fungicides are used; and cover crops, including nitrogen-fixing legumes like Australian pea, help control the vines' tendency to vigor. The Willakenzie soils are relatively deep at Beaux Frères but very well drained.

Fruit sales to other wineries were terminated after the 1992 harvest.

WINEMAKING

The reputation of Beaux Frères has been predicated on a ripe-picked, well-extracted, black-fruit style. Picking is done in quarter-ton bins, and the fruit is hand sorted at the winery. Following a five-day cold soak in two- and four-ton unjacketed stainless steel fermentors, heat plates are used to kick-start the alcoholic fermentation, which relies primarily on resident yeast. Cooling flags are then used to flatten the fermentation's naturally bell-shaped curve and keep the maximum juice temperature around 85 degrees Fahrenheit. Punchdowns are done twice daily until the must is approximately dry; extended maceration continues until the entire vatting has lasted for 19 to 21 days. After pressing, the wine is barreled without settling.

With the exception of the 1993 and 1995 vintages, every vintage of Beaux Frères until 1999 was raised in 100 percent new, heavy-toast François Frères barrels. Beginning with the 1999 vintage, the norm became 80 percent new wood, medium to medium-plus toast, and barrels made from three-year air-dried staves. Malolactic fermentation is left to begin spontaneously, and often does not finish until the spring after the vintage. The wines are not racked until just before bottling, which is done in the autumn or winter after the vintage. There is no fining or filtration.

THE WINES

From 1991 to 1995, Beaux Frères made only one wine each year, entirely from estate fruit. In 1996—confronted with a demand from some customers for a lighter-weight, less-extracted wine, "less like a zinfandel or a syrah," in Etzel's phrase—Parker and Etzel launched Belles Soeurs. Etzel is at pains to point out that Belles Soeurs is not a second label but wine of a different style; however, the winery's own copy describes Beaux Frères as the "flagship" wine. Initially, barrels of Beaux Frères estate wine exhibiting lighter color, lower alcohol, and less black-fruit character were selected for the Belles Soeurs program. Beginning in 1998, however, non-estate fruit was purchased expressly for Belles Soeurs. In 1998, this fruit came entirely from the Shea Vineyard, and that year's edition of Belles Soeurs was a Shea vineyard-designated wine. In 1999, fruit was acquired from both Shea and Archery Summit, and two Belles Soeurs wines were made: a vineyard-designated Shea bottling, and a Yamhill County Cuvée, which contained some Shea, some Beaux Frères, and all of the Archery Summit fruit. In 2000, fruit was purchased from Temperance Hill and Muirfield as well as Shea, and four vineyard-designated Belles Soeurs wines were made, including a Belles Soeurs Beaux Frères Vineyard.

My experience with Beaux Frères and Belles Soeurs pinots is limited to two wines from the 1999 vintage and barrel samples from the 2000 vintage.

TASTING NOTES

Beaux Frères 1999 (tasted in 2001): Saturated, barely transparent, dark purplish-black; cola, blackberries, and some black cherry on the nose; more black fruit in the mouth, with graphite and barrel char; chewy, fat wine, very full-bodied and slightly grippy, medium-long finish.

Belles Soeurs Yamhill County Cuvée 1999 (tasted in 2001): Transparent, medium-dark black-red; explosive nose of red fruits and highly aromatic flowers, including geranium; cranberry, plum, earth, smoke, infused rose petals, and merbromin on the palate; high-toned and angular, slightly grippy, medium-length.

PRACTICAL INFORMATION

Although both Beaux Frères and Belles Soeurs are nationally distributed by Robert Kacher Selections, self-distributed in Oregon, and exported to nine countries, 70 percent is sold directly to individual customers in reciprocal states. The wines are allocated and sell out promptly. The winery is open to the public over the Memorial Day and Thanksgiving weekends only; 503-537-1137.

BLUE MOUNTAIN VINEYARD AND CELLARS

Okanagan Falls, British Columbia

About midway between the United States border and Kelowna, the Okanagan River empties into Vaseaux Lake. Determined to make a life in agriculture, Ian and Jane Mavety purchased land there in 1971, in a breathtakingly beautiful site on the north-eastern side of the valley, surrounded by a wilderness preserve. Their crop of choice was hybrid wine grapes, which were sold to nearby commercial wineries. After a decade of experience with hybrids, Blue Mountain Vineyard was completely replanted to vinifera varieties in 1985, leading the wave of change that transformed the entire Okanagan wine industry at the end of that decade. Then, in 1991, the Mavetys began to make their own wine. In 1998 fruit sales to other wineries ceased, and Blue Mountain became an all-estate operation.

The estate vineyard consists of 65 planted acres, of which 22 are pinot noir. The pinot is set out in seven blocks, each of which is picked and vinified separately. Soils are mostly loamy sand with varying admixtures of rock, and slopes range from about 2 percent to 7 percent. Rows are two meters apart, and intervine spacing is either one meter or 1.25 meters. The oldest pinot was planted in 1985, but most was set out in 1990 and 1991, followed by smaller plantings in 1998 and 2002. The scion material is entirely Dijon clones—113, 114, 115, 667, and 777—sourced directly from French nurseries approved by Agriculture Canada. In this location, Mavety explains, the ideal pinot noir vintage is "warm but not hot," with veraison at the end of the first week in August and harvest between September 20 and September 25. Sustainable land management is practiced, so there is minimal use of chemical agents in the vineyard. Green harvesting is rigorous, and yields are limited to about 2.5 tons per acre.

WINEMAKING

Ian Mavety is his own winemaker and self-taught, though he worked alongside a professionally trained winemaker and enologist during the first two vintages made at Blue Mountain, and he retains Rafael Brisbois, the onetime sparkling-wine maker at Iron Horse Vineyards (see the profile later in this section), as a consultant. Mavety finds that his pinot noir usually displays ripe flavors by the time sugars have reached 22 Brix, so he can usually pick between 22 and 23 Brix. In warm years, however, sugar accumulation outpaces flavor development, and he is forced to wait until the sugars have reached 24 Brix before harvesting. The fruit is partially destemmed and fermented in 2,000-gallon open-top tanks. After two or three days of natural cool soak, the must is inoculated with laboratory yeast. Punchdowns are done by hand twice daily, and the fermentation temperature normally peaks at just under 90 degrees Fahrenheit. Mavety presses after five to seven days of postfermentation maceration and reunifies the press fraction with the free-run juice.

A majority of the barrels are Mercurey, though he "keeps trying others"; they are used for four wines, so 25 percent of the cooperage is new each year. Malolactic fermentations are induced by inoculation, though Mavety says he has experimented with some uninoculated lots. The pinots stay in barrel for 14 months and are racked once after the malolactic fermentation has finished and once more before bottling. There is no fining, and the 2000 vintage was unfiltered. Other vintages are allowed to "dribble through a coarse filter." Up to 16 or 17 months of bottle-aging precede release.

THE WINES

Blue Mountain makes two pinots in each vintage—a regular bottling and a reserve. The latter is made from lots judged better and more structured. The winery's terminology for these wines is Cream Label and Stripe Label, respectively. The wines display very complex flower-dominated aromatics and considerable elegance, but often take time to open in the glass.

TASTING NOTES

2000 Cream Label (tasted prerelease in 2002): Transparent, medium, very red garnet; dried leaves, cherry, and raspberry aromas, with a hint of earth; infused, wilted rose petals, more raspberry, tar, and white pepper on the palate; full-bodied but medium-weight, medium-long, silken finish.

1999 Stripe Label (tasted in 2002): Transparent, light to medium garnet; complex nose of wilted roses, toffee, candy bar, and wild raspberry; raspberry, mint, white pepper, and a hint of mocha in the mouth; light- to medium-weight but very long and elegant, suede-textured.

1997 Stripe Label (tasted in 2002): Transparent, light to medium garnet; dried leaves and petals plus earth on the nose; rose water, raspberry, mint, smoke, and white pepper with hints of clove and mocha in the mouth; elegant, light- to medium-weight wine, long and silken.

1996 Stripe Label (tasted in 2002): Transparent, medium garnet; slightly evolved nose of dried leaves and flower petals with earth, forest floor, and strong mushroom notes; raspberry, earth, wet slate, black pepper, and a bit of barrel char on the palate; slightly grippy with very fine-grained tannins but overall still silken, light- to medium-weight, medium-long finish. This wine was made from the coldest and wettest vintage on record at Blue Mountain, picked the second week of October between 21.5 and 22 Brix.

PRACTICAL INFORMATION

Blue Mountain makes about 2,000 cases of pinot noir annually, which represents about one-third of the winery's total production. Production is slated to rise to about 3,000 cases when the 2002 plantings are in full production. In British Columbia, the wines are sold directly to consumers and to restaurants, where Blue Mountain is well represented on the finest lists in Vancouver and Victoria. The wines are also distributed, in very small quantities, in Washington State and California, via Cavatappi Distribuzione and Intralink Group, respectively. An onsite wine shop and tasting room are open by appointment; the spectacular and captivatingly beautiful site should not be missed; 250-497-8244.

BREWER-CLIFTON

Lompoc, California

Brewer-Clifton is an unusual wine project in almost every way. It is a partnership of two winemakers, who share responsibilities for fruit sourcing, winemaking, marketing, and sales more or less 50–50. The design principle is for fruit taken from multiple Santa Barbara sources to be vinified separately but *identically,* to eliminate all factors that could obscure the fingerprint of the vineyard, and thus to showcase *terroir.* Finally, a key feature in the winemaking is 100 percent whole-cluster fermentations, which are now greatly out of favor almost everywhere, except among hard-core traditionalists in Burgundy.

Greg Brewer is a former French instructor at the University of California, Santa Barbara, who reinvented himself as a winemaker before his thirtieth birthday. His day job is to make the wines at Melville Vineyards. Steve Clifton is a onetime musician and restaurateur who similarly retooled, learning winemaking on the job at Rancho Sisquoc. In 1996, Brewer was the assistant winemaker at Santa Barbara Winery and Clifton at Beckmen Vineyards, both blend-oriented houses, when they resolved to launch a label dedicated entirely to small lots of vineyard-designated chardonnay and pinot noir. The project was itinerant until 1999, when the partners acquired inelegant but dedicated space in the Lompoc "wine ghetto."

In 1996, Brewer-Clifton made just one pinot, with fruit sourced from the Santa Maria Hills vineyard. In 1997, Julia's fruit from Cambria became the second vineyard-designate. In 1999, Brewer-Clifton became one of the first clients for pinot noir grown at Melville Vineyards, where so-called fruit clients now get a third of each crop. In 2000, Clos Pepe and Rozak Ranch, just west of Melville and less than a mile from each other, were added to the lineup. The Melville block is a 1997 planting of equal parts Dijon 114 and 115, in six-foot rows with four feet between vines. At Clos Pepe, the Brewer-Clifton fruit is entirely Dijon 115, from a south-facing slope on the vineyard's knoll, also planted in 1997. Rozak Ranch is extremely sandy soil in a very windy site, planted in 1994 to Dijon clones 114, 115, and 777. In each case, Brewer-Clifton contracts for fruit from designated rows, which are consistent from year to year.

Following the 2000 vintage, the partners decided to focus exclusively on vineyard sites in the new Santa Rita Hills appellation, and thus to give up on Julia's and Santa Maria Hills. Custom plantings of pinot have been put in for Brewer-Clifton at Mount Carmel and at Fess Parker's Ashley's vineyard; the latter debuted in the Brewer-Clifton portfolio in 2002. Clifton explains that in selecting vineyard sources for the Brewer-Clifton program, he is looking for "extreme situations." These can be climatically extreme (that is to say, the coolest sites) or geologically extreme (Rozak Ranch is practically a sand dune).

WINEMAKING

Picking decisions are focused on what Clifton calls "the human perception of physiological ripeness," by which he means, inter alia, slight puckering of the grape skins and no pulp sticking to the seeds. Among the numeric indicators, the winemakers want to see a pH of at least 3.1 before picking, and they will allow sugars to rise as high as 25.8 Brix if necessary. Rigorous sorting is done to remove damaged clusters, leaves, and miscellaneous detritus, first on the tractors during the pick, and subsequently on a sorting table at the winery. Fermentations take place in 1.5-ton double-height plastic-lined fruit bins. The fruit is kept 100 percent whole cluster, and no enzymes are used. A five- to seven-day prefermentation maceration occurs in a 36-degree Fahrenheit refrigerated room. The fermentors are then removed from the cold room, allowed to warm up for 24 hours, and inoculated with yeast. (Consistent use of a single laboratory yeast is one more way to eliminate any possible variations in winemaking technique. In the beginning, the winemakers used Assmannshausen yeast, but they felt it had a tendency to generate too much spice. Beginning with the 2000 vintage, they switched to RC 212, which seems, they say, to heighten the wines' fruit profiles and to generate more color—an obvious advantage in the whole-cluster environment.) Fermentations are long and cool, peaking in the high 70s or low 80s, and postfermentation maceration can last up to two weeks, making for total vattings of 28 to 31 days. (Again, to minimize winery-related variables, Brewer-Clifton tries, in each vintage, to impose exactly the same length of vatting on all its pinots.) The must is then bucketed to an old-fashioned basket press, and bucketed again—free-run juice and press fraction alike—from press to barrel. The winemakers believe the "pop of oxygen" the wine gets from bucketing eliminates reduction in barrel, so Brewer-Clifton wines can stay on their gross lees, without sulfur, until the first full moon in June after the vintage, when the first racking takes place.

Sirugue custom-makes Brewer-Clifton's barrels, using a mix of Tronçais, Allier, and Vosges wood in *each* barrel, so that even a one-barrel lot can be seasoned with a mixture of wood from the three forests, and to eliminate any differences in barrel treatment from wine to wine. One-third of the barrels are new each year. A second racking occurs after the first full moon in July, and the wines are bottled in August, by hand. There is no fining or filtration. The wines are released either the October after the vintage or the following January.

THE WINES

My experience with Brewer-Clifton pinots is limited to the 2000 vintage, tasted at release in October 2001, and the 2001 Rozak Ranch and Clos Pepe wines, tasted as barrel samples. The five 2000 pinots are dramatically different from one another—in terms of color, weight, length, aromas, and flavors—but all are complex, and none is tough from either the extended maceration or the hallmark use of whole clusters. In many ways, Brewer-Clifton pinots are surprising and counterintuitive. For example, the two youngest plantings—Clos Pepe and Melville—from nearly adjacent ranches, produced, respectively, the lightest and most angular wine, and the darkest and richest.

TASTING NOTES

2000 Clos Pepe Vineyard (tasted at release in 2001): Transparent, medium ruby; strong aromas of blackberry followed by an infusion of rose petal in the mouth; notes of cedar, resin, mint, and black pepper; modest tannic grip, but the tannins are fine-grained; medium-weight, considerable length.

2000 Julia's Vineyard (tasted at release in 2001): Transparent, medium black-red; nose of smoked meat, tar, and mocha; brambles, tobacco, and chocolate in the mouth; dense, chewy wine with rich mouthfeel, velvety texture, and fine-grained tannin.

2000 Melville Vineyard (tasted at release in 2001): Barely transparent, saturated medium-dark black-red; aromas of black fruits, strawberry, earth, and smoked meat; black cherry, mint, toasted spices, black pepper, and chocolate in the mouth; very stuffed, dense wine that is also cunningly bright; rich, velvety mouthfeel, considerable length.

2000 Rozak Ranch (tasted at release in 2001): Again transparent, medium ruby; nose of violets and raspberry; black fruits, tar, mocha, vanilla, and slate on the palate; complex, medium grip, medium-length.

2000 Santa Maria Hills (tasted at release in 2001): Transparent, medium black-red; aromas of dried leaves, eucalyptus, and menthol; sweet core of black fruits, fruit candy, tea, and cola; notes of clove and allspice; very silky and elegant wine from 30-year-old vines.

PRACTICAL INFORMATION

Brewer-Clifton made about 700 cases of pinot noir in 2000 and has a target of just 1,200. There are similar quantities and targets for chardonnay. Most of the wine is sold to restaurants and mailing-list customers, but the winery tries to retain "at least one retailer" in each major market. Visits by advance appointment only; 805-452-5609.

BRICK HOUSE WINE COMPANY

Newberg, Oregon

Doug Tunnell's first career, in television news, involved postings in Bonn and Paris, among other places, in the 1980s. In an hour on the autobahn he could get from Bonn to vineyards in the Ahr, Mosel, and Rheingau; an hour by high-speed train took him from Paris to Burgundy. He grew passionate about wine. When he learned that Burgundy *négociant* Robert Drouhin had purchased land in Oregon, a stone's throw from his grandfather's farm outside McMinnville, he resolved to forsake television news, return to his Oregon roots, and reinvent himself as a grape grower. In 1989 he purchased 40 acres of declining hazelnut orchard on Ribbon Ridge, overlooking the Chehalem Valley. The property included a pleasant brick house, built in the 1920s by the engineer who had dredged the port of Portland, and a barn used to accommodate goats, ponies, and (unintentionally) barn owls. In 1990, Tunnell ripped out 16 acres of walnut and hazelnut trees and planted 10.5 acres of pinot noir. The brick house gave its name to the vineyard. In 1993, realizing that plain grape growing was not financially viable, he converted the barn into a low-tech winery (carefully retaining its farm barn ambience, however, down to bales of hay used for seating) and engaged Steve Doerner of Cristom Vineyards to custom-crush the first vintage of Brick House pinot. Gradually Tunnell himself learned to make the wines, absorbing insights informally from Doerner and other neighbors, including Beaux Frères' Michael Etzel, Cameron's John Paul, John Thomas, and Mark Vlossak.

Vineyard consultant Joel Meyers, Eyrie's onetime vineyard manager, guided the 1990 planting at Brick House: unusually dense (for the time) eight-foot rows with one meter between vines; 100 percent nursery-sourced UCD 4. The first crop, in 1992, was sold to Amity Vineyards. From 1993 to 2002 Tunnell shared the crop, variously, with Cameron, St. Innocent, and Archery Summit, all of which made Brick House vineyard-designates from time to time during the 1990s. St. Innocent's last Brick House fruit was supplied in 2000; Cameron continued to buy fruit until 2002, and both used it to make vineyard-designated wines. Cristom also received small quantities of Brick House fruit during the 1990s, but used it in blends. In 1995 Tunnell planted three additional blocks of pinot, just slightly more widely spaced than the first blocks, north and east of the barn cum winery. These blocks, which cumulate to nine acres of Dijon 113, 114, and 115, produced their first crop in 1998. The soils throughout the estate are thin Willakenzie clay-loam, and farming practices have been resolutely organic from the outset. The topsoil in the Dijon blocks is even thinner than in the UCD 4 blocks, hence the decision to reduce the density from one meter to 4.5 feet between vines. Yields are derisory. The UCD 4 blocks rarely produce more than a half-ton per acre; the Dijon blocks now yield a little over one ton per acre.

WINEMAKING

Tunnell picks pinot as close to 24 degrees Brix as possible, while taking care that the stems (of which a maximum of 50 percent are retained in the fermentation) are well lignified and that pH remains under 3.35. The fermentors are 5.5- by five-foot cylindrical open-tops ingeniously mounted on waist-high wheeled platforms designed in such a way that Tunnell can move the containers rather than the wine, that gravity can be used to transfer wine to barrels, and that one person with a forklift can, if necessary, perform all winery operations. Fermentations are allowed to begin naturally with resident yeast, but in the cool Oregon autumn the result can be a natural cold soak lasting seven or eight days. Thereafter Tunnell likes the fermentation to peak at quite a warm temperature, and will even warm his fermentors to maintain temperature as the fermentation subsides. But the generous use of stems also extends the fermentation time, so that the total vatting can last as long as 18 days. When the must is dry, and sometimes even a bit before, Tunnell presses and racks to barrel. The press fraction is kept separate and used for Clos Ladybug, Brick House's second label.

The barrel regime involves 50 percent new oak, mostly from Claude Gillet in St.-Romain and from Séguin Moreau, but Tunnell also uses up to 15 percent Oregon oak coopered by Radoux. (Tunnell says the downside of Oregon oak is that, at worst, it can impart a taste of oak resin; at its best, he believes it adds notes of balsam.) Brick House is also an aggressive purchaser of used, one-year barrels, primarily high-end François Frères barrels with toasted heads, from neighboring Beaux Frères. The half-new protocol, plus the purchase of one-year barrels, gives Tunnell an almost constant surplus of wood, which enables him to rotate barrels, or to transfer some one-year barrels into the gamay program, where no new wood is used. Generally, the pinots are not racked until bottling time, unless extreme funkiness develops. The Cuvée du Tonnelier and Cinquante are bottled after 14 months in barrel; Les Dijonnais gets 16 months in wood. Egg-white fining is sometimes done to take the edge off harsh tannins, but the wines are not filtered.

THE WINES

From 1993 through 1997, Brick House produced a single pinot noir called Cuvée du Tonnelier. (*Tunnell* is in fact an anglicization of *tonnelier,* French for "cooper," so the name translates both as the cooper's cuvée and as Tunnell's cuvée.) I have not tasted these wines, except for the 1997. In 1998, when the Dijon clones began to bear, Tunnell began production of a second pinot, called Les Dijonnais. In 1999, six barrels of 100 percent UCD 4, chosen for their special texture and richness but coincidentally from a lot made with 50 percent whole clusters, were separately bottled as Cinquante. At the same time, some Dijon clone fruit was blended into the Cuvée du Tonnelier, primarily clones 113 and 115, leaving the 114 to anchor Les Dijonnais. In 2001, Tunnell was slightly disenchanted with the lots that normally comprise Les Dijonnais. These lots, plus some of the Pommard lots, were therefore redirected to make, for the first time, a Willamette Valley cuvée. Sold at a slightly lower price point, it seems likely to persist, at least for the duration of the soft economy. In 2002, the fruit from one section of the UCD 4 block (where the soil is Jorylike and strewn with granitic rock) was blended with small quantities of UCD 4 from the sedimentary soils and some Dijon fruit and bottled as Evelyn's Cuvée, named for Tunnell's mother. The future of Evelyn's Cuvée was uncertain at the time of writing, but Tunnell detects a special *terroir* in the anchor section of vineyard, so this cuvée could be made in 2003 and beyond. Meanwhile, in 2002, Les Dijonnais returned to the Brick House portfolio.

Brick House pinots are all succulent, evergreen wines with deep colors, moderate extraction, and good length, but the dry-farmed Willakenzie soils make for substantial tannins. From warmer vintages, all bear and deserve aging.

TASTING NOTES

1999 Cinquante (tasted twice in 2001: once prerelease, once after): Saturated, medium-dark ruby and not quite limpid; cranberry and evergreen aromas; black fruits, cedar, coffee, and chocolate with a hint of tobacco; richer midpalate than the Tonnelier; very chewy; still quite tannic, medium- to heavyweight wine, long.

1999 Cuvée du Tonnelier (tasted prerelease in 2001): Transparent, medium blue-red; nose of cranberry, spruce, and pine; black fruit, resin, and tar on the palate; hint of chocolate; silken texture, long.

1999 Les Dijonnais (tasted prerelease in 2001): Transparent, black-red; strong nose of violets; juicy red and black fruits with blueberry, hints of cola, allspice, and eucalyptus, with cedar and vanilla; decidedly tannic, rich, linen-textured wine.

1998 Les Dijonnais (tasted in 2001): Saturated, deep black-red; aromas of evergreen, vanilla, and red beet; mint, smoke, red licorice, and maybe even marijuana, plus black fruits in the mouth; sweet, richly textured, slightly tannic wine with plummy flavors and a long finish.

PRACTICAL INFORMATION

Brick House wines are available in restaurants and to mailing-list customers. Because of very limited production (less than 1,600 cases total in 1999), the wines are allocated and usually sell out soon after release. Like many other Willamette Valley wineries, Brick House runs an open house on the days after Thanksgiving. Individuals able to visit the winery then can taste the next year's release and preorder; 503-538-5136.

BROADLEY VINEYARDS AND WINERY

Monroe, Oregon

Craig Broadley's conversion from a career in book publishing and distribution to serious, small-scale winemaking began in the early 1970s and revolved around an unlikely trio of institutions: Berkeley's legendary Chez Panisse restaurant, San Francisco's City Lights bookstore and publishers, and Kermit Lynch Wine Merchant. At Chez Panisse, just a block from home, the Broadleys developed a taste for food and wine. Kermit Lynch's Burgundies, from makers who were just beginning to break with *négociants* and bottle their own wines, became favorites. And City Lights, Broadley's employer, was amenable to a book distribution scheme based not in San Francisco but in rural Oregon. Broadley completed the first year of course work in the University of California, Davis's viticulture and enology program. He and his wife then sought out Oregon's pinot pioneers and looked for property in the Willamette Valley. In 1977 they moved from Berkeley to Eugene, and in 1982 they planted their first five acres of vineyard on a northeast-facing slope near Monroe, a farm town with one main street and ceaseless truck traffic, northwest of Eugene.

Broadley's estate vineyard has now grown to 30 acres, wrapped around the northern end of an 850-foot hill. The first planting in 1982 was followed by a second 12-acre installment in 1983, several subsequent small additions, and about seven acres planted since 1996. The 1980s plantings were roughly three-quarters UCD 5 and one-quarter UCD 2A; the most recent increments have been done with Dijon 113, 114, 115, and 777. Spacing is mostly 11-foot rows with four feet between vines, and the trellising, atypically, is lyre-shaped. Although the site is primarily a northeast-facing slope, the planted parcels are mostly oriented east or southeast. This southern end of the Willamette Valley is warmer than the northwestern quadrant where most pinot vineyards are now concentrated, so the Broadleys deliberately chose northern and eastern exposures, to capture the proverbial cooler sites in a warmer climate. The vineyard is farmed and harvested in blocks that correspond to speed of fruit ripening. The first blocks to be harvested are those facing north and northeast; the last to be picked face southeast. Since the early 1990s, Broadley has also purchased fruit from other vineyards in the southern Willamette Valley—especially Whybra Vineyard, which is just 900 feet from his own estate, but also from Alpine Vineyard, a few miles due west, and Walnut Ridge Vineyard in Lane County. The "winery" is a converted Pontiac dealership on Monroe's main drag. Craig Broadley now shares the winemaking duties with his son Morgan, who was raised around the vineyard and winery, and Craig's wife, Claudia, and Morgan's wife, Jessica, are also active members of the self-proclaimed "mom and pop" crew.

WINEMAKING

Purchased grapes are generally picked at approximately 24 Brix and completely destemmed. Estate fruit is a different matter. It is frequently picked at slightly lower sugar but has enjoyed, because of the site, a longer hang time. Broadley finds that the extended hang time makes for riper stems and seeds, so this fruit is used almost entirely in whole clusters. A walk-in cooler is employed to chill the picked fruit. Fermentors are a combination of small stainless steel and 650-gallon wooden open-tops. Transferred from the cooler to the fermentors, the fruit is allowed to warm up slowly. When the grapes are healthy, indigenous fermentations are tolerated, but Broadley does not hesitate to use one or more of several laboratory yeasts on hand if there is a reason to get the fermentation going quickly. The must is first pumped over, then "walked down" by foot, and finally punched down by hand. Broadley aims for peak fermentation temperatures between 88 and 90 degrees Fahrenheit. The must is invariably chaptalized, even when the grapes have been picked at 24 Brix, at least to replace the plus-or-minus half-percent of potential alcohol that is lost to evaporation in open-top fermentation; the sugar is added as the natural fermentation is winding down, to extend its length. He finds the stainless steel tanks are usually dry in about 18 days, but the whole-cluster lots in wooden fermentors, which never go completely dry, are pressed after about three and a half weeks, on the basis of taste. The purchased fruit may be pressed just before dryness, at dryness, or a few days later, to obtain tannins that are substantial but not aggressive. The juice may go directly to barrel or first settle overnight in tank. Whenever possible, the press fraction is immediately reunified with the free-run juice from the same fermentor, but the press fraction from tannic lots may be segregated.

Barrels are a mix of Gillet, Rousseau, and Saury; Broadley says he prefers the combination of these three to any single cooperage. For the Claudia's Choice and Marcile Lorraine bottlings (see below), 100 percent new wood is used, and for the reserve, anywhere between 25 percent and 100 percent. Malolactic fermentation usually happens spontaneously, but often does not complete until April or May. The wines are racked once thereafter, at which point barrels provisionally earmarked for the Claudia's Choice and Marcile Lorraine bottlings are culled, and some are redirected to the reserve wine. The reserve and Marcile Lorraine are bottled in November, 13 to 15 months after the vintage; Claudia's choice stays in barrel until the following spring. There is no fining and no filtration.

THE WINES

The 1980s pinot noir program at Broadley was based primarily on estate fruit, though small quantities of grapes were also purchased. The best barrels went into a reserve wine; the next-best went into a vintage-dated Oregon Pinot Noir, and a nonvintage blend was occasionally made with leftovers. The current program was born in the early 1990s. Claudia's Choice, the Broadleys' flagship wine and their "objective" throughout the 1980s, debuted in 1994, when the owners believed they had enough volume of top-quality wine to justify a separate bottling. Ostensibly a selection of the darkest and most intense barrels, Claudia's Choice has turned out to be almost a block-designate, made from the midslope and lower-slope portions of the original 1982 and 1983 plantings. Marcile Lorraine is another block-designate, made from two acres at the top of the old vineyard, plus some adjacent younger vines; it was first made in 1996. In addition, beginning in 2000, Broadley has picked *a single barrel* from among those set aside for the combination of Claudia's and Marcile, which is bottled separately as Olivia.

The balance of the estate fruit and all of the purchased grapes go to make what is now called Willamette Valley Pinot Noir Reserve. For now, everything the Broadleys grow or buy is used and bottled under their own label; wine is not sold in bulk, nor is there a second label. Broadley is at pains to explain that he is "not afraid of tannin" and deliberately makes "highly individualistic" wines. The wines are broad-shouldered, concentrated, and fleshy. In my experience they are also very layered, medium-weight, and complex, and the much-advertised tannins are tame, well behaved, and fine-grained.

TASTING NOTES

2000 Olivia (tasted prerelease in 2001): Transparent, medium-dark garnet; nose of dark cherry and smoke; very sweet, borderline cherry candy midpalate; slightly tannic, well structured, and precocious, with a medium-long finish.

1999 Claudia's Choice (tasted in 2001): Transparent, medium-dark black-red; aromas of barrel char and dark fruit; sweet black fruit in the mouth, with hints of tree bark, candied orange peel, and wood smoke; medium-weight, linen-textured, and very long. Very fine.

1999 Marcile Lorraine (tasted in 2001): Transparent, very deep black-red; dark fruit, dusty pinecone, and tar on the nose; brighter-toned fruit than Claudia's, with layers of black raspberry and dark cherry, along with a hint of mocha; very fine-grained tannin but still emery-textured wine, medium-weight, and long.

1997 Claudia's Choice (tasted in 2001): Transparent, medium mahogany; tar, pinecone, and forest floor dominate the nose; more tar in the mouth, with dark cherry fruit; rich, silken, and long, with subtle tannins.

PRACTICAL INFORMATION

Broadley makes only pinot noir, and just short of 3,000 cases annually. Although production could increase when the younger blocks of estate fruit come on-line, and from additional purchased fruit, the plan is to remain at the 3,000-case level instead, to become even choosier about barrels destined for the Broadley name, and to develop a new program to dispose of deselected lots. The wines are sold through a small number of retail accounts, to restaurants in selected markets, and to mailing-list customers. There are several open-house days each year, which are an opportunity to purchase wines on a prerelease basis; otherwise, visits by appointment only; 541-847-5934.

BYRON VINEYARD AND WINERY
Santa Maria, California

Ken Brown spent his first years after college selling computers and real estate, reading wine books, and making wine at home. In 1974 he went back to school (at California State University, Fresno) in viticulture and enology and directed the research program for the school's vineyard and winery. He became the winemaker at Zaca Mesa in 1977. Increasingly focused on Burgundian varieties, Brown and several partners established Byron Vineyard and Winery on a small, ten-acre parcel adjacent to the historic Tepusquet Vineyard in 1984. The barnlike wood-shingle winery that they built in time for that year's harvest still stands, used today primarily for barrel storage, offices, and a tasting room.

Byron's pinot program began with grapes purchased from the 1973 plantings at Tepusquet, as well as from the Sierra Madre vineyard, planted in 1974 and located about seven miles west, on the southern side of the Santa Maria River. (On Byron's tiny estate parcel, Brown and his partners planted only chardonnay.) The same two vineyards provided the fruit for the 1984, 1985, and 1986 vintages of Byron's main release of pinot (which was variously labeled Central Coast, Santa Barbara County, and eventually Santa Maria Valley). A reserve wine was made from 100 percent Sierra Madre fruit. In 1987, 1988, and 1989, the Central Coast wine was made from a combination of Sierra Madre and Sanford & Benedict grapes, and the reserve wine evolved into a barrel selection from the same sources.

Between 1988 and 1990, however, three interlocking transactions rearranged the pieces of the puzzle. First, in 1988, Robert Mondavi and San Francisco attorney Jess Jackson purchased the financially ailing Tepusquet Vineyard, which they subsequently divided. Then, in 1989, Brown successfully negotiated the purchase of Uriel Nielson's 1964 vineyard, just upslope from the Tepusquet Vineyard. Finally, in 1990, Mondavi purchased Byron. Effective with the 1990 vintage, Byron discontinued its use of Sanford & Benedict fruit, focusing again (as it had before 1987) entirely on its Santa Maria Valley sources. Byron's 1990 through 1996 vintages of pinot were made from a combination of Nielson (briefly and confusingly renamed Byron Vineyard), Tepusquet (now owned by Mondavi), and Sierra Madre grapes, though an extensive replanting program at Nielson, begun in 1991, pulled large sections of this vineyard out of service for several years. In 1996, a reserve wine was made from the old vines at Tepusquet and Sierra Madre, and the first vineyard-designated pinot—christened Byron Vineyard—was crafted from the 1991 replantings at Nielson. Also in 1996, Mondavi was able to purchase the Sierra Madre vineyard, on which strength Byron began to bottle a Sierra Madre vineyard-designated wine in 1997, and to abandon the reserve program. In 1996, Byron abandoned use of Byron as a vineyard name, reviving Nielson; but the new Nielson name was extended (in 1998) to include the Mondavi-owned parts of the old Tepusquet Vineyard, which Uriel Nielson never owned. Simultaneously, one four-acre section of Nielson was christened Monument Hill, which now produces a separate bottling. Monument Hill is a slice across the first two blocks to be planted at high density in shallow soils at the upper, western end of the vineyard. The combination of shallow soils and strong westerly winds appears to decrease both berry size and yield, and to increase intensity.

Most of the vines at Sierra Madre are still

the original 1974 plantings of UCD 4, plus "some mysterious selections that have never been identified," spaced seven feet by 12, on a well-drained sandy-loam mesa west of Dominion Road, on the southern side of the Santa Maria River. Additional plantings were done in 1997, mostly of Dijon 113, 114, 115, 667, and 777 but including California field selections as well, with densities ranging from 1,400 to 4,400 vines per acre. There are also old pinot vines (primarily UCD 4) in the Tepusquet (a.k.a. East Mesa) portion of the Nielson vineyard, where the shallow soils contain more loam and less sand. Yields from the old vines are low, averaging about 2.75 tons per acre. All of the Nielson part of the Nielson vineyard (and some blocks of the former Tepusquet) has now been replanted (in 1991, 1995, and 1997) to Dijon clones; UCD 1A, 2A, 9, 16, and 23; and a field selection from Sanford & Benedict. Multiple planting densities have been used for experimental purposes, but none is less than 1,200 vines per acre, and the row orientation has been changed from east-west (parallel to the river and across the slope) to north-south. All vines are vertically trellised. Byron's pinot program uses only parts of each vineyard; the balance of the fruit is used in the Mondavi Coastal program. Brown explains that Byron gets first pick from both vineyards. From Sierra Madre this means, for now, the older vines; from Nielson the choice is mostly the vines that were planted in 1991 and 1992.

WINEMAKING

Brown picks ripe enough to avoid hard tannins and "simple strawberry" flavors, when a good percentage of the seeds are dark, and when the vine's basal leaves just begin to yellow. In general, the grapes at this point have a sugar level between not much less than 24 Brix and not much more than 25. Fruit is sorted rigorously—in the vineyard before harvest, in the vineyard again during the pick itself, and (using custom-designed tables) on the crushpad—to eliminate second-crop clusters, botrytis, and leaves. Stems are generally discarded because, according to Brown, "the stems seldom lignify enough to add a positive influence" and can sometimes add a "harder, green tannin profile." The largest fermentors are six-ton stainless steel open-tops, but some lots are fermented in small plastic bins. To make sure the small bins develop sufficient heat, they are placed in a warm room. Native yeast fermentations usually start after about four to five days of cold soak, and about half of the pinot fermentations rely entirely on native yeast. (Nielson vineyard lots generally finish well with native yeast; Sierra Madre is more often inoculated.) Brown finds that native-yeast fermentations "promote less fruit expression, but tend to produce wines of greater complexity." Native yeast is therefore the protocol of choice with old-vines fruit, which has "more complexity potential." The juice temperature is allowed to rise to about 86 degrees Fahrenheit before the chilling jackets are activated. The must is pressed at dryness, or the maceration is extended for as much as seven additional days, depending on the vintage. Extended maceration is generally permitted only in warm years, when there are few green seeds. The basket press's natural tendency to filter the juice sometimes makes tank settling unnecessary, in which case the wine can go directly from press to barrel. Malolactic inoculation occurs during pressing.

The barrels are 60 percent to 70 percent François Frères; the balance are Remond or Boutes (a Bordeaux-based cooper not often used with pinot), along with small quantities of a half-dozen others that are tried out each year. About 25 percent new wood is used for the Santa Maria Valley wine; the vineyard-designates see closer to 40 percent. Sierra Madre and Santa Maria Valley wines are bottled after nine to ten months in barrel; the Nielson wines spend closer to 16 months in wood. About 80 percent of lots are egg-white fined for tannin management (especially Nielson fruit), but most lots are not filtered.

THE WINES

Among Santa Maria Valley pinots, Byron's are uncommonly elegant and rewarding. The Sierra Madre bottlings seem especially silken and softly spicy; the Nielson bottlings are often more richly fruity and earthen. The former, however, have consistently been made from the oldest vines, which are now enviably mature, while the latter (in recent years) have privileged the new plantings (and clones) set out in the early 1990s. My only experience with a "mature" vintage (1996) was impressive, suggesting that the wines can age very attractively.

TASTING NOTES

2000 Nielson Vineyard (tasted in 2003): Transparent, medium crimson-garnet; distinctive aromas of fir, balsam, and tar over very ripe fruit; very sweet and soft on the palate, with flavors of cherry cola; medium-rich and medium-long with a satin texture.

2000 Sierra Madre Vineyard (tasted in 2003): Brilliant, medium black-red with crimson highlights; aromatic flowers, resin, infused roots, and cardamom; concentrated flavors of sweet dark cherry with soft Indonesian spice, tamarind, and white pepper; medium-weight and medium-length, elegant and silken.

1999 Nielson Vineyard (tasted in 2001): Very transparent, medium black-red; nose strongly marked with forest-floor aromas; sweet fruit core with sarsaparilla, allspice, clove, and cinnamon, notes of Szechuan pepper and star anise; long and complex.

1999 Santa Maria Valley (tasted in 2001): Transparent, medium black-red; nose of black fruit, leather, and animal; medium-length.

1999 Sierra Madre Vineyard (tasted in 2001): Transparent, medium black-red; slightly closed; licorice, black cherry, and soft spice on the palate; medium-weight and medium-length.

1998 Sierra Madre Vineyard (tasted twice in 2001): Medium-dark black-red, transparent but saturated color; aromas of daphne, moss, dried leaves, and forest floor with hints of animal; flavors of dehydrated cherry, plums, hard spice, clove, black pepper, and earth; texture of rough silk, fine tannins, light- to medium-weight, and modest alcohol.

1996 Sierra Madre Vineyard (tasted in 2003): Transparent, medium-dark reddish mahogany; leather and cabinet-shop aromas with Penja pepper (a white pepper from the Cameroon that is pungent but rich, woodsy, and earthy) on the nose; spicy pepper over ripe, dark fruit on the palate; mouthcoating and substantial but resolutely elegant; medium-weight and very long, velvety with a hint of grip. Very fine.

PRACTICAL INFORMATION

Byron pinots are nationally distributed, and even the vineyard-designates (except for Monument Hill) are made in moderately generous quantities. The onsite tasting room is open daily except for major holidays. Special arrangements are needed to visit the handsome new winery building, built of rough-sawn cedar with a zinc roof and tucked into the side of the San Rafael foothills, which was designed by architect Scott Johnson and completed in 1996 (Johnson was also the architect for San Francisco's landmark Transamerica Building, and the Opus One winery in the Napa Valley); 805-937-7288.

CALERA WINE COMPANY

Hollister, California

Josh Jensen, a Bay Area dentist's son who discovered good Burgundy while reading for a master's degree in anthropology at Oxford, is one of the authentic pioneers of pinot noir in North America. Convinced from the outset that "dirt, low yield, and barrels" were the keys to great pinot, and passionately dedicated to the proposition that the right dirt was the same limestone-rich soil that underlies the slopes of the Côte d'Or, Jensen chose the loneliest course of any North American pioneer. Since there is very little limestone in California, his Calera Wine Company was, until very recently, many miles from any other winery, on a site originally developed to house a rock-crushing plant. His vineyards—which are a half-hour's crawl uphill from the winery via miles of steep, sinuous dirt track, across cattle guards and through farm gates—occupy an appellation of their own. The only antecedent enterprise in these parts, 90 miles south of San Francisco in San Benito County, was the lime kiln, abandoned but still standing, that has given its name to Calera and figures on its label. To this day, the vineyard coexists with deer, wild boar, rattlesnakes, rabbits, skunks, and tarantulas. Appointments can be made to visit, but Calera is too far off the beaten wine routes to attract more than a handful of wine tourists.

Jensen's search for California's limestone soil began in the early 1970s. Having discovered Mount Harlan, battled for ownership, and prevailed over water-grasping neighbors, Jensen planted his first three vineyards—all to pinot noir—in 1975. These were two five-acre parcels facing each other north and south of Indian Creek—Selleck, south- and southwest-facing and named for the dentist colleague of Jensen's father whose connoisseurship had first introduced Jensen to the pleasures of wine; and Reed, north- and northeast-facing and named for Jensen's first and only nonfamily partner in the Calera venture—and a 14-acre parcel laid out in four differently exposed and differently oriented blocks, which was named Jensen in honor of Jensen *père*. Nine years later, in 1984, a fourth parcel of pinot noir was planted overlooking Harlan Creek, a stone's throw from the first three. This one was named for Everett Mills, a colorful local character who had been instrumental in helping Jensen find his limestone soil and winery site.

Jensen testifies that he was deeply influenced by Chalone Vineyard's founder, Dick Graff, who was "a stickler for the highest quality and for traditional Burgundian methods." Jensen liked Graff's Chalone pinot noirs so much that he used field-selected Chalone budwood for all of the 1975 plantings—save for two-thirds of Jensen, which was planted to an unknown nursery clone. (Stories persist in the industry that Jensen was one of the importers behind the so-called new plantings at Chalone, so that his supposed Chalone selection was in fact none other than a second-generation import from Burgundy; but these stories cannot be confirmed.) Cleaving to natural practices, Jensen chose St. George for rootstock. In 1984, believing that there was no reason to tamper with success, he took budwood from Selleck to plant Mills, but the Mills vines were own-rooted. Additional pinot was planted in a block that bridges the rise between Jensen and Mills in 1997, and a new block, also unnamed, was planted in 1998 north of the lime kiln, in rocky soil overlooking Harlan Creek. There Jensen permitted himself to try some new-generation rootstocks like 3309 and 110-R. The first fruit from the 1997 field was harvested in 2000; the 1998 planting yielded a first crop in 2002. Planting density for the first four vineyards is six feet between vines in ten-foot rows, and the historical yield (1982–1997) is barely 1.5 tons to the acre. The 1997 and 1998 fields are twice as dense, mostly four feet in 7.5-foot rows, but some steeper sections are five feet between vines in eight-foot rows.

When the brand was established in 1975, Calera made zinfandel from purchased grapes.

This practice continued until 1986. The year 1978 marked the first, albeit small, harvest from the three small original vineyards on Mount Harlan; in 1980 Jensen got his first commercially significant crop, enough for about 370 cases. The breakthrough vintage, according to Jensen's memory, was 1982, from which vintage the Selleck Vineyard pinot won a platinum medal in the American Wine Competition, and the Jensen Vineyard was named Best American Pinot Noir in a competition sponsored by the American Restaurant Association. In retrospect, Jensen thinks the 1978 through 1981 vintages were hampered by his view at the time, shaped by Burgundian advice, that pinot noir should be harvested at about 22 degrees Brix, to yield finished wine with approximately 12 percent alcohol. "We were trying so hard," he recalls, "to be sure the wines were not pruny." In "a major winemaking shift," Calera began picking riper in 1982, which allowed the wines to finish about 13 percent to 13.5 percent alcohol—which in Jensen's view improved them dramatically.

WINEMAKING

Unsurprisingly, Jensen follows a classical, almost old-fashioned Burgundian protocol. Fermentations take place in 2,000-gallon open-top tanks, and (very uncharacteristically for the New World) all the stems are used. In fact, Calera does not own a crusher-destemmer, which Jensen describes as a "doomsday machine." Grape clusters are tipped from picking bins directly into the fermentors. There is no cold soak save for the couple of days it takes the must to warm sufficiently that fermentation can start naturally, with resident yeast. Calera "almost always" adds acid and never bleeds the must. The vatting normally lasts about 14 days at a maximum temperature of about 86 degrees Fahrenheit. The pomace is bladder-pressed when the must is dry; the press fraction is immediately reassembled with the free-run juice, and the Mount Harlan wines go into about 30 percent new oak. (Only 10 percent new oak is used for the Central Coast blend.)

Eighty-five percent of the cooperage is François Frères CF (for Central France) barrels, but a small amount of other cooperage is used "for curiosity value." The Central Coast blend is kept in barrel for 11 to 12 months, while the vineyard-designated wines spend 15 to 16 months in wood. The wines are not racked until bottling, nor are they filtered; however, each barrel is fined with one or two egg whites "for clarity or to help manage tannin."

Steve Doerner, a biochemist without formal training in enology, was Calera's winemaker from 1979 to 1991, when he moved to Cristom in Oregon, but Jensen and Doerner collaborated on all key decisions throughout his tenure. Diana Vita, a Cornell graduate in enology, joined the Calera team in 1987, beginning what Jensen calls "major-winemaking-decisions-by-committee-of-three," which continues to this day. Vita is now the winery manager, with responsibility for "institutional memory" and the "maintenance of house style." Following Doerner's departure, the winemaker title was held by Sara Steiner from 1992 to 1995, and by New Zealander Belinda Gould from 1997 through the 2000 vintage. In 2000, Jensen reclaimed the winemaker title for himself but engaged Terry Culton, a veteran of Wild Horse, Edmeades, and Willamette Valley Vineyards, as his assistant. Culton now handles all day-to-day winemaking tasks.

THE WINES

Calera's single-vineyard wines are generally dark, complex, saturated wines. They are also very structured—in a way that is common among wines from mountain vineyards—and angular. They are not, however, heavyweight wines; the inherent elegance of pinot is maintained. Jensen says plainly that these flagship wines are usually "backward" and "really don't taste that great" until they are three or four years old. The Selleck and Mills bottlings are not even released until three years after the vintage; Reed and Jensen are typically held for three and a half or four years; the winery recommends drinking them six to 12 years after the vintage. The Central Coast blend, by contrast, is designed to be ready young. With only a handful of exceptions, all the Mount Harlan fruit goes into the single-vineyard bottlings, and the Central Coast wine is made almost entirely from purchased fruit. In 1993 some lots from three of the four estate vineyards were declassified into a Central Coast Reserve wine, and in 1997, another high-yield year, about 1,200 cases of Calera Mélange Mount Harlan were made from declassified, lighter lots. In other vintages an occasional barrel is declassified into the Central Coast blend.

Most of the fruit for the Central Coast blend comes from four vineyards: the San Ysidro vineyard outside Gilroy in Santa Clara County, Laetitia in Arroyo Grande, Wente in Arroyo Seco, and Gimelli, less than a mile from Calera's winery in San Benito County. Pinot noir accounts for about 60 percent of Calera's total production, which also includes chardonnay and viognier; the percentage will increase slightly when the 1997 and 1998 blocks are in full production.

TASTING NOTES

1999 Central Coast (tasted in 2002): Very transparent, brilliant ruby; strong aromas of earth, moss, and barnyard with some ripe, dark fruit; dark fruit again in the mouth, with notes of earth, spice, barrel char, and a hint of nuts; medium-weight and long, with a silken finish.

1999 Jensen Vineyard (tasted in 2003 from a half-bottle): Color similar to the 1999 Mills, below; aromas of earth and forest floor; flavors of cherry, resin, tar, and white pepper with some barrel char; medium-weight and full-bodied, texture of fine emery, and long.

1999 Mills Vineyard (tasted in 2003 from a half-bottle): Brilliant, medium black-red; potpourri, minty menthol, and leather on the nose; tar, tobacco, licorice, clove, and cherry on the palate; medium-weight, concentrated, slightly grippy, suede-textured, and medium-long.

1999 Reed Vineyard (tasted in 2003 from a half-bottle): Similar color again; raspberry, tea leaves, and geranium on the nose; blackberry, clove, resin, and cola in the mouth; slightly sweeter than the other 1999s; full-bodied, suede-textured, and long.

1999 Selleck Vineyard (tasted in 2003 from a half-bottle): Similar color again; complex nose of toffee, leather, forest floor, and cured meat with hints of nut; black fruit, tobacco, briar, and toasted clove on the palate; exceptionally full-bodied, velvety, and long.

1998 Central Coast (tasted in 2001): Very transparent, medium ruby; bramble, tar, leather, and floral aromas overlay wet underbrush; slightly sweet on the palate with cherry, tar, and soft spice; light- to medium-weight and medium-length, with the texture of soft cotton.

1997 Jensen Vineyard (tasted in 2001 from a half-bottle): Transparent, medium black-red tinged with mahogany; slightly closed nose marked primarily with rose petal; wet slate and black fruit on the palate; dominantly mineral; medium-weight, very long, and the most tannic of the vineyard-designates in this vintage.

1997 Mills Vineyard (tasted in 2001 from a half-bottle): Very transparent, medium reddish mahogany; pungent floral nose; dried flowers, spice, white pepper, and tangerine peel wrapped around very fine-grained tannins; medium-weight and long.

1997 Reed Vineyard (tasted in 2001 from a half-bottle): Transparent, light to medium mahogany; aromas of camphor, leather, and shoe polish; very fine-grained tannins, black pepper, roasted spice, smoke, and wet slate in the mouth; medium-weight, long, and fine.

1997 Selleck Vineyard (tasted in 2001 from a half-bottle): Very transparent, medium black-red tinged with mahogany; hint of animal and roasted, soft sweet spice on the nose; in the mouth, a sweet fruit core surrounded with nuts, clove, pepper, and cherry wood; rich, complex wine, still slightly tannic, long and fine.

1996 Jensen Vineyard (tasted in 2000): Saturated black-red wine, barely transparent; nose and palate of raspberry and dark black fruits, flavors of tree bark, earth, and leather; resinous notes including eucalyptus and tar; tannic, long.

1992 Jensen Vineyard (tasted in 2002): Transparent, medium terra-cotta; aromas of leather and toasted spice; very ripe fruit, camphor, eucalyptus, and menthol on the palate; medium-weight and medium-length, silken.

1989 Jensen Vineyard (tasted in 2000): Very dark, saturated terra-cotta color; nose of stewed black fruit and cola; leather, resin, allspice, and chocolate on the palate; still tannic and dense.

1985 Selleck (tasted in 2000): Transparent, terra-cotta color; resin, leather, and an overall briary impression on the nose; cooked black fruits, fruit candy, and cola on the palate; mostly resolved tannins, medium-weight, and very long.

PRACTICAL INFORMATION

Calera wines are distributed in 47 states and 15 countries. Depending on the vintage, the Mount Harlan vineyards generally produce 600 to 1,600 cases each. Since about 15,000 cases of the Central Coast wine are made, it is much more widely available, but the single-vineyard wines are also sold in stores and restaurants in all Calera's markets, albeit in smaller quantities. All Calera wines can also be ordered directly from the winery. Visits are by appointment only; 831-637-9170.

CAMERON WINERY

Dundee, Oregon

John Paul began his professional life with a doctorate in oceanography and a staff research job in plant biochemistry. His winemaking career commenced, a bit later, with the 1978 crush at Sokol Blosser Winery, followed by four years at Carneros Creek, some time "kicking around" in Burgundy, and six months in New Zealand. Paul took several lessons from this early experience: first, that Los Carneros was too warm for "his kind of pinot"; second, that his kind of winery had to start and stay small—3,500 to 5,000 cases—and compensate for its small size by self-distributing; and third, that New Zealand's domestic wine market, in the early 1980s, was too weak to support self-distribution. So in 1984, Paul moved his family to Portland, Oregon, purchased land near Dundee, and made Cameron's first vintage. The fruit for this vintage was purchased from Bill and Julia Wayne's Abbey Ridge Vineyard in exchange for shares in Cameron, birthing a partnership now in its twentieth year.

Abbey Ridge is one of the oldest vineyards in the Dundee Hills. The first block was planted in 1976; subsequent plantings were done in 1984 and 1990. There are 22 planted acres total. The site is a southwest-facing slope at the northwestern end of the hills, high and cool at 650 feet. The 1977 and 1984 plantings were own-rooted UCD 2A and 4, plus a field selection from Charles Coury's vineyard, set in nine-foot rows with six feet between vines. In 1990, a 1.5-acre section, now called Arley's Leap, was planted with budwood from Cameron's "estate" parcel (see below). Before 1984, Abbey Ridge pinot was sold primarily to The Eyrie Vineyards (see the profile later in this section) and to Adelsheim; now about 85 percent goes into Cameron wines. Small quantities of fruit from the 1984 block are, however, sold to Ken Wright Cellars (see the profile later in this section) and Westrey, both of which also make vineyard-designated wines from Abbey Ridge.

Cameron's estate vineyard, on Worden Hill Road above the town of Dundee, is a former filbert orchard now called Clos Electrique, for its electrified peripheral fence. Paul cleared the filberts and planted two acres of pinot noir immediately after purchasing the property in 1984, using "ten clones," including Dijon 113, 114, and 115. Paul will not identify the other plant material, but it can be presumed to have originated out of state, and probably came from several of California's heritage vineyards. Clos Electrique, like Abbey Ridge, was planted nine feet by six; the soil is typical of the region, iron-rich Jory. Chardonnay was planted at Clos Electrique in 1987, and small bits of Italian varieties were added in 2000.

Although the estate and Abbey Ridge are sufficient for most of Cameron's pinot program, Paul also purchased fruit from Brick House (see the profile earlier in this section) from 1993 through 2002 and from Croft Vineyard between 1997 and 2000. Croft is in the foothills of the Coast Ranges, southwest of Salem.

WINEMAKING

Paul makes the decision to pick his pinot using the usual combination of visual clues (browning seeds and yellowing basal leaves), taste, and numbers. He watches pH carefully, considering the uptick from 3.1 to 3.2 to be an indicator that the vines are beginning to shut down. He thinks the mechanism governing the uptick may be the commencing breakdown of the grapes' skin cells. He destems completely with an Amos crusher-destemmer, but crushes only about 20 percent of the berries. Fermentors are 6.5-foot-diameter stainless steel open-tops—"if you lie down on the bottom, you can just touch the sides with your hands and feet"—about four feet in height. These dimensions are important to Paul's program, which involves not only conventional plunging but also foot-treading of the vats. Alcoholic fermentation is preceded by a long, natural cold soak, lasting from seven to ten days, before the must warms up sufficiently to wake up the native yeasts, on which Paul relies exclusively. Once started, the fermentation takes only five or six additional days. Clos Electrique and Abbey Ridge are pressed when the must is dry; Brick House and Croft, which are grown in thin sedimentary soils with a tendency to high tannins, are pressed when the must is only half dry.

Paul uses some Dargaud & Jaeglé and Mercurey barrels, but has developed a strong preference for two small coopers, Claude Gillet and Michel Toutant. Both Gillet and Toutant make in-person visits to Cameron annually, taste the wines, and custom-make barrels to fit the profile of each wine. Paul uses between 50 percent and 60 percent new wood for the first year's *élevage* of Clos Electrique and Brick House, but only about 10 percent for Abbey Ridge. In fact, the grapes from the oldest vines at Abbey Ridge are often vinified with no new wood at all. Paul is inclined to ignore lots that display slight to moderate reduction, finding that reduction often contributes to the development of desirable leather and mushroom aromas in the end; but he will add copper to barrels that are aggressively reduced. The July after the vintage, the wines are racked and transferred to neutral wood. Lots destined for vineyard-designated bottlings spend another full year in the neutral wood, whereupon they are racked again and bottled, without fining or filtration. From the balance, Paul blends first a Willamette Valley cuvée and finally a nonvintage wine; both are bottled 18 to 20 months after the vintage. Wines are usually held three to five months after bottling before release.

THE WINES

Cameron generally makes four vineyard-designates: Abbey Ridge, Arley's Leap, Clos Electrique, and Brick House. From 1997 to 2000, a single-vineyard wine was also made from Croft Vineyard fruit. A first pick of declassified barrels is repurposed for the Willamette Valley cuvée. The remainder is blended, sometimes with wine from the next vintage, to make a nonvintage bottling, which is sold to Portland restaurants for just $100 per case. The long barrel-aging regime creates wines of considerable complexity and elegance that age exceptionally well; pressing Brick House and Croft before dryness tames otherwise aggressive tannins. The Abbey Ridge wine, in almost every vintage, is a personal favorite.

TASTING NOTES

1999 Arley's Leap (tasted prerelease in 2001): Transparent, dark purplish-black; aromas of black fruits and cola; deep, dark, intensely wound black fruit in the mouth, with slate, licorice, and coffee; rich wine with a long finish.

1999 Croft Vineyard (tasted prerelease in 2001): Transparent, medium-dark black-red; huge nose of cranberry and violets, plus fudge and chocolate brownies; black fruits and chocolate in the mouth; slaty, mineral finish; velvety texture, medium-weight and medium-length.

1998 Abbey Ridge (tasted in 2001): Transparent, deep black-red; earth, rose petal, and dried herbs on the nose; beet, tree bark, slate, clove, and cinnamon overlaying deep, rich black cherry and tea, with a hint of roasted chestnut and sweetness in the midpalate; long and lingering with a linen texture. Very fine.

PRACTICAL INFORMATION

True to the self-distribution model with which he began, Paul sells three-quarters of Cameron's production personally, in Portland, where it is found on many good restaurant lists. Much of the balance is sold via mailing list to customers in reciprocal states. Except for the Thanksgiving weekend open house, the winery is not open to the public; 503-538-0336.

CARNEROS CREEK WINERY

Napa, California

Francis Mahoney, a native San Franciscan drawn to the wine trade by postcollegiate travels in Europe and seasoned with experience in importing European wines and managing vines for Mayacamas Vineyards, purchased a ravine in the ranchland of Los Carneros in 1972. The hilly terrain and rocky subsoils reminded him of Burgundy; the morning fog and cool days seemed to assure a long growing season. Construction of a winery building began in 1973. Although Louis Martini had preceded him in Carneros and André Tchelistcheff encouraged him, Mahoney's venture was still a pioneering effort, waged against the balance of specialists' opinions. From the outset, pinot noir was the heart and raison d'être of Carneros Creek, even though zinfandel, cabernet, and petite sirah made from purchased grapes paid the bills until the estate pinot vineyards became established.

Suspecting that, after soil and climate, clones might be the third most important factor in making great pinot, Mahoney simultaneously planted about seven acres to best-bet clones selected for their performance in other vineyards, and a 1.5-acre plot to tiny, experimental replications of 20 clones and field selections. This second plot, known variously as the Clonal Selection Plot and the Carneros Creek Clonal Trial, was a seminal event in the evolution of North American pinot noir, even though it was ultimately overtaken by interest in the clones that became available from France in the 1990s. In addition to providing systematic comparative data on clonal performance, and budwood for dozens of other vineyards throughout California, the most successful selections in the trial were chosen for subsequent vineyard development at Carneros Creek itself.

In the 1980s and 1990s, Mahoney planted vineyards around his residence on Dealy Lane, east of the winery; on a 37-acre site on the upslope side of Dealy Lane, known sometimes as Las Lomas and sometimes as the Mahoney Vineyard; and finally at Las Brisas, a 95-acre site consisting of gently sloping sand and gravel, on Ramel Road. Because Las Lomas is a warmish site for Carneros, Mahoney eventually planted a bit of syrah in its warmest northwestern corner. Las Brisas, however, was planted entirely to various selections of pinot noir, chosen primarily on the strength of their performance in the trial. Carneros Creek's pinot program also expanded beyond the estate model with which it had begun, as Mahoney launched two programs designed to produce substantial volumes of entry-level wines, called Côte de Carneros and Fleur de Carneros, made primarily from purchased fruit.

In 1998, to finance a further expansion, Carneros Creek secured investment from Bill Hambrecht, a San Francisco–based investment banker with several decades of close involvement with California wine. This infusion of funds was followed, rather rapidly, by a whirlwind of changes. Melissa Moravec, who had managed Mahoney's clonal trials in the 1980s and served as cowinemaker since 1989, departed. Mahoney himself "retired." Hambrecht acquired most of Mahoney's remaining interest in the winery, while Mahoney retained ownership of all the vineyards except the original ten-acre winery parcel. Scott Rich, who had been the day-to-day winemaker at Etude, took over Carneros Creek's winemaking duties in 2001, with a mandate to reverse the 1998 expansion and reposition the brand. He eliminated, at least for the 2001 vintage, Carneros Creek's Fleur de Carneros label, and sold a good many lots into the bulk wine market. Barely a year after his appointment, Rich was succeeded by Ken Foster, longtime winemaker at David Bruce. As of this writing, Carneros Creek continues to acquire fruit from the Mahoney Vineyards Management Company on a long-term contract, but is in the process of adjusting its purchases of pinot from other Carneros vineyards. In addition, at least for the immediate future, Carneros Creek will custom-crush the so-called Mahoney Estate wine—about 400 cases each of pinot noir and chardonnay made from the eastern end of the Mahoney (Las Lomas) Vineyard—but this wine will no longer carry the Carneros Creek name.

Meanwhile, Francis Mahoney has preserved his pioneering interest in the clones of pinot noir. A third phase of the clonal trial was being planned at the end of 2002, designed to test the interaction of clones and rootstocks and to see how well the best selections from the old trial perform against "new" selections, propagated from mother vines used in the trial, that have been treated and rereleased by Foundation Plant Services at Davis.

WINEMAKING

As a large producer of pinot noir made in several styles and sold at different price points, and often struggling against budgetary and space limitations, Carneros Creek followed several winemaking protocols both simultaneously and successively during the 1990s. In general, grapes were completely destemmed, inoculated after a day, and fermented for ten days to two weeks. The must was pressed at dryness and moved promptly to barrel. Mahoney and Moravec avoided racking as far as possible and did not fine the wines, but they always filtered before bottling. The cellar was filled with an assortment of open-top fermentors and closed tanks, including two giant tanks equipped with internal, pneumatically operated plungers. When Rich arrived in 2001, he began work to redesign the crushpad so that fruit could be moved into the fermentors without pumping, cut the largest fermentors down to a capacity of ten tons, and purchased a large number of new five- by eight-foot open-tops. In the large tanks, he replaced pumpovers with a rack-and-return pattern. He began to retain a small percentage of whole clusters, and cut the use of laboratory yeast to about one-quarter of the manufacturer's recommended dose. He stretched the prefermentation maceration period from 24 hours to three days, and doubled the percentage of new wood in the cellar. He began an effort to match barrel choices to individual lots of wine, aiming for "seamless integration of barrels and fruit," and eliminated several infelicitous combinations. As efforts to reposition the brand continue, it seems likely that Ken Foster will make additional changes.

THE WINES

Until 2001, the Carneros Creek portfolio consisted of two wines based on purchased fruit, the Fleur de Carneros that Mahoney usually described as "Pinot 101," and Côte de Carneros, a somewhat more serious and weightier wine, but one always blended for vintage-to-vintage consistency and to be "typical" of the Los Carneros appellation. Fleur de Carneros debuted in 1986; the first vintage of Côte de Carneros was made in 1995. Alongside these high-volume products, Carneros Creek also made (beginning in 1983) a basic estate pinot called Los Carneros, a second estate wine dubbed Las Piedras, and (in selected vintages) a premium bottling called Signature Reserve. Unsurprisingly, the estate wines were blessed with most of the winery's new barrels, while Fleur was raised entirely in neutral wood. With the 2001 vintage, Fleur has been discontinued, at least temporarily; Côte de Carneros has been redefined to rely primarily on estate (i.e., Mahoney Vineyards Management Company) fruit; and three premium, vineyard-designated wines will occupy the brand's top tier. Historically, the Carneros Creek estate wines have been complex, medium- to full-bodied renderings capable of aging felicitously, while the Fleur and Côte de Carneros bottlings have been, for the most part, fairly simple, varietally correct wines. Wines made in and after 2001 will be a new story.

TASTING NOTES

2000 Côte de Carneros (tasted in 2002): Transparent, medium garnet; expansive nose of smoke, black cherry, and violets; sweet, round, and soft in the mouth with ripe cherry, wet stone, and a hint of orange peel; medium-weight and medium-length, relatively full-bodied, modestly structured, texture of rough silk.

2000 Fleur de Carneros (tasted in 2002): Very transparent, light to medium garnet; slightly floral nose with some raspberry, smoke, and a hint of forest floor; strawberry and raspberry in the mouth; simple, lightweight, soft, and silky, medium-length.

2000 Los Carneros (tasted in 2002): Transparent, medium-dark oxblood; aromas of dark fruit, citrus peel, and nuts; black cherry, allspice, and graphite on the palate with notes of barrel char and slate; medium-weight and medium-length with very fine-grained tannins and a slightly hot finish.

1999 Los Carneros (tasted in 2002): Transparent, medium garnet with coral highlights;

nose of black fruits, peppery spice, and cooked carrots; toast, tar, and pepper overlaying black fruit and black licorice in the mouth; medium-weight and medium-length, suede-textured.

1999 Signature Reserve (tasted in 2002): Transparent, medium black-red; aromas of sweet, ripe cherries, smoke, and tar; berry fruit, barrel char, white pepper, and briar on the palate; slightly grippy, silken, and long.

1998 Fleur de Carneros (tasted in 2000): Very transparent, medium garnet color; aromatic with flowers, resin, and black fruits; dose of black pepper; light-bodied.

1998 Las Piedras "Mahoney Estate" (tasted in 2000): Deep, black-red wine tinged with blue; rich nose of cherry, raspberry, and black fruits; mineral and mint notes with a touch of funk; balanced wine with a long finish of rough velvet; fine.

1998 Los Carneros (tasted in 2000): Transparent, black-garnet color; cherry and black fruit; mint, clove, and black pepper flavors, with notes of cedar; concentrated and full-bodied.

1997 Côte de Carneros (tasted in 2000): Transparent, black-red; cherry-berry aromas, some pepper; medium-bodied wine, slightly hollow in the midpalate, finished slightly hot.

1995 25th Anniversary Signature Reserve (tasted in 2000): Saturated color tinged with terra-cotta; explosive nose of violets, plum, prune, and pepper; black fruits, cola, chocolate, cedar; sweet, full, soft, and long.

PRACTICAL INFORMATION

Fleur de Carneros, Côte de Carneros, and Los Carneros are all nationally distributed. The 1999 Signature Reserve and the 2002 Las Brisas and Las Lomas bottlings are destined for distribution to selected markets nationwide. Mahoney Estate wines and the 2001 Sangiacomo vineyard-designate will be available in the winery's spacious new tasting room, open daily; 707-253-9464.

CASA CARNEROS

Napa, California

Casa Carneros is the personal pinot noir project of Melissa Moravec, cowinemaker at Carneros Creek until 2001, and her husband, Kurt Reaume. It is seven acres of vineyard on Bayview Avenue in the southeastern corner of the Carneros appellation, planted in 1989. The flag-shaped parcel consists of about 50 north-south-oriented rows on a gentle south-facing slope, commanding an impressive view of San Pablo Bay. The top of the property is so heavily strewn with rock that Moravec describes grape growing in this section as "nearly hydroponic"; the bottom of the vineyard is Haire clay-loam. Now perfectly manicured and tidily cover-cropped, with each row's end post color-coded by clone, the vineyard bears little witness to the exhausted pastureland, rat-infested barns, and derelict cars that greeted Moravec and Reaume when they purchased the land in 1984. To undo the decades of damage, Moravec farms sustainably, preferring, for example, to lose a few grapes than to poison birds. "We steward this land," she says pointedly; "we only own it on paper."

Although Moravec and Reaume initially intended to plant merlot and chardonnay, their affection for pinot was strong enough to overcome their business doubts, so Casa Carneros became an all-pinot project right from the beginning, though a small amount of merlot was made in 1996 from purchased grapes. The choice of plant material was influenced by Moravec's invaluable, hands-on experience supervising the Carneros Creek clonal trials in the mid 1980s and by her clear intention, at least for some years, to sell most of the fruit. Given booming demand from producers of sparkling wine, she planted some UCD 18 and UCD 23 despite a personal preference for "heavier, denser, and broodier" selections. There was also a healthy chunk of UCD 5 (heat-treated Pommard) and UCD 12, plus field selections from Swan, Hanzell, Chalone, and nearby St. Clair. In many cases Moravec took her plant material personally and directly from the clonal trial block at Carneros Creek, choosing only vines that displayed true-to-clone typicity, then carefully handing only one selection at a time to her vineyard manager, to avoid any possibility of confusion during grafting. This great care—plus the expertise derived from six years' experience with the clonal trial block—has made Casa Carneros a favorite source of budwood when younger California vineyards are planted.

Although Casa Carneros was planted to be a 30-ton vineyard, low yields have kept production closer to 20 tons in most years. Of this about half has gone into Casa Carneros's own wine, a single blend of the eight planted "clones"; the balance has been sold to Etude, MacRostie, Bouchaine, Carneros Creek, and a handful of home winemakers. Beginning in 2001, with Moravec able to spend more of her time on the Casa Carneros project, the share of fruit sold to other producers declined.

WINEMAKING

Moravec picks Casa expensively: as many as seven picks are made in the tiny seven-acre vineyard. The fruit is normally 100 percent destemmed, though a small quantity of stems is very occasionally added back if Moravec likes their smell. ("Apple pie spices" are good; "green and vegetable" smells are not.) Fermentation takes place in small, half-ton fruit bins, with a brief natural prefermentation maceration. Moravec normally relies on resident yeast for Casa wine and rarely experiences stuck fermentations, but will inoculate with RC212 if necessary. Generally, she believes that multiple-organism fermentations produce complexity. During fermentation, the cap is punched down three times daily; if the temperature gets too high, she will add a fourth punchdown. Generally, Moravec presses at dryness, but maceration is sometimes extended for very tannic lots. The press fraction is reintegrated.

About 40 percent new barrels are used each year from as many as 15 coopers—Moravec experiments constantly and tries new coopers regularly. Once the wine is in barrel, Moravec minimizes manipulation. The wine spends 15 to 19 months in wood, and is generally racked just once before bottling, unless high tannin argues for a second racking, as it did in 1997. Typically, Casa pinot is both fined and filtered, though a few early vintages were "unintentionally unfiltered" when the wine refused to pass cleanly through the pads, and the pads were then removed.

Casa pinots were made at Carneros Creek until 2002, when Moravec acquired her own small facility in American Canyon.

THE WINES

Since the first vintage in 1991, Casa Carneros has produced just one blend of pinot each year. It is typically a dark, rich, extracted wine, exhibiting dense fruit on a large frame, that benefits from several years of bottle age and is generally better suited to meat and cheese than to salmon. Vintages since 1995 have been made from the full range of clones and selections planted at Casa; earlier vintages used a smaller palette and are slightly less complete wines.

TASTING NOTES

1998 Los Carneros (tasted in 2001): Transparent, medium-dark black-red; petroleum, tar, and geranium on the nose; bright fruit and some chocolate in the mouth; tannic, chewy, and long.

1997 Los Carneros (tasted in 2001): Transparent, very dark black-red; nose of moss, wet earth, black fruit, and cassis; huge wine in the mouth, very tannic and mineral, with texture approaching Carborundum. This vintage spent the longest time in barrel of any wine made to date at Casa and received a 65 percent share of new oak; but it is still immense and needs time.

1996 Los Carneros (tasted in 2001): Transparent, medium black-red; aromas of black raspberry and beeswax; sweet core of black fruits with tea, wet stone, rose petal, and tobacco; tannic finish just beginning to evolve toward velvet; long. A personal favorite among all the vintages of Casa.

1995 Los Carneros (tasted in 2001): Transparent, medium black-red, touched with terracotta; tea, resin, and ripe fruits on the nose; bramble, earth, and toasted cinnamon on the palate; somewhat angular tannins in a full-bodied wine; long.

1994 Los Carneros (tasted in 2001): Saturated, dark mahogany color; slightly closed with a hint of citrus peel; chocolate, sweet raspberry, leather, black tea, and roasted spice on the palate; glycerol and tannin in the finish; medium- to heavyweight wine; long.

1993 Los Carneros (tasted in 2001): Saturated, dark mahogany; nose of ultraripe fruit, dried currants, and petroleum; mint, wet stone, and flint in the mouth; lush midpalate and chewy but also mineral; tannins resolving to velvet.

1992 Los Carneros (tasted in 2001): Saturated, very dark mahogany; huge, pungent nose redolent of cedar and furniture polish; sweet core of plum and black fruits, plus earth; dense and long.

1991 Los Carneros (tasted in 2001): Saturated, medium-dark mahogany; nose of moss, forest floor, and leather; bright black cherry fruit in the mouth, with pepper, mint, and wet stone; tannins resolving to velvet; medium-length.

PRACTICAL INFORMATION

Casa Carneros pinots are distributed to restaurants and selected retail accounts in New York, Chicago, and California. For consumers, the best source is the winery, which welcomes communications but is currently unable to accept visitors; 707-257-8713.

CHALONE VINEYARD

Soledad, California

When the son of a French homesteader planted the first wine grapes in the isolated, chaparral-covered highlands southeast of Soledad in the 1890s, his choice was no stranger than the vineyard enterprises undertaken by scores of other French, Italian, German, and even English immigrants to the Golden State. Lucien Charles Tamm's vineyard was less than six miles as the crow flies from Mission Nuestra Señora de la Soledad, where vines had been planted a century earlier. By 1860, as commercial winemaking replaced the original mission vineyards, more than 50,000 vines had been planted in Monterey County as a whole. But the Tamm plantings, and a neighboring vineyard planted beginning about 1920 by one Francis William Silvear—an asthmatic as much fascinated by California wildflowers as he was by wine—remained stubbornly isolated: 1,800 feet above the valley floor, a long, serpentine drive from Soledad on a road not paved until the 1980s, off the power grid until 1987, and a very long way from most stirrings in California wine. Nonetheless Silvear, who had planted a very unlikely quartet of varieties—pinot blanc, chardonnay, chenin blanc, and pinot noir—sold his grapes far afield in the 1930s. His customers included Wente, Almaden, Mirassou, and, perhaps most significantly, Beaulieu, where he apparently became good friends with Georges de Latour and André Tchelistcheff. The evidence is ambiguous, but the pinot budwood for Beaulieu's second vineyard, called BV 2, may have been sourced from Silvear.

In the 1960s Silvear's vineyard, sold and resold several times, was renamed for nearby Mount Chalone, and the first estate-bottled wines were released under the Chalone label. Then, over a period of two decades, nearly everyone who was anyone in the California wine business filtered in and out of the Chalone story. Philip Togni, a Montpellier-trained winemaker. Rodney Strong, a retired dancer and choreographer. Berkeley restaurateur Narsai David. Sacramento food and wine merchant Daryl Corti. Banker turned winemaker Dick Graff. The 1969, 1970, and 1971 vintages of Chalone pinot noir, made by Graff—who learned winemaking mostly on the job following some coursework at the University of California, Davis—exploded on the California wine scene to rave reviews and established the reputation of Chalone, still an arid, isolated outpost nearly overpowered by hungry deer and pesky rattlesnakes, as one of the first makers of fine pinot noir in the New World. Eventually Chalone, Inc. (predecessor of today's Chalone Wine Group), went on to spawn or acquire wine properties from Napa to San Luis Obispo, to attract investment from the Rothschilds of Bordeaux, and to become the first publicly traded wine company in America. To this day, Chalone's shareholders are its wine club. They are invited to an annual members-only bash on the ranch, and are offered special bottlings.

Although it is unlikely that Chalone's original stewards knew the facts, the estate inhabits an almost unique geology in California. Throughout most of California, the gradual slippage of the Pacific Plate under the North American Plate has hidden deep in the earth most of the marine deposits formed when the seas retreated from the land. Limestone soils near the surface are consequently rare and widely scattered. But in the Gavilan Range on the eastern side of the Salinas Valley, an extensive tract of limestone and calcium carbonate lies near the surface, overlaid with a relatively thin coating of volcanic topsoil. What is now the Chalone AVA—8,650 acres of hilly terrain between seven and eight miles due east of Soledad, mostly above the 1,800-foot contour—consists of poor, low-acid soils that geologically resemble the main wine lands of Europe, except that the appellation is painfully dry, receiving only about ten inches of rainfall annually. An aerial view of the AVA suggests three slightly skewed rectangles joined along part of their long sides. The surface lies entirely within Monterey County, except for small incursions into San Benito County at three points on the appellation's irregular eastern edge. The Chalone Wine Group owns 950 acres, including all but a few acres of the vineyard surface in the AVA.

Chalone now farms just over 100 acres of pinot noir in ten separate, noncontiguous blocks, the oldest of which was planted, in 12-foot rows with 12 feet between vines, in 1946. Chalone calls this 2.2-acre block, on the southern side of the access road from Highway 146, part of its Lower Vineyard. Now that the old Martin Ray vineyard at Mount Eden has been pulled out, this is the oldest pinot still producing anywhere in North America. The source and identity of the scion material are unknown, but the rootstock is St. George. There are also 27 acres of pinot noir in the MacWood Vineyard; a six- by ten-foot planting laid out in 1972 and 1973, again on St. George, and again with budwood of unknown origin; and 6.4 acres in the Strip Vineyard, planted in 1985. Another six acres were planted in six different blocks at various times between 1990 and 2000 in the so-called Lowest,

Vista, Graff, and Tower Vineyards. The upper portion of Vista has barely any topsoil at all—the surface is almost pure limestone rubble. Vine spacings in these blocks vary—the tightest are four feet by eight—and the plant material is a variety of Dijon clones, plus UCD 4 and Swan selection from Dehlinger.

There are persistent stories that budwood brought at various times from France found a home at Chalone. In some versions, the home was permanent, and MacWood, for example, is said by some to be planted to a suitcase clone. In other versions, Chalone was only a waystation for the imported budwood, which was subsequently transported to other California vineyards. At this point, none of these stories can be confirmed with certainty.

Philip Togni is considered Chalone's first winemaker, having made the first vintages of wine to carry the Chalone name, in 1960, 1961, and 1962. Dick Graff became a partner in the company owning Chalone in 1964, headed immediately for Davis to study viticulture and enology, and became Chalone's winemaker in 1966. Graff and his family were able to buy out the other owners in 1969, which was the first vintage of Chalone made under his complete control. After 1972, Dick Graff seems to have shared winemaking responsibilities with his two younger brothers, John and Peter, at least until Peter was officially named winemaker in 1978. In 1983 Peter was succeeded by Michel Michaud. Fifteen years later, in 1998, the reins were passed to Dan Karlsen. Karlsen is a marine biologist who previously made wine at Dehlinger, Domaine Carneros (where he played a key role in establishing the still pinot program), and Estancia. In general, Chalone has used all of its estate-grown fruit, but some pinot grown at Chalone has been redirected toward other Chalone Wine Group wines, including Echelon, and some fruit was sold to David Bruce between 1993 and 1997.

WINEMAKING

Karlsen has strong and sometimes untraditional views about pinot noir, arguing that it is "not chemistry, but hedonism," that cold soaks are "baloney," and that most California wines get not "overoaked" but "underwined." He suggests that there is no reason to green harvest in California, as long as the clusters ripen evenly, because there is always enough heat to ripen whatever sets. He believes that pinot noir is not ripe "until there is no pulp left," which does not happen in California at less than 25 to 26 Brix. At Chalone, he argues, it is important to "embrace the region" and to adjust farming to suit it. Accordingly, he has *increased* the crop load since his arrival in order to slow down the vines' maturity and increase hang time. Having picked very ripe, he sulfurs the grapes, inoculates, and usually adds acid to drive the pH down from 4.0-plus to 3.8. Fermentors are ten-ton stainless steel cylinders and four-ton wax-lined redwood open-tops brought from Dehlinger via Domaine Carneros. Up to 10 percent whole clusters may be used "if they taste good." Half of the punchdowns are done by hand and half pneumatically, and the fermentation runs for eight to ten days with peak temperatures in the high 90s Fahrenheit. The must is pressed when it is nearly dry and settled in tank for 24 hours. Free-run juice and the press fraction are combined.

About one-third of the barrels are new, primarily Cadus and François Frères, and Karlsen uses a small number of puncheons to supplement the usual *pièces,* in the fashion of Dehlinger. Malolactic fermentation happens without inoculation. The pinots spend ten to 11 months in wood, and are racked once in the late winter after the vintage and once more at bottling. Karlsen does not fine, but he filters before bottling, in part because he has a self-proclaimed "zero tolerance" for brettanomyces.

THE WINES

During the 1960s, pinot was bottled under the Chalone Vineyard label from 1960 through 1962, and again after 1966. In most years there was just a single bottling, though Gavilan was sometimes used as a second label, and a reserve program was inaugurated about 1979. The reserve program, which persisted until 1996, privileged the property's oldest vines, was generally bottled unfiltered, and was supposed to have been sold primarily to Chalone, Inc.'s shareholders. According to Karlsen, who has tasted extensively in the winery's library, the reserve wines rarely lasted as well as the regular bottlings—a circumstance he blames on diseased vines and lack of filtration. As early as 1969, the main release attracted extravagantly positive reviews, and many vintages from the early 1970s are said to be still stunning and alive. By contrast, the winery is not proud of its late 1980s and early 1990s efforts—regular or reserve. In Karlsen's view, these vintages were picked too early. They were also criticized in the wine press for mustiness, which Karlsen believes to have resulted from an overhumidified cellar, which is said to have been "black with mold" when he arrived in 1998. As of this writing, a block-designate is planned for the 2002 vintage, derived from the high-limestone Vista Vineyard, but Karlsen is not sure this wine will be superior to the usual estate release—just different. Chalone pinots inspired several other California producers, and Chalone selections have been taken to plant other vineyards; but my personal experience with these pinots is limited to the vintages since 1999, and an isolated taste of the 1978. The recent vintages are ripe-picked, black-fruited wines with deep flavors.

TASTING NOTES

2001 Estate (tasted in 2003): Transparent, medium oxblood; aromas of ripe plum, beetroot, and resiny chaparral; smoky, ripe black fruit with peppery spice on the palate; satin midpalate with a slightly grippy finish; medium-weight with a warm and medium-long finish.

2000 Estate (tasted in 2003): Transparent, deep magenta; licorice and ripe cherry on the nose; sweet and moderately concentrated on the palate, with flavors of coffee, cinnamon, and mesquite; nearly silken but not without fine-grained tannin; medium-long.

1999 Estate (tasted in 2001): Brilliant, medium, slightly blackish-red; cardamom, sweet spice, and wet earth; sweet red and black fruit, cranberry, oak, vanilla, and barrel char, with mossy highlights on the palate; mineral finish, slightly grippy texture, and medium-length.

1978 Estate (tasted in 2001 from a half-bottle): Dark mahogany red, color shrinking back slightly from the meniscus; nose of tanned leather; briary, resinous palate with a hint of chocolate; still grippy with unresolved tannin, but concentrated and long to finish. Past its prime but still sound. This vintage was made from 100 percent whole-cluster fruit.

PRACTICAL INFORMATION

Chalone pinot noir is nationally distributed to both retail and restaurant accounts, and can be purchased from the winery directly. An onsite tasting room is open to the public on Saturdays and Sundays, and by appointment on other days of the week; 831-678-1717.

CHEHALEM WINES

Newberg, Oregon

Harry Peterson-Nedry, a North Carolina–born chemist whose first career was centered in high-tech manufacturing, created the Chehalem brand in 1990 to market wines made from his family's Ridgecrest estate, on Ribbon Ridge. Chehalem's first wine was the 1990 vintage of Ridgecrest Pinot Noir, released in 1993. Also in 1993, Willamette Valley natives Bill and Cathy Stoller became co-owners of Chehalem, and in 1995 the partners purchased the former Veritas Winery, on Highway 99W just northeast of Newberg, as their production facility. Vintages before 1995 had been made in a 1,000-square-foot brick outbuilding adjacent to Peterson-Nedry's home in downtown Newberg.

Chehalem now sources pinot noir from three vineyards: Ridgecrest, still owned by the Peterson-Nedrys; Corral Creek, adjacent to the ex-Veritas winery and acquired concurrently by Peterson-Nedry; and Stoller, a large property near Lafayette, owned separately by the Stollers. Ridgecrest is the most mature of the three vineyards, having been planted in 1982 on the site of nineteenth-century walnut and prune orchards involuntarily converted into cow pasture by a legendary storm in the 1960s. Ridgecrest is now 37 acres of grapes on a 72-acre site. The oldest vines were planted six feet by ten, but spacing was tightened to 4.5 feet by ten in 1985, and to four feet by eight in 1989 and 1990. The vineyard is at altitudes ranging from 450 to 600 feet, sloping southward, on both sides of Ribbon Ridge Road. Like the rest of Ribbon Ridge, the soil series is Willakenzie clay-loam; the Ridgecrest subseries of this soil is now dubbed Wellsdale. The site produces concentrated black-toned pinot with overtones of wild bramble and cassis, as long as its yield is managed to something around two tons per acre.

Corral Creek is a lower-elevation site, mostly between 200 and 450 feet, toward the base of Parrett Mountain, that was planted in 1983 and 1984, with some replanting in 1991 when a large block of riesling was replaced with pinot noir. (Ironically, some of the vines are now being regrafted to riesling as Peterson-Nedry discovers how well it can perform in this site.) The clonal composition of the vineyard is not entirely clear, but it seems to consist primarily of own-rooted UCD 5 and UCD 2A; spacing is five feet by ten. The soils are shallow Laurelwood series—a brownish clay-loam. Shallower and higher-elevation parts of the vineyard are drip-irrigated at the end of the growing season; the rest is dry-farmed. Chehalem now uses about two-thirds of the fruit from Corral Creek; the balance is sold to Andrew Rich, J. K. Carrière, Hatcher Wine Works, La Bête, and Brooks Wines. In most years it is used, Peterson-Nedry says, to add "structure and brightness" to blends, but in exceptional years it produces "a perfectly balanced wine" in its own right, and some lots are then vineyard-designated.

The youngest of the vineyards is Stoller, which produced its first crop in 1996. Stoller is a 350-acre site of which 110 acres are now planted (80 to pinot noir), on a south-facing slope overlooking Lafayette, in the iron-rich Jory soil (here lightly laced with Nekia series) that is typical of Dundee's Red Hills. Before the Stollers began its transformation into vineyard, this property was dedicated to a combination of turkey farming and cereal crops. The site is exceptionally vigorous—Peterson-Nedry calls it "almost a factory for fruit"—and was tightly planted to compensate. Even with aggressive pruning, however, yields can still top 4 tons per acre. Unlike Ridgecrest and Corral Creek, Stoller is planted entirely on rootstock and is completely drip-irrigated. Dijon clones account for two-thirds of the 80 acres of pinot. These properties make Stoller pinot less dense and deep than fruit from Ridgecrest, exhibiting lower acid and higher pH and tending to emphasize the roundness, femininity, and precocity often associated with the southern half of the Côte d'Or. Pinot fruit from Stoller is sold to Argyle, Domaine Drouhin, and Penner-Ash, as well as being used by Chehalem. Beginning in

2001, a small amount was separately vinified from select blocks in anticipation of a new winery likely to be ready for the 2004 harvest; it will be sold under a new Stoller Vineyards brand.

From 1996 through 2002, winemaking duties at Chehalem were shared by Peterson-Nedry and Cheryl Francis, a Los Angeles native with a biology degree from Lewis and Clark College and on-the-job training in Oregon and New Zealand. Francis departed before the harvest in 2003 to launch her own brand, Francis Tannahill. Patrice Rion, of Domaine Daniel Rion in Prémeaux-Prissey, consulted for Chehalem in the mid 1990s, and the property's top cuvée is named in his honor.

WINEMAKING

Conveniently, Chehalem's three vineyards ripen sequentially, beginning with Stoller, followed closely by Corral Creek. Ridgecrest, largely for reasons of its elevation, is always the last to ripen. Peterson-Nedry says Chehalem is usually "late to pick," waiting until the cluster "begins to look a little sad, and grapes fall off when you shake it," and "our palates say that acids, sugars, and flavors are all in balance"—usually meaning sugars above 24 Brix and a pH around 3.2. Chehalem will tolerate low acids if that is what's needed to obtain ripe flavors, and will sometimes add back a bit of acid if natural acidity has fallen too low. Leaving a few experimental vattings and most of the Ridgecrest fruit aside, the fruit is fully destemmed but the berries are not crushed, and a prefermentation cold soak lasts for five to ten days without punch-downs. Fermentors are in four-, five-, and eight-ton sizes, mostly stainless steel and mostly jacketed. In "clean" years with no rot or botrytis, the winemakers rely on native yeasts; otherwise they "blast" the vats with commercial yeast. Enzymes are sometimes used, on a lot-specific basis, to help manage aggressive tannins, compensate for cold soaks that must be foreshortened, or help "unwind fruit." Temperature manipulation begins after the fermentation is well started, and is aimed at a slow build toward a juice-temperature peak around 88 degrees Fahrenheit. Chehalem generally presses as soon as the must is dry, though the winemakers continue to experiment with varying lengths of prefermentation and postfermentation maceration. The press fraction is normally used in Chehalem's blended pinot (see below), but in some years some of it is reunified with the vineyard-designated wines from which it came. Inoculation is done to start malolactic fermentation, sometimes in the drain tank from the fermentors, sometimes in barrel.

Peterson-Nedry does not want his wines to be cooper-marked, so the barrel regime involves six to eight coopers, wood from several French forests, and a mix of toast levels and stave ages. The property's big wines spend up to 14 months in barrel; others are bottled after 11 to 12 months in wood. The winemakers have not liked the "fruit loss" they have perceived when they have held wine in wood longer than 14 months. Lot-specific decisions are made as to racking, with a preference for avoiding manipulations until the final blends are made and bottled. Prior to bottling, lots are selectively fined or filtered, or both. Typically, the high-tannin Ridgecrest lots benefit from some egg-white fining, and barrels destined for the 3 Vineyards blend (see below) are both fined and filtered in "needy" vintages. Rion Reserve lots (see below) are usually bottled unfined and unfiltered. If the market permits, Chehalem will hold finished wines 12 months after bottling before release, but it has been known to release some pinots with as little as two months' bottle age.

THE WINES

In 1990, 1991, and 1992, Chehalem made only one pinot, and this entirely from Ridgecrest fruit. In 1993, there were two Ridgecrest cuvées: one "regular" and one made from 100 percent UCD 2A. The property's flagship wine, Rion Reserve, was launched in 1994. Rion Reserve is a barrel selection from Ridgecrest, not of the biggest and brawniest lots but of barrels displaying uncommon elegance, silkiness, and length. In 1996, following the acquisition of the Corral Creek vineyard and the first harvest from Stoller, Chehalem's 3 Vineyard blend was born, and (exceptionally) one barrel of Stoller was used in the Rion Reserve. Some lots of Stoller pinot were then vineyard-designated in 1997, and a Stoller Vineyard bottling has been made in all subsequent years. Selected lots of Corral Creek were vineyard-designated in 1998, 2000, and 2001. Each year, barrels (of Ridgecrest) destined for Rion Reserve are selected out first; then barrels are earmarked for the two or three vineyard-designates; remaining lots are used for the 3 Vineyard blend. Since 1998, micro-lots of experimental pinot have also been made from Bethel Heights and Rex Hill's Jacob Hart vineyard, pursuant to an exchange program among the three wineries. All lots are used; nothing is bulked out. Within the limits of each vintage, Chehalem pinots tend toward relatively forward fruit, medium to deep colors, and considerable length; they have generally enjoyed a good deal of critical acclaim. The first vintages of Rion Reserve, now approaching maturity, are especially rewarding.

TASTING NOTES

2000 Corral Creek Vineyard (tasted in 2002): Transparent, medium black-red; sage, thyme, cherry, and lacquer aromas; sweet and simultaneously dry mouthfeel; cherry, barrel char; a hint of mocha and considerable minerality on the finish; very grippy, medium-weight, and long.

2000 Stoller Vineyard (tasted in 2002): Transparent, medium black-red; aromas of black cherry, woodsmoke, and coal tar; dark fruit and wet slate in the mouth; round, dry, and slightly austere, medium-weight and medium-long finish with a linenlike texture.

2000 3 Vineyards (tasted in 2002): Transparent, medium-dark black-red; some geranium on the nose; bright red fruit on the palate, mineral and granitic; accents of spice and black pepper; relatively fine-grained tannins, medium-weight and medium-length.

1999 Ridgecrest (tasted twice, in 2001 and 2002): Saturated, dark black-red; nose of earth, briar, bramble, black cherry, and smoke, with the faintest hint of citrus peel; an infusion of rose and violet petals in the mouth, surrounding a core of huckleberries and other sweet black fruit, hints of black pepper and spice; velvety but still grippy, full-bodied, and long.

1999 Rion Reserve (tasted prerelease in 2001 and again in 2002): Barely transparent, very dark black-red; wild, brambly berries like marionberry on the nose with hints of evergreen, dusty cherry, and smoke; rich, almost unctuous, berry-laden flavors with hints of nuts, graphite, and barrel char; accents of clove, mint, licorice, coffee, bay leaf, and bitter chocolate; rich, full-bodied, nearly chewy, velour-textured wine; long and fine. This edition of Rion Reserve was made using 15 percent whole clusters. Very promising; needs time.

1999 Stoller Vineyard (tasted twice in 2001): Transparent, medium-hued, slightly blackish-red; earthy and herbal aromas overlaying cranberry and cherry; sweet black cherry with some plum in the mouth and just a hint of furniture polish, leather, and minty earth tones; slightly tannic, medium-weight, texture of rough silk.

1999 3 Vineyards (tasted prerelease in 2001): Transparent, medium-dark black-red; violets, black fruit, and earth on the nose; more black fruit, black pepper, and smoke on the palate; medium-weight and medium-length.

1997 Rion Reserve (tasted twice, in 2000 and 2001): Transparent, light to medium black-red; truffle, mushroom, and resin on the nose; tar, leather, and fine, well-articulated spices in the mouth; light- to medium-weight wine, but very silken and lingering.

1996 Rion Reserve (tasted in 2001): Very transparent, light to medium bright red with terra-cotta highlights; wild strawberry and leather aromas; cherry, tar, and leather with hints of mushroom and meat in the mouth; lingering flavors of smoke on the finish; texture of rough silk, long, fine.

PRACTICAL INFORMATION

Chehalem produces about 12,000 cases of wine annually, of which 60 percent is pinot noir. The wines are nationally distributed and can also be mail-ordered from the winery. The winery, on Highway 99W northwest of Newberg, is open to the public on the usual Thanksgiving and Memorial Day weekends, and otherwise by appointment; 503-538-4700.

CRISTOM VINEYARDS

Salem, Oregon

Cristom was created in 1992 when Pennsylvanians Paul and Eileen Gerrie purchased an abandoned vineyard and failing winery on Spring Valley Road, on the eastern side of the Eola Hills. The Gerries recruited Steve Doerner, who was then winemaker at Josh Jensen's Calera Wine Company (see the Calera profile earlier in this section), to pursue their ambitions with Burgundian varieties. Doerner, a biochemist trained at the University of California, Davis, who recalls that he was "only mildly curious about wine" when he was hired at Calera, is still Cristom's winemaker a decade later. The first wines were made entirely from purchased fruit, sourced from well-known vineyards elsewhere in the Eola Hills, but the abandoned estate vineyard was also simultaneously restored, and it returned to production in 1994. Additional vineyard acreage was planted on the Spring Valley Road site beginning in 1993.

Cristom's estate vineyards now contain about 42 acres of pinot noir, in four individually named parcels. The restored vineyard is about eight acres of widely spaced vines, laid out in north-south rows on a mostly east-facing slope astride the 500-foot contour. This parcel was originally planted in the early 1980s when the property was known as Mirassou Cellars, the Oregon wine project launched by a cousin of the San Jose–based Mirassou wine family. The plant material was UCD 2A, 5, and 13, taken presumably from Mirassou's vineyards in Monterey County, and the vines were set out on their own roots. The 2A and 5 have been retained, but the 13 was converted to a combination of Dijon 115 and 777 in 1997. This parcel, rechristened Marjorie, yields barely 1.75 tons per acre. The new vineyards, named Louise, Jessie, and Eileen, were planted beginning in 1993, 1994, and 1996, respectively. All are vertically trellised, dense plantings measuring 1.75 meters between rows and one meter between vines. All include some UCD 5 and a preponderance of Dijon 113, 114, 115, and 777 on rootstock. All are pruned to a single cane of about eight buds plus a two-bud renewal spur, and are green-harvested to yield about two tons per acre. Louise, which has now grown to 11 planted acres, is downslope from Marjorie on gentle south- and southeast-facing slopes, and displays both north-south and east-west row orientations. Jessie is also about 11 acres, planted in east-west rows on a steep slope south of Louise and Marjorie, its low end about 300 feet above the valley floor, but rising to 500 feet at the top. Eileen is the hilltop parcel, at between 600 and 700 feet, and consists of 12 planted acres. The soils throughout are the iron-rich, basalt-based, volcanic series typical of the Eola Hills, and the vineyards ripen from the bottom of the hill to the top, reflecting the cooler temperatures associated with higher altitude.

Cristom's main sources of purchased fruit (for pinot noir) are the Seven Springs and Canary Hill vineyards, both nearby. Both have been used right from the first vintage in 1992. Fruit has also been acquired from the Freedom Hill vineyard since 1993; from Temperance Hill from 1992 through 1999; and from Shea Vineyard in 1998 and 1999. Occasional bits have come from John Thomas, Beaux Frères, Arcus (see Archery Summit Estate), and Knudsen. For the disposition of this fruit, see below.

WINEMAKING

"The definition of a good vintage," Doerner asserts, "is being able to *choose* when you pick the grapes." He explains that in Oregon the winegrower's hand can be forced at higher elevations, and he refuses to pick grapes that are wet, preferring to let them dry if necessary on the vine. The result is that Brix at picking can range from as low as 19 to as high as 26, but in this *terroir* Doerner finds that he can usually obtain good physiological ripeness at relatively low levels of sugar accumulation. Cristom's fermentors range in size from as small as eight-tenths of a ton to as large as seven tons; Doerner's "favorite" is a six-foot-by-six-foot, five-ton stainless steel open-top. He uses about 50 percent whole clusters and permits a four- to five-day ambient cold soak until the primary fermentation begins naturally with resident yeast. Occasionally, Doerner has added a bit of commercial yeast after the primary fermentation has started naturally. He has also been known to add a bit of acid to some lots in some vintages, if necessary to balance the wine. Acid also has the effect of making "the environment slightly hostile for the yeast" and thus slows down the fermentation. He chaptalizes more often than not, because "dribbling" a bit of sugar into the must near the end of the fermentation extends the fermentation time. *Saignée* is practiced occasionally when there is an especially high ratio of juice to solids. Hand punchdowns are routine, and the fermentation temperature is kept under 86 degrees Fahrenheit—again to extend the length of fermentation. The wine is pressed as soon as the cap begins to fall, which is usually after about 15 to 20 days of vatting. The press fraction is reunified with the free-run juice, and the wine goes straight from press to barrel, without settling.

About 35 percent new barrels are used overall, but the vineyard-designated and reserve wines (see below) see a disproportionate share of them. Barrels are purchased from eight coopers—François Frères, Remond, Sirugue, Mercurey, Séguin Moreau, Meyrieux, Rousseau, and Cadus—and there is also a bit of Oregon oak coopered by François Frères. Malolactic bacteria are introduced into the barrels via the topping wine. Doerner says his racking trials have convinced him that "less is more"—fewer rackings produce wine with better body *and less sediment*—so racking is confined to a minimum. The barrels destined for the vineyard-designated and reserve wines are selected in September after the vintage, and the reserve wines spend an additional six months in wood. Egg-white fining for "polish" is standard—Doerner says it can even make the wine "creamy"—but there is no filtration. Six months of bottle-aging precedes release.

THE WINES

A Willamette Valley blend (a.k.a. Mt. Jefferson Cuvée) and a reserve wine have been made in every vintage since 1992. Until the estate vineyard was restored to production in 1994, the Willamette Valley wine and the reserve were both made exclusively from purchased fruit; more recently, estate fruit is also used in these programs. The first vineyard-designated Marjorie was made in 1994; Louise debuted in 1996, Jessie in 1998, and Eileen in 2000. As an ensemble, Cristom pinots are medium-bodied and elegant wines with considerable aromatic complexity, which is probably attributable to a combination of long resident-yeast fermentations and some use of stems. Of the vineyard-designates, Marjorie tends to be the biggest wine, while Jessie can display the greatest aromatic subtlety.

TASTING NOTES

2000 Eileen Vineyard (tasted in 2003): Brilliant, deep oxblood-ruby; exotic aromas of incense, sandalwood, and dark black fruit; explosive sweet fruit on the palate, with blackberry, black pepper, and hints of balsam; considerable minerality on the midpalate; slightly grippy tending toward velvet, mouthcoating, long, and medium-plus weight.

2000 Jessie Vineyard (tasted in 2003): Transparent, medium black-red; barrel char, blackberry, plus hints of barbecue and soy on the nose; black fruit and minerals in the mouth; sweet but austere and slightly grippy; full-bodied, long, and medium-weight.

2000 Louise Vineyard (tasted in 2003): Transparent, medium black-red; dense and earthy aromas with hints of beetroot; resin, sage, and barrel char on the palate; moderately grippy but fine-grained, rich and mouthcoating on the midpalate; finishes like crushed velvet.

2000 Marjorie Vineyard (tasted in 2003): Brilliant, medium black-red; aromas of black cherry, fig, and rose petal; dark fruit, cola, black pepper; slate, and some minty evergreen in the mouth; slightly grippy, medium-weight, and intense but still angular; rather long.

2000 Mt. Jefferson Cuvée (tasted in 2003): Transparent, medium black-red; dominant blackberry and black currant aromas; fruit-forward on the palate with sweet, rich cherry and blackberry, plus black pepper and toasted spice; grippy attack and suedelike finish with intense and slightly resinous fruit on the midpalate; medium-weight and medium-length.

2000 Reserve (tasted in 2003): Transparent, medium ruby; spicy floral elements overlay dark fruit on the nose; sweet fruit, licorice, and barrel char in the mouth with hints of clove and star anise; fine-grained tannins, medium-plus weight, texture of rough silk.

1999 Jessie Vineyard (tasted in 2001): Transparent, medium-dark black-red; floral nose redolent of rose and lavender plus notes of cigar box; sweet, brambly, chewy cherry, blackberry, and red currant fruit; slightly grippy and very long.

1999 Louise Vineyard (tasted in 2001): Transparent, medium black-red; aromas of sarsaparilla, rhubarb, and even nuts; sweet black fruit, cola, tree bark, soft spice, and black pepper on the palate; slightly mineral finish, medium-weight, lengthy finish.

1999 Marjorie Vineyard (tasted in 2001): Transparent, medium-dark black-red; nose of predominantly black fruit with hints of carrot, rose petal, and bay laurel; sweet in the mouth, with smoke, vanilla, cherry, and some spice; fairly concentrated, medium-long, and satiny.

1999 Reserve (tasted in 2001 from a half-bottle): Transparent, medium black-red; aromas of caramel and blackberry with a suggestion of mint; cherry and wet slate in the mouth, with a hint of candied tangerine peel; medium-weight and medium-length.

1998 Reserve (tasted in 2001 from a half-bottle): Again transparent, medium black-red; aromas of pinecone, caramel, rose petals, and potpourri; sweet core of black fruit and black licorice; very fine-grained tannins, mineral finish, and medium-length.

1997 Reserve (tasted in 2001 from a half-bottle): Transparent, medium-dark mahogany; berry fruit, resin, tangerine peel, and Monterey jack cheese on the nose; black fruit, leather, and slate in the mouth; very fine-grained tannins producing a sensation of velvet on the finish, medium-weight, long.

PRACTICAL INFORMATION

Cristom wines are nationally distributed, but the vineyard-designates are best obtained from the winery. An onsite tasting room is open daily except during the winter months; 503-375-3068.

CRONIN VINEYARDS

Woodside, California

Cronin Vineyards is a microboutique enterprise in a residential neighborhood about one mile from the village center of Portola Valley. There are 1.5 acres of chardonnay and cabernet sauvignon, the converted garage and basement of Duane Cronin's postwar ranch house, and an oak grove that shades the crushpad each year at harvest. To provide cellar space, Cronin's basement has been expanded 60 feet into the hillside. In this low-tech environment, Cronin (who was an engineer for IBM until he retired in 1990) has made tiny quantities of pinot noir and small lots of other wines since 1980. The town of Woodside, which has jurisdiction, limits his total wine production to 2,100 cases, of which pinot noir now represents about 13 percent.

Cronin is a self-taught winemaker with a few University of California, Davis, extension classes and the now-defunct Napa Valley School of Cellaring to his credit. His winemaking operation is stubbornly unprofitable, but Cronin finds it "a lot of fun" and vows to persist "as long as I can afford it." Over the years, he has sourced pinot from four vineyards: Ventana, in Monterey County, from 1980 to 1989; Peter Martin Ray since 1987; San Ysidro in Santa Clara County, which also supplies fruit for Calera's Central Coast blend, since 1989; and Matteson/Ciardella, near Aptos, from 1994 to 1997. The Ventana and San Ysidro wines have always been separately bottled and vineyard-designated; the Peter Martin Ray and Matteson wines were sometimes blended, in whole or in part, to make a Santa Cruz Mountains bottling.

The anchor of the pinot program is the Peter Martin Ray vineyard on Table Mountain, which lies just below Martin Ray's original hilltop site (which now belongs to Mount Eden Vineyards) and adjacent to other Mount Eden plantings. These vines are now about 30 years old, widely spaced, dry-farmed, vertical trunk and spur pruned, and produce barely two tons per acre in a generous year. The vineyard, which was planted to field selections from the original Martin Ray plot supplemented with budwood from Winery Lake Vineyard in Los Carneros, produces deeply aromatic and intensely flavored fruit. Cronin says that he would like to increase his production of pinot noir but finds it hard to compete for the dribble of top-quality Santa Cruz Mountains fruit that is available. His best expansion play is to plant two acres of pinot on his own property in Woodside, but this long-discussed project has never materialized.

WINEMAKING

Cronin ferments in double-height plastic-lined plywood containers—"inexpensive and easy," he observes. Temperature control is limited to moving the fermentors in and out of direct sun and suspending buckets of ice water in the must if more cool is desired. Up to 50 percent whole clusters are used if the stems have sufficiently lignified, and some Assmannshausen yeast is added after the native yeast gets started. Fermentation takes about 14 days, and the must macerates for an additional week after the cap falls. An old basket press with a water-filled bladder is used to press gently, whereafter press and free-run juice are reassembled.

Cronin uses 50 percent new Allier barrels from François Frères, along with Allier and Vosges barrels from Damy; he finds these barrels impart the most "smoky, bacon character." The barrel regime is an exceptionally long 24 months, and the wines are then held in bottle an additional 18 to 24 months before release. Thus Cronin pinots hit the market at least two years after most others, which is said to confuse many retailers. At the beginning of 2003, the 1997 still had not been released. There is no fining or filtration.

THE WINES

Cronin pinots are medium- to full-bodied, extremely aromatic wines. Despite significant extraction, they are never heavy and are resolutely elegant. Because of the long barreling and prerelease bottle aging, the wines are more evolved at release than most California pinots and prone to show a bit of tile color at the edge. The wines hold up quite well, however, with the 1980, 1982, 1985, 1987, 1990, and 1992 said to have been in good condition at the end of the century. My personal experience does not go further back than 1987, which was tasted (see below) in 2003. I personally like Cronin wines, but they are not for palates devoted to forward fruit.

TASTING NOTES

1998 Peter Martin Ray Vineyard (tasted in 2003): Brilliant, medium garnet with orange-terra-cotta highlights; resin and merbromin on the nose; tar, tobacco, and orange peel on the palate; elegant and complex, medium-weight, silken, and long.

1996 Peter Martin Ray Vineyard (tasted in 2000): Transparent, ruby-terra-cotta color; roasted fruit and cola aromas; strong notes of eucalyptus, menthol, resin, star anise, and even merbromin, plus meat and bacon; sweet, medium body, long, distinctive.

1996 Santa Clara County San Ysidro District (tasted in 2003): Transparent, medium black-red; rose petal with a hint of charcuterie on the nose; mint, cola, anise, and cedar on the palate; slightly sweet, medium-weight, silken, and quite long.

1995 Santa Cruz Mountains (tasted in 2002): Transparent, medium terra-cotta-mahogany; plummy, mocha-tinged fruit with toasted spices on the nose; rich and mentholated on the palate, with notes of candle wax and mesquite charcoal; slightly sweet and mouth-coating but still angular, concentrated, long, and spicy.

1994 Santa Cruz Mountains (tasted in 2003): Transparent, medium black-red with terra-cotta highlights; aromas of filé, root beer, roasted nuts, earth, mushrooms, and incense; flavors of earth, resin, root beer, fir, briar, and some clove; medium-weight but full-bodied, chamois-textured with a hint of grip.

1991 Peter Martin Ray Vineyard (tasted in 2003): Transparent, light to medium terra-cotta; rose petal, incense, nuts, and a hint of orange peel; tree bark, cedar, white pepper, and merbromin in the mouth; light- to medium-weight with a hint of grip, medium-length, and suede-textured.

1987 Santa Cruz Mountains (tasted in 2003): Transparent, medium tile, still reddish at the center but pale orange at the rim; talc, dried herbs, truffles, and resin on the nose; camphor, tobacco, earth, licorice, and white pepper on the palate, with hints of iodine and evergreen; medium-weight and medium-length, satiny and elegant. Now past its peak but still impressive.

PRACTICAL INFORMATION

Tiny production limits distribution. Outside the San Francisco Bay area, aside from a few restaurant accounts, the winery's mailing list may be a customer's best option. Mailing-list customers who meet certain minimum purchase criteria are periodically invited to taste through the winery's library of older vintages and receive invitations to open houses several times a year. If the client finds a few bottles of some older vintage appealing, Cronin will come up with a price! All visits by appointment only, no tasting room; 650-851-1452.

DAVID BRUCE WINERY

Saratoga, California

David Bruce, the son of staunch teetotalers, discovered wine through an interest in cooking while he was enrolled at Stanford University's school of medicine. "I first tasted wine," he explained in an interview with wine historian Charles Sullivan, "to see if it really was fit to enjoy with food." Bruce then bought the relatively few trade books about wine that were available in the 1950s. Alexis Lichine's description of Richebourg in *The Wines of France*—that it had a "noble robe"—so fascinated Bruce that he bought a bottle "to see what in the world Lichine was talking about." According to Bruce, the Richebourg experience riveted his attention on pinot noir and led him to Martin Ray, who included Bruce for a time on the guest list for his bacchanalian harvest festivities. Ray's relative success with pinot noir—Bruce remembers Ray's pinots besting Domaine de la Romanée-Conti wines in his own comparative tastings—focused Bruce's sights on the Santa Cruz Mountains. Back in the San Francisco Bay area after doing his medical residency in Oregon, Bruce bought, cleared, and planted the 40-acre parcel where his winery stands today, and established a medical practice in dermatology nearby, in Los Gatos.

David Bruce's estate vineyard is on the upslope side of Bear Creek Road, facing south and southwest toward Monterey Bay, at approximately 2,200 feet above sea level. The poorest soils, of yellowish weathered and weathering sandstone, are on the high edge of the vineyard; somewhat richer loam prevails downhill, but vine vigor is uniformly low. Even so, some green harvesting is done to reduce yields. In some years, the green harvesting is done primarily to promote even ripening. Bruce's first plantings, laid out in four blocks—one each of pinot noir, cabernet sauvignon, chardonnay, and riesling—were done by hand beginning in 1962. The cabernet was pulled out in the 1970s; riesling survived into the 1980s. Budwood for the pinot vineyard came from Martin Ray and from Wente's increase block in Arroyo Seco, and the last of these vines succumbed to a combination of phylloxera and Pierce's disease in 1994. (The last vintage of pinot noir made entirely from the first-generation vines was 1992.) In 1993–1994, a second-generation planting was begun using some budwood saved from the Noble Hill Vineyard on Zayante Road, which had been planted in the 1980s with cuttings from the old Bruce estate, plus nursery-sourced Swan, a field selection from Cambria, UCD 5 and 13, and Dijon 115, 667, and 777. To buffer the vineyard from a recurrence of Pierce's disease, trees were cleared well beyond the vineyard's edge. By 2001, just over nine acres of pinot noir were in production in 16 hillside blocks, spaced five feet between vines, in eight- or ten-foot rows depending on the degree of slope.

In remarks made to a symposium on *terroir* in 2002, Bruce recalled that he had found it hard to make a good pinot noir in the 1960s and had been "forced" to work with other varieties until he learned "how individual varieties work differently." In his recollection, the David Bruce brand was known in the 1960s primarily for its zinfandel, and in the 1970s for its chardonnay; it did not begin making "consistent" pinot noirs until the 1980s. During the 1970s, perhaps as part of the learning process, Bruce sourced pinot from well beyond the estate vineyard. Pinot noir was purchased from vineyards in Monterey and San Luis Obispo counties beginning in 1977, from Sonoma County from about 1990 onward, and more recently from other Santa Cruz Mountains sites. These last include the R-R Ranch, a cool, fog-influenced site on the Santa Cruz side of the mountains at about 800 feet; Split Rail Vineyard, at around 1,700 feet overlooking Watsonville; Branciforte Creek, near Scotts Valley; and the Kent Barrie vineyard on Summit Road. This palette has fed, variously, a multicounty label called Vintner's Select; a Central Coast blend; appellation wines from Sonoma County, Russian River, and the Santa Cruz Mountains; and a scattering of vineyard-designates.

Although Bruce and members of his family remain directly involved with the winery, the principal winemakers from 1991 to 2002 were Ken Foster and Anthony Craig, both formed on the job. (In June 2002, Foster left to assume winemaking responsibilities at Carneros Creek.)

WINEMAKING

At the Bear Creek Road facility, pinot noir is made entirely in small, two-ton open-top fermentors, just over five feet tall and four feet in diameter. Stems were gradually eliminated between 1993 and 1997, though Foster admitted to some mixed feelings about the zero-stems regime. On the one hand, he observed, "most stems in California are just not ripe enough" and lead to a taste of stemminess as the wine ages; on the other, stems brighten flavors and reinforce structure. Fermentations are started with Assmannshausen yeast, which tends to be a slow starter, keeping the fermentation temperature fairly cool for the first 48 to 72 hours. Thereafter the temperature rises rapidly into the mid 90s Fahrenheit, with the cap near 100 degrees, and the vatting lasts eight to nine days. Through most of the 1980s, punchdowns were done by hand and foot; this quaint practice was replaced in 1990 with a custom-designed pneumatic *pige* and occasional use of rack and return. Foster generally pressed before the must was completely dry, settled briefly in tanks, and then went to barrel.

In the early 1990s, American oak was used exclusively, but French and Eastern European oak were gradually introduced in the second half of the decade. By the 1998 vintage, the Santa Cruz Mountains wines were finished entirely in French barrels—Foster found that American oak "seems to get in the way of Santa Cruz Mountains fruit"—but about 12 percent of the barrels used to age the Sonoma County wines are still American oak. A single racking is sometimes done about midway through the barrel-aging process; otherwise the wines are not racked until bottling. David Bruce pinots are rarely fined—"only to solve a problem"—and were unfiltered until the mid 1990s. Since then, a coarse pad filtration has been standard, primarily to enhance visual clarity. The Central Coast blend, made in a separate facility at San Luis Obispo, is crafted quite differently. There the format is large eight- and 12-ton fermentors. There is a three-day cold soak at the front end, and the must is pressed at 5 degrees Brix. About 8 percent of the barrels are American oak; only 16 percent are new.

THE WINES

Although the estate vineyard was the historical anchor for David Bruce pinot, the winery's pinot program has depended overwhelmingly on purchased fruit for a decade. A Russian River cuvée has been made since 1991, and a Santa Cruz Mountains blend since 1992. The Central Coast program now dwarfs the balance of the winery's production, having grown from 9,000 cases in 1996 to 31,000 cases in 2000, outgrowing the capacity of the Bear Creek Road facility and requiring the acquisition of additional space in San Luis Obispo. The appellation bottlings are also produced in substantial quantities—roughly 5,200 cases of each. At the end of the 1990s the winery also introduced very small lots of non-estate vineyard-designated wines, primarily for mailing-list and tasting room customers.

My experience with David Bruce pinots is limited to recent vintages. These are very highly extracted, deeply colored wines, made from very ripe fruit, with relatively high levels of finished alcohol.

TASTING NOTES

1999 Brosseau Vineyard (tasted in 2001): Saturated, medium-dark black-red; vanilla, camphor, cedar, and very black fruit on the nose; sweet, black cherry fruit with mocha and hard spice in the mouth; fat, chewy, borderline velvety wine with a long, warm finish. Brosseau vineyard is within the Chalone appellation.

1999 Estate Vineyard (tasted in 2001): Transparent, medium-dark black-red; aromas of licorice, tar, and leather; sweet cherry, toasted cinnamon, Indonesian spices, and tobacco in the mouth; some grip but generally soft wine, velvety finish, medium-length.

1999 Russian River Valley (tasted in 2001): Transparent, medium-dark black-red; smoky and vaguely spicy nose; sweet fruit core, some fruit candy, tree bark, and mineral flavors; supple and medium-long but warm, tannin and alcohol both linger on the finish.

1999 Santa Cruz Mountains (tasted in 2001): Saturated but still transparent, medium-dark black-red; toast and nutmeg on the nose; very sweet core of dark cherry fruit, more nutmeg and tree bark, with a hint of sandalwood and orange peel; supple wine, slightly silken, medium-length.

PRACTICAL INFORMATION

Apart from the vineyard-designated wines, David Bruce pinots are nationally distributed. A mail-order Pinot Only, Please program has been created especially to distribute the small lots of vineyard-designated wines. There is an onsite tasting room on Bear Creek Road, open daily; 800-397-9972.

DAVIS BYNUM WINES

Healdsburg, California

When Davis Bynum converted an abandoned hops kiln into a modern winery during the summer of 1973, he established the first wine production facility on Russian River's Westside Road, antedating luminaries like Williams Selyem and Rochioli. A journalist by profession, Bynum had nonetheless amassed substantial wine credentials prior to his debut in the Russian River valley. Like his father before him, he had judged wine for the California State Fair and the Los Angeles County Fair. He had made wine at home. In 1965 he operated a storefront facility in Albany, California, where he made some wines from scratch—from grapes he bought from Robert Mondavi—blended and bottled others, and sold a large percentage of his product in gallon and half-gallon jugs, catering to a clientele of academics and graduate students with limited budgets. In 1967 Bynum purchased 26 acres of vineyard in Napa, on the site that is now Whitehall Lane Vineyards, but turned his sights to Sonoma when authorities in Napa imposed a moratorium on the construction of new wineries. In Sonoma, Bynum was also able to get some good advice and hands-on assistance from his friend Robert Stemmler, a German immigrant who had established a small winery in nearby Dry Creek.

The conversion of the hops kiln was a blitzkrieg project. Contractors, family, and friends conspired to get the work done in four short months. The winery was hooked up to electric power the same day the crush began in late August 1973. The first red grapes crushed in the new winery were pinot noir from Joe Rochioli's nearby ranch, for which Bynum paid the then-princely sum of $400 a ton. The resulting wine—1973 Davis Bynum Pinot Noir, "produced from grapes grown in the vineyard of Joseph Rochioli, Jr. which overlooks the Russian River"—was a benchmark: the first year Rochioli's pinot was made as a varietal wine, the first wine of any kind to carry the words *Russian River* on its label, and (along with Joe Swan's 1973 pinot noir) the first vineyard-designated pinot from Russian River.

Davis Bynum Wines is an unusual intersection of personal relationships, businesses, and winemaking talent. Davis himself was a self-taught winemaker. He passed what he knew to his son Hampton through old-fashioned apprenticeship. One of Hampton's college buddies was Gary Farrell, who liked helping Hampton at the hops kiln turned winery when he was not busy with his day job—which, as he was fresh from college, was house painting. Farrell eventually became Davis Bynum's winemaker—his on-the-job training supplemented with course work and seminars at the University of California, Davis. Meanwhile, Bynum's neighbor Will McIlroy, a grape grower and Davis-trained enologist, became the winery's source for chardonnay and gewürztraminer grapes, and in due season also Farrell's cowinemaker. A handshake and friendship with Rochioli assured Bynum a supply of what became the most prized pinot fruit in the Russian River valley, even after Rochioli and his son Tom established their own winery and label. Bynum's converted hops kiln also provided a home to Gary Farrell Wines from 1982 to 2000, when Farrell's own facility was finally ready for business. In 2000 Bynum hired David Georges, a Davis-trained viticulturist with experience in Los Carneros and Washington State, to replace Farrell, who remains associated with Davis Bynum as consulting winemaker.

Until 1984, Bynum's profits went to improvements and expansion of the winery's physical plant, and all grapes were purchased from independent growers. From 1973 to 1975, Rochioli was Bynum's exclusive source for pinot noir. Allen Ranch (see the Williams Selyem profile) was added in 1976 and has been used continuously since. Fruit from Rick Moshin's vineyard (on Westside Road south of Wohler Bridge) made its debut in the 1980s and has been used intermittently since. In addition, fruit has been sourced from the Oehlman Vineyard (on Vine Hill Road in Laguna Ridge, near Kistler) since 1995, and from Saralee's Vineyard since 1997. Several other sources, including the Poplar Vineyard near Mark West Winery on Eastside Road, Balverne, Kaiser, Garrison Ranch, and Bacigalupi, were used experimentally during the 1980s and 1990s. In 1990, however, father and son commenced planting pinot on their own land, high above the winery buildings at an altitude of about 280 feet. There, on a butte commanding spectacular views across the Russian River valley to the Mayacamas Range, the so-called Lindleys' Knoll vineyard (Davis Bynum's father's name was Lindley; Davis's first forename is Lindley, and one granddaughter is also Lindley) includes nine acres of pinot noir, planted in ten-foot rows with five feet between vines. About 2.75 acres are UCD 4, two acres are Dijon clones, and 1.75 acres are UCD 2A; the balance is about equally divided between UCD 16, UCD 13, and a field selection, said to be Mount Eden, from the Moshin vineyard. The soil is mostly Sobrante series decomposed shale with some volcanic ash, red-black in color at the surface, low vigor, and extremely well drained; it is farmed organically, with special attention to polyculture and insectary plantings on the vineyard's periphery.

WINEMAKING

Hampton Bynum says winemaking at Bynum hasn't changed dramatically since the first vintage in 1973, though stem retention has been slowly eliminated. Fermentation is done in small, 2.5-ton open-tops, with hand punch-downs. A 36-hour cold soak is permitted before the must is inoculated with laboratory yeast. Bynum fermentations are fast and fairly hot: four or five days at 90 to 95 degrees Fahrenheit. After fermentation, the wine settles for several weeks before it is pressed off the lees, at which time free-run and gentle-press juice are blended.

About 20 percent new oak is used on the Russian River valley blend, and 33 percent for the Rochioli wine. Russian River is bottled after about ten months in barrel; the Rochioli gets 13 to 14 months. The wine is racked before bottling, but neither fined nor filtered. Former winemaker Farrell says he did his share of "fooling around" with yeast strains, malolactic bacteria, barrels from various coopers, and longer prefermentation soaks, but came to agree with most contemporary pinot makers that the big determinants of quality are grown in the vineyard, not made in the winery.

THE WINES

From 1973 to 1976, Davis Bynum made a single pinot only, entirely from Rochioli fruit and labeled simply "Pinot Noir, Sonoma." In 1977 or 1978 (the winery's records are incomplete), fruit from the Allen Ranch entered the mix, and the resulting Sonoma Westside Road pinot noir replaced Pinot Noir, Sonoma. A reserve pinot debuted in 1980, featuring the Rochioli and Allen Ranch fruit that had previously made the reputation of the Sonoma and Sonoma Westside Road cuvées; at the same time, the latter was re-designated Russian River Valley, and its fruit was more widely sourced. Later in the 1980s, the Reserve rubric was abandoned in favor of Limited Release and Limited Edition. These were barrel selections of the most age-worthy lots available to the winery, and were sourced from as many as six vineyards per vintage.

Simultaneously, the Russian River wine evolved into a home for Bynum's lighter lots and was crafted for early drinking. Much of the impetus for the Russian River Valley bottling, which was produced in considerable quantities, was Bynum's arrangement, in those years, with a national marketing company, which used the Bynum name for "a lot of wines that were blended and bottled outside the winery"; the reserve wines were, in fact, Bynum's only serious pinots. Meanwhile, in 1991, Le Pinot emerged as a de facto vineyard-designated wine, made entirely from Rochioli's East Block. Davis Bynum pinots (apart from the Russian River bottlings of the late 1980s and early 1990s) are generally well colored, medium-bodied wines that age well. Despite Bynum's historical position as the original Westside Road pioneer and Farrell's stellar winemaking reputation, Bynum pinots have rarely enjoyed the same critical acclaim that attends Farrell's own wines, Williams Selyem and Rochioli. Part of the explanation may be marketplace confusion resulting from association of the Davis Bynum name with early-maturing, high-volume wines during the late 1980s. My own experience suggests some unevenness in the track record over the years, as fruit supplies have come and gone, and some blending choices have perhaps given less than optimal results. Whatever the explanation, savvy consumers will take full advantage of the anomaly, because the best Bynum pinots are very good indeed.

TASTING NOTES

1999 Bynum and Moshin Vineyards (tasted three times in 2001 and 2002): Transparent, medium-dark black-red; aromas quite different each time tasted, first prune and raisin, then rose petal and cardamom, most recently camphorwood; sweet, dark berry fruit in the mouth with hints of pepper, clove, and allspice; very soft, fine-grained tannins in a long finish. Half and half Moshin and Lindleys' Knoll.

1999 Le Pinot (tasted in 2002): Transparent, deep black-purple; nose of very ripe Italian plum and mocha with a hint of evergreen; sweet, chewy, clove- and coffee-flavored black fruits in the mouth; substantial weight and length, complex.

1999 Lindleys' Knoll Estate Best 4 Barrels (tasted in 2002): Transparent, medium-dark black-red; nose of marzipan and cherry candy; deep and dark on the palate, with black fruit, tree bark, and bramble; considerable tannin and length, texture of rough silk.

1999 Russian River Valley (tasted in 2002): Very transparent, medium black-red; explosive nose of black cherry, blackberry, and beets; infused black fruit, clove, and pepper in the mouth; medium-weight and medium-length. Made from equal shares of Lindleys' Knoll and Oehlman fruit, plus 24 percent Allen Ranch.

1998 Le Pinot (tasted in 2002): Transparent, dark black-red; aromas of bramble, geranium, cinnamon, and spice; black fruits, mocha, chocolate, slate, and minerals in the mouth; linen-textured, well-structured, long-finishing wine.

1997 Le Pinot (tasted in 1999): Transparent, black-red; aromas of leather, tar, meat, clove, and smoke; cherry, black fruit, and fig in the mouth; a rich edition of East Block wine with soft tannins and velvet texture.

1996 Russian River Valley Limited Edition (tasted in 1999): Transparent, black-red; nose of dried rose petals, leaves, and berries; some black pepper on the palate; firm tannins, linen-textured. A special bottling of the best lots of this troublesome vintage, from the Rochioli and Allen vineyards, Saralee's vineyard, and Bynum's estate vineyard.

1995 Le Pinot (tasted in 1999): Dark, black-red; leather, tobacco, and dried leaf nose; touch of earth and forest floor, cinnamon and chocolate; firm tannins, velvet texture. Quite open and evolved aromatically. Farrell's favorite among all Davis Bynum pinots from 1973 to 1995, and exceptional in my book, but scored in the low 80s by *Wine & Spirits* in 1998.

1994 Limited Edition (tasted in 2002): Transparent, light black-red; somewhat closed; dried cherry, black licorice, and cinnamon in the mouth; chewy and somewhat tannic with considerable minerality, medium-long. Predominantly Allen Ranch fruit, blended with roughly equal percentages of Rochioli, Lindleys' Knoll, Moshin, Oehlman, and Bacigalupi.

1992 Limited Edition (tasted in 2002): Transparent, medium ruby, now tiling; vaguely floral nose with some red berry notes; strawberry-raspberry flavors with a hint of clove; structured wine, linen-textured, medium-length. An atypical wine for Bynum, or perhaps an atypical bottle, made from 42 percent Moshin and 32 percent Allen Ranch, with lesser amounts of Rochioli, Kaiser, and Balverne fruit.

1991 Limited Edition (tasted in 2002): Brilliant, terra-cotta with a still-red core; raspberries and rose petals on the nose; raspberry and cherry in the mouth, with red licorice and some coffee; slightly sweet, soft, and silky; elegant, medium-weight wine with a long finish. Made from 30 percent Allen Ranch and 25 percent Davis (see Porter Creek) Vineyard, with smaller amounts of Rochioli, Balverne, Bacigalupi, and Moshin.

1985 Artist Series Limited Release (tasted in 2002): Brilliant and beautiful, medium terra-cotta color; dried cherries and mushroom aromas; more mushrooms, plus shoe polish, mercaptan, and black pepper in the mouth;

long, aromatic, silken, and elegant wine. A personal favorite; 85 percent Allen Ranch, 10 percent Poplar Vineyard, and 5 percent Rochioli.

1984 Pinot Noir Reserve (tasted in 2002): Transparent, medium-dark terra-cotta; wax and shoe polish aromatics; dried cherries, caramel, and camphor on the palate; chewy wine with still noticeable though tame tannins, medium-weight and long. Made from 70 percent Allen Ranch and 30 percent Rochioli.

1982 Reserve (tasted in 2002): Medium-dark terra-cotta with some suspended sediment; nose of caramel, mushroom, and underbrush; very evolved flavors of camphorwood, dried fruit, and tree bark; medium-weight and medium-length. Made from 60 percent Allen Ranch and 40 percent Rochioli.

1980 Reserve (tasted in 2002): Transparent, medium terra-cotta; explosive nose of camphorwood and dried flowers; fading dried cherry in the mouth, plus caramel; still structured and very satisfying for its age. Roughly half and half Rochioli and Allen fruit.

1978 Sonoma Westside Road (tasted in 2002): Terra-cotta tending toward brown, not entirely limpid; earth and dried plums on the nose; slightly sweet and chewy in the mouth, with flavors of earth and dried leaves; medium-weight and lingering. Two-thirds Rochioli, one-third Allen Ranch.

1975 Sonoma (tasted in 2002): Transparent, medium terra-cotta; dark aromas of earth and dried plums; dried leaves and fading cherry-raspberry fruit, with leather and still a hint of clove in the mouth; medium-weight and medium-length, very satisfying.

1973 Sonoma (one of the last known bottles from this vintage, tasted in 2002): Transparent though not quite limpid, light to medium terra-cotta with an orange rim; truffles, bergamot, boot polish, and vaguely cheeselike aromas; dried leaves, infused faded flowers, leather, and mentholated raspberry with just a hint of residual sweetness; nice length but fading.

PRACTICAL INFORMATION

Bynum pinots are nationally distributed, but the limited release and vineyard-designated wines may be more readily available from the winery direct. An onsite tasting room is open seven days; 707-433-5852.

DOMAINE CARNEROS

Napa, California

Domaine Carneros occupies a 138-acre ranch at the corner of Duhig Road and the Carneros Highway. First planted to vines in 1982 by the Allen family of Sequoia Grove Vineyards with advice from Tony Soter, the property was purchased in 1986 by a joint venture dedicated to Champagne-method sparkling wine, involving Champagne Taittinger and its U.S. importer, Kobrand Corporation. The joint venture adopted the Domaine Carneros name and immediately began construction of the incongruous but eye-catching rococo château-winery that now overlooks the highway, an American reincarnation of the Château de la Marquetterie in Reims. Eileen Crane—a veteran of Domaine Chandon and Gloria Ferrer, with the unusual preface of an early career teaching nutrition and a diploma from The Culinary Institute of America before she was trained in viticulture and enology at the University of California, Davis—has been Domaine Carneros's winemaker and managing director from the beginning.

Several stories are told about Domaine Carneros's entry into the still-wine arena. In one version, Crane developed a personal interest in pinot during her term as president of the Carneros Quality Alliance. This was in 1986, when the alliance sponsored research intended to differentiate Carneros-grown pinots from those of other regions. In this version of the story, Claude Taittinger, initially skeptical, grew supportive when the first vintage of still pinot, served to fellow board members of the Relais & Châteaux hotel group, was a huge success—notwithstanding the impertinent inquiry from one of the *convives* "whether fruit extract had been added to the wine." In another version, the foray into pinot noir began as a side project to create noncommercial quantities of still red wine for the Taittinger family, which expanded fortuitously when the wines turned out better than expected. In yet a third version, assistant winemaker Dan Karlsen, recruited to Domaine Carneros from Dehlinger Winery in the early 1990s, "developed the winery's new and notable Pinot Noir line." Whatever the interplay of events and roles, Domaine Carneros was the first of the major sparkling-wine houses to make a serious and successful commitment to still pinot noir, and its production of pinot grew steadily through the 1990s, reaching 20 percent of total output in 2000.

About half of the 60 acres of pinot noir planted on the original "estate" vineyard are now used for still wine, as is about 30 percent of the 56-acre Pompadour Vineyard on Napa Road. A third vineyard, called La Rocaille—on the southern side of the Carneros Highway between Cuttings Wharf Road and Stanly Road—was purchased in 1994 specifically for still pinot. The original estate vineyard is a roughly triangular site bounded by Highway 121, Duhig Road, and Huichica Creek. Pinot is planted there on the steep north- and west-facing slopes, in thin Diablo clay-loam, at elevations between 100 and 150 feet. The original vines were field selections and UCD 13. The UCD 13 came from nurseries and from Carneros Creek. The field selections were from Newlan, just north of Napa on Highway 29, which originally came from Swan; from Smith-Madrone, so it is actually UCD 5; and from Madonna, which makes it a mix of UCD clones via Wente and Mont St. John in Oakville. Some Swan selection was added in 1991, and small quantities of Dijon clones have been planted more recently, primarily to replace vines lost to phylloxera. Until 1992, some fruit from this vineyard was sold to Etude and other makers; since then, Domaine Carneros has used 100 percent of its estate-grown pinot.

Pompadour, Domaine Carneros's second vineyard, is a flat, rectangular, 56-acre parcel, quite different from the estate, used primarily for sparkling wine. The block of Pompadour used for still wine is primarily Swan selection. It is at the vineyard's northern end, where the soils are relatively light and loamy.

La Rocaille, the third site, was entirely replanted in 1995 and 1996, aside from a small block of old merlot. This gentle, east-facing slope, with the lightest, loamiest soils of the three, was planted with budwood taken from the Swan, Smith-Madrone, and Madonna blocks in the original estate vineyard. Domaine Carneros's heavy reliance on field-selected heritage "clones" is unusual in Los Carneros.

In 2003, Domaine Carneros completed a new pinot-only production facility behind the château, featuring temperature- and humidity-controlled barrel rooms and mechanically assisted punchdown devices.

WINEMAKING

Crane picks grapes for flavor, but the harvest usually begins when sugar has reached 23.5 to 24 Brix. She relies on preharvest triage in the vineyard, rather than a sorting table in the winery, to eliminate undesirable fruit. Clusters are completely destemmed but not crushed, and transferred to seven- by seven-foot open-top fermentors. Four to five days of cold soak at 55 degrees Fahrenheit, enforced with dry ice and the fermentors' cooling jackets if necessary, precedes inoculation with Assmannshausen and other laboratory yeasts. Punchdowns are done four times a day for eight to 12 days to get relatively "saturated colors and rich flavors." When the must is dry, it is pressed, settled in tank, and transferred to barrel. The press fraction is kept separate and is typically "used elsewhere."

Barrels are about 45 percent new and are a mix of François Frères, Cadus, Billon, and Radoux. The wine spends about 11 months in barrel and is racked once before bottling. Crane sometimes fines for tannin management. She also filters routinely, asserting that "filtration is a very good thing" because "it ensures that the customer gets what the winemaker intended, not a wine spoiled by microorganisms." Wines are bottle-aged for six months before release.

THE WINES

Every year since 1993, Domaine Carneros has made two still pinots: a regular bottling called Carneros Pinot Noir and about 1,000 cases of a limited release called The Famous Gate, which is available only at the winery. (In 1992, The Famous Gate was the *only* release.) Both wines are usually fairly dark in color and show a dominance of sweet, black fruit flavors with soft, spicy overtones. The Famous Gate consists of a higher proportion of Swan selection fruit that has been raised in François Frères barrels, the combination of which seems to produce (at least in the Domaine Carneros *terroirs*) flavors of smoky bacon. Tasted vertically in 2000, the vintages since 1994 showed considerable variation. This variation is surely attributable in part to what Crane calls "minor modifications in procedure" as the winemaking team has "gained experience" with pinot noir. Given the replantings on the estate vineyard and the introduction of fruit from Pompadour, there have also been fruit source modifications throughout the decade. Crane finds the wines "of a piece" from 1993 to 1995, then "more gutsy, vibrant, and balanced from 1996 through 1999." Analytically, 1996 is the high-alcohol wine at 14.3 percent—other vintages hover around 13.8. My personal favorite (see below) is the 1995 Carneros. In 2001, a third pinot was added to the Domaine Carneros lineup. Dubbed Avant-Garde, it is (like The Famous Gate) available only at the winery, sells for half the price of Domaine Carneros's Carneros bottling, and is intended for early drinking. In the 2002 vintage, Domaine Carneros produced 7,000 cases of the Carneros cuvée, 2,500 cases of Avant-Garde, and 1,700 cases of The Famous Gate. With the combination of its new all-pinot facility behind the château and long-term leases with options to purchase on additional vineyards, the brand expects to double its total production of still pinot over the coming decade while growing its commitment to sparkling wine.

TASTING NOTES

1998 Carneros (tasted in 2000): Transparent, dark black-red; rose petal aromas; black cherry and other black fruits; licorice and black pepper, plus vanilla; elegant and fleshy, with considerable tannin; good balance.

1997 Carneros (tasted in 2000): Transparent, black-red, a bit lighter than the 1998; sweet black fruit and fruit candy; more mineral than flesh.

1996 Carneros (tasted in 2000): Again deep black-red; quite floral on the nose; black cherry, black fruit, and fruit candy; bacon, licorice and black pepper, some chocolate and smoke; sweet, full-bodied wine with velvety texture.

1995 Carneros (tasted in 2000): Transparent, garnet with a touch of terra-cotta thanks to maturity; again cherry and black fruit with licorice and black pepper; decidedly smoky; aromatic, notes of resin; very clean, elegant, long, mineral-flavored wine, silken and balanced. A personal favorite.

1995 The Famous Gate (tasted in 2000): Transparent, medium to dark mahogany; distinctive nose of evergreen, iodine, and peat; leather, tobacco, tar, very black cherry, and mercurochrome flavors; sweet midpalate; long, mouthcoating, and fine.

1994 Carneros (tasted in 2000): Transparent, dark garnet, with tiling at the edge; characteristic dark cherry, black fruit, and fruit candy with a touch of cola; meat and bacon with leather flavors developing with age; a sweet, candied orange peel note on the finish; very fine.

PRACTICAL INFORMATION

Domaine Carneros's Carneros cuvée is nationally distributed by Kobrand. The Famous Gate and Avant-Garde are available only at the winery. A spacious tasting room in the "château" is open daily; 707-257-0101.

DOMAINE DROUHIN OREGON

Dundee, Oregon

Burgundy *négociant* Robert Drouhin has been involved with Oregon pinot noir almost from the outset—albeit unintentionally. Several Drouhin wines were among the pinots bested by The Eyrie Vineyards' 1975 South Block Reserve when the latter was entered in a Paris tasting organized by *GaultMillau* magazine in 1979. When Drouhin orchestrated a rematch the following year, presumably hoping to redeem the tarnished reputation of fine Burgundies, the Eyrie wine placed second in an all-Drouhin field. Five years later, Drouhin decided that Oregon might be just the place for his daughter, the first member of her family to be university trained in enology, to do an internship. Various Oregonian friendships ensued. Véronique Drouhin worked the summer and harvest of 1986 at Adelsheim, Eyrie, and Bethel Heights. David Adelsheim then told Robert Drouhin that some "interesting" property had come on the market just a stone's throw from Eyrie. And so, in 1987, Maison Joseph Drouhin—one of Burgundy's most respected houses and proprietor of almost priceless vineyards in Musigny, Clos de Bèze, and Griotte-Chambertin—birthed Domaine Drouhin Oregon, 98 acres of south-facing slope in the Red Hills of Dundee. Additional land was purchased in the 1990s, bringing the plantable total to 140 acres, and a state-of-the-art gravity-flow winery, dug partially into the hillside, was constructed in 1989. To this day, DDO (as it is called in the trade) is the only significant Burgundian investment in North American pinot noir.

Although Robert Drouhin visited Oregon as early as 1961 and says he was struck even then by the climatic and geographic similarities to the Côte d'Or, his mature interest in Oregon was, he asserts, "fundamentally intellectual." An Oregon project forced him to rethink his Burgundian orientations. Why, he says he asked himself, do Burgundians plant at high density? Why do they fertilize their vineyards? Why, in this century, do they trellis their vines? And then, if the vigneron were unfettered by Burgundy's "history, regulations and *mentalité*," how should these practices be adapted for Oregon? As the Oregon vineyard was planned, Robert placed Véronique (now Véronique Drouhin-Boss) in charge. Decisions were made to plant both sparsely (though what here is called sparse is actually one meter by 1.8) and densely (at one meter by 1.3 meters), to provide a basis for comparison; and to plant some vines own-rooted in the Oregon style of the day and others on resistant rootstock—again for comparison. Drouhin imported cellar equipment from Burgundy, along with Oregon's first row-straddling *enjambeur* tractor. Various of Oregon's pioneer winemakers were already experimenting simultaneously with rootstocks, planting densities, and cellar techniques, so it is not quite accurate to say, as some have reported, that DDO revolutionized either Oregon's viticulture or its winemaking. Nevertheless, the simple fact that Drouhin had chosen to invest in Oregon gave other vintners confidence in the future and attracted many new players to the field.

Although the earliest plantings at DDO were own-rooted UCD 2A and 5, sourced from nurseries, DDO soon developed its own mother block for rootstocks, and converted to Dijon clones as scion material in 1990. Dijon 115 and 777 account for the majority of the post-1990 plantings.

WINEMAKING

Although pinot is picked by taste at DDO, the preference is to aim for modest finished alcohol, between 12.9 and 13.8. Small percentages of whole-cluster fruit are sometimes used, but the default protocol is to destem the fruit completely. The winery is equipped with fermentors in several sizes, designed to accommodate lots as small as 500 gallons and as large as 3,500 gallons. The smaller fermentors are jacketed stainless steel open-tops; the largest are custom-designed horizontal tanks equipped with rotary blades. Apart from a few experimental lots, fermentations rely on resident yeast and are not preceded by a cold soak unless the grapes have arrived warm at the winery. Total vatting time ranges from 12 to 21 days, of which the alcoholic fermentation takes from four to ten, with temperatures peaking just over 90 degrees Fahrenheit. In this protocol, postfermentation macerations can last as long as ten days, depending on the vintage.

About 90 percent of barrels come from the in-house stocks of Joseph Drouhin in Beaune, which are bought as unmilled wood and custom-coopered for Drouhin by François Frères. Ten percent come from other sources, including at the moment a few Hungarian oak barrels, for experimental purposes. In the late 1980s Drouhin-Boss used up to 40 percent new wood, but she has now backed off to about 18 percent. Pinots spend 11 to 12 months in barrel, during which time they are racked once, and then once more to tank before bottling. In some vintages as many as half of the lots may be fined; in other vintages fining is avoided altogether. A light filtration with diatomaceous earth precedes bottling. The Oregon cuvée (see below) is held nine months before release; Cuvée Laurène gets a hefty 21 months of bottle-aging.

THE WINES

The 1988 and 1989 vintages of DDO were made entirely from purchased fruit, sourced from eight Willamette Valley vineyards, and were exceptionally well received by the wine press. As the estate fruit began to come online in 1990, four of the eight sources were abandoned, but DDO has continued to purchase fruit from Seven Springs Vineyard and from three of its immediate neighbors in the Red Hills: Knudsen, Durant, and Stoller. A reserve wine, called Cuvée Laurène in honor of Drouhin-Boss's first daughter and made each year since 1992, is produced entirely from estate fruit and represents a barrel selection of lots exhibiting particular depth and complexity. The DDO pinots are elegant, medium-weight wines that display considerable vintage-to-vintage consistency anchored with aromas of red and black berries; Cuvée Laurène generally shows more structure than the Oregon cuvée. Although Laurène is built with age-worthiness in mind, both wines appear to age handsomely for at least a decade. In 1999, DDO added a third pinot to its portfolio, Cuvée Louise Drouhin, named for Drouhin-Boss's youngest daughter. Production of this cuvée is limited to eight barrels, selected to privilege elegance and silken texture.

TASTING NOTES

2000 Oregon (tasted in 2003): Brilliant, almost iridescent medium black-red; aromas of raspberry with hints of smoke and gremolata; minerals, graphite, black raspberry, and black pepper on the palate; medium-weight, structured, and suedelike with a faint hint of chewing tobacco on the finish.

1999 Cuvée Laurène (tasted in 2003): Brilliant, medium black-red; chalk, raspberry, and floral aromas; dark fruit, tea, barrel char, black pepper, and a hint of tangerine peel on the palate; mineral and mouthcoating, suedelike, slight grip of very fine tannin, long.

1999 Oregon (tasted twice in 2001): Transparent, medium garnet; wild cherry and black raspberry on the nose, with cedar, toast, geranium, and rose hips; red fruit with slate, toasted cinnamon, and a hint of white pepper in the mouth; medium-weight and medium-length, silken.

1998 Cuvée Laurène (tasted in 2001): Transparent, medium-dark black-red; aromas of cherry, blackberry, violets, and smoke; flavors of fruit-infused black tea; moderately sweet core with some discernible tannin, medium-length and medium-weight with the texture of rough silk.

1994 Cuvée Laurène (tasted in 2003): Dark, saturated black-red; sweet black cherry and black licorice, with tea and infused flowers; elegant, moderately rich, smoky, and long, medium-weight, and satin-textured.

1992 Oregon (tasted in 2002): Very transparent, medium mahogany, still brick-red in the center; aromas of camphorwood, leather, candle wax, mint, herbs, and dried currants; in the mouth, fading ripe cherry, licorice, bay leaf, smoke, and slate; medium-weight, very long and silken, very fine. A personal favorite.

PRACTICAL INFORMATION

Most of the DDO wines are nationally distributed by Dreyfus, Ashby and Company and marketed in selected international markets by Maison Joseph Drouhin. There are about 10,000 cases of Oregon cuvée annually, and about 2,000 of Cuvée Laurène. Cuvée Louise Drouhin is available only at the winery and by direct mail or Web order. Visits to the winery can be arranged with advance notice; 503-864-2700.

DOMAINE SERENE

Dayton, Oregon

Domaine Serene is the wine project of a Minnesota couple, Ken and Grace Evenstad, who had the good fortune to bring pharmaceutical wealth to their passion for Burgundian grape varieties. It is also the second of the three brands with which Ken Wright was closely involved, overlapping with his last years at Panther Creek and with the first years of Ken Wright Cellars. (Wright, however, never had any equity interest in Domaine Serene.)

The first releases of Domaine Serene, beginning in 1990, were made at Panther Creek, using fruit Wright sourced. In the early vintages fruit came, inter alia, from the Carter, Canary Hill, and Freedom Hill vineyards, along with Beaux Frères, Knudsen, and Kircher. This last vineyard was eventually purchased by the Evenstads; see below. In 1990 the Evenstads made their first purchase of land in the Red Hills of Dundee, a 42-acre west-facing parcel on the southernmost of the three Dundee hills. The first estate vineyard, called Mark Bradford, was planted there in 1993: just over 11 acres of UCD 4 and 2A, spaced eight feet by four, high on the slope, between 640 and 760 feet. Nine acres of nearby east-facing slope named in honor of Grace Evenstad, a tad lower than Mark Bradford, were planted to Dijon 667 and 777 in 1994; these were followed by six acres of

Dijon 667 and 777 as well as UCD 4, called Gold Eagle, in 1997; and 4.4 acres of Dijon 667 and 777, called Fleur de Lis, in 1998. Meanwhile, a third land acquisition, in 1997, brought the former Kircher vineyard, upslope from the service road that leads to the aforementioned plantings, into the estate. This parcel—some 13 acres of own-rooted UCD 2A and 4 from which Domaine Serene had previously sourced fruit, renamed Côte Sud to describe its orientation—was the site for additional planting from 1999 through 2001 (again Dijon 667 and UCD 4). Spacing throughout has respected the eight-foot by four-foot beginnings, for which the target yield is two tons per acre; but the average as of this writing is just 1.68. Soils throughout are Jory series: weathered, crumbly, reddish basalt. Collectively, these parcels are known as Evenstad Estate. One mile north, on a sister slope, 20 additional acres facing south and west have been planted to Dijon clones. This parcel, called Winery Hill, is also the site for Domaine Serene's new five-level gravity-flow winery, which was completed in time for the 2001 harvest. The Evenstads also purchased 90 acres on Jerusalem Hill, on the east side of the Eola Hills, of which 32 acres have been planted to pinot noir. Together the three sites bring Domaine Serene's holdings of planted pinot to an impressive 100-plus acres.

The first estate fruit, from the Mark Bradford vineyard, entered the Domaine Serene program in 1995. Since then, estate fruit has played an increasingly important role, rising to about 70 percent of all fruit in 1999, and is projected to account for 90 percent of the brand's need by 2005. At that point, Domaine Serene's production of pinot noir should be about 15,000 cases annually. A small amount of chardonnay is also made.

Tony Rynders, a University of California, Davis, graduate with experience at Mirassou, Argyle, and Washington's Hogue Cellars, the last as red-wine maker, took over as winemaker in August 1998. Rynders blended the 1997 vintage and made the 1998 from scratch. Like many of his contemporaries, he is vineyard-driven—committed to dense plantings, low yield, and dry-farming.

WINEMAKING

Rynders is a believer in rigorous fruit thinning during the growing season. Domaine Serene practices two or three thinnings during the season—one early pass in July to reduce crop in the heaviest vineyards, and one or two green thinnings before veraison. Rigorous sorting is also done on the crushpad. There Rynders removes any leaves and second-crop clusters that have been picked with the fruit, as well as clusters that have been affected by rot. He likes a large percentage of whole berries "to moderate tannins," but uses very few whole clusters. His fermentors are small, 1.25-ton cylindrical stainless steel open-tops, enabling him to keep every clone from every block separate. A longish four- to six-day cold soak is enforced with dry ice and sulfur dioxide. Following the cold soak, the tanks are warmed to 65 to 70 degrees Fahrenheit and inoculated with selected yeasts. A custom-built pneumatic device facilitates twice-daily punchdowns. With fermentation temperatures generally peaking in the high 80s or low 90s, the must is usually dry six to 12 days after the cold soak began. If Rynders detects rough tannins in any cuvée, he will press before the must is completely dry and allow the fermentation to finish in wood. The free-run and light press juices are kept separate, but some of the press fraction is used in the Reserve/Yamhill Cuvée (see below) wine.

In the interest of complexity, barrels from about a dozen coopers are used. Although Rynders employs 75 percent new barrels each year, he does not like oaky flavors, eschews heavy toast and toasted heads, and prewashes new barrels with hot water. He likes some barrels with a partially Bordelais pedigree—Sylvain, a Burgundy-shape made in Bordeaux, and Vicard, a Bordeaux-based firm that also operates in Burgundy—which, he says, "seem to impart less smoke and toast to the wines." Once the wine is in barrel, Rynders finds that a "very antioxidative environment," with little or no racking and sulfur dioxide as needed, results in better wood integration. Domaine Serene wines are neither fined nor filtered. Barrel time ranges from about 11 to 16 months, depending on vintage and wine type. Rynders insists that there is "no recipe," and that "the wines let us know when they are ready." After bottling, the wines are held for eight to 18 additional months before release.

THE WINES

Domaine Serene's flagship wine is the Evenstad Reserve. This cuvée, of which about 1,300 cases were made in 1998, is blended first, from the first choice among all available lots, selecting for size, concentration, complexity, and finesse. Generally these lots tend to have been raised in new barrels, so the overall percentage of new wood in the Evenstad Reserve can run about 90 percent. This wine is always bottled after the next year's harvest. Although Evenstad Reserve was and is an evolving wine—having been made perforce entirely from purchased fruit at the outset, but sustained with 70 percent estate fruit by 1999—it is also the winery's main emphasis and main vector for growth. A second wine has always been blended from the remaining lots. Until 1998, this second wine was (rather confusingly) also called Reserve, without a modifier. Effective with the 1999 vintage, this wine has been helpfully rechristened Yamhill Cuvée. Since his arrival in 1998, Rynders has sought to sharpen the stylistic differences between the two wines, bottling the second wine earlier and featuring lots with forward fruit character. In addition to the two blends, a Mark Bradford vineyard-designate was made in 1996, 1998, and 1999, and a Grace Vineyard bottling was released from the 1998 and 1999 vintages. The policy is to make vineyard-designates only in very small quantities, only in superior vintages, and only when lots can be spared from the Evenstad Reserve cuvée without any adverse impact on its quality.

The reputation of Domaine Serene pinots is for large, intense, and complex wines; my experience is unfortunately limited to just two finished wines from the 1998 and 1999 vintages, and to unblended components of the 2000 vintage.

TASTING NOTES

1999 Yamhill Cuvée (tasted in 2001): Transparent, medium-deep, bluish-red; nose of cranberry, strawberry, and tea; berry fruit and slate in the mouth; aftertastes of fennel and light brown sugar; medium-length, soft-finishing wine.

1998 Evenstad Reserve (tasted in 2001): Transparent, medium black-red wine; leather and black tea aromas; black cherry, cherry preserves, raspberry cordial, and leather in the mouth; notes of slate, black pepper, and clove, plus an unusual faint accent of tart citrus peel and cured green olive; medium-weight, very soft, plush wine.

PRACTICAL INFORMATION

Domaine Serene pinots are distributed to 28 markets in the United States, Canada, the United Kingdom, and Japan and can be purchased from the winery directly. The winery is not currently open to the public except for open houses held on the Memorial Day and Thanksgiving weekends; 503-864-4600.

DR. KONSTANTIN FRANK'S VINIFERA WINE CELLARS

Hammondsport, New York

In any other pinot-friendly region, a producer doing business as Vinifera Wine Cellars would seem curiously redundant. But in upstate New York, the name of Dr. Konstantin Frank's winery is a useful reminder that Frank was, only a generation and a half ago, a genuine pioneer. His old blocks of pinot noir, planted in 1959, 1960, and 1961, are older than all California plantings still in production save two: the 1946 block at Chalone and the 1953 block at Hanzell. When he planted these first vines, along with several other varieties of vinifera, on a beautiful bluff overlooking Keuka Lake, New York's wine industry was firmly anchored in native American varieties and hybrids, and experimentation with vinifera was regarded as the height of folly. But Frank persisted, succeeded, birthed a family business that is now in its third generation, and set the course—in riesling and pinot noir—that has finally emerged as the mainstream of the Finger Lakes region's wine. When *Wine Spectator* magazine created a 54-person Hall of Fame to celebrate its 25th anniversary in 2001, Frank was the only individual in the United States wine industry outside California to be named.

Frank immigrated to America in 1951 with no money and little English but a doctorate from the University of Odessa, in the Ukraine, in plant science. His dissertation had been focused specifically on growing vinifera in a cold climate, and the Ukraine displayed extremes of temperature that dwarfed anything on the record books in upstate New York. The story is that Frank worked briefly in Brooklyn after landing on American shores, then bought a bus ticket to Geneva, New York—where he knew the state and Cornell University operated an agricultural experiment station—tried unsuccessfully to stimulate Geneva professors' interest in growing vinifera, and landed a job hoeing blueberries and sweeping floors instead. About 1956, the story continues, Frank chanced to meet Charles Fournier, Gold Seal Wine Company's enologist, when Fournier attended a conference at the Geneva station. It was apparently helpful that Frank spoke much better French than English, and that Fournier, who was a native of Champagne, had a predisposition to vinifera. In any case, Fournier forthwith hired Frank as Gold Seal's director of vineyard research, and the work on vinifera in New York State began seriously. In 1959, Frank began planting the vineyard that was to become the basis for Vinifera Wine Cellars, which he founded in 1962 while he was still working a day job at Gold Seal. Frank's son Willy succeeded his father in 1985. His grandson Frederick, who earned a bachelor's degree in agriculture at Cornell University and then studied viticulture and enology at Geisenheim in Germany, has been president of the firm since 1993; Willy Frank remains as chairman.

Frank's original nine-acre pinot noir vineyard was planted on a steeply sloping hillside on Keuka Lake's western shore, about five miles north of Hammondsport. The soil is fractured shale surmounting bedrock shale—quite typical of the Finger Lakes region. Vines are spaced nine feet by six—which was an unusually dense planting for its day—and the vineyard has recently been converted from sprawl to vertical trellis. The plant material is said to be two clones that Fournier and Frank imported "from Burgundy" at the end of the 1950s, allegedly via the Department of Agriculture's quarantine facility at Beltsville, Maryland. Willy Frank remembers that "nine" clones were originally imported and given trials at Gold Seal, and that his father "eliminated seven of the nine." Apparently the two best were chosen for his own plantings. One of them is now known locally as Clone 7—presumably the seventh of the original nine. Cuttings of Clone 7 have been provided to other Finger Lakes growers, and plantings of it are now fairly widespread. The other best of the Frank imports appears to exist only in Frank's own vineyard.

As an aside, it is unclear whether the so-called Geneva clone of pinot noir, which is now also popular in the Finger Lakes, was another of the Frank-Fournier imports. Willy and Fred Frank do not claim it. Bob Pool, the main viticulturist at the New York State Agricultural Experiment Station, who claims credit for naming it Geneva "because I didn't want anyone else to take the blame," says 20-year-old vines of it were growing in the station's vineyard when he arrived in 1974. This account would square with an import date sometime in the 1950s. It is said to resemble a Champagne clone, however, while the Frank-Fournier imports are supposed to have come from Burgundy. But then, given that Fournier was a Champenois, there is reason to wonder whether all the plant material they imported did in fact come from Burgundy. Whatever the truth of the matter, both Clone 7 and the Geneva clone have displayed good tolerance of cold winters and fair resistance to mildew, which is an endemic local problem, and both have been used extensively at other vineyards in the region.

Pinot noir yields at Frank's estate range between 1.5 and two tons per acre. Three additional acres of pinot were planted in 1990, to Dijon 113 and 115, as well as something called Clone V, which may have been imported through Canada. In addition to the estate fruit, Vinifera also purchases between ten and 15 tons of pinot noir from vineyards on the western side of Seneca Lake.

WINEMAKING

Although Frederick Frank has winemaking credentials, the property is unusual among Finger Lakes region wineries for employing a succession of full-time, professionally trained makers, and more recently also interns from the main European wine schools. Currently the winemakers are Morton Hallgren, trained at Montpellier, and Mark Veraguth, who was trained at the University of California, Davis. Pinot is picked between 22 and 23 Brix, and Frank says they prefer not to chaptalize. Grapes are completely destemmed and fermented in unjacketed stainless steel open-tops seven feet in diameter and four feet tall. A one- to two-day cold soak precedes six to ten days of primary fermentation with peak temperatures around 85 degrees Fahrenheit. The must is pressed at dryness, and the heavier press fraction is usually directed into the Fleur de Pinot Noir bottling; see below. The juice is sometimes settled in tank, and sometimes pumped directly into barrels.

Barrels are mostly François Frères and Remond, but there are also "lots of bits." Barrels are used for four years, so there are roughly equal fractions of new, one-year-old, two-year-old, and three-year-old cooperage. The so-called new barrels are used for a single vintage of chardonnay before being repurposed for the pinot program, however. Until 2000, malolactic inoculation was done in the settling tank. Effective in 2001, it is being done in barrel, and the barrels are stored in a heated room until the secondary fermentation completes. Racking is done once or twice. Lots destined for the Fleur wine are bottled after just six months in wood. At pressing, the winemakers decide which lots will be used to make the Salmon Run wine (see below). When this decision is made, these lots are transferred to tanks for malolactic fermentation and held there until the previous vintage is bottled, which liberates additional cooperage. The wines are fined "as needed" for tannin management and are filtered several times.

THE WINES

In recent years, three pinots have been made at Dr. Frank's. The benchmark wine is called simply Dr. Konstantin Frank and consists entirely of fruit from the 40-year-old estate planting. Fruit from the younger estate parcel and purchased fruit are used for the Salmon Run bottling, which debuted in 1998, and for the Fleur de Pinot Noir wine, which was first made in 1993. The Fleur de Pinot Noir is not vintage-dated. Unsurprisingly, Fleur (despite the lack of vintage-dating) and Salmon Run vary considerably in weight, density, and interest depending on the vintage, but both tend toward lightweight and quaffable editions of pinot. The Dr. Konstantin Frank is a much more serious, medium-weight and sometimes rather concentrated, wine that can develop considerable complexity with a bit of bottle age. It ages exceptionally well, with vintages from the 1960s reported to be still in good condition.

TASTING NOTES

NV Fleur de Pinot Noir (2001 edition, tasted prerelease in 2002): Transparent, medium-dark black-red; smoky, briary black-fruit nose; strong cherry, black licorice, and black pepper on the palate; medium-weight, full-bodied, and concentrated, medium-length and suede-textured. Very promising.

2000 Dr. Konstantin Frank (tasted in 2002): Brilliant, light to medium garnet; cherry, animal, and leather on the nose; raspberry, black pepper, clove, and minerality on the palate; slightly sweet with a hint of candy; light- to medium-weight, moderately concentrated, medium-length, and satin-textured.

1999 Dr. Konstantin Frank (tasted in 2002): Transparent, medium garnet; cherry, raspberry, and rose petal on the nose with spicy gingerbread notes; more raspberry, cherry, and even cassis in the mouth, plus resin, leather, tobacco, and clove; slightly sweet, medium-weight, and full-bodied, slightly grippy, medium-long finish.

1995 Dr. Konstantin Frank (tasted in 2002): Brilliant, medium mahogany; aromas of dark cherry, resin, and leather with a hint of nuts; black fruits, black pepper, clove, cinnamon, minerals, and tree bark in the mouth; chewy and somewhat tannic, concentrated and medium-long; finishes like rough suede with emery edges.

1990 Dr. Konstantin Frank (tasted in 2002): Uncorked with insufficient time to settle, therefore cloudy with suspended sediment; distinctive nose of sweet orange peel, leather, and cherrywood furniture; orange peel, mint, black pepper, and cinnamon with notes of camphor, caramel, cigar box, and briar; medium-weight and full-bodied, suede-textured and long.

PRACTICAL INFORMATION

Vinifera Wine Cellars is primarily a riesling house where pinot noir accounts for only about 3,000 to 4,000 cases out of a total production of 46,000. Distribution covers 20 states, with major emphasis on the New York City, Boston, and Charleston markets. An onsite tasting room, open seven days a week, overlooks the vineyards and Keuka Lake; 607-868-4884.

DUTTON-GOLDFIELD WINES

Graton, California

Dutton-Goldfield is a partnership between veteran winemaker Dan Goldfield and Steve Dutton, whose much-respected family owns and farms more than five dozen of the best vineyard parcels in western Sonoma County. Goldfield is a Philadelphian originally, whose brother is said to have introduced him to pinot noir through a tasting of 1969 Burgundies. Trained first at Brandeis in chemistry and philosophy, and then at the University of California, Davis, in enology, Goldfield worked at Robert Mondavi, Schramsberg, and La Crema, then a small Sonoma-based chardonnay and pinot house. When La Crema was acquired by Kendall-Jackson in 1994, Goldfield went with the deal—"the toy in the crackerjack box," he says—and subsequently became the founding winemaker for the Jackson family's nearby Hartford Court venture. The Dutton-Goldfield project was begun in 1998.

The inaugural release of Dutton-Goldfield was 342 cases of Russian River valley pinot, and about the same amount of chardonnay, both from the 1998 vintage. The pinot was based on fruit from Dutton's Widdoes Ranch on Sullivan Road and the Jewel Ranch, just north of Graton, both in the heart of Green Valley; the balance of the Jewel Ranch pinot went to another Dutton family venture, Sebastopol Vineyards.

In 1999, the Russian River/Dutton Ranch cuvée was made again from Jewel and Widdoes fruit, joined with fruit from the Morelli Lane Vineyard (primarily a centenary zinfandel vineyard, but now farmed to include a few acres of pinot as well) just east of Occidental and the Green Valley Vineyard, on Green Valley Road just west of the Gravenstein Highway. The same year, a vineyard-designate was also made, from Freestone Hill Vineyard, an extremely cool site that the Duttons farm for Ted Clancy, overlooking the hamlet of Freestone. Freestone Hill is an eight-acre, south-facing slope, planted eight feet by five in north-south rows to UCD 2A and Dijon clones 114, 115, 667, and 777.

In 2000, two additional vineyard-designates were added to the Dutton-Goldfield list: the Maurice Galante Vineyard on Cherry Ridge Road northwest of Sebastopol, a ten-acre, east-facing slope planted to Dijon clones and UCD 4; and the so-called Devil's Gulch Vineyard, near Nicasio in Marin County. The latter is not a Dutton vineyard, but Goldfield had experience with its fruit in his days at La Crema. Owned and farmed by Mark Pasternak, Devil's Gulch pinot has been used in some years for Champagne-method sparkling wines made by Kalin Cellars; but Dutton-Goldfield receives fruit only from a new block, planted in 1996 on a very steep, terraced hillside, with five feet between vines and two rows on each terrace. The block is 11 acres, planted entirely to Dijon 114, 115, 667, and 777, and its yield is so far derisory. Some Galante fruit is also used in the Russian River/Dutton Ranch blend.

In 2001, Dutton-Goldfield also received fruit from the McDougall Vineyard in a remote corner of the Sonoma Coast appellation, where Seaview and Tin Barn roads intersect, north of David Hirsch's vineyard and just inland from Camp Meeting Ridge. McDougall consists of two blocks of vines on a south-facing ridge that Warren Dutton planted in 1998 to Dijon 114 and 115. Although Dutton-Goldfield, by the terms of the partnership, has first rights of refusal on all Dutton Ranch fruit as existing contracts with other wineries expire, as well as on all new plantings, Goldfield is satisfied that the vineyards he has now selected give him the palette he needs for the foreseeable future.

The 1998 vintage was made at Windsor Oaks while Goldfield was still finishing his obligations at La Crema and Hartford Court. In 1999, the partners leased space sufficient for 10,000 cases at Martini & Prati. Goldfield spends most of his time now on Dutton-Goldfield wines, but also consults for Alderbrook and Rutz Cellars.

WINEMAKING

Goldfield picks pinot when the skins taste "soft rather than bitter," which can be anywhere between 23 and 25 Brix. He has experimented with enzymes, but has found that in general they increase the "harshness" of cool-climate pinot. He uses whole berries but no stems, enforces a prefermentation cold soak for five to six days with dry ice "to get skin extract without the bitterness that comes from the seed tannins," punches down during both cold soak and alcoholic fermentation, and seeks to achieve peak fermentation temperatures of between 85 and 90 degrees Fahrenheit. Some fermentors are inoculated with an assortment of cultured yeasts, including a syrah yeast that Goldfield likes; others are left to bubble on their own. The 1998 vintage was made in fruit bins; beginning in 1999 the bins were replaced with temperature-controlled five-ton stainless steel fermentors. Unlike many makers, Goldfield holds the completely fermented must for four to seven days of postfermentation maceration, arguing that this step creates "more delicacy and spiciness." Inoculation to kick-start the malolactic fermentation is sometimes done, but is normally not necessary. About one-third of the press juice is sold off; the balance is blended with the free-run juice.

About 40 percent new barrels are used, with Séguin Moreau the favored supplier. Goldfield says he chooses barrels for "nuttiness" rather than "smokiness or meatiness," and is especially partial to new barrels that have been used just briefly for a chardonnay fermentation before being rededicated, in the same vintage, to pinot noir. This trick is possible only in a very cold mesoclimate; pinot otherwise ripens before chardonnay. From this point, the wine is little disturbed until bottling, which occurs before the following harvest. Deselected lots are culled. There is no fining ever, and generally no filtration. "The vineyard where you have to do the least makes the best wine," observes Goldfield. "Winemakers ought to get more credit when they make a good $15 bottle out of juice that would otherwise have made pretty feeble wine."

THE WINES

Dutton-Goldfield's main release, the Russian River/Dutton Ranch cuvée, anchored with Widdoes Ranch fruit, is crafted to emphasize red fruit flavors and to be drinkable at release. The vineyard-designates tend to be denser wines, tending toward the black end of the fruit spectrum, though the lone release to date of Devil's Gulch is an elegant, low-alcohol rendering that appeals to palates accustomed to Burgundies. The combination of relatively long cold soak and short barrel time tends to emphasize succulent fruit.

TASTING NOTES

2000 Devil's Gulch (tasted twice in 2002): Transparent, light to medium garnet; explosive nose of cranberry, blueberry, and bramble with some geranium, daphne, tea, and smoke; bright and layered on the palate with flavors of mint, eucalyptus, licorice, white pepper, and a hint of nutmeg; elegant, light- to medium-weight, medium-length wine with the texture of satin.

2000 Dutton Ranch (tasted twice in 2002): Transparent, medium black-red; nose of black raspberry, cherry, and blueberry, with faint notes of evergreen and minted beets; sweet fruit core marked with soft spice, cedar, mint, and vanilla; very fine-grained tannins but still grippy at the end, texture of crushed velvet, medium-weight, with a medium-long finish.

2000 Freestone Hill Vineyard (tasted twice in 2002): Transparent, medium-dark black-red with oxblood highlights; nose of lightly minted boysenberries; sweet mouth of dark cherries, black fruits, and fruit candy with a hint of cola; accents of black pepper, bay laurel, tobacco, and mocha; mouthcoating but structured, medium-rich wine with the texture of heavy silk, fine-grained tannins, long.

2000 Maurice Galante Vineyard (tasted twice, in 2002 and 2003): Transparent, but dense, deep purplish red; evergreen and slightly floral aromas against a backdrop of black fruits and beetroot; very sweet blackberry jam with cinnamon, mocha, and smoke in the mouth; rich, stuffed, chewy wine, still intense and velvety, but less tannic than the Freestone Hill.

1999 Dutton Ranch (tasted in 2002): Transparent, medium-dark black-red; floral nose featuring lilac and roses; strawberry, cherry, and raspberry palate accented with mint, resin, and licorice; very intense flavors; rough silken texture, medium-weight.

1998 Green Valley Dutton Ranch (tasted in 2001): Transparent, medium-dark black-red wine; well saturated; nose of blueberries and cranberry; some bramble, wild berries, lilac, nutmeg, and allspice; mouthfeel is more velour than silk; bright acidity, soft finish.

PRACTICAL INFORMATION

In 2000, Dutton-Goldfield produced about 3,500 cases of wine, of which about 60 percent was pinot noir. The goal is two-thirds pinot to one-third chardonnay, with just a bit of old-vines zinfandel from Morelli Lane thrown in on the side. A well-received syrah from the Cherry Ridge vineyard was also made in 2000. The wines are distributed in selected markets nationwide and can be found on some restaurant lists. Wines are available to mailing-list customers in reciprocal states. There is currently no tasting room, but plans are afoot; 707-823-3887.

EDMEADES WINERY

Philo, California

Dr. Donald Edmeades, a Pasadena cardiologist, is generally credited with having planted the first successful vineyard in the Anderson Valley in what locals like to call "modern times." This reputation is a nice tribute to a man who gainsaid all contemporary advice to advance a project he himself called "Edmeades' folly," but it is not very precise. Italian Swiss Colony's Boonville vineyard preceded Edmeades by 20 years, and Edmeades's estate vineyard was never really successful until it was completely replanted—a decade and a half after his death. His largest planting, of French colombard, almost never ripened; his cabernet sauvignon fared only slightly better. Throughout the late 1960s and early 1970s, Edmeades's son Deron sold the cabernet and gewürztraminer to whoever would buy it, which was usually John Parducci. He also worked with Ted Bennett (who invested in the Edmeades venture in 1974, a year after purchasing the nearby property that he was transforming into Navarro Vineyards; see the profile later in this section) to build a winemaking facility at Edmeades; and with Jed Steele, then fresh from his master's in enology at the University of California, Davis, to produce a deacidified colombard called Rain Wine. As the partners struggled to build a brand, Steele neglected the estate vineyard in favor of wines he could make from good purchased fruit. A decent reputation was developed for cabernet sauvignon made from various Mendocino sources, including the Carney vineyard in Boonville, but the star wines were zinfandels made from warmer sites off the valley floor in what is now the Mendocino Ridge appellation: DuPratt, Ciapusci, and Zeni. Following Steele's departure in 1983, the remaining partners searched for a buyer. Kendall-Jackson bought Edmeades in 1988.

The first pinot was probably planted at Edmeades about 1980. No one seems to know for sure whether it was an entirely new planting or existing vines were grafted. A small block of old vines remains today, just southwest of the winery building, which may (or may not) be a survival from that first planting. The origin of the plant material is unknown. Jackson's plantings of pinot date from 1989 and 1990: about 30 acres on sandy, clay-loam soil with rocky sections, on benchland that slopes down to the Navarro River. The plantings there are lyre and vertically trellised eight-foot rows, with five feet between vines. The main scion material is UCD 4 sourced from Jackson's Cambria property in the Santa Maria Valley; some blocks were budded over to Dijon 115 in 1999. Edmeades planted a second pinot vineyard, called Falk, in 2000, down-valley from the original estate, from which the first fruit was expected in 2003. Edmeades also purchases pinot from several sources. One is a vineyard owned by Brad Wiley, who was a partner in Edmeades prior to its acquisition by Jackson. This vineyard, which is so far down the valley that its chardonnay ripens only enough to make sparkling wine, is planted to UCD 4 and to Dijon 667 and 777. In various vintages of the 1990s, pinot was also purchased from the Corby, Dennison, Langley, Donnelly Creek, and Savoy vineyards. Wine from some purchased fruit and some estate fruit has sometimes found its way into other Kendall-Jackson pinots, notably La Crema.

Edmeades Winery's winemaker since 1993 has been Van Williamson, a dedicated fly fisherman and onetime beer drinker who worked at Chateau Montelena following his graduation from the enology program at California State University, Fresno, and subsequently as winemaker for Greenwood Ridge from 1988 to 1993.

WINEMAKING

Edmeades's pinots are made in a low-tech facility following minimalist protocols. Williamson hand harvests in small bins and destems completely, but has removed the rollers from his destemmer-crusher so that most of the fruit goes into fermentors as whole berries. Fermentors are fruit bins and converted horizontal dairy tanks. A natural cold soak lasts four days until fermentation begins with resident yeast. No acid is added to the must. Neither is the must bled—"If you bled it, the wine would be clumsy," says Williamson. During the cold soak, punchdowns are done once a day, then once fermentation has started, twice daily in the bins and thrice daily in the dairy tanks. Fermentation usually takes about six days, and the temperature tends to max in the mid 80s Fahrenheit. Once dry, the wine is pressed directly to barrels without settling. The heavy press fraction is set aside. Sometimes it is reintegrated, but more often it is blended into zinfandel or shipped out entirely.

Barrels are ISC (an American cooperage based in Missouri) light char, Latour house toast, and Dargaud & Jaeglé medium-plus toast. Williamson has renounced heavy-toast barrels, observing that they tend to rob the wine of color, but he refuses even to "wash out the dust" from new barrels, in order to obtain maximal smokiness. The percentage of new oak varies with the vintage. In 1998 and 1999 it was high; in 2000 it fell to 50 percent. Malolactic fermentation proceeds naturally without inoculation. The wine stays in barrel for about ten months, during which time it is not racked unless "there is a *lot* of funk." Basically, says Williamson, "we like funk." The wine is racked out of barrel at bottling, and the residue is left in the barrels for the following year's zinfandel. There is no fining or filtration, ever. Williamson believes in his low-tech approach, but he does want a basket press, and he thinks larger fermentors (such as his repurposed dairy tanks) do a better job of producing "connected, linear, middle-ground flavors" than the one-ton fruit bins. Edmeades pinots are bottle-aged for 12-plus months before release.

THE WINES

Since 1993, Edmeades has released only one pinot noir in each vintage, except in 1994, when two wines were made. In 1993, the single release was a vineyard-designated pinot from the Dennison Vineyard in Boonville. In 1994, Edmeades made both an Anderson Crest wine, entirely from estate fruit, and an Anderson Valley wine, which utilized purchased as well as estate fruit. The blended Anderson Valley bottling continued in 1995 and 1996. In 1997 and 1998, only an estate wine was released. In 1999, 2000, and 2001, purchased fruit was used again in the Edmeades release, making it again Anderson Valley on the label. Pinot noir represents about 4,000 cases, or about one-fifth of the winery's total output. The wine has varied in style as fruit sources have changed through the 1990s. The 1994 and 1996 vintages were especially impressive. Edmeades pinots can be late bloomers, taking a few years in bottle before they come together.

TASTING NOTES

1999 Anderson Valley (tasted twice, in 2001 and 2002): Transparent, medium garnet, just very slightly hazy; cotton candy and very ripe red fruit with a bit of farmyard and a hint of peppermint on the nose; fruit candy, licorice, milk chocolate, barrel char, earth, pepper, and some clove in the mouth; slate dominant in 2001 but less apparent in 2002; medium-weight, slightly grippy, full-bodied, mouthcoating, and medium-long wine.

1998 Anderson Valley (tasted in 2002): Transparent, light to medium garnet; nose split between very ripe red fruit and floral properties, especially roses and potpourri, plus a bit of caramelized citrus and brown butter; earth, charcuterie, and barrel char on the palate; medium-weight but mouthcoating and lingering, perhaps thanks to high alcohol; full-bodied, hint of grip, medium-long.

1997 Anderson Valley (tasted in 2002): Transparent, medium garnet with a hint of tile; very ripe plums and dried leaves with a hint of peppermint on the nose; cherry, rich, wet earth, black pepper, merbromin, and evergreen on the palate; full-bodied, medium-length, moderately concentrated, texture of rough silk.

1996 Anderson Valley (tasted in 2001): Nearly transparent, rich blood-red color, moderately evolved; resin and black cherry on the nose; black fruits, cola, more resin, smoke, and earth flavors; rich, fleshy wine, long and velvety.

1995 Anderson Valley (tasted in 2002): Brilliant, light to medium black-red with crimson highlights; aromas of cooked rhubarb, cherry pie, wild strawberries, and tea; earth, resin, cola, black pepper, and cherry in the mouth, with some tree bark and briar; concentrated, full-bodied, very slightly grippy, long, suede-textured wine.

1994 Anderson Crest Vineyard (tasted in 2002): Brilliant, medium-dark black-red with an edge of terra-cotta; very ripe red fruit, carpentry solvents, resin, and black licorice on the nose; more red fruit, earth, black tea, and barrel char, plus hints of mocha and tree bark on the palate; sweet, grippy, mouthcoating, and concentrated; very long, with a texture between emery and velvet.

1994 Anderson Valley (tasted in 2002): Intense, medium black-red; distinctive nose of Asian aromatics, including sandalwood, star anise, and soy, with a bit of strawberry jam; licorice, earth, mocha, and cinnamon in the mouth; full-bodied, concentrated, and slightly grippy with tree bark on the finish; long and suede-textured. A personal favorite.

PRACTICAL INFORMATION

Edmeades pinots are nationally distributed. Visits are possible by appointment only; 707-895-3232.

EL MOLINO WINERY

St. Helena, California

Reginald Oliver's childhood scoutmaster was George Cooper, a NASA test pilot who eventually founded Cooper-Garrod Estate vineyards near Saratoga. Under Cooper's influence, Oliver purchased a wine press while he was still a teenager. Twenty-six years later, following a Wall Street career that gave him "time to think and read about wine, and the financial resources to afford La Tâche and other Burgundies," he restored a tiny nineteenth-century house and winery that had belonged to his aunt, three miles north of St. Helena. The venerable El Molino winery was then repurposed to produce fine pinot noir and chardonnay beginning in 1987, long after pinot noir had all but disappeared from midvalley Napa. The winery now makes about 2,000 cases annually, of which 800 to 1,000 are pinot noir.

A one-acre test vineyard is co-located with the winery. Oliver also purchased several acres of prime cabernet vineyard on the eastern side of Highway 29, south of Rutherford Cross Road. Perversely, Oliver pulled out the cabernet and, between 1991 and 1999, planted four acres of pinot noir. The scion material is a combination of UCD 5 selected from Bouchaine and Saintsbury; Dijon 113, 115, and 777; a field selection "from Abbott Williams in Carneros" that Oliver has dubbed "El Molino"; and cuttings from Larry Hyde's Los Carneros vineyard said to have come from Bouzeron, near Chagny, just beyond the southern end of the Côte d'Or. Of the lot, the El Molino selection is the last to ripen, according to Oliver. The planting, called the Star Vineyard, is (perversely again) in east-west rows, with spacing that ranges from three feet between vines in six-foot rows to six feet between vines in eight-foot rows. Until 2000, El Molino also purchased pinot noir fruit, primarily from Larry Hyde and from CVI (CVI acquired part of the old Stanly ranch circa 1982 and expanded the vineyard surface), both in Los Carneros, and this fruit constituted as much as 20 percent of the total blend. Some fruit purchases may continue, according to Oliver, in "bad" years.

Oliver challenges the prevailing view that pinot noir can be grown successfully only in the state's coolest mesoclimates, arguing that warmer sites work fine as long as the nights stay cool. The only reason pinot noir has disappeared from midvalley Napa, he asserts, is economics. "You cannot use expensive land for a variety that yields only three tons per acre."

WINEMAKING

From the outset, Oliver has been his own winemaker. He harvests in successive *tris,* uses about 75 percent whole-cluster fruit, and relies entirely on resident yeast. The Rutherford vineyard is typically picked at just over 24 Brix; Carneros fruit, picked "about the same time," may show sugar as high as 26 Brix. Fermentors are 1.5-ton, cube-shaped, unjacketed stainless steel open-tops, which were custom-built for El Molino. The must is never bled and there is no use of enzymes, but Oliver will occasionally acidify to be sure the finished pH stays below 3.65. Free-run juice goes directly to barrel when the must is dry; solids are pressed in a basket press; the press juice is also used in the cuvée.

Barrels are all made with three-year air-dried wood from the Tronçais and other Allier forests and coopered by François Frères. Approximately 75 percent new wood is used annually; the rest of the barrels are one year old. The pinot spends a long 18 months in barrel ("I want two full winters," Oliver explains), is racked once after malolactic fermentation has completed, and is egg-white fined and lightly pad filtered before bottling. After bottling, El Molino pinot is held another

16 months in bottle before release, which occurs almost three years after the vintage.

THE WINES

El Molino pinots are medium-weight, elegant wines with considerable aromatic complexity and a generally silky texture. Aromatic properties vary considerably from year to year, reflecting vintage variation and the evolution of El Molino's fruit sources. Vintages as old as 1984 were still showing well in 2003.

TASTING NOTES

1999 Napa Valley (tasted prerelease in 2001 and again in 2003): Transparent, medium garnet; aromas of gingerbread and cherry in 2001, more briar and balsam with dark fruit in 2003; wild berries, cola, allspice, and black pepper in the mouth; concentrated and grippy in 2001, unctuous and smooth in 2003; polished, satin, and long.

1998 Napa Valley (tasted in 2001): Transparent, medium-deep magenta; evergreen aromas with high-toned fruit and a hint of leather on the nose; cherry, black fruits, cola, tar, and a hint of mocha on the palate; medium-weight and very slightly grippy, long and silken.

1994 Napa Valley (tasted in 2003): Brilliant, medium garnet; wild strawberries, cherries, resin, and white pepper on the nose; nuts, briar, and vanilla with a hint of cola on the palate; midpalate texture approaching satin, but grippy on the finish.

1990 Napa Valley (tasted in 2003): Brilliant, medium black-red with terra-cotta at the rim; camphor, menthol, and leather aromas; ripe and rich in the mouth, with orange peel and black licorice; medium-weight and medium-length, silken. A personal favorite.

1988 Napa Valley (tasted in 2003): Transparent, medium mahogany; wild strawberry, rose hips, and herbs on the nose; mushrooms, resin, and merbromin on the palate; concentrated, medium-long, and silken.

1985 Napa Valley (tasted in 2003): Fading terra-cotta; aromas of strawberry and wild raspberry; flavors of cream cooked with a vanilla bean; sound but past its prime.

1984 Napa Valley (tasted in 2003): Transparent, light terra-cotta; leather, truffles, and furniture polish on the nose; resin and tobacco in the mouth; light- to medium-weight but medium-plus length, satin-textured.

PRACTICAL INFORMATION

El Molino pinots are nationally distributed and show up on serious restaurant lists in most major markets. Because of very limited production, retail sources are limited. Mail order is available from the winery. Visits are by advance appointment only; 707-963-3632.

ETUDE WINES

Napa, California

Most wine brands are named eponymously or for some geographical or historical consideration. Others get made-up or mythological names. Very few are named for their purpose. When Tony Soter decided to tackle pinot noir in the early 1980s, he called his project Etude—the French noun for "study." Soter was mindful that *étude* is also used to denote a genre of musical practice composition designed to challenge both composer and performer. An alumnus of Stag's Leap, Spring Mountain, and Chappellet with a formidable reputation as a consulting winemaker, Soter approached pinot noir as a learning exercise. He describes pinot as a "quixotic and unforgiving grape" with "transparency," which makes it, he argues, "the best vehicle for learning about *all* red wine."

Soter launched Etude in 1982. He produced just 500 cases of wine that year, using fruit from Bruce Newlan's vineyard on Darms Lane, south of Yountville. Despite the growing emphasis, even then, on cool sites for good pinot, Soter's early vintages were made from fruit sourced in the midvalley and from Mount Veeder. He argues that the fruit then available from Los Carneros was "not convincingly superior," having been farmed, in general, to produce a neutral base wine for sparkling houses. "There was so much lacking in most pinot efforts anywhere in California," he says now, "that a focus on *place* at the expense of technique did not seem the best way to address its shortcomings." Despite the climate, working with midvalley fruit was, he recalls, "not a struggle," and the results were thought to be "pretty good" for the time. By 1986, however, Soter had found more and better resources in Los Carneros, and he has used Carneros fruit ever since. Over the years, Etude has sourced pinot from some of the best-known independent growers there, including Larry Hyde and Lee Hudson; from Domaine Carneros (which was planted in accordance with Soter's suggestions); and from Domaine Chandon, Artesa, Adastra, Cuvaison, and Casa Carneros. If any of these sources is the anchor for Etude's pinot program, it must be Lee Hudson's vineyard, in rolling, loamy land laced with creeks on the northern side of the Carneros Highway just east of the county line.

Since 1986, Etude's keystone program has been a blended Carneros cuvée. To maximize its quality, Soter has aggressively declassified lots that, once made, did not measure up. After he began using per-acre contracts to persuade his growers to reduce yields, irrigate less, and pick later—in 1996—he found that the percentage of declassified lots decreased from as much as a third in the 1980s to less than 10 percent in 1999, which reinforced his conviction that farming is a crucial factor in winemaking. During this period, Soter also developed an affinity for what he calls "heirloom" clones, by which he means genuine clones and other selections whose common characteristic is that they do *not* meet, in his view, "standard criteria" for pinot noir. Soter's heirlooms are Calera, Chalone, and Swan selections, along with some recent illicit imports from Burgundy. To showcase these selections better, Etude made several editions of an Heirloom cuvée in the late 1990s. Etude also found time, in the late 1980s and early 1990s, to begin producing wines from the "other" pinot grapes—pinot gris, pinot meunier, and pinot blanc—and a bit of cabernet sauvignon, the "yang" foil to the "yin" of pinot noir. Total production increased very gradually to 9,000 cases in 2000, and the staff grew to a grand total of four people.

Soter was the hands-on winemaker until 1994, when the reins were passed for one year to Eric Hamacher (see the Hamacher Wines profile); Scott Rich (see Talisman Wines) took over from 1996 through 2000. Brian Mox currently assists Soter. Picking and blending decisions have remained consistently in Soter's hands. Etude was sold to Beringer Blass Wine Estates in September 2001. Soter now divides his time between Etude and Soter Vineyards, his new Oregon project.

WINEMAKING

Soter's picking decision hinges primarily on the condition of the vine and on his general rule that, as long as the condition of the vine is not declining, the fruit is probably getting better. "As long as the vine is showing signs of stamina," he says, "it can go further before picking." This approach translates to a fairly wide numbers window: sugars as low as 23 Brix or as high as 25.9, and pH anywhere between 3.3 and 3.6. Winery staff supplement picking crews in the vineyard at harvest, so fruit sorting can take place in the vineyard. The utilization of whole cluster varies, but hovers between 20 and 30 percent, depending on seed and stem maturity. Generally Soter finds that stems cannot be used from vineyards that have experienced, in any given vintage, a curtailed vegetative cycle; such stems do not lignify. A wide assortment of fermentors is used, ranging from one-ton fruit bins to six-ton jacketed stainless steel cylinders, some of which are repurposed dairy tanks. Soter believes that fermentors for pinot noir should not be larger than six tons and should always be wider than they are tall, because these properties ensure a high cap-to-juice ratio. The high ratio assists in its turn with what Soter calls "the challenge of differential extraction. . . . You want to get color and fruit and some tannin," he explains, "but there are phenolics you do *not* want, and you want minimal seed tannins." Etude has evolved a yeast-addition technique aimed at cofermentation. To encourage resident yeast, sulfur dioxide and chilling are both avoided. At the same time, Soter inoculates with one-quarter of the manufacturer's recommended dose of laboratory yeast, which, he finds, induces a slow fermentation approximating the natural course of native yeast. The result is a natural prefermentation soak lasting three to four days; a primary fermentation lasting another four to five days, during which time temperatures climb into the 90s Fahrenheit; and one to two weeks of postfermentation maceration—for a total vatting lasting up to 25 days. The must is both punched down and pumped over. After pressing, the wine is settled for three to five days. Some blending occurs at this time, and some dubious lots are culled.

The unusual barrel regime relies entirely on thin-stave, Bordelais *barriques* from Tonnelerie Nadalie, of which 60 percent are new each year. These barrels are an artifact of Soter's cabernet days, but the thin staves seem to improve concentration, and Etude likes their distinctive fingerprint on pinot. Just before the next vintage, the wines are racked. Lots destined for the Heirloom program are returned to barrel for additional aging; the Carneros cuvée is bottled. Etude rarely fines or filters, but the occasional cloudy lot may be fined lightly with Eisenglas, and rare lots demonstrating bacterial activity are filtered. The wines get nine to ten months of bottle-aging before release.

As befits a study project, Etude's wine-making has evolved with time. Soter argues, however, that the changes have been mostly in the nature of refinements, with "first principles" largely confirmed by experience. Small fermentation vessels, punchdowns, hot fermentations, and malolactic fermentations induced in the barrel have been constants. The quarter-strength yeast regime is a recent innovation, however, and *saignée,* to concentrate the must, is now rare. In 1994 and 1995, a very small percentage of pinot meunier was added to the blend; since 1996 the wines have been 100 percent pinot noir.

THE WINES

Etude Carneros Pinot Noir was made regularly and exclusively until 1995. In 1995, believing that the winery commanded enough fruit that the Carneros wine would not suffer if some batches were held aside for a special program, Soter and Rich made several one-barrel prototypes for the Heirloom program from Hudson, Hyde, and Domaine Chandon fruit. About 400 cases of an Heirloom "blend" were then made in 1996, 1997, 1998, and 2000, featuring heirloom blocks from these and other Carneros vineyards. In 1996, an American cuvée, made from a blend of Carneros and Oregon fruit, was also released. As of this writing, a Hudson vineyard-designate is to be released from the 2001 vintage. Because 60 percent of the Carneros bottling goes to restaurants where it will inevitably be consumed young, slightly lighter lots are privileged for this blend. The Heirloom family is a different beast entirely: these wines are complex, layered, nuanced, spicy, and sometimes tight in their youth. However, all Etude pinots have an engaging mouthfeel of very fine-grained tannin.

TASTING NOTES

1998 Carneros (tasted twice, in 2000 and 2001): Transparent, medium black-red; nose of black cherry, cassis, and (distinctively) red beets; in the mouth, cherry fruit with notes of leather, earth, mint, moss, and sassafras; vanilla and smoke from the Nadalie barrels; very fine tannins, medium-long wine with the texture of crinkled velvet.

1997 Heirloom (tasted in 2001): Transparent, medium black-red; notes of animal and earth on the nose; sweet core of cherry and black fruits; flavors of leather, resin, furniture polish; notes of sweet moss, mushroom, graphite, milk chocolate, and licorice; some tree bark on the finish; very mouthcoating and long, medium-weight wine. A personal favorite.

1996 Heirloom (tasted in 2000): Transparent, medium black-red color evolving toward mahogany and terra-cotta; aromas and flavors of tar, resin, leather, tobacco, and Indonesian spice; very bright flavors; medium-length and medium-bodied.

1995 Hudson Vineyard (tasted in 2001): Transparent, medium red with a terra-cotta edge; open, evolved nose of leather and animal with a hint of cardamom and stewed plum; plum and black fruits in the mouth; sweet core marked with leather, mushroom, licorice, allspice, and black pepper; some smoke and vanilla; still bright acidity, medium-length, brooding wine. Very rewarding. (This wine and the one below were prototypes for the Heirloom program.)

1995 Hyde Vineyard (tasted in 2000): Transparent, medium black-red; forward aromas of strawberry and plum; sweet cola on the midpalate; notes of oriental spice; velvety, long.

1994 Carneros (tasted in 2001): Transparent, medium mahogany; aromas of leather and damson plum jam; sweet fruit core with cardamom and nutmeg; creamy mouthfeel; texture of heavy upholstery silk, medium-weight, and long.

PRACTICAL INFORMATION

The Carneros cuvée is nationally distributed; the winery is the best source for the Heirloom and vineyard-designates. Visits to Etude's teal-colored "faux château" on Big Ranch Road north of Napa are by appointment only. Etude is looking for land in Carneros, however—both to plant, at last, an *estate* vineyard of heirloom selections and to build a new winery; 707-257-5300.

EVESHAM WOOD WINERY

Salem, Oregon

Russ Raney was in Germany on a collegiate study-abroad program when he discovered wine. He subsequently apprenticed at Weingut Erbhof Tesch in Langenlonsheim, in the Nahe valley just upstream from its confluence with the Rhine, and earned a degree in viticulture and enology from the state technical school of the Rhine Palatinate (Rheinpfalz), in Bad Kreuznach. After five years selling wines in St. Louis, Missouri, Raney and his wife searched the Willamette Valley for sites well suited to the Burgundian and Alsatian varieties they preferred; Raney also worked for two years for the Adams Winery in Portland. In 1986 the Raneys launched Evesham Wood Winery, named for the vale of Evesham in the English Cotswolds, of which the Willamette Valley landscape reminded them. Their first release was a 1986 pinot noir made from purchased fruit. Simultaneously, they planted eight acres of vineyard on the northern edge of Salem, in an area known locally as Spring Valley, and built a vaguely Tudor-style house overlooking the vineyard and the river beyond. In 1991, a small, full-function winery was built under the house, and Evesham Wood's production was transferred to the estate.

The estate vineyard, called Le Puits Sec, is

a gentle, east-facing slope on the Willamette River side of the Eola Hills, between the 300-foot and 420-foot contours. The shallow, rocky soils are iron-rich Nekia and Jory series, of volcanic origin. The 1986 planting, which included three acres of pinot noir, was laid out in seven-foot east-west rows, with four feet between vines; in a subsequent planting, the intervine spacing was tightened to three feet. In 1999, two acres of 1986 chardonnay were grafted to pinot, bringing total pinot acreage to seven. Of this, about 4.5 acres are own-rooted UCD 4 or 5 sourced from the Adams vineyard; the balance is mostly Dijon 113 and 115, with very small amounts of 114 and 777. In 2001 an additional one-acre parcel provisionally called the northwest field was added. It is a three-foot by six-foot planting of Dijon 777. The Dijon plantings are grafted to either 3309 or 101–14 rootstock. Le Puits Sec normally yields about 2.25 tons per acre. Evesham Wood also purchases pinot noir from other Willamette Valley vineyards, mostly in the Eola Hills, but fruit has been sourced from as far north as the Shea Vineyard near Yamhill (for more on Shea, see chapter 4, "The Willamette Valley") and from as far south as the Mahonia vineyard in the southern Salem Hills.

WINEMAKING

Raney ferments primarily in double-height fruit bins, but also uses one 1,100-gallon open-top stainless steel fermentor. The fruit is entirely destemmed, and the rollers are set to retain approximately 25 percent whole berries. A prefermentation cold soak lasts three to five days, and it is sometimes enforced with blocks of dry ice to maintain a must temperature of about 50 degrees Fahrenheit. The primary fermentation is started with an inoculation of proprietary yeast on the fifth or sixth day of the vatting. The proprietary yeast was propagated from a bottle of Henri Jayer's 1985 vintage, which Raney likes for its "fine and silky texture." Raney sometimes adds acid and sometimes chaptalizes, depending on the vineyard source of the fruit. The estate pinot never requires added sugar, according to Raney, whereas the Temperance Hill fruit often does. He chaptalizes only when Brix at harvest is below 22.5. Pumpovers are done twice daily until the cap is firm; thereafter punchdowns occur once or twice each day; and fermentation temperatures peak at 93 to 95 degrees. Malolactic fermentation is induced about halfway through the primary fermentation. A single daily punchdown continues through four to five days of post-fermentation maceration. The must is pressed at the end of 18 to 21 days' vatting and settled in tank for 24 to 48 hours. The press fraction is blended back "for structure."

Use of new wood varies by cuvée. The Willamette Valley blend gets less than 10 percent new oak; most others see 60 percent to 65 percent in "typical" vintages. In recent years, Evesham Wood has sourced barrels exclusively from François Frères—Raney says he "considers other factors to be more important than barrel variety in achieving complexity in pinot noir." The wines are racked once in May or June after the vintage, and once again at bottling. The Willamette Valley cuvée (see below) is bottled after about ten months in barrel; other cuvées remain in wood until early spring two years after the vintage. There is no use of concentrators or enzymes and no filtration, but wines are occasionally egg-white fined for tannin management. The Willamette Valley bottling is released in February; other bottlings are held until the second autumn after the vintage.

THE WINES

Evesham Wood's main release of pinot noir is a Willamette Valley bottling, whose fruit sources have changed over time. The 1986 bottling was made from Seven Springs and Freedom Hill fruit; the 1987, 1988, and 1989 editions relied on Seven Springs and Temperance Hill fruit. From 1990 to 1996, O'Connor Vineyard fruit joined the blend; estate fruit has been used intermittently since 1995. The 1997 Willamette Valley was made from Seven Springs, Temperance Hill, and estate fruit; the 1998 contained some Shea Vineyard fruit, but no estate. The Collada vineyard became the anchor for the Willamette Valley bottling in 1999. Meanwhile, as early as 1987, single-vineyard wines began to appear in the Evesham Wood portfolio. Some Seven Springs wine was made as a de facto vineyard-designate—labeled Eola Hills—in 1987; formally vineyard-designated Seven Springs bottlings were done in 1989, 1992, 1994, 1996, 1998, and 1999. Single-vineyard bottlings of Temperance Hill were issued in 1994 and 1998; of Mahonia in 1995 and each year since; and of Shea in 1998 and 1999. Cuvée J (named in honor of Henri Jayer) debuted in 1989. J is Raney's selection of his best barrels, whether from a single vineyard or a blend of several, and has been made in every vintage since. A 100 percent estate pinot noir, released in 1990, 1992, 1994, 1997, 1998, and 1999 and designated Le Puits Sec after 1997, completes the list. Barrels destined for the Willamette Valley bottling are identified at the time of the first racking, and are bottled early (see above); single-vineyard wines account for most of the remainder, except that Cuvée J barrels are selected out at the very end, just before the second round of bottling. In 2001, Evesham Wood will grow enough pinot noir to make about 1,000 cases of finished wine; purchased fruit will be sufficient to make another 1,200 cases. Evesham Wood pinots are generally medium-weight wines, with considerable aromatic complexity, elegance, and personality, and textures that vary widely from site to site and year to year.

TASTING NOTES

2000 Willamette Valley (tasted in 2002): Transparent, bright ruby red; aromas of green tea, herbs, wilting flowers, stems, and pine resin; on the palate, slightly sweet strawberry overlaying toast; both herbaceous and cotton-candy notes; light to medium body and medium-length, with a hint of minerality on the finish.

1999 Cuvée J (tasted in 2002): Transparent, medium ruby; wild cherry and briar on the nose; black cherry, briar, and considerable minerality in the mouth; medium-weight, ripe, concentrated, chalky, subtle, and long.

1999 Mahonia Vineyard (tasted in 2002): Transparent, medium black-red; nose of dried leaves and flower petals, with a hint of cured green olives; considerable minerality on the palate with sensations of chalk; black raspberry fruit; light- to medium-weight and medium-length; very slightly grippy but with fine-grained tannins.

PRACTICAL INFORMATION

Evesham Wood pinots are nationally distributed but are never in very generous supply, so most retail outlets report that they sell out quickly. Visitors need advance appointments except on the conventional Willamette Valley open house weekends at Thanksgiving and Memorial Day; 503-371-8478.

THE EYRIE VINEYARDS

McMinnville, Oregon

Three decades after his first pioneering vintage, David Lett—known to various people in the wine trade as Papa Pinot—continues, in his own phrase, to "sail to windward." In 1966, armed with a degree from the University of California, Davis, some observational experience in Burgundy, and convictions born of examining climates similar to Burgundy's in the New World, Lett moved from California to Oregon and planted the Willamette Valley's first few acres of pinot noir. In 1970, he made 115 cases of wine from his young vines, but the wine was so thin and pale that he called it Spring Wine rather than pinot and sold it—with difficulty—for $2.65 a bottle.

Just half a decade later, however, Lett succeeded so well with pinot noir that his 1975 South Block Reserve bested all but one Burgundy at two blind tastings in Paris and established the potential of Oregon pinot beyond a reasonable doubt. Lett's choices—south-facing hillside sites, a mix of UCD 2A and 5 clones, and quasiorganic farming—established the model for the first generation of Oregon pinot noir cultivation and attracted a small but steady trickle of coconspirators to the Willamette Valley. Gradually Lett and his cohorts, working with secondhand equipment and improvisations worthy of Rube Goldberg, established a pinot-oriented wine industry where walnuts, prunes, and cherries had previously flourished.

Lett's original vineyard, which gave its name to the business, is 20 acres of south-facing slope (of which 6.5 are pinot) between Dundee and Lafayette, in the so-called Red Hills of Dundee. The soil there is iron-rich Jory and Woodburn series clay-loam, and the vineyard is planted in a combination of east-west and north-south rows, between about 220 feet and 400 feet above sea level. The vines are loosely spaced six feet by ten and farmed without herbicides, pesticides, or systemic fungicides. The plant material at Eyrie is a combination of 70 percent own-rooted UCD 2A and 5, purchased from California increase blocks, and 30 percent own-rooted UCD 18. The first four acres were planted incrementally in 1966, 1967, and 1968; an additional 2.5 acres went into the ground in 1970. The so-called South Block, from which some of Eyrie's best pinots have been made, is nine-tenths of an acre of this vineyard, which also happens to be entirely UCD 2A. (Lett is a great fan of 2A, which has fallen from favor with many Oregon winemakers.)

The second of Lett's vineyards is Stonehedge, planted in 1979 and 1980, uphill from the first. It has two acres of pinot noir in a total planting of 15 acres, again a mix of UCD 2A and 5, and again in a checkerboard of row orientations. Stonehedge is very rocky Jory soil, above 720 feet. Lett varied the vine spacing here: part of the pinot is very tightly spaced at one meter by 1.5; the balance is six feet by ten.

During the late '80s, Lett acquired and planted two additional vineyards in the Red Hills. Rolling Green Farm is 4.9 acres of pinot noir (plus an acre of pinot gris) planted ten feet by four in north-south rows, at around 600 feet. The scion material is half UCD 2A and half UCD 5. Three Sisters, lower in elevation and thus earlier to ripen, has 4.2 acres of pinot noir in a total planting of 16 acres. Three Sisters' vine spacing is ten feet by four; the scion material once again is UCD 2A and 5. In a good year, yields on all four vineyards amount to just over two tons per acre. Until the two youngest of the four Eyrie vineyards came on-line in 1991, Lett also purchased pinot noir fruit from Abbey Ridge (see the Cameron Winery profile).

Eyrie's production facility is a windowless converted turkey processing plant at the edge of McMinnville, used since the very beginning in 1970. In 1969 Lett commissioned plans for a modern winery to be built on the site of his estate vineyard. The architect's renderings for this unbuilt project still hang on his office wall. They testify to the unwillingness of Oregon's banks, at the end of the 1960s, to invest in the state's fledgling wine business.

WINEMAKING

The secret, says Lett, "is to get pinot noir off the vine at *the* moment of ripeness." Generally, doing so means picking early, to achieve the brilliant, aromatic, and varietally distinctive pinots that Lett likes. Fermentations occur in four- by four- by two-foot plastic bins, using no stems but mostly whole berries. Lett believes it is "ill-advised to load pinot noir with a bunch of tannins." The must is inoculated with Pasteur champagne yeast because "too many off-flavors come from wild yeast." Lett has never added acid, but he chaptalized in 1984 and "here and there" since. Lett would rather pick a bit earlier and chaptalize, he explains, than risk a substantial uptick in pH and "loss of varietal character" with a later pick. Punchdowns are done every four hours. The must is pressed at dryness using a Wilmes press; the clones and vineyards are segregated, but the press fraction of each lot is reintegrated with free-run juice from the same lot.

The unconventional barrel regime uses almost entirely *neutral* oak. Some of Lett's barrels, purchased in 1970, are still in use; an occasional new barrel is purchased from Tonnellerie de Bourgogne. Lett maintains that "the idea of flavoring wine with oak is ridiculous" and that "cutting down an old tree to make three barrels to use for three years is not ecologically correct." Malolactic fermentation occurs spontaneously in barrel, where the plain estate wine (see below) spends 12 months. The estate reserve wines spend 18 to 24 months in wood. Racking is minimal; the wines are not fined, and only a few lots are filtered. In the "old days," says Lett, the pinots spent an additional two years in bottle before being released, but since 1998 release has followed closely on the heels of bottling. Lett confesses to having experimented with enzymes, but (unlike many of his Oregon winemaker colleagues) regards concentrators as "heresy."

THE WINES

From 1970 to 1990, Eyrie's main pinot was a Willamette Valley bottling, made entirely from the original estate vineyard until 1982 and then from a combination of the estate vineyards and Abbey Ridge. An estate bottling debuted in 1979, using fruit from the three younger estate parcels—Rolling Green Farm, Stonehedge, and Three Sisters. Meanwhile, South Block Reserve (from the south block of the original vineyard) was inaugurated in 1975 and has been made in every vintage except 1977, 1978, 1979, and 1984. The balance of the original estate vineyard goes into an estate reserve bottling.

Early vintages of Eyrie pinot attracted very positive critical attention for their "intensity of flavor" and "comparability with fine Burgundies." They were often described as "revolutionary" wines and set New World benchmarks for the variety. In the 1990s, however, as tastes changed toward weightier renderings of pinot noir, it became fashionable to criticize Eyrie's reds, or even to dismiss them as "has-been" efforts. It is unfair to do so and reflects a regrettable confusion, even among winegrowers themselves, between style and quality. Eyrie's pinots are transparent, gossamer, almost weightless wines, brimming with aromatic elegance, built to unfold very gradually with the passage of time. They age exceptionally well, with several vintages from the '70s and early '80s still showing beautifully.

TASTING NOTES

1999 Estate (tasted in 2001): Very transparent, light to medium garnet; aromas of mushroom and earth; raspberry, wild strawberry, and white pepper in the mouth; light- to medium-weight, considerable length.

1996 Reserve (tasted in 2001): Transparent, light black-red; rose petal and wild fruit aromas; raspberry and wild strawberry in the mouth, with accents of tangerine peel, leather, and black pepper; light- to medium-weight, long, and silken.

1989 Reserve (tasted in 2001): Very transparent, light to medium black-red, tinged with terra-cotta; fruit aromas and flavors giving way to faded flowers, mushroom, white pepper, and truffle; still brightly acid, light- to medium-weight wine with a silken finish.

1984 Reserve (tasted in 2001): Very transparent, light reddish terra-cotta; nose of earth and forest floor; resin, camphor, and white pepper in the mouth; a slightly feeble finish with hints of tree bark. A cool and rainy season required substantial additions of sugar; very respectable considering the vintage.

1976 South Block Reserve (tasted in 2001): Barely transparent, saturated mahogany-red with bits of deposit in suspension; earthy nose; big, chewy wine with hints of orange peel and chocolate; still some unresolved tannin, very grand, long, and fine. Unusual vintage for Eyrie. Only a few bottles of this venerable old-timer still exist.

PRACTICAL INFORMATION

Eyrie pinot noirs account for about 3,000 cases in a total production of 8,000 to 10,000 cases. The wines are distributed nationally by Dreyfus, Ashby and Company. The winery is open to visitors on the Thanksgiving and Memorial Day weekends only; 503-472-6315.

FIDDLEHEAD CELLARS

Davis, California

Enology, for Kathy Joseph, was "an escape" from medical school. Headed toward medicine, she had a solid undergraduate background in microbiology and biochemistry. After she worked a summer in Simi Winery's tasting room and learned tasting from the much-respected Zelma Long, her undergraduate work was repurposed as the foundation for a graduate degree in viticulture and enology. Following some early work experience at Long Vineyards and Joseph Phelps, as well as five vintages at Robert Pecota, Joseph created the Fiddlehead brand in 1989, dedicated to pinot noir and sauvignon blanc. Her model was a 3,000-case winery with access to fruit from regions that had been "proven by pioneers" but retained "significant growth potential still on the horizon"; long-term contracts with growers; and production at custom-crush facilities. For pinot noir, this framework led her not to Los Carneros or Russian River, which seemed already "too crowded," but to Oregon's Willamette Valley and Santa Barbara County. Fiddlehead's first release was 100 cases of 1989 pinot from the venerable Sierra Madre Vineyard southeast of Santa Maria, now owned by Robert Mondavi. The first Willamette Valley wine was made in 1991.

In 1996, departing from the original purchased-fruit and custom-crush model, Joseph purchased 133 acres of field-crop and hillside land between Santa Rosa Road and the Santa Ynez River, across the road from the historic Sanford & Benedict vineyard. To develop this large parcel (100 of the 133 acres have now been planted), Joseph and her Fiddlehead partners created a separate vineyard company owned equally with Beringer, hired Coastal Vineyard Care as onsite managers, and reached agreement to split the fruit from each parcel equally with Beringer and to share fruit from Fiddlehead's half with a handful of Santa Barbara wineries, including The Gainey Vineyard, The Hitching Post Wines, and Bonaccorsi Wine Company. The soils in this vineyard, now called Fiddlestix, are mainly Botella and Gazos series clay-loams developed from sandstone and shale-derived alluvia. Of the two, the Gazos soils are shallower and underlaid with bedrock shale. The planting, which was carried out over a four-year period from 1998 to 2001, is mostly north-south-oriented seven-foot rows with four feet between vines (except when an off-angle orientation or slightly different spacing was deemed to respect soil types better). Most of Fiddlestix is very gently sloping benchland, but the eastern end of the vineyard is an impressive, steep-sided knoll. The scion material is roughly one-third UCD 4 and 5, one-third Dijon 113 and 115, and one-third Dijon 667 and 777; the 2001 plantings consist mostly of the trademarked ENTAV versions of 115 and 777.

Fiddlestix produced enough fruit to make 300 cases of wine in 2000 and 1,500 cases in 2001. When the vineyard is in full production, Fiddlehead may choose to retain enough Fiddlestix fruit for as many as 5,000 cases.

Fiddlehead's Willamette Valley wine is made at Yamhill Valley Vineyards, using fruit from the Elton and Seven Springs vineyards in the Eola Hills, as well as from Yamhill Valley Vineyards itself. The Elton and Seven Springs arrangements are per-acre contracts. Seven Springs is a well-known supplier to Adelsheim, Domaine Drouhin Oregon, Cristom, and St. Innocent; Fiddlehead's Seven Springs fruit comes from a designated four-acre block. Elton, the oldest block, planted in 1983, is split between Fiddlehead and Ken Wright Cellars. In Santa Barbara, production was itinerant until 2003, when a dedicated facility was inaugurated in the Lompoc wine ghetto. Itinerant, indeed, describes Fiddlehead overall, with fruit sources a thousand miles apart and offices midway between, in Davis, California.

WINEMAKING

Joseph picks fruit "strictly based on taste," looking for the shift from "simple fruit flavors to complexity," and is sensitive to the uptick in pH that occurs (more or less) when the juice becomes more viscous. Typically, these indicators translate to sugar levels between 23 and 24.8 Brix. Fermentors are four-foot cubical fruit bins. Joseph used about 25 percent whole clusters in early vintages, but she now destems completely. Cold soaking is lot-specific. The Yamhill Valley Vineyards fruit is never cold soaked; other lots may soak for two to four days. All lots are inoculated, using a variety of yeast strains, to start the alcoholic fermentation. Joseph adds neither acid (to the Santa Barbara wine) nor sugar (to the Oregon wine), but will sometimes coferment a lot that is high in natural sugar with one that is low. Punchdowns are done two or three times daily at the outset, and Joseph likes fermentation juice temperatures to peak in the high 80s or low 90s Fahrenheit. Pressing is generally done when the must is dry, except for the Yamhill Valley fruit, which is pressed off slightly sweet. A light press fraction is reintegrated.

Each year, between 35 percent and 45 percent new barrels are used. Although a variety of coopers are used, Séguin Moreau and Cadus are favorites, for their contribution to the wines' aromas and textures. Malolactic fermentations are induced with a second inoculation, after which the wines spend 12 to 15 months in wood, are sometimes racked after malo is complete but sometimes not until bottling, and are generally bottled without fining or filtration. Another year of bottle-aging precedes release.

THE WINES

Joseph says she "cares most about texture" and likes "midpalate weight and a long finish." Without exception, the Fiddlehead pinots I have tasted display exceptional length and plush textures reminiscent of upholstery silk or velvet. They are never heavy, though sometimes quite darkly colored, and age rewardingly. A Santa Maria Valley wine was made from 1989 to 1993, exclusively from Sierra Madre fruit, but was labeled as a vineyard-designate only in 1989. A second Santa Maria Valley wine was made from Santa Maria Hills fruit in 1997 only. The Willamette Valley bottling, made each year since 1991, was joined by an Elton vineyard-designate in 2000. Fiddlehead's first estate wine, from the Fiddlestix Vineyard in Santa Rita Hills, debuted in 2000, replacing the Santa Maria Valley wine. In 2001, Joseph crafted two pinots from Fiddlestix, a mainstream offering called Seven Twenty Eight (for the 7.28 mile marker on Santa Rosa Road that landmarks her driveway) and a selection of the fattest barrels, called Lollapalooza.

TASTING NOTES

2001 Seven Twenty Eight (tasted in 2003): Transparent, medium-dark garnet; game, vanilla, and dried-leaf aromas; lacquer, gum camphor, essence of fruit, cinnamon, and clove on the palate; medium-weight, moderately concentrated, long and silken.

2000 Santa Rita Hills (tasted prerelease in 2002): Relatively saturated but still transparent, medium-dark black-red; strong aromas of black raspberry; infused violets, vanilla, and smoke join black fruits in the mouth; very soft velvet, very long.

1999 Willamette Valley (tasted prerelease in 2002): Nearly saturated, transparent black-red; daphne blossoms, nuts, and ripe blueberries on the nose; infused violets and rose petal with more blueberry, strong licorice, and a hint of cedar in the mouth; a big, rich, velvety wine that (in Joseph's phrase) "pushes the limit of fruit density desirable in pinot noir."

1998 Willamette Valley (tasted in 2002): Nearly saturated, dark black-red color; aromas of blueberry, huckleberry, and mint; black fruits, allspice, and peppery star anise on the palate; round, dusty tannins in a long-finishing, velvety wine.

1997 Santa Maria Valley (tasted in 2002): Transparent, medium terra-cotta; mint, menthol, and camphor on the nose; allspice, chocolate, and root beer in the mouth; long, soft, and velvety.

1993 Willamette Valley (tasted in 2002): Transparent, dark black-red, slightly tiling; very dense aromatics so tightly knit that the component aromas are difficult to differentiate; licorice, tobacco, white pepper, and cinnamon in the mouth; rich, long, and velvety.

1992 Santa Maria Valley (tasted in 2002): Transparent, medium brick-red; nose of potpourri; slightly sweet core of black berry fruit with resin, tobacco, clove, and cinnamon; silken and extremely long.

1992 Willamette Valley (tasted in 2002): Transparent but nearly saturated, dark terra-cotta; aromas of dried Italian plums, wet fur, and cedar chest; cola, wet slate, chocolate, and black cherry on the palate; rich, soft, and long.

1990 Santa Maria Valley (tasted in 2002): Transparent, medium terra-cotta; rose petal, potpourri, and dried fallen leaves on the nose, with a hint of white truffle; resin, tar, tobacco, and black pepper overlaying dried black raspberry; extremely long, pretty, and silken. A personal favorite.

1989 Santa Maria Valley Sierra Madre Vineyard (tasted in 2002): Saturated but still transparent, reddish terra-cotta; nose of bay leaf and other herbs, with resin and camphor; dried cherries and figs with tobacco and mocha on the palate; very long and smooth, with the texture of rough silk.

PRACTICAL INFORMATION

Fiddlehead pinots are sold directly to some retailers and restaurants in California, and via distributors in about 20 markets, including New York, Chicago, Hawaii, the Carolinas, and Oregon. A mailing list and wine club are the best source for limited releases, library wines, and large-format bottlings. Joseph's itinerant lifestyle makes visits nearly impossible, but special arrangements can sometimes be made to see the new winemaking "headquarters" in Lompoc; 530-756-4550.

FLOWERS VINEYARD AND WINERY

Cazadero, California

Walt and Joan Flowers were veterans of the wholesale nursery business in Pennsylvania when they found themselves increasingly fascinated by wine. In the 1980s, as they traveled regularly from Pennsylvania to Oregon to inspect or purchase stock for their nursery, they began making side trips to Napa and Sonoma. They were enamored of red Burgundy and became impressed by Jensen and Selleck pinots from Calera. When they finally decided they wanted to buy a vineyard, the love of pinot drew them west from Napa and Healdsburg to cool, pinot-friendly sites near the coast. In 1989, an advertisement in *Wine Spectator* for "321 acres with vineyard potential" attracted them to Camp Meeting Ridge, a sometime summer retreat site for various religious groups atop the first ridge inland from the ocean, between Jenner and Fort Ross. This was the proverbial warm site in a cool climate that seemed made to order for pinot noir: full sun pretty much all day; moderate daytime high temperatures and cool nights; and from a nurseryman's point of view, "lousy" soils. So in 1991, after extensive investigations and with advice from Andy Bledsoe, Robert Mondavi's viticulturist, the Flowerses began planting the first of 35 acres of their spectacular site to vineyard, 1,200 to 1,400 feet above sea level, in Franciscan clay-loam soils irrigated with water from the south fork of the Gualala River.

The first pinot noir was planted in 1991, and planting or replanting has continued progressively nearly every year since, except between 1995 and 1997. Blocks are laid out on the ridge top itself, on a gentle northwest-facing slope below, and on steeper slopes facing south and southeast. The original rows were oriented east-west; newer plantings are set out in north-south rows, to capture about 60 percent of the morning sunlight and to warm up the soil, while minimizing direct exposure to hot afternoon sun. Clones were selected for rot resistance and open-cluster morphology: two Swan selections, one from Dehlinger and one from Carneros; three Calera selections, all from the Hyde vineyard in Los Carneros; nursery-sourced UCD 1A, 2A, and 4, as well as some UCD 23; plus Dijon 113 and 115. Three spacings were used, all relatively tight: meter by meter, four-foot intervals in seven-foot rows, and five-foot intervals in eight-foot rows. The meter-by-meter blocks, unsurprisingly, produce a slightly higher yield per acre than those more sparsely planted, but total yield has fluctuated wildly from year to year, from as little as 0.71 ton per acre to as much as 2.67 tons.

The first vintages of wine from Camp Meeting Ridge (1994, 1995, and 1996) were made at Kistler, but by 1997 the Flowerses had completed construction of the first modern winery in the true Sonoma Coast—a handsome gravity-fed facility tucked discreetly into the hillside behind a centenary oak tree. Greg La Follette, who began his career working with André Tchelistcheff at Beaulieu and was thereafter founding winemaker at Hartford Court, served as Flowers's winemaker from 1996 to 2000, before "retiring" to a consulting role and to the launch of his own label (see Tandem Winery, in "Producers to Watch"). La Follette remains a passionate advocate for the extreme Sonoma Coast, which he discovered during his time at Hartford Court. It is, he says, "where God meant for pinot to be grown. The sun is high quality, but the fog creates a refrigerator just below the vineyard." La Follette was succeeded in July 2000 by Hugh Chappelle, who previously served at Madrona in the foothills of the Sierra Nevada, and by assistant winemaker Ross Cobb, who worked for two years at Williams Selyem.

Four miles away from Camp Meeting Ridge as the crow flies, the Flowerses acquired a second vineyard site in 1997. This ridge top, provisionally called Flowers Ranch, is even higher than Camp Meeting Ridge, ranging between the 1,650-foot and 1,875-foot contours. There, in rocky soil formed from decomposing red shale, they began planting another 50 acres of pinot noir in 1998, from which the first grapes were harvested in 2001. Again, the clonal assortment is large—Dijon 115, Calera, and UCD 23 budwood from Camp Meeting Ridge; Swan selection from Carneros Creek and Dehlinger; plus nursery-sourced Dijon 667 and 777—on three rootstocks (101–14, 3309, and 420A). No meter-by-meter plantings were attempted at this site, considering the lower-vigor soils; four-foot intervals in seven-foot rows were used instead. Walt Flowers describes the acquisition of this property as an effort to "control the destiny" of his brand.

In addition to the two estate vineyards, the Flowerses farm and manage parts of three additional vineyards, all substantially devoted to pinot noir, under long-term contracts. They also source pinot noir from several vineyards that they do not own or farm.

WINEMAKING

(The following information about winemaking at Flowers is based on conversations with Greg La Follette, who served from 1996 through 2000. At the time of writing, Walt Flowers confirmed that no major changes had been made since, though Chappelle and Cobb "were making small adjustments in the vineyard to smooth out tannins without losing complexity." In the 1999 vintage and afterward, the winery increased the time allowed for bottle-aging before the wines were released.) During and after his tenure at Flowers, La Follette spoke eloquently and engagingly about "listening to the vine," "understanding its language," and "seeing flavors." This dialogue with the vines continued throughout the year, but much of it was performed in the service of determining the best possible time to pick each vine. (Flowers's crews typically make two or three trips through the vineyard over a period of a week or more, so picking can be done almost vine by vine.) La Follette believed visual measures of the fruit's physiological ripeness were of crucial importance. These clues include how much of the berry sticks to the stem when it is pulled away, how firm and crunchy the seeds are when one bites down on them, whether the shoot tips are becoming crispy, and whether the skins are becoming papery and yield color easily. "Listening" to these clues may trigger a decision to pick when the sugar is as low as 22 Brix or as high as 27. La Follette preferred to "let the vineyard hang longer and cull out the raisins than pick before the grapes are physiologically ripe." Imperfect fruit was dropped in the vineyard; perfect fruit was sorted for lignified stems on the crushpad. The percentage of whole cluster used depended entirely on the availability of well-lignified stems, and could therefore range from zero to about 33 percent. (At Camp Meeting Ridge, the Calera selections and Dijon 115 appear to lignify best.)

Most good winemakers explain to interlocutors that they do not operate by recipe, but Flowers's approach shifts widely from lot to lot and from year to year. Cold soaks may be skipped entirely or extended for as much as 14 days, based on prior experience with particular blocks and clones. (Generally, the less the tannins are resolved, the shorter the cold soak.) Fermentations are done in jacketed stainless steel open-tops. The winery is operated to ensure the propagation of a healthy population of resident yeast and bacteria, so most fermentations (including the malolactic fermentations in barrel) begin naturally without inoculation. La Follette believed that aromatic complexity depends in part on compounds created by yeasts that are about to die, which favors multiple resident yeasts over any single laboratory yeast. The must is punched down by hand. Flowers's natural fermentations may take as long as 12 days to finish. When the tannins were hard, La Follette tried to keep the fermentation temperature under 82 degrees Fahrenheit; when they were soft, he would let the temperature rise to about 88 degrees. In either case, he believed, the cap must get hot to build "cedar and tobacco aromas." Hard tannins also dictate pressing before the must is dry and finishing the fermentation in barrels. Flowers's basket press works very gently, so the first and second press fractions can usually be recombined with the free-run juice; subsequent fractions are evaluated lot by lot.

The barrel regime involves heavy use of new wood, and some pinot is finished in barrels that have seen one fermentation of chardonnay. Barrels are acquired from most major coopers, but François Frères and Remond account for the lion's share. Pinots spend eight to 16 months in wood and are not racked until bottling. Flowers avoids both fining and filtration if possible, in the belief that good vineyard and crushpad practices generally eliminate the need for either.

THE WINES

Although Flowers was conceived as an estate operation focused on the home vineyard at Camp Meeting Ridge, its portfolio was expanded in the late 1990s to include a blended wine made primarily from purchased fruit and a variable array of vineyard-designated wines from non-estate vineyards. In 1997, the winery made a Sonoma Coast cuvée and a vineyard-designated wine from David Hirsch's nearby ranch, which is easily seen from the deck of the Flowerses' house at Camp Meeting Ridge. A vineyard-designate from the Pisoni vineyard in the Santa Lucia Highlands was made in 1998 and 1999. Three vintages of vineyard-designated wine were made from a Sangiacomo parcel in Los Carneros and from the Van der Kamp Vineyard on Sonoma Mountain from 1998 through 2000. The debut vintage of a vineyard-designated pinot from the Flowerses' leased block of the Keefer Ranch also occurred in 2000.

In 2001, responding to persistently inconsistent production at Camp Meeting Ridge and to the first crop from Flowers Ranch, the winery launched a second blended Sonoma Coast cuvée, christened Andreen-Gale (for the Flowerses' mothers' maiden names). This first release of Andreen-Gale was crafted from seven vineyards, mostly in the true Sonoma Coast area, and is firmly anchored with estate fruit from both Flowers Ranch and Camp Meeting Ridge. The "plain" Sonoma Coast bottling relies on the same vineyards plus three more. All inhabit the Sonoma Coast AVA (including its overlap with Green Valley), but some lie outside the true coast area. The 2001 Andreen-Gale, not released at the time of writing, is said to emphasize black fruit flavors and minerality, while the profile of the Sonoma Coast wine has been redrawn to feature red-toned fruit. Estate fruit feeds one other program—a reserve-type wine called Camp Meeting Ridge Moon Select, named for the Flowerses' Pennsylvania-based nursery business. It was made from selected barrels in 1996 and 1997, and perhaps was to be made again for the 2002 vintage. The winery has indicated that it expects to focus henceforth almost entirely on Sonoma Coast vineyards at the expense of vineyard-designated wines from other areas. At the same time, the goal is that Andreen-Gale will evolve "within several years" into an all-estate cuvée like Camp Meeting Ridge.

In my experience, Flowers pinots (especially Sonoma Coast wines; see the contrast with Pisoni Vineyard in its profile later in this section) are deeply colored, very saturated wines, with the relatively low pH–high acid backbone typical of mountain-grown wines, and reasonably well managed tannins. They also display racy aromatics that often characterize the true Sonoma Coast.

TASTING NOTES

2000 Camp Meeting Ridge (tasted in 2002): Brilliant, medium garnet; aromas of cola, sarsaparilla, cardamom, and wild black fruit; sweet dark cherry in the mouth, with licorice, black pepper, barrel char, some sweet spice, and graphite; medium-weight, mouthcoating and intense, some grip, relatively silken, long.

2000 Keefer Ranch (tasted in 2002): Transparent but nearly saturated, medium-dark black-red; pronounced aroma of very ripe blueberries; dark, black fruit with infused violets, some black licorice, and considerable minerality; mouthcoating midpalate, concentrated, grippy, and long.

2000 Sonoma Coast (tasted in 2002): Transparent, medium-dark black-red; earth, forest floor, and bramble on the nose; cinnamon, allspice, black pepper, and dark cherry fruit with hints of barrel char in the mouth; grippy, rich, mouthcoating, and borderline velvety, medium-length and medium-weight.

1999 Camp Meeting Ridge (tasted in 2002): Transparent, medium garnet turning to terracotta; pronounced aromas of briar, bright berry, geranium, and wet lacquer; layers of black fruits, tar, Thai spices, tobacco, and pepper on the palate; rich midpalate, mouthcoating, medium-long, and medium-weight, with a very slightly grippy finish.

1999 Van der Kamp Vineyard (tasted in 2002): Transparent, medium black-red; very ripe quasitropical fruit overlaid with wet moss, mint, and fragrant flowers; distinctive palate of peppery black fruit, spicy air-dried pork and tobacco; soft midpalate with grip at the end, full, mouthcoating, long, linen-textured, and fine.

1998 Camp Meeting Ridge (tasted prerelease in 2000): Deep, inky, almost purple color; cardamom nose; orange peel, star anise, and generous Bing cherry in the mouth; some floral highlights; substantial but fairly polished tannins.

1998 Pisoni Vineyard (tasted in 2001): Transparent, medium garnet; huge nose of cranberry, blueberry, with a hint of green vegetable and bacon fat; cardamom, tea, black currants, and black pepper in the mouth; dusty, mineral finish, long and linen-textured.

1998 Sonoma Coast (tasted in 2000): Very transparent, dark garnet; bright, briary blueberry and cranberry nose, with notes of weeds and chaparral and a faint touch of orange peel; brewed black tea with smoke and leather on the palate; not quite rustic, but a dominance of wild flavors, slightly astringent and persistent tannins; lingering wine.

1998 Van der Kamp Vineyard (tasted in 2001): Transparent, medium black-red with bluish highlights; nose of cranberry, blueberry, and leather; very structured, mineral-flavored wine with notes of coffee and lean spice; linen-textured, medium-long.

1997 Hirsch Vineyard (tasted in 2001): Saturated, dark mahogany; slightly evolved nose redolent of cherry furniture; flavors of black cherry, menthol, eucalyptus, clove, and Darjeeling tea; long, firm wine with gradually resolving tannins.

1996 Camp Meeting Ridge (tasted in 2000): Deep, saturated black-red wine; bay leaf, orange peel, and characteristic cardamom aromas; black fruit and toasted Indonesian spice with some tree bark on the palate; very approachable, sweet, velvety wine that finishes long.

PRACTICAL INFORMATION

The Camp Meeting Ridge and Sonoma Coast wines are nationally distributed. However, nearly half of the Camp Meeting Ridge cuvée is sold directly through the winery's mailing list, as are all of the vineyard-designates and the Moon Select. Visits by advance appointment only; 707-847-3661.

FOXEN VINEYARD AND WINERY

Los Olivos, California

Foxen was established in 1987 by Dick Doré and Bill Wathen on a corner of the horse and cattle ranch midway between Santa Maria and Los Olivos where Doré was raised. Doré, whose first career was in banking, had become enamored of wine when he and his family lived for 18 months in Europe during the mid 1970s. Wathen, another native of the southern Central Coast, found his way to wine through a degree in fruit science from California State Polytechnic University at San Luis Obispo, work for Santa Barbara viticultural pioneers Louis Lucas and Dale Hampton, and four years as the vineyard manager for Chalone. The winery is named for Doré's great-great-grandfather Benjamin Foxen, an English sea captain who purchased Rancho Tinaquaic from the government of Mexico in 1837. The logo, a slightly asymmetrical anchor, was the cattle brand for Foxen's ranch. The winery buildings, on the northern side of Foxen Canyon Road, are century-old, repurposed ranch structures that give new meaning to the word *rustic.* Foxen has long since outgrown these historic premises, and plans for a new winery are in the works.

Although Doré and Wathen made a dribble of home wine in 1985 and 1986, the first commercial release came in 1987, made entirely from purchased fruit. From 1987 until 1990, only one pinot noir was made, labeled Santa Maria Valley, using grapes from two vineyards on the Santa Maria Mesa. The 1987 and 1989 editions were 100 percent Sierra Madre fruit; the 1988 vintage came entirely from Santa Maria Hills. Bien Nacido fruit entered the Santa Maria Valley blend in 1990, and anchored it after 1991. The 1992 through 1995 editions were blends of Bien Nacido, Sierra Madre, and Gold Coast; beginning in 1996, fruit was also obtained from Julia's at Cambria. A vineyard-designate program was launched alongside the Santa Maria Valley wine in 1991, using grapes from the Sanford & Benedict vineyard. A vineyard-designated wine from the Bien Nacido Vineyard then debuted in 1994, using fruit from Block Q. In 1997, Foxen entered into a custom planting agreement at Bien Nacido for Block 8, a south-facing slope laid out in eight-foot rows with 3.5 feet between vines, using a combination of Dijon 113 and 115, UCD 2A and 4, and Mount Eden selection sourced from Sanford & Benedict. Block 8 produced its first crop in 1999 and completely replaced Block Q in Foxen's Bien Nacido program in 2001. The last vintage of Foxen's Sanford & Benedict wine was 1999, but in 2002 Foxen began to acquire fruit from the newly planted Sea Smoke Vineyard, about one mile as the crow flies from Sanford & Benedict, so a Sea Smoke vineyard-designate will replace Sanford & Benedict as the Santa Ynez Valley–sourced pinot in the Foxen lineup.

WINEMAKING

Wathen says his winemaking has changed substantially since the first vintages in the late 1980s. He now picks riper, cold soaks, eschews stems, and adds enzymes. Brix at harvest is usually between 24.5 and 25. The fermentors are two- and four-ton stainless steel open-tops. Cold soak lasts from three to five days, during which time enzymes are added, both to boost color and to aid in clarifying the wine later on. Each fermentor is inoculated with laboratory yeast as the cold soak ends. Three or four days of pumpovers are then followed by three or four days of hand punchdowns—Wathen says he likes to pump over "until I begin to see seeds." Fermentation temperatures peak in the high 80s

Fahrenheit, and Wathen will heat the fermentors if necessary to sustain temperatures in this range. He inoculates for malolactic fermentation and presses before the must goes dry. Free-run juice goes directly to barrel; press juice is used only in the Santa Maria Valley wine, and only after settling in tank.

Foxen uses all François Frères barrels, either medium or medium-plus toast. The Santa Maria Valley wine sees about 10 percent new wood and is bottled at the end of ten months; vineyard-designates are raised in 50 percent to 75 percent new barrels for 16 months. Lots that will be used for the vineyard-designates are identified in the spring after each vintage, when a single racking is done; the Santa Maria Valley blend is made from deselected barrels. Wines are not usually fined, and filtration is done only "when it is necessary for stability." The Santa Maria blend is released immediately after bottling; vineyard-designates are held for four to six months before release.

THE WINES

Unsurprisingly, given the evolution of fruit sources and changes in winemaking protocols, Foxen's pinots display a range of styles and personalities. This diversity is especially evident with the Santa Maria Valley and Bien Nacido bottlings, which have the longest histories and greatest fruit-source variation. Farming at Bien Nacido has also changed over time—Block Q was converted from sprawl to vertical trellis in 1998—and these changes have affected the wines' style. Vintages since 1997 are slightly weightier than earlier editions and a bit higher in alcohol, but Foxen pinots generally remain medium-weight wines with considerable aromatic interest.

TASTING NOTES

2000 Santa Maria Valley (tasted in 2002): Transparent, medium black-red; violets and roses with hints of nuts and cocoa butter on the nose; jammy black fruit, with black pepper, clove, and suggestions of tar and chocolate on the palate; full-bodied, almost creamy, moderately concentrated wine, medium-length with a satin finish.

1999 Bien Nacido Vineyard (tasted twice, in 2001 and 2002): Transparent, medium black-red; aromas of peppery flowers and butterscotch; black cherry, blackberry, black pepper, black tea, tar, tobacco, and earth on the palate; medium-weight and concentrated, slightly sweet and grippy, medium-long, crushed velvet texture.

1999 Julia's Vineyard (tasted twice, in 2001 and 2002): Transparent, medium black-red; herbal and black fruit nose; Morello cherry, mint, licorice, and pepper in the mouth, with suggestions of milk chocolate and cedar; large-framed and moderately concentrated, medium-length.

1999 Sanford & Benedict (tasted in 2001): Transparent, medium black-red; aromas and flavors of ripe plum, resin, allspice, and smoke; grippy, medium-length wine with the texture of crushed velvet.

1999 Santa Maria Valley (tasted twice, in 2001 and 2002): Transparent, medium black-red; red fruit aromas with hints of hard spice and oyster sauce; pepper, cinnamon, orange peel, resin, and light soy sauce in the mouth; slightly sweet, relatively lightweight, and slightly grippy with a suedelike texture.

1998 Santa Maria Valley (tasted in 2002): Transparent, medium garnet; nuts, soy, earth, and black fruit aromas; more earth, tar, resin, black pepper, spice, and a hint of coffee on the palate; full-bodied, sweet, concentrated, and slightly chewy, medium-length and roughly silken.

1997 Bien Nacido (tasted in 2002): Transparent, medium black-red; alluring nose of citrus flowers, honeysuckle, geranium, and smoke overlaying cherry fruit and a hint of roasted nuts; infused flowers and cherry with a bit of mocha on the palate; slightly chewy and angular, emery-textured, long, and high-toned.

1997 Santa Maria Valley (tasted in 2002): Transparent, light to medium terra-cotta with amber highlights; fragrant flowers, merbromin, and mocha on the nose; fading raspberry, earth, tar, infused flowers, and mushroom on the palate, with a hint of orange peel; light- to medium-weight and satin-textured, relatively mouthcoating, long, and elegant.

1996 Bien Nacido Vineyard (tasted in 2002): Transparent, medium black-red, tiling at the edge; aldehydes and citrus dominate the nose; cherry, cassis, root beer, mint, mocha, black pepper, and earth on the palate; evergreen and briar on the finish; slightly sweet and grippy, medium-weight and medium-length, texture of crushed velvet.

1996 Santa Maria Valley (tasted in 2002): Brilliant, light to medium garnet; nose of wild strawberries dressed with very old balsamic vinegar; black and white pepper, cinnamon, resin, and a bit of chocolate on the palate; very sweet core and full-bodied; medium-long and suede-textured. From a high-yield year; the must was bled to increase concentration.

1995 Bien Nacido Vineyard (tasted in 2002): Transparent, medium terra-cotta; citrus and citronella on the nose; wild strawberry, resin, tobacco, and cedar in the mouth; medium-weight and medium-length, slightly sweet and grippy, silken.

1995 Santa Maria Valley (tasted in 2002): Transparent, light to medium garnet; aromas of fading cherry, dried flowers, dried leaves, and a hint of light soy; very resinated and leathery flavors with evolved fruit, mint, tobacco, and cinnamon in the mouth; sweet and full-bodied, medium to long finish, suedelike.

1994 Bien Nacido Vineyard (tasted in 2002): Brilliant, medium garnet; earth, animal, and forest floor aromas with a bit of wild strawberry; black licorice, clove, white pepper, smoke, and vanilla on the palate; sweet, medium-weight and very slightly grippy, medium-length with a satin finish.

1994 Santa Maria Valley (tasted in 2002): Transparent, light to medium garnet; wild strawberry and raspberry on both nose and palate, plus red licorice, tar, forest floor, and merbromin; slightly sweet, light- to medium-weight, medium-length, and roughly silken.

1993 Santa Maria Valley (tasted in 2002): Slightly hazy, light to medium garnet, now tiling; fading fruit with dried leaves and petals on the nose; wild strawberry and raspberry with white pepper, leather, resin, and clove on the palate; light- to medium-weight and angular, medium-length, and silken.

1992 Santa Maria Valley (tasted in 2002): Transparent, light to medium terra-cotta, but still quite red; aromas of dried flowers, resin, and forest floor; cherry and raspberry with white pepper, cedar, and cinnamon in the mouth; light- to medium-weight with simultaneous viscosity, grip, and lingering fruit sweetness; medium-length and satin-textured; quite evolved but very pretty. A personal favorite.

1991 Santa Maria Valley (tasted in 2002): Slightly hazy, light to medium terra-cotta; dried leaves and petals overlay fading raspberry; mint, resin, and white pepper in the mouth; light- to medium-weight and medium-length, silken and still very slightly grippy.

1990 Santa Maria Valley (tasted in 2002): Hazy, light to medium terra-cotta; prune, leather, and a hint of truffle oil on the nose; fading wild raspberry, tobacco, white pepper, and clove on the palate; lightweight, medium-length, and satin-textured.

PRACTICAL INFORMATION

Pinot noir accounts for about 4,000 of Foxen's total annual production of 15,000 cases. Three-quarters of the pinot is the Santa Maria Valley blend; the vineyard-designates are made in lots of 400 to 800 cases. Occasionally, very tiny lots of other vineyard-designates are made for Foxen's wine club members. Except for these club-only wines, the pinots are nationally distributed. The tasting room is a convenient stop on the scenic Foxen Canyon route between the Santa Maria and Santa Ynez valleys and is open daily most of the year; 805-937-4251.

GARY FARRELL WINES

Healdsburg, California

Gary Farrell created his eponymous wine brand in 1982, albeit on a Lilliputian scale, while his full-time job was making wine for Davis Bynum (see the profile earlier in this section). Gary Farrell wines were then crafted side by side with Davis Bynum ones in Bynum's converted hops barn until 2000, when Farrell moved to his own purpose-built facility on a spectacular hilltop overlooking the Russian River, one mile downstream from Wohler Bridge. In fact, Gary Farrell Wines and Rochioli Vineyard and Winery debuted simultaneously in 1982, and Farrell was the winemaker for both. Joe Rochioli Jr. had sold his entire crop of pinot noir to Davis Bynum from 1973 through 1981; but in 1982, anticipating the construction of a winery on his own property, he asked that part of the crop be made under the Rochioli name, on what is known in the trade as a custom-crush basis. Simultaneously, Bynum and Rochioli agreed that Farrell could purchase a tiny lot of the same fruit—enough to make two barrels of wine—for a project bearing *his* name.

It was these 50 cases of 1982 pinot noir from Rochioli's West Block and the North Hill of Allen Ranch that launched Gary Farrell Wines. Gradually, production inched up from 50 cases in 1982 to 11,000 in 1999, filling every nook and cranny of Bynum's premises before the move to new and separate facilities. Until the move, Gary Farrell Wines was, in Farrell's own phrase, "the brand that cash flow built," the proceeds from the sale of each vintage financing the purchase of grapes and barrels for the next. An investment by Bill Hambrecht, a veteran player in the ultrapremium sector of California's wine business—he bought a 20 percent ownership share in Farrell's business—was instrumental in financing the new winery. In 1996, Farrell planted a 25-acre estate vineyard on Starr Ridge, on the eastern side of the Middle Reach not far from the current western boundary of the Chalk Hill AVA, all but four acres of which are pinot noir. The main scion material is Dijon 115, but there are also small amounts of Dijon 114 and 777, plus UCD 4, planted in seven-foot rows with four feet between vines. A second estate vineyard was set out in 2000 between Ross Road and the Gravenstein Highway near Iron Horse, of which approximately 12 acres are devoted to the Dijon 115 and 777 clones of pinot noir.

Gary Farrell Wines has made a Russian River Valley pinot noir every year since 1982, and small quantities of vineyard-designated pinots every year since 1985, except in 1989, 1993, and 1996, when the only pinot was the Russian River Valley blend. The blend has typically been anchored with fruit from the hillside blocks at Allen Ranch, which are also the source for Williams Selyem's Allen Ranch bottling. Other components of the blend are Rochioli's River Block (see Rochioli Vineyard and Winery and Williams Selyem), Olivet Lane (see also Merry Edwards Wines and Williams Selyem), the Stiling Vineyard on Vine Hill Road between Kistler and Dehlinger (whence Farrell gets primarily Swan selection planted in the late 1980s), and occasionally a bit of Bien Nacido Block Q (see chapter 4, "The Southern Central Coast"). Bien Nacido, of course, is not a Russian River vineyard, but the quantities used in Farrell's blend—in those years when any at all is used—fall within permitted limits for designated appellation wines. In recent years, some fruit from Farrell's two estate vineyards have also been used in the blend.

During the 1980s, Allen Ranch was the most frequently vineyard-designated wine, but the fruit for the vineyard-designated lots was typically from Allen's Tri-Corner block, not the hillside blocks used in the blend. Similarly, when Rochioli wine was made as a vineyard-designate, the lots used were from Rochioli's East or West block, or both, not from the River Block used in the blend. Lots of Olivet Lane and Bien Nacido have also been vineyard-designated in some vintages, as have lots of Stiling in 1997 and 1998, and Starr Ridge in 2000 and 2001.

WINEMAKING

Farrell's house style emphasizes elegance and balance. To this end, he picks most fruit at lower levels of sugar accumulation than many others do—usually less than 24.2 Brix—and avoids vineyards whose grapes show incomplete flavor development at these levels. He harvests fruit beginning at dawn and always finishes before 11:00 A.M. He believes in rigorous sorting to remove leaves, second-crop and underripe berries, as well as the occasional bit of rot, and has configured a 29-foot-long elevated belt, whose speed is controlled by the sorters, on an exterior but entirely roofed crushpad to facilitate the process. Throughput is intentionally slow: only about three bins per hour. Until it reaches the fermentors, the fruit is moved entirely by belts to minimize bruising, and is entirely destemmed. Farrell argues that it is "not exciting to mass-produce wine in big tanks": the soul of Gary Farrell Wines is genuinely tiny lots, which are handled separately until their potential is clear. Pinot is fermented in a virtual farm of small, five-foot-tall by 6.5-foot-diameter jacketed stainless steel open-tops, most of which are filled less than half full. In 2002, 240 tons of fruit were handled as 105 separate lots! (Occasionally, a fruit bin will be used for an extremely tiny lot, but Farrell is partial to the temperature control he is able to enforce in the jacketed stainless fermentors.) A longish, 45-degree Fahrenheit cold soak (up to seven days) is maintained with a combination of the tank jackets and blanketings of dry ice. The fermentors are then heated to 60 degrees for yeasting, punched down three times daily during the alcoholic fermentation, and pressed when or just before the must is dry. The wine is then settled in tank, separated from the gross lees, and inoculated for malolactic fermentation before being barreled.

An average of 33 percent to 45 percent new French oak is used, primarily from François Frères, Séguin Moreau, and Rousseau. A first racking is done after the malolactic fermentation has finished. The Russian River Valley blend is created just before the next harvest and bottled immediately. Lots destined for vineyard-designation are held longer in wood.

Farrell is at pains to explain that the Russian River wine is always privileged in the course of blending trials and decisions. Vineyard-designated wines are contingent: they are made only when, and to the extent that, lots of extraordinary quality remain unused after the winery has made a Russian River blend that "we are excited about." As a practical matter, however, the twin processes of identifying lots destined for blending and others that have obvious vineyard-designation potential proceed in parallel, and some consolidations based on these judgments are made as early as the first racking. There is no enzyme use or fining, but minimal filtration is done when it is "appropriate." During the years that Gary Farrell and Davis Bynum wines were made at the Bynum facility, there were no significant technical differences between the two winemaking protocols, save for somewhat more intensive use of new oak on the Farrell wines. In his new winery, however, Farrell has a variety of tools at his disposal that he says he "had always wanted" but simply did not have before: belts rather than screws, gravity in lieu of pumps, temperature-controlled fermentors, and ambient temperature control in all tank and barrel rooms.

THE WINES

Gary Farrell enjoys an enviable reputation among fellow winemakers, wine writers, and consumers. References to his mastery, perfectionism, and talent are legion. His pinots, in particular, attract a great deal of approbation for consistency, finesse, complexity, and, in the words of one writer, "cultivated elegance." It is both interesting and reassuring that this acclaim comes in spite of Farrell's determination to avoid the excesses of ripeness and extraction that some critics seem otherwise to prefer. In my experience, Gary Farrell pinots are medium-weight wines with medium to deep black-red color, great transparency, generally soft tannins, and genuinely impressive elegance. There is transparency and definition to the flavors, which never seem muddled, and the wines are fruit-sweet without ever being heavy or seeming to have been picked overripe. I have not tasted wines earlier than the 1997 vintage.

TASTING NOTES

2000 Olivet Lane Vineyard (tasted in 2003): Brilliant, medium crimson with ruby highlights; daphne and cherry-blossom aromas with a hint of minty potpourri; sweet Bing cherry and Italian plum with hints of soft spice, resin, balsam, and mesquite; grippy but fine-textured, rather like coarse velvet, nearly chewy but still midweight; mouthcoating and long.

2000 Russian River Valley (tasted in 2002): Brilliant, medium garnet; demonstrative nose of potpourri, black cherry, earth, tree bark, and pepper; sweet in the mouth, with red and black cherry, resin, tea, and a hint of barrel char; light- to medium-weight, very elegant, precise, and angular, satin-textured but structured, medium-length.

1998 Olivet Lane (tasted in 2000): Transparent, medium-dark black-red; firm, brooding wine with dominant dark fruit, cinnamon, and black pepper; medium-weight, fine-grained tannins, velvety, and long.

1998 Russian River Valley (tasted early spring 2000): Transparent, intense medium-dark black-red; raspberry, cherry, and dried flowers on the nose; blackberry and sweet cherry in the mouth; medium-weight and medium-length, silken.

1997 Allen Vineyard (tasted in 1999): Transparent, medium-dark black-red; spice-scented cherry fruit on the nose; Bing cherry, clove, tree bark, fennel, and plum in the mouth, with notes of animal and leather; medium-weight and mouthcoating, velvety and long; very fine.

PRACTICAL INFORMATION

About half of Farrell's now 14,000-case production is pinot noir, and the Russian River Valley bottling accounts for at least 70 percent of the pinot. In lesser years, it is Farrell's only pinot. This bottling is nationally distributed. The vineyard-designated wines are usually available only to selected restaurant accounts and to mailing-list and tasting room customers. The elegant tasting room in architect Rich McCrea's beautiful stone, tile, and wood building is open by advance appointment; 707-473-2900.

GLORIA FERRER CHAMPAGNE CAVES

Sonoma, California

Gloria Ferrer is the American wine project of Grup Freixenet, the well-regarded Penedes-based *cava* producer whose Carta Nevada and Cordon Negro labels are known around the world. The Carneros project began in 1982, dedicated exclusively to Champagne-method sparkling wine, which was made at Quail Ridge and Chateau St. Jean until 1986. In 1983, the Ferrer family bought a 160-acre ranch at the western edge of the Carneros appellation, about four miles southwest of Sonoma. Another 90-acre parcel, between the first and the Carneros Highway, was purchased in 1986. Between 1984 and 1989, 200 acres of chardonnay and pinot noir were planted there, on what is now called the Home Ranch, in mostly flat clay-loam soils irregularly laced with gravel and in loamier, lower-vigor soils at the toe of the rolling, east-facing hills. The pinot went into Block D, bordering the Carneros Highway, now re-christened Aurora Break; Block B, now called Wind Gap; and, more recently, Blocks E, F, and G, immediately around the winery buildings and above them on the hillside. Row orientation was northeast-southwest, following the natural slope of the land, and vine spacings were originally ten feet by five. Various pieces of E, F, and G now carry the names Wingo Vista, Pedragal, Dolores, Carmen Pilar, and Eagles Fledge. These parcels are known collectively as Gravel Knob and were the source of a block-designated pinot in 2000. The large Spanish-style winery was built in 1986.

Responding in part to a softness in demand for sparkling wine at the end of the 1980s and in part to his conviction that some of the estate fruit had the guts to make good still wines, winemaker Bob Iantosca began thinking about still pinot noir in 1989 and 1990. He was sure, he remembers now, that the property could make good chardonnay but thought pinot noir was more of a gamble. His business plan included an instant exit strategy: the pinot could be sold off in bulk without any financial loss if, once made, he and the Ferrers decided it really wasn't good enough to release. This did not happen, however. A few hundred cases of still pinot, made from the relatively mature vines in Block D, were produced in 1991, and Gloria Ferrer has made still pinot ever since. By 1999 production had increased to 5,000 cases, and it doubled from 1999 to 2000. The facility is now sized for about 120,000 cases of sparkling wine and 30,000 to 40,000 cases of table wine, so pinot production could reach 20,000 to 25,000 cases without encountering space limitations.

Because 175 acres of the Home Ranch plantings were done on nonresistant rootstock, interplanting and replanting began in 1992, and continue. In addition, Gloria Ferrer has leased and planted a small hillside parcel upslope of the winery and leased 100 acres of the Circle Bar Ranch, less than a mile to the southwest. Despite its proximity and similar range of elevations, Circle Bar is very different from the Home Ranch, with substantially thinner, lighter, stone- and gravel-strewn soils (primarily Pajaro and Laniger series) in hilly swales and saddles that bode well for still-wine fruit. Ninety acres of pinot noir were planted at Circle Bar in 1997 and 1998, in 19 very heterogeneously sized and irregularly shaped blocks fitted around the natural contours of the land. Row orientations at Circle Bar follow, variously, soils, prevailing wind, and topography; and vine spacings have been tightened to eight feet by five or six. In 2000 a block-designated pinot was made from one of these blocks, christened Rust Rock Terrace, a chunk of volcanic soil planted to UCD 2A, Dijon 115, and Colmar 538.

Although Gloria Ferrer's still pinot program now relies primarily on fruit from its hillier blocks and will increasingly privilege blocks on the Circle Bar Ranch as more of these plantings come onstream, the pinot program here was designed to complement the sparkling program in perpetuity. To choose scion wood for replanting and new plantings, Iantosca designed extensive clonal trials and selected clones that performed well, in these sites at least, for both still and sparkling wine. This criterion has led to unusual choices. The largest vine populations are now a field selection from Trefethen, UCD 32 (one of the Roederer clones, from Chouilly in Champagne), and Colmar 538—also known as CTPS 162 and UCD 48. Elsewhere (except at Greenwood Ridge in Anderson Valley) the Roederer clones have not been favored for still pinot, and the Colmar clone has been almost ignored for both still and sparkling pinot as a result of poor performance when it underwent trials in Oregon during the 1980s. At Gloria Ferrer UCD 32 seems to produce, of itself, a nearly complete wine, with deep color, dark fruit flavors, and aromas of leather, furniture polish, and cherry jam. Colmar 538, while less complete, gives distinctive aromas of tea leaves, fruitcake, and gingerbread. Other, more popular clones and selections, including UCD 2A, 4, and 13 and Dijon 115, along with some rarities like UCD 56 (CTPS 927 via British Columbia and Champagne) and 58 (CTPS 779 via British Columbia and Champagne), are also planted on the two ranches. Atypically, Gloria Ferrer has *not* planted Dijon 667 or 777, which have emerged as must-haves for most winegrowers in California and Oregon. Small amounts (here *small* means five or ten tons) of pinot fruit are sometimes sold off to other wineries.

WINEMAKING

Pinot for still wine is picked as far as possible between 23.5 and 24.5 Brix, usually around mid September. Some second-crop fruit (i.e., fruit passed over when the first pick for sparkling wine was done in August) is also used for still wine. Second-crop fruit tends to show smaller clusters than first-crop, have a high skin-to-juice ratio, and be a good blending tool, according to Iantosca, though care must be exercised to ensure that the second-crop berries have not raisined. Pinot is completely destemmed and the stems discarded. Several types and sizes of fermentors are used—stainless steel tanks, open-tops, and rotary fermentors—and some of the tanks are equipped with automatic punchdown devices. To optimize for round mouthfeel, Iantosca first tried to extend the length of the primary fermentation, but pinot noir's natural tendency to ferment quickly when whole clusters are not used drove him to stretch out the front and back ends of the vatting instead. The typical vatting now starts with three days of 55-degree Fahrenheit cold soak and ends with one to three days of postfermentation maceration, though some lots are pressed before they are dry. The alcoholic fermentation is started with several yeasts chosen to minimize color absorption; punchdowns or pumpovers are executed three times daily (more often in the rotary fermentors); and juice temperatures peak above 90 degrees. After pressing, the wine is settled in tank overnight and then inoculated for malolactic fermentation; it goes to barrel fairly clean. The press fraction is segregated, cleaned up, sometimes racked, and usually blended back, but occasionally sold off.

About one-third of the barrels are new each year and are mostly Damy, Cadus, Billon, and François Frères, toasted medium or medium-plus. Iantosca is also experimenting with a few Hungarian oak barrels. The lots are evaluated in February or March after the vintage to make the main Carneros blend; then Iantosca "has some fun" with what's left, creating blends for the other lots. The wine stays in barrel for nine months without racking, except for special lots, which spend up to 14 months in wood. The Carneros blend is coarse pad filtered, but Iantosca tries not to filter the smaller lots. The pinots are bottle-aged for 12 months before release.

THE WINES

About four-fifths of Gloria Ferrer's pinot production is a blend of lots from the Home and Circle Bar ranches designated Carneros, which has been made annually since 1991 and is nationally distributed. (About 2,000 cases of a Sonoma County wine are also made, but sold exclusively to chain accounts.) Since its debut in 1998, the flagship wine has been José S. Ferrer Selection, named in honor of Gloria's husband; it is sold to restaurants and mailing-list customers and at the winery. The José S. Ferrer is a barrel selection from four blocks of the Home Vineyard, planted respectively to Trefethen selection, UCD 13 and 32, and Colmar 538; and two blocks of Circle Bar Ranch, planted to Dijon 115 and UCD 2A. Vintages of Gloria Ferrer pinot up to and including 1997 were relatively lightweight wines with slightly herbal properties; beginning with the 1998 vintage, with newer plantings coming on-line, the fruit is sweeter, the hue has deepened, and the wines' palate weight has increased. The José S. Ferrer Selection tends toward spiciness with overtones of smoke and considerable weight. The two block-designates made in 2000 showed exceptionally well in early tastings, combining elegance and minerality with admirable complexity, and less fat than José Ferrer.

TASTING NOTES

2000 Gravel Knob Vineyard (tasted twice in 2003): Brilliant, medium garnet with rosy highlights; potpourri, spicy game, white pepper, dried cranberries, and cedar on the nose; sweet raspberry, cherry, licorice, sage, and peppery spice in the mouth, with some tea and toffee; hint of grip, some minerality, suedelike, medium-weight, and medium-plus length.

2000 José S. Ferrer Selection (tasted in 2003): Transparent, medium oxblood with pinkish-orange highlights; dark fruit and smoke aromas with hints of forest floor and evergreen; sweet, round, and full-bodied in the mouth, with five-spice, dark cherry, and graphite; medium-plus weight, emery texture tending toward rough velvet, medium-long.

2000 Rust Rock Terrace Vineyard (tasted twice in 2003): Transparent, medium rosy-garnet; aromas of rose petals and talc overlay black raspberry; black fruit, black pepper, spice, tar, incense, and camphor in the mouth; satin, structured, medium-weight, mouth-coating and long, with a noticeably mineral finish.

1999 Carneros (tasted in 2001): Transparent, medium black-red; nose of black cherry, raspberry, and licorice; more cherry and smoke flavors in the mouth; slightly creamy texture, light to medium body, and medium-length.

1999 José S. Ferrer Selection (tasted twice in 2001): Transparent, medium garnet; black fruit, currants, smoke, and evergreen on the nose; red and black fruits with red licorice, tar, and sweet, soft spice on the palate; medium-length and medium-weight, texture hovering between fine linen and silk.

1998 Carneros (tasted twice in 2001): Transparent, medium black-red; nose of cherries, earth, and mushrooms; flavors of sweet fruit, clove, cinnamon, cherry candy, and furniture polish; dense, spicy, moderately weighty wine; finishes long.

1998 José S. Ferrer Selection (tasted twice in 2001): Transparent, medium black-red with a bit of brick; aromas of Bing cherries and black fruits; petroleum, char, toasted spice, wet earth, chocolate, and black pepper overlay fruit in the mouth; soft, supple wine with medium body, medium-length.

1996 Carneros (tasted in 2001): Transparent, light to medium black-red; huge and evolved nose of resin, old furniture, animal, and mushroom; cherry-cranberry fruit and tar in the mouth with a touch of graphite; light- to medium-weight wine with a short to medium-length finish.

1994 Carneros (tasted in 2001): Very transparent, light terra-cotta; truffled mushrooms on the nose; fruit core still sweet but making a predominantly herbal impression; short-finishing, lightweight wine with interesting aromatics, silken.

PRACTICAL INFORMATION
The winery is the best source for the José S. Ferrer Selection and the block-designates. A wine club provides access to library and limited-release wines. The onsite tasting room is open seven days; 707-933-1931.

GREENWOOD RIDGE VINEYARDS

Philo, California

There are many unlikely biographies and serendipitous stories on the way to lives and careers in winemaking, but Allan Green's story still stands out. Besides making wine, Green is also an internationally successful graphic designer, a regular rock 'n' roll disc jockey, and a passionate collector of wine cans. That's right, wine *cans.* He is also the son of Aaron G. Green, a San Francisco architect once affiliated with Frank Lloyd Wright, who designed his house, winery, and tasting room; and son also of an anesthesiologist mother with an abiding interest in the health benefits of wine. His brother, a filmmaker, was the inadvertent catalyst for the family's wine venture. Seized with enthusiasm for the post-hippie back-to-the-land movement, Frank Green encouraged his family to purchase 275 remote acres of ranchland on Greenwood Road in 1971—for weekend retreats. Allan Green spent enough time on the ranch to play softball with some of Anderson Valley's wine pioneers and to become infected with the idea that grape growing could be, well, cool. When Tony and Gretchen Husch decided to sell the warm-weather vineyard parcel they owned adjacent to the Greens' property, the Greens acquired three acres of cabernet and two and a half acres each of merlot and riesling. Jed Steele, a softball chum, talked Green through his first years as a home winemaker. Greenwood Ridge was bonded in 1980.

In view of its relatively warm ridge-top location, pinot noir was an unlikely variety for Greenwood Ridge. But when Van Williamson was hired as winemaker in 1989, he "*really* wanted to make some pinot," and Roederer Estate (which had planted a large vineyard but had a narrow pick window for sparkling wine) was happy to sell off a few tons of "late-harvest" fruit for still wine. Greenwood Ridge's pinot program therefore debuted as a non-estate program, and it continued thus until 1999. The fruit source was consistently UCD 32 from Roederer, eventually augmented with UCD 13 from the Corby Vineyard and small quantities of fruit from the Weir Vineyard in the Yorkville Highlands AVA, except in the 1990 vintage, when grapes were purchased instead from Christine Woods. Gradually taken with the variety, Green decided to plant his own pinot noir vineyard in 1996, despite the relative warmth of his site. Four acres were developed southwest of the winery, at an elevation of about 1,400 feet, well above the fog line and commanding a stunning view of nearby ridge tops. The pinot vineyard is planted in east-west-oriented eight-foot rows with five feet between vines, and the scion material is an unusual half and half combination of Dijon 115 and UCD 32, with just a bit of UCD 23 (Mariafeld) "for color and seasoning." Enough fruit was harvested from the estate vineyard in 1999 to make a first release of estate pinot noir, while the purchased fruit went into Greenwood Ridge's Anderson Valley bottling. Even though it is, for the moment, the *only* pinot noir to carry the new designation, Green decided that the property's estate pinot should be labeled as a Mendocino Ridge wine. This decision reflects Green's loyalty to the new Mendocino Ridge AVA, which he helped create, though primarily in the service of warm-climate varieties like merlot, cabernet, and zinfandel, which do badly on the floor of Anderson Valley but thrive on the warm ridge tops. Production of the Anderson Valley bottling was terminated after the 2000 vintage.

WINEMAKING

Not wishing to grow his total production beyond about 7,500 cases and essentially unable to afford a full-time winemaker on that scale, Green resumed winemaking duties himself when Williamson left in 1993. He ferments in horizontal, open-top dairy tanks, first destemming completely and then using a combination of whole and slightly crushed berries. He "likes" a two-day cold soak but cannot chill all of his tanks simultaneously, so he sometimes gets less. He then lets the temperature rise naturally, and inoculates with laboratory yeast. With punchdowns three or four times a day, Greenwood Ridge's fermentations generally last five to six days at or below 90 degrees Fahrenheit. Cool air temperatures in October usually keep the fermentation temperature down naturally. The target is to press into tank when the must reaches about 2 degrees Brix, introducing malolactic bacteria simultaneously so that the beginning of the malolactic fermentation overlaps the end of the alcoholic conversion. The press fraction is reunified with the free-run juice (Green says he used to keep it separate but found it always tasted just fine in the end) and allowed to settle in tank for as little as four days or as long as three weeks before going to barrel.

Greenwood Ridge is a two-cooper-shop—Dargaud & Jaeglé and François Frères. Green likes the "different kind of smokiness" in the Dargaud barrels. He racks to tank for blending in July following the vintage, and bottles at the end of the summer. He finds fining is generally not needed, but he uses coarse pad filters for clarity. Historically, the pinots have been bottle-aged for six months before release, but the new Mendocino Ridge wine will be held for a full year.

THE WINES

Although pinot noir represents only about one-sixth of Greenwood Ridge's total production, it has acquired a loyal following and attracted very favorable reviews. The wines show considerable complexity and typically exhibit notes of evergreen, cedar, or balsam. They are medium-weight wines that drink well early but also seem to age respectably, though I have had limited personal experience with older vintages.

TASTING NOTES

2000 Anderson Valley (tasted in 2002): Transparent, light to medium ruby; aromas of red berry fruit and smoke with hints of herbs, mint, and bay laurel; cherry, strawberry, licorice, cola, leather, and complex South Asian spice in the mouth; medium-weight and medium-length, mouthfilling and suedelike.

2000 Mendocino Ridge Estate (tasted in 2002): Nearly saturated, blood-red color and very slightly hazy; beetroot, balsam, and pine tar on the nose; black cherry, peppery clove, and a hint of barrel char on the palate; moderately concentrated and medium-length, satin-textured wine with some grip on the finish.

1999 Anderson Valley (tasted in 2002): Transparent, medium black-red; pine and mint aromas; raspberry, cherry, and white and black pepper in the mouth, with a hint of cola and minerals; fleshy wine, medium-weight and medium-length.

1999 Mendocino Ridge Estate (tasted in 2002): Transparent, medium-dark black-red; tea, blackberries, plums, and macerated herbs on the nose; very sweet, cherry and plum flavors on the palate with distinctive notes of spruce and nutmeg and a hint of meat; medium-length and medium-weight.

1998 Anderson Valley (tasted in 2001): Transparent, medium black-red; aromas of evergreen, peppermint, and black fruit; red and black fruit with Asian spice, smoke, and a hint of sandalwood on the palate; softly but noticeably tannic, medium-weight, medium-long, the texture of rough silk, but more sober than the 1997 vintage, below.

1997 Anderson Valley (tasted in 2001): Transparent, medium ruby; strawberry jam, balsam, cedar, and licorice on the nose; sweet mouth of cassis, strawberry, and blackberry seasoned with smoke and vanilla; medium-weight, textured like rough silk, long, charming.

PRACTICAL INFORMATION

One-third of Greenwood Ridge pinot is sold from the tasting room, an unconventional redwood polygon on Highway 128 next to Navarro Vineyards, and by mail order. Of the balance, 80 percent is distributed in California. Because Green prefers "a good distributor in a minor market to a bad distributor in a large market," he is absent from several large markets, including Florida and Texas. Arrangements to visit the winery and vineyard, which are 25 minutes uphill from the tasting room, must be made in advance, but the tasting room is open daily; 707-895-2002.

HAMACHER WINES

Carlton, Oregon

Eric Hamacher is a 1960s child who discovered wine while his contemporaries were consuming six-packs of standard American beer. Raised on California's Monterey Peninsula, he studied viticulture and enology at the University of California, Davis, in the 1980s. Because his roommate was an Oregonian, a few bottles of Oregon pinot noir infiltrated their regular weekly tastings of French Burgundies. In 1987 he worked the crush at Rex Hill and fell decisively in love with Oregon. "I saw," he recalls, "Oregon's incredible *potential* for pinot noir." What was missing, he thought, was "consistency." He liked what he calls Oregon's "Wild West" culture: a second generation of arrivistes who "looked at the Ponzis and at Dick Erath and said, 'Wow, me too.'" After the 1987 harvest he returned to California to "make some money"; he worked briefly as a research enologist for Robert Mondavi, studying the effects of sunlight on various chemicals, and put in four years at Chalone and a year for Tony Soter at Etude (see the profile earlier in this section). He remembers the year at Etude as an incredible learning experience: such a "cocktail" of projects, consultants, and winemakers that every day was "like being in school."

Hamacher returned to Oregon in 1995 to launch his own brand and to marry Luisa Ponzi, whom he had met at the Steamboat pinot noir conference in 1992. From the outset, by necessity, he was involved with various winery facilities projects and with campaigns to modify Oregon law so that multiple wineries could share a single physical facility. This involvement culminated in the creation of the Carlton Winemakers Studio, a built-from-scratch, 15,000-square-foot facility designed to accommodate multiple independent boutique-scale winemakers, which opened on the eve of harvest in 2002. The studio has deservedly attracted huge attention. The project has been explicitly green from the outset, incorporating passive solar technology, high-efficiency windows, and captured rainwater from roof runoff with efficient, gravity-based production capabilities, top-of-the-line equipment, and dedication to the sort of environment in which small makers can craft wines of the highest quality, simultaneously and side by side. In its first harvest, the studio was home to eight winemakers, including Andrew Rich Wines, Penner-Ash Wine Cellars, and Soter Vineyards, as well as Hamacher. The Hamacher label was launched with the 1995 vintage, dedicated exclusively to chardonnay and pinot noir. The 1995, 1996, and 1997 vintages were made at the Medici Winery in Newberg; 1998, 1999, and 2000 at Lemelson outside Carlton; and 2001 at Adelsheim. Hamacher was the main designer for the Carlton Winemakers Studio, as he was for Medici and Lemelson earlier. He has now established a considerable reputation, not only as a winemaker, but as a winery planner.

Hamacher's pinot noir is a single blend from a handful of Willamette Valley vineyards, most of them within the confines of Yamhill County. The consistent sources are the Durant Vineyard, a 1973 planting of own-rooted UCD 4 in the Dundee Hills; and Manuela, a 15-year-old vineyard uphill from Abetina (see Ponzi Vineyards) near the top of Chehalem Mountain. In 1995, Hamacher also sourced fruit from three other vineyards; in 2001 he used five additional sites, and two more came onstream in 2002. Like his onetime mentor Tony Soter, Hamacher argues strongly for what he calls "aggressive" farming but "conservative" cropping. Over the years he has dropped vineyards that would not, or could not, farm to his specifications. He is also a strong advocate for blending over vineyard-designation, arguing that most Oregon vineyards are too young to display consistent *terroir* and that most winemakers have too little experience with individual sites to showcase site specificity appropriately. That said, he *almost* regrets blending Durant fruit, which seems to him complex and complete on its own.

WINEMAKING

Because of Oregon's marginal climate, Hamacher believes in a "super" sorting table designed to feed the destemmer as evenly as possible. He destems almost completely and prefers medium-size, four-ton fermentors with excellent heating and chilling capabilities. Most winemakers, Hamacher asserts, "follow the temperature curve Mother Nature provides." Hamacher's fermentors give him the opportunity to achieve higher fermentation temperatures faster, but then to cool the must for a longer and more extended finish. This schema translates to a short cold soak on the front end, but at least five days of postfermentation maceration. To avoid what Hamacher calls "forward, fruit-sweet character," the wine is not pressed or barreled until the must is fully dry.

Cooperage is mixed but primarily Sirugue barrels whose staves have been air-dried for three years—Hamacher likes Sirugue's "clove-cinnamon spiciness"—of which about 35 percent are new each year. The pinots spend 18 to 20 months in barrel, and are racked once barrel-to-barrel using compressed air after malolactic fermentation has completed and once more when the blends are made prior to bottling. Blending is an elaborate process; Hamacher tries out as many as three dozen possible blends before narrowing the field, and he often ends up declassifying many lots. Declassified lots are finished and bottled, but sold under private labels. (In 1995 and 1997, Hamacher declassified *half* of his lots, finding that these vintages had been too weak to tolerate the percentage of new wood he had used.) Hamacher fines or filters, or both, if necessary, though he prefers to avoid these processes.

THE WINES

Hamacher is guided by two main stylistic parameters. First, he seeks what he calls "complete, elegant, and supple" wines. He believes that texture is paramount with pinot, and he aims for what he calls "liquid silk." Second, he insists on "embracing the vintage," by which he means that style is subordinated to vintage variations. The 1995 and 1997 wines are therefore quite different from the 1998s and 1999s. Each of the four vintages I have tasted has been impressive for its integration, balance, and elegance.

TASTING NOTES

2000 Oregon (tasted in 2003): Transparent, medium black-red; aromas of tea and red fruit just veering toward black; delicately rich on the palate with minerality and flavors of lead pencil; very slightly grippy, medium-weight and medium-length.

1999 Oregon (tasted in 2002): Transparent, medium black-red; briar, rhubarb, cranberry, and rose petal on the nose; flavors of spice and dark red fruit with smoke, fine-grained tannin, and graphite; slightly grippy, medium-weight, flannel-textured, deeply flavored, and medium-long.

1998 Oregon (tasted in 2002): Transparent, medium garnet; strongly floral aromas with undertones of strawberry and dried leaves; strawberry and red cherry on the palate, with slate, moss, and black pepper; light- to medium-weight and slightly grippy but elegant, medium-length with a texture of very fine-grained emery.

1997 Oregon (tasted in 2002): Brilliant, medium black-red with terra-cotta highlights; coffee, toast, and spice on the nose; on the palate, bright and slightly tart cherry fruit with hints of citrus peel, resin, and cinnamon; structured, silken and medium-length, light- to medium-weight.

PRACTICAL INFORMATION

Hamacher pinots are nationally distributed and widely represented on good restaurant lists. A tasting room and retail sales room in the Carlton Winemakers Studio is open Thursday through Sunday; 503-852-7200.

HANDLEY CELLARS

Philo, California

Milla Handley entered the University of California, Davis, intending to study art. Six years later, she graduated with a degree in fermentation science, one of the first such degrees awarded to a woman. After three years with the legendary Dick Arrowood at Chateau St. Jean, she moved to Anderson Valley in 1978, working first at Edmeades for Jed Steele. In 1982, she obtained a bond for the converted cellar in her house, northwest of Philo (now the premises for Claudia Springs Winery), and made 250 cases of Handley North Coast chardonnay from a combination of Mendocino and Dry Creek Valley fruit. The wine won awards, and Handley Cellars was launched.

Pinot noir came rather later, after the debut of sparkling wine and several vintages of sauvignon blanc. In 1983, Handley went to Burgundy and found she "really liked the wine." In 1986, she planted four acres of pinot on the former Holmes Ranch, a long stone's throw from the house cum winery. In 1989, the second crop from this vineyard, which had previously been picked for sparkling wine, was used to make an experimental batch of still pinot. The exercise was repeated in 1990. In 1991, the first "real" Handley pinot noir was made. Then the four acres of estate pinot noir grew to 12. Handley later augmented her supply of estate fruit with grapes purchased from the Floodgate vineyard (in 1997, 1998, and 1999), Carol Pratt's little vineyard above Philo, and the Corby vineyard, where Greenwood Road meets Highway 128. By 1998, pinot noir accounted for more than 2,000 cases, or about 15 percent of Handley's total production. In 1999, two additional acres were planted at the 900-foot elevation above the current winery; two more followed in 2001.

The original parcel of estate pinot noir, southeast of the winery building on a mostly south-facing slope, is UCD 13 on a vertical trellis, planted in north-south-oriented ten-foot rows with six feet between vines. This mature vineyard is irrigated, but in fact takes very little water. A second block, planted in 1990, is lyre-trellised UCD 2A in northeast-southwest rows. In the newest plantings, Handley is working with Dijon clones. The estate fruit is divided between a small Estate Reserve bottling (about 200 cases) made in 1992, 1993, 1995, 1996, 1998, 1999, and 2001, and an Anderson Valley cuvée (1,000 to 2,100 cases, depending on the vintage), in which purchased fruit is also used. A blend of pinot noir and pinot meunier, called Cuvée Primo, was also made in 1997 and 1999, composed of "odd lots" of pinot noir that "did not fit," plus pinot meunier purchased from the Floodgate Vineyard. In 2000, Handley also purchased pinot from River Road Vineyard in the Santa Lucia Highlands, which was vinified separately.

WINEMAKING

Handley and cowinemaker Deny Dudzik tend to pick pinot between 23.5 and 24.5 Brix, depending on taste. They ferment in cylindrical stainless steel tanks and converted horizontal open-top dairy tanks that hold about five tons. They have largely abandoned whole clusters, and now use no stems unless they are "very ripe." A cold prefermentation maceration lasts one or two days, and Colorpro enzymes are added to stabilize extracted color. Handley is moving toward resident yeast fermentation, but some lots are still inoculated, and nutrients are added even if there is no inoculation, in order to establish a healthy yeast population. In 2000, for the first time, the must derived from the estate UCD 2A was bled to increase concentration. Punchdowns are done three times daily, and pumpovers sometimes once, during a plus-or-minus 12-day fermentation, with peak temperatures about 90 degrees Fahrenheit. The must is pressed at dryness, and settled for three or four days to avoid racking later. Malolactic bacteria are normally introduced in tank during settling.

The wine then goes to barrel—mostly Latour and Cadus, with some François Frères, Mercurey, and Séguin Moreau, between 25 percent and 30 percent of which are new. The wines are returned to tank in late July or early August after the vintage, retasted, and blended. The reserve, which is usually a selection from the stock of newer barrels, is then sometimes returned to barrel for another few months, and subsequently bottled unfiltered. The Anderson Valley cuvée is bottled directly from tank and may be filtered—unless it is completely dry, visually clear, and biologically sound. Occasionally, lots from the Pratt vineyard are fined for tannin management. The Anderson Valley cuvée is bottle-aged for 12 months before release; the reserve gets 18 months. Handley observes that if she racked more often or could wait longer before release, she might filter less, but she is determined that her wines be clear.

THE WINES

The reputation of Handley pinots grew steadily in the second half of the 1990s, buttressed by favorable reviews and competition medals. The wines are bright, fruit-driven, complex, and moderately long. The 2000 edition seems especially successful, with distinctive aromatics, elegance, and balance.

TASTING NOTES

2000 Anderson Valley (tasted in 2003): Transparent, medium-dark black-red; cherry, raspberry, and dried ancho chiles on the nose; rich, dark blackberry fruit with licorice and smoky dried peppers on the palate; structured with some grip, satin, medium-weight, long, and elegant. Very fine.

2000 Santa Lucia Highlands River Road Vineyard (tasted in 2003): Transparent, medium garnet; aromas of dusty potpourri and peppery geranium; deep cherry fruit with some minerality; chalky, chamois-textured, medium-weight and medium-length.

1998 Anderson Valley (tasted twice in 2001): Transparent, medium black-red; violets, leather, raspberry, cherry, and vanilla on the nose; black fruits, cola, slate, and smoke in the mouth; quite plump, some unresolved tannin, light- to medium-weight, medium-long finish.

1996 Estate Reserve (tasted in 2002): Transparent, medium black-red, tiling at the edge; cherries and orange peel on the nose; black cherry, pepper, anise, and a hint of leather in the mouth; medium-weight and medium-length, with the texture of rough silk.

1995 Anderson Valley (tasted in 2001): Medium terra-cotta red; aromas of leather and geranium; slightly sweet in the mouth, with a minerality suggestive of wet slate, and hints of orange peel and orange blossom; medium-weight and fairly long, attractive and lingering flavors.

1995 Estate Reserve (tasted twice in 2001): Transparent but dark black-red; leather, black fruits, caramel, coffee, and pipe tobacco; some tart blueberry and a hint of lemon peel on the finish; medium-weight and medium-length.

1991 Anderson Valley (tasted in 2001): Transparent, medium garnet, tiling at the rim; ample nose of leather, licorice, flower petals, and cherry; sweet licorice and red fruits with a kiss of soft, sweet spice in the mouth; evolved and elegant; light- to medium-weight and medium-length, exceptional balance and charm.

PRACTICAL INFORMATION

Handley pinots are available in most markets, though the reserve and the offbeat Cuvée Primo may be easier to acquire directly from the winery. Handley's tasting room, unusually decorated with folk art the family has collected around the world, is an attractive, modern facility with fabulous views of rolling vineyard and ample picnic facilities. It is set on the highway west of Philo and is open daily; 800-733-3151.

HANZELL VINEYARDS

Sonoma, California

Hanzell occupies 200 acres in the foothills of the Mayacamas Range above Boyes Hot Springs to the west and Sonoma to the south. Often described as a "jewel" or "millionaire's plaything," Hanzell gives the impression of a well-manicured estate dedicated to gracious living, where the owners just happened to plant a few acres of vines. The winery building was explicitly modeled on a courtyard facade in Burgundy's Clos de Vougeot. Without this referent, it resembles an elegant small barn, its entrances turned discreetly away from the "farm" and residence. James D. Zellerbach, a San Francisco forest products magnate, acquired this property in 1952, preceding his appointment as United States ambassador to Italy, both to serve as a country home and as a venue for his aspirations to produce in California chardonnay and pinot noir as good as Burgundy's.

Zellerbach planted the first eight acres of vines and built the handsome wood and stone winery, which was designed with the assistance of his first winemaker, former Gallo researcher Brad Webb. A half-century later, it is hard not to be amazed by Zellerbach's and Webb's radical departures from the prevailing principles of winemaking and winery design. Save for an initial uphill pump from the crushpad to the fermentors, the winery is largely gravity-flow. A row of small, shallow, rectangular, temperature-controlled stainless steel fermentors (custom-made for Zellerbach by a foundry in Fresno) meets virtually all the requirements of today's exacting maker of small-lot pinot. Zellerbach and Webb made space for a "cellar" of French oak barrels on the ground floor, following the example of Martin Ray, but leading by more than a decade nearly everyone else in California wine.

Zellerbach's original pinot vineyard sits on a saddle of land downhill from the winery. There were originally two blocks of pinot noir here, planted in 1953 and 1957, both using eight-foot intervals in arc-shaped 12-foot rows on a well-drained, mostly south-facing clay-loam slope that looks more fertile than it is in fact. The provenance of Hanzell's scion material is not entirely clear. In the most likely scenario, it is Mount Eden selection via the Stelling vineyard in Napa. In another version of the story, however, the budwood Hanzell took from Stelling is said to have come from the old Inglenook planting in St. Helena via the university's experimental vineyard at Oakville. The vineyard was dry-farmed until the mid 1970s, when drought conditions led to the installation of drip irrigation. The 1957 block was replanted to chardonnay in 1998, but the 1953 block is still in production for pinot. (This 4.04-acre block is believed to be the second-oldest producing pinot vineyard in North America—only the 1946 block at Chalone is older.) In 1976, a second pinot vineyard—named de Brye in honor of Hanzell's new owners post-1973—was planted on another south-facing slope east of the original blocks. Budwood was taken from the 1953 and 1957 blocks for de Brye, but the row spacing was tightened to ten feet by eight. Most recently, a third planting of pinot, called Sessions Vineyard, has been developed near the property's eastern edge, on an east-facing slope overlooking Norrbom Road. There the vine spacing has been tightened again, this time to six-foot intervals in eight-foot rows, and only part of the budwood was taken from the older blocks. The rest of this vineyard is dedicated to "experiments" with a variety of California field selections, Davis clones, and Dijon clones. Some fruit was harvested from Sessions Vineyard in 2001, and was being evaluated at the time of this writing. Yield from the mature blocks ranges from one (for the 1953 block) to two tons per acre.

On the whole, Sonoma Valley is better known for cabernet and zinfandel than for pinot noir, and much of the valley is believed to be too warm for pinot. But Hanzell, close to the valley's southern end, is ventilated with some marine air from Los Carneros and the Petaluma Gap, and cooled a bit by its 800 feet of altitude. Daytime high temperatures several degrees cooler than on the western side of Los Carneros are not unusual. Overnight lows during the summer average in the low 60s. No one knows now whether mesoclimatic considerations were an important criterion in Zellerbach's choice of site, but harvest dates at Hanzell are not much earlier than for most of Carneros, and the fruit attains good physiological ripeness at approximately 25 degrees Brix. Sessions thinks the site may have been cooler 50 years ago than it is now—he remembers two substantial snows in the 1970s but only the lightest dusting in the 1990s. The same "global warming" observation has been made about other parts of Napa and Sonoma.

If the Hanzell story is remarkable in part for Zellerbach's and Webb's prescience and for Zellerbach's willingness to invest in expensive solutions at a time when there was little money in the California wine business, it is remarkable also for its historical continuities. Across three ownerships, the objectives have never changed and the scale of its operation has never been significantly expanded. Webb's association with Hanzell lasted almost 20 years. Ken Giles (who went on to the winemaking job at Mount Veeder Winery) and Tom Dehlinger represent a brief interregnum from 1967 through 1972, but then Bob Sessions, who had been the winemaker at Mayacamas Vineyards, signed on in 1973. In a consulting capacity, Webb overlapped with Sessions, transmitting methodological and stylistic parameters. Now Sessions's son Ben has assumed responsibility for sales and marketing, while Daniel Docher—a native of Clermont-Ferrand and 1986 graduate of the Ecole nationale d'ingénieurs des travaux agricoles de Bordeaux, who has worked at Hanzell since 1995—has been named winemaker. In his turn, Sessions is now consulting winemaker.

WINEMAKING

Bob Sessions reports that in his tenure at Hanzell, he experimented with virtually all known parameters for making pinot noir, but generally returned more or less to where he began, with the regime Zellerbach and Webb devised in the 1950s. The only real exception is the use now of between 15 percent and 20 percent whole clusters, which were avoided entirely at the outset but have been de rigueur since the late 1980s. At Hanzell, apart from the whole-cluster lots, pinot noir is crushed and pumped into the custom-designed, jacketed, one-ton rectangular fermentors, inoculated right away, and sometimes acidulated. The must is punched down by hand and fermented for seven to ten days at very cool temperatures—generally under 80 degrees Fahrenheit. The must is sometimes bled to increase concentration. Arguing that "the worst time to press is around dryness," Sessions usually presses with a bit of remaining sugar, but will sometimes permit a post-fermentation maceration instead "if the right flavors are lacking." Atypically, the new wine is not merely settled in tank but left there for at least the duration of the malolactic fermentation. There is no oak contact until the spring, summer, or even autumn after the vintage, when the wine is finally moved from tank to barrel.

The barrel regime is unusual and conservative. Barrels are almost 100 percent medium-toast *pièces* from Sirugue (Sessions says they give "a subtle complement to the wine"), 25 percent to 30 percent new, and used until they are three-plus years old. The pinot spends a full two years in barrel, is rarely racked except at bottling, is sometimes fined "to take the edge off," and put through a coarse pad filter. Another 12 months of bottle-aging precede release, which occurs about three and a half years after the vintage.

THE WINES

A single release of pinot noir, always the product of barrel selection with deselected lots sold off, and always made entirely from estate fruit, has been produced every year since 1956. The sole exceptions are the 1963 and 1964 vintages, which (following Zellerbach's death in 1963) were sold, via an intermediary, to Joe Heitz, who bottled them as Heitz Cellars Pinot Noir. Hanzell pinots are curiously controversial. In the 1960s and 1970s, the wines enjoyed considerable acclaim and sold out quickly to waiting connoisseurs, but the Vintners Club tasting notes from the period 1973 to 1987 are by no means universally complimentary. Some observers say the wines declined in the 1980s; others argue that they were simply eclipsed by the emergence of newer cult wines. Occasionally, they are described as "portlike," which comparison may contain an element of truth—if the reference is to the aromatic properties of very fine, 20-year tawny. The Hanzell pinots I have tasted, including a substantial selection of older vintages, have been consistently rewarding. They display medium to deep color and complex flavors and aromas, and they age very slowly. Mineral flavors are often more dominant than fruit, though some tasters believe that the wines of the 1990s have been more fruit-driven than earlier vintages. Sessions likes to say, and puts it well, that "fruit is just sharing the space" with other properties in the wines. The 1965 and 1966 vintages, tasted in 2002, testify eloquently to the structure and age-worthiness of these exceptional wines.

TASTING NOTES

1998 Sonoma Valley (tasted in 2002): Transparent, medium black-red; aromas of tobacco, mushroom, and black cherry; tar, earth, black licorice, evergreen, and black pepper in the mouth; medium-weight, concentrated, chewy, grippy, and tannic, emery-textured and very long.

1997 Sonoma Valley (tasted twice, in 2001 and 2002): Transparent, medium red with faint terra-cotta highlights; nose of rose petal and potpourri, with some black cherry and blackberry fruit; leather, licorice, chocolate, slate, and briar in the mouth; vanilla from the cooperage; slightly tannic, concentrated and grippy, long.

1994 Sonoma Valley (tasted in 2002): Transparent, medium black-red; nose of rose petal and black fruits; tobacco, earth, forest floor, evergreen, tree bark, clove, and black pepper on the palate; medium-weight, concentrated and grippy, emery-textured and long.

1991 Sonoma Valley (tasted in 2002): Transparent, medium black-red, tiling at the rim; aromas of black licorice and leather; earth, tobacco, clove, and merbromin, with some dried leaves on the palate; medium-weight, full-bodied and slightly grippy, long and emery-textured. The youngest vintage to show substantial evolution during a vertical tasting in 2002.

1990 Sonoma Valley (tasted in 2002): Color like the 1991; nose of black tea; blackberry, earth, meat, leather, tree bark, black pepper, and smoke in the mouth; full-bodied and grippy, but medium-weight, long, with a suedelike finish.

1989 Sonoma Valley (tasted in 2002): Color again like the 1991; aromas of rose petals, bay leaves, and mothballs; dominant black fruits with earth, tobacco, black pepper, and smoke on the palate; medium-weight, concentrated and grippy, emery-textured.

1986 Sonoma Valley (tasted in 2002): Transparent, medium black-red, now tiling; camphor, mint, and mothballs on the nose; characteristic tobacco, earth, and black pepper joined with tar and clove; concentrated and still grippy, finishes long.

1984 Sonoma Valley (tasted in 2002): Transparent, dark black-red with highlights of terra-cotta; big, explosive nose of cinnamon, black pepper, wet slate, and smoke with hints of black licorice and vintage port; very mineral in the mouth, with deep earth tones, spicy raspberries, and some barrel char; still grippy, with a texture alternating between fine emery and velvet, long, fine.

1981 Sonoma Valley (tasted in 2002): Transparent, medium terra-cotta; aromas of dried leaves, camphor, and shoe polish; briar, smoke, earth, forest floor, black licorice, black pepper, and clove on the palate; medium-weight, full-bodied, and concentrated, medium-long and suede-textured.

1980 Sonoma Valley (tasted in 2001): Transparent, deeply colored, blood-red center, tiling rim, almost mahogany; flavors and aromas of leather, tobacco, cinnamon, earth, and mushroom; slate, chocolate, and tree bark in the mouth; kirschwasser on the finish; very mature with still a bit of tannic grip, complex, and long.

1979 Sonoma Valley (tasted in 2002): Transparent, medium terra-cotta; uncharacteristic nose hinting of nuts and funk; black raspberry, cherry, tea, tobacco, earth, black pepper, and leather in the mouth; medium-weight, concentrated and chewy, long and velvety.

1976 Sonoma Valley (tasted in 2002): Uncharacteristically dark color, splitting the difference between garnet and terra-cotta; hint of prune and dried currants on the nose; a slightly sweet mouth tasting of blackberry jam, cola, tar, earth, and leather; some tree bark; medium-weight, concentrated and chewy, long and velvety.

1966 Sonoma Valley (tasted in 2002): Transparent, dark, blackish tile; aromas of dried leaves, forest floor, black fruits, and cola; licorice, iodine, white pepper, and clove, plus char; medium-weight, full, and chewy, sweet and concentrated, long and suedelike.

1965 Sonoma Valley (tasted in 2002): Transparent, medium to dark tile; aromas of Tootsie Roll, toffee, and roasted nuts; cola and black tea join tobacco, mushroom, earth, clove, pepper, and chocolate in the mouth; slightly sweet and chewy, long and suedelike. A personal favorite.

PRACTICAL INFORMATION

Pinot noir accounts for one-third of Hanzell's total production, or about 1,000 cases. It is nationally distributed, sold at the winery, and available by mailing list. There is no dedicated hospitality staff at this tiny operation, so visits are by appointment only; 800-393-4999.

HARTFORD FAMILY WINERY

Forestville, California

Hartford Family Winery (which did business as Hartford Court until 1999) was created in 1994 by Don Hartford. Hartford is the son of strawberry farmers in western Massachusetts; he once taught English as a second language in Spain, and then practiced law in San Jose, San Francisco, and Tokyo. He came to wine through the law and by marriage: his wife, Jennifer, is Jess Jackson's daughter. Don, Jennifer, and Jennifer's sister Laura Jackson-Giron own Hartford Family Winery, which is supported by Jackson Family Farms, an independent marketing, public relations, and vineyard management company established in 2000 by Jackson *père.* Jackson Family Farms also provides management support to Cambria in Santa Maria and Edmeades in Anderson Valley and is run separately from Kendall-Jackson Wine Estates Ltd., Jess Jackson's large, international, multilabel, multitier business widely known as K-J.

Hartford Family Winery's first winemaker was Dan Goldfield (see the Dutton-Goldfield Wines profile), who had entered the Jackson wine universe when Kendall-Jackson acquired the undercapitalized but Burgundy-oriented La Crema Winery in 1993. When Goldfield left to create his own label in 1997, he was succeeded briefly by Bob Cabral, who left to take the winemaking reins at Williams Selyem. In his turn, Cabral was succeeded by Mike Sullivan, a winemaker trained at California State University, Fresno, with experience at DeLoach, Chappellet, and Landmark, who had served briefly at La Crema before moving to the Hartford Family Winery in 1998. Hartford Family Winery, from the outset, was oriented to tiny lots of very high-end, single-vineyard pinots and chardonnays, made under the Hartford Court label. The winery also makes blended zinfandels, chardonnays, and a single pinot noir that are labeled Hartford *tout court.* For the record, La Crema, both before and after its acquisition by Jackson, has remained focused on rather larger quantities of pinot and chardonnay, blended into regional wines sporting the Russian River, Sonoma Coast, and Anderson Valley appellations. Some fruit sources originally contracted to La Crema were also transferred to the Hartford labels, notably the 25-year-old Arrendell Vineyard on Atascadero Creek northwest of Sebastopol, which Hartford purchased outright in 1997. The production facility is a newish, rambling building on Martinelli Lane in the heart of Green Valley that was originally built (but never really used) by Domaine Laurier.

In 1999, Hartford Court produced a total of approximately 2,400 cases of six single-vineyard pinot noirs from parcels in Mendocino, Sonoma, and Marin counties, as well as from the Napa side of Los Carneros. Production of the Hartford blended pinot amounted to about 4,000 cases. The winery owns two of the parcels used in the single-vineyard program: the aforementioned Arrendell, a cold, low-lying site planted to Martini clone, where frost alarms have been known to sound in August; and the Carneros vineyard, called Sevens Bench in honor of the 667 and 777 Dijon clones tightly planted there, on the eastern side of Duhig Road opposite Robert Mondavi. The other wines depend on purchased fruit, including a section of the Savoy Vineyard in Anderson Valley that Hartford Court calls Velvet Sisters; Devil's Gulch near Nicasio in Marin County, a marginal site situated about 900 feet above sea level and planted to Mount Eden selection; Warren Dutton's Sanchietti Vineyard, just upslope from Arrendell; and a cool, late-ripening parcel south of Sebastopol that was used in 1998 and 1999 to make a wine called Jennifer's, named in honor of Don's wife and partner. Jennifer's is a single-vineyard wine in fact, though it carries a proprietary name. The scion material is a combination of UCD 2A, UCD 23, and Dijon 115. Hartford Court has also purchased and planted (entirely to pinot noir) a large parcel near Annapolis in the true Sonoma Coast, due to begin bearing in 2004.

The business plan for Hartford Family Winery calls for increasing production of the single-vineyard wines to a total of approximately 4,000 cases by 2005 (roughly 400 cases each of ten wines) and to about 5,000 cases of the Hartford blend. Hartford and Sullivan believe the greatest growth potential for the single-vineyard wines lies in Russian River and on the extreme Sonoma Coast, where they are acquiring and planting vineyard whenever opportunity knocks. Hartford has already planted pinot near Annapolis, south of Jenner near Coastlands, on Harrison Ridge Road on the western edge of the Russian River Valley appellation, on Piner Road west of Santa Rosa, and on Ross Road northwest of Sebastopol, overlooking Iron Horse. The first harvest from the Ross Road property was made in 2002.

WINEMAKING

Hartford Family Winery emphasizes low yields, which Sullivan defines as a maximum of four pounds per vine, and *terroirs* that are distinctive expressions of site. Fruit is hand sorted both in the vineyard and at the winery to remove both botrytis and sunburn. Uncharacteristically, Sullivan also insists on good aesthetic appearance: "If you wouldn't eat it, we don't use it," he says. The fruit is completely destemmed and all stems discarded. Four- and six-ton fermentors are used. A long, eight- to ten-day cold soak is practiced, with a combination of cooling jackets and dry ice used to ensure that the must temperature remains at 50 degrees Fahrenheit. Alcoholic fermentations are allowed to begin with resident yeast. Some cuvées, like Sevens Bench, escape without any inoculation; others are inoculated in the interest of obtaining "higher-toned fruit," but Sullivan does not believe that yeasts are a hugely significant choice in winemaking. Fermentation temperature is generally capped at 85 to 90 degrees "to avoid volatilizing too many esters." Punchdowns continue throughout the cold soak and fermentation phases. Pressing, using a Marzola basket press, can occur at approximately 2 or 3 degrees Brix, or when the must is dry. Until the 2000 vintage, the press juice was discarded; the post-2000 regimen involves wait and see.

Depending on vintage, between 30 percent and 70 percent new barrels are used, and Sullivan seeks to avoid "aromas of butterscotch, vanilla, and soot." Barrels are sourced from a wide selection of coopers, including François Frères, Billon, Séguin Moreau, Cadus, and Remond, as well as Latour for the Jennifer's bottling. Velvet Sisters spends 11 months in barrel; other wines stay in barrel for 13 months. Very small lots are racked just once before bottling; larger lots are racked twice. The wines are neither fined nor filtered.

THE WINES

My experience with Hartford Court pinots is limited to the 1999 vintage, tasted in-bottle but prerelease in 2000, and the 2000 vintage, tasted a year after release, in 2003. The 1999 wines were big, highly extracted, tannic, and nearly opaque. The 2000s showed rather differently, displaying tamer tannins, medium weights, and greater charm. The differences certainly reflect the vintages in part, along with an additional 18 months of bottle-aging, but some winemaking changes may also be at work. Sullivan argues that the size of his wines is dictated by the fruit (he says that Jennifer's, the most enormous of the wines, is made with "the least extractive technique"), but there is also a house style at work, imposed by very ripe picking, an unusually long cold soak, and a clear preference for fruit sources that have the capability to yield saturated wines. In addition to the vineyard-designated wines (and Jennifer's), all of which are bottled under the Hartford Court name, the winery makes a blended pinot noir called Hartford Sonoma Coast from estate and non-estate fruit.

TASTING NOTES

2000 Arrendell Vineyard (tasted in 2003): Brilliant, medium-deep black-red with rose highlights; earth and floral aromatics; cherry and allspice in the mouth; sweet, full-flavored, and substantial but still medium-weight and medium-length, slightly grippy on the finish but evolving toward velvety texture.

2000 Marin (tasted in 2003): Nearly saturated, deep magenta; explosive nose of ripe plums and beetroot, with hints of mint and toast; black fruit, fir balsam, more mint, and barrel char in the mouth; sweet and rich, medium-long and warm, with the texture of rough silk.

2000 Sevens Bench Vineyard (tasted in 2003): Saturated, deep ruby; fading rich rose and ripe plum aromas, with a hint of grilled fennel; very sweet in the mouth with cherry and pepper; nearly viscous, mouthcoating, slightly grapey, and long, with a bit of grip at the end.

2000 Velvet Sisters Vineyard (tasted in 2003): Transparent, medium garnet; cherry, raspberry, and potpourri on the nose; intense, high-toned fruit, graphite, and black pepper on the palate; structured, slightly granular, medium-weight, and long, with a texture similar to raw silk.

1999 Arrendell Vineyard (tasted prerelease in 2000): Dense, opaque wine; nose of evergreen, thyme, and wild berries; resin and tar in the mouth, with overtones of stick cinnamon and clove; quite tannic.

1999 Dutton Ranch—Sanchietti Vineyard (tasted prerelease in 2000): Again, dark and dense; blueberries, cola, mint, and resin on the nose and palate, with notes of sandalwood; extremely tannic, texture of burlap.

1999 Jennifer's (tasted prerelease in 2000): Opaque, nearly purple and a visual ringer for syrah; wild berries, boysenberries, cola, cinnamon, and chocolate; very sweet, tannic, and massive.

1999 Marin (tasted prerelease in 2000): Dense, nearly opaque, black-red wine; blackberry, mirabelle plum, and cola; very sweet; some earth, clove, and cedar; rather tannic, but the finish is velvety.

1999 Sevens Bench (tasted prerelease in 2000): Dense, opaque, black-red wine; aromas of raspberry; roasted coffee bean, burnt caramel, pomegranate, and cola on the palate; huge fruit core; appealing velvet texture, least tannic of the 1999s.

1999 Velvet Sisters Vineyard (tasted prerelease in 2000): Barely transparent, very black wine; explosive nose of violets and brown sugar; cola and resin on the palate; some licorice; midpalate sweetness; long, warm finish.

PRACTICAL INFORMATION

Eighty-five percent of Hartford Family Winery's small production is sold in California; to five major national markets; and to the

United Kingdom, Switzerland, Canada, and Japan. Direct sales to a mailing list and to Web site customers account for the other 15 percent. A tasting room opened in 2002 and can be visited seven days a week; 707-887-1756.

HUSCH VINEYARDS

Philo, California

When Tony Husch, a Harvard-educated urban planner, bought a 60-acre ranch in Anderson Valley in 1968, he retreated symbolically from the city to the land. When he then planted eight of the 60 acres to gewürztraminer, chardonnay, and pinot noir, he unleashed a slow but remarkably durable revolution. Except for Donald Edmeades's earlier block of gewürztraminer, these were the first plantings of the grape varieties destined to make the reputation of Anderson Valley. Three years later, having decided to make wine from his own grapes, he established Anderson Valley's first bonded winery and made its first estate-bottled wine.

Across 30 vintages, most of Husch's 1968 block of pinot has remained in production, used exclusively for varietally designated, estate-bottled pinot noir. Since Husch himself sold the business in 1979, much of the credit for this remarkable consistency goes to Hugo Oswald Jr., a Williams College graduate who married into a pear-farming business in California's Santa Clara Valley in the 1950s, and subsequently relocated to Ukiah when the area around Santa Clara became nearly paved with housing tracts and silicon. Oswald purchased Husch, consolidated its operations with his La Ribera Ranch in Talmage, and then invested repeatedly in facilities and additional land. Husch was his own winemaker at the outset; Al White, now the vineyard manager, made the 1979 vintage; Hugo Oswald's son H. A. Oswald III was responsible for 1980 through 1983; Mark Thies served as winemaker from 1984 through 1994. Fritz Meier, with the unusual (for America) background of Geisenheim training in enology, joined Thies as assistant winemaker in 1987 and was named winemaker in 1994. Meier was succeeded, in July 2001, by Zachary Rasmuson, a graduate of St. John's University in Maryland and a veteran of Stag's Leap Wine Cellars and Robert Sinskey Vineyards. Although pinot noir accounts for only about 15 percent of Husch's total production, it is the main product made in the Anderson Valley facility and, along with gewürztraminer, gets most of Rasmuson's attention. Husch's sauvignon blanc and chardonnay are made at the La Ribera facility.

The original estate vineyard on the Nunn Ranch, halfway between Philo and Navarro, was planted on a modest south-facing slope, rising up from the northeastern bank of the Navarro River. Known in-house simply as Husch, this site consists of three blocks originally planted with scion material from Wente's Arroyo Seco vineyard. Interplanting with Dijon 667 began in 2001. The uppermost block, called Knoll, is planted on the best-drained, shallow, shale-laden soil. A second block, unimaginatively called Middle, occupies a steeper portion of the site. The third block, called Meadow, has been withdrawn from the pinot program and replanted to chardonnay. From 1988 through the mid 1990s, 22 additional acres of pinot were planted on the nearby Day Ranch after this property was acquired by Hugo's son Ken Oswald. Here, the Apple Hill (1.6 acres) and East (2.8 acres) blocks were planted to UCD 15; Highway block (four acres) to UCD 16; Main block (10.1 acres) to a combination of UCD 13 and 15; and Tony's block to UCD 32. (Tony's bears no relation to Tony Husch; it takes its name from Tony Sanchez, the Day Ranch foreman.) The average yield on these blocks is about five tons per acre, which is high for Anderson Valley.

Day Ranch fruit made its first appearance in Husch pinot with the 1991 vintage. Gradually, as the crop increased and pinot noir production could grow from about 500 cases to more than 4,000, Day Ranch fruit came to dominate Husch's main bottling, called simply Anderson Valley. In 1992, Meier introduced a second bottling, called Reserve. Through the 1990s, the Reserve sponged up most of the fruit from the old estate vineyard. Interestingly, despite the higher yield on the Day Ranch and the quite different clonal mix, the Anderson Valley wine, tasted in 2001, does not seem to have departed radically from its historic roots. "Only time will tell," Meier said in 2000, "how much different *terroirs* impact the wines." Meanwhile, effective with the 1999 vintage, the reserve program has been abandoned in favor of two block-designated wines: one from the Knoll block on the old Husch estate, and another from the Apple Hill block on Day Ranch. Both of these wines were made in 1999 and 2001; in 2000 the Knoll block did not distinguish itself, so Apple Hill was the only block-designated wine made that year.

An ownership change in 2003 separated the winery and Tony Husch's original plantings from the Day Ranch. Beginning with this vintage, the winery will supplement its historic Husch and Day Ranch sources for the Anderson Valley cuvée with fruit from the Ferrington and Wiley vineyards, and will return the Reserve rubric to designating a barrel-selection of estate lots, primarily from the Knoll block.

WINEMAKING

Meier liked to pick for seed maturity. The seeds, he said, should "taste nutty" before the grapes are picked. Fermentations are done in fruit bins. About 5 percent whole clusters are layered on the bottom of each bin; whole and crushed berries go on top. After 24 hours, each bin is inoculated with one of three laboratory yeasts, and punchdowns are done by hand. The must is pressed when sugars near zero, and the hard press fraction is discarded or used for generic red wine. Rather than go directly to barrel like most pinot makers, Meier preferred to finish the primary fermentation—and the malolactic fermentation—in stainless steel tanks, where he also established the blends. Rasmuson has modified this practice, effective with the 2001 vintage. The wine is now settled for three to five days after pressing, and malolactic fermentations are done in barrel. The Anderson Valley bottling spends nine to ten months in barrel; the block-designates, like the Reserve before them, spend 18. The wines are then racked back to tank, blended again, filtered with diatomaceous earth, and bottled.

The coopers of choice are Bouchard, Cadus, and François Frères. Historically, 50 percent new oak was used for the Reserve and between 17 percent and 20 percent for the Anderson Valley wine; at the time of writing, these figures were to increase to about 60 percent for the block-designates and 30 percent to 35 percent for the Anderson Valley beginning in 2001. Barrels are used until they are four or five years old.

THE WINES

Husch pinots are generally understated, medium-weight, elegant wines that do not always show well in their youth but age faithfully and gracefully. In general, their texture is more silky than plush. The Reserve (and now the vineyard-designates) is distinguished from the Anderson Valley bottling by somewhat greater weight and softer mouthfeel, along with a core of sweeter fruit. All Husch pinots exhibit great complexity, which increases with a few years of bottle-aging. Meier believed (and I agree) that Husch pinots do not "come together" until they are five to seven years old, though prerelease tastings of the 1999 and 2000 block-designated wines were very impressive. In a vertical tasting early in 2001 of 17 vintages between 1979 and 1998, only one wine was in serious decline, and vintages as old as 1982 were showing wonderfully.

TASTING NOTES

2000 Anderson Valley (tasted in 2003): Brilliant medium garnet; intense nose of cedar and spice; cherry, clove, black pepper, and fir balsam in the mouth; bright flavors with soft tannins; almost satin with a bit of very fine emery, medium-weight and quite long.

2000 Apple Hill Vineyard (tasted prerelease in 2002): Transparent, medium magenta with ruby highlights; earth, coffee, caramel, black fruit, and dried roses on the nose; cherry, blackberry, fragrant black pepper, and some hard spice in the mouth; elegant, medium-weight and medium-length, with a hint of graphite on a silken finish.

1999 Anderson Valley (tasted in 2003): Brilliant, medium ruby with rose highlights; aromas of dried petals, dried leaves, and toasted spices; sweet on the palate, with cherry, smoke, earth, and allspice; some grip, rather like rough velvet; medium-weight.

1999 Apple Hill Vineyard (tasted in 2002): Brilliant, medium garnet with terra-cotta highlights; earth, herbs, and a hint of nuts on the nose; dark cherry, blackberry, tar, clove, and black pepper on the palate, with suggestions of mocha, infused flowers, and rose water; intense, concentrated, persistent, and long, medium-weight, texture of rough silk.

1999 Knoll (tasted prerelease in 2002): Brilliant, medium black-red with crimson highlights; earth, ink, dark spice, and black fruit on the nose with a hint of bay laurel; huge and velvety in the mouth, with black fruit flavors, resin, tar, clove, barrel char, black pepper, and graphite; unwraps slowly, finishes long and very slightly grippy. A personal favorite.

1998 Anderson Valley (tasted in 2001): Transparent, light to medium black-red; black cherry and leather nose; black fruits, mint, and black pepper on the palate; medium-weight, linen-textured.

1997 Anderson Valley (tasted in 2001): Transparent, light black-red; slightly closed; rose petals on the nose; cherry in the midpalate, tobacco at the end; medium-weight, silken.

1996 Anderson Valley (tasted in 2001): Transparent, medium black-red; closed again; sweet, cherry-dominated midpalate; mint and herbs; slightly tannic, medium-weight.

1995 Anderson Valley (tasted in 2001): Very transparent, medium ruby with a hint of terra-cotta at the edge; leather, earth, and olive on the nose; some smoke and bacon, also licorice; slightly tannic, texture spanning velvet and linen, long.

1994 Anderson Valley (tasted in 2001): Very transparent, light garnet; very leathery nose; sweet cherry and black fruit midpalate; some licorice; silken.

1993 Anderson Valley (tasted in 2001): Transparent, medium black-red tinged with terra-cotta; evolved nose of leather and animal; more leather, tree bark, earth, and slate in the mouth, with hints of both chocolate and vanilla; sinuous, silken, high-glycerol wine. Very fine.

1991 Anderson Valley (tasted in 2001): Transparent, but darker than the 1993, again with a hint of terra-cotta; leather and a touch of prune on the nose; sweet, almost chewy mouth of plummy, cherry fruit; mint, earth, clove, and vanilla; unusually rich for Husch, velvety, long.

1990 Anderson Valley (tasted in 2001): Very transparent, red and terra-cotta; nose of rose petals and leather; then notes of ripe fruit, raisins, earth, and chocolate; texturally rich like the 1991, but lighter-weight and more elegant.

1989 Anderson Valley (tasted in 2001): Light

red robe, tiling at the edges; flavors and aromas of leather, earth, and black pepper; finishes with caramel; slightly angular but long, linen-textured.

1988 Anderson Valley (tasted in 2001): Ruby-terra-cotta color; earth, herbs, and caramel nose; milk chocolate in the mouth; linen-textured, very long.

1987 Anderson Valley (tasted in 2001): Very evolved terra-cotta color; animal, forest floor, cardamomlike sweet spices; hint of mint at the finish; medium-weight.

1986 Anderson Valley (tasted in 2001): Light to medium terra-cotta with some bright red at the core; coffee and leather aromas; very sweet, mouthfilling midpalate; finishes with tobacco and black pepper; very long and very fine.

1985 Anderson Valley (tasted in 2001): Medium terra-cotta color; nose of raisins and prunes; thinning, tart wine with now-naked tannins; in decline.

1983 Anderson Valley (tasted in 2001): Transparent, medium terra-cotta; leather and resin with a hint of raisin; very open and evolved; tree bark and bitter spice on the finish; medium-weight.

1982 Anderson Valley (tasted in 2001): Transparent, medium red and terra-cotta; nose of leather and caramel; lots of tar and resin in the mouth; rich, long, elegant. Very fine.

1980 Anderson Valley (tasted in 2001): Dark, black-red wine, slightly browning; dense and barely transparent; nose of bay leaf and herbs; dried apricots and tar; huge wine, still tannic. What is going on here? The answer: in this vintage, some cabernet sauvignon press juice was added to beef up the pinot!

1979 Anderson Valley (tasted in 2001): Again dense, red and terra-cotta; raisin, tar; still unresolved tannins, very long. Another instance of doctoring with cabernet press.

PRACTICAL INFORMATION

Husch pinots are nationally distributed, though the new block-designated wines will be found more easily at the winery. A tasting room occupies the repurposed sheep shed where Tony Husch established Anderson Valley's first bonded winery back in 1969. Located on Highway 128 just west of Philo, the tasting room is open daily; 800-554-8724.

IRON HORSE VINEYARDS

Sebastopol, California

Iron Horse sits astride Green Valley Creek about eight miles north of Sebastopol, far removed from most other stirrings in the Russian River valley until the 1990s. The ranch was "discovered" in 1971 by Rodney Strong, whose Windsor Vineyards brand secured an option to buy it. Strong tapped Forrest Tancer, a Berkeley graduate who had grown up on a farm and vineyard in the Alexander Valley and learned winemaking on the job at Windsor Vineyards, to redevelop the ranch as vineyard. When Windsor Vineyards was caught in the general recession and wine bust of the mid 1970s and was unable to exercise its option, Iron Horse was put up for sale. Barry Sterling, an attorney with an international practice in Los Angeles and Paris, and his wife, Audrey, who had previously considered purchasing a château in the Haut-Médoc, heard about the offering at a dinner party in Los Angeles. Despite a driving winter rainstorm, their first visit to Iron Horse was, it is said, love at first sight. The Sterlings bought the ranch and hired Tancer, who became their vineyardist, winemaker, and eventually partner. Vineyard totaling 100 acres, evenly divided between chardonnay and pinot noir, was partially replanted, comprehensively trellised, and provided with sophisticated irrigation. The rest of the story is very engagingly told by the Sterlings' daughter Joy in her 1993 book, *A Cultivated Life.* Relocated to Sonoma from an early career in broadcast journalism, Joy Sterling turned her own talents to marketing and public relations for the winery. In 1990, she and Tancer were married.

The great majority of Iron Horse's estate-grown grapes go into very fine sparkling wine, on which the reputation of the brand has been built. There is also a crisp, elegant still chardonnay. (Warm-climate varieties grown on Tancer's T-T Ranch in Alexander Valley, marked "proprietor-grown," are also made and bottled as Iron Horse wines.) Throughout the 1980s, Tancer experimented with small lots of still pinot noir. The 1980 has a legendary reputation in the family, and those made in 1985, 1986, 1987, and 1988 from a rocky, low-yielding knoll near the winery building called Block G are said to have been especially good. In 1985, hopes for a new generation of still pinot were pinned on the south-facing slope of a butte about a quarter-mile northeast of the winery. This so-called Block Q—which from the winery looks like the back of an armadillo—is a magnificent 3.5-acre site overlooking Green Valley Creek where the Sterlings' son Laurence had once imagined building a house. Tancer selected UCD 5 from the Adelsheim Vineyard in Oregon for Q and, following the style of the mid 1980s, planted about 800 vines to the acre. Unlike the rest of the Iron Horse vineyard, which is very friable Goldridge soils, Block Q is Josephine soil, weathered from a geologically older material, once uplifted from seabed, that is richer both in iron and in clay. From the outset, Block Q demanded patience; the vines were slow to become established there. It also displays a propensity for angular, high-tannin wines. Nonetheless, in 1995, the Iron Horse Estate pinot was made entirely from Block Q.

At the end of the 1980s, as part of a short-lived joint venture with the French champagne firm of Laurent Perrier, pinot was also planted in declining apple orchard along Thomas Road, on the high western side of the ranch. These plantings of UCD 13, known around Iron Horse as the P blocks, were originally intended for the production of sparkling wine. Surprisingly, the P blocks have now become Iron Horse's main source for still pinot. In the late summer of 1996, when Tancer and newly arrived winemaker David Munksgard walked the vineyard, they observed that especially tight clusters of small berries seemed to dominate in the P6 block, and that the berries were especially tasty, which seemed to them auspicious for a still-wine project. A quick review of the contract with Laurent Perrier having revealed no obstacle to the use of Block P fruit for still wine, they dedicated half of the 1996 P6 crop to this end. This fruit produced the inaugural vintage of Iron Horse's first block-designated pinot, the Thomas Road cuvée.

Pleased with the Thomas Road wine and then also liberated by the demise of the joint venture with Laurent Perrier, the winemakers transferred *all* Block P production to the still pinot program in 1997. The 1997 Estate pinot was produced from blocks P2, P7, P9, and part of P6, plus Block Q; the 1997 Thomas Road again came from the rest of P6. The methodology changed between 1996 and 1997, however: the 1996 was a vineyard-designate from the outset; the 1997 was a vineyard-designate in the end, but it developed from a reserve-program protocol. The winemakers chose their favorite barrels to make Thomas Road in 1997; it just happened, they report, that their chosen barrels were all from P6. It also just happened, they say, that the chosen barrels were all new, giving Thomas Road an especially smoky profile. In 1998, however, the reserve-program protocol produced a different result: the winemakers' preferred barrels included a few from Blocks P2 and P9 as well as P6 (P2 and P9 are vinified together because P9, less than one acre, is too small to ferment separately), so the 1998 Thomas Road became a blend of the three blocks. In most vintages, P6 produces exceptionally intense wine, and it is emerging as the anchor for the Thomas Road program.

In sum, from uneven beginnings in the 1980s, making as much as 800 cases in years when Mother Nature could be persuaded to cooperate to none at all in off years, Iron Horse has taken advantage of its new plantings to create an entirely new pinot program in the 1990s. There are now about 3,500 cases of regular estate pinot each year, plus a few hundred cases of Thomas Road. In 2000, a second block-designated wine debuted: the Corral Vineyard bottling made from Block N, southeast of the winery buildings. Each year, the blocks are made separately, and decisions about separate vineyard-designation are reserved until the very end. Of the 87 acres of pinot noir now planted at Iron Horse, about 20 are currently dedicated to still wine.

WINEMAKING

Deliberately experimenting to get better fruit expression, and to obtain soft tannins even in warm years when sugars spike up before the grapes are physiologically mature, Tancer and Munksgard adopted a new, untraditional, and decidedly interventionist protocol in 1997. Enough of "letting the wine make itself"—a proposition of which Munksgard disapproves. The new Iron Horse protocol is unabashedly manipulative: a long cold soak on the front end, then a low-temperature fermentation, pumpovers rather than punchdowns, and finally primary fermentations that finish in barrel, like chardonnay. Cold-water jacketing and layers of dry-ice pellets are used to make sure the grapes macerate for seven full days before the yeasts wake up, so that the extractive properties of water and acid, not alcohol, work first. On the seventh day, the must is heated and inoculated with laboratory yeast, and then fermented for about five days in closed tanks. A rack-and-return system is used to keep the must in contact with the skins during fermentation. During the pumpovers, the winemakers evaluate aromas and flavors. When the fermentation is between 70 percent and 80 percent complete, the juice is drawn off the skins and transferred to barrel, where the fermentation finishes in contact with wood. Fermentation temperature rarely exceeds 70 degrees Fahrenheit. Further intervention comes in the form of lees stirring and racking. The wines then spend upward of ten months in mostly new, medium-toast barrels with toasted heads from a variety of French coopers, of which Sansaud's cognac barrel is now the favorite. They are not fined, and only coarsely bug filtered before bottling.

Tancer argues that in California's environment of warmer weather and earlier harvest, a cold prefermentation maceration may simply mimic the cellar conditions that often occur naturally at harvesttime in Burgundy: fruit harvested in cool weather and brought into cold cellars under gray skies. But neither Tancer nor Munksgard has any interest in imitating Burgundy. "We have different fruit, and we are trying to do something different here," says Tancer.

THE WINES

Until 1996, Iron Horse produced only a single cuvée of pinot noir in each vintage, with the exception of a trickle of so-called Cuvée R, made intermittently in the 1980s. The fruit source for the Estate pinot changed, however, as Block Q and the various P blocks came onstream, and Block G, Tancer's favorite for still pinot in the mid 1980s, was returned to sparkling-wine production. From 1996 to 1998, Iron Horse made both an Estate pinot and a Thomas Road cuvée; in 1999 only an Estate pinot was made, and in 2000 a Corral Vineyard cuvée joined the Estate and Thomas Road duo. I have no experience with Iron Horse pinots before 1996. The 1996 debut vintage of the Thomas Road cuvée—an elegant, medium-weight wine that (in pinot-typical Jekyll and Hyde fashion) actually *gained* both weight and complexity four years after the vintage—was consistently a personal favorite, through multiple tastings, between 1997 and 2001. Since 1997, Iron Horse pinots have been a bit heavier and darker than the 1996 editions, with a more complex aromatic profile and more fruit-based juiciness.

TASTING NOTES

2000 Corral Vineyard (tasted twice, in 2001 and 2002): Transparent, medium black-red with amber highlights; in 2001 showing herbal aromas plus tea and toast, in 2002 a huge and distinctive nose of gingerbread, orange peel, musk, and flowers; black cherries, wet slate, and rose water in the mouth, with some barrel char and bay leaf; slightly grippy; medium-long, medium-weight, texture of fine emery.

2000 Estate (tasted in 2002): Very transparent, medium black-red; balsam, fir, mint, sassafras, and roses on the nose; evergreen and spearmint flavors in the mouth, with white pepper, raspberry, cherry, and a hint of cinnamon; medium-weight and medium-length, satin finish.

2000 Thomas Road (tasted in 2002): Transparent, medium ruby; aromas of very ripe cherries with hints of mocha and smoke; cherries, black licorice, cocoa, vanilla, and some soft spice on the palate; finishes simultaneously slightly sweet and slightly grippy, concentrated flavors, medium-weight, and suedelike texture.

1999 Estate (tasted in 2002): Brilliant, medium black-red with oxblood tones; slightly minty, cherry-fruit nose, with some meat, sausage, and shoe polish; cherry and infused flowers in the mouth, plus barrel char, Indonesian spice, black licorice, and roasted nuts; medium-weight and medium-length, silken finish.

1998 Estate (tasted in 2002): Transparent, medium black-red; high-toned floral aromas with slightly funky black fruit and a hint of mint; slightly sweet on the palate with black cherry, black fruits, graphite, black pepper, clove, and barrel char; some grip, concentrated, medium-weight and medium-length, the texture of rough, heavy upholstery silk.

1998 Thomas Road (tasted prerelease in 1999 and again in 2002): Dense and saturated prerelease; then very transparent, medium black-red with orange highlights in 2002; cherry, dried leaves, mixed spice, and smoke on the nose; sweet cherry and black fruits in the mouth, with notes of cinnamon, clove, and black licorice and a hint of cola; slightly grippy, full-bodied, medium-weight and medium-length, emerylike finish.

1997 Estate (tasted in 1999): Transparent, black-red; cherry, fruit candy, and cola; some menthol and resin; medium-weight and medium-length.

1997 Thomas Road (tasted in 1998 and 1999): Transparent, medium-dark black-red; lots of smoke on the nose; huge fruit and cherry candy on the palate; flavors of tar and eucalyptus. The winery chose to release this atypical high-alcohol, low-acid wine one full year later than normal.

1996 Thomas Road (tasted repeatedly in 1997, 1998, 1999, and 2001): Bright medium red color, very transparent; flavors of cherry and cherry cola (more cola as the wine matures), a light seasoning of cinnamon and allspice, markedly but pleasantly smoky from the medium-toast barrels; more weight and complex flavors with time; soft and silky. A personal favorite.

PRACTICAL INFORMATION
Iron Horse pinots are nationally distributed, but the vineyard-designated wines are more easily obtained directly from the winery. The site is spectacular, and an outdoor tasting "bar" is usually open in season, but it is best to call ahead during the off-season; 707-895-1507.

JOSEPH SWAN VINEYARDS

Forestville, California

Joseph Swan was a commercial pilot, amateur artist, avid reader, and the first boutique producer of estate-grown pinot noir in the Russian River valley. The son of teetotaler parents in North Dakota, he read about wine as a child and became fascinated. Swan's first "wine" was reportedly made from rhubarb crushed in the wringer of his mother's washing machine and fermented in a small crock that was hidden in the family's attic. Rather later, he is supposed to have made zinfandel in Utah, and to have planted a vineyard in the foothills of the Sierra Nevada. In 1967, at the age of 45, he bought a farm on Laguna Road in the Russian River valley: 13 acres of old zinfandel, some fruit trees and pasture, a barn, and a centenary house that had once housed the post office, telephone exchange, and general store for the now-extinct hamlet called Trenton. The property looked good to Swan. It looked as if it ought to be good for vineyard. It wasn't flat. And the soil was poor: one to three feet of decomposed sandstone surmounting bedrock.

Swan made wine from the existing zinfandel vines in 1968. In 1969, cognizant of the pioneer plantings at Bacigalupi and Rochioli and encouraged by his friend and mentor, André Tchelistcheff, he began replanting the dying zin vineyard to chardonnay and pinot noir. (Later he also planted a bit of cabernet sauvignon and cabernet franc. The cabernet sauvignon still exists, and has its fans.) The source of Swan budwood has been a matter of some dispute, since Swan is quoted variously by other growers who later obtained *their* cuttings from him; in fact, the wood almost certainly came from Martin Ray, albeit following an unlikely path. (This matter is covered in detail in chapter 5.)

Swan's first block of pinot, planted in 1969, was done in the fashion of the day, in 12-foot rows with six-foot intervine spacing, on a south-facing slope. A second block, south of the first but facing north, was planted in 1974 with slightly tighter six- by ten-foot spacing. The very shallow topsoil is the same Goldridge series that prevails across a large portion of Laguna Ridge, but here, near the northern edge of the formation, it forms an especially thin layer. In 1973, from the 1969 planting, Swan produced a pinot of legendary beauty. Those who had the chance to taste it in its prime say it had balance, elegance, and "Burgundian complexity." Along with the wine Davis Bynum (see the profile earlier in this section) made the same year from Joe Rochioli's fruit, it was a benchmark in the evolution of Russian River pinot noir.

Swan's models for Russian River pinot were always French. He traveled often to France and interviewed Burgundian vignerons exhaustively. He seems to have believed that "if it was French, it had to be good." Swan is said to have walked his vineyard whenever he received visitors from Burgundy; and if a knowledgeable visitor raised critical questions about the appearance of a particular vine, Swan immediately marked it for removal after harvest. Happily, he seems to have learned a number of good lessons from his French travels: a vineyard should be small enough that a single person could tend it; the winery should be small enough that one winemaker could maintain complete control; and low-production vines planted in low-vigor soil should be pruned and thinned rigorously. Swan's first vintages were made in the cellar of the old farmhouse, then in the adjacent barn. In 1974, Swan built the present winery building, which has come to be called "the tin shed." With only a few amenities added over time—wider doors, a lab, a bathroom, and a concrete crushpad in back—the tin shed is still in use.

Since Swan's death in 1989, winemaking has been in the hands of his son-in-law, Rod Berglund. Berglund, the founding winemaker at La Crema Vinera (now known as La Crema), who credits Swan as the inspiration for his choice of winemaking as a career, has kept faith with the founder on all basic matters: boutique size, consummate attention to the vineyard, and ceaseless experimentation. Swan, Berglund remembers, was "always thinking, always evolving." He has also expanded Swan's practice of purchasing fruit to make non-estate wines, including several non-estate pinots, and has begun the process of replanting the estate vineyard. In 1996, 3.5 of the 8.5 acres of pinot noir on the estate were replanted, using primarily the estate's own budwood, plus Dijon 113, 114, 115, 667, and 777. Vine spacing was dramatically tightened to one meter by two. It is too early to know how much the tighter spacing will increase the vineyard's notoriously parsimonious yield.

Other Swan vineyard-designated pinots have been made from Saralee's Vineyard and Lone Redwood Ranch in the Russian River valley, and from the Steiner and Wolfspierre vineyards on Sonoma Mountain. Saralee Kunde's eponymous vineyard, near the Sonoma County airport, is planted—for demonstration purposes and as a source of budwood—to no less than 100 grape varieties. Herculean farming measures are employed to compensate for a high water table. From 1996 through 1999, Berglund used just a single row of Dijon clone pinot vines from Saralee's—115, 667, and 777—that was originally planted in 1991 as pinot meunier and subsequently grafted. In 2000 he obtained additional fruit from other parts of the vineyard, including some Dijon 114 and Dijon 777, along with UCD 4 and 37. The 2001 edition also includes some UCD 29.

A vineyard-designated pinot was made from Lone Redwood Ranch fruit in 1995, 1997, and 1998. This vineyard, first planted to pinot in the 1960s, abuts the southern edge of the Sonoma County airport. Old-vines fruit was used exclusively to make the 1995 Lone Redwood, and a 50–50 blend of old vines and younger Dijon clones was used in 1997. In 1998 Berglund decided to rely entirely on a block of Dijon clones, which makes a deeper, darker, and richer wine.

Dave Steiner's wind-cooled, north-facing vineyard on Sonoma Mountain, overlooking Bennett Valley, was the source of fruit for a beautiful run of vineyard-designated Swan pinots from 1992 through 2000. The blocks earmarked for Swan were planted in 1989 in rocky, volcanic soil, using budwood from the Trenton Estate Vineyard.

In some vintages during the 1990s, when Berglund has found the wine from individual vineyards incomplete as stand-alone wine, he has also produced blended pinots. In 1994, there was a Sonoma Mountain pinot made from a combination of fruit from Steiner and neighboring Wolfspierre, just across Sonoma Mountain Road from the former. In 1996, Lone Redwood Ranch and Hopkins River Ranch (on Eastside Road in Middle Reach) fruit was blended to create a Russian River valley cuvée. In 1999, Berglund made a Cuvée de Trois from Saralee's and Lone Redwood fruit, plus the first crop from the young 1996 vines on the Trenton Estate Vineyard. A second edition of Cuvée de Trois was made in 2000, using the UCD 4 fruit from Saralee's, again the young-vines fruit from the estate, plus a small percentage of Steiner.

New sources will come on-line shortly. As of this writing, Berglund is working closely with the owners of spectacular land on the lower slopes of Black Mountain, west of the Middle Reach, planted in 1998 as Great Oak Vineyard. The scion material there is partly Dijon clones and partly budwood from Trenton Estate. Berglund has also agreed to manage other Russian River valley vineyards in return for a share of their fruit. Beginning in 2001, however, Swan was exclusively a Russian River valley house, having discontinued the purchase of fruit from Sonoma Mountain.

WINEMAKING

Winemaking at Joseph Swan is fairly traditional and does not change radically from year to year. The prefermentation maceration lasts two to three days, and the entire vatting continues for three to three and a half weeks. The Estate pinot almost always relies on resident yeast; other pinots may be inoculated, depending on the vintage and the condition of the fruit. The usage of whole clusters rose to 100 percent in the late 1980s but has since dropped back to between 15 percent and 20 percent; berries in the destemmed fruit are kept whole as far as possible. Berglund punches down in open-top fermentors during the primary fermentation, which usually tops out at 90 to 93 degrees Fahrenheit. Toward the end of the vatting, when most of the action is postfermentation maceration, the cap is manipulated just enough to keep it wet and the wine safe. The use of some whole clusters means that some residual fermentation continues until the wine is barreled.

Pinots spend nine to 15 months in various combinations of new barrels with one-, two-, and three-year-old ones. The Estate pinot gets half to two-thirds new oak, depending on the vintage; other pinots take anywhere between 5 percent and 50 percent. The wines are racked once before bottling, and are rarely fined and never filtered. The barrels are a combination of Remond house toast and François Frères medium to medium-plus toast, using wood sourced from the Tronçais and Bretanges forests as well as forests in the Allier and Vosges. Berglund says he is more inclined to "push the envelope" with the Estate wine than he is with pinots made from purchased fruit, partially because he knows better how to read the vineyard, and partially because he is reconciled to this wine taking longer to come together. Pushing the envelope means more new barrels, more whole clusters in warm years, and longer fermentations.

THE WINES

Joseph Swan pinots are made in lots so tiny that they give a new dimension to the term *boutique.* A single barrel, or two, may be all that's made. With its small size and parsimonious yield, the estate vineyard has never made more than a few hundred cases of pinot—and even less in recent vintages, while part of the vineyard is out of production for replanting. The wines are the antithesis of house style: each vineyard and each vintage is allowed self-expression—which is an article of faith for Berglund, who insists that "at all cost, winemaking must not obscure the vineyard." In general, however, Swan pinots show more minerality and nuance than bold fruit, and they are never heavily extracted. The flagship wine is the Estate pinot noir, now called the Trenton Estate Vineyard, thus far made entirely from the original 1969 and 1974 plantings. In most years, the Estate wines are angular, tannic, and a touch backward in their youth, but open up and soften two to four years after the vintage, displaying an avalanche of fruit, earth flavors, and pepper. Ten years of positive evolution before the wine peaks is not unusual, and several vintages from the 1970s are still in good condition. When *Wine Spectator* reviewed the 1990 vintage on release in 1992, it scored poorly.

Rereviewed five years later, it scored 94 and ranked best of the vintage. In 1995, there were 260 cases of Estate pinot; in 1999 fewer than 160. Some vintages (like 1996), which show a bit more youthful charm (and therefore garner better reviews on release), sell out quickly. Others (like 1995) remain available for four to five years. Joseph Swan's Estate pinot is not a cult wine. By current standards, it is not expensive. But for nearly three decades, it has helped to define what New World pinot can and cannot be.

Among Swan's non-estate pinots, I have been especially impressed with the Steiner Vineyard wines, which combine the structure derived from montane soils with a panoply of flavors; and with the 1997 Lone Redwood Ranch, a North American incarnation of Côte de Nuits Villages from a lightweight year.

TASTING NOTES

2000 Cuvée de Trois (tasted in 2002): Light to medium garnet; aromas of smoke, wintergreen, dark cherry, and earth; more cherry in the mouth, mixed with black raspberry, mint, and white pepper; light- to medium-weight, medium-length, texture of very fine emery.

2000 Saralee's Vineyard (tasted in 2002): Very slightly hazy, light to medium garnet; rose petals, red licorice, and black raspberry on the nose; more black raspberry on the palate, with hints of soft spice, cherry candy, earth, and caramel; medium-weight, silken texture, soft with glycerol, quite long.

2000 Steiner Vineyard (tasted in 2003): Transparent, medium garnet; earth, underbrush, forest floor, orange blossom, and resin aromas; tea, spice, black pepper, and wet slate in the mouth; structured and mineral, slightly grippy, and textured like fine emery.

1999 Steiner Vineyard (tasted twice, in 2001 and 2003): Very transparent, light to medium garnet; nose of wild raspberries, mushroom, and truffles; some fading flowers, wet moss, and beef jerky in 2003; resin, earth, leather, black pepper, and bay leaf in the mouth; light- to medium-weight wine with a long, linenlike texture and engaging complexity.

1999 Trenton Estate Vineyard (tasted in 2002): Transparent, light to medium black-red; aromas of violets, smoke, roses, and dark cherries; sweet in the mouth with black raspberry, white pepper, and licorice and a hint of minerality; chamois-textured, medium-weight and medium-length.

1998 Steiner Vineyard (tasted in 2001): Very transparent, light to medium ruby; black raspberry nose with some cherry; more fruit-forward than the 1999 Steiner; notes of cola, eucalyptus, cedary chocolate, and licorice; more characteristic black pepper; some fine-grained tannin, linen-textured, medium to long finish.

1997 Lone Redwood Ranch (tasted repeatedly in 1999, 2000, and 2001): Like Saralee's, the color is light, bright, and extremely transparent tile-red; perfume of white truffles, leather, forest floor, and roses; licorice, wild strawberry, and cherry on the palate; very svelte, elegant, and aromatically interesting wine; some bottles fading in 2001. A personal favorite.

1997 Saralee's Vineyard (tasted in 1999): Light, bright tile-red; mushroom and forest-floor nose, then wild strawberry and bright cherry; a light seasoning of black pepper and spice; lightweight, elegant, and aromatic.

1997 Steiner Vineyard (tasted in 2001): Transparent, medium garnet; aromas of mace, nutmeg, and India ink; black fruits, tar, and tobacco in the mouth; mineral flavors and black pepper overlaying sweet fruit; very fine-grained tannins, same linen texture, long.

1997 Trenton Estate Vineyard (tasted in 2002): Transparent, medium black-red; aromas of blackberry and violets, with hints of briar and roasted beets; core of sweet dark fruit in the mouth and very peppery, with some tobacco and freshly ground espresso; concentrated and very long, texture simultaneously creamy and very fine emery.

1997 Trenton Estate Vineyard Pentagon Reserve (tasted in 2002): Saturated, slightly hazy, medium-dark black-red with oxblood and terra-cotta highlights; nose of very ripe fruit with hints of root vegetables; intensely sweet plum and blackberry fruit on the palate, with very dense and deep notes of allspice, black pepper, mint, cigar box, and wet slate; very full and concentrated, slightly grippy, long and velvety.

1996 Estate (tasted in 2000): Dense, oxblood red with a hint of terra-cotta and slightly hazy with suspended sediment; lavender and rose petal on the nose; lavender pastilles, infused flowers, white pepper, and a hint of orange peel in the mouth; sweet fruit core; substantially weighty wine, chewy but still elegant, long.

1995 Estate (tasted in 1999): Medium-dark black-red; nose of black fruits, resin, tar, underbrush, and smoke; cherry, black pepper, and hard spice on the palate. Large-framed and chewy but elegantly balanced, acid and tannin still very present, barely evolved.

1994 Estate (tasted in 2002): Transparent, deep oxblood; explosive nose of blackberry, spice, and black pepper, with a hint of resin; very ripe black fruit in the mouth, with more pepper and allspice; structured and mineral, full and concentrated, stuffed but elegant, long. A personal favorite.

1993 Estate (tasted in 2002): Brilliant, light to medium, very reddish garnet with hints of tile; potpourri, forest floor, and smoke on the nose; peppery spice, furniture polish, fading dark fruit, and minerality; still very slightly grippy, full-bodied, angular, silky, and long.

1991 Estate (tasted in 1999): Medium black-red color with no hint of tiling; earth, forest floor, and truffle nose; eucalyptus, black fruit, black pepper, and allspice on the palate; mouthcoating and still evolving.

PRACTICAL INFORMATION

Swan pinots are available at the winery, by mailing list, through selected retailers, and in restaurants, but many of the microlots sell out quickly. The winery is open for tasting most weekends; 707-573-3747.

J WINE COMPANY

Healdsburg, California

In the early 1970s, Tom Jordan—an oil entrepreneur from Colorado—purchased almost 1,600 acres of prune orchard and oak woodland on the southern side of the Alexander Valley. There he planted a vineyard, built a grand château, and established Jordan Vineyards and Winery. Rather quickly, Jordan developed a good reputation for Sonoma cabernet and chardonnay. In 1986, two years after his daughter Judy graduated from Stanford with a degree in applied earth science, father and daughter entered into a new partnership to make sparkling wine, using space in the existing winery. The new company, called J for Judy, gradually acquired land suitable for cool-climate chardonnay and pinot noir in the Russian River valley and co-marketed its successful sparkling wine with the Jordan brand. Judy Jordan held key positions in the Jordan Vineyards company. When the market for sparkling wine softened in the early 1990s, J winemaker Oded Shakked convinced Judy to experiment with two barrels of still pinot noir. The still pinot was initially no easier to sell than the sparkling wine, but winemaker and proprietor both liked it, so the die was cast, though J continues to make very well respected bottle-fermented sparkling wine as well.

In 1996, having outgrown its back-door arrangements with Jordan, J was poised to build a winery of its own. Land had been acquired, plans drawn, and ground almost broken when the former Piper Sonoma winery came on the market, along with 110 acres of Russian River vineyard, of which 90 were planted to pinot noir. The winery was a near-nightmare of deferred maintenance and a floor plan that reflected French ideas about management and staffing hierarchies, but the hundred-plus acres of prime vineyard were, according to Shakked, "too good to miss." J abandoned its building plan, acquired the Piper Sonoma property, and turned its energies from new construction to extensive remodeling. Production of J wines moved from the Jordan winery to the erstwhile Piper facility in 1997, and an attractively redesigned tasting room opened to the public in October 1999. It is unusual among tasting rooms in offering bits of finger food—gravlax, duck rillettes, and pecorino cheese, for example—chosen to illustrate the pairing of each wine with comestibles.

With the acquisition of Piper Sonoma's vineyards, primarily on the eastern side of the river, and soaring demand for pinot, J's production of still pinot rose from the experimental two barrels (50 cases) of the 1994 vintage to nearly 4,000 cases three years later. In 1998, according to Shakked, J committed to becoming a major player in Russian River pinot noir, and production increased to 12,000 cases.

Winemaker Shakked has crafted J wines almost from the beginning. In a world in which unusual biographies are fairly commonplace, Shakked's story is still unique. A passionate surfer born in Israel, he discovered fine wine while shooting the curl along the French coast near Bordeaux. His palate was formed in France, he lived for a time in Uruguay, and he eventually learned winemaking at the University of California, Davis. Shakked claims that "good karma" landed him at J. Scanning the employment ads in *Wines and Vines* one day in 1988, he closed his eyes and let his finger fall at random. After two years as a cellar hand, Shakked became J's winemaker in 1990. He came to J with a well-developed passion for pinot noir, having made tiny quantities for himself every year since 1986. The fruit he was picking from J's Nicole's Vineyard (see below) for sparkling wine was, he says now, "screaming" to be made into a still red. That, even more than the soft market for sparklers, led him to push for a still pinot program at J.

The fruit for J's still pinot noir comes from five noncontiguous Russian River sites: two along Mark West Creek at the southern end of the Middle Reach, two along Eastside Road in the heart of the Middle Reach, and one on Westside Road south of Wohler Bridge. These are, variously, river-bottom, benchland, and hillside vineyards, planted to no less than 12 selections of scion material on a half-dozen rootstocks. The vines are generally young, and some blocks were still being replanted at the time of this writing. The oldest vines (acquired with the purchase of Piper) date to 1972. In addition to Nicole's and Robert Thomas (see below), J's pinot vineyards are referred to internally as Shirley's, Nick and Nonny's, and Teardrop. Multiple lots are blended to produce J's Russian River Valley bottling, which accounts for more than 80 percent of total production. Certain lots made from older vines at Nicole's, a hillside vineyard 150 feet above the valley floor with a commanding view of the river, are bottled separately as a vineyard-designated wine. These lots always include about half of Block 4, a 21-acre parcel of UCD 2A that Shakked obtained from Domaine Chandon's nursery in Los Carneros. The surface soil in Block 4 (and parts of adjacent blocks at Nicole's) is visibly red Goldridge series, similar to soils in the Laguna Ridge area of the Russian River valley but unusual on the eastern side of the Middle Reach. The combination of red Goldridge-series soil, naturally low yield, and UCD 2A appears to produce a distinctively earthy character tinged with meatiness.

J's second vineyard-designated wine comes from the 23-acre Robert Thomas Vineyard south of Wohler Bridge. There, a combination of Dijon 113 and 115, UCD 32, and budwood selected from Rochioli's UCD 4 vines was planted fairly densely on the benchland portion of the vineyard in 1994. (Fruit from the lower portion of the vineyard, where the rich alluvial soils produce higher yields, is used for the Russian River Valley blend and for sparkling wine.) Primarily because of its low elevation, Robert Thomas is an especially cool site where fruit ripens almost three weeks later than in vineyards in the heart of the Middle Reach. The combination of longer hang time, yields capped at about four tons per acre, and Rochioli budwood appears to create a wine of considerable concentration, spiciness characteristic of the Middle Reach's west side, and velvety softness. Only about 12 percent of the Robert Thomas fruit goes into the vineyard-designated wine.

WINEMAKING

Shakked picks his fruit at relatively low Brix to keep the alcohol in the finished wine under 14.5 percent, and generally closer to 13.5 percent. He destems everything except part of Nicole's vineyard, which is fermented as whole clusters; no enzymes are added to the fermentations. One-, 2.5-, and 7.5-ton open-top fermentors are used as far as possible, but some lots ferment in large ten- and 19-ton closed tanks. Four days of cold soak precede fermentation, which is jump-started with a combination of Williams Selyem and Assmannshausen yeasts. The cap is punched down in the open-tops; pumpover is the only solution in the closed tanks. The must is pressed at dryness, and there is no postfermentation maceration.

A combination of free-run and light press juice goes into 30 percent to 35 percent new medium-plus-toast barrels with toasted heads from Séguin Moreau, Mercurey, and François Frères. Shakked tells his barrel purveyors that he is looking for barrels that can impart flavors of meat and sausage rather than vanilla and butterscotch. The Russian River Valley blend spends ten months in barrel before bottling; the vineyard-designates get 15 months. Shakked says he "tries" not to filter but sometimes practices a light pad filtration, and always passes the wine through a coarse "bug-catcher" type of sieve before bottling. No fining is done; the only exception was in 1995, when Shakked mistakenly fermented too high a percentage of whole clusters, generating too much tannin.

THE WINES

Nicole's Vineyard was J's first pinot noir, and the only pinot made in the 1994 and 1995 vintages. The Russian River blend debuted in 1996 and has been made each year since, as has Nicole's. The Robert Thomas bottling was introduced in 1997. All J pinots are elegant, quintessential pinots that display great finesse and cascading layers of flavor, in a light- to medium-weight frame. The wines are also transparent, brilliant, and unsaturated. The Russian River bottling typically showcases high-toned fruit and floral notes; Nicole's has a tendency to feature charcuterie; and Robert Thomas is distinctively though elegantly spicy. The wines tend to divide reviewers, some of whom find them "dead ringers for Burgundy," while others are critical of their feminine structure and unsaturated robe.

TASTING NOTES

1999 Robert Thomas Vineyard (tasted in 2002): Transparent, light to medium garnet; earth, moss, air-dried beef, rose petals, and black cherry aromas; more cherry, smoke, cloves, and pickling spice in the mouth, overlaying considerable minerality; very slightly sweet, light- to medium-weight, medium-length, and suedelike texture.

1999 Russian River Valley (tasted in 2002): Brilliant, shimmering, light to medium mahogany-tinged red; nose of black cherry, red licorice, charcuterie, and barrel char; cherry, black raspberry, smoke, and licorice on the palate; light- to medium-weight and medium-length, very slightly grippy with a texture between suede and silk.

1998 Nicole's Vineyard (tasted in 2001): Hazy, medium black-red; briar, seasoned meat, rose petals, and a hint of root beer on the nose; black raspberry, black pepper, and barrel char in the mouth, with hints of spice and coffee; medium-weight but relatively lean, coarsely silken and long.

1998 Robert Thomas Vineyard (tasted in 2001): Transparent, medium black-red; floral aromas with hints of macadamia nut and vegetables; Indonesian spice in the mouth, with licorice, merbromin, and white pepper; medium-weight and medium-length, with a silken texture.

1997 Nicole's Vineyard (tasted twice in 1999): Transparent, light garnet; still the trademark meat and truffle, but this vintage shows more smoke, anise, eucalyptus, and tar than the 1996 or 1998; medium-weight and long, texture of polished cotton.

1997 Robert Thomas Vineyard (tasted multiple times in 2000 and 2001): Very transparent, light to medium black-red; dried mixed herbs, sausage, leather, and smoke on the nose; dark cherry, meat, and black pepper in the mouth; long, silken, light-weight, and elegant.

1997 Russian River Valley (tasted in 1999): Transparent, light garnet; cherries, rose petals, and smoke on the nose; more cherry in the mouth, plus hints of tea, licorice, and fennel; medium-weight and medium-length, silken.

1996 Nicole's Vineyard (tasted twice in 1999): Transparent, pale black-red; cherry, blackberry, truffle, forest floor, meat, sausage, hints of caramelized brown sugar on both nose and palate, plus roasted tea; silken and elegant. In this vintage, a small percentage of the wine was made in closed tanks.

PRACTICAL INFORMATION

The Russian River Valley and Nicole's bottlings are distributed nationwide, but the Robert Thomas vineyard-designate is sold only at the tasting room and to mail-order customers. The tasting room, open daily, offers sophisticated, bite-sized comestibles conceived and prepared by professional chefs, as well as sit-down food and wine tasting options; 707-431-3646.

KEN WRIGHT CELLARS

Carlton, Oregon

Ken Wright is engaging and passionate about pinot noir and an indefatigable champion of its Oregonian editions. He is also almost an icon among its many producers, having created, from scratch, no less than three brands of persistently high reputation: Panther Creek, Domaine Serene, and Ken Wright Cellars. At one point when Wright was the winemaker for both Domaine Serene and Ken Wright Cellars, those houses (which then cohabited) were simultaneously Robert M. Parker's choices for Oregon's two outstanding producers of pinot noir.

Wright's road to wine is no less likely than a score of others. He says he was "hooked" on pinot while waiting tables in Lexington, Kentucky, working his way through college. The restaurant's owner was determined to educate his waitstaff about wine and repeatedly broke out a few of his best bottles for systematic tastings. Struck with the discovery that Domaine de la Romanée-Conti was "infinitely more interesting than Lancer's," Wright transferred from the University of Kentucky to the viticulture program at the University of California, Davis, and embarked—albeit with no financial assets—on a career in wine. After eight years making, in his own phrase, "very average" pinot noir for wineries in California's Central Coast, he moved to Oregon, waited tables again to make ends meet, and launched Panther Creek in 1986 with just ten barrels of wine.

Within a few years, Wright was transformed from a skillful blender into a champion of vineyard-designation. By the time he founded Ken Wright Cellars in 1994, vineyard-designation had become the core of his program. In some vintages, as many as 12 individually designated pinots have been made under the Ken Wright Cellars imprimatur, entirely from purchased fruit, and from sites scattered throughout the northwestern quadrant of the Willamette Valley. In the Red Hills, Wright has sourced fruit from Abbey Ridge (see the Cameron Winery profile for details), Arcus (see Archery Summit Estate), and Nysa, a dense planting of UCD 2A and 5 between Domaine Drouhin and Archery Summit, set out in 1990. In the Eola Hills, Wright gets fruit from Canary Hill, about ten miles west of Salem, where UCD 5 was planted in 1982 and 1983; from the nearby Carter Vineyard, where Wright's parcel is 100 percent old UCD 2A; and from Elton, a 1983 planting of own-rooted UCD 5 overlooking the hamlet of Hopewell. Near the winery in Carlton, the persistent sources are Guadalupe, a 1989 planting of UCD 5 spaced seven feet by five in exceptionally well-drained shallow dirt where volcanic soils transition to sedimentary material; Shea, which is described in chapter 4's section on the Willamette Valley; McCrone, a dense planting of Dijon 115 set out in 1992 that typically displays dense black fruit flavors and considerable power; and Wahle, an old UCD 5 vineyard that yields spicy, cassis-flavored wine. Since 1996, Wright has also purchased UCD 5 fruit from Whistling Ridge Vineyard on Ribbon Ridge, adjacent to Beaux Frères, where vines were planted in 1990 spaced seven feet by five, and where typical aromas involve blackberries, earth, and cola. In the McMinnville foothills area, Wright uses fruit from three designated acres of the Meredith Mitchell Vineyard, a widely spaced 1988 planting of UCD 5 in especially shallow sedimentary soils surmounting basaltic mother rock.

Wright pioneered the use of acreage contracts with growers to maximize his control over green harvesting decisions, pick date, and yield. In some cases his contracts are now long-term lease agreements. In 1999 Wright was finally able to begin planting an estate vineyard, called Savoya, on Blackburn Road east of Yamhill. On this 40-acre parcel, Wright planted 17 acres of pinot over a three-year period and harvested a first crop in 2002. Nearby, on an east-west-oriented ridge east of Carlton, Wright also began planting the Abbott Claim Vineyard in 2001. This ridge, which Wright shares with Soter Wines, displays sedimentary soils of remarkably consistent depth. In 2001 and 2002, 17 acres were planted there.

WINEMAKING

Asserting that "there is no human way to sort fruit in the vineyard," Wright insists on a meticulous sorting regimen in which eight to ten people are deployed around a shaker table. The objective is to eliminate "every leaf, whether brown or green; every bit of mold; and all second-crop berries." The sorted fruit is then destemmed—apart from between 3 percent and 10 percent whole clusters, which are layered on the bottom of each fermentor—but not crushed. Wright prefers to ferment in plastic fruit bins, but he also uses some three-ton stainless steel tanks. Since 1994, he has practiced a five-day cold soak, enforced with a single application of dry ice. After the ice has evaporated, he uses an inserted flag (a flat, rectangular panel laced with tubes that is used to warm or chill the must by circulating hot or cold water through the tubes) to warm the must to about 60 degrees Fahrenheit, at which point, for some lots but not others, he adds commercial yeasts. Several yeast strains may be employed, but only one is introduced per fermentor. The choice whether to inoculate or rely on native yeast is (like nearly everything else at Ken Wright Cellars) site-specific. During the cold soak, the must is left pretty much alone. One or two punchdowns per day are done once fermentation starts, and the fermentation temperature peaks in the high 80s. Wright does not bleed the must—he compares this procedure to doing surgery with a hacksaw and says it can make the wines tannic. He will, however, use an evaporator to increase concentration in rainy years. He has abandoned postfermentation maceration, having found that it often produced bitterness. The must is pressed when dry, and the press fraction is reintegrated unless the pH is high, in which case it may be kept separate.

Barrels are between 65 percent and 70 percent new; the balance is one year old. Wright likes Vosges wood for the "sweetness" it imparts to the wine; he uses mostly house-toast barrels from Cadus and Sirugue, in roughly equal percentages. Malolactic fermentation is started by inoculation with Hansen freeze-dried bacteria, though this practice may change once a resident yeast population has become established in the new facility, completed in 1998. The wine is racked once at bottling, is neither fined nor filtered, and is bottled before the next year's vintage. Release occurs at the annual Thanksgiving open house.

THE WINES

Wright's large portfolio of vineyard-designated wines unfolds as follows. In 1994, he made pinots from Freedom Hill Vineyard, Abbey Heights Vineyard (which was renamed Guadalupe the following year), Canary Hill Vineyard, Carter Vineyard, and Shea Vineyard. In 1995, he added Kircher, which was then purchased by Domaine Serene. The 1996 vintage saw the debut of his Abbey Ridge, Whistling Ridge, and McCrone bottlings. Elton Vineyard joined the lineup in 1997. In 1998, Wright began a four-year run with Archery Summit's Arcus Vineyard and began acquiring fruit also from the Nysa and Wahle vineyards. The Meredith Mitchell Vineyard in the McMinnville foothills debuted in 2001. With the exceptions of Kircher, which was made for one year only, in 1995; Abbey Ridge, which was not made in 1997; Whistling Ridge, which was relinquished after the 2000 harvest; and Arcus, which was no longer available after 2001, Wright has stuck with every vineyard he has tried, and each new vineyard has been an addition to his lineup.

Wright criticizes many New World pinots, including those he himself made in the late 1970s and early 1980s, for their lack of "middle" or "plushness." Unsurprisingly, recent vintages of Ken Wright Cellars are big wines by Oregon standards: very dark, sometimes opaque, sometimes tannic but always on a large frame, and often plush. Even in rainy years, Wright's use of an evaporator keeps the wines fairly dark and concentrated. Considerable cellaring usually improves the wines, some of which (Wahle is a notable exception) can be tough in their youth. Unfortunately, my experience with Ken Wright pinots is limited to the 1999 vintage.

TASTING NOTES

1999 Canary Hill (tasted in 2001): Transparent, deep black-red; some violets and cherry on the nose but partially closed; cherry, plum, cola, and black fruits, with resin, tobacco, licorice, and cinnamon bark; notes of cedar and vanilla; medium- to full-bodied and long, but relatively approachable.

1999 Guadalupe Vineyard (tasted in 2001): Opaque, inky wine; nose of violets; black fruits, ink, and cola flavors with a sweet mid-palate; accents of mint, resin, and licorice; chocolate and tannin at the end; long and linen-textured.

1999 McCrone Vineyard (tasted in 2001): Transparent, medium-dark black-red; slate, rose petal, berry stems, and strawberry on the nose; sweet berry fruit on the palate, with hints of green tea and foliage; some grip but predominantly soft, light in weight, and medium-length.

1999 Nysa Vineyard (tasted in 2001): Nearly opaque, reddish-black; nose of tea, India ink, and black cherry; flavors of resin, leather, and earth; tightly knit, structured wine, finishes rich.

1999 Shea Vineyard (tasted twice, in 2001 and 2002): Nearly opaque, reddish-black; black fruits, plum, beetroot, rose petal, and cola; borderline notes of prune; slate, India ink, and chocolate on the palate, with some unresolved tannin; medium-weight, velvety, and long.

1999 Wahle Vineyard (tasted in 2001): Transparent, light to medium ruby; aromas of raspberry, smoke, cassis, and bramble; vanilla, berry fruit, and a hint of tar in the mouth; light to medium body, medium-length, gossamer structure, and a silken finish.

PRACTICAL INFORMATION

Pinot noir represents about 85 percent of total production. Most wines are made in tiny lots of 90 to 400 cases. Sixty percent is sold directly to consumers through an annual tasting of the just-made vintage held Thanksgiving weekend. In-state retail and restaurant accounts get another 20 percent of production. The remaining 20 percent is allocated to distributors. Consumers wanting Ken Wright wines are well advised to head for Carlton, Oregon, on Thanksgiving weekend, absent tight and friendly relations with a well-connected retailer. Except for Thanksgiving weekend, visits are by appointment only; 800-571-6825.

LAMOREAUX LANDING WINE CELLARS

Lodi, New York

In his own youth, Mark Wagner's father grew native American grape varieties on the eastern shore of New York's Seneca Lake and sold his crop to Welch's for grape juice. In the 1950s, the focus of Wagner *père*'s interests shifted to French-American hybrids, most of which he sold to The Taylor Wine Company. Taylor based virtually all of its business on the production of "uncomplicated" wines made from hybrids and combinations of hybrids with native American grapes, sold as Sauterne, Rhine wine, Sherry, and Champagne. But when Wagner *fils* was still a teenager, he began to taste "real" wines, including German rieslings, Alsatian gewürztraminers, and red Burgundies. He remembers "falling in love with these wines," noticing that "you tasted a different thing" with every whiff and sniff. After his father's untimely death in 1978—and against the backdrop of Taylor's sale to Coca-Cola in 1977, which decimated the market for hybrid grapes in the Finger Lakes—Mark Wagner began planting vinifera varieties in the family's vineyards. Even though the state's official advice to grape growers counterindicated vinifera, warning that it might not survive the region's long, frigid winters, Wagner's choice worked out well. His first crop of chardonnay sold for $1,500 per ton and was hugely profitable. By the end of the 1990s, Wagner's stake in vinifera varieties had risen to half of his planted acreage.

Wagner's first pinot noir was planted in 1982, in north-south-oriented nine-foot rows with seven feet between vines. Wagner does not know for sure what scion material was used, but thinks it was probably a combination of Geneva and Clone 7. (See the profile of Dr. Konstantin Frank's Vinifera Wine Cellars for more information about pinot clones in New York State.) A second block of pinot was planted in 1988, similarly oriented and spaced, but the scion material this time was UCD 13. A third block, planted to UCD 23 in 2000, brought his total investment in pinot noir to 7.5 acres. The soils are all glacial till mixtures of silt, loam, and gravel, and yield is managed to about two tons per acre. Lamoreaux Landing Wine Cellars was created in 1990 to produce wines from the vinifera portion of Wagner's vineyards. The mainstays of this production are barrel-fermented chardonnay, riesling, and merlot, plus a blended white and a blended red wine; but a small amount of pinot noir has been made in every vintage since 1990—except 1997—and pinot production stood at about 500 cases in 2002. (Lamoreaux Landing's 1997 pinot noir was blended with some of the following year's wine and released as a nonvintage blend.) As the 2000 block of pinot comes into full production in 2003 and 2004, production will increase to between 700 and 750 cases annually.

In 1992, Wagner built a handsome new home for Lamoreaux Landing overlooking his vineyards, on Highway 414 south of the town of Lodi. California architect Bruce Corson was the architect for this facility, a tall, L-shaped, multilevel building whose main entrance is a neoclassical four-column facade surmounted by a triangular pediment. The result, which combines American barn with Greek temple executed in wood, has won awards from the American Institute of Architects.

WINEMAKING

Wagner finds he picks pinot noir between 21 and 24 Brix, and can "sometimes" get full flavors even at 21. He destems completely, ferments in four-foot cubical fruit bins, and typically inoculates with commercial yeast to start the alcoholic fermentation. The must is chaptalized in cool, wet years like 2000; in warmer years the natural sugar accumulation is ample. In 2000, Wagner began moving fermentors outside at night to allow for a few days of cold soak before inoculation. Punchdowns are standard, though pumpovers are also done in some vintages. Primary fermentations last eight to ten days, and the must is pressed either at dryness or after a few days of post-fermentation maceration. Wagner siphons off as much juice as possible from each fermentor and keeps it separate; the balance of the must is pressed. The two fractions from each fermentor are barreled separately and may or may not be reassembled when the final blend is made. Inoculation for malolactic fermentation occurs in tank, before the wine is transferred to barrel.

Until 1999, Lamoreaux Landing pinots were raised entirely in American oak. In 2000, Wagner converted to French cooperage, mostly from Remond. The new barrels are sometimes seasoned with a barrel fermentation of chardonnay before being used for pinot noir. The wines spend nine to 12 months in wood before bottling, during which time they are racked twice. They are both fined and filtered. Six to eight months of bottle-aging precede release.

Lamoreaux Landing's winemaker from 1991 until 1999 was Rob Thomas, who remains as a consultant but now devotes most of his time to a separate venture nearby called Shalestone Vineyards. Effective with the 1999 vintage, Wagner began to function as his own winemaker, but he is assisted by a cellarmaster.

THE WINES

A single bottling of pinot noir has been made in each vintage, with declassified lots redirected to the winery's Estate Red blend, though a reserve wine may be made from the 2001 vintage. My experience with Lamoreaux Landing pinots is limited to the vintages from 1997 through 2000. These are quite fleshy and full-bodied by Finger Lakes standards and have shown extremely well in comparative tastings alongside pinots from Oregon, California, and the Okanagan. The wines are also aromatically complex, despite the use of American barrels through 1999.

TASTING NOTES

2000 Pinot Noir (tasted twice in 2002): Transparent, medium garnet; highly aromatic, floral nose with hints of camphor; very complex palate of cherry candy, resin, tobacco, earth, and black tea; concentrated and full-bodied, with noticeable glycerol, satin-textured, long.

1999 Pinot Noir (tasted in 2002): Transparent, medium garnet; dried leaves with some cherry and hints of tobacco on the nose; flavors of tobacco and earth on the palate; full-bodied, sweet, and concentrated, satin-textured, long.

1998 Pinot Noir (tasted in 2002): Transparent, medium garnet; resin, clove, and black pepper on the nose; cherry, tobacco, and some raisin in the mouth; medium-weight, full-bodied, and sweet, texture of suede turning to velvet, long.

NV [1997–1998] Pinot Noir (tasted in 2002): Transparent, light to medium garnet; raspberry, white pepper, and leather aromas, with a hint of cassis and truffle; raspberry and cherry, with smoke, cherry candy, and some clove on the palate; light- to medium-weight wine, firm structure, satin finish, and long.

PRACTICAL INFORMATION

Because of limited production and New York State laws, Lamoreaux Landing pinots are not widely available. There is some in-state retail distribution, and the wines appear on restaurant lists in the Finger Lakes area. However, the winery will ship to consumers both in-state and out-of-state, directly and via "shipping connections." The winery, open daily, houses a handsome high-ceilinged tasting room overlooking the vineyards and lake; 607-582-6011.

LANE TANNER WINES

Santa Maria, California

In 1980, André Tchelistcheff inadvertently recruited Lane Tanner into the wine business. A chemist whose first career was focused on air pollution control, Tanner was temping in Konocti Winery's laboratory, in her hometown of Kelseyville, California—and considering alternative careers—when Tchelistcheff arrived on a consulting visit. As Tanner tells the story, her temporary employers, presumably reluctant to tell their illustrious consultant that, in fact, they employed no dedicated lab staff, introduced her to Tchelistcheff as "the new enologist." A year later, on Tchelistcheff's recommendation, Tanner became an enologist for real at Firestone Vineyard in Santa Barbara, and in 1984 commenced making wines for The Hitching Post, then the private label of a Buellton steakhouse.

In 1989 she launched her own wine project, which was dedicated entirely to pinot noir until 1996, when she reluctantly (and briefly) diversified into syrah. Over the years, Tanner has sourced pinot from most of Santa Barbara County's best pinot vineyards, including Sierra Madre, Bien Nacido, Julia's (Cambria), and Sanford & Benedict, using long-term contracts wherever possible to guarantee consistent access to specific rows of fruit. The wines are made at the Central Coast Wine facility in Santa Maria.

WINEMAKING

Tanner is an early picker of pinot noir, sometimes taking fruit off the vine at as low as 21.5 Brix and generating wines with relatively low pH and high total acidity, at which levels the aromas are, she believes, "more exciting." (That said, she picked later in 2000 and 2001.) She ferments barely crushed but completely destemmed berries in double-height plastic-lined plywood fruit bins, using a bit of dry ice and argon but no sulfur to ensure one or two days of prefermentation cold soak. The alcoholic fermentation is kicked off with an inoculation of Assmannshausen yeast, which Tanner describes as "a slow grower" that "never sticks" and "does not infringe on the flavor of the fruit." Punchdowns are done three or four times daily at the beginning of the fermentation, but the frequency decreases as the fermentation slows down. Tanner inoculates for malolactic fermentation and presses very gently just before the cap sinks, always leaving a bit of juice for some other (and less fussy) winemaker.

Barrels are two-year air-dried, medium-toast *pièces* from François Frères, of which just 20 percent are new each year. The wines are racked once the February after the vintage, barrel to tank and tank back to barrel for uniformity, and once again before bottling, which occurs the August after the vintage. The wines are not fined, but are coarse pad filtered for visual clarity. The Santa Maria Valley cuvée (see below) is released in October; other wines are held until January of the second year after the vintage. The Santa Maria Valley cuvée is blended with 5 percent syrah "just to make it different"; the others are 100 percent pinot noir. No enzymes are used.

THE WINES

In 1989 Lane Tanner made two pinots: a Santa Barbara County cuvée made entirely from Sierra Madre fruit, and a Benedict vineyard-designate from Sanford & Benedict fruit. In 1990 there was only one wine, from Sierra Madre. In 1991 and 1992, the Santa Barbara County bottling was made mainly from Sierra Madre fruit, but with a touch of Bien Nacido added "for color"; from 1993 through 1996, this bottling was replaced by a Sierra Madre Plateau wine that used fruit from the Gold Coast Vineyard as well as Sierra Madre. Simultaneously, from 1991 through 1994, a Sanford & Benedict vineyard-designate was also made. The 1993 vintage saw the debut of a vineyard-designated Bien Nacido cuvée, which has been made annually ever since, from UCD 4 fruit in Bien Nacido's Block N; and 1996 was the first vintage of a Julia's Vineyard wine, which also continues. Tanner's Santa Maria Valley cuvée, made from Bien Nacido Blocks X, Y, and Z, plus the aforementioned 5 percent syrah, debuted in 1997 and was made for four vintages. In 2000, Tanner added her first Santa Rita Hills wine, from a block planted, as she specified, to an unusual combination of UCD 2A, 9, and 16, in the Melville Vineyard on Highway 246.

Lane Tanner pinots are generally light- to medium-weight wines with strong aromatic profiles, suave textures, and considerable length. Tanner sometimes describes her pinots as "chick wines," to differentiate them (quite properly) from some blockbuster exemplars of the pinot genre. Their relatively high levels of acid ensure age-worthiness and make them especially good as food wines.

TASTING NOTES

2000 Bien Nacido Vineyard (tasted in 2001): Transparent, medium black-red; aromas of earth, cherries, and black fruits; very sweet fruit in the mouth, with tobacco, mushroom, black tea, and signature black pepper; rich and velvety.

2000 Julia's Vineyard (tasted in 2001): Transparent, medium-dark black-red; intense nose of dark cherries and India ink; licorice, tobacco, cola, and black fruit on the palate, with a hint of smoke; uncharacteristically dense and chewy wine for Lane Tanner, rich and velvety.

2000 Melville Vineyard (tasted in 2001): Very transparent, medium black-red; distinctive floral nose combining camellia, lilac, and lavender; cherries, earth, licorice, and wet stone on the palate; rich wine with the texture of fine linen.

2000 Santa Maria Valley (tasted in 2001): Transparent, light to medium black-red; strawberries and a hint of mint on the nose; berry fruit, characteristic Bien Nacido black pepper, and soft allspice in the mouth; light to medium body, silken.

1995 Bien Nacido Vineyard (tasted in 2001): Transparent, light to medium terra-cotta; aromas of camphor, herbs, and menthol; resinous and minty on the palate, with black pepper and dried cherry fruit; tannic, chewy, and long, rich texture of crinkled velvet.

1993 Bien Nacido Vineyard (tasted in 2001): Transparent, very reddish terra-cotta; nose of resin and leather, with a whiff of tobacco; black berries, cola, and fruit candy in the mouth, with hints of black pepper, allspice, and smoke; medium-weight and very long, with a silken finish. A personal favorite.

1993 Sierra Madre Plateau (tasted in 2001): Transparent, light to medium terra-cotta; aromas of rose petal and wild strawberry; leather, mushroom, and red licorice in the mouth; light- to medium-weight wine with bright acidity and a long, silken finish.

1991 Sanford & Benedict Vineyard (tasted in 2001): Transparent, medium terra-cotta; resin and furniture polish on the nose; leather, tobacco, earth, clove, and cedar in the mouth, plus wet slate; substantial lingering tannins despite an extra six months in wood at the outset, velvety.

PRACTICAL INFORMATION

In 2000, there were about 500 cases each of the Bien Nacido and Santa Maria Valley cuvées, a bit less of Julia's, and fewer than 150 cases of Melville. Distribution is to restaurants and a few retailers in selected markets. As the Melville block comes into full production, Tanner's annual throughput could double to about 3,000 cases. The winery is not open to the public, but the wines can be tasted at Los Olivos Wine and Spirits Emporium in Los Olivos; 805-929-1826.

LITTORAI WINES

St. Helena, California

The path from suburban Westchester County in New York, where he grew up, to winemaking on Napa's Howell Mountain took Ted Lemon through an undergraduate major in French literature at Brown University, a junior year abroad in France, a postgraduate fellowship to study enology at the university in Dijon, and apprenticeships at Domaine Dujac, Domaine Roumier, and Domaine Bruno Clair. In 1982, Lemon was hired to make wine for the house of Guy Roulot in Meursault—as far as anyone knows, the first and only time an American has been employed, not as a consultant or harvest worker, but as *the winemaker and vineyard manager,* by a reputed Burgundy firm. Back from France in 1984, Lemon became the founding winemaker for Napa-based Chateau Woltner.

In 1991 and 1992, he traveled up and down the Pacific Coast, from Oregon to Santa Barbara, examining vineyards and tasting extensively, searching for fruit on which to base a label of his own. He found himself drawn to what he calls the "true" North Coast, located within a few miles of the ocean north and south of the Russian River and in Anderson Valley. The quality of the fruit from these sites impressed him, he recalls, "even when the wines were not especially well made." In 1992 Lemon left Chateau Woltner to begin a consulting career, working inter alia with several wineries, including Franciscan Estates' Estancia operation and Oregon's Archery Summit, that aspired to make top-quality pinot noir. In 1993, Lemon and his wife, Heidi, founded Littorai—a plural derivative of Latin *littor,* meaning "coasts"—a boutique-size project dedicated to coastal pinot noir and chardonnay.

Littorai's first pinot noir was the 1993 One Acre, Lemon's designation for a piece of Rich Savoy's Deer Meadow Ranch, at 1,600 feet on the crest of a northwest-facing ridge on the northeastern side of the Anderson Valley, above Boonville. This vineyard was planted in 1986 in nine-foot rows with three feet between vines, in shallow loamy soil overlaying uplifted marine sandstone. The scion material is UCD 13 and 2A clones, along with Mount Eden selection, and the yield ranges from two to 3.5 tons per acre. In 1995, Littorai added a second Anderson Valley vineyard to its pinot portfolio: Savoy's main ranch, on the northern side of Highway 128, west of Philo. There Littorai gets fruit from blocks planted in 1991, 1992, and 1993 at the toe of the hill, in Boont and Pinole loam soil overlaying Franciscan shale. The plant material is a mix of Dijon 114 and 115 and UCD 4, plus Swan selections.

Also in 1995, Littorai began sourcing pinot noir from David Hirsch's well-known vineyard northeast of Jenner, in the Sonoma Coast AVA. Because of the aggressive topography and noncontiguous plantings at Hirsch, the property's various blocks are more like separate vineyards. Littorai's pinot comes from Block 5, an east-facing slope on Josephine loam strewn with dark brown pebbles, planted six feet by nine to UCD 4 on AxR1 rootstock in 1991; and from Block 6, a north-facing slope of Hugo gravelly, gray loam planted in 1995 to Dijon 114 along with smaller parcels of UCD 4 and Swan selection. Until the 2000 vintage, Littorai also sourced fruit from Block 7, a south-facing, relatively flat site, where Martin Ray/Mount Eden selection has been planted in black-colored, high-clay loam. Additionally, Littorai gets fruit from Block 9, again south-facing but at lower altitude, again Martin Ray/Mount Eden selection and Dijon 114, but on 9C rootstock.

In 1997, Littorai began sourcing pinot from the Thieriot Vineyard, a two-acre parcel at 1,200 feet between the Fay and Tannery Creek drainages, overlooking the town of Bodega Bay, five miles from the ocean. There, in a thin layer of Goldridge sandy loam surmounting fractured sandstone, Cameron Thieriot planted Swan selection in 1991 and Dijon 114, 777, and 667, along with UCD 4, in 1994. Littorai now has a 25-year lease on this site. Finally, in 2001 Littorai also began to purchase fruit from a custom-planted block in the Cerise Vineyard, not far from Deer Meadow Ranch in Anderson Valley. All of Littorai's pinot contracts are per-acre agreements, so Lemon has considerable control over viticultural choices.

Littorai's production facility is the Black-Sears Winery on Howell Mountain, where space is shared with Black-Sears and the Howell Mountain Winery. Elegant underground barrel cellars were constructed there in 2001.

WINEMAKING

Lemon tailors winemaking to the vineyard and the vintage, paying particular attention to tannin management. Fruit is sorted repeatedly: in the vineyard before harvest, at the destemmer, and again between the destemmer and the fermentor. Whole-cluster percentage varies from wine to wine and year to year and is taste-based, but is always lower in cool years. The fermentors are all jacketed stainless steel and mostly open-tops, ranging in size from 400 to 1,200 gallons. Nevertheless, Lemon argues that closed-top tanks can be an advantage in the case of very small volumes, because they help both to sustain temperature and to maintain an anaerobic environment, and he purchased a few in 1999. Because Littorai's vineyards are some distance from the winery, the fruit is picked into refrigerated trucks, where it is chilled to 45 degrees Fahrenheit. On the crushpad the fruit typically gains about five degrees, going into the fermentors at about 50 degrees. Lemon then seeks to maintain the 50-degree temperature during a three- to ten-day cold soak, and thereafter begins to warm the fermentors. The resident yeasts on which Littorai relies tend to start slowly and spike late—a fermentation curve that Lemon finds conducive to good palate length. Hand punchdowns are de rigueur, but Lemon may taper off their frequency, convert to pumpover, or desist altogether when he is confronted with tannic lots. At one extreme, he may press before the must is dry and go directly to barrel without settling the juice, or (at the other extreme) he may permit as much as seven to ten days of postfermentation maceration before pressing. (Lemon believes that long periods of extended maceration are not good for pinot, in general.) In early editions of Littorai, the press juice was reassembled; now press wines are generally excluded and bulked out.

On average, about 50 percent of barrels are new, but the mix varies considerably from wine to wine. (Despite its overall precocity, One Acre [see below] seems to benefit from a high percentage of new oak.) Most of the cooperage comes from François Frères, Remond, and Rousseau; medium to medium-plus toast is favored, and there is a preference for a mix of barrels that have been air-aged two years rather than three. If the malolactic fermentation does not take off naturally, Lemon inoculates. Unless the wine is massive, it is not racked until bottling. Littorai pinots have not been fined since 1997, and the 1993 One Acre was the only wine ever filtered. Wines spend 11 to 15 months in barrel—as necessary to polymerize the tannins. Release date is two years after the vintage.

THE WINES

The fruit sources for Littorai's four vineyard-designated pinots have been consistent, except that Block 6 was added to Blocks 5, 7, and 9 at Hirsch beginning in 1996; a block of Dijon 115 was exchanged for a block of UCD 13 at Savoy beginning in 1996; and the UCD 4 block was added to the Swan block at Thieriot in 1998. In 1997, tiny quantities of Hirsch Blocks 5, 7, and 9 were bottled separately. These wines have been misunderstood in some circles as super-vineyard-designates; in fact the block-designates were kept separate for analytic purposes only. In 2001, for the first time and perhaps also for the last, Littorai also blended a few barrels of Hirsch and Thieriot to make a Sonoma Coast bottling.

Overall, Littorai pinots are very elegant, medium-weight, deeply flavored wines, each of which showcases its respective *terroir.* Aromas and flavors are always nuanced, layered, and complex, and there is always much more at work than fruit. Lemon has chosen sites where optimal flavor development occurs at very reasonable levels of sugar accumulation, so only a few of the finished wines exceed 14 percent alcohol. Savoy has a tendency to brilliant cherry fruit and chewiness, Thieriot to spiciness, and One Acre to dried flowers and exotic berries. Hirsch is the most tannic, wildest, and smokiest of the lot, and generally the last to soften.

TASTING NOTES

1999 One Acre (tasted in 2002): Transparent, medium ruby red; exotic nose of nutmeg and hazelnut; cherry, cantaloupe, cocoa, and wild berries in the mouth; medium-long finish, silken texture, medium-weight, very fine. A personal favorite.

1999 Savoy Vineyard (tasted in 2002): Transparent, medium-dark black-red; nose of mocha, mothballs, nuts, moss, and underbrush; still slightly closed; flavors of cherry, earth, cinnamon, mercaptin, and exotic soft spices with hints of infused lavender, a sweet core of black fruits and currants, plus some black pepper and licorice; medium-weight and elegant, very deep flavors, linen texture with fine-grained tannins still noticeable, long.

1999 Thieriot Vineyard (tasted prerelease in 2001): Transparent, medium black-red; intense nose of black cherries and plums; more cherries and toasted spice in the mouth, with notes of chocolate, game, and orange peel; long, complex, structured, charming. In this vintage, some third-crop UCD 4 fruit was used, and 10 percent whole clusters.

1998 Hirsch Vineyard (tasted in 2001): Transparent, medium-dark black-red; cranberry, evergreen, and syrah pepper on the nose; cola, milk chocolate, and vanilla in the mouth; rich, tannic wine with the texture of crushed velvet.

1998 Thieriot Vineyard (tasted in 2001): Transparent, medium-dark black-red; cranberry and rose petal on the nose; sweet core of plum, cherry, and cola; notes of licorice, cardamom, and dense, roasted Indian spices; long, medium-bodied, velvety. This vintage of Thieriot was made with zero whole-cluster fruit and mostly second-crop UCD 4.

1997 Hirsch Vineyard (tasted in 2001): Transparent, medium-dark black-red; nose of rose petals and dark cherry, with aromatic resin and mahogany-furniture overtones; mint, eucalyptus, licorice, and black pepper, some soft south Asian spice; full-bodied, moderately tannic, velvety.

1997 One Acre (tasted twice in 2001): Transparent, medium-dark oxblood red; exotic nose of lingonberry, aromatic herbs, and lilac, with hints of lemon peel, violets, leather, and tobacco; soft spice including cardamom in the mouth, plus assorted berries, cherry, candle wax, and leather; dark fruit flavors; hints of pepper and licorice; medium-weight, textured like rough linen, and very long. Another personal favorite.

1997 Savoy Vineyard (tasted in 2003): Transparent, medium-dark garnet with a slightly orange rim; very open nose of flowers and blackberry; very concentrated and grippy in the mouth, with mineral, graphite, slate, and other black flavors; medium-length and medium-weight but austere.

1997 Thieriot Vineyard (tasted in 2001): Transparent, medium black-red; nose of wet fur and earth; flavors of sweet dark cherry, orange peel, and clove; chewy tannins, substantial length. This vintage of Thieriot was made entirely from Swan selection fruit, and one-quarter of the fruit was left in whole-cluster form.

PRACTICAL INFORMATION

Littorai pinots are made in lots of 200 to 600 cases, depending on the vintage, and are sold exclusively to restaurants and mailing-list customers. The wines are now generally allocated. All wines (except the 2001 Sonoma Coast) sell for about the same per-bottle price. The winery is closed to the public; 707-963-4762.

MARIMAR TORRES ESTATE

Sebastopol, California

Marimar Torres is the youngest child and only daughter of Miguel Torres, the distinguished winemaker and entrepreneur who built Bodegas Torres—a Catalan firm anchored in the Penedes—into the largest family-owned wine business in Spain. Known internationally for proprietary blends like Viña Sol, Sangre de Toro, and Gran Coronas,

Bodegas Torres was founded in the middle of the nineteenth century, when Miguel's great-granduncle worked his way to the Americas as a cabin boy, and then parlayed a fortuitous investment in Cuban oil into the beginnings of a wine empire.

Marimar joined the family firm in 1967, armed with a degree in business and economics from the University of Barcelona and fluency in six languages. She worked initially as export director, and then as Torres's resident representative in North America. Following a four-year marriage to wine writer Robert Finigan, the youngest Torres undertook to persuade her father that the family should expand its business beyond Spain and Chile to include grape growing and winemaking in California. At the time Marimar was not especially passionate about pinot noir, and the family's experience elsewhere was concentrated in warm-climate varieties; but the purchase in 1983 of a 56-acre parcel west of Graton, just ten miles as the crow flies from the Pacific Coast, argued for a wine program focused on pinot and chardonnay. About the same time, Torres began work on the first of two books about Spanish cuisine, which have become classics.

Torres's so-called Don Miguel vineyard, named in honor of Marimar's father, is a narrow, northeast-southwest-oriented parcel fronting on Graton Road about halfway between Graton and Occidental. The upslope, which faces mostly eastward, is fairly steep, gaining about 400 feet from roadside to hilltop. The soils are almost entirely Goldridge loam, reddish in some spots, yellowish in others. The first 14 acres of pinot noir were planted in 1988 and 1989; 2.5 acres were added between 1992 and 1994. Ten additional acres of pinot were added in 1995, 1996, and 1997, at which time four acres of chardonnay were also grafted to pinot. A small (0.9-acre) block, planted meter by meter, was set out in 2000.

The 1980s plantings were made with field-selected budwood from various North Coast sources. For the six acres planted in 1988, Torres used wood from the Eliot Vineyard on Big Ranch Road in Napa that was first dubbed Beringer Selection because the Eliot plantings were said to have been made, circa 1972, with budwood obtained from Beringer Brothers. (Since Beringer had obtained its budwood in the mid 1960s from FPMS, Eliot selection is probably one—or a mix of several—of California's first certified clones.) Torres has now abandoned the Beringer designation and rechristened this selection Cristina 88. (Marimar's daughter, Cristina, was born the year the vines were planted.) The balance of the 1980s plantings were Swan selection from Dehlinger, Lee selection from Iron Horse, and UCD 4 from Adelsheim in Oregon via Saintsbury. Dijon 115, 667, and 777 were added in the 1990s, along with more Swan and UCD 4 propagated from the 1980s plantings. It is worth noting that Dijon clones 667 and 777, bred in France for their capacity to ripen early, are among the latest ripeners at this site—only Lee selection ripens later than Dijon 667. Typical spacing is 2,000 vines per acre, though several blocks are set out meter by meter. Yields are about three tons per acre. (Conveniently, at 2,000 vines per acre, a three-ton yield translates exactly to three pounds of fruit per vine.)

A mustard-yellow Catalan farmhouse–style winery was built near the bottom of the property in 1991 and 1992. At that time the Don Miguel Vineyard was projected to yield 10,000 cases annually of pinot and chardonnay combined, and the winery was scaled to handle as much as 15,000. In fact, yields have been erratic, owing to notoriously cold springs and consequent uneven fruit sets. This uneconomical variability led Torres to acquire and plant some additional acreage contiguous to the Don Miguel site and then, in 2000, to acquire more property in rugged terrain near Freestone, where ten acres of pinot were planted in 2002. The new vineyard, which has been named Doña Margarita in honor of Marimar's mother, will be used to grow the winery's total production to about 20,000 cases, which will require minor expansion of the production facilities.

The winegrowing team is now composed of Torres, technical director Bill Dyer, cellarmaster Tony Britton, and vineyard manager Ventura Albor.

WINEMAKING

The Torres Estate fruit is usually destemmed and slightly crushed before going into three sizes (3.5-, seven-, and nine-ton) of open-top stainless steel fermentors. Cellarmaster Tony Britton finds that the Lee selection fruit, which is normally the last to be picked, sometimes exhibits genuinely ripe stems, and in this case some whole clusters are layered on the bottom of the relevant fermentor. A three-day cold soak precedes inoculation with Assmannshausen yeast. The alcoholic fermentation then continues for approximately seven days, with the thermostats set to begin cooling at 85 degrees Fahrenheit—meaning that, according to Britton, the tank centers probably peak at 90 degrees. Punchdowns are done two or three times per day. The must is pressed at dryness, and the press fraction is recombined with the free-run juice.

The barrel regime is 100 percent French oak, about one-third of which is new each year. Until 1998, the largest share of barrels was purchased from François Frères, but the main sources of cooperage since 1998 have been Rousseau (which Britton finds similar to François Frères), Radoux, and Séguin Moreau. All lots are inoculated to initiate the malolactic fermentation, and the wine spends a minimum of ten months in barrel. (The 1999 vintage remained in barrel for 14 months.) A first racking is done as soon as the malolactic fermentation is over "so that the wine will not need to be filtered," and the blend is also established at this time. A second racking is done prior to bottling. The 1997 vintage was fined with egg whites both for clarity and for tannin management, but there has been no filtration since 1996. A few barrels are sometimes deselected and sold off, but in general the winemaking team has liked the "natural" blend of all fruit from the vineyard better than any choice-based blends. The wine is held in bottle for 12 months before release.

THE WINES

Marimar Torres Estate pinots are medium-weight wines that finish long and exhibit considerable complexity—though the components of their complexity vary from vintage to vintage. Vintages through 1995 were based exclusively on the California heritage selections planted in 1988 and 1989; since 1996 an increasing minority percentage of Dijon-clone fruit has been used. Some critics have preferred the post-1995 wines, which have also been unfiltered; but see my notes below. Because almost 10 percent of production is exported (via the Torres family connection) to European markets, the wines attract substantial and quite positive attention from the British wine press. Except in 1992, when a few lots, mostly UCD 4, were held out for a so-called Vineyard Selection, only one pinot has been produced each year. The winemaking team tastes regularly for the possibility that a few lots will stand out enough to justify a special bottling, however, and admits to being periodically tempted by lots of UCD 4. It is interesting that, despite the substantial changes associated with the availability of fruit (especially Dijon clones) from the 1990s plantings, the team finds, each year, that a blend of the whole, with no special selection *or* deselection, works best. This, Torres argues, is the advantage of having planted the vineyard in two main phases. "We were able to plant," she says, "exactly what would benefit the wine."

TASTING NOTES

1999 Don Miguel Vineyard (tasted in 2002): Transparent, medium black-red; aromas and flavors of dark cherry and lightly resinated briar, with hints of root beer, sarsaparilla, orange peel, black pepper, and allspice; some grip but predominantly rough silk, medium-weight and long.

1998 Don Miguel Vineyard (tasted in 2000): Transparent, medium-dark black-red; violets, raspberry, cherry, and hints of fig on the nose; simultaneously sweet and tannic; accents of mint, black pepper, and a tangy form of cinnamon; long.

1997 Don Miguel Vineyard (tasted in 2000): Transparent, medium-dark, more red than black; nose of tree bark, raspberry, and black cherry; sweeter core than the 1998; again hints of mint and black pepper, but here also clove and cardamom; flavors of chocolate crème brûlée; tannic but very mouthcoating and long.

1995 Don Miguel Vineyard (tasted in 2000): Transparent, medium black-red; aromas of sweet orange blossom, herb, and tar; black fruit and slate flavors, with a bit of tobacco, mushroom, black pepper, and clove; still tannic but silken and lingering.

1992 Don Miguel Vineyard Selection (tasted in 2000): Very transparent, light to medium garnet with a tinge of terra-cotta; nose of cherry and licorice, with toffee cream; hint of animal; some toasted spice, pepper, tobacco, mushroom, chocolate, and slate; medium-weight and silken, clean and layered flavors, well-preserved and lingering. A personal favorite.

PRACTICAL INFORMATION

Production fluctuates between approximately 4,000 and 6,000 cases annually, which are distributed to most markets and to Europe. Current releases may also be mail-ordered directly from the winery. Tours may be arranged by appointment; 707-823-4365.

McKINLAY VINEYARDS

Newberg, Oregon

Matt and Holly Kinne live on the south-facing slope of Parrett Mountain, the southernmost peak of the Chehalem Mountains, between Newberg and Wilsonville. The deck of their house overlooks 20 acres of vineyard planted and tended, more or less, with their own hands. McKinlay Vineyards' crushpad is outside, on the northern side of the house. The rest of the winery is the house's cellar, just as in Burgundy. Matt Kinne does not commute. He still purchases some fruit, but only from vineyards within a five-minute drive or so. He maintains a low profile but makes some of Oregon's best pinot noir.

The Kinnes started planting the "estate" vineyard behind the house in 1990. Five acres at the top of the property, where the soils are shallowest, were planted first; then four acres just below the first five. The vines were in eight-foot rows, oriented northwest-southeast, with five-foot intervine spacing. At first they were interested in both pinot and chardonnay, and made chardonnay for several vintages; but beginning in 1996, the chardonnay vines in these first blocks were grafted to pinot noir, and additional pinot was planted in new blocks. Spacing in the new blocks was tightened to six feet by one meter, but the six-foot rows have demonstrated too much tendency to rot, so McKinlay has now settled on seven-foot row spacings for future plantings.

The scion material is a combination of UCD 5 field-selected from the Adelsheim and Adams vineyards in Chehalem Valley; UCD 2A and 30 from Abbey Ridge (see the Cameron Winery profile for details); a field selection from Charles Coury's vineyard (then called Laurel Ridge; see Cameron Winery) near Forest Grove, which Coury is reputed to have imported personally from Burgundy about 1965; about four acres of a field selection from Hanzell, chosen personally by Matt Kinne; and (most recently) Dijon 114, 115, 667, and 777. Of these, the Hanzell and Coury selections are visibly virused, shy-bearing vines, whose small clusters and small berries give less juice per pound than the UCD clones. The vineyard is dry-farmed and rarely produces more than 1.5 tons per acre.

The Kinnes have also planted a dozen acres of leased land that fronts on Earlwood Road, and they purchase fruit from an old-vines vineyard they call Marquis (the owner, Matt explains, "looks like a European marquis"), half a mile uphill from the estate; and from La Cantera, which is adjacent to Rex Hill. La Cantera fruit has been used since 1993. Marquis, which Matt describes as "our little chunk of Musigny," became available to McKinlay in 1994. Vintages of McKinlay before 1994 were made entirely from purchased fruit sourced elsewhere in the Willamette Valley. The 1988 vintage was made entirely from the Zena Vineyard in the Eola Hills. From 1990 through 1992, the Kinnes bought fruit from Beaux Frères; in 1990, 1992, and 1993 from Cooper Mountain (west of Beaverton, not far from Ponzi); and in 1991 and 1992 also from Eola Springs Vineyard. Since 1995, however, all fruit has come from the estate and its neighbors, Marquis and La Cantera, giving recent vintages more consistency. Matt Kinne's formal winemaking education derives from a single year at the University of California, Davis, in 1984–1985, and from on-the-job experience at Hanzell immediately thereafter. He explains that winemaking has always come to him "naturally," but he has had to work hard to learn farming. "I am a kid from the suburbs," he says, "and my thumbs are not green." However, the Kinnes did *everything* in the estate vineyard until a few years ago, and they still do all the wire work and hedging. He walks the vineyard every day.

WINEMAKING

Matt Kinne focuses on pH to tell him when to pick. A upward spike in pH, from just over 3.0 to about 3.2, is "an indicator that the plant is done." Generally, he is inclined to pick early, when natural acidity is fairly high, and will always pick before rain if it's humanly possible, even if it means taking fruit that is less than ideally ripe. After a brief flirtation with whole-cluster fermentation in his first vintage (1987), Kinne renounced stems entirely. He uses a proportion of whole berries but believes that breaking at least some of the berries can promote the formation of glycerols, which he likes. The fermentors are plastic fruit bins and small wooden open-tops; the only control over temperature involves moving them indoors from the crush-pad, or back outside. The estate vineyard, which is the first to be picked, generally cold soaks for six to eight days before fermentation begins naturally with resident yeast; La Cantera, which is picked later, generally soaks only three to four days, since the cellar's yeast population has by then built up. Kinne punches down three times a day during the cold soak, then cuts back to twice daily after the primary fermentation has begun. Once the Brix sinks below 2.0, the cap is manipulated just enough to keep it wet. The must is usually dry on day 16 or 17, but a postfermentation maceration continues for several additional days, until the wine's phenolics move "farther and farther back in the mouth." Kinne then presses, bucketing solids into the press with a Chinese wonton skimmer, and settles briefly in tank. He reassembles the press fraction, which he claims to like better than the free-run juice.

Kinne also likes neutral barrels and believes that between 20 percent and 25 percent of each wine should be raised free from the influence of oak. After a period of purchasing one- and two-year-old barrels from Beaux Frères and other wineries, Kinne has now settled on a regime that involves purchasing just 25 percent new wood each year, and no used barrels at all. Because malolactic fermentations are natural and sometimes start late, especially if the winter is cold, Kinne frequently does not bottle until after the next vintage, in which case he will buy additional "ancient" barrels from a neighbor to handle the holdover. Domaine Drouhin is a favored source. Kinne explains that he has changed McKinlay's style twice, first by abandoning stems after his first vintage, in 1987, was too tannic for the marketplace; and again in 1996, when infatuation with European wines and experience tasting older wines tipped the scales back again, leading him to higher acidities, slightly longer fermentations, and a renewed emphasis on structure.

THE WINES

In most vintages, McKinlay makes two blends. Special Selection is made from richer, denser, and darker barrels; the Willamette Valley designation is used for a blend of lots that display "less than reserve caliber." In some warmer years, McKinlay's entire production has gone into Special Selection; in other vintages there has been only a Willamette Valley cuvée. The 1987, 1988, 1989, and 1992 vintages were Willamette Valley–only years; in 1993, 1995, 1998, and 1999, all barrels were made into Special Selection. In other vintages, both wines were produced. In 1998, Kinne flirted with modified vineyard-designates. The Special Selection was made from 90 percent estate fruit; a Quarry label "focused" on fruit from La Cantera; and a Ladd Hill bottling was similarly focused on fruit from the Marquis vineyard. Kinne says he cannot bring himself to do real vineyard-designates when "10 to 15 percent of something else can make the wine so much better." He does not exclude the possibility, however, that an estate wine, probably high in phenolics, may be made at some point in the future.

Because my experience with McKinlay pinots is confined to very recent vintages on the one hand, and on the other to a single vertical tasting of wines from the late 1980s and early 1990s—thus overlapping Kinne's "fat, soft, endearing" period and his most recent "more-structure-is-a-good-thing" period, along with considerable evolution in fruit sources—it is hard to generalize about these wines. Kinne says he believes pinot should emphasize red fruits rather than black (strawberry, raspberry, and cherry rather than blueberry or boysenberry), but my tasting notes repeatedly feature black-fruit flavors and aromas. The wines from 1988 through 1994 have all aged beautifully, despite the "supple" style parameter Kinne says he imposed on himself during this period. I find a strong floral component in the recent vintages, possibly deriving from the *terroirs* of Ladd Hill. But every McKinlay pinot I have tasted has been complex and fine.

TASTING NOTES

2000 Ladd Hill (tasted in 2003): Transparent, medium garnet; chalk, black raspberry, and briar on the nose; slightly sweet red and black berries in the mouth, with strong minerality; mouthcoating but structured, suede-textured and long.

2000 Special Selection (tasted in 2003): Transparent, medium garnet with rosy-orange highlights; slightly closed nose with some raspberry, anise, smoke, and a hint of camphor; cherry, raspberry, clove, black pepper, and tangerine peel in the mouth; bitter-spice finish; grippy, high-toned, structured, and mineral, medium-weight, not yet together, medium-long.

2000 Willamette Valley (tasted in 2003): Very transparent, light to medium ruby; flower-box nose combining earth, flowers, and orange peel; strong berry flavors, very juicy; forward fruit, short- to medium-length.

1999 Special Selection (tasted twice in 2001,

once from a half-bottle): Transparent, light to medium black-red; slightly closed; flavors of black fruit, smoke, mint, leather, and tree bark; angular wine, but very long. From the half-bottle, showing white pepper, tangerine peel, and gardenia on the nose; and displaying smoke and ink on the palate.

1994 Special Selection (tasted from magnum in 2001): Transparent, medium black-red; lightly fruity nose against a background of mineral and slate; soft, blended spices on the palate, with some earth and a hint of leather; medium-weight but very long finish, showing barely a hint of six years' bottle age.

1992 Willamette Valley (tasted in 2001): Transparent, medium black-red; black fruits, currants, and tree bark on the nose; slightly tannic in the mouth, with flavors of clove, nutmeg, soft cinnamon, and a touch of black pepper; hints of licorice and leather; a long, soft wine, showing beautifully.

1991 Special Selection (tasted from magnum in 2001): Transparent, medium-dark black-red; explosive nose of boysenberry pie; sweet core of red fruit, with black pepper and a hint of chocolate; very long and elegant.

1988 Willamette Valley (tasted in 2001): Transparent, tiling, but still medium-dark; aromas of leather and mushroom, with a whiff of plain barnyard funk; roasted cherries in the mouth; hints of menthol, root beer, and truffles; medium-weight, long, and fine.

PRACTICAL INFORMATION

McKinlay's production is now about 1,000 cases and will grow to approximately 1,500 when the newest plantings are in full production. The wines are distributed in 12 markets nationwide and by mailing list. They are well represented in Portland's best restaurants, including Wildwood, Paley's Place, the Heathman Hotel, Ivy House, and Cuveron. The winery may be visited by appointment only, except on the Memorial Day and Thanksgiving weekends; 503-625-2534.

MERRY EDWARDS WINES

Windsor, California

Merry Edwards is something of a legend in the California wine business and was a pioneer with pinot noir from the outset. An avid cook and food scientist whose fascination with yeast led her from bread to beer and then to wine, she was an amateur winemaker even before she graduated from the University of California, Berkeley, with a degree in physiology. Fascinated to discover, soon thereafter, that formal coursework and "real" academic degrees were offered in her avocation, she enrolled in the then-obscure program at the University of California, Davis, where she earned a master's degree in food science with an emphasis in enology in 1973. Her class was the first to graduate women, and Edwards was the only one of her female classmates to pursue winemaking as a career.

As a winemaker, she is credited with the development of two well-respected California brands: Mount Eden Vineyards in the Santa Cruz Mountains and Matanzas Creek Winery in Sonoma's Bennett Valley. Subsequent ventures in the mid and late 1980s—a family enterprise called The Merry Vintners, and Domaine Laurier, the child of an ill-fated investment company that built the winery now used by Hartford Family Wines—both succumbed to economic recession, but Edwards worked successfully throughout the 1990s as a consultant to various California wineries, including Liparita, Nelson Estate, Lambert Bridge, B. R. Cohn, and Pellegrini Family.

Edwards made legendary pinot noir at Mount Eden. The 1974, 1975, and 1976 vintages of this wine, along with the 1973 made by Dick Graff, were turnaround benchmarks as pinot noir clawed its way back from the qualitative nadir of the late 1960s and early 1970s. She also made pinot for three of the seven years she worked at Matanzas Creek, using fruit from Quail Hill in the Russian River valley. In 1997 Edwards launched a new all-pinot venture called Meredith Vineyard Estate, a privately held corporation created to underwrite the planting of her Meredith Estate vineyard and the production of Merry Edwards Wines. In that year, she purchased fruit from several mature vineyards around Russian River and planted a 24-acre parcel just outside the current periphery of the appellation, on Burnside Road southwest of Sebastopol. The mature sources were the Klopp Ranch on Laguna Road, a 1989 planting of Swan selection and UCD 4 in the Laguna Ridge section of Russian River; Robert Pellegrini's Olivet Lane Vineyard, planted in 1972 (see also the Williams Selyem and Gary Farrell Wines profiles); and Windsor Gardens, a stand of 33-year-old UCD 13 leased by Lee Martinelli, on doomed land slated for redevelopment as tract housing north of the Sonoma County airport. Fruit from the Dutton family's Jewell vineyard near Sebastopol was used in 1998 only, but Edwards continues to source pinot from the other three vineyards. Olivet Lane fruit has been used to make a vineyard-designated wine every year; in 1999 vineyard-designates were also made from Klopp Ranch and Windsor Gardens fruit. With the 2000 vintage, Klopp Ranch has emerged as the anchor for Edwards's Russian River Valley blend (see below).

Meanwhile, Meredith Estate vineyard—a cool but south-facing slope heavily influenced by marine air flows through the Petaluma Gap that was planted to Dijon 115, 667, and 777, plus Swan and UCD 37, a certified clone Edwards personally selected from Mount Eden during her tenure there—produced its first significant crop in 2000, from which ten barrels were selected as the inaugural bottling of Meredith Estate wine. In 2001, having finally downsized her consulting business, Edwards planted a second estate vineyard, bearing her husband's name. This Coopersmith Vineyard is 9.5 acres of south- and southeast-facing hillside where the Gravenstein Highway intersects Graton Road, in Goldridge series soil. There Edwards set out more UCD 37, along with Dijon 828 sourced from Archery Summit in Oregon, configuring the vineyard in eight-foot rows with five-foot spacing between vines. The first small crop was harvested in 2003.

Edwards was among the first California winemakers to recognize the importance of clonal selection, the first to observe clonal research and field trials in Burgundy, and the first person to teach a seminar on clonal selection at Davis. She credits the availability of new French clones, alongside earlier imports that are now field selections in California, with part of the overall improvement in California wine quality, and argues that this difference applies particularly to pinot noir. She also believes that vertical trellising has played a major role in the betterment of California pinots, arguing that fruit well exposed to sunlight ripens more evenly, colors better, and resists disease more effectively. At Olivet Lane, she persuaded Bob Pellegrini to retrofit his previously sprawling vines to a vertical trellis. The 1997 through 1999 vintages of Merry Edwards were made at Lambert Bridge and Michel Schlumberger in Dry Creek Valley; the 2000 vintage was made at Taft Street Winery in Sebastopol. A new facility that Edwards was instrumental in designing on the Olivet Lane property was ready for the harvest in 2001.

WINEMAKING

Edwards picks by taste, and says she finds that Russian River pinot generally tastes ripe somewhere between 24 and 25.5 Brix. Rows destined for vineyard-designation, identified before harvest, are segregated, fermented in 4.5- and five-ton stainless steel open-tops, and punched down manually or with the aid of pneumatic *piges.* The rest of the fruit, which is used in the Russian River blend, is fermented in conventional ten-ton tanks, in which juice from the bottom of the tank is pumped over the cap. Interestingly, this difference in technique, often described as fundamental, seems to have only a modest impact on the style of the resulting wines, though the vineyard-designated wines usually exhibit more complex flavor profiles, which *may* be attributable in part to the subtleties of extraction that are associated with hand punchdowns. (Separately, making an exceptionally good-value pinot for Bob Pellegrini's Olivet Lane Vineyard label, Edwards has experimented with rotary fermentors. Although the rotaries will not accommodate whole clusters and sometimes involve losses "in layers of complexity," Edwards likes the rotaries' ability to "enhance forward fruit" and finds they seem to work well with Martini clones.) For the Merry Edwards Wines, Edwards likes to use a significant percentage of whole clusters, cold soaks for two to three days using dry ice and the tanks' chilling jackets, and prefers relatively warm fermentations. She inoculates using a combination of D-254 and Assmannshausen yeast. "I like to be in control," Edwards admits, ascribing her conservatism to long experience as a consultant. "You take fewer risks when it is someone else's wine," she observes. Edwards argues that "if you get grapes really ripe, you must add acid," and she does. The must is generally pressed at dryness, though macerations were extended on some lots in 2001. After pressing, the wine is settled one or two days in tank to separate the gross lees. Free-run juice and the press fraction are combined.

Barrel regimes are tailored to each cuvée—"with time," Edwards explains, "it becomes clear that certain barrels work better for certain wines." Across the board, she uses only new and one-year-old barrels from four cooperages—François Frères, Dargaud & Jaeglé, Mercurey, and Remond. The barrels are ordered in several different toastings. The Russian River Valley cuvée sees about 60 percent new oak from a mix of the four coopers; about the same percentage has been used for the first two vintages of the estate wine, but in this case most of the barrels are Mercurey. The Klopp Ranch wine, invariably large-framed and "flashy," is finished in about 78 percent new oak from the mix of coopers; Olivet Lane sees about 85 percent, also from the mix. For Windsor Gardens, an especially rich-textured wine, Edwards prefers Dargaud & Jaeglé barrels and finds that 80 percent new wood works best. Distribution of toast levels among the wines varies; this Edwards describes as "a moving target." Lees are sometimes stirred in barrel, but the wines are not racked until bottling—just before the next vintage. The goal is to make wine "on the front end" so that fining is unnecessary at the end, but Edwards will fine her pinots if the wine is excessively tannic. Coarse pad filtering is practiced to "remove the big chunks only," and experiments are done continuously to compare filtered and unfiltered lots.

THE WINES

Edwards describes her ideal pinot noir with words like *luscious, opulent,* and *concentrated.* Her emphasis on "perfectly ripe fruit" and a high percentage of new oak yields big wines; relatively intensive use of whole clusters and aggressive cluster thinning also ensure that some are, by pinot standards, relatively tannic. Nor is Edwards shy about the much-debated matter of color, arguing (controversially) that deeply colored pinot is a "marketplace necessity." Although she was not around to taste them, Edwards says she has "a mental image" of what old Burgundies were like, and these "ideal" old Burgundies serve her as a model. From the very first vintage, Edwards's wines have received high praise from the wine press—not least from the *New York Times'* incorruptible Frank Prial—and from fellow winemakers, one of whom described her 1997 Russian River Valley cuvée as his image of the "perfect" California pinot noir.

TASTING NOTES

2000 Klopp Ranch (tasted in 2002): Transparent, medium-dark magenta; rose petal, dark cherry, Penja pepper, and Italian plum on the nose; very ripe dark fruit with cinnamon and slate in the mouth; rich, mouthcoating, and velvety but grippy, long.

2000 Meredith Estate Vineyard 2000 (tasted in 2002): Transparent, deep oxblood; aromas of deep black cherry, beetroot, and licorice; very ripe fruit in the mouth, with overtones of wet slate and allspice; texture of very fine emery and substantially tannic, but rich and medium-long.

2000 Olivet Lane (tasted in 2002): Brilliant, medium-deep garnet; very ripe cherry-plum fruit with spiced beets on the nose; in the mouth, sweet dark cherry with hints of hard spice, black licorice, plum candy, and resin; medium-weight and quite long, with fine-grained tannin and the texture of crushed velvet.

2000 Russian River Valley (tasted in 2002): Transparent, very dark garnet with crimson highlights; aromas of balsam, charcuterie, and bay laurel; sweet, dark cherry fruit in the mouth, with black licorice, slate, graphite, mocha, and barrel char; mouthcoating and concentrated, slightly grippy but still velvety, very long.

2000 Windsor Gardens (tasted in 2002): Transparent but nearly saturated, dark black-red; aromas of dark berry fruit wrapped in pickling spices with black pepper and some vanilla; slightly sweet dark cherry, with graphite and freshly toasted clove; full-bodied and chamois-textured with some grip, medium-weight, and medium-length.

1999 Klopp Ranch (tasted in 2002): Transparent but nearly saturated, dark black-red; nose of beetroot, very ripe plums, and tobacco; slow to open; very sweet on the palate, with bright flavors of licorice, black cherry, smoke, and a hint of orange peel; very fine-grained tannin, already resolving; slightly chewy, full-bodied, and very long. Made from a block of Swan selection vines.

1999 Olivet Lane Vineyard (tasted in 2002): Transparent, medium black-red; unusual but seductive nose of sea foam, iodine, and salt marsh against a backdrop of wild cherries; sweet cherry fruit with tree bark, cinnamon, and clove in the mouth; medium-weight, very fine-grained tannins, medium-long. Made from the oldest vines at Olivet Lane, on the western side of the vineyard.

1999 Russian River Valley (tasted in 2002): Transparent, brilliant, medium-dark black-red; on the nose, violets, toasted sweet spice, and the aromas of a caramel and nut candy bar; sweet core of blackberry and black cherry in the mouth, plus an infusion of black currants, smoke, tar, and toasted spice; evident, plush tannins, borderline velvety, medium-rich texture and weight, long.

1999 Windsor Gardens (tasted twice, in 2001 and 2002): Transparent, medium-dark ruby; tea, ink, a hint of nut, and root vegetable on the nose; black English Breakfast tea, India ink, blueberry, and blackberry on the palate; texturally soft like fine velvet, medium-rich, very long, elegant, and fine. A personal favorite.

1998 Olivet Lane Vineyard (tasted in 2001): Transparent, dark black-red; aromas of black cherry and bramble, with a whiff of gardenia and lavender; slightly sweet core of cherry and ripe plums; strong flavors of Carborundum and lead pencil; chewy, tannic, dense, and long.

1998 Russian River Valley (tasted in 2001): Transparent, medium black-red; daphne, nut, and lemon peel aromas; very sweet dark cherry on the palate, with cinnamon, Indonesian spices, and infused rose petals; long and medium-weight with some very fine-grained tannin.

1997 Olivet Lane Vineyard (tasted thrice, in 1999, 2001, and 2002): Substantially changed from 1999 to 2001; deep black-red in 1999, medium garnet two years later; strong aromas of black fruit jam and cola in 1999; more toast, cardamom, rose petal, and white pepper by 2001; tobacco, coffee, and cocoa flavors persisting; earthy flavors emerging by 2001; enormous body and considerable tannin in 1999; soft, silken, and sweet but still tannic in 2001; in 2002, dominant black fruit again, with sweet spice; now a very plush mouthfeel with dark mouthcoating spice, hints of smoke and sausage; dense and very long, with undertones of coffee and tobacco and a velvety but still grippy finish. *New York Times* columnist Frank Prial loved this wine from the outset, describing it as "considerably more attractive than wines twice its price."

1997 Russian River Valley (tasted several times in 1999, 2000, and 2001): Transparent, medium-dark, black-red wine; nose of violets, ripe plum, and black fruit with hints of merbromin; more cherry and plum on the palate, plus cinnamon, allspice, nutmeg, and slate, with a bit of smoke and herbs; quite tannic when first tasted in 1999, softening slightly by 2001; medium-weight wine with the texture of rough velvet. Still young; may improve for another decade.

PRACTICAL INFORMATION

Merry Edwards's pinots are found on fine restaurant lists around the country and can be ordered directly from the winery. The winery has made arrangements to ship into most states. The wines are not, however, available through conventional retail channels. The winery is currently not open to the public; 888-388-9050.

MOUNT EDEN VINEYARDS

Saratoga, California

About two air miles south of the Stevens Creek Reservoir, at the very edge of Silicon Valley's suburban sprawl, Table Mountain rises 2,000 feet above the town of Saratoga, in the shape of a U open to the east. La Cresta, Paul Masson's mountain winery—now empty of wine but a favorite site for executive events, weddings, and summer concerts—is on the southern side of the U. A narrow, vertiginous dirt road snakes up the northern (and much higher) side of the mountain, where, beginning in 1943, Masson's protégé Martin Ray cleared enough chaparral and poison oak to make room for five small vineyards of cabernet sauvignon, chardonnay, and pinot noir; two houses; and a winery. The houses were the venue for Ray's interminable and infamous bacchanalian fests, attended variously by academics from the University of California, Davis, screen stars from Hollywood, aspiring winemakers, and others willing to endure Ray's filibusters about all and sundry but most especially, we are told, about the pitiful state of American wine, his own excepted.

Ray's years on Table Mountain, chronicled in 1993 by his widow, Eleanor, in *Vineyards in the Sky,* were apparently a more or less constant struggle against the elements, destructive fires, insufficient insurance, inadequate financial resources, and personal enemies. In the 1960s Ray conceived the idea of simultaneously financing new vineyard development and surrounding himself with a "club of compatible people" by selling shares in an enterprise he called Mount Eden Vineyards. Almost from the outset, however, Ray quarreled with his investors, eventually setting off waves and counterwaves of litigation. When the legal dust settled in 1971, the original hilltop vineyard Ray had planted in 1943 and the hilltop ranch house, with its wide verandahs overlooking Santa Clara Valley, plus considerable acreage lower on the mountain, had all passed to a subset of the investors, while Ray and his family retained a second house on the midslope between the two, along with a small vineyard downslope from the house. (This small vineyard now belongs to Ray's stepson, Peter Martin Ray, who sells its fruit to Mount Eden and to a handful of small Santa Cruz Mountains vintners. The pinot noir is split between Mount Eden and Cronin Vineyards; see Cronin's profile earlier in this section.)

From these tumultuous beginnings, Mount Eden Vineyards, first a partnership, then a corporation, produced its first vintage of pinot noir in 1972, using fruit from Martin Ray's 29-year-old vines. Chalone founder Dick Graff was the winemaker for a single vintage; he was followed by his brother, Peter Graff. The baton then passed to Merry Edwards, who established the brand's reputation for voluptuous, mineral-laced chardonnay, and later to Bill Anderson and Fred Peterson. For the past 22 vintages, Jeffrey Patterson has made the wines. An autodidact in wine matters who supported his postcollegiate self-study of fine wine with odd jobs painting houses and repairing cars, Patterson has brought a steady hand, a huge passion, and a site-specific dedication to Mount Eden's wines. Patterson and his family live in the hilltop house.

There are now seven pinot vineyards at Mount Eden, counting the one that is actually owned by Peter Martin Ray. Five of the original seven acres of hilltop vineyard have been replanted to pinot noir: one acre to cuttings taken from the original planting, in 1996; one acre each to Dijon 115, 667, and 777, planted in 1998; and another acre of the Old Mount Chardonnay Vineyard to Dijon 115, planted in 1999. In other words, most of Ray's original hilltop pinot, which had been sourced from La Cresta and grafted to rootstock by a local nursery, was kept in production until 1997, and the acre replanted in 1996 will preserve the original Paul Masson pedigree indefinitely. The hilltop vineyards share a moderate, east-facing slope of friable, well-drained Franciscan shale. (Martin Ray likened the shale to "fine Parmesan cheese" for its granularity and tendency to fracture simultaneously in orthogonal directions.) Yield was down to a measly quarter-ton per acre on the hilltop before the old vines were removed. The higher density of the new plantings (1,800 vines to the acre) and the health of younger, unvirused vines will boost that figure, but the thin mountaintop soil will always limit vigor on the summit. The other two vineyards are 400 feet downslope, on the northern side of the access road. One is the 1.5-acre Peter Martin Ray vineyard already discussed. It is a sparsely planted parcel—ten-foot rows with ten feet between vines, untrellised—and the budwood was a field selection from Winery Lake Vineyard in Los Carneros. The other vineyard is a one-acre parcel set in ten-foot rows with six-foot intervine spacing, whose scion material was taken from the hilltop site. The soils in these lower vineyards contain a bit more clay, so the yield is slightly higher, ranging from one to three tons per acre. Together the seven vineyards produce only enough fruit for about 400 to 600 cases of wine, which makes pinot noir less than 4 percent of Mount Eden's total production. (The rest of Mount Eden's program is chardonnay and cabernet sauvignon.) A single bottling of pinot has been made each year since 1972, except for 1992, when no pinot was released, and 1997, when 200 cases of a wonderful Cuvée des Vieilles Vignes was separately bottled, to honor the last vintage from Ray's original planting.

Mount Eden has been a favored source when pinot growers elsewhere in California have field-selected budwood. It has been known variously as the Paul Masson selection, the Martin Ray selection, and the Mount Eden selection; additionally, budwood taken from Mount Eden by Merry Edwards has been released by FPMS as UCD 37. In these pages, I have standardized the nomenclature for the field selections as Mount Eden, but UCD 37 is still UCD 37.

WINEMAKING

Pinot is usually picked at Mount Eden during the first half of September at Brix levels ranging from 23 to 25. Patterson ferments in 120-gallon bins and 1,000-gallon stainless steel open-tops. The 1995 and 1998 vintages were made in tank, the 1996 and 1997 in bins. Like many pinot makers, Patterson has changed course in his use of stems. His predecessors had followed a 100 percent whole-cluster protocol, but in 1983, Patterson eliminated stems entirely. Now he crushes the majority of his fruit, but uses between 5 percent and 10 percent whole berries, "some of which have stems"—so the must is getting a light seasoning of stems. "It's a moving target," he asserts. He is also experimenting with cold soaks, which run for as few as two days to as many as seven. Fermentation is jump-started with Assmannshausen and Burgundian yeasts, and acid is added to the must about two years out of three, to compensate for high levels of juice potassium. The must is punched down four times daily, and the primary fermentation normally takes about seven days. Patterson favors a fairly hot alcoholic fermentation (between 85 and 90 degrees Fahrenheit) to gain "earth, mushroom, and cheese flavors, and some sexiness," but he argues that fermentation temperature is a stylistic rather than a qualitative parameter with pinot. Two to five days of postfermentation maceration are permitted before the must is pressed with a membrane Europress and sent to barrel, where the malolactic fermentation is allowed to begin naturally. The press fraction is settled in tanks before being reintegrated with the barreled wine.

Patterson uses 50 percent new barrels, mostly medium-plus-toast François Frères. Barrel time is a fairly long 18 to 20 months because Patterson finds that "the wine is better when it goes over a second winter in wood. . . . You lose some fruit," he admits, "but you gain a lot in secondary flavors." One racking is performed after malolactic fermentation has ended; a second is done at bottling. There has been no fining since 1984, but Patterson sometimes filters to control brettanomyces.

THE WINES

The 1990s Mount Eden pinots have been complex, elegant, medium-bodied wines with jammy berry flavors up front and an avalanche of minty, earthy, and meaty notes on the midpalate and finish. I have no personal experience with older vintages, but others report that the wines usually age very well, peaking ten to 15 years after the vintage. The 1997 Cuvée des Vieilles Vignes, the only Mount Eden pinot of the decade to be made exclusively from Martin Ray's old vines, is a fine testament to the quality of this historic vineyard.

TASTING NOTES

1997 Cuvée des Vieilles Vignes (tasted twice in 2000 and a third time in 2002): Transparent, light to medium garnet, tiling; berries, fruit candy, mint, mushroom, bacon, leather, and black pepper variously on the nose and palate; notes of licorice, allspice, and chocolate; lingering, elegant, silken wine. The last vintage for Martin Ray's half-century-old vines.

1997 Estate (tasted in 2000): Transparent, brick-red; nose of roses and raw meat; cherry, mint, resin, and black pepper in the mouth; some smoke; long, light- to medium-weight, linen-textured wine.

1996 Estate (tasted in 2000): Saturated but still transparent, black-red; complex nose of smoke, berries, leather, mushroom, and earth;

mint, truffle, and black pepper in the mouth; some of the secondary flavors attributable to brettanomyces; sweet, chewy, rich wine, long and velvety. A personal favorite.

1995 Estate (tasted in 2000): Transparent, medium black-red; blackberry, violets, mint, and chocolate on the nose and palate; noticeably tannic, medium-bodied, and silken.

PRACTICAL INFORMATION

Mount Eden pinot is nationally distributed and available by mailing list, but with only about 400 cases made, supply is short. Quantities should increase a bit when the hilltop vineyard comes back into full production. Visits are by appointment only; 408-867-5832.

NAVARRO VINEYARDS

Philo, California

Ted Bennett and Deborah Cahn, husband and wife, moved to Anderson Valley in 1974. They had sold a successful retail business in the Bay Area but shared strong counterculture values. In Anderson Valley they raised sheep, and they even paid the obstetrician who delivered their first child with lambs. They also planted grapes: gewürztraminer and pinot noir. Bennett loved gewürztraminer. As for the pinot, well, he remembers needing a red grape that could ripen in a cool mesoclimate. A quarter-century later, having outlasted Anderson Valley's other wine pioneers, Bennett and Cahn are still planting grapes, raising animals, and selling most of their wine from the tasting room they built on Highway 128. They still make more white wine than red, but pinot noir has become a substantial part of their business.

Bennett made his first pinots under the Edmeades label—he was an early investor in Edmeades—in 1975 and 1976. The grapes for these wines were sourced from the Redwood Valley, northeast of Ukiah. In 1977, fruit from the same source was used to make Navarro Mendocino Pinot Noir, which was the first pinot to carry the Navarro name. Meanwhile, the four acres of pinot Bennett had planted on the Navarro Ranch in 1975—the block is now called South Hill—began to bear, and an estate pinot debuted in 1978.

Testifying to the winery's early emphasis on gewürztraminer and its relative success in the marketplace, Navarro did not increase its investment in pinot noir until 1990. At that point, Bennett planted a new block called Hammer-Olsen, which consisted of 3.5 acres of UCD 13 and three acres of a field selection from Chalone, plus 1.5 additional acres of the same UCD 4 that had been planted on South Hill. In 1992 the Hammer-Olsen planting was expanded to include an acre of Dijon 115. By 1995, when it was obvious that pinot noir was now *very* marketable, Navarro began an ambitious planting program, crawling gradually up the hillside that marks the northeastern boundary of the Anderson Valley appellation. Upper Garden Spot was planted in 1995: a 3.9-acre block devoted primarily to Dijon 115, with some 113 and 114. At the same time the 1.3-acre Lower Garden Spot was planted to UCD 4. In 1996, the Omega vineyard, 1.8 acres between the 400- and 600-foot elevation contours, was planted to Dijon 667 on 3309 rootstock. Another 1.3 acres of Dijon 667 was planted on a site called Fox Point at the 1,000-foot elevation; and 2.2 acres, called Middle Ridge, ranging from 1,000 to 1,300 feet, were planted to Dijon 114 and 777. The following year the so-called Upper Marking Corral (remember that this property was originally a sheep ranch), at 1,500 feet on mostly rocky, thin soil, was planted to 5.5 acres of Dijon 113, 114, and 115 along with a bit of UCD 4. The 1998 project was the Lower Marking Corral: 2.3 acres of Dijon 115 and 667 on 101–14 rootstock, Dijon 777 on

3309, and Clone 459 on St. George. The 459 was replaced in 2001 with Clone 238. Navarro also became a buyer of Anderson Valley pinot noir, acquiring fruit from its next-door neighbor on Highway 128, Valley Foothills vineyard, and from the Bemposto and Savoy vineyards nearby.

This expansion means that Navarro now farms about 30 acres of estate-grown pinot noir and contracts for about 15 more. Together, they provide a rich palette for blending, involving no fewer than 11 selections on eight rootstocks in 13 discrete sites. Blending, indeed, has become Navarro's approach to pinot noir. Although Bennett maintains that it took ten years' experience before Navarro was able to make a pinot that "really excited us," the original South Hill planting still provides the anchor for the property's reserve wine, called Deep End Blend. Arguing that "*terroir* is a winemaking tool, not an end in itself," Navarro winemaker Jim Klein explains that the allocation of lots among Navarro's three pinot releases changes from year to year, and that wind and temperature may favor first one site, then another. Klein—a Southern Californian and onetime certified public accountant who did course work at the University of California, Davis, and made wine in both Santa Barbara and Israel—has been at Navarro since 1992.

WINEMAKING

Klein says that a "smorgasbord" of factors shapes Navarro's decisions about picking: the numbers, of course; how the fruit tastes; whether the seeds have lignified; and always, whether there is rain in the forecast. He is a strong believer that grapes should be sorted in the field, and that it is far better to invest in multiple pickings than to invest in sorting tables at the winery. Navarro used to ferment with about 15 percent whole clusters; now the grapes are completely destemmed. The must is cold soaked in fruit bins and small stainless steel open-tops for three to five days. The fruit arrives cool, having been picked at night, but the chill is reinforced by circulating cold water in the tank jackets and by layering dry ice in the fruit bins. Fermentation usually starts spontaneously, but Klein inoculates all lots anyway, using a Bordeaux red yeast. To minimize bitterness from seed tannins, he likes to press well before the must is dry and move the wine to tank. If it is clean, he will transfer it from tank to barrel when sugar is still about 1 or 2 degrees Brix; or he will let the fermentation finish completely in tank and do one clean racking before barreling the wine. Either way, the wine is still turgid and a little foamy when it gets to barrel.

Klein gets 95 percent of the winery's barrel stock for pinot from Remond, coopered from forests in the Allier. For the Deep End Blend and Anderson Valley wines, one-third of the barrels are new each year. Malolactic fermentation is started by inoculation, in barrel. Some barrels finish secondary fermentation as early as November; others subside for the winter and finish in the spring. Klein likes to keep the wine on its lees until spring anyway, and will simply stir the lees (rather than rack) if he detects reduction. A single racking, to tank, is then done just before bottling. Klein always fines with egg whites, both for clarity and for tannin management (he calls this step "polishing" and says it gives the wine "a touch of sheen"). In most vintages, some of the Anderson Valley blend is bottled unfiltered (and is so labeled), but Klein and Bennett are not great fans of brettanomyces, so they will filter with pads or cartridges if they detect signs of it. Navarro pinots are bottled before the next vintage for pragmatic reasons.

THE WINES

Navarro makes three pinots: about 200 cases of a reserve called Deep End Blend, about 4,000 cases of an Anderson Valley bottling called Méthode à l'Ancienne, and a variable quantity of Pinot Mendocino. The reserve is mostly or all estate-grown fruit—normally the fruit that has ripened last, and has therefore benefited from the longest hang time. Estate and purchased fruit are used in the Anderson Valley wine. Pinot Mendocino is made from declassified lots of estate and purchased Anderson Valley fruit, plus, almost always, fruit from the Potter or Redwood valley, or both. The latter is normally acquired to make pinot noir grape juice, a nonalcoholic Navarro specialty, but some of it is repurposed into Pinot Mendocino. The two high-end wines are classic Anderson Valley pinots, dominated by bright cherry and with generally fairly high acid, that rarely show optimally until three to five years after the vintage but hold up quite well thereafter. Nor should Pinot Mendocino be neglected. Sold for a very modest price, it varies by vintage but is frequently delicious light pinot noir, perfect for warm weather and salmon and much more enjoyable than most Bourgogne Rouge.

TASTING NOTES

1999 Anderson Valley (tasted in 2001): Transparent, medium-dark blackish-red; violets, cherry, and cassis on the nose; more cherry, resin, slate, and tobacco in the mouth; angular but elegant, medium-long.

1999 Deep End Blend (tasted in 2002): Dense, dark, saturated black-red with a hint of terra-cotta at the rim; earthy and mossy on the nose, with a hint of wet underbrush, wild black fruit, and balsam; spicy corned beef in the mouth with very ripe black fruit; sweet and full-bodied, very slightly chewy and mouthcoating, wrapped, layered wine with the texture of chamois.

1998 Anderson Valley (tasted twice, in 2000 and 2001): Transparent, medium black-red; characteristic perfume of violets; very sweet cherry and black fruits on the palate, along with resin, leather, mint, licorice, and black pepper; round, silken, and long.

1998 Deep End Blend (tasted in 2001): Inky but transparent, dark black-red; violets again, plus resin and leather; sweet core of cherry, cola, and tree bark; some chocolate and vanilla; big, soft, full-bodied, brooding wine.

1997 Anderson Valley (tasted in 2001): Transparent, medium black-red; violets joined with rose petal and slate; black cherries and blackberries; resin, licorice, and soft Asian spice; high glycerol gives the wine an unctuous quality; lingering.

1997 Deep End Blend (tasted in 2001): Transparent, medium-dark black-red; leather on the nose; deep black fruits, cola, resin, tar, and earthy flavors, with hints of allspice and chocolate; silken texture, more angular than the Anderson Valley bottling of the same year.

1996 Anderson Valley (tasted twice, in 2000 and 2001): Transparent, light to medium garnet; fairly closed; dried rose petals, black fruit, mint, and resin on the nose, with smoky highlights; flavors of sweet licorice and cardamom; medium-length.

1996 Deep End Blend (tasted in 2001): Dark, inky, transparent; nose of very black fruit conserve; hints of leather and caramel; hugely sweet midpalate of crème caramel, cherries, and plums, with hints of tar; glycerol, medium-long finish.

1994 Anderson Valley (tasted in 2000): Transparent, dark black-red; aromas of dark cherries, black fruits, and cola; quite sweet on the palate, characteristic resin joined here with strong clove, cinnamon, allspice, and vanilla; rich, linen-textured and long; fine.

1994 South Hill (tasted in 2000): Transparent, but ultra-dark; sweet cherry on the nose; black fruits, resin, chocolate, and spice; dense, rich, mouthcoating; fine. An unusual release for Navarro; a vineyard-designate raised in 100 percent new Remond barrels.

1993 Anderson Valley (tasted in 2000): Transparent, medium black-red; rose petal nose; cherry and resin against a background of clove and allspice in the mouth; medium-weight and medium-length.

1992 Anderson Valley (tasted in 2000): Transparent, medium ruby; plum, black fruits, and prune on the nose and palate; resin as usual, plus clove, cinnamon, and allspice; medium-weight, linen-textured.

PRACTICAL INFORMATION

Most Navarro wine is sold from the tasting room, which is open daily, or to mailing-list customers, and pinot accounts for about one-fifth of the winery's total production. Eighty percent of the Deep End Blend is sold as futures. The unfiltered batch of the Anderson Valley bottling is sold locally or to nearby restaurants. The winery's newsletter is uncommonly informative; 800-537-9463.

THE OJAI VINEYARD

Ojai, California

The Ojai Vineyard is Adam and Helen Tolmach's small, family-owned wine project in the hilly canyon that ascends from the Pacific Coast at Ventura to the pretty resort town of Ojai. The Tolmachs planted a syrah vineyard there in 1981, but it succumbed to Pierce's disease in 1995 and has not been replanted. The Ojai Vineyard label was launched in 1983, based on estate-grown syrah and purchased sauvignon blanc; the wines were made in Los Olivos, where Adam Tolmach and Jim Clendenen were partners in Au Bon Climat. After their partnership was dissolved in 1991, Tolmach added pinot noir to the Ojai Vineyard portfolio, sourcing fruit from the Bien Nacido vineyard. Now Tolmach makes four vineyard-designated pinots, and pinot noir accounts for about 20 percent of the company's 6,000-case production. Tolmach was trained at the University of California, Davis, and was the enologist at Zaca Mesa Winery before he and Clendenen founded Au Bon Climat in 1982.

WINEMAKING

Since 1998, The Ojai Vineyard has been able to purchase all of its pinot noir on per-acre contracts. Tolmach likes to pick pinot at about 24 Brix in relatively cooler sites. He finds that warmer sites may not develop full flavors until the Brix has risen to 25.5, and this level is, in his view, problematically high. His fermentors are unjacketed 3.5-ton stainless steel open-tops. He now destems completely, having discovered that stems tended to drive up the must's pH, forcing him to acidify, and that the added acid then caused "bad tastes." A cool room facilitates a four- to six-day cold soak before the alcoholic fermentation is started, usually by inoculation. Enzymes are used to simplify clarification later; fermentation temperature peaks between 90 and 95 degrees Fahrenheit; and the must is dry within four to six days. After a short time in tank to settle the grossest lees, the wine goes to barrel fairly dirty.

The barrels are mostly François Frères, though some Remond barrels are also used, and about 60 percent to 75 percent are new; but Tolmach steams the new barrels briefly before they are filled "to minimize wood flavors." The cellar is kept quite cool, so malolactic fermentation is usually slow to start and long to finish. Tolmach says he likes the wine's flavors better if it is held in barrel until after the next harvest, so the usual regime is about 15 months. Ideally, he says, he never racks, and generally avoids both fining and filtration. He has also learned to minimize the use of sulfur throughout the winemaking process. Not only does sulfur, in his experience, affect pinot noir's flavors more than it affects other varieties; it also tends to block the wine's tannins from absorbing oxygen, which in turn makes the wines harder. Once in bottle, the Bien Nacido wine (see below) is held for four to six months before release, while the Pisoni

Vineyard bottling is held back for ten to 12 months.

THE WINES

All Ojai Vineyard pinot noirs are vineyard-designated. The Bien Nacido bottling has been made every year since 1991, and a Pisoni Vineyard wine debuted in 1996. Two new vineyards in the new Santa Rita Hills appellation, Clos Pepe and Melville, were added to the portfolio in 2000 and 2001, respectively. At Bien Nacido, Ojai's fruit comes from the eastern end of Block Q, a widely spaced planting of UCD 13 converted to a vertical trellis system in 1993. Ojai's pinots are relatively large-framed, darkly colored, saturated wines that display considerable tannin when they are young. They often divide reviewers, some of whom believe Ojai makes, year in and year out, the best Bien Nacido, Clos Pepe, and Pisoni pinots in the marketplace; others find the wines too "syrahlike."

TASTING NOTES

2000 Bien Nacido Vineyard (tasted in 2002): Transparent, dark, black-purple; aromas of ripe tomato, beetroot, and plum; very sweet dark fruit on the palate, with overtones of black pepper, black tea, India ink, and resin; very fine-grained tannins but still grippy, with a long, chewy finish.

2000 Clos Pepe Vineyard (tasted in 2002): Brilliant, saturated, dark purple-red; aromas of wild berries and geraniums; minty berry fruits with black pepper and minerality in the mouth; big, mouthcoating, long, and very tannic, almost reminiscent of syrah.

2000 Pisoni Vineyard (tasted in 2002): Brilliant but very saturated, inky black-red; violets, blackberry, and a hint of white pepper on the nose; sweet and slightly nutty on the palate, with a core of wild berry fruit and bramble, and hints of lead pencil and soft spice; relatively approachable tannins, big, slightly chewy, long, and velvety.

1997 Bien Nacido Vineyard (tasted in 1999): Transparent, medium-dark black-red; leather, smoke, wet earth, and forest floor aromas; hard spice and very ripe, dark fruit in the mouth; dense and weighty.

1997 Pisoni Vineyard (tasted in 1999): Saturated, black-red wine, not quite limpid; violets, mushroom, wet fur, and wet earth aromas; mint and black fruits on the palate; sweet, full-bodied, long, and velvety.

1994 Bien Nacido Vineyard (tasted in 2002): Saturated, deep black-red turning to terracotta at the rim; spruce and other evergreen aromas; slightly sweet fruit core, with notes of green olive, clove, cinnamon, merbromin, and black pepper on the palate; silken texture and long finish.

PRACTICAL INFORMATION

The Ojai Vineyard's pinots are distributed to most major markets and can be ordered directly from the winery. The winery is not open for tours or tastings; 805-649-1674.

PANTHER CREEK CELLARS

McMinnville, Oregon

Ken Wright (see the Ken Wright Cellars profile) created Panther Creek Cellars in 1986. When an ill-fated partnership subsequently ended in an acrimonious dispute, Ron Kaplan—a midwestern lawyer with some French culinary training and a taste for Burgundies—purchased the brand in the summer of 1994. Since 1990, it has occupied a repurposed power station in uptown McMinnville that looks surprisingly like a bank. Panther Creek does not own vineyards but sources fruit, on a row- or block-specific basis, from a small list of mostly well-known and much-respected sites in the Willamette Valley. Most of the production is pinot noir, but a bit of chardonnay and melon are also made.

When Kaplan acquired Panther Creek, he asked St. Innocent partner and winemaker Mark Vlossak to assume overall responsibility for winemaking, while Michael Stevenson, who had worked harvests at St. Innocent and at Flynn, signed on as cellarmaster. In 1999, Vlossak withdrew to consultant-only status, and Stevenson, who trained entirely on the job, became Panther Creek's full-time winemaker.

WINEMAKING

Stevenson says that Panther Creek tries not to "micromanage" its growers, instead establishing relationships with growers who share its philosophy. Picking decisions are made "on flavor," and the harvested fruit is completely hand sorted on the crushpad to eliminate leaves, second-crop fruit, and botrytis. Until 1999, the sorted fruit was completely crushed and pumped into fermentors; now gentle and partial crushing leaves between 30 percent and 40 percent of the berries uncrushed and as much as 17 percent in whole clusters. Fermentors are a mix of nine-ton stainless steel open-tops seven feet in diameter, six-ton open-tops six feet in diameter, and double-height fruit bins. After taking over in 1999, Stevenson increased the length of the prefermentation cold soak, going from between one and three days to between five and seven, though this parameter remains vintage-dependent. Fermentations are started with multiple strains of laboratory yeast, all of which are chosen for their slow action. Until 2001, the must was left alone during the cold soak; now punchdowns are started during this phase. Ten-day fermentations followed by one to three days of postfermentation maceration have been replaced, in 2002, with somewhat shorter fermentations and pressing as soon as the must is dry. Increasingly, Stevenson finds that the wines are adequately structured by the time the primary fermentation has finished, so that extended maceration is not useful.

Fermentation temperatures are allowed to creep into the high 80s or low 90s Fahrenheit, but Stevenson prefers to avoid temperatures above 93 degrees. The winery employs a Willmes membrane press, and settles the wine in tank before racking it to barrel. The press fraction is sometimes separated from the free-run juice and sometimes not; Stevenson anticipates that he may enforce separation more often in the future.

Although barrels from Sylvain, Séguin Moreau, and Cadus predominate, Panther Creek relies on a growing mix of coopers and prefers three-year air-dried wood that is toasted medium-plus or heavy. Stevenson explains that he is now seeking to maximize the reuse of barrels previously used for one or two wines, and to reduce both the percentage of barrels that are new and the percentage that have seen three or more wines. In this protocol, new wood use amounts to between 30 percent and 45 percent of total cooperage. Malolactic fermentations are left to start and finish naturally, and the wines are racked after the secondary fermentation has finished. Pinots spend ten to 16 months in wood before bottling. There is generally no fining or filtration, but coarse pad filtration is practiced "as necessary." Only about four months of bottle-aging precede release, thanks to space and business considerations.

THE WINES

In the 1980s, Panther Creek made primarily blended wines. Beginning about 1990, Wright turned increasingly toward vineyard-designation. When the brand changed hands in 1994, both programs were continued. Under the current ownership, vineyard-designated wines have been made from the Freedom Hill, Shea, and Bednarik (a small plot northwest of Gaston) vineyards in every vintage. In addition, a vineyard-designated wine made from Nysa Vineyard fruit debuted in 1997, and a vineyard-designated Youngberg Hill wine joined the lineup in 2000. From 1999 through 2001, Panther Creek also made vineyard-designated wines from two Archery Summit vineyards, Red Hills Estate and Arcus.

On the blends side, both a Reserve and a Willamette Valley bottling were crafted in every vintage through 1999, except for 1998, when no Willamette Valley wine was made. The composition of both has varied in each vintage, but Freedom Hill's UCD 2A fruit typically anchors the Reserve wine, and Shea's role has increased gradually but steadily since 1995. Effective with the 2000 vintage, the Willamette Valley and Reserve programs were discontinued in favor of a single blended wine, now called Winemaker's Cuvée, which bears only an Oregon designation. The anchor for this wine is a new fruit source for Panther Creek, the Melrose Vineyard northwest of Roseburg, in the Umpqua Valley. This 1990, 11- by seven-foot planting of UCD 23 is on the western bank of the Umpqua River, on relatively flat land, and is machine harvested. The combination of machine harvesting and higher yields deriving from warmer temperatures, deeper soils, and a productive clone gives, according to Stevenson, fruit with a "good cost-to-quality ratio." The balance of Winemaker's Cuvée comes from Panther Creek's Willamette Valley fruit sources. The Winemaker's Cuvée is blended first, however, and absorbs as much of the Willamette Valley wines as, in Stevenson and Kaplan's opinion, it needs to be first-rate, even if the volume of wines available for vineyard-designated bottlings is reduced.

Among the vineyard-designates, Freedom Hill is almost always the monster wine, demanding the most time before it softens, while Bednarik exhibits the most persistently exotic flavor profile. In my experience, vintages up to and including 1999 were very considerably extracted, large-framed wines that were often tough in their youth; vintages since 2000 are still structured but significantly more approachable.

TASTING NOTES

2001 Winemaker's Cuvée (tasted in 2003): Transparent, light to medium garnet; pine needles, raspberry, and vanilla-butterscotch on the nose; white pepper, raspberry, cherry, and resin in the mouth, with graphite and barrel char on the finish; medium-weight and medium-length, chamois-textured, and structured.

2000 Freedom Hill Vineyard (tasted in 2003): Transparent, medium garnet; chalky potpourri aromas superimposed on red berries; dark fruit and graphite in the mouth, with hints of cinnamon and black tea; austere and grippy, emery-textured, and medium-weight.

2000 Youngberg Hill Vineyard (tasted in 2003): Transparent, deep, rosy crimson; floral nose with notes of menthol and tarragon; cherry, black pepper, cedar, and minerals in the mouth; medium-weight with a silken midpalate and grippy finish, approachable, structured, and medium-long.

1999 Willamette Valley (tasted in 2001): Barely transparent, medium-dark black-red; menthol and resin on the nose; cinnamon, tree bark, and bitter chocolate in the mouth; grippy and tannic, medium-weight, and long.

1996 Freedom Hill Vineyard (tasted in 2001): Transparent, medium-deep ruby-oxblood; dark fruit, hard spice, and black pepper aromas; some red fruit, spice, tree bark, slate, and minerals on the palate; medium-weight, tannic, and long.

1995 Reserve (tasted in 2001): Transparent, medium garnet with mahogany highlights; dark-skinned plum and roasted vegetables on the nose; slate, tree bark, and cinnamon on the palate; brightly flavored, still young, and dominantly mineral; medium-weight, tannic, and very long.

1994 Bednarik Vineyard (tasted in 2001): Saturated, dark black-red turning to mahogany; candle wax and furniture polish aromas; chewy in the mouth, with plummy fruit, dark chocolate, earth, tree bark, and black pepper; medium- to heavyweight, velvety, and long.

PRACTICAL INFORMATION

Panther Creek produces about 7,500 cases a year, of which just over 6,000 are pinot noir. The pinots are nationally distributed to both retail and restaurant accounts, and the winery strives for broad distribution within the limits of availability. In the Pacific Northwest, for example, Panther Creek wines are readily available at Fred Meyer stores. Consumers can also purchase wines directly from the winery, and futures are offered for sale twice each year. Like most Willamette Valley wineries, Panther Creek is open to the public on the Thanksgiving and Memorial Day weekends; unlike many others, it also welcomes visitors throughout the year, as long as they make appointments in advance; 503-472-8080.

PATZ & HALL WINE COMPANY

Napa, California

Donald and Heather Patz, James Hall, and Anne Moses created the Patz & Hall Wine Company in 1988, focused initially on chardonnay made from purchased fruit, and operated on about the same scale as a medium-size *propriétaire-récoltant* in the Côte d'Or. Hall and Moses are the winemaking side of the venture, with experience (between them) at Flora Springs, Honig, Far Niente, Spring Mountain, and Marimar Torres; the two Patzes contribute hands-on expertise in sales and marketing. The two men met when they both worked at Flora Springs, as national sales manager and assistant winemaker, respectively, in the mid 1980s. A 1985 Flora Springs experiment called Leaping Lizards, involving the Musqué clone of chardonnay finished with full malolactic fermentation but not filtered, was part of the inspiration for the partners' new venture.

In the tradition of this experiment, Patz & Hall focused from the outset on the importance of clones and selections, of gentle handling as a determinant of aging potential, and of the circumstances in which wines can be safely bottled without filtration. From the first release in 1988, the brand made only chardonnay until 1995, when the first pinot noir was added to its offerings. Patz explains that they considered other red varieties initially, but "were very interested in how [pinot noir] was improving all over the cooler areas of California."

Pinot fruit was purchased from the Aquarius Ranch, a 1992 planting on the downslope side of Westside Road near Porter Creek, in the Russian River valley, in 1995, and was made and bottled as Russian River Valley pinot noir. A Russian River Valley bottling was then made in each subsequent vintage except in 1999 (see below), but the fruit sources have evolved considerably. In 1996 and 1997, the wine was a blend of lots from Aquarius Ranch and Saralee's Richard's Grove vineyard. In 1998, Saralee's Richard's Grove was the sole source. The 1999 edition, though anchored with Russian River valley fruit, contained enough wine from Patz & Hall's Mount Veeder source that it was bottled as a Sonoma County wine. The Russian River sources in 1999 were Saralee's Buggy Patch parcel, planted to a mix of UCD 2A and UCD 23; Catie's Corner vineyard near Windsor; and Keefer Ranch, a Green Valley site planted entirely to Dijon clones that is also used by Flowers and Tandem. The 2000 Russian River was once again anchored with the Buggy Patch parcel of Saralee's Vineyard, plus Catie's Corner, Keefer Ranch, and a block called Pie Shaped Piece farmed by Lee Martinelli; Mount Veeder fruit was also used. With the 2001 vintage, use of the Mount Veeder fruit was discontinued, and the Vin Alchemy (Keefer Ranch) and Thomas Road (Dutton Ranch) vineyards were added to the mix of Saralee's, Catie's Corner, and Pie Shaped Piece. In 2002, the blended wine was rechristened Sonoma Coast, reflecting the use of a substantial quantity of fruit from Peay Vineyards near Annapolis and the McDougall Vineyard north of Flowers, complementing the Russian River and Green Valley sources that anchored the 2001 blend. A fourth vineyard-designate also debuted in 2002, from the Burnside Road vineyard west of Graton.

Meanwhile, in 1996, the partners began purchasing fruit from Larry Hyde's Los Carneros vineyard, which emerged as Patz & Hall's first vineyard-designated pinot. In 1997, vineyard-designated wines from the Pisoni Vineyard in the Santa Lucia Highlands and the Alder Springs Vineyard, a 2,100-foot site near the hamlet of Laytonville in Mendocino County, about seven miles from the Pacific Coast, were also introduced. With the exceptions of Hyde and Pisoni, the common characteristic of Patz & Hall's fruit sources for pinot is relatively young plantings of Dijon clones. Hyde is mostly Swan and Calera selections, with some Dijon 113; see chapter 4's section "The Greater Salinas Valley" for information on the source or sources of plant material at Pisoni.

WINEMAKING

Hall explains that "no single factor" governs the picking decision, but he defines *mature grapes* in terms of "mature tannins," "ripe seeds," and good acidity. His subsequent decisions about length of fermentation, punchdowns, and fermentation temperature all revolve, he says, around the type, quantity, and maturity of tannins in the fruit. That said, Hall finds that he usually ends up picking pinot between 24 and 25 Brix. Fruit is sorted on the crushpad to remove leaves, second-crop fruit, green clusters, and botrytis. Somewhere between 5 percent and 25 percent whole clusters are then layered on the bottom of each fermentor, with the exact percentage dependent on acid levels, stem maturity, how much red-fruit aroma is typical of the vineyard, and how much tannin can be tolerated in the specific vintage. Destemmed grapes, poured directly from macro bins, are then layered on top of the whole clusters. The combination of whole clusters and whole berries promotes slower fermentations at higher temperatures, which Hall finds conducive to "better tannin extraction" with "softer and more complex tannin polymers." The fermentors are very wide open-tops that handle four to six tons each. There is only the briefest of cold soaks, since primary fermentations usually start within two days. Inoculation with RC 212 yeast is typical. Hall adds acid if the finished wine will have a pH value higher than 3.7, and "often" also adds a color-extraction enzyme. The must is pumped over on the first day of primary fermentation and then punched down three to five times daily, but sometimes a mix of punchdowns and pumpovers is practiced, depending on the condition of the berries and how the tannins are being extracted. Peak juice temperatures during fermentation range between 80 and 84 degrees Fahrenheit, and Hall uses heaters to maintain this temperature even toward the end of the fermentation, which lasts seven to 12 days. The must is usually pressed at about zero Brix, goes into barrel with all the lees the day after pressing, and finishes its primary fermentation in wood. Malolactic starter is added in barrel six to eight weeks later. Various methods are used to compensate for what Hall admits are "high Brix levels."

Preferred coopers are François Frères, Séguin Moreau, and Meyrieux, but small numbers of other barrels are also used. With François Frères, Patz & Hall purchases stave wood in advance, which is air-dried for three years before being coopered, making for "more sweet spice" and "less drying oak tannins." Between 55 percent and 80 percent new wood is used, depending on the weight of each wine—by which Hall means that the barrels in Patz & Hall's pinot program are either new or used previously just for chardonnay. The wines are left on their lees until one month before bottling, with weekly stirrings before and during the malolactic fermentation. At this point the wines are racked off their lees and immediately returned to barrel for a final month in clean wood. Total barrel time is ten to 11 months, followed by seven to 12 months of bottle-aging before release. The wines are rarely fined and, so far, never filtered. While the winemaking operations are generally consistent, Hall adjusts how and when each is applied based on the characteristics of the vintage and the vineyard.

THE WINES

Patz & Hall pinots are medium-weight and elegant, with uncharacteristically strong minerality. Alder Springs is the most distinctive of the vineyard-designates; Hyde is perhaps the most elegant and nuanced; Pisoni is the ripe monster of the tribe.

TASTING NOTES

2001 Alder Springs Vineyard (tasted in 2002): Transparent, medium black-red; very open nose of black cherry, nutmeg, smoke, and black pepper; sweet orange peel and spice-laced cherry on the palate; vaguely exotic; mouthcoating midpalate; grippy, medium-weight, and long, with the texture of fine emery.

2001 Hyde Vineyard (tasted in 2002): Brilliant garnet with coral highlights; earth, forest floor, and dark cherry on the nose; sweet, with red cherry, raspberry, resin, and some hard spice, along with a hint of wintergreen, on the palate; mouthcoating and medium-weight; high-toned and elegant, silken and medium-long.

2001 Pisoni Vineyard (tasted in 2003): Transparent but nearly saturated, deep black-red; aromas of violets and dark cherry with a hint of geranium; sweet, black fruit flavors in the mouth, with cherry cola, graphite, barrel char, cinnamon, and strong black tea; grippy but still soft, like crushed velvet, mouthcoating with fine-grained tannins, rich and long.

2001 Russian River Valley (tasted in 2002): Very transparent, medium garnet; black cherry, smoke, and rose petal aromas; sweet and slightly mineral on the palate, with flavors of black cherry, roasted beetroot, and black pepper; medium-weight and medium-length, silken, and slightly grippy.

2000 Alder Springs Vineyard (tasted in 2002): Brilliant, medium black-red with rose-colored highlights; earth and spice on the nose, with hints of cured meat, camphor, and dark fruit; very spicy fruit on the palate, with clove, black cherry, and mineral notes; mouthcoating and medium-weight, some barrel char on the finish, texture of very fine-grained emery, long.

2000 Hyde Vineyard (tasted in 2002): Brilliant, medium garnet; earthy and woodsy aromas, with a hint of mint and potpourri; cherry and red berries on the palate, with some smoke, orange, and rose water, and hints of spice and citrus; structured, high-toned, and angular, medium-weight and medium-length.

2000 Pisoni Vineyard (tasted in 2002): Transparent, medium-dark black-red; dark fruit aromas, with elements of coffee, mace, smoke, and tropical flowers; very sweet, with dark cherry and Italian plum fruit on the palate and hints of clove, earth, and root beer; slightly peppery, very ripe, and tastes warm; full-bodied and long, mouthcoating, texture of heavy upholstery silk.

2000 Russian River Valley (tasted in 2002): Brilliant, light to medium garnet; earthy spice, black raspberry, and very subtle black truffle on the nose; sweet, delicate black fruit flavors in the mouth, with Tellicherry pepper; medium-weight and almost mouthcoating, suedelike texture with a hint of slate and grip, long finish.

1996 Hyde Vineyard (tasted in 2002): Brilliant, medium garnet with crimson highlights; aromas of dusty flowers, with tar, smoke, raspberry, and a hint of walnut; fruit-infused black tea in the mouth; very slightly sweet, with undertones of mineral, pepper, and mocha; suedelike texture, medium-weight, some grip, and a touch of glycerol, medium-long.

PRACTICAL INFORMATION

Pinot noir accounts for about 5,000 cases of Patz & Hall's total annual production of 14,000 cases; the balance is chardonnay. The wines are nationally distributed and exported to Canada, France, Japan, Singapore, and the United Kingdom. Sales and tasting are possible every day except Tuesday at the Vintner's Collective in Napa. The winery also operates a mailing list and ships directly to customers in reciprocal states; 707-265-7700.

PONZI VINEYARDS

Beaverton, Oregon

When Dick Ponzi left a lucrative career in mechanical and aeronautical engineering—he designed rockets, jet fighters, and rides for California's Disneyland—to grow grapes in Oregon, there were just four wineries in the entire state. "If you had made a business plan," he likes to recall, "you would not have started." In 1969 he and his wife, Nancy, planted their first vines on a 20-acre parcel in the Tualatin Valley, just half an hour's drive from downtown Portland. Being close to Portland was important; they thought Portland would be the winery's main market. The next year they founded Ponzi Vineyards; in 1974 they produced their first four barrels of pinot noir.

Ponzi's estate vineyard, which includes two acres of pinot noir, is close to the meandering Tualatin River, on relatively flat, deep, sandy benchland soils in the Hillsboro loam series. The pinot is own-rooted UCD 4 from Wente's Arroyo Seco increase block, and UCD 18 from another increase block farmed by Mirassou. The original spacing was seven feet between vines in nine-foot rows, but this density was doubled by interplanting in 1980. The winery, which is just east of the vineyard, is an attractively expanded and remodeled edition of the family's first house in Oregon, built more or less with their own hands.

In 1981 the Ponzis were able to purchase a 20-acre parcel ten miles west of their estate, at the crest of the Chehalem Mountains, facing southeast and commanding a beautiful view of the Cascades. Two acres of this parcel had been planted in 1975 as a joint venture of the state's fledgling wine industry with Oregon State University, for trials of various clones of pinot noir. This vineyard, named Abetina for its surrounding stand of fir trees, is planted in eight-foot rows with four feet between vines, own-rooted, in Laurelwood series soil. Madrona, the Ponzis' third vineyard, is ten acres just downslope from Abetina in identical soil, of which eight acres were planted in 1985 exclusively to own-rooted UCD 4.

In 1991, the Ponzis were able to expand again, acquiring a 65-acre parcel on Highway 219 between Scholls and Newberg, which they christened Aurora for its spectacular views of the dawn. Aurora is another southeast-facing site on gently rolling hills of Laurelwood soils, at elevations ranging from 300 to 600 feet. Over the decade between 1991 and 2001, roughly half of Aurora was planted to Dijon clones 113, 114, 115, and 777, as well as UCD 4, using several spacings ranging from four by eight feet to one by 1.5 meters, and using (on an experimental basis) several rootstocks as well as own-rooted plants. Except for part of Aurora, which was drip-irrigated in 2000, the Ponzis' vineyards are dry-farmed and LIVE (Low Impact Viticulture and Enology) certified. Dick Ponzi believes the jury is still out on vine spacing for pinot noir, but he has a strong bias toward own-rooted vineyards, to the extent that phylloxera can be kept at bay.

In addition to the four estate vineyards, Ponzi has purchased fruit from other vineyards for its pinot program. Durant Vineyard, directly below Domaine Drouhin in the Dundee Hills, and Temperance Hill vineyard in the Eola Hills have been consistent sources, but pinot has also been purchased from the Winter's Hill and Linda Vista vineyards. Dick Ponzi explains that the winery "is always looking for new vineyards and sites" and seeks to use a wide range of fruit sources for its blends.

The youngest son of immigrant Italian parents, Ponzi learned the basics of winemaking as a child and functioned as his own winemaker until he passed the reins to his daughter Luisa, following her return from wine-related studies in France in 1993. He also leveraged his professional training as an engineer to design and fabricate the winery's first press, rebuild its first tractor, and pioneer—long before they became de rigueur—gravity-driven protocols for moving wine. For her part, Luisa spent six months at Beaune's Centre de formation professionnelle et de promotion agricole (CFPPA) and did an internship at Domaine Roumier.

While the close-knit character of Oregon's pioneer winegrowing group in the 1970s and 1980s birthed many mutual influences on style and method, it can be argued that Ponzi more than any other is responsible for the combination of generosity and high-toned elegance that typifies the majority of Oregon pinots today.

WINEMAKING

"The first ten years," says Dick Ponzi, "we tried every possible combination of winemaking techniques." The list of tried and discarded manipulations includes use of a high percentage of whole clusters, destemming and then returning stems to the fermentors, very long macerations, and fermentations at very high temperatures. Now, with adjustments to fit each vineyard and vintage, the general practice is to sort the incoming fruit by hand on a stainless steel table, destem it completely—though a small percentage of whole clusters is used in warm years when the stems are truly ripe—and cold soak for about seven days without sulfur dioxide. Luisa Ponzi uses both 1.5-ton bins and three-ton jacketed stainless steel open-tops, but is developing a preference for the latter. Fermentation starts naturally with resident yeast, and the goal is a nice bell-shaped fermentation curve. Lots destined for the Willamette Valley blend are pressed before the must is dry; other lots are allowed to finish fermenting and macerate postfermentation before they are pressed. The hard press fraction is kept separate and excluded from both the Willamette Valley and the Reserve programs.

Overall, about 50 percent of barrels are new. Until 2000, Luisa Ponzi used mostly François Frères barrels; beginning with the 2001 vintage, the majority share is an eclectic assortment, but 100 percent French oak. The Willamette Valley blend stays in barrel for 11 months, gets just a single racking, and is bottled before the next vintage. Reserve wines are also racked at the 11-month mark but are returned to barrel for another six-plus months, at which point they are racked again and bottled. Ponzi pinots are not filtered, but some barrels are egg-white fined for clarity. The wines are held six to seven months in bottle before release.

Luisa Ponzi's experience in Burgundy is

responsible for various winemaking changes after 1993, including introduction of the sorting table, the shift to resident yeast fermentation, and racking pushed with plain compressed air rather than inert gas. The Ponzis now feel that the bit of air is beneficial. In fact, they suspect that too anaerobic an environment can actually weaken the wine, jeopardizing its potential for age.

THE WINES

In most vintages, Ponzi has made two pinots: a Willamette Valley blend and a Reserve blend. Although the reserve program is nominally a barrel selection privileging slightly darker, weightier, and more complex lots, the Ponzis' 30-plus years of experience with many of their fruit sources have led to the Reserve wine being regularly anchored, even before individual barrels are evaluated, in the Abetina and Madrona vineyards, supplemented with purchased fruit from Linda Vista. The Willamette Valley wine claims most of the remaining estate fruit and fruit purchased from the Eola Hills. In 1998, Ponzi produced its first vineyard-designated pinot noir, from the historic Abetina Vineyard, but in small enough quantity that some Abetina fruit remained for the reserve blend. The year 2001 saw the debut of Tavola, Ponzi's entry into the arena of very moderately priced pinot noir, made mostly from purchased fruit blended with Aurora vineyard grapes. All Ponzi pinots I have tasted have been both fruit-intensive and mildly spicy. They are enjoyable young but (in most vintages) also age superbly. This duality has become a Ponzi mantra. Both father and daughter insist that a good pinot should show "all the components" of great pinot young, and should demonstrate "integration" with age. Fortunately, the winery has maintained a substantial library of older vintages, so vertical tastings are possible.

TASTING NOTES

1998 Abetina Vineyard (tasted in 2001): Transparent, medium-dark, very blackish red; complex nose of camphor, cocoa, and rose petal potpourri; leather and resin reminiscent of a baseball glove; cedar and maple sugar, plus soft spice and black pepper that emerges on the finish; velvety and lingering. Very fine.

1998 Reserve (tasted in 2001): Transparent, medium-dark black-red; slightly closed, with some chocolate and cocoa on the nose; ripe black fruits, black pepper, and allspice on the palate; fat wine with substantial glycerol and supple tannins, medium-weight, and the texture of worn velvet.

1998 Willamette Valley (tasted in 2001): Transparent, medium-dark black-red; nose of black fruits, earth, and mushrooms; blueberries and blackberries on the palate, with hints of smoke, licorice, cedar, maple sugar, and white pepper; medium-weight and medium-length.

1990 Reserve (tasted in 2001): Transparent, medium red with terra-cotta edge; tar, leather, and tobacco on the nose; considerable core of sweet black fruits; hint of black pepper; long and roughly silken.

1980 Reserve (tasted in 2001): Transparent, and now the color of mahogany furniture; nose of leather and furniture polish; more leather with tobacco and white pepper on the palate; long, silken finish.

PRACTICAL INFORMATION

Ponzi wines are nationally distributed by Wilson Daniels, Ltd., though the Abetina vineyard-designate will necessarily be in short supply. There is an onsite tasting room at the estate vineyard near Scholls, and Ponzi wines are also poured in the family-owned Ponzi Wine Bar tasting room and the Dundee Bistro, both housed under the same roof and open daily; 503-628-1227.

PORTER CREEK VINEYARDS

Healdsburg, California

Porter Creek is a 34-acre ranch on Westside Road, about one-half mile upstream from Wohler Bridge, now almost completely surrounded by Gallo's Twin Valley Vineyard. Reached by an unpaved driveway and untouched by wine-biz glitz, it looks and feels like an outpost. Production is tiny. Porter Creek, however, produces two of the Russian River valley's most underrated vineyard-designated pinots.

George Davis bought Porter Creek in 1979 as a career change. For 20 years he had designed and built sailboats in Berkeley, Maui, and Southern California. His plan, when he moved, was to grow and sell grapes. Two parcels on the Porter Creek property had already been planted to pinot noir, but the variety was not much in demand, so Davis planted a bit of chardonnay to supplement the pinot. The hilly site was a parsimonious producer, however, and even the chardonnay remained persistently unprofitable. So in 1982, Davis decided to make his own wine, hoping to improve the economics of his career change. Like so many others in Russian River during the early years, he was a self-taught winemaker. He was also self-financing. Porter Creek grew slowly: a barn converted to winery, new French oak barrels purchased one by one, refrigerated storage space cobbled together from old freestanding insulated storage units, a roof finally constructed over the crushpad area to minimize the infiltration of leaves and dust into the open-top fermentors. To this day the winery's tasting facility is a modest, tin-roofed farmhouse alongside a dusty driveway; the only seating space is a bench outside the front door.

Before the 1997 vintage, Davis decided to concentrate his personal energies on the vineyard and passed the winemaking role to his son Alex. The younger Davis grew up surrounded by grapes, wine, and neighboring winemakers and graduated from the viticulture and enology program at California State University, Fresno. He apprenticed at Sonoma-Cutrer, a benchmark producer of large-volume chardonnay, which was something of a mecca for visiting European wine folk. Using Sonoma-Cutrer contacts, Alex Davis soon took off for France, bent on experience with handmade, tiny-volume, top-quality wines. He could scarcely have picked a better mentor than Christophe Roumier of Domaine Georges Roumier in Chambolle-Musigny, one of Burgundy's leading young lights and, in his late 30s, just half a generation older than Davis. Roumier's *premier cru* wines (Chambolle Les Cras and Chambolle Les Amoureuses) and his *grand cru* wines from Le Musigny, Bonnes-Mares, and Clos Vougeot have acquired cult status in Burgundy, owing to a combination of winemaking prowess and ultrameticulous attention to vineyard management. Davis also repeated the enology curriculum he had already completed in Fresno, this time in French, at the Université de Bourgogne, and spent an additional year working for the Rhône house of Guigal, where he developed a taste for syrah as well.

The French experience made him a devout *terroiriste.* He argues, quite properly, that *terroir* is not enough explored in the New World. "We don't know," he observes, "which *terroirs* will produce wines that are better young, and which will produce something age-worthy. Even Bonnes-Mares can be very linear in its youth." And demonstrating a plainspoken modesty uncharacteristic of the California wine business, Davis says candidly, "If Porter Creek turns out to be a great site for pinot noir, we will have to admit to dumb luck."

There are two pinot vineyards at Porter Creek, called simply Creekside and Hillside. Hillside, a moderately steep five-acre parcel of 24-year-old vines on fine-particle clay soil at an altitude of 175 to 200 feet, yields a measly 1.25 tons to the acre—enough for about 300 cases of wine. This vineyard is never profitable, and Davis now wonders if it should not, in time, be replanted to syrah. For the moment it is UCD 13 on St. George rootstock, planted sparsely in the fashion of its day—about 450 vines to the acre, but gradually coaxed from California sprawl to a semblance of verticality. Because it sits above the fog line, Hillside ripens early.

Creekside vineyard straddles the creek at the entrance to the property, is sloped very gently, and displays black topsoils. It is about 60 percent UCD 13, but here on AxR1; the balance is a combination of UCD 4 or 5—no one knows which—and 2A. Spacing, a bit tighter than in Hillside, is a little over 500 vines to the acre; yield is 2.5 to three tons per acre, for a total production, in a good year, of almost 800 cases.

Both vineyards are almost completely dry-farmed and cover-cropped, with minimal use of pesticides and herbicides. Virused vines and some intrusion of Pierce's disease have occasioned a bit of interplanting and vine replacements in recent years, done always with Dijon clones (114, 667, and 777) on 110R rootstock. Between one and two acres of Creekside have been replanted. In addition, about one acre of George's Hill, the chardonnay vineyard, has been interplanted with pinot noir. Until these vines come into production, Davis will not decide how to use the fruit. Meanwhile, late in 2002, Porter Creek reached agreement with E. and J. Gallo to exchange the Creekside vineyard for a hillside block on Gallo's adjacent Twin Valley Ranch, so that Gallo can use the Creekside parcel for an access road. The new block was planted in 1997, planted eight feet by five in thin, rocky soil underlaid with fractured shale. The scion material is all UCD 2A, and the rows are oriented northeast-southwest, reducing sunburn during the hottest part of the day. This land swap means that 2001 was the last vintage for Porter Creek's venerable Creekside wine, and that 2002 marked the debut of a new wine in the Porter Creek pinot program.

WINEMAKING

Winemaking at Porter Creek is low-tech and straightforward. Grapes are picked when the stems crack audibly when they are snapped and they no longer taste bitter when chewed. The Hillside vineyard (see below) is typically picked between 22 and 23 Brix; Creekside was picked between 23 and 24. The Hillside fruit is usually completely destemmed, but as much as 20 percent of the Creekside harvest was fermented as whole clusters. Fermentors are six-foot unjacketed stainless steel open-tops. The fruit comes in cold and usually macerates three to four days before fermentation begins naturally with resident yeasts; there is no addition of enzymes. (The reliance on resident yeast is an innovation that Alex Davis learned from Roumier. A few cans of lab yeast left from earlier vintages sit on a shelf, unused.) Davis rarely adds acid, but when exceptionally warm weather drives sugar levels too high, acid goes in before fermentation begins. The primary fermentation generally lasts about 12 days at 86 to 92 degrees Fahrenheit. Davis both punches down and pumps over. If the fermentation gets too warm—he has not invested yet in the luxury of cold-water jackets for his open-tops—Davis just pumps the must briefly into a nearby jacketed tank, cools it down, and then returns it to the fermentor. Both free-run and press juice go into the cuvée, but each is handled separately.

Generally about 25 percent new oak is used—Cadus and Rousseau are the favored coopers—and the wine stays in barrel for about 11 months, though the Hillside vineyard, a more austere wine, sometimes requires as much as 18 months in wood. Davis racks once or twice after a natural malolactic fermentation has finished, does not filter, and occasionally fines with egg white for suppleness. Davis subscribes to the unconventional idea that pinots made with *some* air contact may display increased resistance to oxidation later in life, making them more age-worthy. This hypothesis reinforces Davis's belief in open-top fermentations, and means that he sometimes racks with compressed air rather than inert gas.

THE WINES

Creekside and Hillside are made as two separate, vineyard-designated wines. Both are elegant, midweight wines of admirable complexity. Hillside is the more austere of the two but also the more complex, usually marked by aromas of potpourri and dried flowers. Creekside is more forward and fruit-driven, and usually more appealing on release. Hillside is a stellar ager, but Creekside also aged well in many vintages.

TASTING NOTES

2000 Creekside Vineyard (tasted in 2002): Transparent, medium black-red; roses and violets on the nose, with some black raspberry and smoke; more raspberry mixed with cherry and spice on the palate; medium-weight, full-bodied, and slightly grippy, linen-textured, and medium-long.

2000 Hillside Vineyard (tasted in 2002): Brilliant, medium black-red; aromas of faded roses, dried leaves, and dried petals with some raspberry; very concentrated black fruits on the palate, with hints of mint, black pepper, clove, and allspice; medium-weight and slightly grippy, texture of rough silk, long.

1999 Hillside Vineyard (tasted in 2002): Transparent, medium garnet but very slightly hazy; aromatic with dried leaves and flowers, roses and violets, dark raspberry, and a hint of herb; substantially mineral on the palate, again herbal, with some barrel char; soft, powdery, light- to medium-weight and medium-length.

1997 Creekside Vineyard (tasted in 1999): Transparent, dark black-red; full of black cherries and cola, marked by the same black pepper and clove notes that often appear in low-altitude Westside Road pinots; soft, rich, and silken.

1997 Hillside Vineyard (tasted twice, in 1999 and 2001): In 1999, transparent, medium garnet; perfume of dried rose petals; cherry, berries, cola, and orange peel with a hint of chocolate on the palate; sinuous, delicate, and finely structured. In 2001, slightly tiling at the rim; rose petal perfume now mixed with lavender, leather, and cardamom; tar, camphor, and cigar tobacco, with maturing fruit in the mouth; medium-weight and silken, very fine.

1994 Creekside Vineyard (tasted in 1999): Still dark black-red; redolent of Bing cherries, black pepper, and clove; dominant fruit, exquisite balance, still slightly grippy, evolving slowly, velvety, and long.

PRACTICAL INFORMATION

Since the 1997 vintage, Porter Creek wines have been distributed nationwide by Neal Rosenthal, a much-respected merchant who concentrates most of his attention on fine Burgundies. Wines are also available from the onsite tasting room, which is open daily, and via a mailing list. Hillside sells out fairly quickly following its spring release each year; 707-433-6321.

RICHARD LONGORIA WINES

Los Olivos, California

Richard Longoria's wine credentials go back to 1974, when he worked at the historic Buena Vista Winery in Sonoma. Two years later, he became cellar foreman for The Firestone Vineyard near Los Olivos. Experience at Chappellet in Napa, J. Carey, and The Gainey Vineyard (the last as its founding winemaker) followed. Meanwhile, he and his wife established Richard Longoria Wines in 1982, producing just 500 cases of pinot noir and chardonnay. The family business finally grew into a full-time project at the end of the 1990s, simultaneously inhabiting an unglamorous production facility in Lompoc and a quaint tasting room on the main street of Los Olivos.

Richard Longoria Wines has produced pinot noir in every vintage since 1982, except for 1990 and 1992, but the ebb and flow of fruit sources illustrates the vicissitudes visited upon small, landless Santa Barbara–based producers until very recently. The legendary Sierra Madre Vineyard southeast of Santa Maria was the anchor for the earliest vintages, from 1982 through 1986. Longoria's 1982, 1983, and 1984 Santa Maria Valley bottlings were 100 percent Sierra Madre fruit; a Santa Maria Hills vineyard-designated wine was also made in 1983. Reflecting Longoria's demanding new assignment as winemaker for The Gainey Vineyard beginning in February 1985 and some avowed frustration with fruit sources, his release letter for the 1984 vintage announced that it would be his last effort under the Longoria label; but the retreat was short-lived. Pinot noir was made in 1985 after all. In that vintage and the next, however, the pinot carried a Santa Barbara County designation on the label, confirming that the fruit was sourced in both the Santa Maria and the Santa Ynez valleys (1985 was a combination of Sierra Madre and Sanford & Benedict; 1986 was widely sourced). In 1987, Longoria made two pinots, a Santa Maria Valley wine once again sourced entirely from Sierra Madre, and a Santa Ynez Valley–Benedict Vineyard wine. In 1988 and 1989, the only pinot was a Santa Ynez Valley wine sourced from Sanford & Benedict. In 1991, the Santa Maria Valley rubric returned, made from a combination of Sierra Madre and (for the first time since 1986) Bien Nacido fruit. The year 1993 marked the beginning of vineyard-designated wines from Bien Nacido Blocks G and N, and these have been made in every vintage since, except that in 1997 the fruit from Block G was kept separate and bottled as a block-designated, lighter-weight wine.

At the end of the millennium, much of Longoria's attention turned to the newly approved Santa Rita Hills AVA, close to his production facility in Lompoc. He was the architect of a project to plant a new vineyard called Fe Ciega, at around the 400-foot contour on the northern bank of the Santa Ynez River, in 1998. This 7.75-acre parcel consists of two blocks, one laid out in east-west rows to accommodate topography, the other oriented north-south. Vines are spaced four feet apart in eight-foot rows, and the scion material is evenly divided among UCD 5, Dijon 115, and Dijon 667. While waiting for this vineyard to begin bearing in 2001, Longoria also began to acquire fruit from the nearby Mount Carmel Vineyard, the balance of whose pinot noir goes to Babcock Vineyards. Sanford & Benedict also returned to the list of source vineyards for pinot in 2002. These sources enabled Longoria to reduce his commitment at Bien Nacido, where his rows of Block G were released after the 2000 harvest. The emphasis is now firmly on vineyard-designated wines, but Longoria will make a blended Santa Rita Hills wine from time to time from some combination of declassified lots of Mount Carmel, Fe Ciega, and Sanford & Benedict.

WINEMAKING

Longoria is one of the many winemakers who say they pick by flavor, but he admits that until the mid 1990s, he tried to pick at sugar levels lower than 24 Brix. This choice put him, he recalls "in the middle position" for picking at Sierra Madre and Bien Nacido—later than early birds like Lane Tanner, but earlier than many very-ripe-fruit makers. Since the mid 1990s, he has been more tolerant of higher sugars. He fermented entirely in fruit bins through 2001, but added one small, two-ton stainless steel tank to his cellar in 2002. He destems completely, allows about two days of cellar-temperature "cool soak," and inoculates with various laboratory yeasts, usually Assmannshausen. Fermentation temperatures usually peak in the high 80s Fahrenheit. Longoria admits that a few degrees warmer might be better, but a fruit bin is not large enough to build juice temperatures much higher than 90 degrees. He normally delays pressing until about five days after the primary fermentation has completed, reunifies the free-run and press fractions, and settles briefly in tank.

A mix of medium-toast barrels from François Frères, Remond, and Billon is used; Dargaud & Jaeglé was an earlier favorite but has now been phased out of service. About one-third of the barrels are new each year, though the new Santa Rita Hills wines are seeing a bit larger fraction of new wood. A few barrels are inoculated to kick off the malolactic fermentation; this is usually sufficient to start the rest. The pinots spend 11 or 12 months in barrel and are not racked until time for bottling, just before the next harvest. Egg-white fining and one-micron pad filtration are standard. The Bien Nacido bottling is released after about four months of bottle-aging; the Santa Rita Hills wines are held about eight months before release.

THE WINES

Longoria pinots are elegant, medium-weight wines with considerable complexity and depth of flavor. Early vintages were, by contemporary standards, relatively low in alcohol. In my experience with the older vintages, which is limited to a few bottles, they also age in ways that increase their initial complexity and give huge satisfaction. To the extent that the 2000 Mount Carmel is a harbinger of Longoria's forthcoming Santa Rita Hills pinots, these will be darker and denser wines than their mostly Santa Maria Valley–derived predecessors.

TASTING NOTES

2000 Bien Nacido Vineyard (tasted in 2002): Transparent, medium black-red; strong aromas of rose petal, potpourri, and wild strawberry; more sweet strawberry in the mouth, plus cherry and cassis; hints of mint, black pepper, and minerals; medium-weight and medium-length, satin-textured.

2000 Mount Carmel Vineyard (tasted in 2002): Saturated, medium-dark black-red; nose of black fruit and smoke; rich, black fruit on the palate, with earth, resin, evergreen, and briar; dense, sweet, and concentrated; medium-weight and considerable length, suede-textured.

1996 Bien Nacido Vineyard (tasted in 2002): Transparent, light to medium reddish terracotta; huge nose of earth, dried leaves, and flowers, with hints of peanut oil and briar; slightly sweet cherry and cassis in the mouth, with strong notes of cola, tar, and black pepper; some milk chocolate creaminess; medium-weight, full-bodied, satin-textured, and long.

1987 Benedict Vineyard (tasted in 2002): Brilliant, medium-dark black-red, barely evolved; complex nose of earth, leather, tree sap, roses, violets, and dried leaves; black fruits, cola, cinnamon, tree bark, and tobacco, with a hint of orange peel in the mouth; concentrated, still grippy and slightly chewy, still young. Very fine.

1983 Santa Maria Valley (tasted in 2002): Transparent, light to medium terra-cotta; aromas of leather, malt, and soy; a hint of wild strawberry still in the mouth, but primarily mint, tobacco, resin, white pepper, and even white truffle oil; astonishingly sweet, bright, lively, silken, and long.

PRACTICAL INFORMATION

About 2,000 out of Longoria's total production of 4,000 cases are pinot noir. By 2004, half of this wine was to come from the Fe Ciega Vineyard. The wines are distributed to most major markets and can be ordered directly from the winery. There is a wine club for periodic shipments. The tasting room in Los Olivos, which includes a pleasant garden patio, is open daily except Tuesdays; 866-759-4637.

ROBERT SINSKEY VINEYARDS

Napa, California

Robert Sinskey, a Los Angeles ophthalmologist, was one of the original investing partners in Acacia Winery (see the profile earlier in this section). After his initial investment when the Acacia partnership was created in 1980, Sinskey also provided capital to finance an intended but stillborn expansion (into Bordelais varieties) in 1984. Alongside these investments, he purchased land near Acacia's new facility on Las Amigas Road in 1982, where he planted chardonnay and pinot noir the following year, planning to sell grapes to Acacia for its vineyard-designation program.

The sales never happened. Acacia sailed into troubled waters at mid-decade and was sold to Chalone, Inc. in 1986. At this point Sinskey's investment in Acacia's forthcoming expansion was "exchanged" for a piece of that expansion—a five-acre parcel of volcanic shale and rocky clay in Napa's Stag's Leap district, where he built a state-of-the-art winery in 1988. This transaction explains how Robert Sinskey, always a Burgundy-focused producer with extensive holdings in Los Carneros, came to be domiciled in the heart of Napa's cab country and to make a benchmark cabernet sauvignon on the side.

As the winery was completed, Sinskey appealed to his son, a New York–trained photographer, to "take a six-month vacation" and "make a business and distribution plan" for Robert Sinskey wines. Rob Sinskey took over management of the winery and, in effect, never looked back. Fifteen years later, he is the winery's general manager, "daydream believer," and evangelist. In 1997, Sinskey *fils* married Maria Helm, then the executive chef at San Francisco's Plumpjack Café, who became the nexus of a tight alliance between cuisine and Sinskey wines, and eventually culinary director for the winery.

Sinskey's original plantings of pinot noir—about 15 acres on the southwestern corner of Las Amigas and Milton roads, and facing the northern side of Las Amigas—are part of what the winery now calls the Three Amigos vineyards. These were in ten-foot rows with four feet between vines, in the Haire series clay-loam soils typical of the area, using scion material from the Iund and St. Clair vineyards. In 1988 Sinskey acquired a second Carneros vineyard, called Vandal, close to the northern edge of the appellation, due west of the city of Napa. Eighteen acres of pinot noir were planted there, using nursery-sourced UCD 4 and St. Clair selection taken from the Las Amigas Road vineyards. Nine more acres of pinot were planted on a property known as the Capa Ranch, on Buhman Avenue near Henry Road, in 1993. This west-facing site is the warmest and most precocious of Sinskey's Carneros vineyards. It is laid out in eight-foot rows with six feet between vines—except that one block of Dijon 115 was planted meter by meter—to UCD 4 and field selections from Hanzell and Chalone. Then, in 1996 and 1997, more land was acquired on the eastern side of Old Sonoma Road south of Saintsbury's Brown Ranch, dubbed simply O.S.R. Vineyard for Old Sonoma Road. Thirteen acres of pinot noir were planted there (alongside a similar quantity of merlot)—Dijon 114 and 115 as well as UCD 4. At the same time, more land was purchased adjacent to the old plantings on Las Amigas Road, which was now dubbed Three Amigos. Some of this acreage was also planted to pinot noir. Expansion continuing, Sinskey planted more pinot on the Sonoma side of Los Carneros in 2001 and 2002, in a vineyard on Ramal Road just east of Carneros Creek's Las Brisas vineyard. The winery calls this parcel Scintilla Sonoma.

In 1990, alarmed by the spread of phylloxera in neighboring vineyards and by the dead, wormless look of his own earth, Rob Sinskey began the slow conversion of Sinskey's vineyards from chemical herbicides and nitrogen-based fertilizers to sustainable and organic viticultural practices. This change, according to the principals, has produced more consistent year-by-year yields, longer hang times, healthier late-season development, better-colored grapes, more intensely flavored wines, and better expression of *terroir.*

Winemaker Jeff Virnig joined the Sinskey team in 1988, initially as assistant to then winemaker Joe Cafaro. A 1984 graduate of California State Polytechnic University, San Luis Obispo, with a degree in agricultural business management, Virnig had learned winemaking on the job at Mayacamas and Joseph Phelps. He has been Sinskey's winemaker since 1991.

WINEMAKING

Virnig and Sinskey *fils,* a bit like David Lett in Oregon, take the road less traveled. They are champions of elegance, proponents of wine that combines well with food, and enemies of the competitions that measure wine quality in terms of point scores. It follows that Virnig picks pinot early, typically between 22.5 and 24.5 Brix. Since 1998, the fermentors have been mostly 8.8- and 6.5-ton open-tops, though some lots are fermented in half-ton fruit bins, and a few closed tanks remain. A two- to three-day cool soak not enforced with tank jackets or dry ice typically precedes the onset of fermentation, which may be powered entirely by resident yeasts or buttressed with additions of Wädenswil 46 or RA 17. Because of its early-ripening character, the Capa Ranch fruit sometimes demands acidification, but otherwise acid additions are avoided, and there is no use of enzymes. Punchdowns are done in all the open-top fermentors (and cap irrigation is practiced in a few closed-top tanks) until sugars reach 1 percent or less, at which point the must is pressed. Depending on the vintage, the press fraction may be fined or not, and is then reassembled with the free-run juice.

One-, two-, three-, and four-year-old barrels are used to raise the wine, and between 25 percent and 30 percent of barrels are new each year. François Frères is Sinskey's "base cooperage," but barrels are also purchased from Taransaud and from the boutique operations of Michel Toutant and Claude Gillet. Sinskey and Virnig say the "sweet spot" in their barrel regime is a one-year-old barrel coopered from Bertranges wood by François Frères. Malolactic starter is added when the pressed wine is barreled, and malolactic fermentation has usually ended before Christmas. Racking is done "as needed"—twice or three times. Blends are made in June after the vintage, but the wines usually stay in barrel until January or February of the second year after the vintage. "One or two lots out of ten" are generally fined with egg whites, and crossflow filtration has been practiced since 1999. Twelve to 24 months of bottle-aging precede release.

THE WINES

Sinskey has made an estate-grown Los Carneros of Napa Valley pinot in every vintage since 1987, except for 1989. (Sinskey's 1986 first release of pinot noir was made from purchased fruit.) Until 1990, the Los Carneros wine was made entirely from Las Amigas Road fruit. In 1991, Vandal Vineyard fruit entered the blend, as did Capa Ranch fruit beginning in 1996. Meanwhile, in 1990 for one vintage and again after 1993, Sinskey also began making a Reserve bottling alongside the Los Carneros wine. In 1998, the Reserve was renamed Four Vineyards. Under both names, it has been a barrel selection anchored with fruit from the Las Amigas Road vineyards.

Beginning with the 2001 vintage, Sinskey launched an array of single-vineyard wines: Three Amigos, Vandal Vineyard, and Capa Ranch. (Three Amigos and Vandal were also made in 2002; Capa was not.) The single-vineyard wines debuted at the expense of the Four Vineyards program, whose volume was substantially reduced after the 2000 vintage. In 2003, a small vertical tasting of Sinskey pinots from the 1990s testified to the persistent elegance and satiny texture of these wines, and to a rich palate of secondary flavors happily unmasked by dominant fruit or high alcohol. The 2001 single-vineyard wines were also impressive, showing brilliant colors and dramatic *terroir-* and clone-based differences.

TASTING NOTES

2001 Capa Ranch (tasted prerelease in 2003): Slightly darker-hued than the other 2001s; game and sausage on the nose, followed by black fruit on the palate with an intensely sweet core; texture of fine emery.

2001 Three Amigos (tasted prerelease in 2003): Color similar to the Vandal; animal and underbrush aromas; very sweet black raspberry fruit plus earth and tobacco in the mouth; medium-weight, medium-length.

2001 Vandal Vineyard (tasted prerelease in 2003): Brilliant, medium black-red; mint and high-toned cherry with some stems on the nose; mint and bramble in the mouth; medium-weight again, and substantial length.

2000 Four Vineyards (tasted in 2003): Brilliant light to medium garnet; slightly closed; tea, cherry, raspberry, and fragrant earth on the palate; somewhat austere overall, light- to medium-weight, and satin-textured.

1999 Four Vineyards (tasted in 2003): Color similar to the 2000; dominantly floral nose, with tea and other fragrant dried leaves; cherry, black fruit, mint, and white pepper in the mouth, with a bit of merbromin and vanilla; substantially concentrated, medium-weight, and satin-textured.

1996 Reserve (tasted in 2003): Brilliant garnet with even color from rim to rim; aromas of dried flowers and wild strawberries; more strawberry plus raspberry on the palate; complementary flavors of resin, red licorice, and black pepper; medium-weight and satin-textured.

1993 Los Carneros of Napa Valley (tasted from a magnum in 2003): Brilliant garnet, just barely tiling; rose petal aromas with dried currants and a hint of animal; strawberry and raspberry in the mouth, with mint, white pepper, and iodine; concentrated and elegant, drinking beautifully, satin-textured.

PRACTICAL INFORMATION

Pinot noir accounts for just less than half of Robert Sinskey's total production of 25,000 cases. The Los Carneros and Four Vineyards wines are nationally distributed. Some of the new single-vineyard wines will be also, but small-volume lots may be reserved for selected restaurant accounts and for tasting room and mailing-list sales. A tasting room in the handsome modern winery is open daily, and the winery operates a program of special events, including guest-chef cooking classes and occasional multicourse dinners paired with Sinskey wines; 800-869-2030.

ROCHIOLI VINEYARD AND WINERY

Healdsburg, California

Joseph Rochioli Jr.'s 160-acre estate on Westside Road, about seven miles from Healdsburg, is the nexus of Russian River Valley pinot noir. For more than three decades, his vineyards have provided fruit for some of the area's most talented pinot makers, including Davis Bynum, Gary Farrell, Burt Williams, and his own son Tom, whose collective craftsmanship is substantially responsible for the appellation's impressive reputation. Budwood from his so-called West Block has been the basis for important plantings in neighboring vineyards. The adjacent Allen Ranch—which Rochioli also farms, exactly as he farms his own—is Williams Selyem's home turf. And the eight acres of pinot that Rochioli planted on his own ranch at the end of the 1960s are today, virus and phylloxera notwithstanding, the benchmark for rich, complex pinot from the western side of the Middle Reach.

The beginnings were scarcely grand. Joe's father, Joseph Rochioli Sr., had leased the present estate in the 1930s, before he accumulated the resources to purchase it outright. He sold its yield of zinfandel grapes, hops, and hay for cash and raised nearly everything the family needed to live—fruits, vegetables, pigs, and chickens—plus a few cows and horses, alongside the cash crops. When the hops business deteriorated in the 1950s, he replaced the hops with Blue Lake green beans and then, as the market for wine grapes improved, interplanted the beans with vinifera—mostly colombard and cabernet sauvignon. In 1959, he planted ten acres of sauvignon blanc close to the center of the ranch, a block that is still in production. "The colombard and cabernet were the wrong choices," Joe Jr. says now. "But in 1960 we didn't even know what Region we were in. I had no clue. No one else had a clue, either. I got the University of California farm adviser to put in a weather station in 1962."

By the time his father died in 1966, Joe Jr. had learned Russian River's cool-weather truth, so in 1968 he began the process of replacing the colombard and cabernet with pinot noir and chardonnay. When his first crop of pinot was picked in 1971, however, winemakers were scarcely standing in line. Joe Jr. says he was forced to sell that harvest and the next to Martini & Prati, who "sent it on to Gallo," where it seems to have finished ignominiously in Hearty Burgundy. But the picture brightened substantially in 1973. Former San Francisco newspaperman Davis Bynum (see the Davis Bynum Wines profile earlier in this section) purchased a nearby hops kiln, transformed it into a modern winery, purchased Rochioli's entire crop of pinot, vinified it as a varietal wine, and put Rochioli's name on the label. Beginning in 1979, some fruit was also sold to Williams Selyem, which made it genuinely famous.

In 1976, Joe Jr. briefly tried his own hand at winemaking, working in Davis Bynum's facility, where he made 1,000 cases each of pinot noir and chardonnay under a label called Fenton Acres. (I am not aware of any tasting notes for these wines.) In 1982, Rochioli agreed to sell a very small quantity of pinot to Gary Farrell, Davis Bynum's winemaker, for a project that would carry Farrell's name, and Farrell agreed to make 150 cases of pinot noir on a custom-crush basis to launch the Rochioli brand. Soon thereafter Joe Jr.'s son Tom returned to the family farm from a short-lived career in banking. He applied his training in business and finance to plans for a new 10,000-case winery and home for Rochioli wines, which was built on the Rochioli estate in 1985. To his father's surprise, Tom also reinvented himself as a hands-on winemaker, so the custom-crush arrangement with Farrell and Bynum was allowed to expire, making Rochioli both an estate winery and an all-in-the-family enterprise.

The estate vineyard now consists of approximately 128 planted acres, of which half is pinot noir. The oldest pinot vines are in the East Block, four acres planted in 1968, and the West Block, another four acres set out the following year. The scion material for East Block is said to be a combination of UCD 4 and a field selection taken from a vineyard "south of St. Helena on the east side of Route 29" whose particulars Joe Jr. can no longer recall. The budwood for West Block was acquired from Karl Wente. Joe Jr. thinks he remembers being told that these cuttings came from Wente's estate vineyard in Livermore, and before that directly from France, but Karl's son Phil believes this scenario is unlikely. He thinks any budwood obtained from Wente at the end of the 1960s would have been taken from the winery's increase block in Arroyo Seco—which was planted entirely to UCD selections. Indeed, several winegrowers familiar with West Block fruit believe it is morphologically consistent with UCD 4; but others disagree, leaving the matter of provenance open.

Both East and West blocks are east-facing deep alluvial soil, though West Block is slightly higher ground and less vigorous; the vines were planted, in the style of the day, in widely spaced 14-foot rows with eight feet between vines. The vines sprawl, and the rootstock is nonresistant AxR1. East Block yields about four tons per acre; West Block typically produces less than three. No more pinot was planted at Rochioli until 1985, when a rise between West Block and Westside Road was planted to cuttings from the West Block vines. These 2.2 acres of rocky soil are called Little Hill. In the mid 1990s, 13 acres between East Block and the river, called River Block, were planted with cuttings taken from West Block, as were 2.8 acres on the uphill side of Westside Road. (This was the first pinot noir planted on the western side of the road, which had hitherto been used only for cabernet, zinfandel, gamay, and chardonnay.) More pinot was added at the end of the 1990s and in 2000, in several blocks on both sides of Westside Road, using (variously) cuttings from West Block, Swan selection, and nursery-sourced Dijon 115 and 777.

Collectively, Rochioli calls the blocks on the uphill side of Westside Road the Sweetwater Ranch. A 3.7-acre block, called Three Corner for its triangular shape, is Rochioli's southernmost vineyard, bordering Little Hill and West Block on their southern edge. This 1974 planting of nursery-sourced UCD 4, planted in 12-foot rows with eight feet between vines and laid out uncharacteristically in east-west rather than north-south rows, was part of the Allen Ranch until 1999, when Howard Allen deeded it to Rochioli. Joe Jr. says the gift was a thank-you for his two decades of stewardship over Allen's vineyards.

East Block fruit is the basis for the Rochioli pinots made by Bynum called Le Pinot, as well as Rochioli's own East Block vineyard-designate (see below). A mix of East Block, West Block, and Three Corner Vineyard fruit has also been sold to Farrell, who has made the components into single-vineyard wines or blended them to create a Rochioli–Allen Vineyards blend. Some West Block and Three Corner fruit was sold to Williams Selyem until 1997. Williams Selyem used most of the West Block grapes for a vineyard-designated wine called simply Rochioli Vineyard, and bottled most of the Three Corner as Allen Ranch–Tricorner Vineyard. Since 1997, the only Rochioli fruit sold to Williams Selyem comes from the younger River Block planting.

West Block is the most reputed of the Rochioli blocks, which explains its use as a source of budwood for several younger blocks. Some winemakers, including Farrell, refer to it as Rochioli's "mother block." East Block, however, has a reputation for making the longest-lived of the Rochioli wines.

WINEMAKING

(The winery provided the following information about its winemaking protocols in response to written questions, but declined requests for further information.) Picking decisions are based on "visual maturity and stats." The fruit is sorted both in the vineyard and on the crushpad. Fermentations are done in three-ton open-top tanks. A three-day cold soak precedes inoculation with a combination of Montrachet and Assmannshausen yeasts. The winery has tried enzyme additions "experimentally" but regards them as "not yet proven." The primary fermentation normally takes eight to ten days at temperatures in the low 80s Fahrenheit, during which time the cap is plunged three times daily. Malolactic inoculation is done in the fermentors. Wines are barreled directly from the fermentors without settling, and there is no postfermentation maceration.

Barrels are all French oak and preponderantly medium-plus toast from François Frères. The percentage of new oak used for each wine varies from 30 percent to 100 percent, with "top vineyards" getting a greater share of the new barrels. All wines spend 15 months in barrel, are racked once prior to bottling, are never fined, and are rarely filtered. The estate blend is held three months after bottling before release; the single-vineyard wines are held for eight.

THE WINES

An Estate pinot noir has been made under the Rochioli label in every vintage since 1982, in quantities ranging from just 150 cases in the first years to about 2,500 cases in the most generous of recent vintages. A Reserve wine was made in 1986, 1989, 1990, and 1991 from a selection of West Block lots; something called Special Selection was made just once, in 1988, also from West Block lots. The now-famous block-designates debuted in 1992, effectively replacing the Reserve program. A West Block wine and a Three Corner Vineyard wine have been made in every vintage since. A block-designated wine from East Block was made in 1993, 1994, and every year since 1997; a vineyard-designated wine from the Little Hill Vineyard debuted in 1995. In 1997 and 1999, small quantities of vineyard-designated wine were also made from purchased fruit—in 1999 from J Wine Company's Nicole's Vineyard—but these are the only exceptions to an all-estate policy for Rochioli wines. Although my own tasting experience is limited, Rochioli pinots have a reputation for stylistic consistency, deep color, and medium to full body with a strong fruit and spice profile. My experience confirms both the medium-weight and the strong spice parameters.

In recent years the Estate blend has been anchored with fruit from River Block and Little Hill (between them, these two vineyards account for 70 percent of the blend), plus declassified lots from the other estate parcels. This picture—including the list of block-designated wines itself—is subject to change as the nearly 35 acres of pinot noir planted in 1999 and 2000, much of it Dijon clones, comes into full bearing in 2002 and beyond.

By convention, the winery labels the Estate blend as "Rochioli" and the single-vineyard wines as "J. Rochioli."

TASTING NOTES

During the research for this book, the winery made only three wines available for tasting.

1997 Estate (tasted in 1999): Transparent, deep black-red; aromas of Bing cherries and blackberries; cinnamon and coffee on the palate; medium-weight and long.

1997 West Block (tasted in 1999): Beautifully transparent but deeply tinted, black-red wine; cherries, black fruit, and smoke on the nose, plus notes of tobacco and leather; black fruit and cinnamon in the mouth; rich, long, and suede-textured.

1996 Estate (tasted in 1999): Medium black-red; aromas of dried leaves and rose petals; plums and orange peel in the mouth; rather light and volatile, possibly a flawed bottle.

PRACTICAL INFORMATION

Block-designated wines (typically made in lots of 100 to 400 cases) are sold by mailing list and to selected restaurant accounts and are allocated. The Estate wine is nationally distributed and sold at the winery. A handsome tasting room, large outdoor deck, and flagstone patio command a stunning view of the Middle Reach and are open daily; 707-433-2305.

RODNEY STRONG VINEYARDS

Healdsburg, California

Rodney Strong is perhaps the only successful dancer of classical ballet who has made a second, and mostly successful, career in wine. Born to a winemaking family in the Rheingau, Strong returned to wine when, at the age of 33, he created a storefront firm in Tiburon that specialized in small lots of custom-labeled wines. In 1962 he purchased a winemaking operation between Windsor and Healdsburg and began to acquire vineyard land throughout Sonoma County. By the early 1970s Strong owned no less than 6,500 acres and had built one of California's first wine production facilities designed from the ground up for tourism: an avant-garde structure shaped vaguely like an incomplete pyramid, at the corner of Eastside Road and Old Redwood Highway.

The wine glut of the mid 1970s nearly ruined Strong's business, however. Although most of his vineyards were sold and investors assumed a majority interest in the remaining enterprise, there was still room for a joint venture with Piper-Heidsieck in 1980, dedicated to the production of Champagne-method sparkling wine. This partnership resulted in the construction of a second winery next door to the pyramid that was subsequently sold to J Wine Company. In 1989 Tom Klein—a Stanford M.B.A. with farm roots in the Central Valley near Stockton, who knew Strong from an earlier management consulting assignment—purchased the company from its then owner, Guinness American, Inc. Production octupled during the 1990s to 460,000 cases of Sonoma County wines in 1999—including a much-respected cabernet sauvignon from the Alexander Valley, and about 36,000 cases of Russian River valley pinot noir.

Strong planted his first pinot noir about 1967 in what is now called the River East vineyard. The plant material was a field selection from Louis Martini's plantings on the Stanly ranch. The pinot program then began in the 1970s, albeit somewhat erratically, with some fruit from River East and some from the Iron Horse vineyard near Sebastopol, which Strong then controlled. Strong seems to have believed that any "serious" winery would produce pinot noir perforce, and an additional 80 acres of pinot (mostly UCD selections from Wente's increase block) were planted on the western side of the Middle Reach, in a parcel now known simply as River West. This vineyard has since been sold but remains under long-term contract. Still, pinot noir was a hard sell in the 1970s, and most of Strong's pinot fruit ended up in a rosé wine, which was sold, it is said, "by the truckload." Fortuitously, Strong's sparkling-wine venture with Piper-Heidsieck had an almost bottomless appetite for pinot fruit, reducing the still pinot program to modest (and therefore salable) dimensions throughout the 1980s and into the early 1990s.

While the River East vineyard was the sole source of fruit, Rodney Strong pinots were labeled Russian River Valley River East Vineyard; the "River East Vineyard" part of the designation was dropped when the River West plantings came on-line. With still pinot finally popular and the Piper-Heidsieck venture sold, most of River East (except the legacy Martini block) was replanted, and in 1997 55 acres of pinot noir were planted in a third vineyard site, called Kate's vineyard, on Piner Road west of Santa Rosa. There the plant material is UCD 2A, 4, 17, and 23. Vintages through 1999 are a blend of River East and River West; Kate's vineyard fruit entered the blend in 2000. Rodney Strong grows all of its pinot fruit and produces only "estate" pinot noir.

Rodney Strong's operation has been blessed with a succession of skilled winemakers, including Dick Arrowood, who went on to Chateau St. Jean, and, since 1979, Rick Sayre. In the 1970s Sayre worked at Simi, where the *éminence grise* was then André Tchelistcheff, recently retired from Beaulieu. Simi struggled to produce good pinots in this period, handicapped by fruit grown in the warm Alexander Valley, but Sayre had the benefit of Tchelistcheff's perspective on pinot noir, and the opportunity to work with a coterie of amazingly talented young winemakers at Simi.

WINEMAKING

Rodney Strong pinots are made in large, 28-ton stainless steel tanks, where the cap is pumped over, not punched down. Sayre argues the minority view that, in his experience, punchdowns and open-tops do *not* make better pinot. In fact, beginning in 1999, Sayre has even used rotary fermentors for part of the pinot production, though he admits that they were purchased primarily for cabernet and merlot and have a tendency to ferment "too hot and too fast" for pinot. In a further departure from classical pinot protocol, Sayre adds a small percentage of syrah to most lots, mostly for color, but also in the belief that good syrah "can have the same meaty quality" as good pinot. Sayre inoculates with lab yeast on the second day after crush, but he keeps the tanks chilled to about 55 degrees Fahrenheit until the fourth or fifth day to ensure that fermentation starts slowly and to obtain good color extraction. Thereafter fermentation temperature is allowed to rise to about 85 degrees, and the must is pressed when it is nearly dry. One day to one week is allowed for settling in tank, whereupon the wine is barreled.

Here again, the Sayre regime is unusual. About 15 percent American oak is used "for mouthfeel." French barrels are purchased from François Frères and two Charente-based coopers, Tonnellerie Marchive and Tonnellerie Vicard; 40 percent new oak is used on the Estate wine, and 70 percent on the Reserve. The lees are stirred "to soften tannins" and because Sayre finds that this step helps to produce a desirable "gamy, meaty character." The wines spend 11 to 13 months in barrel and are fined and filtered "only if necessary." Sayre explains that fining and filtration trials are done every year but that the unfined and unfiltered "control" lot is usually preferred. The 1998 Estate was lightly fined to soften the tannins. Between 2 percent and 5 percent of syrah is blended with the pinot. After 21 vintages at Rodney Strong, Sayre says he is "still learning a lot" about pinot noir.

THE WINES

Rodney Strong's Estate pinot is typically a straightforward, medium-weight, fruit-driven wine that is modestly marked by oak. The Reserve, made for the first time in 1997 with a preponderance of Wente selection fruit from River West, is a bit heavier and darker, with more complexity and more tannin. The Estate is a good example of pinot that is made in large volume from relatively vigorous vineyards, seasoned with syrah and some American oak. The result is eminently serviceable. I have no experience with mature vintages of the Estate wine.

TASTING NOTES

2000 Russian River Valley (tasted in 2002): Brilliant, light to medium garnet; roses, white pepper, and cherry on the nose, with a whiff of animal; in the mouth, orange-flower water, sweet cherry, and strawberry, with black pepper, barrel char, and graphite; mostly silken but some grip, finishes slightly austere and dry, medium-weight and medium-length.

1999 Reserve (tasted in 2002): Very transparent, medium garnet with pinkish-orange highlights; cured meat, cranberry, and orange-flower water on the nose, with a hint of peppermint; slightly sweet red cherry in the mouth, with some spice, glycerol, and wet slate on the finish; soft midpalate with a slightly grippy edge, finishes warm, medium-weight, and moderately long.

1998 Estate (tasted in 2000): Transparent, light to medium ruby-red; nose of red and black fruits, with animal notes; flavors of vanilla, brown sugar, and smoke; medium-length, soft texture.

1998 Reserve (tasted prerelease in 2000): Transparent black-red; complex nose of violets, smoke, and animal; a very sweet midpalate of strawberry, cherry, and fruit candy; some meat and spice; quite concentrated, still tannic, needs time.

1997 Reserve (tasted in 2000): Transparent, medium black-red; somewhat closed; notes of black cherry, resin, licorice, cinnamon, and cedar; smoky and moderately tannic. The winery admits to some prerelease reservations about this wine, which was alarmingly slow to evolve. Although it was finally released early in 2000, more bottle age is in order.

PRACTICAL INFORMATION

Thanks to the large production, the Estate wine is readily available in all markets, and may sometimes be found discounted. "Ours," says the winery, "is the pinot you can actually find." The Reserve, of which about 1,000 cases were produced in 1997 and 1998, and 1,200 in 1999, is scarcer but not allocated. An onsite tasting room and attractive picnic area are open seven days a week; 707-431-1533.

SAINTSBURY

Napa, California

Saintsbury, named for the English man of letters who wrote *Notes on a Cellar-Book,* was founded in 1981 by David Graves and Dick Ward, two winemakers trained at the University of California, Davis, who dedicated themselves explicitly to proving that the contemporaneous critics were wrong—that genuinely good pinot noir really could be made in California. For the first five years, Saintsbury worked entirely with fruit purchased from other growers in Los Carneros, including Winery Lake, CV Investors, and Zach Berkowitz. In 1986 the partners planted their first estate vineyard (12.5 acres), adjacent to the present winery buildings at the corner of Dealy Lane and Los Carneros Avenue, which they now call the Saintsbury Home Ranch. Ten acres were added on leased land near the RMS Brandy Distillery in 1991, and 24 acres were planted on Los Carneros Avenue in 1992. Also in 1992, Saintsbury acquired the 40-acre Brown Ranch on Old Sonoma Road, in the Carneros banana belt, where the soils are sandier, rockier, and lower in clay.

The original estate vineyard on Los Carneros Avenue is a low-density planting of UCD 5 from the Adelsheim vineyard in Oregon, with some field selections from the nearby St. Clair vineyard. In contrast, Brown Ranch is more densely planted, and the scion material is Dijon 115, 667, and 777. The combination of Dijon clones and partially volcanic soils causes Brown Ranch to throw fruit with dark, black flavors, while the original estate fruit tends toward the red flavors of strawberry and cherry.

The year 1995 was a watershed for all Saintsbury pinots. Brown Ranch fruit then began to dominate all the wines save the Garnet blend (see below), bringing the stamp of a new *terroir* and a change in clonal composition. About the same time, Saintsbury made fundamental changes to its farming and irrigation programs. Chemical additives were minimized, and the emphasis shifted toward compost, cover crops, and mulching to maintain the vines' health. Irrigation was rescheduled from the beginning of the growing season to the tail end, changing the flavor curve and making for brighter fruit flavors overall. Since 1995, the vines have not been irrigated until after veraison.

Byron Kosuge, a Davis-trained enologist who began college as an English major, was Saintsbury's winemaker from 1991 to 2000. Mark West, who joined the staff in 1998 as assistant winemaker with the unusual qualification of a Ph.D. from the Johns Hopkins School of Medicine, was named winemaker in 2001.

WINEMAKING

Saintsbury is one of many producers that claim to pick "by taste." Once the fruit is picked, the mantra here as elsewhere is to handle it *gently.* Through the 1997 vintage, fermentations were carried out in tanks with pumpovers. The first open-top fermentors were installed in 1998. About one-eighth of the stems are used, and the destemmer-crusher is adjusted so that about 30 percent of berries enter the tank intact. A prefermentation cold soak lasts between two and three days, and the "yeast strategy" is "pretty catholic": sometimes native yeasts are allowed to take their course; sometimes various laboratory yeasts are added. This approach yields, according to Graves, "an interesting palette of wines for blending." Graves says that Saintsbury is now "much less interested" in adding acid than it was in the past, because the incoming fruit has "generally better chemistry"—owing primarily to the changes in the irrigation calendar and to better soils management. The must is always bled to increase concentration and to produce a few hundred cases of Vin Gris. The press fraction is handled separately and racked more often, but is eventually reunified with the free-run juice, except that no press juice is used in the Reserve or Brown Ranch bottlings (see below).

Barrels are primarily Nevers and Allier wood coopered by François Frères and Séguin Moreau, "because these coopers tend to age their wood longer, and longer-aged wood produces softer and less astringent wines." Garnet ends up being made from lots that are about 25 percent new wood; the various Brown Ranch lots see closer to 50 percent new barrels. Malolactic fermentations occur in barrel, and are generally finished in February. After about five months in barrel, the lots are tasted, and those chosen for the Garnet blend are finished early. The remaining lots spend a total of about 16 months in barrel, are assembled with one racking, and are generally not fined. Only barrel bottoms were filtered until the winery introduced cross-flow filtration in 2003.

THE WINES

About 35,000 cases of pinot noir are now produced annually—up from a mere 3,000 in 1981. More than half of total pinot production is a Carneros blend, since 1995 heavily anchored with fruit from Brown Ranch. In addition, about 7,000 cases of Garnet pinot noir are made, mostly from fruit purchased from a dozen independent growers in Carneros but with a small admixture of Monterey County grapes. The high-end wines are a Carneros Reserve, 85 percent derived from Brown Ranch fruit since 1995, and a Brown Ranch vineyard-designate, first produced in the 1997 vintage. Graves says the vineyard-designate was his response to the profusion of expensive single-vineyard bottlings from boutique producers, and a reflection of his determination to prove that Saintsbury could do just as well and sell the wine for just as much.

The Garnet blend, which has been made since 1983, is many critics' choice for a good "entry-level" pinot. It is expressly crafted to be relatively light in color, with fresh, forward fruit and an open, perfumed nose. Most of the fruit for Garnet is acquired from non-estate growers, most of them in Los Carneros, but some fruit is also sourced from Monterey County.

Despite vintage variations (1998 and 1999 were both late harvests with a preponderance of ripening occurring under autumnal rather than summer weather), the fruit-source and irrigation-regime changes at Saintsbury make the post-1994 vintages more of a piece than their predecessors. It is also worth noting that the open-top fermentors that made their debut in 1998 have a greater capacity to preserve primary fruit character than conventional tanks.

TASTING NOTES

2001 Carneros (tasted in 2003): Transparent, medium black-red; aromas of dusty rose, potpourri, and berries; cherry and strawberry in the mouth, with bits of root vegetables and red licorice; some grip, texture of rough suede, medium-weight and medium-length.

2000 Carneros Reserve (tasted in 2002): Brilliant, oxblood with rose highlights; dark fruit, earth, violets, and carpenter-shop aromas; dark cherry, graphite, infused violets, and barrel char in the mouth; rich, mouth-coating, and chewy, large-framed and warm, grippy but very fine-grained tannins, medium-plus weight, suede-textured, and long.

1999 Brown Ranch (tasted in 2003): Deep, luminous garnet; earth, woodsy cinnamon, and raw meat on the nose; spicy mocha, sweet black cherry, and wet slate in the mouth; medium-weight, rich, and long.

1999 Carneros (tasted in 2001): Transparent, deep black-red; nose of earthy clay and cherries; cherry, citrus peel, toasted cinnamon, and India ink in the mouth; very ripe, loosely structured, medium-length.

1999 Carneros Reserve (tasted in 2002): Transparent, medium ruby; aromas of black fruit, black pepper, and vanilla; sweet black cherry and black raspberry on the palate, with tree bark and barrel char; grippy with fine-grained but still slightly mouth-drying tannins, moderately full-bodied, medium-weight, and medium-length.

1998 Carneros Reserve (tasted in 2000): Very transparent, medium black-red; aromas and flavors of cherry fruit with overtones of tobacco, earth, black pepper, cinnamon, and chocolate; tree bark on the finish, noticeably tannic; a big, well-stuffed, rich wine.

1997 Brown Ranch (tasted in 2002): Transparent, deep black-crimson; violets, root beer, black cherry, and a hint of pipe tobacco on the nose; cola, tar, tree bark, and sarsaparilla in the mouth; mouthcoating, stuffed, and almost chewy, texture of rough velvet but with some grip, rich and long.

1995 Carneros Reserve (tasted in 2000): Very transparent, medium-dark garnet; earth and forest floor on the nose; cherry and black fruit with (again) cinnamon and chocolate in the mouth; still somewhat tannic, linen-textured wine, medium-length.

1994 Carneros Reserve (tasted in 2000): Very transparent, medium garnet; rose petal, black cherry, and leather in both bouquet and palate; simpler fruit than the post-1995 wines, and less spice; noticeable glycerol, silken, medium-length.

PRACTICAL INFORMATION

Saintsbury pinots are nationally distributed and exported to several markets. The winery does not have a tasting room or employ a hospitality staff, so appointments to visit must be made in advance; 707-252-0592.

SANFORD WINERY

Buellton, California

Richard Sanford's wartime service in Vietnam drove him to seek a civilian career working close to the earth and caring for the landscape. Travels in France birthed a passion for viticulture and fine Burgundies. In 1970 he began driving the back roads of coastal California, looking for the perfect spot to grow cool-climate grapes. In 1971, he and partner Michael Benedict purchased a 600-acre ranch on Santa Rosa Road between Buellton and Lompoc, where they planted, in various increments, about 130 acres of cabernet, merlot, riesling, chardonnay, and pinot noir. Five years later, the partners harvested their first crop and made their first wines, using portable electric power and gas lamps, in an old rustic barn uphill from the vineyard. The first fermentors, made of wood, are said to have been built in a friend's hot-tub factory.

When the 1976 estate-grown Sanford & Benedict pinot noir was released in 1978, the acclaim was instantaneous. Five vintages of this wine were made before the partnership was dissolved in 1980. Sanford then left to make wines under a new, Sanford-only label, while Benedict sold Sanford & Benedict fruit to Byron, Au Bon Climat, and other local winemakers. The new Sanford Winery established a reputation for chardonnay, sauvignon blanc, and pinot noir made from purchased fruit, which was vinified at Edna Valley Winery in 1981 and 1982, and after 1983 in a Buellton warehouse. In 1983 Sanford and his wife purchased a second ranch, El Jabali, on Santa Rosa Road, three miles east of the Sanford & Benedict vineyard. The property was used primarily for entertaining and for a tasting room, but a small vineyard was also planted, giving Sanford a bit of estate fruit. In 1988, Benedict and his remaining partners sold the original vineyard to a British couple acting silently on Sanford's behalf, giving Sanford Winery access, beginning in 1990, to the vines from which the first vintages of Sanford & Benedict had been made in the 1970s. Nevertheless, Sanford Winery uses only a minority share of the Sanford & Benedict fruit. Fruit clients have included Lane Tanner, Au Bon Climat, and Foxen, among others.

Today's Sanford & Benedict vineyard dedicates about 45 acres to pinot noir. It is a well-drained, north-facing hillside parcel of relatively deep clay-loam and shaley clay-loam mixed heavily with chert. The original plantings were own-rooted, east-west-oriented rows spaced ten feet by 12, unirrigated and organically farmed. The pinot plant material is a combination of cuttings from Mount Eden Vineyard and nursery-sourced UCD 18. The cabernet and merlot were soon grafted over to pinot noir, and the riesling to chardonnay. In 1999 a new block of pinot was planted on an especially rock-strewn upslope, this time vertically trellised, on rootstock, and entirely Dijon 667 and 777. There are also about six acres of "experimental" pinot gris and viognier. When Sanford & Benedict was dry-farmed, the yield hovered, parsimoniously, around three-quarters of a ton per acre; after irrigation was installed in 1988, it soared to nearly five tons. As the old vines have become self-regulating and vineyard practices have been tuned, yield has settled in at between two and 2.5 tons per acre.

In 1995, Sanford purchased the 485-acre ranch just west of Sanford & Benedict. This southwestern corner section of the original Rancho Santa Rosa land grant has been given its own name: La Rinconada. About 120 acres were planted there in 1995 and 1996, of which approximately half are pinot noir. This is a modern planting, in eight-foot north-south rows with four-foot intervine spacing, vertically trellised. The scion material is mostly Dijon clones, but there is also some UCD 2A and 4, along with some Mount Eden from Sanford & Benedict. La Rinconada is also the site for Sanford's spectacular new winery, constructed from recycled quarried dolomite, old-growth timber from sawmills in Oregon and Washington, and adobe bricks that were manufactured onsite. Across the river, on a south-facing slope, a fourth ranch, called La Viña, was planted in 2000.

Sanford's winemaker is Bruno D'Alfonso, trained at the University of California, Davis, who was assistant winemaker at Edna Valley Winery from 1980 to 1983.

WINEMAKING

D'Alfonso likes to pick pinot "when the seeds go brown," which is normally between 24.5 and 25.5 Brix. Fermentors are ten- by five-foot and eight- by five-foot jacketed stainless steel open-tops. The fruit is 100 percent destemmed, cold soaked for four days, treated with enzymes to enhance the wine's ultimate clarity, and inoculated to begin fermentation. D'Alfonso likes a relatively cool fermentation (85 to 90 degrees Fahrenheit) "to preserve delicate flavors," during which time he punches down twice daily and occasionally pumps over. He presses early, when the must is between 4 and 5 Brix ("everything you need to get from the skins you have by this time"), and settles overnight.

The fermentation finishes in barrel, usually about three weeks from crush. One hundred percent new wood is used for the vineyard-designated wines, less for the Santa Barbara County blend. There is no preponderant cooper—Sirugue, François Frères, Remond, Damy, and others are used—but D'Alfonso is developing a preference for Sirugue, which, in his opinion, integrates best with the wine. (Interestingly, although the Sirugue barrels are medium toast, D'Alfonso—atypically—orders light toast from François Frères and Damy.) Malolactic fermentation occurs without inoculation. The wines are racked once after the malolactic fermentation has completed, at which time the blends are made. Another racking occurs prior to bottling, which happens during the wine's second winter. There is no filtration (D'Alfonso says the enzyme treatment during the cold soak has eliminated the need for it), but the wines may be fined with Eisenglas "for polish."

THE WINES

Proclaiming that he likes his coffee dark and his women brunette, D'Alfonso strives for "sexy, sensuous, delicate pinots that are full of flavor and fruit." Indeed, Sanford's are aromatically forward and fruit-driven wines, exhibiting relatively dark, saturated color and alcohol levels generally above 14 percent. A blended Santa Barbara County bottling has been made from the beginning, in 1981. This wine used to rely primarily on purchased fruit, much of it from Bien Nacido, some (within the legal limit) from Mendocino County, plus a bit of fruit from the "home" El Jabali Ranch. Beginning with the 2001 vintage, enough fruit from La Rinconada and Sanford & Benedict was available to support the program, and the purchase of fruit was discontinued. Since 1990, a vineyard-designated Sanford & Benedict bottling has been made each year, and a vineyard-designated La Rinconada was inaugurated in 1999. Both are actually barrel selections at this writing, but La Rinconada increasingly features fruit from those blocks that were planted to Dijon clones; and the Sanford & Benedict bottling, beginning with the 2000 vintage, was made exclusively from that vineyard's young vines, which are primarily Dijon 667 and 777. D'Alfonso is an ardent believer that clones "are the biggest determinant of character" in pinot and—ironically for someone with access to his pick of fruit from the oldest and most respected vineyard in the Santa Rita Hills—a self-proclaimed nonbeliever in *terroir.*

TASTING NOTES

1999 La Rinconada (tasted in 2001): Saturated, black-red; violets and blueberries on the nose; deep cherry and plum on the palate, with notes of meat, cinnamon, black pepper, and cedar; a very packed, rich wine with round tannins and velvety finish.

1999 Sanford & Benedict Vineyard (tasted in 2001): Transparent, dark furniture red; nose of violets, chocolate, and fruit; very cherry mouth with some fruit candy, cola, and resin, along with notes of cinnamon and cocoa and a touch of black pepper; rich texture and soft tannins.

1998 Sanford & Benedict Vineyard (tasted in 2001): Transparent, medium black-red; nose of lavender, cherry blossoms, leather, and tar; bright cherry and berry flavors, with notes of cola and black pepper; medium-weight, long finish.

PRACTICAL INFORMATION

Sanford currently makes about 50,000 cases of wine annually, of which fewer than 20,000 are pinot noir. Production is expected to increase to about 80,000 cases now that the new winery and vineyards are on-line. The wines are nationally distributed. There is a tasting room on El Jabali Ranch that is open daily; 805-688-3300.

SIDURI WINES

Santa Rosa, California

Adam and Dianna Lee met at Neiman Marcus in Dallas when he was the store's wine buyer and she the food buyer. They married and moved to California in 1993 "to do something in wine." After a year working in tasting rooms, the Lees wrote a one-acre contract with the Rose Vineyard in Anderson Valley, hauled the grapes to rented space at Lambert Bridge in Dry Creek, and made the first four and a half barrels of Siduri pinot noir. Their formal training in winemaking was limited to Dianna's one course in viticulture at Sonoma State and a weekend course at the University of California, Davis; but they liked their first pinot. When they heard that Robert M. Parker Jr. was a guest at the Meadowood Resort in nearby Napa in 1995, they decided to leave a sample bottle with the concierge. Parker loved the wine.

In 1995, the Lees added to their portfolio fruit from the Muirfield Vineyard in Oregon and from David Hirsch's much-admired vineyard in Sonoma Coast, beginning their evolution toward the longest and most geographically extensive list of single-vineyard pinots made by any winery in North America. At the end of the decade, fruit sources ranged from Muirfield, just southwest of Portland; to Cerise, a hillside site above Boonville in the Anderson Valley; to Hirsch and Coastlands in the true Sonoma Coast; to Sapphire Hill, in the Russian River valley; to Van der Kamp, high on Sonoma Mountain; and to

Garys' and Pisoni vineyards in the Santa Lucia Highlands. The 1995, 1996, and 1997 vintages of Siduri were made at deLorimer in Alexander Valley; in 1998 the Lees moved into anonymous but functional warehouse space in a light-industrial park on the northern edge of Santa Rosa.

WINEMAKING

With a single exception, all of Siduri's contracts are per acre rather than per ton, so the Lees have control over matters like leaf pulling, crop thinning, and pick date. In each vineyard, one of them is always present the day before picking begins, to supervise the discarding of any clusters they want to exclude from the crush. The fruit is sorted manually when it arrives in Santa Rosa, mostly to remove leaves from the California fruit and stem rot from Oregon grapes. Adam Lee says that making pinot from Oregon fruit has helped teach him that ripeness must be flavor-based, not sugar-based. "You learn," he explains, "to worry less about sugar." With the Central Coast fruit, in which sugars rise very early, Lee has learned to wait for flavor in the fruit, and to exercise a bit of legerdemain in the cellar to compensate for the high alcohol that results. Fermentations are done in half-ton and one-ton plastic bins, with the larger size preferred in a high-tannin year like 1998. Up to 20 percent of the fruit is left in the form of whole clusters, provided that the stems are sufficiently lignified, and a three- to five-day cold soak is assured with dry ice. One-third of the fermentors are made to rely on resident yeast, another third are inoculated with Assmannshausen, and a final third are inoculated with RC 212. Acid is added if necessary to the California wines; conversely, the Oregon wines are sometimes chaptalized. The Lees do frequent punchdowns during the cold soak and early in the alcoholic fermentation, but then "back off a bit." The must may be pressed and barreled dry, or with a bit of residual sugar. In 1998, some wines were subjected to extended maceration.

Siduri employs between 50 percent and 55 percent new barrels, about 40 percent of which are from François Frères. Latour, Meyrieux, and Remond barrels are also used, along with some Marsannay for the Pisoni Vineyard wine and some Rousseau for the Oregon bottlings. Malolactic fermentation is allowed to begin naturally "unless there is a problem." Depending on vineyard and vintage, Siduri wines spend ten to 17 months in barrel. They are racked only if necessary to clarify the wine, and are not fined or filtered. Commercial success allows the Lees the luxury of bottle-aging before release, so the wines are now typically released the spring or fall of the second year after the vintage.

THE WINES

Siduri is the example that seems to disprove the adage that winemakers learn their craft slowly. But the Lees' story is a bit deceptive. It was part of Adam Lee's "education" as a wine buyer and retailer in Texas that he "got to know" a good many small-scale pinot producers in California and spent prodigious amounts of time querying the likes of Burt Williams and Tom Rochioli about the fine points of winemaking, years before the first Siduri wine was made in 1994. The Siduri style is very transparent, so that site always dominates house style, but the fruit is unquestionably picked very ripe. (At Pisoni, for example, Siduri is one of the last producers to pick.) The wines are generous, sensuous, and complex. Production is now up to 2,300 cases, of which all but a few hundred are vineyard-designates. Beginning in 1998, deselected barrels of vineyard-designated wines were blended to make a California bottling, while the previous Oregon bottling was renamed Muirfield for the vineyard that had always supplied most of its fruit.

TASTING NOTES

1999 Garys' Vineyard (tasted in late 2000 from a magnum): Very transparent, medium black-red; distinctive nose of cardamom; very ripe black fruit and cola in the mouth; notes of spice and cedar; medium-weight and medium-length.

1999 Muirfield Vineyard (tasted in 2000): Barely transparent (the skins got very mature in this vintage), black-red; strong notes of resin, anise, black pepper, and chocolate; very stuffed, concentrated wine, atypically high in alcohol, with significant unresolved tannin.

1999 Pisoni Vineyard (tasted in 2000): Nearly opaque, dark ruby color, with a sapphire edge; violets on the nose; plum and cola in the mouth; a chewy body seasoned with Chinese five-spice; very big, very long, and moderately tannic.

1999 Santa Lucia Highlands (tasted in 2000): Barely transparent, dark blackish-red; black fruits and cola on the nose; strong flavors of meat, chocolate, and vanilla; very gutsy, big wine with considerable tannin and alcohol, long. Mostly fruit from Garys' Vineyard, with a small addition of Pisoni.

1999 Van der Kamp Vineyard (tasted in 2000): Quite different from the 1998 edition (see below); transparent, less saturated, medium black-red; again very briary; sweet core of black fruits and cola; notes of leather and licorice; even balance of tannin and acid; soft, linen-textured wine with considerable length. This vineyard, at 1,700 feet on the north side of Sonoma Mountain, was originally planted in the early 1960s to dry-farmed, head-trained vines of unknown provenance. (For more information on Van der Kamp, see page 112.) The 1999 was made mostly with fruit from the 1986 block.

1998 Coastlands Vineyard (tasted in 2000): Saturated, dense color; black fruits and barnyard on the nose; notes of spruce, cedar, and other evergreens, along with licorice and sweet allspice; general impression of rusticity; well balanced with acid and tannin, linen-textured, long.

1998 Hirsch Vineyard (tasted in 2000): Transparent, deep black-red, with an edge of tile; fruit-cocktail nose tinged with leather and wet fur; black cherries, currants, and raspberries, with some chocolate; rich, chewy, tannic wine picked at higher sugar than the predecessor vintages (24.3 Brix), very concentrated, needs time.

1998 Muirfield Vineyard (tasted in 2000): Transparent, very blackish-red; strong notes of leather and animal on the nose; red and black berries, mushroom, earth, black pepper, and cinnamon in the mouth, with some floral notes; medium-bodied wine with a silken finish and some unresolved tannin.

1998 Pisoni Vineyard (tasted in 2000): Dense black-red color with a hint of tile; cherry, plum, and cola on the nose and palate; sweet, with some clove and bell pepper; appealing already, but needs time.

1998 Van der Kamp Vineyard (tasted in 2000): Barely transparent, dark, inky black-red wine; briary nose with smoky raspberry and a tinge of stewed fruit; licorice, cola, coffee, and clove; considerable smoke and vanilla from the barrel regime; very big and tannic. This vintage of Van der Kamp was made mostly with fruit from the 1952 block.

1997 Hirsch Vineyard (tasted in 2000): Very transparent, brick-red; notes of pine and other evergreens on the nose; characteristic forest floor and black pepper, some chocolate and barnyard; long, silky.

1996 Hirsch Vineyard (tasted in 2000): Transparent, dark brick red; strong nose of chocolate and coffee; mint, earth, forest floor, meat, bright orange peel, and black pepper on the palate and aftertaste; midweight wine, silken texture, complex, fine.

1996 Oregon (tasted in 2000): Very transparent, medium black-red; nose of berries touched with prune and smoke; berries, cola, and forest floor on the palate; light-bodied wine, medium-length.

PRACTICAL INFORMATION

Because Siduri wines are made in small lots and the brand has been blessed with considerable acclaim, the best source of these wines is the winery's mailing list. There is limited distribution to key markets. The winery can be visited by appointment only; 707-578-3882.

TALISMAN WINES

Napa, California

Scott Rich's first career, in the 1980s, was in landscape architecture and environmental planning. In 1989, however—disenamored of work for land developers and the deadlines associated with regulatory approvals—Rich reexamined his interests and priorities, thought seriously about the red Burgundies he had tasted from his father's cellar, and returned to his alma mater, the University of California, Davis. This time he earned a degree in food science, with an emphasis on enology. Following stints as a research enologist for Robert Mondavi's Woodbridge facility and subsequently for R. H. Phillips, Rich was named winemaker for Mont St. John Cellars in 1992. In 1993, Mont St. John agreed that three tons of fruit from its much-respected Madonna Vineyard in Los Carneros could be part of Rich's compensation as winemaker. This was the debut of Rich's own, Carneros-centered pinot noir project, called Talisman.

In 1993 and 1994, Talisman's total production was eight barrels of Madonna Vineyard pinot. In 1995, following Rich's move from Mont St. John to Etude, he began sourcing fruit for the Talisman project from the Truchard Vineyard, not far from Mont St. John. His fruit sources expanded beyond Los Carneros to the Russian River Valley AVA in 1999, and to the Sonoma Coast in 2000. Meanwhile, Rich's day job changed too. He left Etude to assume the winemaking mantle at Carneros Creek Winery in 2001, and then moved to a combination of consulting, winemaking for Bel Air's Moraga Vineyards, and Talisman itself in 2002.

WINEMAKING

Rich says he picks pinot by taste alone. In the Truchard vineyard, owing to viticultural practices, the result is that the fruit is picked very ripe, between 25.5 and 26 Brix. In the Klopp and Thornridge Vineyards, sugars are usually a bit lower when the pick is done. About 25 percent whole clusters are used, and the fermentors are mostly fruit bins, plus one or two eight-ton stainless steel open-tops. Two to three days of ambient cool soak with just a bit of sulfur dioxide precede inoculation with a quarter-strength dose of laboratory yeast. The must is punched down quite vigorously at the beginning of the alcoholic fermentation, when the majority of extraction is aqueous rather than alcoholic; Rich then reduces the frequency of punchdowns as the fermentation continues. He looks for relatively hot peak temperatures, and moves the fruit bins into the sun if that is what's needed to warm things up. A long postfermentation maceration follows, so that the total time from pick to press is 30 to 35 days. Rich no longer separates the press fraction from the free-run juice except in very tannic years, having found that the press fraction's high pH made it difficult to manage independently.

After settling briefly in tank, the wine is barreled, using about 60 percent new wood. Dargaud & Jaeglé is Rich's favorite cooper, but he also uses some Cadus, and he has recently replaced the François Frères barrels used in early vintages of Talisman with Remond. Malolactic starter from Matanzas Creek is added to each barrel. The Carneros and Russian River Valley cuvées spend 12 months in wood, but the new Sonoma Coast cuvée is demanding much more barrel time, ranging from 18 to 24 months. Fining is rare; filtration is done as necessary. When the wine is fined, it is done for clarity but not for tannin management, for which other solutions are preferable, according to Rich. Rich does not filter if he can "sleep comfortably" with the wine unfiltered.

THE WINES

In 1993 and 1994, the only Talisman wine was a Carneros bottling, made entirely from Madonna Vineyard fruit. In 1995, when the Carneros source shifted from Madonna to Truchard, fruit from Truchard's old block of Swan selection was used exclusively. The 1996 Talisman was a blend of Truchard's old Swan block with an old Pommard (UCD 4) block from Domaine Chandon's Carneros vineyards. In 1997 Sasaki's old Pommard block (on the Sonoma side of Carneros) replaced the Domaine Chandon block, blended again with Truchard's Swan. In 1998 and 1999 the Carneros wine was made entirely from Truchard fruit (as it had been in 1995), but in 1998 some UCD 4 was added to the Swan; and in 1999 and 2000, fruit from a new mixed-clone block was also used. The Russian River Valley bottling debuted in 1999, based entirely on fruit from Ted Klopp's Ranch on Laguna Road, a combination of Swan selection, UCD 4, and Dijon 115. As of this writing, the Sonoma Coast wine was to make its first appearance in the 2000 vintage. The fruit source for this wine is another Klopp property, called Thornridge, about three miles due south of Sebastopol on the northeastern side of English Hill. It was planted in 1995, also to a mix of Swan selection, UCD 4, and Dijon 115, in nine-foot rows with six feet between vines, in sandy-loam soil.

My experience with Talisman pinots is confined to the 1999 and 2000 vintages—the latter tasted prerelease. They are visually attractive, moderately colored, complex wines with moderate concentration and considerable length.

TASTING NOTES

2000 Carneros (tasted prerelease in 2002): Very transparent, medium garnet; cherries, black raspberries, tea, and rose petals on the nose; very peppery and spice-enveloped sweet fruit in the mouth, with hints of orange peel, clove, and resin; lingering minerality and charcuterie flavors; moderately concentrated, hint of grip, glycerol-rich finish, texture of rough silk, medium-weight, and long.

2000 Russian River Valley (tasted prerelease in 2002): Brilliant, slightly blackish-red with ruby highlights; dark fruit, earth, and violets on the nose; sweet cherry and slightly minty black fruit on the palate, with hints of clove and black pepper and an undertone of minerality; mouthcoating and full-bodied, very slightly grippy but predominantly velvety, medium-weight and medium-length.

1999 Carneros (tasted in 2002): Brilliant, light to medium garnet with highlights of terra-cotta and coral; tar, cedar, red licorice, and very ripe fruit aromas; mocha, dark cherries, charcuterie, barrel char, and more cedar in the mouth; elegant, structured, and suede-textured, very fine-grained tannins, long.

PRACTICAL INFORMATION

Talisman pinots are sold primarily to mailing-list customers, but there is also limited distribution in California, Massachusetts, North Carolina, and Rhode Island; 707-258-5722. At present, Talisman is unable to receive visitors.

TALLEY VINEYARDS

Arroyo Grande, California

Oliver Talley began farming vegetables in the Arroyo Grande Valley soon after World War II. Three decades later, aware that vineyards had been developed in the nearby Edna and Santa Maria valleys, Oliver's son Don began to explore whether the hillsides above the family's vegetable fields could be successfully planted to wine grapes. In 1981, five quarter-acre test plots were set out with cabernet sauvignon, riesling, chardonnay, pinot noir, and sauvignon blanc. Today, while Talley Farms remains an important player in the field of specialty produce, Talley Vineyards has established a considerable reputation for estate-grown chardonnay and pinot noir. Some grapes of both varieties are also sold to Au Bon Climat (see the profile earlier in this section).

Talley's pinot noir plantings are divided between two vineyards, Rincon and Rosemary's, overseen by Don's son Brian and vineyard manager Rodolfo Romero. Rincon, the site of Don Talley's original test plots, has grown to 86 acres, of which 37 are now pinot noir. The oldest pinot is 3.6 acres of vines on Rincon's West Hillside—a steep, south-facing slope planted six feet by 12 in east-west rows, originally planted as own-rooted sauvignon blanc in 1983 but grafted to pinot noir (UCD 2A) in 1992. Just over five acres of pinot noir were planted on Rincon's East Hillside between 1984 and 1986, similarly spaced but in north-south rows; again the scion material was UCD 2A, and again the vines were mostly own-rooted. The Rincon vineyard is about eight miles from the Pacific Coast and is routinely fog-shrouded until midday; both hillsides consist of shallow, rocky, clay-loam soils. The West Hillside contains some subsurface limestone; the East Hillside is underlaid with fragmented sandstone. These two plantings at Rincon were the basis for Talley's first pinots, beginning in 1986. Planting resumed on the East Hillside of Rincon in 1999, 2000, and 2001, using a combination of UCD 2A selected from Rosemary's vineyard (see below) and Dijon clones 115, 667, and 777, this time on predominantly 101–14 rootstock.

Talley's second vineyard, called Rosemary's after Don Talley's wife, is a slightly cooler hill one mile west of Rincon, almost overlooking Talley Farms' vegetable coolers. The soil at Rosemary's is also underlaid with fragmented sandstone, and the surface layer is mostly a rocky loam weathered in place from the sandstone. The site is cooler than Rincon, and typically ripens a week or two later. There planting began in 1987 on a northwest-facing slope and continued throughout the 1990s, wrapping around the hillside to southwest- and south-facing exposures. The first Rosemary's plantings were, like early Rincon, set out six feet by 12, on a combination of their own roots and AxR1, but vine spacing was tightened to eight feet by four in the 1990s. In 2000, there were about 17 acres of pinot noir at Rosemary's. As at Rincon, the 1990s plantings have been split between field-selected UCD 2A and Dijon clones.

Appropriately for an enterprise founded on farming, the rule at Talley is sustainable viticulture that utilizes onsite compost and cover crops and minimizes the use of pesticides. Yields in both vineyards are managed to between two and 2.5 tons per acre. (Left to its own devices, Rosemary's would yield a bit more than Rincon.)

Talley's winemaker, from the very first vintage in 1986, has been Steve Rasmussen, a Berkeley native trained in enology at the University of California, Davis, with prior experience at Robert Mondavi and Corbett Canyon.

WINEMAKING

Talley pinots are mostly fermented in one-ton, plastic-lined plywood bins, but the winery sometimes also uses a six-ton or a nine-ton stainless steel open-top for pinot. Until 1995, 25 percent whole clusters was the rule; subsequent vintages have been completely destemmed. A four- to five-day cold soak precedes five days of alcoholic fermentation at 85 to 92 degrees Fahrenheit, relying entirely on resident yeast but acidifying as necessary. Punchdowns are done by hand twice daily. The must is pressed when it is dry or just before, and the juice is settled overnight before being barreled.

Malolactic fermentation takes place in barrel without inoculation. The entire barrel room is cold-stabilized for one month each winter. Pinots spend 16 to 17 months in barrel and are racked once during the spring or summer after the vintage. Barrels were all François Frères until 1999, mostly medium- or heavy-toast wood from the Allier and Vosges forests, but Talley has now begun to source some barrels from other coopers on an experimental basis and uses just 35 percent to 40 percent new oak. Rasmussen fines some lots to help manage tannins and finds that fining is more often required with fruit from Rincon than from Rosemary's; but Talley pinots have not been filtered since 1989. Seven months of bottle-aging precede release.

THE WINES

Until 1989, Talley made just one pinot noir in each vintage: an estate bottling derived entirely from Rincon Vineyard fruit. In 1990, Rosemary's fruit entered the estate wine. In 1993, Talley added vineyard-designated Rincon and Rosemary's wines to the portfolio. These wines have gradually evolved into quasi–block selections; Rosemary's is made primarily from 2.6 acres of the oldest, northwest-facing rows, while Rincon is anchored with fruit from the grafted, own-rooted sauvignon blanc vines on West Hillside. Talley pinots are ripe, deeply colored, intensely flavored, and richly textured wines, emphasizing black rather than red fruit characteristics that belie the vineyards' reliance on UCD 2A. In my experience, the wines age well, with the 1991 showing especially well at age ten.

TASTING NOTES

2000 Estate (tasted in 2003): Brilliant, medium garnet; aromas of earth and animal give way to barrel char and wild strawberries; sweet candied cherries and resinated berries in the mouth, with hints of clove; silken, round, medium-rich, and long.

2000 Rincon (tasted in 2003): Transparent, medium black-red; aromas of black fruit and black pepper; sweet and soft on the palate; dark cherry and barrel char, with a slight hint of infused orange blossom; medium-weight and concentrated, polished and suede-textured.

2000 Rosemary's (tasted in 2003): Brilliant, dark crimson; strong aromas of camphor, earth, and evergreen; very sweet black fruit, rich spice, and black pepper; full, round, long, and satin-textured.

1999 Rincon (tasted in 2001): Saturated, very dark black-red wine with just a hint of tile; aromas of dried currants and beeswax; black cherry, cassis, spice, and dried fruits in the mouth; intense, concentrated wine but soft, with the texture of heavy silk.

1999 Rosemary's (tasted in 2001): Saturated, dark, black-red wine, again with just a hint of tile; nose of evergreen and geranium, with a whiff of truffle; big, rich, long, and fine-grained, but without the forward fruit character that typifies this vineyard in most vintages.

1995 Rincon (tasted in 2001): Saturated, dark mahogany; aromas of fig and furniture polish; huge flavors of cherry, cassis, coffee, and resin; fine-grained tannins, long finish.

1994 Rosemary's (tasted in 2001): Saturated, dark mahogany; mocha, meat, cardamom, nutmeg, and evergreen on the nose; resin and soft spice on the palate; soft and long.

1991 Estate (tasted in 2001): Saturated, medium terra-cotta; wet earth, moss, forest floor, fading wild strawberry, and red vermouth aromas; merbromin, pepper, resin, and black fruit in the mouth; medium-weight and structured, long and elegant. A personal favorite.

1990 Estate (tasted in 2001): Transparent, medium-dark reddish mahogany; hints of animal and dried flowers on the nose; coffee, resin, and very evolved fruit in the mouth; slightly sweet core, medium-weight and medium-length.

1989 Estate (tasted in 2001): Transparent, red-mahogany; aromas of leather, gum camphor, and sage; cherry, chocolate, and briary flavors; still grippy but with a tendency toward velvet, chewy, long.

PRACTICAL INFORMATION

In 2000, Talley made about 3,600 cases of pinot noir. In 2001 and 2002, because of short crops, production sank to 2,300 and 1,800 cases, respectively. At this writing, 2003 production is forecast to return to approximately the 2000 levels. Eventually, as the new plantings come on-line, production will trend upward, and pinot may come to represent as much as half of Talley's total. Wines are nationally distributed within the limits of short supply. A new tasting room, open daily, was inaugurated in 2002, featuring a commanding view of the Rincon Vineyard's West Hillside. A subscription program is available to consumers in reciprocal states; 805-489-0446.

TESTAROSSA VINEYARDS

Los Gatos, California

First, Rob and Diana Jensen planted a small cabernet sauvignon vineyard in the yard of their Sunnyvale home and made wine in the garage. Then they attempted to restore an overgrown vineyard in the Santa Cruz Mountains but were defeated by a combination of poison oak and hungry birds. Finally, in 1993, the two software engineers created Testarossa Vineyards on a shoestring. In 1994, the sale of stock in Mountain View–based Veritas Software, which was Rob Jensen's day job; a second mortgage on their primary residence; and a second mortgage on Rob's parents' house combined to generate sufficient cash to finance the purchase of a few tons of chardonnay and enough pinot noir for about 40 cases of wine—from no less a source than the Chalone Vineyard—plus barrels, bottles, and other essential winemaking paraphernalia. Diana retired from *her* Silicon Valley day job to manage Testarossa's affairs, and George Troquato was engaged to make the wines, on a custom-crush basis, at the Cinnabar Winery in Saratoga.

No pinot noir was made in 1995, but the program recommenced in 1996, again with fruit from Chalone. In 1997, the Jensens were able to purchase pinot grapes from Robb Talbott's Sleepy Hollow Vineyard and Gary Pisoni's eponymous vineyard, both in the Santa Lucia Highlands, as well as from Bien Nacido's Block T in Santa Maria, bringing their total output of pinot noir to a commercially visible level. Two years later, in 1999, Testarossa added a third Santa Lucia Highlands vineyard (Garys') to its list of fruit sources and contracted with Bien Nacido to double the vine density in Block T by interplanting the 12-foot rows. Additional vineyards in Santa Lucia Highlands were added in 2000 and 2001.

Simultaneously, Testarossa's pinot horizon expanded northward to the Sonoma Coast and Russian River appellations, though Jensen argues that Santa Lucia Highlands "has the potential to be the best pinot noir–growing area in the country." Fruit was contracted from two new Sonoma vineyards:

Sonatera, near Highway 101 in the Sonoma Coast AVA, and Fritschen, on a hill overlooking Eastside Road in the Russian River Valley AVA. Planting also commenced in 2001 at the Howard Graham Vineyards, an 11-acre parcel in the Russian River Valley AVA between Dehlinger and Iron Horse. Graham is a member of Testarossa's board of directors, and Rob Jensen refers to this parcel as Testarossa's first "estate" vineyard. A few other sources in the southern Central Coast, Monterey, San Benito, and the Santa Cruz Mountains, used briefly during this period but never vineyard-designated, have since been abandoned. The Chalone appellation—now in the guise of Michel Michaud's vineyard—returned to Testarossa's pinot lineup in 2001, and a block of chardonnay at Clos Pepe in the Santa Rita Hills AVA, used for white wine in 1999 and 2000, was grafted to pinot noir (Dijon 115 on 5C rootstock) in time for the 2002 harvest. Of the Sonoma sources, Sonatera came onstream in 2002. As of this writing, Fritschen was due in 2003; Graham should yield its first crop in 2004.

In 1999, Ed Kurzman succeeded Troquato as Testarossa's winemaker. When Kurzman departed after the 2002 harvest, assistant winemaker Bill Brosseau, an enologist trained at the University of California, Davis, whose family has long farmed a small vineyard in the Chalone appellation, was named to replace him. Production moved from Cinnabar to the historic Novitiate Winery in Los Gatos in 1997.

WINEMAKING

Kurzman, Brosseau, and Rob Jensen say that they pick pinot "when the fruit tastes ripe," which can range from a low of 24.5 Brix to a high of about 26.2. (Bien Nacido was picked at 23.5 Brix in 1997.) Fermentors are an assortment of one-, three-, five-, eight-, and ten-ton stainless steel open-tops, with the five-ton size a favorite. The fermentors were custom-made so that only the bottom four feet of each is jacketed, enabling the winemakers to keep the juice cool even as the cap temperature is allowed to rise. Fruit bins are used for overflow lots. The clusters are usually destemmed completely, and three to five days of cool soak (not enforced with jackets or dry ice) precede inoculation. Pectinase is used to increase color extraction. Punchdowns are done several times daily, though the winemakers will reduce the frequency if they feel too much tannin is being extracted. The must is pressed when it goes dry; extended maceration is done on an experimental basis only. Half of the press fraction is immediately reintegrated with the free-run juice; the balance is kept separate. Sometimes this remainder is added back later; sometimes it is sold off.

Testarossa uses between 50 percent and 70 percent new barrels, but the percentage of new barrels used for any particular wine is adjusted after the first racking, based on taste. François Frères accounts for half of the barrel stock; Remond and Cadus are also used in substantial quantity. Malolactic bacteria are introduced either in tank or in barrel. The first racking is done between February and April after the vintage; the second is done just prior to bottling. Testarossa's Palazzio wine (see below) is bottled after ten or 11 months in wood; the other pinots are held until after the following vintage. There is no fining or filtration.

THE WINES

The backbone of Testarossa's pinot program is vineyard-designated wines from each of its source vineyards. They may be made in lots as small as 50 cases, but lots of 200 to 500 cases are more typical. In addition, a blend dubbed Palazzio is made from a large assortment of lots that, according to Jensen, display less site-based typicity than the barrels selected for vineyard-designation. Testarossa describes Palazzio as its "flagship" wine, even though it sells for a lower price than the vineyard-designates, and the company resists any suggestion that the wine is "lesser" or "lighter" in any way. (Lesser and lighter barrels, according to Rob Jensen, are bottled under a second label called Moorewood.) Although some fruit was contracted specifically for Palazzio in the 1999 and 2000 vintages, the program now relies entirely on vineyards that are also vineyard-designated, especially Sleepy Hollow, Garys', Bien Nacido, Rosella's, and Michaud. There are also 150 cases of a "reserve" wine, called Cuvée Niclaire, made from the "very best barrels" in the cellar. The first vintage of Palazzio was made in 2000; Niclaire debuted earlier, in 1997. From 1997 through 1999, Niclaire was based entirely on selected barrels of Pisoni and Sleepy Hollow wine, but in 2000 some barrels of Garys' and Bien Nacido also made their way into the final blend. Among the vineyard-designates, Sleepy Hollow and Pisoni have been made in every vintage since 1997, and Garys' since 1999. The Bien Nacido fruit was bottled as a Santa Maria Valley wine in 1997, but it has been specifically vineyard-designated since 1999.

The common characteristics of the vineyard-designated wines (and Niclaire) are very ripe flavors and a voluptuous mouthfeel that is reminiscent of heavy, draped silk. Aromatic properties vary, but dark fruit flavors laden with cola, mocha, cedar, and chocolate are common. Bien Nacido seems to pick at lower sugars than the Santa Lucia Highlands vineyards and to display a bit more elegance, but Testarossa's pinots are showy wines, crafted to impress. Perhaps unsurprisingly, in view of the fruit sources and the craftsmanship, they have taken an impressive array of awards in comparative tasting environments.

TASTING NOTES

2001 Bien Nacido (tasted prerelease in 2003): Transparent, medium black-red; herbs, rose petal, and cherry aromas; cola, black pepper, and bay laurel on the palate; medium-weight and concentrated, with a long, satin finish.

2001 Garys' Vineyard (tasted prerelease in 2003): Brilliant, medium garnet with pink highlights; aromas of fragrant geranium, dark cherry, and black licorice; very ripe, bright jammy black fruit in the mouth, with smoke and cinnamon; concentrated and full-bodied, with the texture of heavy silk and a slightly grippy finish.

2001 Michaud Vineyard (tasted prerelease in 2003): Brilliant, medium black-red; explosive nose of black fruits, tar, and bramble; huge palate of earth, slate, cinnamon, clove, bitter chocolate, and barrel char; chewy, grippy, and concentrated, finishes long and velvety.

2001 Rosella's Vineyard (tasted prerelease in 2003): Transparent, medium garnet; distinctive nose of camphorwood, vanilla, and ripe Italian plum; intense, extracted evergreen and coal tar with mocha; herbal notes on the finish; chewy, tannic, and concentrated. From the Gary Franscioni home vineyard and named for his wife.

2001 Sleepy Hollow Vineyard (tasted prerelease in 2003): Transparent, medium black-red; aromas of resin and tobacco; very ripe cherry and plum on the palate, with flavors of toasted cinnamon and tree bark; sweet, medium- to heavyweight, borderline chewy, texture of heavy silk.

2000 Palazzio (tasted in 2002): Transparent, medium garnet; rose petal, cola, leather, and a hint of mixed nuts on the nose; meat, black pepper, and smoke on the palate; medium-weight and silken.

1999 Garys' Vineyard (tasted in 2002): Medium-dark black-red; earth and black fruit on the nose; layers of strong flavors in the mouth, including meat, chocolate, cedar, smoke, and merbromin; medium-weight but chewy and long.

1999 Sleepy Hollow Vineyard (tasted in 2002 from a half-bottle): Transparent, medium-dark black-red; aromas of currants and raisins; black cherry, cola, chocolate, cedar, and cinnamon in the mouth; very sweet, smooth, and textured like heavy silk.

1998 Pisoni Vineyard (tasted in 2002): Medium-dark; evergreen, eucalyptus, plum, and licorice aromas; meat, cola, and sweet mocha in the mouth; saturated, medium-plus weight, texture of heavy silk.

PRACTICAL INFORMATION

In 2001, half of Testarossa's 9,000-case total production was pinot noir—divided about evenly between vineyard-designates and Palazzio, plus 150 cases of Niclaire. The winery's business plan calls for an annual increase of about 1,500 cases overall. As of this writing, no decision had been made whether the Sonoma sources that were to come onstream in 2002, 2003, and 2004 would be vineyard-designated or blended. Distribution reaches 20 states, Japan, Germany, and the United Kingdom. A tasting room is open daily in the old Novitiate winery, and open houses are held on several Saturdays each year. Wines are sold directly to mailing-list and Internet customers; 408-354-6150.

THOMAS FOGARTY WINERY

Woodside, California

In the 1970s, Thomas J. Fogarty was a Stanford University professor, cardiovascular surgeon, tireless inventor of medical devices, and home winemaker. Late in the decade, his home winemaking turned serious. He then planted grapes on a 320-acre parcel of mountainous land overlooking the Stanford campus and San Francisco Bay; hired Michael Martella, who trained at California State University, Fresno, to make his wines "professionally"; and built a commercial winery to replace the cabin he had used for his personal efforts. The Thomas Fogarty Winery was bonded in 1981.

The winery describes pinot noir as its flagship wine, though it accounts for less than 7 percent of total production. In 1983, Martella and Fogarty planted two acres of pinot on a knoll adjacent to the winery building, at an elevation of 1,950 feet. Another five-acre block, called Rapley Vineyard, was planted downhill from the winery in 1984, at about 1,750 feet. Both sites are cold (though the lower vineyard is a bit warmer than the hilltop) and ripen late. Early October is considered an early harvest, and picks extending into November are not unusual. The soils are relatively thin sandy loams strewn with shale and fractured sandstone, and both face essentially southeastward. Vines are planted six feet by ten and minimally irrigated. (Martella does not irrigate the deeper soils toward the bottom of the vineyard at all, but the top of the hill requires some water.) Since about 1993, the vines have been trellised à la Scott Henry: four canes rather than two are left on each vine, with two of the canes trained downward rather than up. This approach reduces vigor and seems to produce better fruit in sites that would normally promote high-vigor vines. The plant material was sourced from Wente's Arroyo Seco vineyard and is therefore some mixture of UCD 2A, 4, and 13, with a probable preponderance of UCD 4 and 13. Yield is three to 3.5 tons per acre (though only 1.5 tons in 1998 thanks to persistent fog during flowering), and green harvesting is practiced in most years. Although the estate vineyard has been the heart of Fogarty's pinot program since it came onstream in 1989, a small amount of pinot is purchased from neighboring vineyards in the Santa Cruz Mountains appellation. Before 1989 Fogarty pinot was a different beast entirely, having been sourced from the Winery Lake Vineyard.

WINEMAKING

Martella picks pinot noir over an eight- to ten-day period when it has reached 24 to 25 Brix. He finds that he now picks riper than he did in the early 1990s, largely to avoid the site's tendency to taste a bit herbaceous at lower sugars. The grapes are 100 percent destemmed and the stems are discarded, and between 20 percent and 30 percent of the fruit is not crushed. Martella has gradually increased the percentage of whole berries over time, and he modifies the winemaking protocol from year to year. A combination of 500-gallon stainless steel tanks measuring five feet in diameter and five feet high with double-height fruit bins is used for fermentation. The fruit macerates cold for two days with low-tech temperature controls: soaker hoses are wrapped around the stainless steel tanks to chill them, and the fruit bins are moved outside at night. The must is inoculated to start the alcoholic fermentation, and it generally ferments 15 to 20 days at 85 to 90 degrees Fahrenheit, with manual punch-downs three to four times per day. Pressing generally occurs before the must is completely dry. Lightening of the skins, as fermentation leaches the anthocyanins into the must, is one indication that the time to press has arrived, as are flavors to the taste; but Martella is now also measuring flavor components of the must with gas chromatography and comparing the must analysis with analyses previously done on the unfermented berries. This comparison helps to indicate when the extraction is approaching its "potential." The press fraction is kept separate, but is generally reassembled in the cuvée.

About 75 percent new wood is used, in part to "tame the tannin" but in part, Martella admits, "because I like the flavor of oak." Most barrels are medium-plus toast coopered by François Frères, using wood from forests in the Allier and Vosges. Martella inoculates to start the malolactic fermentation. The wines spend 12 to 16 months in barrel and are generally racked once, the August after the vintage. Martella tried fining for tannin management but found it "didn't work." He filters if laboratory analysis reveals any residual sugar or bacteria. Long bottle-aging is practiced: 12 months for the Santa Cruz Mountains wine, and 24 months for the Estate Reserve.

THE WINES

Fogarty pinots are big, dark, structured wines that are often marked with flavors of both vanilla and chocolate. Alcohols now tend to top 14 percent, but good acidity keeps them in balance, and the tannins are usually omnipresent and firm. The winery's long prerelease bottle-aging regimen helps to soften the wines, but consumers will be rewarded if they cellar for an additional few years. The main release (800 to 1,000 cases) is a Santa Cruz Mountains wine that often contains a small percentage of non-estate fruit. In 1994, 1995, 1996, and 1999, barrels that exhibited especially "strong" fruit were set aside for about 200 cases of an Estate Reserve wine. Martella has found that barrels picked for the reserve frequently represent fruit from the lower part of the Rapley Vineyard, perhaps because this site is slightly warmer than the hilltop and can therefore be picked riper. Two block-designated wines were isolated in the 2002 vintage, from Block B and Block M of Rapley. They effectively replaced the Estate Reserve wine, at least for this vintage.

TASTING NOTES

1999 Estate Reserve (tasted in 2003): Transparent, medium-dark black-red with rose highlights; chocolate, cigar box, and ripe cherry on the nose; very ripe, slightly sweet black fruit on the palate, with wet slate and minerals; mouthcoating and moderately grippy, medium-weight.

1999 Santa Cruz Mountains (tasted prerelease in 2000, and again in 2003): Transparent, medium black-red; briary nose in 2000, more rose and ripe cherry in 2003; black fruit with mint and black pepper in 2000, some cinnamon by 2003; structured, angular wine in which minerality overshadows fruit, big-framed, grippy, and medium-long.

1998 Santa Cruz Mountains (tasted prerelease in 2000, and again in 2003): Very dark black-red; earth, underbrush, and balsamic-marinated fruit on the nose; sweet black fruit on the palate, with wet slate and graphite; some cinnamon and chocolate; grippy and full, emery-textured but still plush, medium-plus weight, long.

1997 Santa Cruz Mountains (tasted in 2000): Transparent, black-red; ripe fruit nose tinged with prune; cola, chocolate, and oak flavors; very tannic and long.

1996 Estate Reserve (tasted in 2000): Transparent, dark black-red wine; rich, sweet black fruit and cola, vanilla, and chocolate; evolutionary notes of leather and forest floor; softening tannins; generously textured wine, with a long, sweet fruit finish.

1995 Estate Reserve (tasted in 2000): Dark black-red; huge, intense black fruit flavors; cola and chocolate; brooding flavors; structured and long.

PRACTICAL INFORMATION

Fogarty pinots are distributed nationwide. An onsite tasting room is open Tuesday through Sunday, and the winery does a considerable business in conferences, weddings, and other events; 800-247-4163.

W. H. SMITH WINES

St. Helena, California

The first wine venture of Bay Area oil and gas man and real estate developer Bill Smith was the successful and much-respected La Jota project: cabernet sauvignon, cabernet franc, and petite syrah grown on Howell Mountain and made in a tiny stone winery built at the turn of the past century. Early in the 1990s, however, Smith found that his personal taste was turning away from cabernet toward Burgundies, and he was seduced by a new challenge. "If you make wine," he explains, "you want to make wine out of the hard-to-do stuff."

So in 1992 he bought a half-ton of pinot from the Hyde Vineyard in Los Carneros and another half-ton from a sparkling-wine vineyard in the Russian River valley, fermented the fruit in half-ton macro bins, and realized that pinot noir "wasn't as tough as I thought." In 1993, he discovered the wild charms of the extreme Sonoma Coast. He bought some more Russian River fruit—this time from the Quail Hill Vineyard—and fruit from Gard Hellenthal, a "timbering" guy who was also tending a small pinot noir vineyard on a remote, unforested ridge top northeast of Jenner. In 1994, 1995, and 1996, Smith's pinot program consisted entirely of a single, vineyard-designated Hellenthal bottling. In 1997, there were three different bottlings, all from Hellenthal grapes: the Hellenthal Vineyard, made from old vines; a Sonoma Coast bottling, made from younger Hellenthal vines; and so-called Little Billy, the lightest wine of the three. In 1998, a short-crop year, Smith reverted to the single bottling of Hellenthal Vineyard; in 1999 and 2000, both Hellenthal and Sonoma Coast were produced again, differentiated as in 1997.

Hellenthal's vineyard is on Creighton Ridge, about 14 tortuous road miles from Fort Ross but barely more than two miles as the crow flies from the Pacific Coast. The oldest vines were planted in 1980: 2.1 acres of Pommard clone taken from an unspecified vineyard in the Santa Cruz Mountains. Budwood from those vines was then used to plant a new, six-acre vineyard in 1992. These blocks are the distinction between Smith's Hellenthal and Sonoma Coast bottlings. Meanwhile, in 1994, Smith made his own purchase of Sonoma Coast land, acquiring 360 hilly acres due north of Hellenthal's property, accessible from King Ridge Road. The soils there seem promising to Smith: a great deal of cross-faulting has superimposed shale, deep soils, and uplifted marine sedimentation. He planted just over 11 acres of this parcel in 1997 and 1998, in six-foot rows with three feet between vines, using entirely Dijon clones—115, 667, and 777. The first estate wine, dubbed Maritime Vineyard, was made in 2002.

WINEMAKING

Although Smith is his own hands-on winemaker, Helen Turley acted as a consultant for the first vintages. Three-quarter-ton bins are used to ferment the grapes, though one 3.5-ton stainless steel open-top tank was introduced in 1999. Smith says he is using stems "less and less" and was "down to 15 percent whole clusters in 2000." A seven-day cold soak is practiced, and fermentation is then allowed to start naturally with resident yeast. The must is punched down by hand, and fermentation lasts about seven days at a peak temperature of 85 to 87 degrees Fahrenheit. The must is pressed when it is dry, and the wine goes into barrel dirty. Press fraction and free-run juice are barreled together.

Wine destined for the Hellenthal bottling is in 100 percent new oak (primarily François Frères and Cadus); one- and two-year-old barrels are retained to raise the Sonoma Coast bottling and Little Billy. The wines are left undisturbed for seven to eight months, at which time they are racked once, and they are bottled two months after racking, without fining or filtration. Release date is January 1 of the second year after harvest.

THE WINES

My experience with W. H. Smith pinot noir is confined to the 1998, 1999, 2000, and 2001 vintages. These wines are quite different, reflecting both the natural variation of vintages at the end of the 1990s and, one suspects, some differences in winemaking protocols. Nevertheless, the Hellenthal site produces some aromatic consistency and considerable complexity.

TASTING NOTES

2001 Hellenthal Vineyard (tasted in 2003): Transparent, medium garnet; black pepper, dried currants, and a bit of cocoa on the nose; a high-spice, low-fruit palate redolent of graphite and Ybarra chocolate; medium-weight and medium-length, angular, slightly grippy, and vaguely bitter on the finish.

2001 Sonoma Coast (tasted in 2003): Brilliant, medium-dark but very black red; very ripe fruit, with rose petals and fig preserves on the nose; sweet, dark cherry in the mouth, with flavors of caramelized sugar and sugar-cured ham; soft with glycerol, medium-weight, and silken.

2000 Hellenthal Vineyard (tasted in 2003): Saturated, dark black-red; nose of chaparral, pungent herbs, and tar; very mineral, dry, peppery, and austere; concentrated, grippy, and long.

1999 Hellenthal Vineyard (tasted in 2001): Very transparent, light to medium garnet; cardamom surrounded with leather and forest-floor aromatics; lots of black pepper and very dark cherry in the mouth; less fleshy and more austere than the 1998; long finish, light- to medium-weight wine.

1998 Hellenthal Vineyard (tasted in 2000): Transparent, medium to dark black-red; nose of violets, cardamom, coriander seed, and mace; slate, tar, tobacco, and dark, sweet fruit, with tree bark and mesquite on both nose and palate; dominance of wild, brambly flavors; linen texture, long, very fine.

PRACTICAL INFORMATION
In most vintages, production is fewer than 1,000 cases. There are some direct sales to restaurants and a few retail accounts, but W. H. Smith wines are sold primarily via mailing list, and visits to the winery are by appointment only; 707-965-9726.

WILLIAMS SELYEM WINES

Healdsburg, California

Williams Selyem is an icon, and the company has had much to do with the emergence of the Russian River valley as a premier site for pinot noir. It was the first pinot-centered "cult" winery in North America, the first producer to make Joe Rochioli's grapes genuinely famous, and one of the first to sell its entire production to fanatically loyal customers by the simple and inexpensive device of a mailing list. Today there are 14,000 names on the winery's list, including restaurants, and 3,000 more on a waiting list. Allocations are small, and all customers, including restaurants, pay the same price. There is no tasting room and no name on the mailbox.

The story of Williams Selyem is the Wine Country equivalent of a modest Silicon Valley startup. Born as a home-winemaking project in a garage in 1979, the brand, its mailing list, and two years' inventory were sold 18 years later for $9 million. When Burt Williams and Ed Selyem, both residents of Forestville, first met in the 1970s, Williams was a pressman for the San Francisco Newspaper Agency. Selyem was the wine buyer for a local supermarket. Enamored of French Burgundies but unable to afford the best exemplars on their salaries, they began making a few barrels of wine in Selyem's garage, beginning with zinfandel from Leno Martinelli's nearby Jackass Hill vineyard. In 1981, advised that the TTB would not ignore their home production indefinitely, they obtained a winery bond as Hacienda del Rio—named for Selyem's house on the Russian River. The previously established but now defunct Hacienda Winery complained about the name, however, so in 1984 the partners shifted to using, simply, their own surnames. Williams, who knew a thing or two about typography from his work in the pressroom, designed a simple black-and-red label on a background of cream-colored paper, adorned with nothing more than a stock ornament of the sort known to typesetters as a dingbat. This logo has never changed.

From the beginning, Williams was the winemaker and Selyem the marketer. They owned no land and worked on a shoestring. They purchased grapes from growers who would grow grapes the way Williams wanted them. Their contracts were a handshake. On the two-hour bus ride between Forestville and his day job in San Francisco each morning and evening, Williams read everything he could find about wine and winemaking. Selyem came up with the then revolutionary idea of selling wine to a mailing list: "Sign up with us, and you will get six bottles of something we make, twice a year." Faithful customers lined up to purchase everything the partners could produce. In 1987, judges at California's state fair picked Williams Selyem's 1985 Rochioli Vineyard pinot noir—the winery's first vineyard-designated pinot noir—as the sweepstakes winner and named Williams Selyem—still operating from a two-car garage on River Road, with converted dairy tanks and an outdoor crushpad—Winery of the Year.

Friend and neighbor Howard Allen, who owned a vineyard on Westside Road adjacent to the Rochioli ranch, leased the partners some old buildings on his property in 1988, which were repurposed as a "real" winery in time for the crush in 1989. By 1992 Williams Selyem was finally self-supporting, and Williams quit his day job. The wines achieved cult status, defined Russian River pinot for many connoisseurs, and set the benchmark by which other American pinots were and are judged. Throughout, says Bob Cabral, Williams Selyem's current winemaker, "it was and is strictly about quality, not about profit. There were no great secrets. No pumps, no filters; just rigorous selection." Williams, it is said, kept meticulous winegrowing notes but was never much concerned if yields were low or production tiny.

Then, less than ten years after construction of the winery, in a move that made front-page news throughout the wine world, Burt Williams and Ed Selyem retired simultaneously, and Williams Selyem was sold to John Dyson, a New York–based connoisseur and investor. No stranger to the wine business, Dyson already owned Millbrook Winery in the Hudson Valley, Villa Pillo in Tuscany, and several hundred acres of grapes on California's Central Coast. Dyson's wife, Kathe, who had met Burt Williams at a winemaker dinner in the early 1990s, had finagled a spot on the Williams Selyem mailing list. Dyson's choice for winemaker, on Williams's recommendation, was Bob Cabral, a veteran of Hartford Court, Alderbrook, Kunde, and DeLoach. Cabral, too, held a spot on the Williams Selyem list (number 576!); he had signed up as a college kid who loved wine.

Williams Selyem's sale was greeted with skepticism in the wine press. Respected sources speculated that the brand might be on the verge of demise. Subsequent vintages, however, were well reviewed. Cabral made few changes to winemaking protocols, and Williams remained, in the end, as a consultant, providing occasional advice, tasting unfinished 1998 and 1999 wines, and sometimes writing tasting notes for the winery's newsletter. The main transition issue—as is typical for landless wineries—was persistence of fruit sources. Some key ones were lost, including Rochioli's West Block and Olivet Lane. Cabral contracted instead with several other Russian River valley sites and the Weir Vineyard in Mendocino's Yorkville Highlands. The winery also began to use pinot noir from Dyson's vineyards on the Central Coast. In a bid to mitigate permanently the vagaries associated with purchased fruit and to generate estate fruit sufficient for 70 percent of Williams Selyem's total production by 2010, Dyson began to acquire land in 1998: 34 acres of pinot noir (and some chardonnay) were planted in eight blocks of sandy, loamy river bottomland near Guerneville in 1999, in seven-foot rows with five feet between vines. The scion material is UCD 4; Dijon 115, 667, and 777; Mount Eden selection via David Bruce; and a "French clone" said to have been imported via Canada, Cornell University, and Dyson's Millbrook Vineyard. The first crop was harvested in 2002; the grapes are intended to feed the appellation wine program (see below). A second parcel has been acquired since, straddling Westside Road about one mile downstream from the winery site. There, between 34 and 38 acres of pinot noir were to be planted in 2003, 2004, and 2005.

For now, Williams Selyem's "home" vineyard remains the Allen Ranch on Westside Road. Although the winery is only a tenant there and the fruit is shared with other wineries—notably Rochioli, Gary Farrell, and Davis Bynum—this property is the brand's single most persistent source of pinot and has produced a vineyard-designate every year since 1987. The ranch occupies hilly former prune orchard and pastureland on the upslope side of Westside Road, about two miles north of Wohler Bridge. The soil is sandy loam weathered in place from sandstone laced with broken volcanic rock. In 1970, UCD 4 was planted there in 12-foot rows with eight-foot intervine spacing; it now yields two to 2.5 tons per acre in a typical year. Williams Selyem's share comes primarily from the property's northern hill, but Williams Selyem also obtains fruit from the southern hill and (until 1997) from a small, triangular parcel on the downslope side of Westside Road (Williams Selyem calls this block Tricorner; Rochioli calls it Three Corner).

Williams Selyem also sources pinot noir from vineyards as far north as Anderson Valley, as far west as Fort Ross, and as far south as San Benito County. Ferrington Vineyard, northwest of Boonville at the warm end of Anderson Valley, has provided fruit since 1992. This vineyard consists of 27 acres of pinot noir on the valley floor, allegedly including some suitcase clones. Weir Vineyard—a cool, fog-strewn site in Yorkville Highlands southeast of Boonville—is another Mendocino County source. Weir is planted to some combination of a suitcase clone and UCD 2A. In the true Sonoma Coast, fruit has been sourced from David Hirsch's vineyard on Bohan-Dillon Road, from Precious Mountain near Fort Ross, and from David and Diane Cobb's Coastlands Vineyard, on very steep hillsides overlooking Bodega Bay. Coastlands consists of several quite different blocks at altitudes ranging from 900 to 1,150 feet above sea level. There are about 15 acres of pinot noir there—UCD 4, 13, and 15, along with several Dijon clones—and the oldest vines date to 1989.

WINEMAKING

Over the years, Williams developed a "formula" for growing pinot noir, which Cabral follows. ("I've never worked so hard in my life not to change something," Dyson was quoted as saying after the purchase.) Crop thinning in the vineyard is aggressive: as much as 30 percent of the clusters are sacrificed for better concentration. Between 10 percent and 25 percent whole clusters are used, depending on the ripeness of the stems and the history of the vineyard. Three to four days of cold soak in open-tops precede the alcoholic fermentation, which is allowed to begin with resident yeast. At this point, when "you can smell" the resident yeast at work, the must is inoculated with a proprietary yeast made for Williams Selyem by a local laboratory, the starter for which came, during the mid 1980s, from a fermentation involving zinfandel from the Jackass Hill Vineyard. The primary fermentation then proceeds rather quickly, taking just five to six days (with punchdowns two to four times daily) to reach zero sugar. The must is immediately pressed, inoculated for malolactic fermentation, and transferred to barrel. The press juice, instead of being barreled separately, is used to top up each free-run barrel.

Cabral uses anywhere from 33 percent to 100 percent new oak, depending on the vineyard and the vintage, and *all* the barrels are François Frères medium toast, with toasted heads. The so-called appellation wines—Russian River Valley, Sonoma Coast, Central Coast, and sometimes also Sonoma and Mendocino County—are bottled after ten to 11 months in wood, but the vineyard-designated wines stay in barrel 14 to 19 months. There is no fining or filtration, and all wines get an additional eight to 12 months of bottle-aging before release.

THE WINES

Williams Selyem pinots are almost always richly flavored and concentrated wines, but the finished wines remain transparent, and the alcohol levels rarely exceed about 14.2 percent. The flagship wines are the vineyard-designates, of which six or more may be made in any single year. The so-called appellation wines command slightly lower prices and are usually the first wines made available to new names on the mailing list. The "appellation" category also includes Sonoma County and Mendocino County bottlings, which combine lots from more than one AVA. The combination of consistent winemaking and uniform use of François Frères barrels creates a strong impression of house style in all the wines. The concentration of the vineyard-designated wines is protected by rigorous barrel-by-barrel selection; deselected barrels of vineyard-designated wines are used as the backbone of the appellation wines. The balance of the appellation wines derive from vineyards judged to have vineyard-designation potential in due season, and (in a few cases) from vineyards sourced specifically for use in these wines. The longest-running vineyard-designate now produced is the Allen Ranch bottling (see above), made every year since 1987; it is followed by Rochioli's River Block (Williams Selyem spells this *Riverblock* on its labels) and Hirsch Vineyard, both made since 1994. Ferrington has been made as a vineyard-designate since 1992; Coastlands since 1995, except in 2000, when an extremely meager yield did not measure up; Precious Mountain since 1996; and Weir since 1999. The vineyard-designated wine that Williams Selyem called simply Rochioli Vineyard—actually fruit from Rochioli's so-called West Block—was made from 1985 through 1997; vineyard-designated Olivet Lane wine was made from 1989 through 1997. Vineyard-designates were made from the Summa Vineyard in 1988, 1991, and 1993; and from the Cohn Vineyard in the Russian River valley, near the boundary with Dry Creek, in 1993 only. A blend labeled Summa and Coastlands was also made in 1993.

The Russian River and Sonoma Coast so-called appellation wines both debuted in 1988. Thereafter the Russian River valley wine was made from 1990 through 1995 and again since 1999, anchored with old-vines fruit from Charles Bacigalupi's Westside Road vineyard, plus declassified barrels of River Block and Allen Ranch. Recent vintages have also used fruit from the Flax vineyard, adjacent to Allen. A Sonoma Coast blend was made from 1988 through 1990, 1993 through 1995, and 1998 through 2000, mostly with declassified barrels of Coastlands and Hirsch but sometimes also with deselected lots of Summa and Precious Mountain. The Sonoma County bottling, made mostly from leftovers after the vineyard-designates and appellation wines were assembled, first appeared in 1984. It was not made again until 1994, but has been made in each vintage since, except in 1995. The Mendocino County bottling, introduced in 1998, is a blend of deselected Ferrington and Weir lots. Williams Selyem's Central Coast wines are a creature of the Dyson era, using fruit from Dyson's vineyards in San Benito County. Selected blocks of Vista Verde vineyard are custom-farmed to low yields for the Williams Selyem program; fruit from Dyson's Mistral Vineyard was also used for three years beginning in 1999. The 1998 edition of Central Coast pinot was made entirely from Vista Verde fruit, as it was again beginning in 2002. Some barrels of Vista Verde were also made as a vineyard-designate in 2000.

In 1998, in Los Angeles, well-known collector Bipin Desai orchestrated a two-day-long vertical tasting of 59 Williams Selyem pinots made between 1981 and 1995. In notes released later by the *Insiders' Wine Line,* virtually every wine in this tasting was judged outstanding, though tasters generally preferred wines from the 1986, 1988, 1991, 1994, and 1995 vintages, and in those years the appellation wines were not judged lesser than the vineyard-designates. Even wines from the 1981 vintage were holding up well. In Cabral's view, Williams Selyem pinots are generally "just beginning to come around" ten to 12 years after the vintage.

TASTING NOTES

2000 Central Coast (tasted in 2002): Transparent, medium ruby-red; on the nose, cured meat, camphor, compost, and funky fruit; dark cherry fruit, barrel char, and mentholated butterscotch on the palate; flavors of roasted summer vegetables; soft and smooth, medium-weight and medium-length. Entirely different from Williams Selyem's North Coast wines.

1999 Coastlands Vineyard (tasted in 2000): Deep, semisaturated black-red; earth, coffee, forest floor, and very ripe black fruit on the nose; deep, black cherry-fruit in the mouth, with hints of plum, barrel char, mocha, bay leaf, and herbs; concentrated, full-bodied, and very slightly grippy, but overall texture still more like rough silk, fairly weighty and long. A personal favorite.

1999 Hirsch Vineyard (tasted in 2002): Transparent, deep, lustrous garnet; mossy, spicy nose, with wet heather and licorice; intense, deep black fruit flavors on the palate, with cinnamon, ink, blackberry preserves, and minerals; concentrated, rich-textured, full-bodied wine with some grip, texture like embroidery.

1999 Russian River Valley (tasted in 2002): Transparent, medium garnet; cinnamon, pepper, slate, rose petal, and dark fruit on the nose; slightly sweet, with infused flowers and spicy fruit on the palate, plus hints of root vegetables, smoke, tangerine peel, and graphite; medium-weight and medium-length, emery-textured, and moderately angular.

1999 Sonoma Coast (tasted in 2000): Transparent, medium black-red; black licorice and daphne-geranium aromas; sweet, plum and cherry fruit in the mouth, with notes of clove and allspice; concentrated and full-bodied, silken-suede texture, medium-weight, and long.

1999 Sonoma County (tasted in 2002): Transparent, medium ruby; dusty floral aromas, with raspberry and cranberry; raspberry, chalk, and white pepper, with a touch of citrus peel, in the mouth; lightweight and medium-length, linear and uncomplicated.

1999 Weir Vineyard (tasted in 2002): Transparent, medium black-red; dark cherry, briar, smoke, and moss on the nose, with a hint of animal; dark fruit, resin, vanilla, graphite, and black pepper in the mouth; medium-weight and moderately grippy, decidedly concentrated, slightly hot, and medium-long.

1998 Allen Ranch (tasted in 2002): Transparent, medium garnet; dried leaves, roses, and earth on the nose, with hints of camphor and acetone; ginger, black cherry, allspice, and barrel char in the mouth; slightly sweet and just a hint green, with some orange peel; mouthcoating, full-bodied, structured, texture of rough silk with a slightly viscous core, medium-long.

1998 Mendocino County (tasted in 2002): Transparent, medium black-red with ruby highlights; Queen Anne cherries, blanched walnuts, and potpourri on the nose; soft Indonesian spice and toast in the mouth; slightly sweet; full-bodied, somewhat chewy and grippy, lush, medium-weight, and long.

1997 Allen Ranch (tasted in 1999): Somewhat closed; cherry and black fruit on the palate, with spicy notes plus chocolate and vanilla; rich, very concentrated, and silken.

1997 Ferrington Vineyard (tasted in 2002): Brilliant, medium black-red with terra-cotta highlights; aromas of rose-lavender potpourri, chalk, and wild strawberry; strawberry, cherry, rhubarb, and white pepper, with some minerality, in the mouth; light- to medium-weight and medium-length, with a soft texture somewhere between chamois and silk.

1997 Hirsch Vineyard (tasted in 2002): Transparent, medium-dark black-red with just a hint of orange at the rim; blackberry, bramble, black pepper, and beetroot on the nose; dense, velvety, and borderline chewy on the palate, with cherry, cinnamon, black licorice, and a hint of resin; fleshy, mouthcoating, and very slightly grippy, very long and fine. A personal favorite.

1997 Riverblock (tasted in 1999): Dark and purple-red; cherries, plum, and cola; hint of fennel, fig, and prune; strongly spicy, with some chocolate; concentrated and tannic.

1997 Rochioli Vineyard (tasted in 1999): Black-red with purple highlights; ultraripe berries and black fruit, plus resin, tar, tobacco, cinnamon, and coffee; soft tannins, velvety.

1996 Allen Ranch (tasted in 1999): Transparent, black-red color; cherry and black fruit nose; hints of leather, forest floor, black pepper, clove, and cinnamon; medium body, creamy texture, simultaneously robust and elegant.

1996 Riverblock (tasted in 1999): Red with a touch of terra-cotta; plum, black fruits, and cola; black pepper, clove, cinnamon, allspice, and cardamom; rich and grippy.

1996 Rochioli Vineyard (tasted in 1999): Transparent, very dark black-red; resin and tar aromas like the 1997; very dense, dominated by berry and black fruit flavors; tannic, fat, and richly textured.

PRACTICAL INFORMATION

At this writing, normal mortals' best shot for tasting Williams Selyem wines is in restaurants. In Sonoma County, John Ash in Santa Rosa and Manzanita in Healdsburg both list the wines. Farther afield, Jardinière in San Francisco, Patina in Los Angeles, and Montrachet in New York all have substantial libraries. Williams Selyem wines, even from recent vintages, also show up regularly in the commercial wine auction market, though for prices considerably above their official release prices. Williams Selyem's annual production of pinot noir is increasing gradually, however, having passed 10,000 cases in 2002 on its way to a business-plan target of 14,000, so names will migrate from the waiting list to the mailing list with each new vintage. Zinfandel and chardonnay, which were phased out when Williams Selyem focused on pinot noir in the 1990s, have been reintroduced. There is no tasting room at the winery and no visiting, but active mailing-list customers may make advance appointments for tours; 707-433-6425.

PRODUCERS TO WATCH

A measure of the contemporary interest in pinot noir, and the enormous acreage that has been planted since the mid 1990s, is the proliferation of producers and labels that have appeared in the marketplace since the 1997 vintage. Some of these are associated with genuinely new winegrowing talent and new or replanted vineyards. Domaine Alfred, a new vineyard and winery on the site of one of Edna Valley's pioneer plantings, comes to mind, as do Stewart Dorman's Adrian Fog label, sourced primarily from Anderson Valley vineyards, and Jim Prosser's J. K. Carrière brand, whose first wines were made in 1998. Sea Smoke Cellars in the Santa Rita Hills is a new label from a newly planted vineyard. Many more involve producers who have expanded their varietal range to encompass pinot, and some are new start-ups by established pinot makers. Anderson Valley's Goldeneye, created by merlot and sauvignon blanc specialist Dan Duckhorn, is a good example of the former, as are the pinots made since 1998 by Hermann J. Wiemer, a riesling specialist and nurseryman in the Finger Lakes. Tandem Winery, Scherrer Winery, Penner-Ash Wine Cellars, Patricia Green Cellars, and Francis Tannahill (a partnership of former Chehalem winemaker Cheryl Francis and former Archery Summit winemaker Sam Tannahill) are instances of the latter. Another large category of new entrants is growers who have chosen to launch their own labels, often on a custom-crush basis, taking advantage of the reputation that their third-party vineyard-designated wines already enjoy. Examples include Oregon's Shea Wine Cellars; David Hirsch's new eponymous winery; the Roar label launched by Garys' Vineyard and Rosella's Vineyard owner Gary Franscioni "in collaboration with" Siduri; McIlroy Cellars, whose wines are made from the family's Aquarius Ranch fruit in the Russian River valley; and Pisoni Vineyards, whose wines—sometimes informally dubbed "Pisoni-Pisoni" for clarity—are made in Copain Wines' facility by Gary Pisoni's son Jeff.

A comprehensive list of newcomers is beyond the scope of this book, but at least the seven described below have made wines of more than routine interest right from the outset.

TANDEM WINERY

Sebastopol, California

Two Gregs, La Follette and Bjornstad, with intersecting careers and continuous association since they worked together at Flowers Vineyard and Winery (see the profile earlier in this section) from 1996 to 2000, founded Tandem in a repurposed fruit-processing plant north of Sebastopol just before the crush in 2000. The first pinots were a 2000 Pisoni Vineyard and 2001s from Van der Kamp Vineyard, Keefer Ranch, Halleck Vineyard, and the Sangiacomo family's 1998 planting on Roberts Road in the Sonoma Coast AVA. The Pisoni wine was discontinued after the 2001 vintage, leaving Tandem to concentrate on North Coast AVAs. La Follette and Bjornstad pick fruit ripe, but the wines are complex, richly layered, and graceful, and La Follette says that he and his partner, "as they grow older," are moving toward less-aggressive extractions. Tandem also operates custom-crush and consulting services for several other new pinot producers, including DuNah, Sapphire Hill, and Londer. The Van der Kamp wines are personal favorites.

SCHERRER WINERY

Sebastopol, California

Fred Scherrer, a winemaker trained at the University of California, Davis, with experience at Fieldstone, Greenwood Ridge (see the profile earlier in this section), and (from 1988 to 1998) Dehlinger, launched his own label in 1991 with zinfandel from his family's vineyard in Alexander Valley. His first pinots debuted in 1999: twin cuvées of Russian River valley wine made from parcels farmed by Sonoma-Cutrer, dubbed Big Brother and Little Sister to evoke their respective weights and stature; a Hirsch Vineyards wine poetically called Diaphanous; and a Sonoma Coast bottling made from a combination of Russian River and Hirsch fruit. Big Brother and Little Sister were collapsed into a single Russian River cuvée in 2000, and two vineyard-designated wines were made from the new Fort Ross Vineyard (on Meyers Grade Road north of Jenner) in 2001. (Scherrer also custom-crushed Fort Ross fruit for the owners' own Fort Ross Vineyard label.) At this writing, Scherrer's pinot sources were to remain volatile until at least 2004, when fruit from Lewis Platt's new Sonoma Coast vineyard becomes available to Scherrer under a long-term contract. The 1999, 2000, and 2001 pinots that I have tasted display tantalizing aromatics, exotic flavors, and very distinctive personalities.

CAMPION WINES

Napa, California

Larry Brooks, the winemaker at Acacia Winery (see the profile earlier in this section) for most of the 1980s and 1990s and subsequently vice president at the Chalone Wine Group, created his own label in 2000, dedicated exclusively to pinot noir. Most production thus far consists of appellation wines from Santa Lucia Highlands, Los Carneros, and Edna Valley, some of which have been de facto single-vineyard efforts. For Campion's first vintage using Edna Valley fruit (from Baileyana's Firepeak Vineyard just south of San Luis Obispo), in 2001, 20 percent of the wine was specifically set aside for a "reserve-quality" Firepeak Vineyard cuvée. The Edna Valley and Firepeak bottlings were both exceptional in this vintage, giving wines of stunning depth and brilliant flavors. (Brooks sometimes coferments small amounts of pinot gris with his pinot noir; see chapter 6.)

SINE QUA NON

Oak View, California

Manfred Krankl, the Austria-born partner in Los Angeles's Campanile restaurant and its bread-oriented spinoff, La Brea Bakery, established his own wine brand in 1994. This project followed several cooperative ventures with established vintners, in both Santa Barbara County and Piedmont, during the early 1990s, dedicated to crafting top-quality house wines for Campanile. Sine Qua Non made its first pinot noir in 1996, using fruit hauled south in refrigerated trucks from Oregon's Shea Vineyard. A Shea Vineyard pinot has been made in every vintage since then and usually represents about one-fifth of Sine Qua Non's total production, but Krankl's practice is to give each vintage a unique proprietary name. Thus 1998 Shea was dubbed Veiled, 1999 Ox, 2000 A Cappella, and 2001 No. 6. Almost without exception, each vintage has been better than its predecessor. Ox and A Cappella have shown impressively in comparative tastings with other vineyard-designated wines from Shea. Beginning in 2002, Krankl also obtained a small quantity of pinot from the Arita Hills vineyard in the Santa Rita Hills AVA, but at this writing he had not yet decided how that fruit would be used.

BONACCORSI WINE COMPANY

Santa Monica, California

Master Sommelier Michael Bonaccorsi, who established a near-legendary reputation as a wine buyer during his tenure at Spago in Beverly Hills, took two years off in 1997 and 1998 to work vineyard and cellar jobs with Christophe Roumier in Chambolle-Musigny and then launched his own label in 1999, about 60 percent dedicated to pinot noir. His first release, Cuvée Douze, was made from grapes purchased from the Santa Maria Hills vineyard. In 2000, the same fruit was labeled simply Santa Barbara County. In 2001, Bonaccorsi purchased pinot from four vineyards—Melville, Gold Coast, Le Bon Climat (see the Au Bon Climat profile), and Santa Maria Hills—the best of which was again sold as a Santa Barbara County bottling, while declassified barrels were bottled as Red Monkey. A new regime debuted in 2002 with appellation wines from Santa Maria Valley and Santa Rita Hills, as well as two vineyard-designated wines from Melville and Fiddlestix (see the Fiddlehead Cellars profile). The 2001 Santa Barbara County seems especially successful, with red-fruit-oriented aromatic complexity and considerable length. All cellar protocols are "evolving," according to Bonaccorsi, as he gains experience with fruit from various southern Central Coast sources.

COPAIN WINES

Santa Rosa, California

Wells Guthrie, who began his wine career as the tasting coordinator for *Wine Spectator,* lived two years in the Rhône Valley (working for Chapoutier and gleaning wisdom from Jean-Louis Chave) before launching his own California label in 1999. Guthrie's pinots are exclusively sourced from Anderson Valley and are always made as single-vineyard wines. The first, in 1999, was a Dennison Vineyard wine. Cerise, Hein (off Guntley Road near Philo), and Hacienda Secoya (on Nash Mill Road) bottlings debuted in 2000. Starting in 2003, Copain also obtained fruit from the Wiley and Keiser vineyards. Quantities are tiny, ranging from as few as 25 cases to an average of about 200 per vineyard-designate, but the wines have established an enviable reputation, so that Copain's facility is also home to several other pinots, including DuMol, McIlroy, and Pisoni, on a custom-crush basis. Copain wines showcase *terroir,* but Guthrie aims for wines that "are not cumbersome to drink" as they generally are picked between 23 and 24.5 Brix. The first vintages of Dennison are personal favorites, displaying a complex nose of dried flowers and leaves and an explosive palate of spicy flavors.

PATRICIA GREEN CELLARS

Newberg, Oregon

Patricia Green, who came to winemaking from a succession of nontraditional careers in the 1980s and then served as winemaker for McMinnville's Torii Mor Winery from 1993 to 2000, acquired the defunct Autumn Wind Winery in 2000 and launched her own brand. Small lots of mostly vineyard-designated pinots from sites in the Dundee Hills, the Yamhill-Carlton District, and Ribbon Ridge—including Green's estate vineyard; the Eason Vineyard, which she manages; and the Shea Vineyard—were made in 2000 and 2001. Even from sedimentary soils, Green coaxes soft, lush, and layered wines that have shown well young, using techniques like lees additions in barrel.

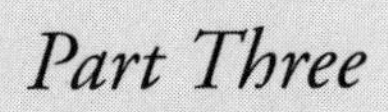

Part Three

ENJOYING PINOT NOIR

Advice for Consumers

FINDING AND BUYING PINOT NOIR

Good pinot noir is not entirely easy to acquire. North American pinot noir priced in the same tier as basic cabernet, merlot, or chardonnay is almost universally unrewarding. Usually pinot in this tier has been made from mediocre or overcropped fruit or was blended with a very perceptible amount of some other grape variety. In a testament to the problem, only two pinot noirs made *Decanter* magazine's 2002 list of the top 50 red wines priced under ten pounds sterling (about $15)—a Mercurey 1er Cru from Domaine Levert and a Kaituna Hills Reserve from Marlborough in New Zealand—while cabernets, Rhône valley reds, and Australian shiraz wines abounded. In the $15 to $20 range, however, pinot choices improve substantially. A number of very good and widely available pinots are priced in this range, including Saintsbury's Garnet bottling, Rodney Strong's Russian River valley blend, Navarro Vineyards' Méthode à l'Ancienne bottling, Husch Vineyards' Anderson Valley cuvée, and Morgan's Santa Lucia Highlands blend. There is also Ramsay, blended differently each year by Kent Rasmussen; Chalone Group's Echelon brand; several (though not all) labels made by E. and J. Gallo; and Sebastiani's Sonoma Coast pinot noir, the 2001 edition of which was well reviewed. Overwhelmingly, however, very good North American pinots, including a majority of the wines described in the preceding pages, are pricey.

Worse, just like high-end Burgundies, they are made in excruciatingly small quantities—especially vineyard-designated wines. Most are present only in so-called selected markets, and many never make even a fleeting appearance on retail shelves. Some are sold exclusively to restaurants and to the winery's mailing-list customers. Canadian wines are barely available in the United States at all, and only a few New York producers have distribution channels beyond the New York State line. At worst, demand so far outstrips supply that the wines are "allocated," which means that they are essentially unavailable to new customers of any stripe and that even existing customers cannot increase the quantity of their purchase from the baseline of a prior year.

The best advice for all consumers without preexisting connections is to use restaurants with good lists of pinot noir to *discover* wines that fit personal tastes and budgets. Wherever possible, it pays to cultivate a local wine merchant who is passionate about pinot noir. It can be useful to contact wineries directly, well in advance of wines' projected release dates. Anyone serious about pinot noir who lives within driving distance of the Willamette Valley should consider visiting those wineries on the Thanksgiving and Memorial Day weekends, when it is often possible to taste barrel samples and purchase futures. Pinot-related events, like the Russian River Winegrowers' Grape to Glass Festival, Oregon's International Pinot Noir Celebration, and the World of Pinot Noir, held each spring in Shell Beach, California, are also good opportunities to taste and sometimes to order wines that are otherwise scarce in the marketplace, or at least to get on a mailing list for the *next* vintage to be released.

Consumers need to know that by the time a wine made in small volume is released, reviewed, and highly rated, it has already sold out. Consumers who covet such bottlings must make arrangements in advance or purchase when, if, and as the wines are offered in commercial auctions or in another secondary market.

On the other hand, chasing high-priced, scarce wines is *not* the only way to enjoy fine pinot noirs from North American producers. Many wonderful wines are made in quantities adequate to meet current demand. Most producers are happy to sell directly to consumers, even at a modest discount, to avoid the much deeper discounts entailed in so-called three-tier distribution. Some even specialize in such arrangements. Furthermore, because scores awarded by critics and magazines lower than 88 points have virtually *zero* impact on price or demand, many excellent wines that (for various reasons) do not show well in large, comparative, blind tastings are readily available to enlightened buyers.

Finally, new small-volume producers of pinot noir emerge every year. Consumers willing to follow a winemaker as he or she leaves a well-known label to create a new brand of his or her own, or to make wine for other brands on a custom-crush basis, can establish rapport with the next cult-status pinot before the cult takes shape.

WHY GOOD PINOT NOIR IS EXPENSIVE

Some wine writers like to assert, or at least to repeat, that pinot is expensive because it is hard to make. This claim is, frankly, nonsense. Good pinot noir is *relatively* expensive because yields are low compared to varieties like cabernet, syrah, and chardonnay; because there is not a lot of land either in Burgundy or in North America where pinot can be grown with really good results; and mostly because, since the early 1990s, demand for many pinots has vastly exceeded the supply *of those specific wines.*

Consider the following: Producer costs that can be allocated easily on a per-bottle basis amount to something between $6 and $12. The single largest cost element is the price of the grapes used. It amounts to about $4 per bottle when pinot noir is purchased for $3,000 per ton, which was a fair average price in 2002 for very good pinot noir from the main regions treated in this book. A few cult vineyards charge premium prices for fruit, sometimes as much as $6,000 per ton, which adds another $4 to the cost per bottle. The next largest per-bottle expense can be oak cooperage, if the producer uses a high percentage of new oak. Figure a per-bottle cost of about $2.30 for barrels if the producer uses 100 percent new French oak, or about 70 cents if the protocol is 33 percent new oak. Bottles, corks, labels, and foils contribute another $1.10 to $1.85 per bottle, bottling about 25 cents, storage before sale 16 to 20 cents, and excise taxes 16 cents. (Very large-volume producers enjoy economies of scale on packaging, however, and cost-saving alternatives to real corks and foils exist.) The producer's remaining costs—which include amortization on equipment and facilities, labor not associated with vineyard work (including the winemaker's compensation), and marketing—are much harder to allocate per bottle because they are enormously affected by the scale of operations and the identity of a given brand; but insiders say that numbers from less than $2 per bottle to about $5 per bottle are credible. All of these expenditures together bring the *cost* of a single bottle of good North American pinot noir, before the winery has made a profit, to somewhere between $8 and $18 per bottle. Allow the winery a modest margin for profit, and it is easy to see why wholesale prices to distributors (which are normally half of the suggested retail price) are rarely less than $10 per bottle and often as high as $20.

These cost factors also demonstrate, however, that there is no cost-based reason for *any* bottle of pinot noir to sell for more than about $30. Prices pegged at $50, $70, and even $100 per bottle are purely a function of limited supply and intense demand for the individual wines involved. Wineries often observe, however, and with considerable justice, that consumers interpret price as a surrogate for quality. Calera Wine Company revealed this perverse logic to its mail-order customers in 2001, explaining that its hitherto reasonable prices were damaging its marketplace reputation and would consequently be raised.

Consumers who discover bargain-priced pinot from otherwise unknown producers should be interested but skeptical. The most common and benevolent explanation for such offerings is that some party to the supply chain has lost money and is selling fruit or declassified wine or stagnant inventory at a loss. Otherwise, the low price is either a reflection of very large-scale production and a producer's willingness to settle for a very thin margin of profit or an indication that some element of the wine's cost has been cut well below prevailing averages. *Caveat emptor.*

Conventional wisdom holds that vintages matter little in California because the weather varies little from year to year, while vintage can be hugely important in Oregon, Burgundy, and upstate New York, where average growing-season temperatures and rainfall can be very different from one year to the next. While there is some truth in the conventional wisdom—a rain-drenched harvest is pretty rare in any of California's pinot-friendly regions—most California winemakers who worked through the 1990s are now likely to say that vintage matters hugely to them. Some even assert that the 1990s varied so widely that they no longer know what a "typical" growing season looks like.

In truth, every vintage is different everywhere, and pinot noir's legendary transparency showcases those differences, just as it does differences in *terroir* and winemaking. Conversely, however, more sophisticated cultivation techniques, rigorous fruit sorting at harvest, and use of devices called concentrators to compensate for harvest rain have taken some of the edge off vintage differences, at least in qualitative terms. Everywhere, some vintages are more challenging than others. Winemakers are fond of asserting that so-called picture-perfect vintages like 1994 (in both Oregon and California) were so unproblematic that colleagues who could not make good wine in such years should have considered changing careers. Conversely, difficult years present hard choices with respect to picking and demand that winemaking protocols be adjusted to fit the profile of the harvested fruit. They tend to challenge neophytes and to reward experienced hands. Enlightened consumers will keep an open mind about vintage assessments, however. Brilliant wines and good values are often produced in so-called lesser vintages, and it is absolutely untrue that such vintages, as a rule, are less age-worthy than "classic," warmer, and riper vintages.

The following is a very brief summary of vintages from 1994 through 2002 in the main regions where North American pinot noir is grown.

- 1994: A dry and sunny March on the North Coast was followed by a cool and windy late spring and early summer, with rain in May. Temperatures were generally moderate, except for a heat spike in early August. Crop levels were about 10 percent below normal, but the vintage produced ripe tannins and good acid levels. Wines are dark, rich, and powerful, especially those from Anderson Valley. Intense, elegant wines were typical in the Russian River valley. This is widely regarded as a classic, perfect year for pinot noir. Quite a rainy year in the southern Central Coast, however, led to uneven results, though some wines from this vintage have evolved charmingly. It was a warm, ripe vintage in Oregon, but hot and dry in the Okanagan River valley, similar to 1998.

- 1995: Uneven fruit set in California's North Coast was followed by a warm summer, producing generally rich, soft wines with considerable forward fruit, complexity, and balance. Yields were very low on the southern Central Coast but gave elegant wines with exotic flavors. A perfect spring and early summer in Oregon were jeopardized by high humidity, late-season rain, and cool temperatures at harvesttime. Growers who waited out the late-September rains were able to harvest in a narrow window of warm, dry weather in early October. Rigorous fruit sorting was the price of quality, and some makers bled the must to increase concentration. Good wines have held well, however, presenting complex aromas and silky textures. A temperate growing season in the Okanagan was followed by an Indian summer in September, which created good pinots with dominant red fruit flavors and considerable spiciness. In New York and Ontario, a warm but not hot year with considerable sunshine and limited rain yielded balanced and naturally ripe wines.

- 1996: This vintage was difficult for pinot noir in most of California. Spring rains led to widespread shatter along the North Coast, making for a smaller than normal crop. An early, hot summer, with many days topping the century mark, created the dilemma of grapes low in flavor if they were picked early, and low in acid if they were left to hang. Some pinots were lean, hard, and tannic, but makers who cut back on extraction produced fine wines with huge aromatic interest, if lesser stuffing. On the southern Central Coast, the weather was more forgiving. Spring rains were less aggressive, and the season was generally long and cool, with overall good results for pinot noir. In Oregon, a cool and rainy May delayed bloom, pushing fruit set into June, which turned out sunny and warm. July and August remained warm, and a cool September allowed flavors to develop well, enabling a ripe and flavorful vintage. The coldest and wettest year in recent memory in the Okanagan delayed picking into mid-October, with sugar levels barely reaching 22 Brix. It was a troublesome year in the Finger Lakes, too: cool and wet, with a large crop load.
- 1997: In California, this precocious year offered an early budbreak and an early harvest, but a long season overall. In most regions the crop was huge, placing a premium on intelligent yield management. It was generally regarded as a good year for pinot in the North Coast and irregular in the southern Central Coast. Many wines were tannic on release, but most of them have softened with age; the Russian River valley and Sonoma Coast wines from 1997 are showing well in 2002. In Oregon, May, July, August, and September were warm, despite a bit of rain in September. Many vintners were skeptical about the vintage at harvest, but with time the wines have displayed elegance and more than routine aromatic interest. In the Okanagan, the vintage was similar to 1999, but cooler. A cool year in New York and Ontario resulted in a tendency to dilution and green flavors when crop loads were not well managed.

- 1998: In California, this was an El Niño year par excellence. A very wet winter persisted into normal springtime, especially in the North Coast, delaying budbreak and causing uneven flowering. Crop levels were consequently low. Despite unusual rains in early September, southern Central Coast vineyards harvested late and ripe, and some pinots from this area are exceptionally rich and fine. Critics have judged the vintage inconsistent. In Oregon, warm temperatures in midspring contributed to an early flowering, but late-spring rains cut the yields in some vineyards. Warm, dry weather in August and September gave intense wines. Hot and dry weather in the Okanagan generated small berries and a high ratio of skin to juice; resulting wines have a very ripe fruit character. A warm and sunny year in New York and Ontario, though not excessively dry, yielded ripe and relatively full-bodied wines.

- 1999: This year was superficially a carbon copy of 1998 in most of California but even cooler, with a longer growing season and a later harvest. Pinot noir was harvested with high sugars, high natural acidity, and ripe flavors, but seeds and stems remained green. A very small crop was produced, with generally good balance and dense flavors. Many wines display intense aromas and flavors and better than average length. It was the third warm, dry year in a row in Oregon, birthing superripe flavors and good structure. The Okanagan had a slightly cooler than normal year, with higher than normal diurnal temperature variation. Warm and dry weather in New York and Ontario produced naturally ripe wines.

- 2000: In California, an early, wet spring was followed by a heat wave in the second half of June and then a cooler than normal summer. The season's roller-coaster character led to an exceptionally early harvest in parts of the southern Central Coast, but to late harvesting at Chalone and in Los Carneros. The year bore a strong similarity to 1997 in the southern Central Coast and was widely perceived as a "return-to-normal year" along the North Coast. Winegrowers found the moderately warm season helped to maintain good levels of natural acid and yielded brown and crunchy seeds. California pinots from this vintage are deemed by some to be deep and rich, by others to be of variable quality. In Oregon, the growing season was similarly long and free of harvest rain; the summer was dry and even-tempered. Yields were up even from the bumper levels of 1998 and 1999. Black fruit flavors predominated, and the wines have rich midpalate textures. One winegrower describes 2000 as "1998 on steroids." In the Okanagan, the vintage was typical, with harvest at the end of September. A cool, wet year in New York and Ontario was offset by a long, sunny fall; makers who limited yield and picked late made some elegant wines.

- 2001: The growing season in most of California was cool but protracted; the autumn rainy season started late, so harvests were not compromised. The southern

Central Coast experienced an exceptionally cool summer with more summer fog than usual, but a heat spell in late September was helpful. Yields were lower than in 2000. *Wine Spectator* asserts that 2001 is "on track to provide more outstanding Pinot Noirs than any vintage in California history." In Oregon, 2001 was a near-drought year, with rainfall less than 50 percent of normal. Budbreak occurred slightly late, and flowering was not uniform, but yields were still slightly above average. There were warm days and cool nights at harvest. The Okanagan saw a warmer than normal growing season, giving big, ripe wines in general, though some growers reported an emphasis on red fruit character. An especially hot and dry year in New York and Ontario delayed the harvest and increased hang time, yielding many naturally ripe pinots that needed no chaptalization.

- 2002: There was a "balanced" growing season in most of California, but it was somewhat cooler than normal. Heat spikes during flowering in the southern Central Coast led to shatter and low yields. There were lower than normal yields elsewhere, too, owing primarily to small berry size. Long hang times produced intense, ripe flavors in North Coast wines. In Oregon, warm days and cool nights prevailed throughout the longer than average growing season, but there was considerable vineyard-to-vineyard variation. Overcast weather at the beginning of October delayed harvesting, but moisture did not compromise the crop. Some vintners reported exceptionally ripe fruit. Dry, even heat in the Okanagan persisted through October, leading to bigger and darker pinots with higher than average levels of alcohol. The Finger Lakes region was drier than usual, with some quantitative losses from cold snaps in April, but above-normal heat accumulation overall yielded ripe wines without chaptalization.

CELLARING OLDER VINTAGES

The same properties of pinot noir that cause its makers grief in the cellar have implications for consumers. Modest levels of tannins and anthocyanins are often good news for the consumer. Because of these, most pinots tend to drink well on or soon after release. Young vintages of pinot are capable of giving much greater hedonistic pleasure than, for example, young vintages of *cru classé* Bordeaux or California cabernet, whose tannin load can be forbidding. One should not conclude, however, that pinots *must* be drunk young; most will reward consumers who can muster a few years' patience. Pinot's legendary transparency—which enables it to show the *terroir* in which it was grown and to bear the mark of cellar treatments good and bad—allows it to be scarred easily in the course of distribution. Consumers must handle it carefully if they aspire to age it, because it will deteriorate rapidly in suboptimal storage conditions. Consumers should not be tempted to cellar pinots in a disused corner of the kitchen or under the attic stairs.

THE BURGUNDY GLASS

Among the various revolutions that have transformed the wine world in the past century, few are more impressive than the emergence of so-called technical tasting and wine appreciation. Emile Peynaud, the French enologist who wrote the benchmark book *Le Goût du vin* in 1980, calls this phenomenon "the intellectualization of wine." Wineglasses—which until this point had been either the simplest of utilitarian vessels or art objects in their own right—became tasting tools, designed to heighten wine appreciation, flatter the properties of individual wine types, or facilitate comparisons among wines. Beakers, heavy cut glass, various applications of color, and bowl shapes that were typically trapezoidal or hyperbolic in cross section, all popular in the nineteenth century, gradually gave way during the middle of the twentieth century to relatively large, thin-walled, undecorated, more or less tulip-shaped glasses, of which the so-called INAO glass, developed and certified by the French Institut national des appellations d'origine contrôlées in the 1970s, is accepted as the objective standard version. The main point of this modern wineglass is a bowl size sufficient to develop aromas when it is one-third or less full, and a "chimney" of empty glass above the wine's poured surface that conducts the wine's aromas toward the taster's nose and palate.

Even as the INAO glass was emerging as a technical standard for comparative tasting, however, it occurred to a few manufacturers of stemware that different wines demanded glasses of *different sizes and shapes,* to flatter their specific organoleptic properties. The Austrian firm of Riedel Glas claims credit for the first glasses to be optimized for individual wine types, but Baccarat Crystal was also an early player, and in the 1950s both firms marketed glasses dedicated to the special enjoyment of red Burgundies. Baccarat's entry was the so-called Romanée-Conti glass, whose bowl was a slightly squashed sphere with only a small top opening. Riedel, claiming to have been influenced by Bauhaus form-follows-function design principles, introduced the Grand Cru Burgundy glass, an enormous 37-ounce vessel with a huge bowl and slightly flared rim, in 1958. Both of these glasses seem to have been inspired by a Burgundy-specific *bistrot* glass that achieved popularity sometime between 1930 and 1950, though the *bistrot* glass was thicker-walled and generally less refined than the Baccarat and Riedel editions. Today most manufacturers serious about wine glassware produce one or more glasses designed specifically for pinot noir, nearly all of which are distinguished by very large bowls and visibly constricted chimneys. The most widely accepted single format is Riedel Glas's Vinum Burgundy glass, which was introduced in 1986, though most winemakers prefer something more like the INAO glass for in-cellar tasting.

Just how much difference glasses make to the taste of wine has been persistently debated, but the overwhelming accumulation of anecdotal evidence suggests that the differences are real and sometimes profound, and probably have a scientific basis. Unsurprisingly, perhaps, given its legendary transparency and aromatic complexity, pinot noir seems to showcase glass-based variation. "No grape," according to Riedel Glas's president, Georg Riedel, "is so sensitive to glass as pinot noir." *New York Times* wine critic Howard Goldberg believes the point was proved in the course of a glass tasting he organized with Riedel at New York's Montrachet Restaurant in 2002, featuring exclusively Riedel's three pinot-specific models. Two red Burgundies—1997 Savigny-les-Beaune Aux Vergelesses from Simon Bize and 1997 Vosne-Romanée Les Beaux Monts from Jean Grivot—were tasted side by side in the three glasses, with differences, according to Goldberg's notes, "so bold as to be shocking." The Grand Cru glass made the Savigny taste "dull" to Goldberg's palate, and heightened the perception of fruit in the Vosne-Romanée, while the Vinum Burgundy glass showcased both wines' earthy and forest-floor properties. In my experience with the several thousand North American pinot noirs tasted for this book, wines *not* tasted from Vinum Burgundy glasses (or close cousins like Spiegelau's pinot noir glass) were almost invariably disadvantaged, sometimes seeming aromatically closed and almost always showing less complexity and nuance.

PAIRING PINOT NOIR WITH FOOD

"The question of what to drink with what you eat," according to *Wine & Spirits* in 2003, "is hot." In fact, the question has drawn increasing attention for at least a decade. As chefs have deepened their personal wine savvy, as restaurants have increasingly employed professionally qualified sommeliers, and as tasting menus precoordinated with dish-specific wines have proliferated, consumers have become more sophisticated about wine and food pairings.

In this evolution, pinot has developed a reputation for being endlessly versatile. Sommeliers, chefs, winemakers, and critics alike call it the food-friendliest of all varieties. According to one commentator, "It pairs as easily with a roasted chicken as with a cheese course, sautéed skate or pâté." It is alleged to "provide clarity" with spicy dishes and to "provide a sweet antidote" to tart sauces like some marinades and vinaigrettes. Sommeliers recommend pinot with an almost endless list of dishes, from lamb and duck to sushi, mushrooms, lasagna, and even cioppino. Shelf-talker labels in the pinot section of one New York City wine shop suggested various of the wines on offer to drink with pork loin, tuna steak, chicken pot pie, Shropshire blue cheese, roast beef on sourdough, or salmon with dill and onion sauce.

This enthusiasm is fair enough, to a point. Pinot's modest tannins give it greater flexibility in food pairings than high-tannin varieties, which call out for the moderating influence of animal fat. The coinvolvement of fruity, spicy, and earthy elements *can* provide a more satisfying counterpoint to some ingredients than many white varieties. Good pinots are complex and distinctive rather than bland, however, and distinctive wines are not endlessly versatile. In my experience and for my palate, pinot noir does *not* go with everything. Pinot noir is usually counterindicated with quite a long list of preparations and seasonings; see below. Individual wines also work well in some combinations, while other wine-specific combinations fail to enhance either member of the pair.

In Burgundy, pinot noir is preeminently paired with game: venison, boar, wild rabbit, pigeon, quail, partridge, and duck. Richard Olney, in his book *Romanée-Conti,* cites memorable combinations like rare roasted woodcock, split and sauced with cognac, served with 1949 La Tâche; and roast grouse served with the 1952 vintage of Domaine de la Romanée-Conti's Grands Echézeaux. In North America, where game is neither common nor popular, the classic pairings are with lamb and, increasingly, salmon. Most red meats are said to work well, subject to certain caveats about their preparation, and chefs and sommeliers successfully pair many fattier fish with pinot. Twenty years ago—when good North American pinot noir was still scarce—one of California's first winery chefs, Inglenook's Barbara Lang, wrote a piece about pinot noir for *Practical Winery* magazine's new department on wine and food, most of whose conclusions still seem reasonable. With lighter-weight pinots, Lang argued in favor of roast chicken and "less gamey" fowl; Cornish game hens, especially if they are stuffed with mushrooms; and salmon, poached or grilled. With "fuller" pinots she advocated fattier foods, like duck and beef filet. "The similar soft but meaty textures in the wine and food fatten one another's flavor," she asserted.

Today's sommeliers generally agree with Lang, though the availability of Asian seasonings, exotic cultivated mushrooms, and a much larger palette of seafoods has complicated things. Chicago-based chef Charlie Trotter, whose book about cooking seafood is organized by the wine varieties with which the dishes can be successfully paired, argues that pinot noir's "ephemeral" and "delicate" properties can make it the "most frustrating wine" to match with seafood, while its soft tannins and high acidity give it (conversely) "the best chance [of any red] with many seafood preparations." Trotter's solutions often involve *cuissons* in which the fish is enriched with a bit of meat or poultry broth or with earthy mushrooms. Raw fish, traditionally consumed with Japanese sake, has evolved into a new canvas for pinot noir. Daisuke Utagawa, proprietor of Washington, D.C.'s Sushi-Ko restaurant, is a strong advocate for pinot noir (at least in the form of red Burgundy) with raw seafood, arguing that the prominence of *umami* in uncooked fish works splendidly with low-tannin red wine. (*Umami* is an untranslatable flavor category in Japanese food, which is said to heighten the palate's sensitivity to bitterness.) In the Pacific Northwest especially, where many chefs have a love affair with fresh, local berries, it is quite common to see pinot noir paired with meat and game dishes sauced with berry reductions, purees, and essences. These matches can be tricky, however. Just as a sweet dessert can hollow out a so-called dessert wine, a fruit-based sauce can overpower the fruit in even a fruity pinot noir. Subtle combinations seem to work well, however, such as marinated pork tenderloin sauced with a plum butter, or breast of squab served with braised figs.

Some commentators draw a distinction between red Burgundies and North American pinots, observing that the traditional affinities between Burgundies and wild game are a function of the greater "gaminess" of Burgundies, and that North American pinots, which are generally more fruit-driven wines, are easier to pair with dishes generally, and especially those with a touch of sweetness. But Mark Ellenbogen, wine director for San Francisco's Slanted Door Restaurant, says that many Asian soy-flavored dishes, which also see the use of one or more sweeteners, tend to marry badly with California-style high-alcohol and oak-rich pinots. The oak-soy combination, he explains, "makes these pinots seem more tannic." Virtually all wine professionals agree that older vintages of serious pinot from either side of the Atlantic demand simple preparations of the food. Richard Olney was partial to roasts, rare beef, and semirare saddle or leg of lamb with "wines of great finesse"; Debbie Zachareas, managing partner at San Francisco's Bacar Restaurant, agrees emphatically, arguing that old pinots are the unique exception to a general rule that complex wines can be paired with complex dishes. "Delicate old wines," she explains, "need to stand on their own and not have the food overpower them." Merry Edwards says she often pours two pinots with the same meal—an older vintage followed by a younger one. In this scenario, the older vintage accompanies "more subtly flavored dishes" like roasted quail, while the younger wine is paired with "heartier fare" like roasted venison or grilled pork tenderloin.

Although conventional wisdom pairs wine and cheese and many people claim to like combinations of, for example, pinot noir and Brie, most taste tests are not especially persuasive. Some sommeliers I consulted believe that washed-rind cheeses (typically those with orange- or russet-colored rinds) can make pinot taste metallic, but cheese expert Juliet Harbutt disagrees. She finds that the "meaty, pungent washed-rind style" is especially well suited to Oregon, California, and New Zealand pinots, which are both "complex" and "mellow." Aubert de Villaine, codirector of Domaine de la Romanée-Conti, says the only cheese he can "accept" with the Domaine's wines is Cîteaux, which falls in the meaty, washed-rind category. De Villaine finds other washed-rind cheeses (like Reblochon) are "not suitable," having "too much pronounced flavor." Harbutt thinks that ewe's-milk cheeses "bring out the best" in pinot noir. A tasting of white and red Burgundies with a large assortment of cheeses—orchestrated by Domaine Charles Thomas in Nuits-St.-Georges in March 2002—in which I participated with some fascination, reached the discomforting conclusion that a superb 1959 Vosne-Romanée Malconsorts tasted a lot better with chocolate than with *any* of the cheeses, though a 1999 Beaune Grèves was a reasonable match for Brillat-Savarin. No fewer than 169 wine-cheese combinations tested by wine educator Karen MacNeil in 2001 (and reported in *Sunset* magazine) produced only nine genuinely exciting alliances overall, and only one of those involved pinot noir. A 1997 Robert Mondavi pinot noir is said to have worked well with French chèvre. In my experience, with only a handful of exceptions, it's just as well to finish off the pinot before the cheese course begins.

My own experience, in countless pinot dinners and tastings done for this book, is that pairing pinot with food in ways that flatter both is certainly no easier than pairing food with any other wine. Arguably, the combination of pinot noir's transparency, the strong mark of different *terroirs,* and the wide variety of winemaking styles actually makes it harder to work with pinot noir than with more opaque and homogeneous varieties like cabernet sauvignon or merlot. More, rather than less, is demanded of the sommelier, chef, and consumer—to know the properties of individual wines, and the details of the food's preparation. Here are the best generalizations I can muster. Most red meat preparations *can* work, as long as dominant and very spicy sauces (green peppercorns, for example) or high-acid, tomato-based sauces are avoided. On the other hand, there are so many other terrific, high-tannin red wines to enjoy with prime rib—wines that do not work well *unless* they are paired with chewy, high-fat meat—that it seems a pity to waste tannin-deficient pinot noir on steak. Most game and poultry *can* work with pinot noir, unless the dish has been prepared with a lot of fruit in general, or citrus in particular, or vinegar. I agree with Charlie Trotter about fish: a bit of meat, meat stock, or mushrooms in the preparation usually makes it pinot-friendlier. Grilling, which creates caramelized or char-related flavors, can sometimes have the same effect. Some fish preparations are counterindicated, however, like sole meunière, salmon *grenobloise,* and tomato-fish dishes like cioppino. Many vegetarian dishes work well with pinot noir, especially mushroom-based dishes, risottos (especially those made with red wine or meat stock), and earthy dishes, like some Parmentiers and *brandades* extended with potatoes. Again, however, vegetarian dishes with tomato-based sauces—especially fresh tomato sauces, like most southern Italian pasta dishes—are counterindicated, as are notorious wine-food mismatches like pinot with artichokes or (sometimes) asparagus.

Generally, the hardest pinots to pair flatteringly with *any* dish are the highly extracted, high-alcohol types. Assuming modest extract and alcohol, the bigger, weightier wines (unsurprisingly) work best with richer foods and more complex preparations. Young, fruit-forward editions of North American pinot do not work as well with very earthy dishes, such as, for example, roast chicken stuffed with mushrooms. On the other hand, a hint of bitterness (braised radicchio, for example) can be a fine counterpoint to a fruit-forward wine. Mushrooms and truffles often argue either for pinots that are intrinsically mineral, earthy, or farmyardy, or for older wines whose secondary aromatics have begun to show. And finally, as indicated earlier, one should pair older vintages invariably with simple preparations in which the natural flavors of the meat, game, or fish predominate over seasonings and sauces.

All this said, veteran wine writer Matt Kramer's dictum is still worth bearing in mind. "All good wines," he wrote in *Wine Spectator* in 1996, "can take care of themselves if the food is even remotely plausible for the wine. The trick is serving a good wine."

The following are a few exceptionally successful marriages of North American pinots with various foods, encountered during the three years spent researching this book:

- A salt-cod *brandade* laced with cream and heirloom potatoes served at Bacar Restaurant in San Francisco, tasted first with Bonaccorsi's 1999 Cuvée Douze and subsequently with Foxen Vineyard's 1997 Bien Nacido Vineyard, both medium-plus-weight, earthy, black-fruited wines. Even though cod is a white-fleshed fish, the earthiness of the potato made this dish a perfect match for the dark-toned and earthy wines. Lighter pinots, also tried with this dish, were less flattering.
- *Toro* and *maguro* (different cuts of ahi tuna) sushi, freshly fished from the Pacific off San Diego by a friend's enterprising son, barely kissed with soy sauce and the tiniest hint of wasabi, served with J Wine Company's 1998 Robert Thomas Vineyard. The unctuous fattiness of the *toro* and *maguro* paired perfectly with this silky, medium-weight, and slightly spicy edition of Robert Thomas.
- Seared duck-gizzard confit, marinated with cognac, thyme, juniper berries, and bay leaves, then cooked in fat, deglazed with kirsch, and seasoned with fennel seeds, prepared at San Francisco's Farallon Restaurant and served with Merry Edwards's 1999 Windsor Gardens Vineyard. The Windsor Gardens old-vines complexity worked magnificently with the layered spiciness and rich texture of the gizzards.
- Braised duck with dried figs and olives, prepared at Sassafras Restaurant in Santa Rosa, California, and served with Siduri's 2000 Garys' Vineyard. The 2000 was only the second harvest from this newly planted vineyard, but the wine's ripe, aromatic assertiveness was a good foil for the preparation, which combined fat, dried fruit, and a slightly tart highlight.
- Pepper- and fennel-crusted salmon with shallot-Madeira sauce and polenta, conceived by Eric Ripert of Le Bernardin in New York, served at home with Chehalem Vineyards' 1997 Rion Reserve. The sauce, which involved both Madeira and veal stock, and the polenta, which was scented with truffled olive oil, were astonishingly friendly to this relatively lightweight, elegant edition of Rion Reserve.
- Risotto made with radicchio, dried and fresh porcini, and a combination of red wine and very hearty chicken stock, cooked at home, served with Littorai Wines' 1996 One Acre Vineyard. The residual bitterness of the radicchio, the earthiness of the porcini, and the creamy texture of the rice worked beautifully with the medium-weight One Acre, which displays an avalanche of subtle, exotic aromatics.

- Pan-roasted veal sirloin with white and romano beans, roasted garlic, asparagus-bacon ragout, and a coarse-grained mustard sauce, prepared at Mirepoix restaurant in Windsor, California, served with Tandem Winery's 2001 Van der Kamp Vineyard. The earthiness of the beans and asparagus married with the earthiness in the wine, while the flavors of charcuterie in the wine were the perfect foil for the bacon, and the veal sirloin itself was just sufficiently lighter than beef to flatter the pinot and counterindicate a gutsier red like syrah.

Pinot Terminology

AOC or AC *(Appellation d'origine contrôlée):* The French system of controlled appellations of origin for wines and some food products debuted in the 1930s. Often described for simplicity as the French equivalent of American AVAs (see below), French appellations are hugely more complicated. While an AVA defines a region only by its geographic perimeter, French AOC regulations stipulate at least which grape varieties may be grown in the appellation and what maximum yield is permitted, and sometimes codify other parameters of winegrowing and winemaking as well. The AOC delineations are especially arcane in Burgundy, where the surface area entitled to an appellation can be very small, and some appellations are nested three and four deep.

appellation: The geographical provenance of a wine. In the United States, the names of states, counties, and American Viticultural Areas (AVAs) can be used as wine appellations, as can Delimited Viticultural Areas (DVAs) in Canada. In France, *appellation* is usually short for *Appellation d'origine contrôlée* (see *AOC,* above). Confusingly, some North American producers have begun to use the phrase *appellation wines* to designate blends made from several vineyards within a single county or AVA. In this usage, they wish to differentiate blended wines from single-vineyard (a.k.a. vineyard-designated) wines. Properly speaking, the single-vineyard wines are appellation wines, too.

AVA (American Viticultural Area): Geographically delimited wine regions in the United States that are neither counties nor states (see *appellation,* above). They are created by petition and approved by the Alcohol and Tobacco Tax and Trade Bureau (TTB)—which was formerly the Bureau of Alcohol, Tobacco and Firearms (ATF)—in the Department of the Treasury. Some AVAs are soundly based on viticulturally relevant criteria; others are seriously heterogeneous and significant primarily as marketing mechanisms.

bleeding: To increase the concentration of a finished wine, or to produce both rosé and red wines from the same batch of grapes, winemakers sometimes elect to remove some lightly colored juice from a fermentation vessel early in the fermentation process. In principle, this has the effect of increasing the skin-to-juice ratio in what remains, enhancing color and extraction. From French *saignée.*

bloom *or* flowering: The second marker in the annual growth cycle of the vine; the point at which the vine flowers and the first small green berries are set.

brettanomyces *or* brett: A type of yeast that occurs naturally wherever wine grapes are handled. If brettanomyces is not eliminated with sulfur dioxide or through filtration, it can persist into finished wine. Controversial, it is sometimes associated with complexity in pinot noir, including the aromas and flavors described as barnyard and forest floor, but many winemakers refer to brettanomyces as a spoilage yeast that can give rise to "mousy" or dirty flavors.

Brix: A numeric value (named for Adolf Brix, a nineteenth-century German scientist) used in North America to express the concentration of dissolved compounds in grape juice. Since 90 percent of this material in ripe grapes is sugar, Brix is usually accepted as a surrogate for the sugar content at harvest and just before it. One degree Brix equates to approximately 18 grams of sugar per liter of juice.

budbreak: The first marker in the annual growth cycle of a grapevine, budbreak is the point at which small green shoots emerge from each bud on the vine. In regions with mild winters and early onset of spring, like the southern Central Coast of California, budbreak occurs early. Early budbreak can be a hazard in regions like the Finger Lakes, however, where damaging frosts can occur as late as May.

budwood: Synonymous with vine cuttings taken for the specific purpose of grafting to rootstock or to an existing vine, or for propagation as a new own-rooted vine plant (see *grafts*). Budwood is fundamental to vegetative propagation, which is the only way to generate new vine plants that are genetically identical to their parents.

cap: When red grapes are fermented, the skins and stems (if the grape clusters were not destemmed in advance) rise to the surface of the fermentation vessel, lifted by their lighter weight and by the constant formation of carbon dioxide in the must, until a raftlike "cap" forms on top of the juice. Because color, flavor, and structure in red wines come from compounds in the skins, it is essential to keep the cap in contact with the juice until the combination of juice and cap is pressed (see *pumpover; punchdown* for two illustrations of "cap management" techniques).

chaptalize: Named for Jean-Antoine Chaptal, an early-nineteenth-century French chemist, chaptalization is the process of adding sugar to grape juice before fermentation or, more commonly, to the must during fermentation. If the concentration of sugar is increased, the finished wine will develop higher alcoholic strength. Chaptalization is common practice with pinot noir in Burgundy and is permitted in New York, Oregon, and Canada.

clones *and* clonal selection: A clone is any population of vines propagated asexually from a single mother vine. Clonal selection is the process of identifying individual, disease-free mother vines that display desirable properties, keeping the cuttings from each potential mother vine separate, and eventually propagating a large population of genetically identical clones. Clonal selection is an alternative to mass selection (*sélection massale* in French) or *field selection* (see below).

cold soak *or* prefermentation maceration: After harvested grapes, destemmed or not and crushed or not, are transferred to the vessel in which they will ferment, sometimes that vessel is kept cold for a period of time in order to delay the onset of fermentation. This first phase of winemaking is called a cold soak or a prefermentation maceration. There are many ways to keep the vessel and its contents cold: some tanks are manufactured with jackets in which cold water can be circulated; dry ice can be layered in with the fruit; or the vessel and its contents can be moved into a refrigerated room. Cold soaking favors aqueous extraction, which is generally associated with fruitier flavors in the finished wine.

concentration; concentrator: Various techniques, processes, and equipment whose effect is to remove water from grapes or from grape must early in the fermentation process. Though controversial, concentration can be an alternative to chaptalization (see *chaptalize,* above) or a remedy for grapes that have been bloated by rain at the end of the growing season.

crushpad: Harvested grapes' first stop at the winery. The crushpad can be as simple as a bit of pavement where the winery moves the grapes, one way or another, from the bins or gondolas in which they arrive from the vineyard into the vessels in which they will be fermented. Most wineries employ destemming machines on the crushpad, or crusher-destemmers, and many also use some kind of sorting table to separate healthy grapes from rot, leaves, and other undesirable material.

custom crush: In North America, many wineries with a bit of extra space and staff agree to make wine, from scratch, for another party. In general, the other party has purchased the fruit independently, owns the wine throughout the process, and is responsible for marketing the finished product. In some instances, the client makes all winemaking decisions, instructing the winery to follow, more or less, his or her recipe. In other cases, the client relies heavily on advice from the host winery. The defining property of a custom crush, however, is that the custom-crushed lots of wine are handled separately throughout and are effectively "made to order." Many new brands of pinot noir have been launched as custom-crush operations in an existing winery.

cuvée: Derived from *cuve,* French for a tank or vat. In France, it has specialized meanings, especially in Champagne. In the Anglophone wine world, its meanings derive from the fact that one tank or vat of wine, of whatever size, is the smallest lot of wine that can be separately handled throughout the winemaking process, and thus develop and maintain a distinct identity. Thus cuvée is often used to denote a batch of wine that is somehow different from other lots made in the same winery in the same vintage. A cuvée may be distinct because it was picked from a special block of vineyard, or was fermented using a different strain of yeast, or followed a different barrel regime, or was left unfiltered at the end when related lots were filtered. Alternatively, in the hands of winemakers who blend, different cuvées may represent different blends from the same overall palette of raw materials.

élevage: The phase of winemaking that begins when the fermented must is drained or pressed and ends when the wine is readied for bottling.

eutypa: A destructive fungal disease that attacks the wood of grapevines, apricots, and some other plants, entering the plant through pruning wounds. Eutypa is especially prevalent in damp or windy conditions.

field selection: A process in which cuttings for propagation are deliberately taken from many mother vines in an effort to privilege and preserve genetic diversity. (By contrast, see *clones* and *clonal selection,* above.)

fining: One of two principal ways to clarify wine before bottling. Fining involves the introduction into the wine of a substance like egg white, whose physical properties attach to suspended particulate matter and drag it out of the wine. Some winemakers say fining also softens aggressively astringent tannins; others believe this use of fining is futile.

FPS (Foundation Plant Services): Called FPMS (Foundation Plant Materials Service) until 2003, FPS is a self-supporting service department of the University of California, Davis. It handles the import and quarantine of various plant materials including vines and cuttings of grapes, maintains a foundation vineyard of grape varieties and selections, and distributes healthy plant materials to nurseries and other customers throughout the United States. It also maintains the registry used in the United States to identify the various clones and selections of grape varieties, including pinot noir. See *UCD numbers.*

free-run juice: At the end of the primary fermentation, when the grape must is drained out of the fermentor, the free-run juice is that portion of the contents of the fermentation vessel which runs off without pressing. Free-run juice accounts for more than half of the contents of each fermentor. The balance is pressed, and the juice expelled from the press is called the *press fraction.* Free-run juice is conventionally accepted as the superior product, but many winemakers like the press fraction for the flavor and concentration it brings to the finished wine.

fruit bin: A large square bin (sometimes called a T-bin), usually about five feet on a side, made of plastic or plywood lined with plastic, conventionally used to store and transport fruits like apples and pears. As is or slightly modified, fruit bins are now commonly used as fermentation vessels by winemakers who work with small lots. A single-height fruit bin will generally accommodate about half a ton of grapes; double-height bins take a full ton.

grafts: Most cultivated grapevines planted since the end of the nineteenth century are grafts of wine-worthy scion material on rootstock species that are resistant to phylloxera. If the rootstock was planted first and the scion material joined to it in the vineyard, the vines are said to be *field grafts.* If the grafting takes place indoors and the vines are planted as prejoined units, the plants are called *bench grafts.*

grand cru; premier cru: These terms are applied to a short list of Burgundy's finest vineyards, with *grand cru* theoretically reserved for just 32 vineyards regarded as the crème de la crème, while *premier cru* applies to the 476 next-best. In Burgundy, unlike Bordeaux, the terms are applied to sites, not to makers or brands. The designations are part of the *Appellation d'origine contrôlée* system (see *AOC,* above), and more stringent requirements (for sugar accumulation and yield management) apply to *grand cru* and *premier cru* wines than to village and regional wines. *Grand cru* and *premier cru* vineyards account for only a tiny fraction of Burgundy's planted surface.

green harvest: The practice of removing and discarding some of a vine's grape clusters before the end of the growing season. Green harvesting is done to reduce yield at harvest, which is thought to improve concentration and quality in the remaining fruit; to hasten ripening, especially in cool sites or unusually cool years; or to eliminate clusters that are lagging the overall ripening process, threatening uneven outcomes when the vineyard is finally picked.

hang time: The elapsed time from the second marker in the annual growth cycle of a grapevine (called bloom, when the first tiny green berries are set) to harvest. Most growers believe longer hang times correlate with more complete flavor development. In North America, hang times for pinot noir range from as few as 13 weeks to as many as 18, depending on region and vintage.

increase block: When FPMS (see *FPS,* above) began distributing disease-free plant material in the 1950s, its small vineyards were unable to furnish enough buds to individual growers to plant entire vineyards. Agreements were therefore made with selected nurseries and wineries to take small quantities of budwood and segregate the vines propagated from those cuttings, so that cuttings taken in their turn from second-, third-, and fourth-generation vines would be as healthy and true to type as the first-generation cuttings from FPMS. The vineyard blocks set aside for this purpose are called certified increase blocks.

lieu-dit: In France, a *lieu-dit* is any spot in the countryside—outside the boundaries of a town or village—known by a persistent and widely accepted name. Burgundy is awash in *lieux-dits,* many of which have given their names to vineyards. Some *lieux-dits* are now used as vineyard names in their own right, particularly among *premier cru* vineyards. Other *lieux-dits* are denominated spots within the surface area set aside for various village wines, and wines from those spots are entitled to be labeled with the name of the village and the name of the *lieu-dit,* creating more granularity in Burgundy's complex naming scheme for wines.

malolactic fermentation: Usually described as a secondary fermentation, it produces no alcohol and may be more easily understood as a natural deacidification of newly made wine. Essentially, malolactic bacteria transform malic (apple) acid, which is tart, into lactic (milk) acid, which is softer. Malolactic transformation can begin during the vatting (see below) or be delayed, naturally or by intervention, until the pressed wine is settled and barreled. Most red wines, including pinot noir, are improved by malolactic fermentation.

mesoclimate *and* microclimate: The differences among *climate, mesoclimate,* and *microclimate* are a little fuzzy, and all three terms are frequently misused in common speech about winegrowing. Properly, *climate* applies to the temperature and weather conditions affecting a region, *mesoclimate* to an individual vineyard or cluster of vineyards that lie essentially cheek by jowl, and *microclimate* to the circumstances surrounding an individual vine.

négociant: One of many French terms for a wine merchant. In Burgundy, the *négociants* are well-established firms based primarily in Beaune and Nuits-St.-Georges whose essential business is to buy grapes or partially made wine from multiple independent growers, and then to create blends of village and regional wines. As more growers finish and bottle their own wines, however, *négociants* have responded by acquiring vineyard of their own, and a number of grower-winemakers have begun to function as *négociants* for their immediate friends and neighbors, making it increasingly difficult to determine who is, and who is not, a *négociant.* Conventionally, about 100 firms in Burgundy are accepted as Les Maisons de négoce.

phenology: Properly, the science of plant development. In common parlance, however, *phenology* is used interchangeably with *phenological development,* which is the timing of various benchmarks in the annual growth cycle of the vine (see *bloom; budbreak; veraison*).

Pierce's disease: A bacterial disease affecting grapevines, spread by small insects called sharpshooters. Epidemic in California since the end of the nineteenth century, Pierce's was first called Anaheim disease, for the part of Southern California it first affected. More recent outbreaks of Pierce's virtually eliminated viticulture in the inland areas south of Los Angeles and destroyed several vineyards in the Santa Cruz Mountains. Pinot noir, alas, seems to be particularly susceptible to Pierce's.

pigeage; pige: Pigeage is French for punchdown (see *pumpover; punchdown,* below). A *pige* is any tool used in punching down.

premier cru. See *grand cru; premier cru*

press fraction. See *free-run juice*

pumpover; punchdown: Two techniques for cap management during fermentation (see *cap,* above). In a pumpover, a pump is used to withdraw juice from beneath the cap and spray it back on top, keeping the cap wet and maintaining contact between juice and skins. In a punchdown, human hands or feet, a simple tamping tool, or a mechanically assisted device are used to push the cap down into the juice.

racking: Moving wine from one container to another—barrel to tank, barrel to barrel, and so on. Because pinot noir oxidizes easily and is easily bruised by rough handling, racking is usually minimized. Nevertheless, at least one racking is usually required before bottling, and racking is the usual remedy for barrel lots that develop funky smells because of very limited contact with air.

reserve: The antecedent terms in French, Italian, and Spanish—*réserve, reserva,* and *riserva*—have some special meanings, but the English term is unregulated and essentially meaningless. Generally, producers use it to identify some form of bottling (see *cuvée,* above) that is special or that the producer would like the consumer to construe as special. *Reserve quality* is used by some producers to describe wines superior to regular, estate, or appellation bottlings.

resident yeast: Yeasts are single-celled organisms belonging to several genera that live in vineyards, wineries, and other places where grapes or wines are handled. Contrary to popular belief, they do not cling to grape skins, but are airborne. These naturally occurring organisms are variously described as *wild yeast, native yeast, ambient yeast, natural yeast,* and *resident yeast.* Such yeasts are an alternative, in fermentations, to cultured, inoculated, or laboratory yeasts, all of which belong to the genus *Saccharomyces.*

saignée. See *bleeding*

scion; scion material: The varietally significant part of a vine plant (see *grafts,* above).

second-crop fruit: After the main flowering and fruit set take place, usually around the beginning of summer, vines sometimes set additional clusters on what viticulturists call lateral shoots. Varieties differ in their propensity to set such clusters; pinot noir's propensity is high. Generally, second-crop fruit competes with first-crop for nutrients, potentially lessening the quality of the latter; it also ripens later, creating the potential for unripe fruit to find its way into picking bins at harvesttime. For these reasons, second-crop fruit is usually removed from the vines well before harvest and discarded, or carefully separated from harvested fruit on the crushpad.

settling: At the end of the vatting, the process of separating red wine from its lees often involves a period of time during which the runoff and pressed wine are held in a tank until some additional solids fall to the bottom and can be eliminated. Wines that are made with no settling step, or with only a short one, are said to go "dirty" to barrel. Winemakers disagree about the merits and demerits of settling.

terroir: A French word with the basic meaning of "rural environment that has some form or degree of cultural impact," *terroir* is used by nearly everyone associated with wine to denote all the physical properties of a site where wine grapes are grown. Soil, slope, orientation, microclimate, and exposure are all elements of *terroir.*

tiling: A change in the color of red wine as it matures: generally, the change from the youthful hues variously described as black-red, ruby, garnet, crimson, and vermilion to colors more commonly associated with clay roof tiles and terra-cotta pots. Tiling is a natural evolution in red wines and can occur anywhere between five and ten years after the vintage, but many wines evolve slowly and show no signs of tiling until they are much older.

toast: The process of forming wooden staves into barrels usually involves heating them over some kind of open fire. The fire chars the inside surface of each stave, creating "toast." In recent decades, as the taste for toast has increased, coopers have produced barrels with differing levels of toast, from light to heavy. Winemakers may specify the level of toast they desire when ordering barrels from most cooperages. Toast levels, in combination with the source of the wood and other factors, affect the flavor of the finished wine. Heavier toast levels are often associated with charred, smoky flavors.

trellis systems; trellising: Various configurations of upright posts and horizontal wires designed to support grapevines during the growing season. Trellis systems are adapted to particular vine training systems. In North America, vineyards planted before about 1980 typically involved rudimentary trellis systems, and the vines were said to "sprawl." New vineyards, at least for pinot noir, are usually trellised to support vertical vine training, especially the version known as vertical shoot positioning (VSP), which is the antithesis of sprawl. Most viticulturists believe that VSP is well adapted to pinot noir and tends to maximize the grower's control over canopy management, sunlight penetration to individual grape clusters, and related parameters. A trellis system called Scott Henry, developed at Oregon's Henry Estate Winery, is sometimes used in high-vigor sites. In this system, four canes are left on each vine, and the shoots from two of the four are trained downward rather than upward, creating two fruiting zones. This configuration appears to discourage vine vigor.

TTB (Alcohol and Tobacco Tax and Trade Bureau): Successor (in 2003) to the ATF or BATF (Bureau of Alcohol, Tobacco and Firearms). This agency, within the United

States Department of the Treasury, interprets and enforces federal laws about wine. The TTB approves all wine labels and administers AVA designations, among other things. The change of name from ATF to TTB reflects the reassignment of authority for firearms to the new Department of Homeland Security.

UCD numbers: Since the 1940s, successive organizations housed at the University of California, Davis, have maintained a registry of grape varieties and subvarietal selections, each of which is numbered. In principle, this is an unambiguous way to identify the various clones and selections of grape varieties: e.g., UCD [Pinot Noir] 1A. UCD 1A can also be rendered as FPMS 1A (see *FPS,* above), but since the name of the unit maintaining the registry has changed over time, *UCD* is the preferred designation.

vatting: Generally, *vatting* refers to the active phase of red winemaking, beginning when the picked grapes are placed in a fermentation vessel and ending when the newly made wine is separated from its lees. In this sense, *vatting* is identical to the French *cuvaison.* However, *vatting* is sometimes also used as a synonym for *cuvée* when the latter is used to denote the contents of a single *cuve* or fermentor.

veraison: The third significant marker in the annual growth cycle of the grapevine, veraison (French *véraison*) is said to occur when the grapes change color, from green to yellow-green in the case of white varieties, and from green to some shade of red-black in the case of red varieties like pinot noir. Color change is associated with a simultaneous increase in berry size and sugar content and a decrease in acidity. At veraison, harvest is usually four to seven weeks away.

vinifera: The species of the genus *Vitis* to which most varieties of wine grapes belong, though wine is sometime also made from other species of the genus. Because vinifera is not native to North America, vinifera varieties have sometimes been known here as *European varieties.* In this sense, they are differentiated from *native varieties* and from *hybrids,* which are crosses of vinifera and nonvinifera varieties.

A Note on Sources

There are few books specifically about pinot noir, and even fewer focused on pinot noir in North America. For what does exist, see Andrew Barr, *Pinot Noir* (New York: Viking, 1992); Cathleen Francisco, *Pinot Noir: A Reference Guide to California and Oregon Pinot Noir* (Sonoma: Wine Key Publications, 1999); and Marq de Villiers, *The Heartbreak Grape: A California Winemaker's Search for the Perfect Pinot Noir* (New York: HarperCollins, 1994). Articles abound, however, in *Wine Spectator, Wine & Spirits, Decanter, Wines & Vines, Practical Winery and Vineyard,* and other periodicals.

Sources used in chapters 1 and 2 include Jancis Robinson, *Vines, Grapes, and Wines* (New York: Alfred A. Knopf, 1986); Roger Dion, *Histoire de la vigne et du vin en France* (Paris: Flammarion, 1959); and Jim Clendenen, "Debunking Pinot Noir Production as the Search for the Holy Grail," *Napa Valley Wine Library Report* (Winter 1990): 4–6. Professor Carole Meredith's groundbreaking work on grape varieties is reported in numerous scientific articles, including "Historical Genetics: The Parentage of Chardonnay, Gamay and Other Wine Grapes of Northeastern France," *Science* 285 (3 September 1999): 1562–1565, and is usefully summarized for the general reader in Carole P. Meredith, "Science as a Window into Wine History," *Bulletin of the American Academy of Arts and Sciences* 56, no. 2 (2003): 54–70. The unorthodox (and generally unaccepted) Austrian view that pinot noir is a cross of schwarzriesling and traminer is reported in Ferdinand Regner et al., "Genetic Relationships among Pinots and Related Cultivars," *American Journal of Enology and Viticulture* 51, no. 1 (2000): 7–14. Professor Raymond Bernard's views were expressed to the author in interviews, letters, and e-mail.

The main English-language sources for the Burgundian experience with pinot are Anthony Hansen, *Burgundy* (London: Faber and Faber, 1985); and Clive Coates, *Côte d'Or: A Celebration of the Great Wines of Burgundy* (Berkeley: University of California Press, 1997). Richard Olney's fascinating *Romanée-Conti: The World's Most Fabled Wine* (New York: Rizzoli, 1995) is richly rooted in primary and secondary French sources. Alexis Lichine's *Wines of France,* 5th ed. (New York: Alfred A. Knopf, 1972), contains good firsthand testimony about the Burgundian wine trade in the 1950s, '60s, and '70s. Kermit Lynch, *Adventures on the Wine Route* (New York: Farrar, Straus and Giroux, 1988), and David Cobbold, *Beaune* (Paris: Flammarion, 2001), are both useful.

Chapter 3, on the history of pinot in North America, relies on a considerable list of secondary sources, some readings in California newspapers from the nineteenth and early twentieth centuries, and typescripts of interviews conducted by the Regional Oral History Office, a division of the Bancroft Library at the University of California, Berkeley. See especially Louis P. Martini, *A Family Winery and the California Wine Industry,* 1984; Louis M. and Louis P. Martini, *Wine Making in the Napa Valley,* 1973; Harold P. Olmo, *Plant Genetics and New Grape Varieties,* 1976; and André Tchelistcheff, *Grapes, Wine and Ecology,* 1983. Important treatments include Thomas Pinney, *A History of Wine in America from the Beginnings to Prohibition* (Berkeley: University of California Press, 1989); Charles Sullivan, *A Companion to California Wine* (Berkeley: University of California Press, 1998); and James T. Lapsley, *Bottled Poetry: Napa Winemaking from Prohibition to the Modern Era* (Berkeley: University of California Press, 1996). A significant nineteenth-century document is University of California–College of Agriculture, *Report of the Viticultural Work during the Seasons 1887–93 with Data Regarding the Vintages of 1894–95* (Sacramento: A. J. Johnston Superintendent State Printing, 1896). Contemporaneous testimony and reflections were also taken from Robert Lawrence Balzer, *California's Best Wines* (Los Angeles: Ward Ritchie Press, 1948); Frona Eunice Wait, *Wines and Vines of California* (Berkeley: Howell-North Books, 1973 [orig. 1889]); Tom Marvel and Frank Schoonmaker, *American Wines* (New York: Duell, Sloan and Pearce, 1941); Bob Thompson, *Notes on a California Cellarbook* (New York: William Morrow, 1988); and Robert Gorman, *Gorman on Premium California Wines* (Berkeley: Ten Speed Press, 1975). *Vintners Club: Fourteen Years of Wine Tastings 1973–1987,* ed. Mary-Ellen McNeil-Draper (San Francisco: Vintners' Press, 1988), is a valuable window on contemporaneous assessments of pinot noir, as are pinot-specific issues of early wine newsletters, including *Connoisseurs' Guide, Robert Lawrence Balzer's Private Guide to Food and Wine,* and Robert Finigan's *Private Guide to Wines.* Some recent history is captured (though not without errors) in Michael Bonadies, "Pinot Noir American Style," *Wine & Spirits* (April 1997): 45–49.

The Special Collections Department at the University of California, Davis, and the New York Public Library both hold important collections of wine lists, menus, tasting announcements, and other ephemera from the first half of the twentieth century. At Davis, the papers of Roy Brady, Maynard Amerine, Leon Adams, and Martin Ray are all rich sources. The menu collection at the New York Public Library contains especially comprehensive documentation of tastings conducted by the Wine and Food Society, Inc.

Chapter 4 draws primarily on extensive interviews with winegrowers and viticulturists in the various regions where pinot noir has emerged as a specialty. An important and underused examination of American wine regions by a professional geographer is John J. Baxevanis, *The Wine Regions of America: Geographical Reflections and Appraisals* (Stroudsburg: Vinifera Wine Growers Journal, 1992). The section on the Russian River valley was substantially informed by Ernest P. Peninou, *History of the Sonoma Viticultural District* (Santa Rosa: Nomis Press, 1998). A number of articles were also helpful, including Rod Smith, "The Russian River Reconsidered," *Wine & Spirits* (August 1996): 20–23; Gerald Asher, "California Pinot Noir: The New Frontier," in his *On Wine* (New York: Random House, 1982), pp. 164–171; "Unique Conditions Spur Carneros Expansion," *Practical Winery and Vineyard* (March–April 1986): 26–29; and Norman S. Roby, "California Pinot Noir," *Vintage Magazine* (January 1982): 3–4. Several unpublished items were also consulted, especially Patrick L. Shabram, "Unique Climatic and Environmental Characteristics of the Proposed Fort Ross–Seaview Viticultural Area," 2001; Charles L. Sullivan, "A Miraculous Intersection: A Short History of Viticulture and Winegrowing in Western Sonoma County," 2001; and Neill Bell, "Anderson Valley—Winegrowing and Winemaking History," undated. Background materials prepared by and for the Carneros Quality Alliance (www.carneros.org) were uncommonly useful. Climatic data came from various sources but were systematically cross-checked with data available on www.weather.com. Phenological data were compiled from data provided by Byron Vineyard and Winery, Babcock Winery and Vineyards, Calera Wine Company, Chalone Vineyard, the Carneros Quality Alliance, Iron Horse Vineyards, Marimar Torres Estate, J Wine Company, Coastlands Vineyard, Roederer Estate, Handley Cellars, Knudsen Vineyard, the Pacific Agri-Food Research Center, and Sheldrake Point Vineyard and Winery.

The best single source of information on the history of California's efforts to procure and distribute clean, true-to-variety grapevines is Lynn Alley and Deborah A. Golino, "The Origins of the Grape Program at Foundation Plant Materials Service," *American Journal of Enology and Viticulture* 51, no. 5 (2000). The Foundation Plant Materials Service (now called Foundation Plant Services) also publishes and distributes a variety of useful publications, including the *FPMS Grape Program Newsletter* and *FPMS Registered, Provisional, Non-Registered and Quarantine Grape Selections.* Unpublished documents held at FPMS—including card files that record each instance of grapevine distribution from FPMS to its customers, loose-leaf binders recording source and treatments for clonal selections, and a vertical file containing copies of correspondence and other materials documenting the history of the university's Jackson field station—are enormously valuable. A good summary of American experience with the clones of pinot noir is Stan Hock, "Clonal Selections: Obstacles and Opportunities with Pinot Noir," *Practical Winery and Vineyard* (May–June 1989): 37–42. Melissa Moravec, "Clonal Evolution at Carneros Creek," *Vineyard and Winery Management* 21, no. 3 (1995): 36–39, is also useful. Much of the information summarized in chapter 5 was gleaned from interviews, correspondence, and e-mail with Raymond Bernard, David Adelsheim, Francis Mahoney, Bob Pool, Deborah Golino, and Susan Nelson-Kluk. It is perhaps important to note that a great deal of folklore and hearsay is repeated about the various clones of pinot noir and that a good deal of this finds its way back into otherwise reliable professional literature. *Caveat lector.*

Many hundreds of conversations with winemakers underpin chapter 6. Useful background is also found in John Gladstones, *Viticulture and Environment* (Adelaide: Winetitles, 1992), and Claude Bourguignon, *Le Sol, la terre et les champs* (Paris: Sang de la Terre, 1989). The numerous references to André Tchelistcheff's "classic" opinions about making pinot noir point to an interview published in *Connoisseurs' Guide* (March–April 1977): 33–36. The quotation from Christophe Tupinier appears in "Quand l'homme fait la loi," *Bourgogne Aujourd'hui* no. 32: 57. It should go almost without saying that a huge amount of unimpeachable information about winegrowing issues, techniques, and procedures is also found in Jancis Robinson, ed., *The Oxford Companion to Wine* (Oxford: Oxford University Press, 1994), under the usual-suspect headings.

Chapter 7 is the most personal chapter in the book, and the least rooted in sources. Frank Prial's comments on Burgundies and American pinot noir are found in his column for the *New York Times,* April 8, 1998. *Wine Spectator*'s so-called Pinot Noir Challenge is reported in the issue dated May 15, 1998.

Index

Note: Boldfaced page numbers denote the main discussions of indexed terms. Personal names and vineyard names are indexed comprehensively throughout the book. Corporate names are indexed where the reference is substantive, except that the names of coopers are indexed only in parts I and III. The proper names of grape varieties other than pinot noir are indexed, but variant names are not. When a winery's name is eponymous, references to the personal name (or names) and the winery usually are combined and listed under the personal name. Wine brands and proprietary wine names that are not also corporate or vineyard names normally are not indexed. Only the main occurrences of viticultural and winemaking terminology are indexed. Geographical names (other than vineyard names) are indexed only when they refer to pinot-producing regions in North America, and then selectively. Other geographical names, including the names of continents, countries, counties, provinces, *départments,* cantons, rivers, lakes, cities, and towns, are not indexed—with only a few exceptions. Historical expressions (e.g., *French Revolution, Middle Ages, Prohibition,* and *Repeal*) are not indexed. Terms that occur constantly because of the book's subject matter, like *pinot noir* and its paranyms, *Burgundy, Bourgogne, Côte d'Or, Côte de Nuits,* and *vinifera,* are not indexed.

C

D

N

T

U

V

W

Designer: Nola Burger
Text: Adobe Garamond
Display: Sackers Gothic
Cartographers: Mark Chambers, Bill Nelson
Compositor: Integrated Composition Systems
Printer and Binder: Thomson-Shore, Inc.